The
Lost Theatres
of
London

The
Lost Theatres
of
London

by Raymond Mander and Joe Mitchenson

*Wherever there is a playhouse
the world will go on not amiss.*
HAZLITT

TAPLINGER PUBLISHING COMPANY
NEW YORK

For
Woody
and
Chris
who were intrigued

Contents

A*

Illustrations

Preface

WHEN WE COMPILED *The Theatres of London*, (first published in 1961, revised and brought up to date in 1963,) we included a number of Lost Theatres which, though still existing as buildings, were no longer used for their original purpose. We have now attempted to record the histories of those central London theatres of the last century which have vanished completely and left little or no visible trace, except a vast confusion of name, identity and location for the casual theatrical enthusiast, to say nothing of the amateur theatrical historian!

The theatres, lost but not gone, included in the previous book are: the Carlton Theatre (Cinema); the Coliseum (Cinema); the Dominion Theatre (Cinema); the Leicester Square Theatre (Cinema); the London Casino (Cinema); the London Hippodrome (the Talk of the Town); the London Pavilion (Cinema); the Lyceum Theatre (Dance Hall); the Playhouse (B.B.C. Studio); the Prince Charles Theatre (Cinema); the Royal Theatre, Kingsway (Cinema); the Windmill Theatre (Cinema and Casino); the Winter Garden Theatre (demolished awaiting compulsory re-building in new office block). The Metropolitan, Edgeware Road became a complete loss when it was demolished in 1963.

In compiling this book we have naturally had recourse to previous writers covering similar ground; *History of the London Stage and its Famous Players* by H. Barton Baker (first published 1889, revised and brought up to date in 1904), and *London's Lost Theatres of the Nineteenth Century* by Erroll Sherson (1925).

There is also much useful information in *Old and New London* by Walter Thornbury and Edward Walford (originally published in parts from 1878-1880). For contemporary reports, mainly quoted in the text, the files of *The Era* and *The Stage* have provided the most valuable source. Other periodicals will be found

credited in the appropriate place, as well as individual books
devoted to particular theatres, etc.

In many cases assembling this book has been a vast task of
clearing up the mass of inaccuracies left behind by previous
writers which were eventually gathered together in *The Oxford
Companion to the Theatre* (1951 and revised, to conspicuously
little effect in 1957). This unfortunately gave renewed vitality,
at least as far as theatre histories were concerned, to a fund of
misinformation in a readily accessible form. A new third edition
appeared in September 1967, and this was said to have been
'thoroughly overhauled and re-set' and 'articles have been revised
or corrected, and, in many cases added to'. Sad to say, at this
juncture judging only the theatre histories, condensation and
so called revision have only made bad worse. Most of the fun-
damental errors still remain to befog the general reader. Strangely
even a correct statement in the earlier editions is now at times
made incorrect!

As Harold Hobson, in his *Sunday Times* review, said:

'The only disadvantage of Phyllis Hartnoll's *The Oxford
Companion to the Theatre* as a bedside book is that it is likely
to keep you awake with laughing. You can dip into it at any page
with a fair confidence of finding some hilarious piece of misinformation . . .'

The lists of Theatres in Allardyce Nicolls' two volumes *Early
and Late Eighteenth Century Drama* (1930 and 1946) are confused
and inaccurate to the point of uselessness.

A great deal of work has also had to be done to clear up the mess
left behind in newspapers and popular magazines by uninformed
journalists and amateur week-end historians.

Most of the trouble with theatrical history of the early
nineteenth century seems to stem from that respected writer,
E. L. Blanchard (1820-1889). He was a prolific playwright and
writer of pantomimes, and spent his life in and around the theatres
of London. Davenport Adams in *A Dictionary of the Drama*
(Volume 1, 1904; unfortunately the only half published covers
A to G) says: 'From an early age he (E. L. Blanchard) had
written on theatrical matters for various newspapers and other
publications including *The Era* (from 1850) and the London
Daily Telegraph (from 1863). He was also a copious contributor to
the *Era Almanac* (from 1868). His 'Diary' (from 1844 to 1888)

edited by Clement Scott and Cecil Howard appeared in 1891.'

Blanchard, like most writers of contemporary history, was apt to rely on his own memory and to use familiar names rather than the correct designation, and once, like any journalist, he had covered a subject, his notes, without revision, were re-used when the necessity again arose. His hand though uncredited, can be seen in many of *The Era* notices of re-openings of theatres, where a brief resumé of their previous history was needed. These were often repeated at later dates and then again served up in articles in the Almanacs. From these much sought after annuals, which cover the period 1868-1919, a great number of the mistakes of Baker, Sherson and their latter day 'raiders' stem, spiced yet again with their own inaccurate, unchecked personal reminiscences.

We lay no claim to have put the whole house of London theatrical history in order, but interested readers will find some well worn 'facts' exploded or revised, and we hope corrected.

In our work we have had the greatest help from Dr. Francis Sheppard, the Editor of the *Survey of London*, who, besides his past work, made available to us the proofs of the latest volumes 33 and 34 (1966) while they were going through the press, so that we could, when our theatres coincided, collate material. The Greater London Council, under whose auspices the Survey is published, have also been of great help through their Architects' (Theatre) Department and the Historic Building Department.

The Westminster Public Library, both at Leicester Place and at Buckingham Palace Road Archives have been tireless in their assistance, searching old Rate Books, etc., to solve finer points of date and ownership. We have had similar help from the Marylebone Public Library Archives; the Holborn Central Library Archives; the Guildhall Library; the R.I.B.A. Library; the Bodleian Library and the British Museum Newspaper Library. To the voices, often anonymous, who have shown great patience with our enquiries we offer our sincere thanks.

Our thanks also to the Enthoven Collection at the Victoria and Albert Museum, George Nash and his staff, Betty Johnson and Tony Latham, and John Hayes of the London Museum.

Our thanks to Norman Marshall for permission to use his history of the Gate Theatre, which it would have been impossible to better or rewrite, and to Molly Veness for her comments and loan of pictures etc. Thanks are also due to Cecil Wilson who hunted out his brother, A. E.'s copies of the *Era Almanac* to fill some of our gaps; Raymond Howarth who gave up his lunch hours to slip into the Guildhall Library for us, at the drop of a hat, to check the files of *The Times*, and to Vera Seaton-Reid for material assistance.

To our two old friends Edward J. Wood and Chris Gannon, to whom this book is dedicated, we offer our thanks for reading it in manuscript and proof and keeping us up to scratch by their enthusiasm during the eighteen months that this book, in one way or another, has been almost part of our daily routine.

Finally, there would be no book unless Mary Quinnell, our 'Quinney', had not learnt to cope with and transcribe our almost indecipherable manuscript, and incidentally had the strength to manage the volumes of *The Era*, awkwardly as large in size as they are small in type.

We wish to thank the libraries and museums for permission to reproduce original watercolours and drawings from their collections which are credited under each individual picture.

Except for the undermentioned sources the remaining pictures are from the authors' Collection.

1. Enthoven Collection, Victoria and Albert Museum 3, 18, 24, 37, 38, 71, 84, 98, 99, 101, 108.
2. National Monuments Record 17, 21, 36, 51, 57, 93, 100
3. Greater London Council, Picture Library 4, 23, 85
4. Guildhall Library 26, 27
5. Holborn Central Library 25
6. Westminster Public Library 13, 47
7. Bristol University Theatre Collection 75
8. B.B.C. Photo Library 86, 89
9. Moss Empires Press Office 30

Raymond Mander and Joe Mitchenson
March 1968

1

The Alhambra Theatre

The Royal Panopticon of Science and Art, The Alhambra Palace, The Alhambra Palace Music Hall, The Royal Alhambra Palace of Varieties, The Royal Alhambra Theatre, The Alhambra Theatre, The Alhambra Theatre Royal, The Theatre Royal Alhambra, The Alhambra Theatre of Varieties

Leicester Square
Numbers 24-27 on the east side with no side or back entrance. Backing on buildings in Castle Street (now Charing Cross Road). Later given a stage door in Hunts Court and an entrance in Charing Cross Road

FIRST BUILDING

Opened as the Royal Panopticon of Science and Art 18 March 1854, closed 1856 and contents dispersed. Converted into the Alhambra Palace, under the management of E. T. Smith. A circus ring installed and opened 3 April 1858.
Under the management of Howes and Cushing's American Circus. Converted into a music hall with stage and proscenium and opened as the Alhambra Palace Music Hall 10 December 1860, with a Music Hall Bill.
Under the management of E. T. Smith.
On obtaining a dramatic licence became the Royal Alhambra Palace of Varieties.
Opened 24 April 1871 with *Oh! My Head*, a farce by F. F. Allen, followed by The Praeger Family and *The Crimson Scarf*, a comic opera by H. B. Farnie, with music by J. E. Legouix and the ballets *The Beauties of the Harem* and *Puella; or, the Fairy and the Evil Genii*. Under the management of Frederick Strange.
Name changed to the Royal Alhambra Theatre 20 May 1872.

(The names the Royal Alhambra Palace, the Alhambra Theatre, the Alhambra Theatre Royal and the Theatre Royal Alhambra also used).
After alterations, re-opened as the Alhambra Theatre, 3 December 1881.
Burnt down 7 December 1882.

SECOND THEATRE

Opened as the Alhambra Theatre Royal 3 December 1883, with *The Golden Ring*, a fairy spectacular opera by George R. Sims, music by Frederic Clay.
Preceded by an opening address spoken by Fred Mervin, specially written by Vernon De Montgomery.
Under the management of William Holland.
Again became a music hall, the Alhambra Theatre of Varieties 18 October 1884, but from 1890 resumed the name Alhambra Theatre, and retained it from then on.
Under the management of Charles Morton.
A new 'grand entrance' and office block in Charing Cross Road built in 1897.
Closed 1 September 1936, and demolished.

THIRD BUILDING

The Odeon (Cinema) opened 2 November 1937 with *The Prisoner of Zenda*.

THERE WAS A PROPOSAL to build a theatre on the east side of Leicester Square, on the site of some empty houses built in the 1670's, numbers 24-27, which were demolished in 1840. Previously there had been a scheme for a 'Casino, Promenade Concert Room, à la Musard', designed by Samuel Beazley, but this was superseded by 1842 by that for a theatre, promoted by Benjamin Webster, the lessee of the Theatre Royal, Haymarket, and J. B. Buckstone, the actor, playwright and manager. Their idea 'to build a new theatre, on a grand scale, to be devoted to the encouragement of English authors,' was doomed when Webster lost a large sum at the Haymarket on the 1847-48 season.

The theatre project turned into one for a circus, which also came to nothing owing to the death of Charles Tulk, the ground landlord, which put the estate into chancery for over two years.

In July 1851 an agreement was signed for the lease of the ground for sixty years, for the building of the Royal Panopticon of Science and Art. This was a project conceived by Edward Clarke, founder of the London Electrical Society, who was deeply interested in promoting exhibitions of Science and Art in London and the provinces. He gathered round him a number of interested, public-spirited and scientific gentlemen who formed the Council, and a Royal Charter was granted by the Queen in February 1850. T. Hayter Lewis was appointed the architect of a building to be in the Moorish idiom. *The Illustrated London News* of 31 January 1852 gave a foretaste of things to come:

> The building now in course of erection on the eastern side of Leicester Square, by the Corporation of the Royal Panopticon of Science and Art, will it is expected, present a finished specimen of the Saracenic style of architecture, a style which has as yet no perfect exemplification in the metropolis; and, while on the one hand the erection in question will attempt to convey to the spectator a model of Moorish grandeur, it will, at the same time, be no servile copy of any existing edifice. The splendid remains at Cairo have afforded much that is now reproduced; and it is from an actual Daguerreotype of one of the mosques that the model of the dome has been taken, whose intrinsic beauty in this instance affords an ample apology for the strict adhesion of the architect to the magnificent original. The imposing *façade* which this structure will present towards Leicester Square will be by no means diminished by the two lofty minarets which rise on either side to a height of upwards of 100 feet; and from which, we understand, it is proposed to exhibit powerful lights.
>
> Passing through the vestibule or entrance, the spectator will be at once ushered into a grand circular hall of a diameter of ninety-seven feet, surrounded by three galleries, placed one above the other in the circumference of the building; and destined, as well as the centre, for the reception of works of

art and industry, models of manufactures and scientific apparatus, and thus to afford the most agreeable opportunity for the sightseer to mingle instruction with amusement. We must not forget, however, to mention that a very considerable space in the great circular hall will be allotted to an extremely large and powerful organ, to be built for the Corporation by Messrs. W. Hill and Co., whose success at Birmingham warrants every expectation which the most sanguine can form as to the compass and execution of the instrument entrusted to their construction.

The other portions of the building, though less striking, will nevertheless be first-rate of their kind; the lecture-rooms, laboratory, and offices will be of such dimensions and finish as will well warrant the beauty of the external edifice.

This strange building was opened to the public, after a private preview at which the Bishop of London read an Opening Prayer, on 18 March 1854. *The Illustrated London News* of the same date noted:

This new 'Institution for Scientific Exhibitions, and for Promoting Discoveries in Arts and Manufactures,' was opened for private inspection yesterday, and on Thursday, and to-day is opened to the public. The building occupies a large space on the centre of the east side of Leicester Square, for many years a great focus of metropolitan exhibitions. The Panopticon, however, belongs to a higher class than the majority of the sights previously located in the Square [Wilde's Globe etc.] . . . The style of the architecture is reputed Saracenic; and its minarets and horse-shoe arches are of that period of art; but its escutcheons, which are prominent features of the elevation, represent the most important branches of the arts and sciences, in the arms of their professors, in addition to the Royal Arms, and the bearings of the Panopticon itself, with the motto, 'Mente et manu.' The site has, moreover, olden scientific repute; for, upon this spot, John Hunter collected his valuable museum, and in one of the adjoining houses was temporarily located 'the National Repository,' some four-and-twenty years since —this being the first 'Polytechnic' Exhibition in the metropolis.

Having passed through the vestibule, which is pleasingly decorated with encaustic tiles and English alabaster, next is the internal porch, 'strictly ornate Saracenic,' and then we reach the Rotunda. The centre of this is occupied with a magnificent fountain, and throughout the circle are two galleries, with ornate fronts, stalls, and richly decorated ceilings. The great central dome is radiant with gold and colour, and through the glass crown a circle of small stars, and a series of semi-circular windows, the vast apartment is lighted. This room is about 97 feet in diameter, and the same in height, and the total cubical contents of the Hall and its recesses are about 500,000 feet; in addition to the space occupied by the boxes and the organ-gallery. At night it will be lighted by lamps of design in keeping with the character of the decorations. The fountain throws up a centre jet to the height of the dome, and eight minor jets, each 40 feet, converging to the centre; the water being obtained from an Artesian well 346 feet deep. The fountain is worked by a powerful pneumatic apparatus, aided by a steam-engine.

In the lower gallery is a Photographic Room, which may be reached by the staircases, or by an ascending carriage up a shaft. Around the Rotunda are the Laboratory and adjoining apparatus-rooms; and, descending, you reach the circular railway, engine-room, &c. North and south are Lecture-rooms. The ventilation and warming are by 'Gurney's Warming Battery,' which is described in the 'Handbook' sold in the establishment. To the same source we refer the reader for the details of the apparatus to be exhibited here to illustrate diving; turning and planing, drilling and boring, the combustion of steel; aurora-borealis and thunder; pin-making and needle-making, and gas cookery; freezing mercury; the liquefaction and solidification of carbonic acid; ballooning under water; galvanism, magnetism, and the electric light; and a large collection of machinery, models, &c. In the first gallery is a 'Royal stand' sumptuously fitted with scarlet and gold.

The east side of the Rotunda is filled from the first gallery with an organ, by Hill and Co., who state that it exceeds in tone and compass every other organ in the metropolis, and the organs of York and Birmingham.

The scheme of the Panopticon promises much for the popular spread of science in its application to the arts and manufactures; to which are to be added the attractions of painting, sculpture, and music; and we shall be happy to record its success.

At first all went well; there were reputed to be over one thousand visitors a day, but it was soon said that the promoters had 'failed to produce a single illustration of their purpose,' and that there was 'a want of proper management, or, indeed, of any management whatever.' Clarke himself was supposed to be the manager of his own brain child, and failure was complete and final, ending in bankruptcy.

In August 1856 the whole premises and contents were advertised for sale by auction, and in May 1857 they were bought by the eccentric showman, E. T. Smith, then the lessee of Drury Lane. He had been a Bow Street runner and had risen to be a reckless theatrical speculator. He bought the whole concern, lock, stock and barrel, for £9,000. It was said to have originally cost over £80,000 to build and equip. Smith sold the contents—the organ went to St. Paul's Cathedral—and changed the name to the Alhambra Palace, in keeping with its Moorish atmosphere. He installed a circus ring in the centre of the building and let it to Howes and Cushing's American Circus, which opened on 3 April 1858. *The Illustrated London News* again reported:

There is the arena in the centre, in which the American athletes and equestrians perform their wonders with a facility and safety that appear still more marvellous. Round them, in immediate relation, are the audience of the pit and stalls placed in the most favourable situations for seeing and hearing. The latter is as important as the former, for the Yankee clown spins many a humorous yarn; and his voluble discourse is needed to connect the scenes in the circus into an intelligible unity. Even in amusements of this kind, that apparently appeal only to the senses, there is a recognised need of an intellectual accompaniment, sometimes to explain and interpret, but more frequently to elevate and give an additional importance, or rather significance, to the natural and physical exhibition. No scheme of popular amusement can be invented in which this necessity does not arise; and hence we may appreciate their moral value. That they have such, the instinct of mankind confesses, and in consequence all attempts of straight-laced Puritanism at their suppression have uniformly failed. Over the pit and stalls the spectator will be gratified with the sight of the boxes and galleries, densely populated—tier above tier of human faces looking down upon the marvellous feats of the arena, and constituting a galaxy of animation not elsewhere to be paralleled. It is indeed a magnificent spectacle of itself, and will for some time command the attendance of thousands, no less from its grandeur than from its novelty.

The circus succeeded, where the arts and sciences had failed, in bringing its Royal Patron to visit the building. In June, Queen Victoria, who throughout her long life could never resist a circus, came to see 'The Horse of Beauty,' Black Eagle, accompanied by the Prince Consort and the royal children. The success of the circus was assured.

Smith had wanted to use the building as a theatre but was refused a licence by the Lord Chamberlain. In October 1858 he succeeded in obtaining a Magistrate's licence for music and dancing. He eventually closed the circus, added a stage with a proscenium (the first in a Music Hall), where the organ had been, and opened as the Alhambra Palace Music Hall on 10 December 1860 with a ballet and music hall programme of the style then coming into vogue. The ground floor was set out with tables at which drinks were served.

The changes are noted in *The Era* 2 December 1860:

This magnificent structure, which, for some weeks past, has been undergoing extensive alterations, will be completed in a few days. The portion of the space formerly known as the organ gallery is now occupied by a stage about seventy feet in depth and about fifty feet in width, and is carried up to the top of the building, a height of nearly one hundred feet. The proscenium and general decorations strictly preserve the Alhambra style of architecture . . . A new mode of lighting has been introduced, consisting of a centre star from the roof, of about seven feet in diameter, surrounded by sixteen others of smaller circumference . . . The dome has been entirely re-decorated, and now presents a much more light

and chaste appearance than formerly. The decoration
consists of a pale blue ground, with stars in gold, surrounded
by rich ornaments of scarlet and gold, the colours gradually
becoming stronger towards the convex portion of the dome.
The front of the galleries have been ornamented in blue,
crimson, cream, white, and gold. The area or ground-floor
has been fitted up with reserved and other seats, as well as
refreshment-counters of various kinds. From the centre of
each there is hung a very tasteful chandelier, in strict harmony
with the general architectural character.

The new music hall was inaugurated with a banquet on
7 December, before it opened to the public on the Monday. *The
Era* 9 December reports:

The opening of this new and magnificent establishment is
now definitely arranged to take place on Monday next, and
the elegance of the decorations, and the extent to which the
comfort of the public has been studied in the general arrangements, begin now to be advantageously apparent. On Friday
afternoon a grand inaugural banquet was given by the
enterprising Proprietor, Mr. E. T. Smith, to celebrate the
commencement of the season at the new and important
institution, which is henceforth to be associated with his
name. Prior to the festival, which formed the great feature of
the gathering, including the most eminent members of the
magistracy, the legal the literary, the theatrical, and the
musical professions, ample opportunity was afforded the
company for a survey of the splendid building, which, thus
metamorphosed, will form a conspicuous portion of the
architectural splendours of the metropolis, as well as a
valuable addition to the amusements provided for its inhabit-
ants . . . The whole of the building has been altered, and the
designs carried out under the superintendence of Mr. William
Beverley; and the proscenium and paintings in the dome have
been executed by the celebrated artists, Messrs. Danson and
Sons, and characteristically comprise in the Rotunda—The
Court of Lions in the Alhambra, the Lion Fight of the Moor,
the Fall of the Moor, Last Sigh of the Moor, Almed on the
Banks of the Darro, and the Last Look on the Vermilion
Tower. The proscenium presents in the compartments;

Tacadora, The Toilet of the Queen, Boar Hunt, Rise of the Moor, Battle of Vega, the Gardens of Sinderaxa, and the Tower of Camaras, Arabel architect, forming in all ten illustrations. The decorations are by Mr. Hurwitz, of Southampton Street, Strand; the stage by Mr. Watts, the builder, assisted by Mr. Barnum and Mr. Tucker; the fittings by Mr. Needham, of Her Majesty's and Drury Lane; the mirrors supplied by Mr. Cooke; the gas-fittings and novel lights by Messrs. Stevens and Sons, of the Southwark Bridge Road, under Mr. William Beverley's superintendence; the cooking and culinary apparatus by Mr. Hart, of Wych-street, Strand; and the entire direction of the refreshment department will be under the control of the experienced public caterer, Mr. James Ellis, formerly proprietor of Cremorne Gardens, and who has lately, in Australia, for years, had the merit of originating and superintending undertakings of similar purpose and magnitude. The musical department will be directed by Mr. James Tully, whose celebrity, as a composer of popular music and a thorough student of his art in its popular aspect, will be an assurance of his being well chosen for the post he occupies. The entire building, which has cost over £120,000, will accommodate, with every comfort, 3,500 persons; and the extensive cellarage, arrangements for the supply of every article of the best quality, and engagements made with the most popular professionals, will justify the Proprietor in his expectation that the Royal Alhambra will sustain an existence as a grand Music Hall which will 'ultimately resolve itself into an institution identified with the moral, social, and intellectual well-being of the permanent and casual population of the metropolis of the British Empire'.

The opening is described the following week:

On Monday evening, when the portals were first thrown open for the admission of the public, as many were compelled to be turned away from the doors as had found ingress to the place, and for succeeding hours as many succeeding hundreds were constrained to postpone their visit for another occasion, or to remain satisfied with the most fugitive glimpse of the splendid interior. . . . The arrangements are, as yet, far from being completed, but enough is indicated to show that, when all the departments of the Concert Hall are fully developed, it will supply a most desirable addition in this locality, to the recreations of the people. For the economical outlay of sixpence, the visitor will find himself in comfortable possession of a commodious seat in a magnificently-appointed and admirably-ventilated hall, with every physical refreshment he may desire obtainable at the lowest rates, and of the best quality, and with a rational and pleasing entertainment superadded for his mental delectation. On the opening night, after the National Anthem had been rendered with striking effect, having been sung, not merely by the vocalists engaged at this establishment, but by the chorus of both Drury Lane and Her Majesty's theatres, there was a general call for the enterprising proprietor, who came forward, and bowed his acknowledgements amidst tumultous cheering. . . . Under the direction of Mr. J. H. Tully, a numerous and effective orchestra performed some of the most popular selections from modern Operas; and the vocal portion of the concert was adequately supported by Miss Emma Heywood, Madame Volkener, Mr. E. Rosenthal, and Mr. W. M. Parkinson, who especially signalised themselves in the performance of favourite *morceaux* from Flotow's favourite Opera of *Martha*. Mr. Seymour Carleton, an admirable imitator of the peculiarities of our popular actors, gave his series of professional photographs, to the great delight of the audience; and in a musical *mélange*, Madame Giulani, Miss Graham, Mrs. Caulfield, Miss Campbell, Miss Rosina Collins, and Messrs. Hermanns, Frank Hall, and Tom Matthews successfully appeared, and contributed to their amusement. A blended entertainment of song and ballet, called 'The Gipsy Haunt,' terminated the programme with satisfactory effect.

These were the days of Léotard, 'the Daring Young man on the Flying Trapeze,' who appeared here in 1861.

In October 1861 Smith sold out to William Wild Jnr, who spent over £7,000 in improvements and carried on with music hall bills and circus. He also exhibited dioramas and presented Blondin, fresh from his crossing of Niagara Falls on a tightrope. This regime did not last long, and Wild sold out to Frederick Strange,

who formed a limited company for the management of the
Alhambra. In *The Era* 25 December 1864 he states his aims and
credentials in an advertisement:

Royal Alhambra Palace, Leicester Square. New Management, New Decorations, and Entirely New Arrangements.

Mr. Frederick Strange, late of the Crystal Palace, has the
honour to announce to his Patrons the Public, that he has
become Sole Lessee and Manager of the Royal Alhambra
Palace. In order to adapt this Magnificent Structure (one of
the Architectural beauties of the Metropolis) to the public
requirements of a first-class 'Temple of the Muses,' an
entire Re-decoration and Re-arrangement became an
important necessity.

Under the talented and combined energies of Mr. J. H.
Rowley, the Architect, of 35, Poultry, E.C., from whose design
and superintendence the whole of the works have been
carried out; Mr. Brass, the Builder; Mr. Homann, the
Decorator; and Mr. Chaffin, the Upholsterer; the Royal
Alhambra Palace will be pronounced one of the most magnificent buildings in Europe.

It would be utterly impossible, in the limits of an ordinary
Advertisement, to detail the singular and costly change that
will present itself to the visitor of the New Alhambra, but
some idea may be arrived at when Mr. Strange assures the
Public that, before the doors are opened on Boxing Night, a
sum of over Ten Thousand Pounds will have been expended
in rendering the place worthy of the support of the Music-
loving community. The Establishment has been adapted to
The Lyric and Terpsichorean Art, and will rank second only
to the Royal English Opera itself.

The lighting of the Palace has been entrusted to the
celebrated Defries. There will be Thirty-nine Crystal
Chandeliers, exclusive of a new and wonderful Prismatic
Illuminator suspended from the great Dome, which will
distribute the rays from nearly Thirteen Hundred different
Lights. The Contract price for this astonishing specimen of
Chandelier production is One Thousand Guineas. In order
that nothing may be wanting to please the eye as well as to
charm the ear, the very extensive Stage has been re-built, and

Effects of the most astonishing and truly magnificent character will be produced by Real Water, one of the features being a wonderful Torrent Cascade. Nor have the domestic comforts been forgotten. A Grand Supper Saloon, furnished in the most luxurious style, will invite the patronage of the visitors, whilst the character of the Refreshments will leave nothing to be desired. Wines of specially-approved Vintages, Spirits of unexceptionable quality, and Cigars of the choicest brands, will commend themselves to the Purchasers. Indeed, in this department, the Lessee feels somewhat confident, and refers with pleasurable pride to his successful career at the Crystal Palace.

As has already been intimated, the resources of the establishment will be directed towards the illustration of Music and the Sister Art. Selections from the finest gems of Modern Opera, interwoven with the marvels of Terpsichorean Stars, supported by a Band and Chorus of One Hundred Performers, will it is hoped place the Royal Alhambra Palace far beyond all similar competitors for public favour.

Amongst the Engagements now being completed will be found the following well known and popular Artistes:

Miss Pearce (Prima Donna), Miss Fanny Harrison, Madame Marie Forbes, Madame Palmyre, Mrs. Burgess, and the Misses Rose Palmer, Agnes Villers, Nelly Corri, Sarah Rowe, Edith Villers, Lowther, Withnall, Powell, &c., &c., &c.

Principal Tenors—Mr. H. De Brenner and Mr. Henry Herbert.

Principal Baritone—Mr. Theodore Distin (From the Royal Italian Opera, Covent Garden). and Messrs. St. Albyn, Vito, Jervis, Lincoln, Hunter, Hines, Parre, Lloyd, Henley, Ashton, &c., &c., &c.

But the Sons of Momus have not been overlooked. The leading character will be that brilliant Australian Constellation, The Great Barlow.

This wonderful and unapproachable Negro Melodist and universal Comic Humorist of the very highest polish, will, for the first time in England, after an absence of fourteen years, act in violent motion and commotion the risible faculties of the audience.

The next Wonder is the Marvellous Eccentric Musical Spider, the Laughter Demon of Paris.

This singularly mirth-provoking being will make his first appearance in England, having been expressly engaged for the boards of the Alhambra. 'Le Petit Blondin' will display his balancing precocity on the Low Rope elevated only a few feet above the level of the audience.

One of the great attractions will be the production, upon a scale of unexampled magnificence, of a Grand Ballet, supported by artists selected from the chief Theatres at home and abroad.

Mdlle Bioletti, from the Grand Opera, Paris, has been expressly engaged as *Première Danseuse* for this establishment.

Mr. Strange hopes that his visitors will feel satisfied that their comfort, convenience, and amusement, have been carefully and minutely studied; for unless that end be attained all other expenditure is misapplied; indeed, that one word, 'comfort,' is the great especial charactcristic of the English people.

The Cities of Continental Europe will furnish the Lessee with some of the principal Artistes of his Company, and he ventures to assert that the Entertainments 'will stand alone in their superiority.'

It will thus be seen that this magnificent structure will have its unrivalled capabilities developed to the fullest extent.

In concluding this his first appeal for Public support in his new undertaking, the Lessee hopefully trusts that his anxiety and labours will be met with success, and that in a building capable of accommodating upwards of 4,000 persons he will have the gratifying plcasure of nightly meeting an audience appreciative of the occasion, and encouraging to himself, to enjoy those Entertainments for which the 'Alhambra' is so super-eminently adapted.

The Doors will be thrown open on Boxing Night (December 26th) at Half-past Seven o'clock.

Musical Director—Mr. J. W. Hird. The Selections and Choruses under the Direction of Mr. J. Caulfield, Jun. Leader of the Band—Mr. Gough.

Stage-Director—Mr. H. Boleno. Sole Proprietor—Mr. Frederick Strange. Prices:—Private Boxes (with Admission

through Private House), One Guinea: Reserved Seats 3s.:
Stalls, 2s: Balcony and Grand Hall, 1s.: Upper Balcony and
Hall, 6d.
    Open every Evening at 7.30. Commence at Eight precisely.
                                  VIVAT REGINA.

Once again called the Royal Alhambra Palace, the pit floor was
covered with orderly rows of tables for food and drink and while
this part of the hall was predominantly masculine, ladies were
admitted unescorted to the upper promenade where 'neatly fitted
up bars and stalls, presided over by the most civil and obliging
demoiselles, offer inducements for the lounger to indulge himself'
—in wine and spirits, it is presumed.
    A fourth gallery was added by the original architect and by 1866
Strange was said to have spent £25,000 on improvements.
    The Alhambra began to acquire a Bohemian notoriety,
which was even the envy of Parisian visitors to London. This
moral freedom in the front of house and the dramatic freedom
of the stage productions was to get Strange into constant trouble.
When he took over he immediately inaugurated the spectacular
and lavish but inartistic ballet for which the Alhambra, the
Empire and other music halls were famed in the second half of the
nineteenth century. They filled the gap between the Romantic
ballet of the 1840's and the advent of the first Russian companies
in the immediate pre-war years. During this period the opera
houses ignored ballet, which could only be seen at the music
halls. Of these the Alhambra was the best London house in
which to show it.
    In the 1860's the legality of the performace of ballet under a
music and dancing licence was extremely doubtful, and in January
1865 a group of lessees of London theatres, anxious to preserve
their privileged position as holders of licences from the Lord
Chamberlain for the performance of 'stage plays,' obtained a
summons against Strange. The Marlborough Street magistrate
decided that the Alhambra ballets involved 'pantomimic action'
and were therefore 'stage plays' which required a licence from the
Lord Chamberlain, and imposed a nominal fine, but this decision
was reversed on appeal to Quarter Sessions. In 1866 a Select
Committee of the House of Commons was appointed to examine
the state of the law on theatrical licences and in the evidence which

he gave to the committee in April, Strange stated that he had recently been summonsed three times and had won his case each time. The committee recommended that it was 'not desirable to continue the existing restrictions which prevent music halls from giving theatrical entertainments,' but no change was made in the law until 1912 when the halls came under the Jurisdiction of the Lord Chamberlain and the 'perpetual series of conflicts' at the Alhambra to which Strange had referred in his evidence continued.

The different construction of the building was part of the cause of dissatisfaction for, as opposed to legitimate theatres, at least one of the saloons now commanded a view of the stage, while from the other vantage points it was possible for a promenader 'to take a view of his fellow-spectators, which is totally unlike anything to be found in an ordinary theatre.'

In December 1866 Strange presented a ballet entitled *Where's the Police?* which was described in the press as 'to all intents and purposes, the comic scene of a pantomime.' Fresh summonses were granted against him, the Marlborough Street magistrate decided that this piece *was* a pantomime, and in June 1867 Strange was fined £240.

While preparations for his Christmas production were in hand Strange organised a 'Grand Bal D'Opéra' for 16 December 1867, with the pit cleared of its tables for dancing. Rivière conducted an orchestra of one hundred performers and there were twelve Masters of Ceremonies. That such 'Continental Amusements' were regarded with suspicion is reflected in the notice it received in *The Illustrated Sporting and Theatrical News* on 12 December:

Prejudice and mistaken notions of morality have caused these brilliant *réunions* to be somewhat coldly viewed by the slow going portion of the British public; but Mr. Strange has exhibited such taste and discrimination, combined with sound judgment, in the magnificent spectacle which greeted our admiring eyes on Monday evening, that the minds of the most fastidious must be disabused of such antiquated ideas. Gorgeous dresses and lovely forms combined to make the scene truly enchanting; and the dancing was simply worthy of the orchestra, which breathed forth most 'voluptuous music,' and was quite sufficient to tempt an anchorite to join in the exciting whirl. It is needless to comment upon the elaborate decorations, which contributed in no small degree to render the hall absolutely entrancing; it will be quite sufficient to say that they were perfect; and those who, after joining in the 'soul-inspiring dance,' sought to refresh the inward man, were enabled to gratify appetites the most wayward, by partaking of a supper worthy of Lucullus. Taken altogether, it was a fête most brilliantly and successfully carried out; and the scene so artistically developed by our artist will give some idea of the pleasurable hours which all enjoyed; and when at last the votaries of the volatile goddess dispersed, and sought the 'dreamy couch,' it was with the wish that Mr. Strange might long live thus to cater for the enjoyment of the public, and, ere long, to give a repetition of the *Bal Masque* at the Alhambra.

Ballet continued to form part of the Alhambra's productions (although 'pantomimic action' was presumably excluded), but at the Middlesex Sessions in October 1870 the police opposed the renewal of Strange's music and dancing licence on grounds of indecency. They alleged that four ladies, the Collonna Troupe, had 'danced the Parisienne Quadrille', or ordinary *'Can Can'*; one of the performers (Sara Wright, 'Wiry Sal') had raised her foot 'higher than her head several times towards the public,' an action which had been 'much applauded.' Despite the fact that the Prince and Princess of Wales had previously witnessed the *Can Can*, danced by Finette in 1868 at the Lyceum (she was later at the Alhambra itself) without complaint, the magistrates agreed with the police and the licence for dancing was not renewed.

Strange immediately presented a series of promenade concerts. The Franco-Prussian War was still proceeding and when two Germans sang *Die Wacht am Rhein* they were greeted by cries of *A bas les Prussiens*. 'A vigorous contest of voices ensued', and a French couple then sang the *Marseillaise* with much the same result, 'but the English, who represented about three-fourths of the audience, drowned the opposition of both sides in rounds of applause' and ultimately the performance was concluded by a Frenchman singing *Rule, Britannia* and waving a Union Jack. The entertainment was regarded as 'highly successful', but in

January 1871 Strange was again fined at Marlborough Street Police Court for infringement of the licensing regulations, and the Theatre was closed.

During the closure Strange obtained, in April, a licence from the Lord Chamberlain for stage plays. (The original music and dancing licence was not again granted till 1884.)

The tables in the pit were cleared away and replaced by seats. A programme of operetta, ballet and variety soon superseded simply by one act farces and opera bouffe, generously interspersed with often excellent ballets, became the staple fare for the next decade.

Strange re-opened as the Royal Alhambra Theatre of Varieties on 24 April 1871. The name was changed again to the Royal Alhambra Theatre in 1872, and during the next ten years various combinations of title were used, including the Alhambra Theatre, the Alhambra Theatre Royal and the Theatre Royal Alhambra. The opening is reviewed in *The Era* 30 April 1871:

The attempt of the Licensing Magistrates to rob the public of the magnificent spectacles, in providing which the Alhambra stood alone and unrivalled, has been frustrated, and on Monday evening, under the new name, and with the Lord Chamberlain's licence, it reopened its doors to an eager crowd, which rapidly filled the splendid edifice in every part, and finally overflowed into the streets, hundreds, for whom not even standing room could be found, being turned from the doors. What wonder! A programme more gigantic or more attractive could scarcely be devised, including, as it did, farce, comic opera, the performance of the world-renowned band, and, greatest attraction of all, the ballet. Before touching upon the entertainments we may remark that the auditorium of the Alhambra has undergone a complete metamorphosis. The rows of tables which filled the basement have given way to a number of elegant and luxurious chairs, as tasteful as they are comfortable. The refreshment bars have disappeared from their wonted sites, and are now to be found in snug nooks and sly corners out of view of the stage. Smoking is conspicuous by its absence, except in the large and commodious smoke-room, formerly known as the supper-rooms. The attractions of the place are thus mainly to be concentrated upon the stage, without sacrificing the desires of those who seek for creature comforts of another kind. The prices, except to the elegant row of stalls to which we have alluded, remain the same, so that an entertainment which, for diversity and excellence, can scarcely be surpassed, is placed within reach of the humblest artisan as well as of the higher classes of society. Farce, as we have said, is included in the programme, and on Monday a sketch of this description, by Mr. F. Allen, and entitled *Oh! My Head*, was produced for the first time. The whole of the performers acquitted themselves admirably, and if a modicum of praise is due to any one in excess of this general remark it is to Miss Minnie Sidney, whose pretty face and vivacious manner appeared to be highly acceptable to the audience. The farce was followed by the appearance of the celebrated Praeger family in their Tyrolean entertainment. The popularity they have deservedly won elsewhere is not likely to suffer diminution here, their clever instrumentation and admirable vocalism being greeted with the heartiest of cheering. The 'Cats' duet,' with which their entertainment concluded, was given with most humorous effect, and we could scarcely help wishing that the tabbies who 'make night hideous' to London sleepers could be taught a lesson out of their musical *répertoire*. The comic opera entitled *The Crimson Scarf*, which was produced, has been written by Mr. H. B. Farnie, with music composed by Mr. J. E. Legouix.

The band—well it is almost as difficult to say anything new of the Alhambra band as of the Alhambra ballets. Its excellences have again and again been pointed out. Its performances would provide a good evening's entertainment unaided, and we must rest content now to chronicle the fact that its magnificent, soul-stirring playing, under the able direction of Jules Rivière, of the prize competition, entitled 'The Battle Field,' which everyone should hear, afforded an amount of delight which found expression in the most enthusiastic cheering. The ballet we have left to the last, not because it is least worthy of notice, but because we have put off as long as possible an attempt to describe that which is almost indescribable. Two exhibitions of this character are now given, the first, entitled *The Beauties of the Harem*, and the

second, *Puella; or, the Fairy and the Evil Genii*. Of course the
new ballets exceed in splendour anything before attempted.
They always do, and, from what we have seen hitherto, there
is nothing so gorgeous and nothing so costly which we may
expect to find placed upon this stage. The *corps de ballet* is as
numerous, as efficient, and let us add as comely as ever, and a
star of the first magnitude has been secured for *première
danseuse* in the person of Mdlle. Rita Sangalli. The appearance
of this lady, of whom report had spoken highly, was awaited
with some eagerness; and the encouraging cheer which
greeted her as in the first-named ballet she bounded on to the
stage grew in intensity as the piece progressed, until at last
her remarkably clever, graceful, and novel movements,
elicited a perfect hurricane of applause. We have used the term
novel advisedly, for it is seldom we find anything which is
unconventional among dancers. But many of Mdlle. Sangalli's
steps are new, at least to the English spectator. Her comely
looks, not less than her undoubted accomplishments, are
sure to gain her a host of admirers, and we are pleased to hail
her first appearance as a triumphant success. In the second
ballet—in which she also appears—she is ably assisted by
Messrs. Raymond and Kellino, the latter gentleman, who
appears as the Evil Geni, displaying a remarkable aptitude
for turning somersaults, jumping through spring traps, and
other feats of agility. The dresses in both ballets are superb,
and the curious effect produced by the mingling of the many
brilliant but harmonising colours, in the complicated mazes
which Mr. Milano has so ingeniously devised for the *corps de
ballet*, was as pleasing as it was novel. In the first ballet the
scenery is magnificent by its very simplicity; and in the
second, in which we have woodland glades and fairy dells
and mystic caverns, ending with a Transformation scene,
which would employ more superlatives than we have at
command, Messrs. Grieve and Son, the artists, have but
added another to the many proofs we have already been
afforded of their acknowledged skill.

Strange left the Alhambra as manager in 1872, his policy having
brought about his downfall, and he died in obscurity in 1879.
He was succeeded by John Baum, acting for the Alhambra

B

Theatre Company Limited, and Variety was dropped from the bills. Baum was followed by Joseph Cave, who was succeeded in 1877 by Charles Morton. William Holland took over in 1881. During most of this period Georges Jacobi was the musical director and Wilhelm began to make his name as a designer and writer of ballets and the firm of costumiers under the designer Alias commenced its long association with the theatre.

The following comic operas were among those produced:

Le Roi Carotte (Offenbach, 1872); *The Black Crook* (Clay, 1872); *La Belle Hélène* (Offenbach, 1873); *Whittington* (Offenbach, 1875); *Le Voyage dans la Lune* (Offenbach, 1876); *Die Fledermaus* (Strauss, 1877); *Orphée aux Enfers* (Offenbach, 1877); *La Fille de Madam Angot* (Lecocq, 1877); *The Grand Duchess* (Offenbach, 1878); *Geneviève de Brabant* (Offenbach, 1878); *La Périchole* (Offenbach, 1878); *La Fille du Tambour Major* (Offenbach, 1880), and many others.

These were the days of the English opera bouffe stars, Kate Santley, Amy Sheridan, Julia Matthews, Emily Soldene and the French importations Cornelie D'Anka and Selina Dolaro. The ballets, usually of considerable length which were interpolated in the operettas, were led by either the Ballerinas Petoldi, Pettri or Palladin, with a strong supporting company and *corps de ballet*.

A full history and list of the ballets of this period and later, at the Alhambra, is told in *The Alhambra Ballet* by Ivor Guest (1949), with an additional list of all the comic opera productions.

In the autumn of 1881 the Theatre closed for re-decoration and re-construction. The re-opening on 2 December was reported:

After being closed for a short time for alterations the Alhambra has been re-opened, and presents so greatly improved an appearance that it is clear those entrusted with the execution of the work must have made the best of their time. As a matter of fact, it seems that the result so satisfactorily attained has only been achieved by the simple process of working night and day, and great credit is due to the contractor, Mr. Deputy Brass, of Old Street, for the manner in which the details have been carried out. The improvements effected largely concern the arrangements for egress, which are

now said to be absolutely perfect, but several important
changes have also been made in various parts of the building,
and the decorations have been renewed, so that the general
aspect is now extremely pleasing. Amongst other points of
interest we may especially note the introduction of the
electric light, for which an exceedingly beautiful Turkish
lantern has been constructed by Messrs. Pitman and Son,
of Newgate Street. The entertainment with which the house
has been re-opened is a revised version of the famous spectacle,
The Black Crook; and familiar as the frequenters of the
Alhambra are with magnificent stage effects, it is seldom that
anything approaching in splendour the present display has
been put before them. The ballets are especially beautiful,
and of these there are three, each of which has its own
peculiar form of beauty to commend it to attention.

The changes also included a widening of the proscenium and the
removal of two of the iron columns supporting the roof. The
Survey of London, Volume 31, gives the following details:

Plans submitted to the Metropolitan Board of Works in
November 1882 show how the Panopticon building had been
finally adapted to function as a music hall. The two eastern
bays of the rotunda were demolished to provide a proscenium
opening to the deep but narrow stage, formed out of the
large lecture hall. In the auditorium the ground floor was
divided into fauteuils, stalls, pit and an extensive promenade.
A range of twenty-four boxes was constructed as a mezzanine
below the first gallery, this becoming a balcony with five
stepped rows of seats. The second gallery was provided with
five stepped rows of benches, and behind the horseshoe arches
of the rotunda, an upper gallery of three rows was constructed,
giving a steep and restricted view of the stage.

After all the name changes it was as the Alhambra Theatre,
plain and simple, that it was almost completely destroyed by fire
on 7 December 1882. *The Era*, 9 December, reported:

On Thursday morning, at a few minutes after one, a fire
broke out in the Alhambra Theatre, Leicester Square, which
has resulted in the total destruction of that popular place of
public amusement. The fire was first discovered by a detective

named Bowden, as he was coming off duty and returning to the Police Section House in Leicester Square, where he resides. The detective, on approaching the theatre, perceived a volume of smoke issuing from three of the windows in the second row, and at once raised an alarm. With some difficulty he succeeded in arousing the resident fireman, who was stationed in the theatre in accordance with a regulation observed in buildings of that description. On being admitted to the interior of the building, the detective was joined by one of the officials attached to the Alhambra, and together they proceeded to examine the rooms. They soon ascertained that the fire had originated in the dress circle of the theatre, for on reaching this part they saw a dense volume of smoke and flame rolling upwards. While Bowden and his companion took steps to secure the books, the fireman proceeded to get his wife and two children out of the theatre, and then directed his attention to the flames, which he endeavoured to subdue by means of a private hose on the premises. All his efforts, however, proved unavailing, and, indeed, so rapidly did the conflagration spread that in an incredibly short space of time he was compelled to make his escape by forcing his way through the flames. The building then appeared to be in one fierce blaze, and by the time the first contingent of the Fire Brigade arrived upon the scene the doomed theatre was wrapped in flames almost from floor to roof. The alarm of fire that had been given soon roused the neighbourhood, and crowds of spectators rapidly rushed to the scene of the conflagration, and blocked in compact mass every avenue of approach to the square in which the theatre stood. It was not long before a powerful body of police from the A, C, E, and S divisions, under Superintendent Dunlop, arrived upon the scene, and were drawn up in a strong and impenetrable cordon round the square and across the thoroughfares leading to the back of the burning building. Throughout the night the police acted with admirable coolness, and succeeded in keeping back the dense crowds collected at every point of vantage. This was fortunate, as not only did it enable the firemen to accomplish their arduous and difficult task unimpeded, but it also saved the public from the risk and peril to which they would have been exposed from the falling debris. When the alarm was once given, no long interval elapsed before the fire-engines were on the spot. First to put in an appearance was the Chandos Street engine, which was quickly followed by the one from King Street and nearly twenty others. Notwithstanding the promptitude displayed on the part of the Fire Brigade authorities, it was evident by the time the steamers got fairly to work that the theatre was irretrievably doomed to destruction. Twenty minutes after the time of the raising of the alarm the building was one raging mass of fire. Huge volumes of smoke, mingling with a column of flame, swept upwards from the burning pile, lighting up with a ruddy glow the houses in the square and the vicinity. The scene was one of terrible grandeur. The engines played upon the blazing pile from front and rear, but no visible effect was for a long time produced. Still the flames belched forth, and still the smoke hung overhead in a dense canopy relieved by myriads of brilliant sparks with which the air was thickened. The fire had probably not been raging more than half an hour when the roof fell in with a loud crash, an event which was followed by the upheaval of a gigantic column of forked flame, which seemed to pierce even the leaden mass above, and lit up the neighbourhood with startling effect. Although the roof had apparently fallen in, the two towers which flank the building north and south continued to remain intact, and it speaks well for the strength and solidity of the masonry when it is mentioned that they did not succumb to the flames, although burning furiously for several hours. Even when the fire had nearly burnt itself out, and when Leicester Square and Soho had again lapsed into comparative darkness, the towers were blazing still, licked by circling wreaths of flame, and shone out like beacons from the smoky obscurity above. So swift was the fire in its career of destruction, so complete was the catastrophe, that time was not permitted to save anything from the theatre. The furniture and fittings, as well as the dresses and properties of those engaged at the theatre, all shared one common fate; while it was at once evident that the theatre was doomed, and consequently the efforts of the brigade were to a great extent directed to preventing the fire spreading to the adjoining houses. Under the able superintendence of

Captain Shaw, who arrived on the spot with praiseworthy promptitude, a steady stream of water was poured upon the back portion of the burning theatre from steamers stationed in Castle Street, Bear Street, and Green Street . . .

Despite all the efforts made, notwithstanding the tremendous volumes of water directed against the flames, the fire still raged with fierce intensity. The central flagstaff fell from the roof into the roadway beneath, and snapped in twain like so much matchwood. Fortunately the firemen manning the escapes and directing the streams of water below had ample notice of the impending downfall, and were thus enabled to withdraw to a safe distance. One of the small flagstaffs subsequently fell, and remained partially attached to the roof, and while in that position was promptly secured by a fireman, who boldly mounted the escape and essayed the dangerous duty. On the southern flank of the theatre the flames never at any time spread to the adjoining house, though it was at one time in great jeopardy. On the north, however, the case was different. Here, when once the fire had taken a strong hold, and had entered into undisputed possession of the ill-fated theatre, the flames soon spread to the roof of the adjoining house, which is fitted up as a Turkish bath. Before the fire could be got under the upper portion of the house was completely gutted, while the next building, which is used as a police-station house, where a number of unattached members of the force reside, was considerably damaged by water, though it did not actually catch fire.

About half-past three it became evident that the water was gradually gaining the mastery over the flames in the northern wing of the theatre which faces the square. Although intermittent tongues of fire darted out and flickered here and there, yet beyond all question the work of destruction had been completed, and all that was inflammable had been destroyed. In the centre, and also the southern wing, however, the fire still raged, and beyond the blackened masses of masonry which stood out gaunt and skeleton-like, the flames still leaped, while one could hear the crash of falling timber and watch the progress of the fire. Yet even here by degrees the fire began to burn itself out, aided of course by the torrents of water being poured on the building, and by four o'clock the fire was finally got under. The theatre, however, stands gutted from roof to floor. The skeleton masonry stands, but not a solitary stick of furniture is left; and all that remains of a splendid interior, with its lavish appointments, is a few charred, broken rafters of the beams, sufficiently stout to resist the all-devouring flames.

Strange to say, while the destruction in the inside of the building has thus been so terribly complete, the exterior decorations of the walls and the entrance to the theatre have almost altogether escaped damage. The ornamental doorway remains practically intact, beyond whatever injury may have been inflicted by smoke and water, while the boards on which are posted the announcements have, strange to say, passed through the ordeal unscathed. As to the origin of the fire, that still remains a complete mystery. The performance took place as usual on Wednesday night, and when the building was left all was then apparently safe. When the fire was discovered, the startling and almost incredible rapidity with which the flames spread over the whole building and clutched it in their deadly grip rendered its preservation impossible.

Mr. William Holland, the manager of the Alhambra, states that the fire was first discovered in the balcony stalls by the firemen employed on the establishment. These men immediately set three hydrants to work, and also closed all the iron doors in the hope of checking the conflagration. Their efforts were, however, of little avail, for the flames spread with a rapidity with which they were unable to cope. Mr. Holland was the last to leave the premises, at about half-past eleven. Previous to doing so all lights and fires were put out. It appears that the only portion of the building saved from the flames is the painting room and Mr. Holland's own office. The whole of the valuable wardrobe which is estimated at £10,000, is destroyed, but fortunately the dresses for the new piece, which was in rehearsal, and was, oddly enough, to be called *King Comet; or, Love of the Flame and Icicle*, had not been delivered. The building and contents were insured for £34,000 in the North British, the Royal, and some other offices. More than 400 persons are, in consequence of the catastrophe, thrown out of employment.

The books, containing what may fairly be called the

archives of the theatre, with all the orchestral scores, were
saved by the bill inspector, Mr. Charles Yates, who, living
near, entered the building and threw the contents of the
library from the window. The musicians having large
instruments, which they are almost compelled to leave behind
them at their own personal risk, have been losers in some
cases to a severe extent. Four double-basses, each worth £60,
have been destroyed. The kettle-drums also sacrificed,
belonged to the theatre.

On Thursday afternoon, although the interior presented a
forlorn and ruinous aspect, no fire could be seen, but the
brigade, knowing that a large incandescent mass still glowed
beneath a blackened crust of charred beams and wreckage,
continued pouring streams of water into the middle of the
area. The auditorium was in form of a Spanish or Byzantine
amphitheatre; and the shapes of Saracenic arches against the
bare and desolate walls have a strange barbaric look. A
curiously suggestive feature is the strange entanglement of
crumpled iron, one huge girder being bent into the rough
form of a horse-shoe. The Hotel Cavour adjoining the theatre
escaped with but slight damage, and M. Oscar Philippe
will be able to carry on his business as usual.

Mr. William Holland, the Alhambra manager, writes that
the directors met on Thursday morning, and instructed their
architect to prepare plans for the immediate rebuilding of the
theatre in such a manner as, while preserving the old beautiful
lines, will embrace all those improvements for the comfort
and safety of the public which experience has suggested. A
movement has already been made to raise a fund for the relief
of the large number of persons suddenly thrown out of
employment by the burning of the Alhambra at a time when
there is no possibility of their finding employment again until
pantomimes have run their course.

The proprietor obtained the freehold of the site after the fire,
and plans for a new theatre were put in hand, with Messrs. Perry
and Reed in charge. They had been the architects responsible for
the 1881 reconstructions. The new theatre was ready for re-
opening on 3 December 1883. *The Era* 10 November gave a
preview of the new theatre:

The new building has been designed in the same style as the old one, but most important modifications have been made in the mode of construction, and in the materials employed. The whole of the floors, galleries, roofs, box divisions, stairs, &c., throughout, before, and behind the scenes, except, of course, the stage, are constructed of Portland cement concrete carried on iron girders, columns, and brackets, which are themselves again deeply embedded in the concrete. To improve the acoustic qualities an under dome of iron and fibrous plaster of very different section to its predecessor has been formed with the most satisfactory result, and singers who have tested the building describe it as 'simply perfect' for sound, easy to sing in, and allowing, in spite of its enormous size, all the *piano* passages to be distinctly heard in every part. The whole of the constructive woodwork of the stage has been painted with asbestos paint, which renders the wood entirely uninflammable. The auditorium will be lighted by one of Strode and Co.'s patent ventilating sun burners, which will have 819 jets, giving a light of upwards of 12,000 standard candles. It will be fixed in the centre of the domed ceiling, and be surrounded by a very handsome grating of pierced iron-work, designed by the architects, which, in addition to the removal of the products of combustion of this very large quantity of gas, will also perfectly ventilate the auditorium. The only sun burner approaching this one in size was made and fixed by Messrs. Strode and Co., at the Michaeloff Theatre, in St. Petersburg, some years ago. In addition to this sun-burner, which will certainly be a very prominent feature, Messrs. Strode and Co. are also constructing and fitting up arrangements of rings, or coronas, of gas jets for illuminating the turrets, which will be lighted instantaneously by the flash-light arrangements so successfully applied by them at the Princess's, Savoy, Strand, Glasgow, Belfast, and at many other theatres in London and the country. These works are being superintended by Mr John Bartlett. Messrs. Vaughan and Brown, gas engineers, of Kirby Street and Farringdon Road, London, E.C., are executing the whole of the other gas arrangements from special designs by the architects—viz., the massive chandeliers and brackets for the auditorium, passages, and entrances. The stage they are also

B*

fitting with their patent flash-light system, which enables
the gas-man at the index-plate to light or extinguish the
whole of the stage arrangements instantaneously. They are
also fitting their improved registered water-joints, and also
large holders and tanks for the lime-light. The whole of the
works are under the personal superintendence of Mr.
Vaughan and their out-door engineer, S. Pemberton. The
passages, stairs and exits have all been made to suit the very
stringent requirements of the Board of Works; and the whole
of the main front consists practically of one door, which will
be shielded by an iron and glass portico extending the length
of the building and projecting to the pavement kerb. The
dimensions of the building are from the front of the curtain to
the back wall, 82 ft. The internal width of the auditorium is
96 ft., and clear of the box fronts, 60 ft.; and the diameter of
the dome is 73 ft. The height from the floor level to the
underside of the dome is 81 ft., and the gross height from the
basement floor to the top of the cupola, 116 ft. The dimensions
of the stage are from curtain to wall, 41 ft.; clear of the wing
walls, 62 ft.; and the proscenium opening, 40 ft. by 40 ft.
The works have been carried out by Mr. W. Brass in twenty-
seven weeks from the date of commencement, from the
designs of Messrs. Perry and Reed, of the Adelphi, architects
to the company; Professor Kennedy acting as consulting
Engineer.'

On 8 December *The Era* gave an account of the opening performance:

Again the Alhambra has opened its doors to enthusiastic
crowds. What was a mere ruin has once more, thanks to the
energy and enterprise of the directors, become a home of
popular entertainment. With true British pluck and spirit,
they did not weep over lost tiers, but, having 'stood fire,' they
met a renewed charge with determination and courage, and in
a space of time really brief, considering the work that had to
be done, the new Alhambra has risen from its ashes with every
promise of enjoying the popularity of yore. Changes of a very
important kind have been made, and, since the Demon Fire
is greatly feared by modern audiences, we noticed with
much satisfaction the many and large doorways which could

in a moment be thrown open for the exit of a panic-stricken crowd. None need apprehend danger at the Alhambra now. The accommodation for a large audience is enormous, and it has been fully tested during the week. Visitors will notice that, while the general lines of the building are preserved, there is some loss of the grace, quaintness, and picturesqueness of the old design. The snug private boxes round the first tier have given place to a dress circle. Possibly some frequenters of the theatre would have preferred the old plan, but the change has doubtless been made for sufficient reasons. At present it must be confessed the solid and massive columns and the huge staircases have a somewhat bare appearance, but as there is still work to be done in the decorative department, we shall be enabled to judge better of the ultimate effect when all is complete. One immense advantage will be immediately recognised. The improved stage, enlarged and fitted with mechanical appliances, capable of spectacular scenes of the most elaborate kind, is certainly calculated to sustain and even increase the reputation of the Alhambra for gorgeous scenic displays. In the course of the performance last Monday evening the ample capabilities of the stage and its remarkable mechanical resources were fully revealed, greatly to the satisfaction of the audience, and during the week all the splendid effects have been presented with still greater completeness, and with the advantage of ending the performance half-an-hour earlier. The new act-drop is characteristic and appropriate, and, when drawn up, the height and width of the stage enable every visitor to see the performance with comfort. The orchestra is also improved, and the lighting of the theatre is sufficiently brilliant. The performance on Monday evening commenced with the National Anthem, after which an address, written by Mr. Vernon De Montgomery, was spoken with excellent effect by Mr. Fred Mervin. We must especially congratulate the directors upon the choice of a piece entirely due to the talents of an English author and composer. When we find that Parisian plays, 'with the naughtiness cut out,' have not enough dramatic merit left to make them acceptable to the public, it is just and right to welcome an author and composer who can produce a work interesting and effective, yet absolutely free from French uncleanness. *The Golden Ring* is as pure a production as ever was placed upon the stage. It is witty, fanciful, and poetical; but the wit has no sting, the fancy has no double meaning, and the poetry is not sensual. It is as innocent as a nursery tale and as pleasant, reviving the kindly fairy tales of our youth, and blending with spirits of Good and Evil and weird unearthly forms, that genial element of everyday life in which Mr. G. R. Sims shines more than any author of our day, and when we consider the extreme difficulty there is in working out a fairy story to blend with the requirements of the Alhambra, it must be frankly declared that Mr. Sims has done his share in *The Golden Ring* with remarkable skill, and has presented a piece in every way up to the Alhambra standard. He has been careful not to overload his book with dialogue, and his lyrics are as fresh and tuneful as any composer could desire. Of the music of Mr. Frederic Clay we can also speak in warm terms of commendation, as we are justified in declaring it to be the most important he has yet composed. Several of the melodies and choruses, and the concerted finales and ballet music, would not disgrace any opera house in Europe.'

After telling the plot and praising the cast, which included Marion Hood, Constance Loseby, Ansley Cook, Fred Mervin and G. A. Honey, the notice goes on:

We must praise the brilliant scenery and commend the exertions of the orchestra warmly. The conductor, M. Rivière, is admirably qualified for his post, and Mr. Viotti Collins is a first violin of the greatest merit. The entire production reflects great credit upon the management, and there is ample evidence that the valuable labours of Mr. William Holland have not been wasted. The Alhambra is evidently well equipped for the coming holiday season.

Despite the statements that the new theatre was a complete re-building, pictures and photographs prove that the original Leicester Square front was retained and restored. The *Survey of London* says:

The party walls were largely rebuilt and a more efficient stage block was constructed, with a working area of some 62 feet wide and 39 feet deep. The surviving iron columns and horseshoe arches of the rotunda were incorporated in a system of partly cantilevered tiers strongly constructed in iron and concrete, and the public parts of the house were largely built of incombustible materials. The auditorium now contained three lyre-fronted tiers—a dress circle of five rows with seven boxes in each arm, an upper circle with five rows in the centre and three in each arm, and a balcony of two rows in a central extension at the back. Seats were provided for 1,800, but the extensive promenades round the stalls and the first two tiers brought the total capacity of the house up to 4,000.

The old interior was deliberately recalled by the Saracenic decorations of the new auditorium, in the elaborate geometrical fret panels of the balcony fronts, the slender cast-iron columns with their honeycomb capitals and elaborate brackets above, and in the ring of horseshoe arches supporting the ceiling, now formed with a cove below the perforated drum of a large saucer-dome, its centre opening to a lantern skylight.

The theatre now had a stage door in Hunts Court, off Castle Street (now Charing Cross Road). The new theatre once more became a music hall, the Alhambra Theatre of Varieties, in October 1884, when the managers were at long last again granted a music and dancing licence at the Middlesex Sessions. From then on variety with two spectacular ballets became the main feature until the advent of revue.

In April 1888 the theatre was again re-decorated, the work being undertaken by Messrs. Campbell Smith & Co., who furnished this account of the re-decorations:

The character of the interior of the dome has been entirely altered by the substitution of a cerulean blue, in several shades, graduating in lines of tint from the base to the summit, the sun-burner there being framed in an elaborate circle of colours, while an Alhambresque frieze in *carton pierre* forms a base, the large cove being ornamented with characteristic work in plaster, coloured. The arches have been filled in with Moorish fretwork, surrounding several panels of stained and illuminated glass. The background of the iron railings, forming the points of the various tiers of circles are painted in a mosaic effect of colour, and the ceilings themselves have been gilded and are now surmounted by polished brass handrails. A change has been effected in the second circle, the iron and concrete ceiling having been covered with *carton pierre*, while a frieze supports the exterior railings. New Alhambresque capitals have been affixed to all the columns. The large open screen facing the second Saloon has also been filled with fretwork and stained glass. The saloon itself has been kept Arab in character, as lending itself to rather bolder treatment than the actual Moorish or Alhambresque and is in quite a different key of colour to the promenade on this floor. Stalactites, rising in tiers, have been affixed to the ceiling of the first circle, and the walls panelled with *carton pierre* and mirrors. The grand staircase and box-office vestibule have been treated in Diaper work in gold and colours, and fitted with stained glass windows. Messrs. Campbell Smith & Co. are the designers and contractors for the whole of the internal and external decorations. The work has been carried out under the supervision of Mr. E. Clark—Architect.

In the summer of 1892, now calling itself the Alhambra Theatre again, a further partial re-construction took place, of which Messrs. Clark & Pollard were the architects.

On 19 December 1892 Hollingshead 'constructed' *Aladdin* as a ballet on a magnificent scale, and we read that a glass curtain was introduced, composed of some 75,000 glass facets held together with 24 miles of wire.

In 1893 Albert Gilmer became manager, but he was succeeded the following year by Alfred Moul. In 1896 future events cast their shadows before them. A topical film of the Derby of that year was shown the day after the race was run at Epsom. Between 1896 and 1898 Robert Paul, the British film pioneer, produced dramas and love stories on the roof of the Alhambra and showed the films in the music hall below!

In 1897, the Jubilee year, the theatre was honoured with nearly a score of royal visits; in this year also a new entrance for booked seats and office block, in the old idiom, was built in Charing Cross Road: the proprietors having acquired some property backing on the theatre. It was built to the design of W. M. Brutton. John Hollingshead writing in *The Tatler* commented:

> The new and lofty Moorish building in the Charing Cross Road, nearly completed, which is like a solid piece of Seville transported to London, is not a Turkish mosque nor a new Jewish synagogue, but a much-needed extension of the Alhambra Palace Theatre, and a new frontage on the eastern side intended to rival the old western frontage in Leicester Square. No one can accuse the directors of hot-headed haste in their architectural developments. When the new entrances, saloons, board-rooms, offices, &c., are opened, the Alhambra will have been in existence, as a public company, more than thirty years, and as a theatre of varieties more than forty years.

This frontage eventually became the main entrance, which was transferred from Leicester Square in 1922.

In 1898 Moul retired and C. Dundas Slater succeeded. G. W. Byng became musical director at this time.

At an Annual General Meeting of shareholders in the early part of 1902 Alfred Moul was invited by shareholders and directors to again assume control, and within a few days returned to be installed as chairman of the Company. One of his first achievements in that position was to engage Landon Ronald as musical director.

Ballet continued to attract, and successes of the early twentieth century included: *Soldiers of the Queen* (1900); *Britannia's Realm* (1902); *The Devil's Forge* (1903); *All the Year Round* (1904); *Parisiana* (1905); *The Queen of Spades* (1907); *Femina* (1910) and *The Dance Dream* and *1830* (1911).

Many famous solo continental dancers made their appearance here, but gradually more prominence was given to spectacular musical and acrobatic acts, suitable for the large house, rather than the solo music hall singer or comedian.

Between 1906 and May 1907 a partial re-construction and a complete and elaborate re-decoration took place, all carried through without the theatre being closed for a single night. And again in 1912 another re-construction under Frank Matcham took place. Moul assumed the dual task of being chairman and managing director, and the general manager from 1911 to 1915 was H. G. Bryan.

As the public succumbed to the Russian dancers who began to come to London, first singly or in pairs, then in 1911 with the full Diaghilev company, so English ballet at the Alhambra, and later the Empire, declined.

Revue haɑ begun to take hold on a lighter theatre-going public, originally at the Empire where it was first seen in 1906, and at the Alhambra when it came under the direction of André Charlot in 1912. *Kill that Fly!* was the first of the new craze on 14 October. It was followed by *8d.-a-Mile* (1913); *Keep Smiling!* (1913), which introduced Lee White; *Not Likely* (1914), which featured Beatrice Lillie and Connie Ediss; *5164 Gerrard* (1915); *Now's the Time* (1915).

In January 1916 Oswald Stoll acquired the Alhambra and in April *The Bing Boys are Here* with Violet Loraine, George Robey and Alfred Lester was produced. This 'Picture of London life in seven panels' adapted from the French was one of the outstanding successes of the war years, and ran for 378 performances. *Round the Map* (1917) followed, and *The Bing Boys on Broadway* (1918) continued the adventures begun in *The Bing Boys are Here*, and ran 562 performances, longer than its more famous predecessor.

In 1919 Serge Diaghilev gave a season of Russian ballets and *La Boutique Fantasque* and *The Three Cornered Hat* were first produced. 1920 and 1921 saw George Robey reigning over the Alhambra with *Johnny Jones (and his Sister Sue)*, 'a Robey salad with a musical dressing', (1920), and *Robey en Casserole* (1921). There was another Diaghilev season in 1921, and a milestone in the history of ballet was set up by the first English production of *The Sleeping Princess*.

It seemed as if the Alhambra was coming back into its own as a home of ballet, but this impression was unfortunately not to last for long. In February 1922 the theatre was closed for a complete overhaul, and Variety, three times daily, returned on 10 April, with a weekly change of bill.

It was in 1923 that Stoll booked the touring revue, *Mr Tower of London* to fill in an odd week. It made the name of Gracie Fields, its star.

In 1925 and 1926 the Royal Variety performances were given here. In 1929 Primo Carnera gave exhibition boxing bouts and then the theatre 'went over' to the cinema for a time with the showing of *All Quiet on the Western Front*, followed by the new craze—'Talkies.'

A successful return to the legitimate was made in August 1931, when *Waltzes from Vienna* started a run of 607 performances (a large false proscenium designed for this production lasted out the life of the theatre). After some failures, de Basil's *Ballets Russes de Monte Carlo* began on 4 July 1933 what proved a record season; they originally came for three weeks and remained for four months, and London saw the now historic ballets *Les Présages*, *Beau Danube* and the 'Baby' ballerinas for the first time, and another Russian ballet craze was born.

There were then a number of flops; a straight play, *The Tudor Wench*, a revival of *Lilac Time*, a season of Popular Shakespeare and a return to variety, to fill the gap in April 1934, before a revival of *The Bing Boys are Here*, which was a dismal failure. Ballet returned with a season of the National Ballet of Lithuania. At last in 1935 *Tulip Time* had a successful run of 427 performances from August.

The final burst of glory for the Alhambra was another ballet season, this time by the René Blum Company, with Fokine as chief choreographer, which ran from May to July 1936. It was then announced that the site had been sold for £600,000 to Oscar Deutsch, the founder of the Odeon Circuit of Cinemas, and another London landmark was to vanish.

The last stage show at the Alhambra was a season given by Dante, the Danish magician, with his 'Great Mystery Spectacle' *Sim-Sala Bim*. This opened on 12 August and the last public performance in the theatre took place on 1 September 1936.

The last audience to assemble in the Alhambra were film extras who, with the cast and technicians, used the interior on Sunday 8 October as a film set for the *Othello* sequences of *Men are not Gods*, which starred Gertrude Lawrence and Miriam Hopkins. Directly after, the housebreakers moved in and by the new year the Alhambra was no more.

An adjoining property (number 23) was added to the site, a passageway through from Leicester Square to Charing Cross Road was made, and on the ground arose the Odeon Cinema, designed by Andrew Mather and Harry Weedon, and seating 2,300. The Odeon opened on 2 November 1937 with *The Prisoner of Zenda*.

The main entrance is still in Leicester Square, the Charing Cross Road section housing an office block separated from the Cinema.

The exterior is simple and has the merit of expressing the building's functions in a design that features a large oblong sign frame above the lofty entrance recess. At the north end is a tower, 120 feet high, which is faced, like the rest of the front, with slabs and slightly raised bands of polished black granite.

2
Daly's Theatre

Cranbourne Street
Leicester Square
On corner of Ryder's Court (now Leicester Court) with stage door in
Lisle Street at rear of building

FIRST BUILDING

Opened 27 June 1893 with *The Taming of the Shrew* by William Shakespeare. Preceded by an introductory address delivered by Ada Rehan, written by Clement Scott, and the National Anthem sung by Lloyd Daubigny and chorus and the Star Spangled Banner sung by Percy Haswell and Lena Loraine with chorus. Under the management of Augustin Daly.
Closed 25 September 1937, and demolished.

SECOND BUILDING

The Warner Theatre (Cinema), opened 12 October 1938, with *The Adventures of Robin Hood*.

DURING FIVE SUMMERS between 1884 and 1891, Augustin Daly, the American producer, brought his company to London, playing at the Lyceum, the Gaiety and other theatres. The great favour with which they were received by the Press suggested the idea that they should have a permanent London home, and for this purpose a theatre—originally to be called the Salisbury—was built by George Edwardes, to be leased to Daly at a cost of £60,000.

The site was leased by Edwardes from the Marquis of Salisbury. Negotiations commenced in 1889. It was bounded by Lisle Street, Ryder's Court and Cranbourne Street. Ryder's Court crossed the land and was widened and straightened (it was later re-named Leicester Court).

The foundation stone was laid appropriately by Ada Rehan, leading lady of the Daly company, on 30 October 1891. The architect was Spencer Chadwick, assisted by C. J. Phipps, and the contractor, Frank Kirk. It was one of the first theatres in London to be built on the cantilever principle.

The Daily Graphic for 28 June 1893 tells us:

The façade in Cranbourne Street is a pleasing relief from the unimposing architecture of most of the London theatres. It has been designed in the Italian Renaissance style, and executed in Ham Hill stone. The ground floor is of the rustic order, and from it rises a Doric base with fluted columns. In the centre of the building is a bold pediment over a series of columns, a design which gives a pleasing dignity to the front. At each end of the façade is a graceful tower with carved figure spandrels representing the muses of song. The whole is crowned by a fine example of the Attic order.

The main entrance of the theatre opens into a handsomely-furnished hall, with a mosaic flooring. A feature of the hall is the American logwood stove, which gives to the entrance a warm and cheering effect. From the entrance-hall a spacious staircase leads to the *foyer*, which arrangement, it is claimed by the architect, is a distinct novelty in theatrical construction. The *foyer* itself has been carried out in an Italian style, with a treatment of gold and blending tints.

On entering the auditorium the first thing to impress the spectator is the bold originality of its outline and decoration. The general scheme of colour is a blending of red, gold, silver and bronze. The circle fronts and boxes have been modelled in such a way as to represent boatloads of sea-nymphs and Cupids in the act of blowing bubbles, which bubbles have been ingeniously converted into electric lights of many tints. The auditorium will seat upwards of twelve hundred persons, and it has been so arranged that the public

will be able to obtain a good view of the stage from all parts
of the house.

The Times added:

a striking feature of the decoration is the number and variety
of the figures shown in relief, in the moulding of which the
plastic hand of Mr. Alfred Gilbert, R.A. is felt.

The Taming of the Shrew was chosen as the opening production
on 27 June 1893. *The Era* reported on 1 July:

A brilliant audience, which included many celebrities in the
legal, literary, and dramatic worlds, assembled in Mr.
Augustin Daly's new theatre in Leicester Square on Tuesday
last, to admire the house, and to witness a performance of
The Taming of the Shrew, with Miss Ada Rehan in the part of
Katharine. After the overture, the rose-coloured, gold-
embroidered curtains separated, and showed a number of
ladies and gentlemen in evening dress, who subsequently,
led by Mr. Lloyd Daubigny, sang 'God Save the Queen,'
the audience, of course, standing, and then Miss Percy
Haswell and Miss Lena Loraine sang the solo part of 'The
Star Spangled Banner,' in which the chorus heartily joined.
Loud and long was the applause which greeted Miss Ada
Rehan, who was visibly affected by the cordiality of the
welcome, but who preserved sufficient composure to repeat,
with exquisite distinctness and deep feeling, the 'Song of
Union,' written for the occasion at the Falls of Niagara, by
Mr. Clement Scott.

In the vestibule, the fine marble floor and the circular
gallery above are most remarkable. In the auditorium has
been made one of the boldest experiments in theatrical
architecture that we have for some time seen. The theory that
colouring and design in the body of a playhouse should be
'kept down' has been entirely abandoned; and instead of the
half-tints and delicate traceries of some theatres, we have
great masses of ruby, Venetian red, dull silver and burnished
gold. Additional warmth is given to the colour-scheme by the
marqueterie panelling with which the walls of the lower part of
the auditorium are covered. The general effect of the scheme
is powerful and impressive. There is fine freedom in the

modelling of the Cupids in boats which adorn each of the circles; and the nobility of aim is well sustained in the dome, with its severe scroll around the sunlight, and its immense winged figures of Fame. The style of most theatres is based on the idea of a drawing-room; Daly's rather recalls the more solid dining or banqueting apartment. In somewhat curious contrast to this solidity are the delicacy and graceful gaiety of the curtain, upon which Miss Ada Rehan is represented seated studying a part from an open book, whilst a dark-haired Cupid endeavours in vain to distract her from her task —an excellent moral, by the way, for any actress. It is only fair to the architect to mention that on Tuesday the impression created by the auditorium, as a whole, was imperfect. Owing to some hitch in the electric lighting apparatus, a great many of the lamps around the circles were extinguished, and the effect was not the same as it would have been with the amount of illumination on which Mr. Spencer Chadwick had relied when he made his plans. Tastes may differ as to the style best suited for the inside of a playhouse, but there can be no two opinions about the manner in which the highly original leading idea has been carried out, or as to the sumptuous style of the upholstery. Daly's Theatre has certainly one of the most original and artistic interiors in London.

During his first season till August, Daly produced *The Hunch-back*, *The Last Word* and *Love in Tandem*. He returned in September till May 1894 with *Dollars and Sense*, *The Forsters*, *The School for Scandal*, *Twelfth Night* and *As You Like It*.

Visits by Eleanora Duse and Sarah Bernhardt and her company followed and in the autumn George Edwardes occupied the theatre with a transfer of *A Gaiety Girl* (from the Prince of Wales'). In January 1895 the Carl Rosa Company gave the first London performance of Humperdinck's opera *Hansel and Gretel*.

Edwardes produced a new musical comedy *An Artist's Model* in February 1895, and so began to lay the foundations of the policy which was to make Daly's Theatre a household word for musicals.

London had not responded to the Americanised classics as Daly had hoped and he only returned once more, in June 1895, after which, though he remained lessee, Daly did not use the theatre again. In September 1898 Edwardes became the sole proprietor. A second edition of *An Artist's Model* opened in September 1895 and was followed by *The Geisha* (which ran for 760 performances, 1896), *A Greek Slave* (1898), *San Toy* (which ran for 768 performances, and was Marie Tempest's last appearance in musical comedy—1899), *A Country Girl* (729 performances, 1902), *The Cingalee* (1904), *The Little Michus* (1905), *The Merveilleuses* (The Lady Dandies) (1906), *The Merry Widow* 1907. The last mentioned was the most triumphant of the series, starring Lily Elsie. It ran for 778 performances from 8 June 1907 until 31 July 1909, and marked the introduction of Viennese operetta to London.

George Edwards was particularly well served by his composers, especially by Sidney Jones, who wrote the music for *An Artist's Model*, *The Geisha*, *A Greek Slave* and *San Toy*. It is perhaps interesting to note that four of them, *The Geisha*, *A Country Girl*, *San Toy* and *The Merry Widow* ran between them a total of ten years!

Continental operetta continued with *The Dollar Princess* (1909), *The Count of Luxemburg* (1911), *Gipsy Love* (1912), and *The Marriage Market* (1913). The great war brought a revival of *A Country Girl* (1914), and *Betty* (1915) which brings us to the year of Edwardes' death in October 1915. He left £49,780. Robert Evett and Mrs. Sherbrook, (Edwardes' daughter) became co-directors and Evett assumed management on behalf of the Edwardes family; the tradition continued with *The Happy Day* (1916), *The Maid of the Mountains* (1917), *A Southern Maid* (1920) and *Sybil* (1921).

The Maid of the Mountains introduced José Collins, daughter of Lottie Collins; it was an all-British production, with a book by Frederick Lonsdale and music by Harold Fraser-Simpson, and enjoyed a run of 1,352 performances. The Trustees sold the theatre to James White, the Stock Exchange gambler, for £200,000 in 1922 (he committed suicide in 1927).

Musical plays still continued, and Evelyn Laye became the leading lady, with *The Lady of the Rose* (1922), *Madame Pompadour* (1923) and *Cleopatra* (1925). Other productions were *Yvonne* (1926), *Peggy Ann* and *The Blue Mazurka* (1927), and revivals of *Lilac Time* (1927 and 1928).

In 1925 the theatre was re-decorated. A brief interruption of the musical comedy tradition was made when Noël Coward's ill-fated play *Sirocco* was produced in November 1927. This was a dismal failure, and an amusing and detailed account of the first night can be read in Coward's *Present Indicative*. *Lady Mary* restored the musical sequence in February 1928 and in 1929 the theatre came under the management of Harry Welchman, with *The White Camellia* and a revival of *The Lady of the Rose*. Later in the year British Amalgamated Theatres Limited bought the theatre. In 1931 and 1932 there was a series of revivals of old musical successes including *The Belle of New York*, *The Geisha*, *Florodora*, *A Country Girl*, *Monsieur Beaucaire*, *La Poupeé*, *San Toy*, *Miss Hook of Holland* and *The Duchess of Dantzig*. In 1933 Seymour Hicks took charge, and *It's You I Want*, *That's a Pretty Thing* and *Vintage Wine* were produced.

The glory of Daly's Theatre was on the wane, and between 1935 and 1937 though a good many plays were seen here, none enjoyed a very long run; amongst them may be mentioned *Tread Softly* (1935), *The Unguarded Hour* (1935) and *St. Helena* (transferred from the Old Vic—1936), as passing 100 performances. One other production is particularly worthy of note—in 1935 *Young England* was transferred here from the Victoria Palace and the Kingsway.

The last curtain dropped at Daly's on a play, *The First Legion* on 25 September 1937. Daly's had been bought by Warner Brothers in order that a cinema might be erected on the site.

The Warner Theatre covers exactly the same area as Daly's, with the addition of some premises in Lisle Street, but a greater sense of space has been obtained by various methods, and whereas in the original theatre stalls were below street level and the circle on street level, in the Warner Theatre the stalls are on street level and the circle above. The space occupied by Daly's stalls was converted into a public reception room and engineering equipment chambers.

The architects of the new building were E. A. Stone and T. R. Somerford.

The exterior of the Warner Theatre is faced with reconstructed marble blocks backed with granite concrete, and treated chemically to preserve the colour of the face—a warm cream colour. The sculptured panels of Sight and Sound are by Bainbridge Copnall.

The new cinema, seating 1,775, was completed one year to the day from the commencement of the demolition of the old building, but the actual opening, with *The Adventures of Robin Hood*, which took place in the presence of the Duke and Duchess of Kent, was held up until 12 October 1938.

The history of Daly's Theatre is told in *Daly's, The Biography of a Theatre* by D. Forbes-Winslow (1944).

3
The Empire Theatre

The Royal London Panorama (Façade), the Pandora Theatre (Foundations)

Leicester Square
Side exit in Leicester Street with stage door in Lisle Street at rear of building

FIRST THEATRE

Opened 17 April 1884 with *Chilperic*, a grand musical spectacle by Florimund Hervé, adapted by Henry Hersee and H. B. Farnie.
Under the management of Alexander Henderson.
Became a music hall, the Empire Theatre of Varieties, 22 December 1887.
Under the management of Augustus Harris and George Edwardes.
New vestibule and side entrance added in Lisle Street. Opened 6 July 1893.
From 1898 onwards known as the Empire Theatre.
Closed 22 January 1927, and demolished.

SECOND BUILDING

The Empire (Cinema), on an enlarged site extending at the side to Leicester Place.
Opened 8 November 1928 with *Trelawny of the Wells*.
Under the management of Metro-Goldwyn-Meyer.
Used for large scale stage dance productions in conjunction with films from 1949 till 1952.
Closed May 1961.

Auditorium reconstructed on two levels. The upper, opened as the Empire (Cinema), 19 December 1962, with *Jumbo*.
Under the management of Metro-Goldwyn-Meyer.
The lower, as a dance hall, the Empire Ballroom, March 1963.
Under the management of Mecca Ltd.

THE SITE ON WHICH the Empire Theatre was built had a long history. Part of it was covered by Saville House, numbers 5 and 6 on the north side of Leicester Square. Originally built as Aylesbury House in 1684, its stables stretched to Lisle Street. After its occupant, Lord Aylesbury, was arrested for high treason, the house was used on and off as a royal residence by the Prince of Wales (George II) and other members of the royal family. It became Saville House when bought by Sir George Saville in 1729. (He had a long lease from Lord Leicester the ground landlord.)

After damage in the Gordon Riots of 1778 the house passed out of the family and was bought, in 1789, with its neighbours numbers 3 and 4, to form the site of the proposed new Opera House which stretched along the whole north side of the square (see the Pantheon, number 16). When the scheme fell through Saville house was eventually partly reconstructed and split up into various shops, warehouses and exhibition rooms. It was here that Mary Linwood exhibited her famous woolwork pictures from 1809. Miscellaneous entertainments are advertised for other parts of the house during the following years.

The Astronomical Panorama (1814), Miller's Mechanical and Beautiful Representations, with musical accompaniment (1815), and in 1823 the Saville Rooms were 'opened for readings, recitations and lectures, also for Evening Concerts.'

The Saville Palace Wine, Concert and Exhibition Rooms were advertised in 1833. Mary Linwood remained with all these numerous entertainments and show rooms around her till her death in 1845. Her Collection was sold and the Linwood Gallery became a theatre called the Walhalla, and used by a Madame Wharton for her *Poses plastiques* (a kind of *tableau vivant*, or early striptease show!) A contemporary account says:

> The establishment became so divided by different interests,
> that few could tell whether it was a theatre, wine vaults, a

billiard-room, a coffee-shop, a gunsmith's, or a Royal
Academy; or, if they could, they never knew, amidst the
ascending and descending steps, and doors and passages,
which one must take to get anywhere . . . A confusion of
sounds further tends to bewilder the visitor: the noise of
everything is heard every where else. The click of billiard-
balls, the music of *poses plastiques*, the thwacking of single-
sticks, the cracking of rifles, and the stamping of delighted
Walhallists, all mingle with each other; and it is only by
taking refuge in the lowest apartment, which partakes of a
coffee-room, a cabin, and a cellar, that you will find
repose.

It was redecorated and reconstructed in 1848 and opened as the
Salle Valentino, where 'two thousand dancers could enjoy the
Fashionable Quadrille, and the Graceful Polka, or the Exciting
Galop.' By 1852 it had become known as the Théâtre des Variétés
or the Leicester Music Hall 'where and in other parts of the
building exhibitions of fencing, wrestling, antique armour,
panoramas, clairvoyance, magic and ventriloquy all found a
stamping-ground.'

The *Survey of London*, volume 34, says:

Between 1846 and 1865 parts of Saville House were known
at various times by the following names: Grand American
Hall, Leicester Music Hall, El Dorado Music Hall and
Café Chantant, Parisian Hall, Royal Living Marionette
Theatre, Royal Victoria Hall, Salle Valentino, Saville Hall,
Saville Hall and Hotel, Saville-House Entertainments,
Saville House Gymnasium, Théâtre des Variétés, and
Walhalla.

Added confusion to theatrical nomenclature was caused when the
name the Sans Souci, or, Theatre of Variety, Saville House, was
used for a troupe of German acrobats in January 1852. The last
theatre of that name, round the corner in Leicester Place, had
been closed in 1835. (See number 23.)

On 28 February 1865 Saville House was burnt down. The fire
started in the basement, where a workman searching for a leak of
gas 'incautiously took a lighted candle with him, and was applying
it along the crevices of some wainscoting when a loud explosion

took place.' The flames spread so rapidly that very soon nothing but the bare walls remained.

Plans for a new building on the site were put in hand by the following June, but these and others which followed came to nothing, and the ruins of Saville House remained standing. Among the proposals made was one for a new theatre, the Denmark Theatre and Winter Garden, named in honour of the Princess of Wales, but the company formed for the purpose in 1869 failed to develop its scheme. At one time a proposed roadway from Oxford Street to join Leicester Square by extending Dean Street across the site was suggested.

It was in 1878 that the Alcazar Company Limited was incorporated for the establishment of a 'Grand Theatre of Varieties, Restaurant and Café,' the Alcazar (a name used later by the Royal Amphitheatre, Holborn in December 1882). Alexander Henderson was to manage the theatre, and contracts were entered into for the purchase of the site, which had been enlarged by the acquisition of three houses in Lisle Street, and which was now cleared of its ruins. Plans for the new building were made by Edward L. Paraire, but this scheme also proved abortive.

The *Survey of London* tells us:

In October 1880 *The Builder* reported that 'A large circular building is at present in course of erection at the rear of the north side of Leicester square . . . which is intended for panoramic purposes'. The architect employed by the French company which sponsored this venture was M. L. Dumoulin of Paris. The principal entrance was along a wide corridor from the north side of the square.

The Royal London Panorama opened on 28 March 1881 with a representation on 15,000 square feet of canvas of 'The Charge of the Light Brigade'. A year later, however, it was announced that the building was to be converted into a theatre, to be known as the Pandora, from designs prepared for the Pandora Theatre Company by Thomas Verity. Building work began in the summer of 1882 (in December a rehearsal call for the actors was announced in *The Era*) but in the spring of 1883 the Pandora Theatre Company entered into liquidation, building was suspended and the property changed hands yet again. According to *The Building News*, work was subsequently resumed under the supervision of different architects, J. and A. E. Bull, the façade to Leicester Square which had been erected for the panorama being retained. In February 1884 it was announced first that the new theatre was to be called the Phoenix, and then the Queen's but when it opened it was as the Empire.

For the Pandora Theatre Company, Verity retained part of the large oval shell of brickwork built for the Panorama, this formed the northern five bays which were demolished to make way for the wide proscenium and stage, and the auditorium was formed inside the remaining horseshoe of seven bays. A ring of cast-iron columns was introduced to support the raking girders of the two shallow tiers, the first containing three rows of seats in front of a range of loges. The second tier, with four rows, was overlooked by a wide promenade, above which was a gallery of seven rows, rising behind the columns of an arcade supporting the oval conical ceiling.

After the failure of the Pandora Company, the unfinished building was completed more or less in accordance with Thomas Verity's plans. The changes were mainly ones of rearrangement, such as the enlargement of the pit and omission of a promenade at stalls level, this feature being transferred to the first tier. Instead of the Chinese scheme originally envisaged, the lavish decorations were mainly in the Second Empire taste.

The Empire Theatre was opened on 17 April 1884 and *The Era* gave a full account of the event and production of *Chilperic*, an operetta by Hervé on 19 April:

There has been some delay in opening the theatre, partly owing to the very positive demands of the Board of Works. Since the gigantic fires we have had of late years, there is a very natural desire on the part of the public for all possible means to be adopted to obtain security in this respect, and we believe that the Empire is better provided for, owing to its roomy and convenient approaches, than any other theatre existing. Some particulars of the auditorium may be welcome, and first we may state that the height of the theatre from the floor to the centre of the roof is fifty-one feet, but the theatre is so broad that the proportions are very graceful. The horse-shoe form is that adopted, and there are four tiers of boxes, there being also a balcony and promenade, as well as a dress circle. This circle is surrounded by private boxes. The style of decoration belongs to the period termed French Renaissance, the predominating colours being cream and gold, contrasted with crimson hangings, and the stall seats are similarly covered. There are one hundred and eighty orchestra stalls and one hundred and eight reserved pit stalls. The pit, with a promenade twelve feet wide, will supply accommodation for five hundred and fifty visitors. The opening of the proscenium is thirty-two feet wide and thirty-five feet high, the supports of the ceiling being caryatides of colossal size giving great effect and boldness to the design. All the tiers and corridors are constructed of fireproof materials. The stage is magnificently adapted for all spectacular purposes, being seventy-seven feet wide, and fifty feet deep. A feature in the construction is comparatively novel in an English theatre, that is the *foyer* so generally popular on the Continent. The *foyer* at the Empire theatre is in reality a splendid saloon nearly fifty feet square. It has a balcony and is thirty-three feet in height. The *foyer* is magnificently embellished, and has a mosaic flooring. Columns of Scagliola marble, with an entablature and dado of black marble, surround the *foyer*, which is also brilliantly illuminated with sunlights. Ultimately the electric light is to be employed for novel effects, as it is already for scenic illusion. It is calculated that the Empire Theatre when used to the full extent of its capacity will seat about three thousand five hundred visitors. But there is not the slightest fear, however well the theatre may be attended, that the visitors will suffer any of the inconveniences unavoidable in some of the older establishments, as in every portion of the house the utmost freedom for exit and entrance has been preserved. In fact, after the visitor has been dazzled and delighted with the splendour and elegance of the auditorium and the graceful form of the entire theatre, the next thing that will attract attention is the airy and expansive effect of the whole. In a theatre devoted to entertainments of a musical and spectacular kind this brilliancy of the auditorium will not be the least of the attractions. Our playgoers now demand greater comfort and convenience than in the barn-like structures and dimly-lighted dramatic temples which their forefathers

frequented, and since the appearance of the theatre itself
does unquestionably exert an important influence on the
minds of modern audiences, the beauty and completeness of
the Empire Theatre ought to go a long way towards securing
the popularity which may reasonably be anticipated for the
splendid establishment in Leicester Square. If we are lost in
astonishment as we recall the magnificence of the auditorium,
we are impressed, if possible, to a greater extent still by the
really wonderful effects produced upon the stage. The
manner in which *Chilperic* is illustrated and decorated may be
said to mark a new departure in the history of stage illusion.
There is something fairylike and dreamlike in the way some
of the scenes are managed, as, for example, the 'Mistletoe
Grove,' in the first act. The scene was an enchanted forest,
the trees and branching foliage, the wild flowers and under-
growth being rendered with magical delicacy and truth to
nature. This was Mr. Ryan's masterpiece; Mr. Grieve being
extremely successful in his splendid interiors especially the
throne-room. Mr. Bruce Smith had his triumphs in the
'Camp of the Goths' and the 'Ramparts of Chilperic's Castle,'
the change of scene being effected with a bewildering rapidity,
causing breathless excitement to the audience, and being
rewarded with a perfect tempest of applause. Then, as a
spectacular display when was anything seen to equal the
electric ballet of Amazons in the last act? Fifty beautiful
ladies, arrayed in armour of exquisite design, after performing
various brilliant evolutions with a precision and grace worthy
of the utmost commendation, halted, and suddenly from their
shields, their helmets, their glittering breastplates, even from
their spears there was seen a dazzling electrical illumination
of the most enchanting kind it is possible to imagine. The
colours were varied and intensely brilliant, and the effect,
contrasted as it was with the shadowy foliage of the distant
forest was absolutely startling in its novelty and splendour.
All London will talk of it when all London has seen it.
Nothing to compare with it of its kind has been witnesssed
on the modern stage. Regarding the performance of the
opera itself there is much to praise, nor need we detain the
reader with the incidents of a plot so familiar as that of
Chilperic, which fourteen years ago at the Lyceum proved a

great attraction. The work is well adapted for spectacular display, and the wooing of Fredegonda by the butterfly monarch, who tires of one beauty as soon as another appears, amused the audience as it has often done before, and the downfall of the capricious fair one, supplanted as she is by a rival, supplies no little entertainment, contrasted with mystical scenes of Druid rites and wonderful military spectacles. Mr. Herbert Standing makes a gallant Chilperic, his comedy experience being of great value in the rendering of the character, while he looks the amorous monarch completely. Mr. Standing has a pleasant baritone voice, and he was much applauded in the music, especially in the 'Butterfly Song,' in which Chilperic describes the sort of monarch he is. Mr. Henry Wardroper was amusing as Siegbert, and the good singing of Mr. Westlake Parry, as the Arch Druid, was of value in the opening scene. M. Paulus, as the Court Jester, introduced a number of French comic ditties, which gained him hearty applause, a certain quaint, eccentric style causing him to be a favourite with the audience. He was several times encored. The Brothers Tacchi convulsed the house by their remarkable and novel performance. One of them sings melodies, accompanied upon the guitar, while the other introduces a series of grotesque imitations, impossible to hear without side-splitting mirth. How this artist produces those extraordinary tones, where they come from, and what they resemble, it is almost impossible to describe. If our readers can fancy a performer having swallowed a bassoon, which continues playing internally, they will get some idea of the grotesque effect produced by these unearthly, but irresistibly funny tones. The artist literally uses his voice as a comic instrument, and it is quite a new musical experience to listen to the astonishing tones produced. We need hardly say that the Brothers Tacchi made a tremendous hit. In fact, they were encored so rapturously that the performance was suspended until they appeared again and startled their hearers with new combinations of eccentric sound. The comic talent of Mr. James T. Powers as a Royal Page was amusingly displayed, and Mr. Harry Paulton revelled in the eccentricities which so delight his admirers as a Grand Factotum to Chilperic. Mr. Paulton was as droll as usual, and was loudly applauded in a medley introducing the titles of all the popular songs of the day. Mdlle. Camille D'Arville, by her graceful appearance, her sprightly acting, and clear, brilliant soprano voice, rendered important aid as Fredegonda. Her rendering of the pretty waltz melody in the first act was greatly applauded, and the vein of sentiment infused into Fredegonda's farewell made the melody all the more pleasing and effective. Mdlle D'Arville will, we have no doubt, be even more successful in her singing when accustomed to the theatre. Miss Agnes Consuelo made an attractive Landry; and Miss Clara Graham as the King of the Goths looked handsome. Miss Katherine Gardner represented the arch Druidess effectively; and Miss Clara Douglass cleverly sustained the character of Brunehaut. The Castilian Princess, who supplants Fredegonda, had a most satisfactory representative in Miss Madge Shirley, and the whimsical rendering of a Spanish duenna, whose native tongue is most laughably twisted with Anglo-Spanish names, enabled Miss Sallie Turner to win cordial applause in return for the merry laughter she evoked. These were some of the chief personages in the opera, which was supplied with some capital dance music by Mr. John S. Hiller, who conducted the orchestra. Mr. Bertrand, who has done wonders in the ballet department, was called to the front, and the services of Mr. Charles H. Stephenson as stage manager must be referred to with commendation, while no praise can be too great for Mr. H. B. Farnie, who has devoted all his skill and experience to the production of the piece in such a manner as to do credit to the theatre. We have next to mention the appearance of two extremely talented dancers. Mdlle. Laurent, from the Grand Opera, Paris, met with a most flattering reception in a grand Spanish ballet. Mdlle. Laurent has a very attractive manner, and this, combined with her youth and grace, will no doubt make her a favourite. Fräulein Hoffachuller, from the Opera House at Vienna, is another danseuse of first-rate ability. Her very elegant and finished dancing recalled to our minds the golden days of the ballet, when Taglioni, Cerito, and other famous artistes, made ballet dancing a truly artistic feature. A novel musical solo was that of Mdlle. Lauge on the *cor de chasse*, or hunting horn, in the last act. This was clever, and was warmly applauded. The crowded audience took every opportunity of testifying their wonder, delight, and enjoyment of the new theatre and the performance, and at the close Messrs. Farnie and Hersee were called to the footlights and greeted with hearty applause; and then, as the vast crowd passed along the beautiful corridors, with artistic attractions meeting their gaze on every side, congratulations were heard from every visitor, and the universal verdict pronounced was that the Empire Theatre had started on its career in a manner worthy of its imperial name. Never in the history of the stage has there been a more brilliantly successful first night, and never has theatrical enterprise more throughly deserved such a reward.

The new theatre did not achieve the success which had been hoped for. Burlesques, operettas and ballets were tried, the latter including versions of *Coppélia* and *Giselle*. In 1885 John Hollingshead tried to improve matters with a mixed programme of farce, variety, and burlesque, with his Gaiety Theatre company, and Marius, in March 1886, followed with a version of Jules Verne's *Round the World in Eighty Days* by Alfred Murray with 'Three grand Ballets, a chorus of 400 and a trained elephant, etc.'

After this nothing seemed to succeed and by the autumn the theatre was closed. The proprietor, Daniel N. de Nicola, tried to turn the theatre into a music hall, but was opposed, when he applied for a licence, by his rivals across the square at the Alhambra. He formed a new company, the Empire Palace Company, with George Edwardes as managing director, had the theatre redecorated by the designers Messrs. Romaine-Walker and Tanner, and re-opened as the Empire Theatre of Varieties, under the joint direction of Edwardes and Augustus Harris, on 22 December 1887. *The Era* 24 December reported:

> The success of the entertainment called 'variety' has induced Messrs. Augustus Harris and George Edwardes to open yet another music hall on a scale of palatial magnificence. The Empire Theatre, after its redecoration and improvements, is, indeed, a 'Palace of Delight,' with its luxurious fauteuils, its plush-covered seats, and its lavishly adorned interior. The general character of the decorations of the auditorium is Persian, and turquoise and indigo blue, rose colour and

crimson, black and gold are mingled with dazzling effect in its ornamentation. The sunlight is a large flower in coloured glass, with the stamens and pistils of electric lights. The columns all round the theatre are white, with characteristic ornament in two blues and gold. This treatment is applied to the various box fronts, using in, as far as possible, the raised ornamentation already existing. The back and ceiling of gallery circle is treated with ruby and gold leather paper. The three other circles, which are architecturally Louis Seize in treatment, are severally rose and gold; blue, white, and gold; and white and gold, the latter with plush panels. The upper circle is lighted by eighteen lamps of Persian design, in coloured glass, with gold frames, and the walls of the private boxes are all covered with a highly enriched gold leather paper. The pit entrance is decorated with Egyptian ornament, leading down to a solid gold leather paper on lower walls, and the white and gold treatment of the ground floor is one of the most characteristic pieces of work in the theatre. Various refreshment-bars and staircases are all treated with special decoration; the foyer—which is pure Renaissance—is entered by a grand staircase, Pompeiian in treatment; the entrance halls are Indian, and are coloured with black and gold and a deep rich crimson. The black and gold striped pilasters here are noteworthy in the general scheme, and the large hall is lighted by specially designed Indian lamps of coloured glass, supported on bronze bases. From the hall entering into the grand circle, one passes through a lovely little Japanese vestibule, with gold frets, bamboos, birds, butterflies, &c., with a specially designed coloured glass Chinese lantern in centre of a golden fretted ceiling. The seating arrangements are excellent, the stalls being especially commodious, the liberal space between their rows permitting ingress and egress without inconvenience. The private boxes at the back of the grand circle are most tastefully and comfortably upholstered, and a wide corridor makes a pleasant promenade, and is, as Artemus Ward would have said, a 'great boon.' In a few weeks' time, when the tints of the decorations have become a little toned and harmonised, and the 'spick and span' glitter quieted down, the general effect of the auditorium will be perfectly artistic, as it is now dazzlingly beautiful. We must not, however, expend all our adjectives of admiration upon the appearance of the interior. In any case, we shall find it difficult enough to find at hand terms sufficiently strong to describe the beauty of the ballets, which are evidently to be the great feature at the Empire. In dealing with *Dilara*, the grand divertissement, which was the ninth item in the programme on Thursday evening we shall relinquish any attempt to describe the ballet in all its lovely details. *Dilara* is in two scenes, one representing an Eastern port, and the second showing the interior of the Caliph's palace. The story of the ballet matters little. The features which remain fixed on the retina of memory, almost wearied by the recollection of so much optic delight, are the solos danced by Mdlle. Rossi, including a shadow dance, which was particularly graceful, and the excellent descriptive pantomime of this artist on several occasions; the ingenious use of palm branches to assist in the formation of a striking tableau; and above all, a grand valse and galop, in which the *corps de ballet* go swinging round, wheeling in lines upon a central pivot, in most exhilarating style. The lightness and gaiety of a troupe of young odalisques was also a pleasant feature of the ballet, and the Signorinas Manneroffer and Santori, and Mdlle. Johnstone, agreeably supported the *première danseuse* by their agility and grace. The effects of colour in the first scene are produced by the admixture of sea-green and chocolate, crimson and white, and blue and purple costumes. There is an entry of Amazons in shining helmets, and a pretty dance by *coryphées*, each bearing on her wrist a white cockatoo, and an entry of juvenile black slaves playing on silver bells. Bronze and pale green, light blue, cream colour and gold, dark blue and brown are mingled with exquisite effect in the second tableau. When we say that the scenery has been painted by Mr. Walter Emden, the dresses designed by M. Wilhelm, and the music composed by M. Hervé, it may be imagined how well-nigh perfect is the result of their combined efforts. The second ballet, *The Sports of England*, is easier to describe than *Dilara*, and is entirely different in character. The idea is to depict in the conventionalised style necessary in ballets the various sports and outdoor recreations of England. Thus we have female representatives of the M.C.C. and Australian

Eleven, yachtsmen, lawn tennis and polo players, shots and
fishermen, hunting-men in pink, football players, the Oxford
and Cambridge crews, cyclists, and 'noble sportsmen' (and
sportswomen) on Derby Day. The boating dances and
hunting chorus gave special satisfaction, and Messrs. Cazaly
and Ridley's comicalities in the fishing picture created much
amusement. Madame Katti Lanner was again responsible for
the arrangement of the dances. M. Hervé's music was exactly
what was required, and the costumes by Miss Fisher and
Messrs. Rouy and Felix were neat and pretty. The reward
of the workers came after the conclusion of *Dilara*, when
Madame Katti Lanner and Mdlle. Rossi and M. Hervé
appeared hand in hand and bowed their acknowledgments.
As the cheers continued, the two ladies after a slight commotion at the wing, succeeded in leading Mr. Augustus Harris
smiling before the curtain, to receive the guerdon of applause
so well earned by his share of the success. The variety
entertainment seemed to be regarded by the audience on
Thursday as subordinate to the spectacular portion of the
evening's amusement, but it nevertheless contained some
features worthy of remark. First, Mr. George Fairbarne
gave his imitations of various music hall singers, including
the topical singer, the late Mr. Fred. Albert, and concluding
with an imitation of Mr. Charles Godfrey. Clark and Barton,
musical comedians, played cleverly on a peal of bells and a
dulcimer, a melodious item of their turn being the performance of 'Massa's in the cold, cold ground,' on belts of
sleigh-bells. Mr. Leo Stormont sang the 'Toreador' song from
Carmen, and Mdlle. Clari sang a *chansonette française*, which
was not very well received. The fact is, unless the air be
specially 'catchy,' an English audience derives little amusement from the hearing of the song, the meaning of which
they do not comprehend; nor did they appreciate Mdlle.
Clairi's peculiar style. Mdlle. Nydia de Bleicken in the same
line was more successful. Her manner and appearance were
refined and pleasing, and she chose the bright and lively
'Petit Bleu,' the spirited tune of which is already familiar
to English ears. Bellonini, a French juggler, besides doing
some neat plate-throwing, introduced a clever poodle, who
swings standing on his hind legs on the trapeze; the Two

Macs were as funny and 'rollicking' as ever; and La Petite Amoros, a clever little girl, who combines contortion with trapeze business, did some surprising feats in both departments. The names of the Arabian trio of French cornet players, and the Estrellas, aerial gymnasts, were also on the programme; and Mr. Charles Godfrey, besides singing a song in the character of an elderly *roué*, contributed a patriotic ditty 'Our Empire', one verse of which alluded to the new enterprise in Leicester Square. An incident of the evening was the appearance of Cyrus and Maud, as it was announced, 'with their performing donkey.' Cyrus played 'The Lost Chord' cleverly on the cornet, but the 'moke' did not put in an appearance, though loud cries of 'Where's the donkey?' greeted this deviation from the programme. In the ninth tableau of the Sports of England, after the performance of the Anciolotti troupe of bicyclists, a very tiny child, a mere baby, was brought on and put upon a cycle. This produced a storm of hisses and hooting, amidst which the poor little thing was removed. Otherwise the whole 'show' passed off without a hitch, and every one appeared to be delighted.

In the Souvenir, *The Empire Past and Present*, published in 1905, the management were able to say:

During the eighteen years of success there have been produced at the Empire a number of splendid Ballets, it is interesting to recall a few of the 'stars' who have scintillated on the boards of the stage here since 1887. Among them were Paulus, Madame Vanoni, Arthur Roberts, Dan Leno (who made his first appearance here at a West End variety theatre, singing 'I'll give him beans to-night'), the Schaffer Troupe, Madame Yvette Guilbert, Madame Palladino, and Madame Juniori. Bicycle Polo was first played at the Empire, and Looping the Loop introduced here for the first time. Then, among other artistes who have appeared at various times, are Amy Roselle, Sims Reeves, R. G. Knowles and Cinquevalli, Mrs. Brown Potter and Marie Lloyd, Vesta Tilley, Edith Helena, Otero, Carl Hertz, Sousa's Band and Strauss' Imperial Orchestra, also Streator's American Zouaves and The Phantom Guards, and last, but not least, that transcendent luminary of ballet, Mdlle Adeline Genée.

In connection with the ballets produced at this theatre, the name of Madame Katti Lanner will always be associated, she having from the earliest days of the premier variety theatre of the world assisted in the perfection of these productions, bringing her unexampled experience to bear upon some of the most beautiful spectacles Europe has ever seen. Another veteran who for many years rendered yeoman service to the Empire was Mons. Leopold Wenzel, of 'Petit Bleu' fame, who, as musical director, contributed so much melody both to the ballets and numberless musical selections performed in the theatre.

On several occasions there have been special performances given at the Empire to which the general public were not admitted; one being the occasion of the visit of the Shah of Persia, on July 4th, 1889; and on another evening, that of August 19th, 1902, when H.I.M. the Shah of Persia, H.R.H. the Prince of Wales, and H.R.H. Prince Arthur of Connaught were present, surrounded by a brilliant suite and an audience present by invitation.

Performers at the Empire have also been commanded to appear before our crowned heads; the company being 'commanded' to Windsor Castle by Her late Majesty Queen Victoria, on November 23rd, 1897, and to Sandringham by our present King, when Prince of Wales, on December 30th, 1897. Mdlle. Adeline Genée has also had the honour of appearing before our King and Queen at Chatsworth and Copenhagen, the former as recently as January 5th, 1905.

After the retirement of Sir Augustus Harris, Mr. George Edwardes remained sole Managing Director, an office he has filled ever since, until, on the death last year of the late lamented Chairman of the Company, Mr. H. N. Tennent, Mr. George Edwardes became the Chairman and Mr. Walter Dickson Managing Director. It is a matter of almost universal knowledge, reaching far beyond theatrical circles, that all the beautiful ballet for which this house is famed have been produced under the personal direction of Mr. Edwardes, and that he still continues such active direction in the matter of ballets and revues.

From the earliest years of the Empire, as the leading theatre of varieties and ballet in London, Mr. Charles

Wilhelm has been associated with its fortunes as practically its sole costume designer, a position which his opportunities here have enabled him to develop into the more exacting and comprehensive one of Deviser of Spectacle. In undertaking to originate a theme suitable for the somewhat limited scope of action allowed in a *divertissement*, to design its scenic setting and its costuming, and to supervise its action, he claims to secure a completeness of *ensemble* and pictorial effect unattainable by other means.

In 1893 a new foyer, and a secondary entrance in Leicester Street were constructed on the ground between the side of the auditorium and the adjacent street. It was built to the design of Frank Verity, and was opened on 6 July 1893. (The exterior still remains, and was used as an exit to the Cinema in 1928; it is now closed and forms the exterior of the Staff Room.)

The Gay Nineties were not without their troubles at the Empire, which, even more than the Alhambra became 'To its Victorian or Edwardian patrons, men about town, gallants from Ouida or Kipling, the most celebrated rendezvous in the world. It bordered on Bohemia and was almost a club. Its social amenities, if such they could be called, included the notorious Promenade, where ladies of the town consorted with the dandies of the time and shocked the entire nation.' In 1894 the London County Council, as a condition of renewal of the music and dancing licence, insisted on the alteration of the promenades, which the Council had been informed had been 'the habitual resort for prostitutes in pursuit of their traffic.'

This was the work of a vigorous American social reformer, Mrs. Ormiston Chant. She and her supporters were designated by their opponents in the Press as 'Prudes on the Prowl!' They had a slight victory, and the London County Council closed the Empire from 27 October to 2 November. When it re-opened canvas screens had been placed between the offending promenade and the auditorium. Resentment at this outrage was expressed by the young Winston Churchill and some fellow cadets from Sandhurst who went to the re-opened Empire and found the canvas screens separating 'the temples of Bacchus and Venus.' It was a rowdy Saturday night audience, and repeated comment at the canvas screens eventually led to action, especially as young

C*

gentlemen with walking sticks had discovered that the screens were as flimsy as they looked. The comedian on the stage was shouted down, in a 'friendly' manner, and the mob proceeded to storm the barricades, pulling down the remainder of the screens with great gusto. 'In these somewhat unvirginal surroundings I now made my maiden speech,' relates Mr. Churchill, regretting that no very accurate report of his speech has been preserved. He recalls that he appealed to sentiment and even passion, and said something like this: 'You have seen us tear down these barricades; see that you pull down those who are responsible for them at the coming election.' The speech elicited 'rapturous applause.' Afterwards the audience paraded in Piccadilly waving pieces of the broken partitions. For years afterwards it was fashionable to boast of having taken part in that night's battle for liberty. George Edwardes magnanimously forgave those who cried 'Long live Edwardes!' and then wrecked his theatre. The full story of this episode is to be found in *Roads to Ruin*, by E. S. Turner from which we quote.

Eventually, on a technical issue, a superior court ruled that the London County Council had exceeded their jurisdiction, and the promenade remained till 1916 when the theatre was no longer a music hall, and changing custom had outdated its use.

Once again, in 1904, the London County Council stepped in and demanded considerable structural alterations, and the Empire was closed from 30 June till 9 October. The work done is described in the Souvenir:

At the end of 1904 the London County Council served requisitions upon the Directors of the Company to make certain improvements in the building for the safety of the public. This entailed structural alterations and involved, practically, removing the interior of the auditorium, as it was found the walls and decorative portions were of soft wood and canvas.

The Directors entrusted the work of remodelling the building to Mr. Frank Verity, with instructions to design a building different to anything existing, and he is to be credited with having produced one of the most palatial, comfortable, elegant, and safe theatres that the metropolis can now boast of, comprising in all its details every modern improvement and device for securing comfort, convenience, and safety.

The Main Entrance and Vestibule is in Leicester Square; the walls and ceilings are decorated in the Empire style of architecture, which, indeed, is that in which the whole of the interior of the new building has been designed.

The First Tier of Box Circle is on the same level as the vestibule. This tier consists of four rows of seats, surrounded by private boxes, the green silk hangings of which give a richness to the lower portion of the theatre. The design of the curve at this level, with one row of seats projecting beyond the line of the tier above it, is in the form of a horseshoe, and is of gilt wrought iron, and from every seat a good and complete view of the stage can be obtained. The Grand Circle Tier is above this level, and is approached by the Grand Staircase direct from the Main Entrance Hall and Vestibule, and will undoubtedly prove a most popular portion of the building, with an entirely uninterrupted view of the stage. The handsome Foyer, 45 feet long, for this tier is at the rear, and approached from this level by another staircase.

The Gallery Tier is approached by a corridor from Lisle Street and a single flight of stairs, and, strange as it may appear, is only about 15 feet above the level of Lisle Street. There is a Fireproof Exit from the gallery on the opposite side, carried right across, but not communicating in any way with, the stage; this will only be used as an extra exit. Descending on either side of the proscenium opening, immediately behind the stage-boxes, is a Staircase, 5 feet wide, which communicates with every portion of the building from the gallery to the orchestra stalls. The more than ample arrangements for exit will enable the audience from every part of the house to leave the theatre without inconvenience in the space of less than three minutes.

One of the greatest changes in the new house will be found in the Parterre, which occupies the whole of the ground floor, and replaces the former fauteuils and pit. The seats in this part of the theatre are Orchestra Stalls, 320 in number, approached by a wide Corridor and Staircase from Leicester Square, and another entrance from Leicester Street, with an additional exit into Lisle Street. In connection with this portion of the theatre, and immediately under the vestibule hall and principal staircase to foyer, is a large Saloon, with spacious retiring rooms and lavatories for gentlemen. The ladies' cloak room is approached from the Leicester Street entrance. Lavatories are also supplied on each level or tier.

The general effect of the auditorium on ascending the principal staircase leading from vestibule is most pleasing.

As one glances round, one cannot but be struck with the warmth, cosiness, and general comfort of the whole building. The acoustic properties have been proved to be admirable. The Proscenium Opening is 32 feet wide and 35 feet high. The ceiling of the auditorium is circular, and finished white. From its centre hangs a handsome electrolier in the Empire Style, containing 540 lights.

This is ample for illuminating the entire theatre, but additional electric torches are provided on the first tier, and on the outer walls of each promenade are electric brackets and pendants. The entire length of the auditorium from proscenium front to back of pit is 83 feet, and the width from wall to wall is 88 feet, whilst the height from orchestra stalls to centre of ceiling is 51 feet.

The system for properly ventilating the auditorium and foyers and keeping the auditorium free from smoke is very elaborate. At the ceiling level of each tier a series of openings lead into flues, which join up in the roof space. At the topmost point the electrically-driven fans are fixed, which draw the vitiated air from all parts of the house. Each fan controls the extraction of air from one half of the building, in order that few or many changes of air can be made as occasion requires. A separate arrangement is made for the stage, an independent fan being fixed for extracting the air from this part of the building. A complete system of heating has also been installed. All entrances are thoroughly heated, and the fresh air for the building being supplied from these sources, is thereby warmed before entering the house, thus preventing draughts.

All the tiers and corridors are of fireproof construction. The wood framings dividing the boxes are of mahogany. The entire building may thus be said to be fire-resisting. All the requirements of the London County Council have been most

strictly carried out, and there will not be found in the whole
of the metropolis a theatre safer or more easily understood in
regard to its exits than the Empire Theatre. With regard to
the stage and the appointments generally behind, everything
has been done for the comfort and convenience of each person
engaged in the building. The dressing rooms, with water laid
on and fitted with lavatories, lockers, and other conveniences,
are numerous and airy. The property room, scene docks,
music and ballet rooms, flies, gridiron, &c., are all models of
their respective kinds, whilst the stage itself is one of the
largest and best in London, being 77 feet wide by 50 feet
deep.

On 9 November 1896 Lumières Moving Pictures were first
shown in London and *Cinématographe* first cast shadows over the
building they were eventually to permanently engulf in 1928.

It was not till October 1905 that the even tenor of the Empire
programme was disturbed. A revue, *Rogues and Vagabonds*
formed part of the programme. This was a new form of entertainment, via the French though of English ancestry, and was to
prove with the Cinemas the biggest enemy of music hall and
variety in the next twenty years. Other similar revues followed,
and by 1911 they were becoming the main part of the programme.
Variety and ballet dwindled, and the last ballet, as a separate
item, was *Pastorale* in 1915, with Phyllis Bedells as the ballerina
(she had followed Lydia Kyasht who reigned from 1908 to 1913).
The full story of the era is told by Ivor Guest in *The Empire Ballet*.
From now on the Empire presented full evening revues and from
1914 Alfred Butt became managing director. The first musical
was *The Lilac Domino*, which ran 747 performances from 1918.
This was followed (after a ballet season by the Diaghilev Company)
by *Irene*, 1920; and *The Rebel Maid*, 1921. Seasons of films filled
in between shows and in 1924 variety returned for a short while,
but there were many short lived musical productions during these
years, which are now quite forgotten. In 1925 Jack Buchanan was
in *Boodle* and in the same year Sybil Thorndike and Lewis
Casson were in a spectacular revival of *Henry VIII*, followed by
The Cenci, but the end of the theatre was near. It was announced
to have been purchased first by the Allen Enterprise Company, a
Canadian Company and then, in August 1925, it was stated to have

been bought by the Metro-Goldwyn Film Corporation. The final stage presentation was an American musical comedy, *Lady be Good*, by George Gershwin, with the Astaires in the cast.

The last performance on the stage of the old theatre was on 22 January 1927, in the presence of the then Prince of Wales (the Duke of Windsor). Genée was also there and came on the stage at the end of the evening. The theatre was then closed for demolition.

One of the stipulations of the sale by Alfred Butt was that a stage must be included in the new cinema which was to be built. Properties in Leicester Place and Lisle Street were bought and added to the original site. The new cinema was designed by Thomas W. Lamb of New York, in association with Frank Matcham. *The Survey of London* says:

> The original Empire Theatre had been planned on a north-to-south axis with the stage north of the auditorium, but the new Empire, built on an enlarged site, was orientated with the stage on the east. Designed by one of the leading American theatre specialists, it introduced transatlantic standards of size, magnificence and luxury to London, in a spaciously planned building, provided with such features as smoking-rooms, cosmetic-rooms, rest-rooms and a large tea-room.
>
> The Portland stone front to Leicester Square is a more scholarly composition than most theatre exteriors. It is, in fact, a large-scaled adaptation of the Venetian-arched motif used by Anmanati for the upper loggia in the second court of the Villa di Papa Giulia in Rome. In the recessed wall behind the central arch and trabeated side openings are windows set within rich frames of polychrome terracotta.
>
> From Leicester Square a deeply recessed screen of six double doors led through an oblong lobby into the large and lofty grand *foyer*. Here the walls were lined with a high dado of walnut panelling, surmounted by an order of scagliola-shafted Corinthian columns and pilasters, spaced to form bays containing arched pseudo-windows glazed with mirrors. Opposite the entrance screen was a marble and metal stair-case, with a wide flight descending centrally to the stalls foyer, between parallel flights rising to an apsed landing, where doors led into the large oblong tea-room, formed within the

void below the circle. The huge auditorium, containing stalls seating for 2,000 and a circle holding 1,500, was sumptuously decorated in the High Renaissance style. The elliptically-arched proscenium, its deep reveal rich with delicate arabesques, was flanked by concave splayed walls, each decorated with grotesque-ornamented panels and Corinthian pilasters flanking a large arch dressed with elaborate draperies, concealing an organ loft. A high dado of walnut panelling extended round the walls, below panels of gold brocade set in rich plasterwork painted in warm tones of brown, ivory and rose, and enriched with much gilding. The large stage was fully equipped for theatrical performances, and rising platforms were provided for the orchestra and organ console.

The cinema was completed and ready for opening by 8 November 1928. The first film was *Trelawney of the Wells*.

The Empire once again became the centre of another form of entertainment with the arrival of the 'Talkies', but changing tastes brought about another turn in the tide for the cinema and in December 1949 the large stage was brought into use with programmes half film and half revue. These spectacular shows mostly consisted of dancing and ballet. Staged by Nat Karson, they ran until 1952, when television was beginning to make itself felt as an opposition to the cinema and Dance Halls were also coming into vogue.

The Empire was closed in May 1961 and the interior completely reconstructed. Within the shell of the cinema two separate buildings were built. Designed by George Coles, these comprised a large dance-hall of two storeys—with a platform and revolving stage—and below it a cinema of the stadium type seating 1,336 designed for presentation of films on a panoramic screen. The entrance front was retained, but completely covered with an electric sign. The original *foyer* was remodelled to form twin entrance halls, the south one serving the Empire cinema, which was opened 19 December 1962 (with *Jumbo*) and the north leading to the Mecca dance-hall, the Empire Ballroom, which opened in March 1963.

4
The Gaiety Theatre

The Strand Musick Hall

Strand

In a block bounded by Wellington Street and Catherine Street, with Exeter Street at the rear

FIRST THEATRE

Opened as the Strand Musick Hall 15 October 1864 with a Promenade Concert consisting of a mixed musical entertainment. Under the management of John Lea.
Closed 2 December 1866.
Completely re-constructed on an enlarged site with entrances and exits in Catherine Street and stage door in Wellington Street.
Opened as the Gaiety Theatre 21 December 1868 with *The Two Harlequins*, as an operetta in one act by Emile Jonas (English words by Gilbert á'Beckett), *On the Cards*, a comedy drama by Alfred Thompson (from the French) and *Robert the Devil; or, The Nun, the Dun and the Son of a Gun*, an operatic extravaganza by W. S. Gilbert.
Under the management of John Hollingshead.
Closed 4 July 1903 and demolished for the Strand (Aldwych and Kingsway) development scheme.

SECOND THEATRE

On a new site at the corner of Aldwych and Strand.

Opened 26 October 1903 with *The Orchid*, a musical play by James T. Tanner, lyrics by Adrian Ross and Percy Greenbank. Music by Ivan Caryll and Lionel Monckton. Additional numbers by Paul Rubens.
Under the management of George Edwardes.

Closed 25 February 1939 but not demolished until 1957.
English Electric House stands on the site.

UNTIL THE TURN of this century the Strand was a narrow thoroughfare along most of its length, about the width it is now at Temple
Bar. A scheme to widen the eastern end of the main artery from
the City to the West End was proposed for many years, but did
not take place until the Strand (Aldwych and Kingsway), development scheme was put into operation in the late nineties.

The area covered by the maze of streets and courts between
St Clement Danes and Catherine Street is dealt with under the
Globe Theatre, the Olympic Theatre and the Opera Comique
(numbers 6, 13 and 14). The westerly end of the scheme involved
the area from Wellington Street North, (Wellington Street South
was the approach to Waterloo Bridge).

There had been earlier improvements in the Strand. The north
side, between St. Clement Danes and Chancery Lane, had been
mostly re-built as the Law Courts, which opened in 1882. At the
beginning of the century when Waterloo Bridge was built (it was
opened in 1817), Wellington Street (south) was constructed to
join the bridge to the Strand, which it met opposite Exeter
Change (Cross's Menagerie), and the entrance of the first Lyceum
Theatre, at number 254, (see *The Theatres of London*). The Change
was pulled down after the Lyceum had been destroyed by fire,
with much adjacent property, in 1830.

A new Lyceum Theatre was built with its frontage on the
western side of Wellington Street (north), now continued across
the Strand to Bow Street into Covent Garden. From the eastern
corner of Wellington Street, on the ground which had been
covered by part of the original Lyceum, numerous miscellaneous
buildings were soon built and this block, to Catherine Street, was
later to contain firstly the Strand Musick Hall and then the first
Gaiety Theatre.

John Hollingshead's *Gaiety Chronicles* (1898) says:

The mouth of Wellington Street North has two blocks of
buildings—one at the west corner, the centre of which is the
Lyceum Theatre, and the other at the east corner, the centre
of which is the Gaiety Theatre. *Thalia* (if I may be allowed

such classical allusions) is represented on one side, and *Melpomene* on the other. The hilly gorge between, too well known to drivers and horses, is the Dardanelles of the drama.

The eastern corner, which has long held, at the back, the historic premises of the *Morning Post*, presented a Strand frontage that was marked out by destiny for a metropolitan place of amusement. The frontage was part of an island of little interest in the history of London—the history of the day before yesterday, and not the records of remote antiquity. The eastern boundary of the property was a festive thoroughfare, where the chimes were heard long after midnight, from Drury Lane Theatre and the (now defunct) Albion Tavern at one end, to the Strand thoroughfare at the other. Old taverns and *à la mode* beef shops abounded, and a private amateur theatre, where many celebrities made their first appearance, which afterwards became a flash night-house called 'Jessop's,' then a printing office, then one of the numerous homes of the Savage Club before it turned its Bohemian coat and cultivated a liking for clean linen and the aristocracy, stood near the middle of the street, where it stands now as the office of the *Echo* newspaper.

The 'private amateur theatre' mentioned by Hollingshead was at number 11 Catherine Street, on the corner of Little Catherine Street, which led through courts to Drury Lane. It is said to have been opened as the Temple of Arts by Moritz, a German conjuror, in 1807 with a mixture of magic, acrobatics and performing animals. *Oxberry's Dramatic Biography*, Volume 3, August 1825, contains the following which gives an account of the theatre at an early date:

> We copy the following from a newspaper, published about twenty years since. Perhaps some of our readers, who are not in the habit of seeing criticisms on themselves, may be amused by a revision of past events.
>
> 'On Tuesday last, some amateurs performed the old comedy of *The Wonder*, in a *new* manner, at a small though neat theatre in Catherine Street, Strand. The gentleman who performed the part of *Felix*, seemed to possess more judgment than powers of execution, and less knowledge of stage-effect than either. He was but indifferently supported by the under-

characters, upon the judicious bustle of which depends the effect of the whole. The *Colonel* and *Frederick* were both respectable, and a *young* boy, in the part of an *old* man, displayed much humour. Of the ladies, a Miss Marsh in *Violante*, deserves the highest praise; she evinced through the whole a superior judgment, and easy and graceful deportment, free from those affections and theatrical artifices, which, amongst the ignorant, are reckoned necessary to gain applause. *Inis* was performed in true vixen-like style; and, upon the whole, the audience, which was respectable appeared much amused. We cannot conclude without observing, that there is much obloquy thrown upon private theatricals, more, we believe, than they in general deserve. We saw no impropriety or indecorum; everything was conducted in a regular and decent manner. One thing we particularly observed—the *frail sisterhood* had no admittance there.'

By October 1809 it had become known as the Minor Theatre and was occupied by another conjuror named Ingleby. It is first mentioned in the annual guide, *The Picture of London* for 1811 (published 1810), under the heading 'Private Theatres':

Upon a small scale may be mentioned those of Tottenham Court Road, Berwick Street, and the Minor Theatre, Catherine Street, Strand; in the two latter of which not less than ten different companies perform. Tickets are delivered gratis by the performers to their friends, and are procured, in their respective neighbourhoods, without much difficulty.

In 1813 it was calling itself Phillipstall's Exhibition Room, after its proprietor who was showing mechanical tricks and optical illusions. In turn it became a school of acting and the Harmonic Theatre in 1816, again managed by a conjuror, Gyngall, an Italian who also exhibited Chinese Shadows, Puppets and a Panorama of London. In between showman managers the amateurs came and went.

The theatre was situated upstairs in the building, and for many years a firm of piano and organ manufacturers occupied the lower floor. For a time, in 1820, it was known as the Théâtre Mécanique, for the exhibition of mechanical figures, but amateurs returned and it became the Argus Subscription Theatre.

Yet another change of name came in September 1823 when the title Theatre of Variety was used for the first time to designate a mixed entertainment. By 1826 it was again the Harmonic Theatre for amateurs and aspiring professionals. A new management in 1830 re-named the theatre yet again the Thespian Institute, where:

> Free Monthly Tickets to be had, and Gentlemen desirous of playing on Private Nights, may learn the Terms of Subscription, by applying at the Theatre. Attendance at the Theatre for Business; from Seven till Eleven o'clock in the Evening. The Theatre to Let for Exhibitions or Lectures. Letters addressed, post paid, will be duly attended to. No Money taken at the Doors. Tickets may be obtained, and places for the Boxes secured, at Mr. Onshyn's Circulating Library, No. 4, Catherine Street, Strand. No Ladies admitted to the Dress Circle with Bonnets.

In 1839 Benjamin Smythson, a provincial actor who had been at the Sans Souci in Leicester Place, (calling it the Vaudeville Subscription Theatre) took over number 11 and added number 12 Catherine Street into the building, re-opening as the Royal Pantheon Theatre (not to be confused with the Oxford Street theatre of the same name, which existed from 1813 to 1814. (see number 16).)

In a short history of this theatre by Malcolm Morley and George Speaight in *Theatre Notebook* (Volume 18, number 4), we are told:

> A narrow passage was anything but a royal approach to the Royal Pantheon. It was dirty and dark, lit only by a single gas jet above the entrance which opened upon a flight of steep stone steps leading to the auditorium. The theatre held about one hundred and fifty persons; sixty in the Pit, forty in the Gallery and sixty in the so designated Boxes lining the interior. Two Private Boxes, like sentry boxes stood on either side of the small stage fourteen feet deep and not much wider. Under the stage was a room spoken of as 'The Saloon.' Here ambitious amateurs talked and evaluated the performances given above, naturally not forgetting their own. Over the fireplace were placed notices of future productions and a list of the parts to be filled, those characters being as it were for sale. Against each role was set down the price

for which it would be allocated to the prentice player. The prices varied according to the occasion. There is a record preserved of the charges made for a performance of *Richard III*. The crook-back king went for £5, Richmond £3, Buckingham £2 10s., Catesby £1, Lord Stanley £1, Norfolk 10s., Ratcliffe 10s, and smaller parts 5s. In all £22 was collected for which sum Smythson provided the theatre, scenery, printing, dresses, gas, etc. . . . .

Female roles were enacted by the very lesser lights of the stage. They were rated as professional actresses and were not expected to pay for any glory they might acquire in portraying epic heroines in Catherine Street. The fledgling males footed the bill and in return received tickets equal in face value to the cash invested. Of the plays selected those by Shakespeare were first and foremost, the emphasis being strongly on tragedy. Hamlets, Macbeths, Romeos and Othellos lined up by the score, waiting to parade their talent, saving their shillings to bring about the momentous moment. A number of these raw recruits were afterwards to distinguish themselves in the profession, William Creswick, Henry Marston, Leigh Murray and Nye Chart, all made their début at the Pantheon.

Several attempts were made to obtain a Magistrate's Licence for the theatre. Official recognition was legally required to allow the place to admit the general public and not be designated a private playhouse, or a supposedly private one. Applications met with refusal, time and time again. At last, in 1839, Smythson secured the coveted Licence. But the policy at the Pantheon remained the same as before, even though now tickets could be sold at the door.

Smythson died in 1841 and the theatre soon closed, though it is listed in the Rate Books as the Little Catherine Street Theatre until 1857. A printer and publisher, Frederick Haxall, took over the lower part of the premises, and in 1843 John Jessop converted the theatre into a coffee house and night haunt, Jessop's Hall or Saloon, which acquired a notorious reputation causing its speedy closure. It became the Royal Victoria Saloon with a Ball Room, serving supper up to 10 p.m., but soon closed.

In the early Eighteen-Sixties Henry St. Maine ran a Dancing Academy at Number 11. The theatre attached to the premises was opened under the management of A. James and rented by the night to Amateur Dramatic Societies. Among the Societies producing plays were the Stirling, the Arundel, the Ellistonian and the Byron. The Gem, as the theatre was now called, opened on September 17 1861, and lasted for only seven months. The Dancing Academy continued.

For a time, from 1862, the Savage Club occupied part of the premises, but members complained of the noise made by the dancing academy in the other part of the building and the Club moved.

In 1863 it became the home of a firm of auctioneers. It was turned into a restaurant in 1864 and eventually became the offices of *The Echo* in 1870, which it remained until this part of Catherine Street was lost in the Strand improvements. The Minor Theatre site is somewhere under Aldwych, outside the Waldorf Hotel.

John Hollingshead's tour of the area continues:

The west side of Catherine Street saw the birth of the *Era* newspaper, a professional journal devoted to the interests of the stage.

At the north-east corner of the block, on the rise of the Wellington Street Hill, was the most interesting building of all—the first public workshop of Charles Dickens. Here *Household Words* was started. The building still exists, unchanged externally; but about ten years ago it was absorbed by the Gaiety Theatre, providing space that had long been much needed for dressing rooms and offices.

Next door to the office of *Household Words*, running from Wellington Street North to Catherine Street, was a narrow passage or arcade of shops, sometimes erroneously called 'Exeter Change', and often confused with the old building in the Strand, which stood where Burleigh Street now stands, and contained Cross's Menagerie. This old, original 'Change' was pulled down early in the present century for Strand improvements, and the only fragment of it remaining is an architectural scroll with a clock-dial, which stands over the shoe-shop next door to the Lyceum pit entrance.

Exeter Arcade was never a commercial success. Its shops were always displaying the legend 'to let', and if a tenant came in one week he generally went out the next, especially if he was asked for rent. Bohemian journals, started by writers who wished to be their own editors and masters of a shop-boy, obtained a 'local habitation and a name' in the *Arcade*. The journals were written in the back parlours, and sold or given away across the counters, under which some of the editors slept at night or in the early morning. At the western mouth of this arcade—in Wellington Street North—was a tall and very narrow building, such as architects call an 'engaged column', with rooms like the rooms of a lighthouse, let to people who required modest chambers.

Next to Exeter Arcade was the historic office of *The Morning Post* much enlarged, having displaced *The Field*, the *Queen* and *The Law Times*. The proprietors, by this move, obtained a great frontage at the Strand corner of Wellington Street. The oldest and quaintest of the buildings which stood on the Strand front of this block, amongst other shops of less importance, was the office of *The Mirror*, that fossil relic of the primary formation of periodical literature.

This important London island, which I have walked round and briefly described, arrived at the time in the early sixties when it had to bow to its inevitable destiny. A music-hall was projected and built, and a portion of the island was bought for the purpose. The entrance was, of course, on the Strand front, as near the centre as possible, and the place was called the Strand Musick Hall.

The Era 16 October 1864 described the building and the opening:

This establishment, which is promoted by a Joint Stock Company (The Strand Musick Hall Company) after numerous delays, opens to the public to-morrow, though probably it will never have a more crowded or attentive audience than at its inauguration last evening.

Continental Gothic is the basis of this eclectic design, and if the architect has succeeded in erecting a structure which, departing from recognised codes, outrages none, he trusts that unity and comprehensiveness in the execution of a difficult task will obtain for him a just appreciation of his work.

The main building as it at present exists, which constitutes

what may be called the Hall proper, covers ground running
E. and W. from opposite the Lyceum Theatre, in Wellington
Street, Strand, to Catherine Street, where it has a present
frontage of seventy feet, from which to Wellington Street
the depth is over a hundred and ten feet.

The Company have acquired the land upon which will
ultimately extend the main building to Exeter Street on the
N., where it will possess a frontage of about sixty feet.

The Hall is approached from the Strand by a building
ninety-six feet long, with a frontage of thirty-six feet to the
Strand, which contains besides the spacious corridors and grand
staircase saloon (forming communications from the Strand
with all parts of the building), commodious and elegant
dining and smoking rooms, with waiters' serving rooms, and
lavatory and dressing rooms for visitors to each; and
immediately communicating with the Hall proper on the
ground, balcony, and box floors, refreshment bars or buffets,
which will be used as luncheon bars and for the service of the
dining-rooms during the day, and as buffets for the use of the
Hall in the evening.

The building has been erected from the designs and details
of Mr. E. Bassett Keeling, of Gray's Inn, and under the
superintendence of himself and Mr. H. H. Collins, the joint
architects to the Company. The whole of the coloured
decorations, which are of a very novel and elaborate character,
have been executed from the special directions of Mr.
Keeling, under whose independent control the whole of the
decorative portions of the building have been carried out.
Among those connected with the building we may mention
that the general contractors were Messrs. Trollope and Sons.
The whole of the gas arrangements have been executed by
Messrs. Defries and Sons. The ventilating apparatus, lifts,
&c., have been under the care of Mr. Wilson W. Phipson,
C.E. All ornamental wrought iron work in the front building is
by Hart and Sons, and the copper foliations are by Brawn,
of Birmingham. The painting and decorations have been
executed by Mr. Geo. Foxley, and the greater portion of the
stone carving has been undertaken by Mr. Tolmie.

The ventilation of the whole structure has received the
greatest attention at the hands of Mr. Wilson W. Phipson,

and it is hoped that a degree of success has been secured which will render the Strand Musick Hall the best ventilated public building in London.

Vocal and Instrumental Operatic Selections will fill a prominent place in the nightly programmes, and will be arranged upon a novel plan, calculated to afford full scope at once for the talent of the singers and for the skill of the orchestral performers. The symphonies of the Great Masters will occasionally be rendered, but at the same time the light and effervescent works of the composers of the hour will receive their full share of attention. The aim of the Directors of the Strand Musick Hall will be to please all tastes, save only those which are depraved. They purpose to enable the classical amateur to revel in the emanations of the loftiest genius—the lover of sparkling dance music to drink in the capering melodies to his heart's content—the worshipper of grand lyric inspirations to depart well satisfied with his treat —the adorer of the simple ballad to feel that he has had his full share of enjoyment—and the patron of comic singing to recognise that his special predilections have not been uncared for. In the last-named department it may be almost needless to say that every feature introduced will be jealously and rigorously scrutinised, and carefully kept free from anything that could shock the most refined taste or grate upon the most delicate susceptibilities.

Smoking and drinking have, in the establishments heretofore called Music Halls, sat elbow to elbow with harmony. The Directors of the Strand Musick Hall have thought it fitting to bestow this designation upon their building, inasmuch as it is a Hall devoted to the performance of music—but as the music given will be of a superior class, they expect from their visitors an equally exalted etiquette. Creature comforts— both nicotian and alcoholic—will be found at the spacious buffets, and in the corridors and saloons which surround the Hall. Visitors will have all the facilities they could desire for their puffings and their potations, but not within the Hall, which is consecrated to music.

From a circular distributed in the Hall by Messrs. Defries we extract the following:

The novel system invented and patented by Messrs. J.

Defries and Sons, who have had the entire management of everything concerning the lighting of the building, will form one of the prominent features of the Hall, and cannot fail to create a total innovation in the system hitherto adopted in lighting Theatres, Concert-rooms, and other large buildings. This new system combines that great *desideratum* of allying with the nearest approach to a soft daylight a system of thorough and complete ventilation throughout the building. Hence to Messrs. J. Defries and Sons is due the full credit of having overcome those difficulties which had hitherto arisen in lighting, and the same time introducing a proper system of ventilation; and their patent is destined to form a new era in the principle of lighting. The numerous audiences which will no doubt visit this new resort of amusement will fully appreciate the beautiful amalgamation of colours produced without there being any show of gas. The light is entirely given from the top of the building, and by a combination of coloured sheets of glass and prisms, a soft and radiant light is thrown into every part of the building. The system of ventilation is so perfect, that a continual current of fresh air is introduced throughout the building, whilst the impure air, as well as the heat, is carried away through the top of the building by the powerful current which is established.

To convey a slight idea of the vast importance of Messrs. J. Defries and Sons' new patent, it will be sufficient to state that there are several thousands of burners. The lighting chamber contains upwards of 350 ventilating tubes, the whole of which are conducted into enormous shafts, in which a proper vacuum has been established, thus causing an unvarying upward current, so that heat as well as the vitiated air is constantly conveyed out of the building. The thorough lighting of all our principal Opera Houses, Theatres, Music Halls, &c., bear full testimony to the vast resources of Messrs. J. Defries & Sons, but they have now in this new method surpassed anything hitherto produced.

The inaugural performance commenced about half-past seven last evening with the National Anthem, by the band only, the ladies who were announced to take the solo parts not appearing. This was followed by the overture from

Masaniello, and, ably as Mr. Kingsbury is known to conduct, it became soon evident that his troops, consisting of some five and twenty instrumentalists, had not been sufficiently drilled—a defect, however, which will no doubt be rectified on future representations. Signor Tito Mattei, pianist to the King of Italy, next appeared and played a Notturno, 'Souvenir d'Italie,' and Grand Valse, 'L'espooizione Italiana,' in a manner which showed him to be a thorough master of his instrument, and he at once made himself a favourite with the audience, maintaining his position in the latter part of the evening in a Fantasia from *Norma*. Mdlle. Molidoff was the first vocalist introduced, being represented as of the principal Concerts of France, Germany, Belgium, &c., and gave a valse with some spirit, though lacking breadth. The lady has a fair mezzo-soprano voice and a good appearance, but seemed nervous, owing, no doubt, to the novelty of singing before a new audience. After 'Gems of the Opera,' i.e. Selections from *Semiramide*, by the band, which, though sometimes uneven, acted better together than in *Masaniello*, Mdlle. Rosa Wilks, of the Conservatoire Royale de Musique, Brussels, gave 'Bel raggio' with some taste and sweetness but her voice, though pure, is wanting in power, or the unfinished state of the Hall had an unfavourable effect upon it. The next *débutante*, Mdlle. Carlotta Mayer, again of France and Belgium, made, however, the success of the evening. Her voice is a rich contralto, and she evidently knows how to use it, and we can fairly predict that she will become a favourite of the public. The band having played the *finale* to the first part, the Persian Story-teller Kisseh Kon appeared in full costume to introduce one of his wonderful relations; and this we must protest against as altogether a mistake—Whitechapel Persian without a scintilla of wit is not suited for a Music (we beg pardon, Musick) Hall which pretends to eclipse all others in the nature of its performances; and the wonderful relation was certainly not equal to the stump orations of other establishments. He was both vulgar and impertinent, and being duly appreciated by the audience, first told them if they did not like him they 'had better go and liquor,' and then bid them good night in a huff. In the second part Mdlle. Wilks confirmed the good opinion formed of her

in the first by her rendering of 'Leggiero Invisible,' and Mdlle.
Mayer on coming forward to sing the favourite Brindisi from
Il Segreto received a welcome such as is rarely accorded
excepting to an old favourite. Mons. Duhem (from Brussels)
gave a cornet solo with variations on Rode's Air, which
proved him a perfect master of his art, and was the real gem
of the evening. Signor Giovanni Adelmann played a violin
solo judiciously and with taste. A terzetta for clarionet,
cornet and euphonium by Messrs. G. Tyler, A. Boulcourt,
and Signor Jannoti was deservedly admired. The various
other performances of the orchestra showed more warmth
and spirit than in the first part, more especially in a Valse,
by Strauss, and a concluding Galop, by Laroche. Taken as a
whole, the house may be said to have opened auspiciously,
though we very much doubt if the entertainments are not a
little too Pretentious or Classic to insure a permanent success.
Mr. Frederick Kingsbury led well, and was repeatedly
applauded, whilst both Mr. Keeling, the clever Architect, and
Mr. Lea, the General Manager, were called to receive the
congratulations of their friends in the course of the evening.

The general appearance of the Hall is good, but the pillars
and fronts of the balconies and boxes are too sombre. The
roof, which is most beautiful by day, does not show to
advantage in the evening, and owing to the peculiar arrangement of the lights much of the beautiful decorations, especially of the ceilings of the balconies, is altogether lost. The
light itself requires some modification, and we would suggest
the taking away of all that portion of the glass roof painted
yellow and substituting plain ground glass, with, perhaps, the
introduction of an occasionally polished star. The waiters and
other officials are in livery, supplied by Messrs. Samuels, and
the whole of the arrangements appear to have been conducted
with taste and judgment. One of the regulations—that of the
non supply of refreshments in the Hall or Balconies—was not
rigidly adhered to last night and we doubt if it can be fully
carried out.

At a quarter to one this morning (Sunday), an alarm of
fire was raised, and the basement part of one of the houses
connected with the Hall in Exeter Street was discovered on

fire. Several engines arrived, and, of course, much excitement prevailed, but the fire was soon extinguished.

The Strand Musick Hall opened to the general public on 17 October.

The man behind the project was Maurice R. Syers, but unfortunately the programmes of music and 'variety' were in advance of their time. In the early sixties the music halls were only just emerging from the bar parlour atmosphere and a more robust entertainment was in vogue generally, though at the Canterbury and the Oxford, Morton was providing good music in his halls.

The Strand Musick Hall provided a hybrid form of entertainment. Promenade concerts with long opera selections as a first half at 8 o-clock followed by music hall turns by the favourites of the day. This failed dismally and Syers tried straightforward music hall with eating, smoking and drinking. 'Jolly' John Nash became the Chairman, but the damage had been done, the public would not respond. The company went into liquidation and the building closed on 2 December 1866. Hollingshead says of the failure:

> For various reasons, in spite of its position, the Strand Musick Hall was a failure from the day of opening. It is always a mistake to go too far ahead of your audience. The architecture of the place had something to do with it. The word *rococo* expresses much, but it never expressed half enough when used in a description of the 'Strand Musick Hall.' A decorator's studio, overloaded with samples picked from all nations, was the only thing the place suggested. I took the late Sir Richard Burton to see it, and he then considered his education thoroughly completed. He had seen many things but never, under one roof, anything like this very remarkable building.

He goes on to say:

> The empty premises were not long without a purchaser, who kept his name concealed, and did not appear to be in any hurry to utilize his property. The secret was well kept, until the proper time arrived to disclose it. By that time all the houses in the eastern section of Exeter Street (south side), including the old Fountain Tavern, but leaving the public-

house at the corner of Catherine Street and Exeter Street; the Arcade, several houses on the west side of Catherine Street, from this corner public-house towards the Strand, excluding *The Era* and *Illustrated Times* offices, and all the shops in the Strand (not many) from the Strand corner of Catherine Street up to *The Field* and *Queen* offices, on each side of the Strand Musick Hall entrance, had been acquired by a mysterious capitalist. The secret purchaser of these properties was Mr. Lionel Lawson, part proprietor of the *Daily Telegraph* newspaper, whose idea was to build a moderately-sized and improved theatre, with a restaurant attached, to be called the Gaiety.

Mr. Lawson employed a rising architect, Mr. C. J. Phipps, who had previously built the Queen's Theatre for him in Long Acre. They went over to Paris together, and took as their model the Théâtre Lyrique, in the Place du Chatelet, copying the projecting balcony, with small private boxes round the back, instead of the old-fashioned 'dress-circle,' kept in a line with the supporting columns. Their theatre was practically open on four sides, though neither the Lord Chamberlain nor the Metropolitan Board of Works insisted, at that time, on any such structural conditions. The plan of the house and its title were settled before I heard that such a theatre was to be erected, and I am not, therefore, entitled to any credit that may attach to its construction. The idea of joining a restaurant to the theatre, where people could dine and walk from their dinner into the playhouse, or, after the performance, could walk from the playhouse into the restaurant to supper, was Mr. Lawson's, not mine.

I first heard of the proposed theatre from Mr. Dion Boucicault, who suggested that I should make an offer for the tenancy. I was on friendly terms with Mr. Lawson, and had written occasionally for *The Daily Telegraph*. I had been the stage director of the Alhambra for nearly three years. I did not pose as a capitalist, particularly before a reputed millionaire and a man of financial genius. I treated my means as a joke, but I got the theatre. A literary friend, of all people, whipped up a small syndicate of companions to support me, and we were duly registered as the 'New Theatres Company, Limited; Capital, £5,000.' The lease was in my name individually, and a board was soon painted and stuck up on the Strand front: 'The Gaiety Theatre. This house, when completed, will be opened under the direction of Mr. John Hollingshead.' Many people who saw the announcement wondered who John Hollingshead was, as my name had never appeared in connexion with the Alhambra. I passed my apprenticeship there anonymously. Many who knew me only knew me as 'one of those writing chaps,' and as 'writing chaps' were common as theatre directors in London as they are in Paris, they were no doubt not inclined to bid much for my chances of success.

The first thing I did was to buy a cylinder writing-desk with plenty of pigeon-holes, a cheap working piano, and a few chairs, including one office-chair, with a seat that revolved on its own axis. These were placed in a large room facing the Strand, the only carpet being mortar dust and broken bricks. It was a room intended to form part of the Strand Musick Hall restaurant, and it commanded a view of the 'works' at the back, where the contractor was digging out the foundations of the future theatre.

Mr. C. J. Phipps, the architect, Mr. Gordon, the scenic artist, and Mr. Robert Bell, the decorator, with the contractors, began their Gaiety labours in the early summer of 1868, allowing about seven months for the completion of the building. The area on which the theatre was to be erected— the front part belonging to the Strand Musick Hall, what was left of it, being devoted to the main passages and staircase, and the back part in Exeter Street to the stage and auditorium was in a very fair sanitary condition. The site was a natural slope, rising from the Strand to the back, so that the ground floor of the theatre was on a level with the first-floor of the frontage.

He tells that:

The total cost of the Gaiety Theatre, as a building, was £15,000. Some allowance must be made for the low rates for labour and material existing in 1868. The original rental, with two of the best stage-boxes in the ground tier, reserved by the landlord, communicating with a small ante-room under the Royal box, and having the use of the private Royal entrance, was £3,500 a year, and this *without bars*, which belonged (and

still belong) to the restaurant's half of the lease. This reservation of the drinking department practically increased the rent
another £1,000 a year—making £4,500 a year. As the tenant,
I paid rates, taxes, insurance, including the land-tax
(redeemed), storage for scenery outside the theatre, and
carriage to and fro, making at least another £1,000 a year.
When, owing to the sudden death of Mr. Lionel Lawson, the
two proprietary boxes were thrown into the theatre, the rent,
by arrangement, was increased another £500 a year, so that I
stood altogether to pay annually about £6,000. The rent of the
theatre, which I punctually paid for eighteen years, according
to my calculations, bought the freehold of the ground from
the Marquis of Exeter, built and furnished the theatre up to
the starting-point, and gave the landlord a bonus of £18,000.

Of the last minute rush to get the theatre opened he says:

About three or four o'clock on the afternoon of Monday,
the 21st of December, 1868, the straggling parts of the little
Gaiety army came together on the Gaiety stage before the
contractor's men had departed. Some of these men pretended
to be at work, and others lingered in the hope of seeing a full
rehearsal. In this they were disappointed. Dresses were tried
on, and their wearers came up or down to the wings, according
to whether they dressed upstairs or down, in the 'flies' or on
the 'mezzanine floor' (pronounced 'mazarine' by theatrical
workmen), paraded before the management, and then left the
scene, after suggestions, in company with one of the wardrobe
sempstresses. The stage-manager, Mr. Robert Soutar,
new to the place, took possession of a Royal ante-room, which
communicated with the stage, and was hardly satisfied with
the explanation that the room belonged to the auditorium
side of the curtain. About twenty minutes past six the last
of the lingering workmen filed out with the implements of their
handicraft, leaving a trail of lime-dust behind them. They
filed off the stage, but not out of the house, and took up a firm
position, with their implements, in the front rows of the upper
balcony. When the acting manager remonstrated with them
before he opened the various doors to the public, they
declined to move, and said they had built the (adjective)
theatre, and they meant to see it opened. The difficulty was

reported to me, and I recognised a certain amount of justice in their contention. They were allowed to remain, and see the (adjective) theatre opened.

The theatre is described in *The Era* 13 December 1868:

This large, elegant, and central Theatre, has been erected on part of the Strand, part of Exeter Street, part of Catherine Street, and part of Wellington Street, and the site of the Strand Musick Hall—a building that has been entirely pulled down for the lobbies of the new house. The site possesses the very marked advantage of approach from the four main thoroughfares before named, and occupies a much larger area than any similar property situated on that great stream of through traffic—the Strand.

A portion of the Strand frontage, lately known as that of the Strand Musick Hall, remains almost as formerly; a few modifications, however, have necessarily been made on the ground storey by the erection of the new entrance, which will form the approach to the principal tiers of the Theatre. The rooms over this entrance, and the new building extending along the Strand, forming the angle of Catherine Street will form the 'Restaurant' entirely distinct from the Theatre, but with a corridor of access from every tier of the Theatre.

As mentioned above, the principal entrance is in the Strand, leading by a few steps to the level of the stalls, and by a spacious octangular staircase to the balcony or grand tier and the upper boxes. Another entrance, also on this level, is in Exeter Street, on the other side of the stalls, which, though designed specially as a private entrance for the Royal Family, is available as an exit-way in case of sudden panic, there being a stone staircase from the entrance to the highest floor of the Theatre, with communication on every level. There is also a corridor running under the back of the pit, solely for the use of the stalls' audience, thus giving access on both sides of the house, and obviating the unpleasantness of having to cross the audience when the performance has commenced.

The entrances to pit and gallery are in Catherine Street, and the stage entrance is in Wellington Street.

The plan of the auditory is quite new to London. It consists of a balcony, the front forming a semicircle, opening out by

D

arms of a contrary flexure to the proscenium column; behind this is a tier of private boxes, with the restu of which the front of the upper boxes radiates; and a gallery above, the front of which form a complete circle. The columns supporting the various tiers are carried up to a sufficient height above the gallery, and from the cap spring a series of arches supporting an elaborate cornice and coved ceiling.

The proscenium pillars are all of solid stone, enriched with carved capitals.

There are five rows of arm-chairs in stalls; a commodious pit; three rows of arm-chair stalls in balcony; four rows of upper box seats, with considerable standing room; twenty-eight private boxes; and a spacious gallery. In all, the capacity of this house is above the average of the London Theatres, and will hold upwards of 2,000 persons.

Every department or division of the audience has its own approach separate from the others; and all the tiers have enclosed corridors at back; one special feature of the arrangements being that there are staircases on both sides of the dress circle, upper boxes, and gallery, with external doors at the bottom of each, and all fire proof. In fact, the whole construction of the building is as nearly as possible fireproof, for not only are all staircases, passages, and corridors of stone or cement, and separated in every case by brick walls, but the several tiers—balcony, upper boxes, and gallery—have no wood in their construction, except the flooring boards; they are entirely built of an iron framework, embedded in and filled between with a solid mass of cement concrete, much on the principle adopted at the Grand Opera and the New Vaudeville Theatre at Paris, which system was adopted there as being the most perfect that could be devised, as by diminishing the amount of inflammable material in a building the risk of its even taking fire is rendered almost impossible, while the prevention of a fire spreading is insured. With the exception of the two Theatres at Paris before mentioned, the 'Gaiety' will be the only Theatre in Europe so constructed.

The ironwork necessary for this construction has been manufactured by Messrs. W. and T. Phillips of the Coal Exchange, at their works in Belgium, and constructed by them at the Theatre, in a very satisfactory manner.

The very elaborate box-fronts, together with the arches and cornices, are executed in patent plaster on canvas, and manufactured and fixed by the patentees, Messrs. George Jackson and Sons, of Rathbone Place, from the architect's designs.

The iron balcony-front was executed by Messrs. Hart, of Wych Street.

The lighting of the auditory is by a powerful sunburner, which will act as an efficient ventilator, manufactured by Messrs. Strode and Co., who have also executed the float-lights. These are of peculiar as well as novel construction, and have only been used before in England at the Queen's Theatre and at Brighton, by the same architect. In the present instance, many modifications have been introduced. The float consists of a series of argand burners reversed, and burning downwards, the products of the combustion being taken away in a large iron cylinder running parallel with the front of the stage, and carried up inside the brickwork behind the proscenium columns. One great advantage gained by this invention is, that the unpleasant vapour screen, which in the old manner was constantly rising between the audience and the scene, is entirely removed, and the performers can now approach the foot-lights without the risk of getting burnt, as a piece of gauze may be placed over the burner without ignition. By an ingenious contrivance, should any of the glasses break, that particular burner falls down and shuts off the gas. The coloured glasses, called mediums, are worked on levers in front of the lights, on the same principle as the switch-lights on railways.

The stage has been constructed by Mr. G. R. Tasker, the Clerk of Works, and is a most elaborate piece of mechanism, admirably contrived and executed, fitted up with several novelties in the way of machinery. There is a depth of some twenty feet under the stage floor, for sinking large scenes, and a height above of fifty feet. All the departments of the stage are very complete. There are green-rooms, managers' rooms, and more than twenty other rooms, for the numerous requirements of a large dramatic company, with wardrobes, property-rooms, carpenters' shops, &c.

The whole of the coloured decoration of the auditory and

the lobbies has been executed by Mr. George Gordon, late of the Bristol and Bath Theatres. It partakes somewhat of the early Romanesque character, thus carrying out the architecture of the house with some of the most beautiful and varied of the Greek forms of ornament introduced. The same gentleman has also painted the act drop, which, unlike that at most Theatres, is intended not as a scene or a picture, but as a part of the decoration of the Theatre. The design is extremely chaste and elegant; and the small vignette in the centre, representing a villa on one of the Italian lakes, is broadly, and at the same time delicately painted.

Perhaps the most noticeable feature of the decoration is the frieze over the proscenium, designed and painted by Mr. H. S. Marks—30 feet long by 4 feet 6 in. deep. It represents a king and queen of mediaeval times, with surrounding courtiers, watching a mask which is being performed before them. On either side this frieze, over the proscenium boxes, are lunettes in the arches—the one on the left represents lyric, and the other epic poetry—designed by the same artist. It is satisfactory to find that these pictures, which are really fine works of art, have been painted by Mr. Marks in no narrow spirit as easel pictures, but as forming a part of, and in a measure subservient to, the general scheme of decoration.

The arm-chairs in stalls and balcony are those designed by the architect, and manufactured by Wadman Brothers, Bath. The chairs for private boxes were made by Mr. Church, of Bath. The curtains have been supplied by Messrs. Hampton, of Pall Mall, and the carpets by Messrs. Tyler, of Long Acre.

The general builder's work has been done by Mr. Simpson; and the gas work (except as mentioned above) by Messrs. J. Jones and Son, of Bow Street.

The opening is recorded in *The Era* 27 December:

After having occupied scarcely more than five months in construction, this elegant new Theatre opened on Monday night, precisely on the very date which had been announced long beforehand. Such a determined resolution to keep faith with the public shows that the Lessee and Manager, Mr. John Hollingshead, has a keen perception of one of the first duties of a caterer for the people, and it may be at once declared

that a more elegant and commodious Theatre has never been
seen in the Metropolis. A description of the building has
already been given in the columns of *The Era*, and we have
now only to chronicle the nature of the novelties produced
on the opening night—novelties which we have the gratification of announcing achieved a success at once decided and
deserved. Soon after dusk an electric light [it's first use on a
public building in this Country] from the summit of the
building flashed down the Strand, the intelligence of the
original announcement being rigidly adhered to, and immediately after the doors were opened the house, no less remarkable for the convenience of its site than for the commodiousness
of its construction and the elegance of its appearance, was
crowded by an audience which comprised all the notabilities
of the several worlds of the Drama, Literature, Science, Art,
and Fashion. Three new pieces were produced on the
occasion, and the completeness with which each was represented indicated the energy of the new Management and the
strenuous exertions which must have been made by all therewith associated. The announcement by the Lessee and
Manager Mr. John Hollingshead, that all box booking, and
other fees would be entirely abolished was found to be
perfectly justified by the experience of every person who
entered the building, and among the pleasant surprises of the
evening was the presentation to each lady who occupied a
seat in the boxes or stalls of a perfumed fan, which spread
forth into a programme, giving a perfect account of the
evening's performances, and supplying all the names of the
characters appearing therein. The National Anthem having
been played by the excellent orchestra, under the direction of
Mr. Kettenus, the entertainments commenced with *The Two
Harlequins*, an operetta by M. Emile Jonas. With the music
of this composer the Parisians have been for some time
familiar. *Les Deux Arlequins*, which Mr. Gilbert à'Beckett has
rendered into English. Mr. Charles Lyall sang the music well,
and acted the part with the necessary spirit. Miss Constance
Loseby (Miss Constance of the London Music Halls) is not
altogether new to the stage. She sang the pretty romance,
'O Columbine, my own for ever!' very expressively. The
operetta is an unquestionable success, and is very well

performed by all engaged, the band, under the direction of
Mr. Kettenus; and the chorus superintended by Mr. J. Pittman. The scene, à la Watteau, is a glimpse of sylvan beauty
realised to perfection by Mr. T. Grieve.

This was succeeded by a new comedy-drama, in three acts,
entitled *On the Cards*, adapted from the five-act *drama*, by
MM. D'Ennery and Bresil, called *L'Escamoteur*. The present
adapter, who, from his response to the demand for the author
at the end of the drama, may be identified with Mr. Alfred
Thompson, the accomplished artist (who also designed the
programme covers). The great recommendation of the piece is
the abundant opportunity afforded Mr. Alfred Wigan for
representing one of those characters in which he has long since
achieved a distinct position. Adolphe Chavillard speaks broken
English, is diverting, pathetic, indignant, compassionate, and
chivalrous, all qualities which Mr. Wigan knows well how to
turn to the best histrionic account. The high finish, extreme
delicacy of delineation, and consummate tact displayed in this
embodiment would alone make Mr. Wigan's name illustrious
in the list of modern actors. Miss Madge Robertson represented the heroine with her usual grace, earnestness, and
intelligence. Miss Marie Litton dressed and acted the small
part of Mrs. Cureton in excellent taste, and Miss Ellen Farren,
received with an enthusiastic burst of welcome, played the
conjuror's assistant, Sprightley, with an archness and
vivacity which proved more than usually delightful. Mr.
H. R. Teesdale, who made his first appearance as the sinister
cousin, Guy Chilstone, showed no lack of self-possession, and
his quiet style of expression shows a performer of good training
and sound discrimination. M. William Stuart, an Englishman
by birth, but who has hitherto been only known as an actor at
the Odéon, Gaiété, and Porte St. Martin Theatres, is a young
comedian with stage features and a very prepossessing
appearance, but his style is not in accordance with British
notions of histrionic art. When he has more successfully overcome his strong French accent, and acquired a little more
ease on the English stage, we shall have, no doubt, to speak
more favourably of his exertions. Always a careful actor, Mr
Maclean proved himself as Sir Gilbert Ethelward, a most
desirable addition to the company. The curtain fell amidst

unqualified applause, and the principal performers were successively recalled. A loudly expressed wish to give a greeting to the new Manager, brought forward Mr. John Hollingshead, who spoke as follows:

'Ladies and Gentlemen,—You will see by the programme that no managerial address was intended, but I am happy to appear before you. I might make an apology for Mr. Grieve— not that he requires one—an artist who, for the last fifty years, has done more than any other for the embellishment of the stage. You will see that though he has had to contend with singular difficulties, he has most effectually and effectively triumphed over them. We only got possession of the stage at six on Saturday evening, and that night took place what may be called our first rehearsal. With regard to the abolition of fees to boxkeepers, &c., I have only to beg of you to assist me in carrying out that arrangement. Giving money to servants who ought to be—and here are—well paid by their employers, places master and man alike in a false position. I can only effectually carry out this system of theatrical reform by your aid, and I hope you will give it me.'

With these few remarks, which were manifestly spoken on the impulse of the moment, Mr. Hollingshead retired amidst renewed plaudits.

Of all subjects for a burlesque the opera of *Robert le Diable* would seem to be the least promising, but Mr. W. S. Gilbert, who has taken the work in hand, and produced a very bright extravaganza, under the title of *Robert the Devil; or, The Nun, the Dun, and the Son of a Gun*, has most successfully managed to render the story amusing. By making fun of the 'fiend father,' who seems quite unable to stand the force of ridicule, Mr. W. S. Gilbert seems to have fairly broken the spell. Notwithstanding the haste with which the piece had been produced no accident occurred, a fact which says something for the care of the Stage-Manager, Mr. Robert Soutar. It must at once be stated that the present extravaganza is characterised by a great improvement. No tune from the Music Halls will be heard during the performance. The composers of the vocal music, which has been so well arranged by Mr. Pittman, bear the illustrious names of Meyerbeer, Hérold, Bellini, and Auber, to say nothing of Offenbach,

Hervé, Jules Javelot, and others. The orchestral music, arranged by M. Kettenus, is also excellently selected and admirably performed. The dresses, designed by Mr. Alfred Thompson, and which are singularly tasteful, have been furnished by Miss Bennett and Mr. Coombes, and the ballet has been well placed under the direction of Miss Collier. The scenes of the port of Palermo and a view of Pandemonium, after the famous Martin picture, are especially effective; and the veteran scenic artist, Mr. Grieve, had to appear in the latter scene, and personally acknowledge the applause of the audience. In a series of five brisk scenes, furnished with a running fire of puns, the author has presented his whimsical perversion of the perilous ordeal to which Robert of Normandy was subjected. For the resuscitation of the nuns we have the animation of the waxwork in Madame Tussaud's famous Chamber of Horrors, and for the mystic branch is substituted a policeman's *baton*. There is a capital stroke of satire in the inscription, 'No eye can see the man who bears this staff.' The burlesque is produced with remarkable completeness in every department, and is admirably played. Miss Ellen Farren is full of fun and animation as Robert, Duke of Normandy. Miss Constance Loseby sings charmingly as Raimbault, the troubadour. Miss Emily Fowler is a most intelligent representative of the peasant girl, Alice, and Mr. R. Barker, who made his first appearance in London as Bertram, the fiend father, seems to be a comedian of much dry drollery. Mr. J. Aldred is amusing as Gobetto, the drunken Sicilian bore, who becomes afterwards Bertram's familar. Mr. J. Robins funnily personates Old Baily in the Chamber of Horrors, and Mr. Everett, Mr. Roe, Miss Ashton, and Miss Grundy are efficient representatives of the other waxwork figures. In the feminine department the company of the Gaiety is unusually strong. Miss Lilian Hastings shows a fine figure off to advantage as the Princess Isabella. Miss A. Tremaine looks handsome as the Prince of Granada, and Miss Henrie and Miss Lister are seen to the fullest personal advantage in the very slight form of costume they wear as Ferdinando and Bertruccio, the two Sicilian nobles. The ballet is a fantastic dance of the *Satanella* kind, in which Mdlle. Anna Bossi, of the Porte St. Martin and the Opera

House of Rio de Janeiro, figures prominently as the *première danseuse*. A grotesque effect is produced by the introduction of a couple of Sprites, cleverly embodied by those agile panto-mimists, Messrs. John D'Auban and John Warde, who execute some nimble movements with amazing quickness and cleverness. The burlesque was throughout warmly received, and Mr. Gilbert appeared, when the curtain fell, to acknow-ledge the applause of the audience. Since the first night some judicious curtailments have improved the drama, the burlesque has benefited by repetition, and the houses have been excellent. There can be little doubt that if the energy which has characterised the enterprise so far be continued through this and succeeding seasons the 'Gaiety' is destined to take a prominent position among the West End Theatres, and to prove most remunerative to those more immediately interested in its pecuniary prosperity.

From the start the Gaiety proved a success and Hollingshead's methods of advertising broke new ground. He put long advertise-ments in the newspapers, abolished the old style playbill and poster, and provided the audience with free programmes, in the early days printed on a fan. In 1871 he introduced matinées (morning performances), as a regular part of theatrical routine, (they had previously been given only for Christmas productions and as charity performances).

In 1877 electric street lighting was first seen in Paris, and the following year when the Gaiety was re-decorated for the first time, during its four week closure, Hollingshead decided to install the new lighting outside his theatre. On 1 August 1878 six electric lamps on the frontage of the Gaiety lit the Strand with electricity for the first time.

Hollingshead's main attraction was Burlesque; a form of topical 'musical', blending Operetta, Music Hall and what we now know as Revue then called Extravaganza. These shows, on fairy tale, operatic or historical subjects, served as a framework for singer and comedian to exploit their particular talents.

Before long the 'Gaiety Quartette', Ellen Farren, Kate Vaughan, Edward Terry and E. W. Royce, dominated the burlesque company.

Hollingshead also presented legitimate operettas by the popular

D*

composers of the day, several by Offenbach had their first production in London at the Gaiety. Farces and dramas filled up the
'Three Tier' Bills then in favour. Famous stars of the legitimate
theatre appeared at the matinées: Charles Mathews, J. L.
Toole, Henry Irving, Samuel Phelps among them. Successful trials were
often transferred to the evening programmes.

The first Gilbert and Sullivan collaboration *Thespis; or, the Gods
Grown Old* was commissioned by Hollingshead for Christmas 1871,
and at times Opera was staged. Santley sang in Auber's *Fra
Diavolo*, Donizetti's *Betly*, *The Daughter of the Regiment*, Delibes'
Lakmé, Verdi's *Rigoletto*: all were staged in the first twenty years
of the theatre's life, as well as Shakespeare, old comedy and
Restoration plays. He brought the Comédie Française to London
for the first time in 1879 and introduced Sarah Bernhardt to
London.

To list all that went on in a theatre of which its manager said
'The stage was never idle for a moment, except during a few hours
of the night and early morning!' would be impossible here.
Hollingshead's great personal love was the Burlesque, and he
referred to his policy of 'Keeping alight the sacred Lamp of
Burlesque' on many occasions from 1880. He told the story of his
theatre in two books: *Gaiety Chronicles* (1898) and *Good Old
Gaiety* (1903). In the former, eighteen closely packed pages list the
productions between the opening in 1868 and 1886, when
Hollingshead retired. He had taken George Edwardes, from the
Savoy Theatre, into partnership in 1885, before he finally gave up
active work at the theatre. Together they presented *Little Jack
Sheppard*, with Nellie Farren and Fred Leslie, and a new Gaiety
team was inaugurated which was to last out the few remaining
years of life left in Burlesque as a form of entertainment.

Edwardes was looking ahead for a new style of entertainment,
though he continued the Burlesque tradition with *Faust up-to-Date*
(1888), *Ruy Blas and the Blasé Roué* (1889), *Carmen up-to-Data*
(1890), *Cinder-Ellen, up too Late* (1891) among others.

A complete interior re-decoration in the Indian style, by
Romaine Walker took place in 1889, but the end of an era was near
both for the theatre and its traditions.

It was the death of Fred Leslie and the illness of Nellie Farren
which postponed the production of *Don Juan*, a new burlesque, in
1892, and decided Edwardes to bring in to the Gaiety from his

other theatre, the Prince of Wales', a new style entertainment he had 'invented' called Musical Comedy. *In Town* had a slight plot, told in modern dress, with songs and dances, quite different from anything which had been staged up to this time. It was first produced on 15 October 1892 and transferred to the Gaiety the following December. Still not quite sure of himself and his invention, Edwardes returned to burlesque and produced *Don Juan* (October 1893), and a revival of *Little Jack Sheppard* (August 1894). Meantime he had had another try at the Prince of Wales' with *A Gaiety Girl* in October 1893, another embryo Musical Comedy.

Fully confident now of his genre he launched his Gaiety 'Girls' with *The Shop Girl* on 24 November 1894, with Ada Reeve, fresh from the music halls, in the title role. It ran 546 performances and Musical Comedy became the order of the day and banished burlesque and comic opera from the theatre. With this new-found success the Gaiety flourished during what was to be its last years.

The long awaited Strand improvements were on their way, but before the theatre was condemned, *My Girl* (1896), *The Circus Girl* (1896), *A Runaway Girl* (1898), *The Messenger Boy* (1900) and *The Toreador* (1901) were produced. These last years were the great days of the Gaiety Girl (the show girls and chorus *not* the leading ladies). The theatre became a shop window for the peerage marriage market, and world famous for its stage door 'Johnnies'.

The leading lights of the era were Ellaline Terriss, Seymour Hicks, Connie Ediss, Edmund Payne, George Grossmith Jun., Gertie Millar and many other household names, some of whom were to bridge the gap to the new Gaiety Theatre which was to come.

The Theatre was finally closed on 4 July 1903. It had survived a little longer than the other theatres—the Globe (see Number 6), the Olympic (see Number 13) and the Opera Comique (see Number 14)—which disappeared in the surrounding chaos of the creation of the new Aldwych and a widened Strand, at the corner of which a new Gaiety was in course of construction. On the final night, before the contents were sold and the theatre dismantled, a nostalgic audience assembled for Act 2 of *The Toreador* and a 'pièce d'occasion' *The Linkman*, which revived memories of the old theatre. After midnight Sir Henry Irving delivered a valedictory speech and everyone sang 'Auld Lang Syne'.

The new Gaiety Theatre, at the corner of Aldwych and the Strand, was ready for opening four months later, and on 26 October 1903, in the presence of King Edward VII and Queen Alexandra, a new musical comedy, *The Orchid*, was produced. *The Era*, 17 October, described the new building:

The site of the New Gaiety Theatre, Strand, which opens on the 24th inst. with the musical comedy, at present entitled *The Orchid Hunt*, consists of 12,800 square feet, and has a frontage of 97 ft. 6in. to the Strand, and a corner frontage of 40ft. and a frontage of 138ft. 6in. to Aldwych in which the stage door is situated. Entering under the dome we find ourselves in a circular columniated crush-room, with retiring-rooms and box-office, from which staircases lead right and left up to the grand circle 'back.' This again leads one right and one left for the full width of the tier, with three entrances thereto and down both sides of it, with additional entrances at the bottom, and midway between them on either side an extra exit on to the street, which obviates the necessity of passing through the crush-room in the event of a panic. This arrangement obtains practically in all parts of the house. Suitable accommodation for both ladies and gentlemen is provided for each part. Below the crush-room is the stall saloon, and above it are the saloons to the grand circle, balcony, and gallery, all following the lines of the crush-room and circular or oval in plan. A special feature has been made of private retiring-rooms or lounges to the private boxes of the stalls and grand circle tiers; those to the latter on the O.P. side become the royal retiring-rooms, with a separate entrance from Aldwych, and with private and separate accommodation. The ranges of boxes and the adjoining retiring-rooms can be respectively thrown into one at will. The entrances and exits to the parts other than the stalls and grand circle are alternately in the Strand and Aldwych. On the north side is provided a convenient and commodious suite of offices for the use of the management. The open colonnade or loggia is approached by two staircases from the gallery level. Great care has been taken in designing the line of the tiers so as to insure a perfect view of the whole of the scene from every seat in the house. The theatre is what is known as a 'three-tier house,' and the seating accommodation is approximately as follows: Gallery, 400; upper circle, 250; dress circle, 180; stalls, 140; pit, 320; private boxes, 48; total 1,338. The chief dimensions are as follows: Auditorium, 60ft. wide by 64ft. deep; proscenium, 30ft. wide by 32ft. high by 36 ft. 6in. deep. Behind the proscenium is a commodious stage 40ft. deep, and of an average width of 80ft., with a mezzanine floor and cellar below. Right and left to the Strand and Aldwych are the stairs leading to the stage exit and entrance and the dressing-rooms, numbering twenty-nine.

The grand but simple proportions of the Italian Renaissance of the Florentine school have supplied the *motif* of the external treatment, sufficient relief for the large wall spaces being found in the large circular-headed windows and niches with their pilasters and pediments. The massiveness of the treatment is well crowned by the open order of coupled Ionic columns, entablature, and balustrade. But the most striking feature is naturally the large dome, 40ft. in diameter and 90ft. above the pavement level, supported by seven pairs of consoles of strong, yet graceful, outline, and surmounted by a figure 17ft. in height. The whole of the façades are executed in Portland stone, with bands of verde antique marble. The internal dome will be constructed of steel and concrete, and finished in gold and colour mosaic. The external dome will be built up in steel and wood and covered with copper. The whole of the construction is as fireproof as is practically possible, and generally consists of cement, greystone and blue lias-lime, brickwork and steel, and concrete floors and roof. The floors are almost exclusively finished in cement, and the roofs (of auditorium) with a double layer of asphalte. The steps throughout are of granolithic. Scagliola will be employed in the columns of the crush-room and foyer, with modelled caps and bases in plaster, and where practicable all architectural decorations will be in plaster. The proscenium is fitted with an improved double thickness asbestos fire-resisting curtain, with patent slip gear at the stage level and at the stage door, as demanded by the London County Council, as well as the usual raising and lowering gear and counter-balance weights, and provision is also made for cooling the curtain by means of a specially designed sprinkler controlled from the stage level or in necessity from the stage door. The circles are constructed in steel and concrete throughout, and so designed as to carry from wall to wall of auditorium without intermediate supports. The main girders of circles vary from 3ft. to 4ft. in depth, and support lighter shaped girders through which cantilevers project 12ft. to 15ft. to the front of circles. The cantilevers are built up with steel plates and angles, and the larger ones have a depth of 2ft. at the fulcrum. The total weight of the three circles when fully loaded is estimated at about 350 tons, and this weight is transmitted to the foundations partly by the brick walls and partly by cast-iron and steel stanchions embedded in the brickwork. The plans of the building in their successive stages had to receive the approval of the following bodies and committees: The Building Act Committee and its departments, the Theatres Committee and its departments, the Lord Chamberlain, the Westminster City Council, the district surveyor, and the New Gaiety Theatre directorate.

The auditorium is flanked with twelve private boxes, with arched loggia over, forming also a constructional feature in carrying the novel vaulted ceiling with its squinch-arch treatment, trumpet-like in general formation for acoustic purposes, and embellished with bold winged figures and modelling by Mr. W. J. Neatby, and three decorative tympanum panels in oils by Buchel, the principal one over the proscenium opening representing Aladdin journeying with his magnificent retinue to his new palace. Upon either side of this arched opening and in the spandrels are two niches containing figure-subjects of Music and Dancing, by Hibbert Binney. The whole of these figures are decorated in colour. The boxes are divided by pilasters and columns, in front of which are conventional figures bearing electric lights. The ceiling over the auditorium is fan-shaped, with the divisions embellished by shells, masks, and swags. The circle fronts are of modelled plaster, principally by Sidney Webb, and are most refined in detail. The mural decorations have a groundwork of old rose, with a raised 'art nouveau' design in gold, cerulean blue, Hooker's green and permanent red being sparingly introduced. The draperies are of pale moss green, richly embroidered, in conformity with the general scheme, the carpets and seats being of similar colour. The retiring-rooms, in the rear of the boxes, are of various colour schemes, in contrast to the auditorium; the royal rooms are in the Georgian style, having a special brocaded fabric on the walls. The crush-room is in the Georgian style, with marble columns with bronze caps and bases supporting a modelled entablature and frieze, and the walls are panelled in hardwood, dull polished, six panels being occupied by full-length portraits of the following Gaiety favourites: Nelly Farren as the Street Arab; Kate Vaughan as Morgiana, in *The Forty Thieves*; Letty Lind as a Dancing Girl; Sylvia Grey, in *Monte Cristo*; Connie Gilchrist, in *The Forty Thieves*, and Ellaline Terriss, in *The Runaway Girl*. The frieze above is plain tinted, and the modelled ceiling is entirely in ivory white. The buffet, occupying a segment of the foyer, is in hardwood; the balcony foyer is panelled in hardwood and tapestry fabric; and the gallery saloon is panelled for the reception of sketches in black and white by well-known artists.

The architects are Messrs. Ernest Rüntz and Geo. M'Lean Ford, and in addition to the general structure the whole of the decorative work and upholstery are from their designs. The contractor is Mr. Henry Lovatt.

The Stage, 29 October described the brilliant opening of the Theatre:

It became known on Saturday and Sunday that Mr. George Edwardes had shifted back to Monday, instead of Tuesday, the opening of the sumptuous new playhouse, with the production of *The Orchid*, to suit Royal convenience; and it was generally understood that, as a frequenter of the old Gaiety, the King was desirous of being present at the first performance in the splendid building on the other side of Catherine Street, at the corner of the rapidly progressing Aldwych. It is no small honour to have a reigning Sovereign among the audience on the first night in a new theatre, and the manager of the Gaiety was properly conscious of the added prestige and *éclat* that would result from so happy a conjuncture. Hence the order went forth that Monday, October 26, 1903, was to witness the 'inauguration' of the successor to the edifice that finally closed its doors on July 4. The

public interest was whetted with the announcement of the
change, and the most patient and ardent of 'Gaiety boys and
girls' began to collect outside the pit and gallery entrances at
an early hour in the morning, most of them having the
endurance to retain their positions throughout a miserable
day of squalls and pouring rain, although many less hardy
and more extravagant playgoers had their places filled
vicariously by District Messenger boys. In the old days, before
the establishment of the queue system, such a procedure
would not have been tolerated. However, all, except those for
whom room could be found, were made happy on the opening
of the doors; and the audience was fully engrossed in studying
the features of the interior of the house, before, at eight
o'clock punctually, Mr. Ivan Caryll arose in the conductor's
chair to direct the playing of the National Anthem, the words
of which were taken up heartily, although, as yet, there were
no signs of the Royal party. After a few minutes, Mr. Joseph
Harker's beautiful act drop went up, displaying Mr. Hawes
Craven's brilliant set of the Countess of Barwick's Horti-
cultural College. The opening chorus was just over when the
familiar figure of the King, accompanied by Queen Alexandra,
who returned on Saturday from her visit to Denmark and
Darmstadt, was seen at the back of the Royal box, which in
this new theatre is placed on the left hand side of the auditorium. A roar of welcome rang out as their Majesties came
forward and took their seats, and so enthusiastic and prolonged was the cheering that both King and Queen, beaming
with delight at the hearty spontaneity of their reception, half
rose in their places, and bowed and smiled repeatedly to their
loyal subjects. The genuine cordiality of the greeting was
apparent, and the directors of the Gaiety could have had no
more 'auspicious' opening to their enterprise. Sir Dighton
Probyn was to be noted among the suite in the box adjoining,
and still farther from the stage was that staunch playgoer,
Mr. Alfred de Rothschild; whilst in a pit-tier box on the
other side was Sir Thomas Lipton. The audience included,
further, a number of theatrical, financial, and other celebrities.

Despite the discomfort which the occupants of the pit and
gallery must have undergone during their tedious hours of
waiting, there was no jarring or discordant note during this

first representation of *The Orchid*, which follows the accepted lines of Gaiety musical plays. The new piece, indeed, though it would bear compression in the second act, made an unquestionable success; and at the close of Monday's performance a friendly reception was given to Mr. James T. Tanner, the author of the interesting and essentially topical book; Mr. Adrian Ross, the chief writer of the neatly-turned lyrics; Messrs. Ivan Caryll and Lionel Monckton, the principal composers concerned; the indefatigable stage director, Mr. Sydney Ellison, who has never done abler or more artistic work than in helping his uncle in the 'production' of *The Orchid*; and, finally, the Gaiety manager himself. There were loud cries for a speech when Mr. Edwardes made his final appearance before the curtain, but he wisely refused to be drawn, although there was mute eloquence in his deep bows and expressive looks of thanks.

The graceful melodies of Mr. Caryll and the piquant, yet always musicianly, strains of Mr. Monckton, whose wife, Miss Gertie Millar, made one of the chief successes of Monday's performance, count for a great deal in the attractiveness of *The Orchid*. Miss Millar, a naive and dainty Violet made a great hit in a clever 'Little Mary' ditty (Leslie Mayne and Monckton), and also in the tuneful 'Come along with me,' ending, oddly but effectively, in a cake-walk for Pierrots, a queer combination. Miss Millar had a Yorkshire millgirl turn, 'Liza Ann,' with Mr. Fred Wright, junior, who gave a grotesquely dramatic rendering of Zaccary's 'From Far Peru' song, with Mr. Caryll's pretty *Bouche fermée* refrain, and did well also in his 'Emperor of Sahara' ditty. Mr. Payne, a delightfully droll Meakin, and Miss Ediss, her old self as Caroline, have been provided with a good duet, 'Fancies' (Greenbank and Monckton), with its jumble of the prosaic and the romantic. Mr. Payne, besides his capital gardening business in 'I do all the dirty work' and his screamingly funny burlesque duel with diverting Mr. Robert Nainby, as the pugnacious Count, has a most successful 'Unemployed' number with Mr. Grossmith, who wrote the pointed words, to music by Mr. Caryll. Somewhat less original is Mr. Grossmith's 'Bedelia' solo, containing various theatrical sallies. Miss Ediss may repeat some of her Old Gaiety triumphs

in 'Up to the advertisement,' with Ross's 'saucy' words to
Monckton's sprightly music, her other solo being 'Fancy
Dress.' Miss Ethel Sydney and Mr. Lionel Mackinder have
not particularly good parts as Josephine and Ronald. They
had a pretty old-style duet, 'A-lack-a-day,' and Miss Sydney,
who worked especially hard in the beautiful representation of
the Proménade des Anglais, act two, scene two, had, among
other things, Caryll's charming 'Nobody and Somebody,'
and Bernard Rolt's 'Rose-a-Rubie.' Miss Gabrielle Ray
danced prettily as Chesterton's private secretary, Thisbe,
and sang passably in pieces by Monckton and Rubens. Mr.
Caryll's concerted numbers were well rendered, the chorus
work being generally excellent. Other roles in *The Orchid*
were filled acceptably by Misses Lydia West, Phyllis
Hatherton, Will Bishop, G. Gregory, C. Brown and H. Lewis.
The dancing throughout was beautifully executed. Mr. A. E.
Dodson and Mr. E. Marshall are stage manager and acting-
manager at the New Gaiety.'

The Orchid ran for 559 performances. The reputation of the
Gaiety as a home of musical comedy continued and increased as the
following productions were staged year by year. *The Spring
Chicken* (1905) 401 performances; *The New Aladdin* (1906) 203
performances; *The Girls of Gottenburg* (1907) 303 performances;
Our Miss Gibbs (1909) 636 performances; the music for all these
was by Ivan Caryll and Lionel Monckton. The number of performances is an indication of how popular was the particular style
created at the Gaiety by George Edwardes during this period.
Subsequent successes prior to the Great War of 1914-1918 were
Peggy (1911) 270 performances; *The Sunshine Girl* (1912) 336
performances; *The Girl on the Film* (1913) 232 performances; and
After the Girl (1914) 105 performances. The last of these was
described as 'A revusical comedy'—a sign of a new trend which
was to develop enormously during the war years.

When war broke out Edwardes was in Germany 'on a cure' and
he was interned for a while. Eventually repatriated, he died a
broken man on 4 October 1915. Meantime his interests were
looked after by Robert Evett, who was mainly concerned with the
series of musical plays at Daly's, and the Gaiety management
passed into the hands of Grossmith joined by Laurillard, and the

Gaiety policy continued unbroken with *To-Night's the Night* (1915) 160 performances; *Theodore and Co.* (1916) 503 performances; *The Beauty Spot* (1917) 152 performances; *Going Up!* (1918) 574 performances; *The Kiss Call* (1919) 176 performances; and a revival of *The Shop Girl* (1920) 327 performances. Maurice Maeterlinck's *The Betrothal* broke the musical comedy sequence in 1921, but bad luck followed and the Gaiety had a series of 'flops'.

Robert Evett left Daly's when it was bought by James White and brought his star leading lady, José Collins, over to the Gaiety. His production of *The Last Waltz* in 1922, which scored 280 performances, was followed in turn by *Catherine* (1923) 217 performances and *Our Nell* (1924) 140 performances. Changing managements produced *Poppy* (1924) 188 performances; *Katja the Dancer* and *The Blue Kitten* (1925) 505 and 140 performances respectively; *Lido Lady* (1926) 259 performances. In 1929 Laddie Cliff commenced a successful regime with *Love Lies* 347 performances; *Darling I Love You* and *The Love Race* (1930) 147 and 237 performances; but *Blue Roses* and *The Millionaire Kid* in 1931 failed and his management ended. His partner, Stanley Lupino, remained to play, with Jessie Matthews, in *Hold my Hand* (1931) 212 performances; Delysia was in *Mother of Pearl* (1933) 181 performances and Laddie Cliff and Stanley Lupino were back again in *Sporting Love* (1934) 302 performances.

The next few years were ones of constant change. Cochran presented *The Ballet Jooss* (1934 and 1935) and Lee Ephriam, *Gay Deceivers* (1935) among other shows. In October 1935 Firth Shephard took over management and presented Leslie Henson in *Seeing Stars*. A new team was formed with Fred Emney and Richard Hearne, and a period of success at last dawned. The first production ran 126 performances, and after a break for *Blackbirds of 1936* came *Swing Along* 311 performances; *Going Greek* (1937) 306 performances; and finally *Running Riot* (1938) 207 performances.

The full history of the later years of the Gaiety are told by W. Macqueen-Pope in *Gaiety, Theatre of Enchantment* (1949).

The last production opened with an air of impending gloom. It had been announced that yet another major road widening and reconstruction scheme would once again call for the demolition of the Gaiety Theatre. During the late thirties a new Waterloo Bridge was under construction and an enlarged approach was planned. This would need the demolition of the Lyceum Theatr (see *The Theatres of London*), as well as the Gaiety, part of whose site was needed. Compulsory orders were made by the L.C.C. who had acquired the ground of both buildings and those near them. The last performance took place on 25 February 1939.

A farce was acted out between the L.C.C. and the Lessees of the Theatre by which the L.C.C. could gain possession of the building still held on a lease. A newspaper announcement appeared which said:

> The musical play, *Running Riot*, was withdrawn from the Gaiety Theatre on Saturday after a run of more than six months. Its successor has not yet been announced, but before the Gaiety Theatre receives its new licence from the Lord Chamberlain certain structural alterations will have to be made, which will include the provision of larger staircases and an improved gallery. The system of ventilation will also have to be changed. The estimated cost of these alterations is said to be well over £10,000.
>
> Mr. A. E. Fournier, one of the directors of Associated Theatre Properties, Limited, who owned the lease, stated on Saturday that the demands were considered to be uneconomic. In view of the money required to carry out the operations suggested and the money spent a few years ago, the question was whether the directors would be justified in effecting further alterations. Mr. Fournier said that the L.C.C had the freehold of the theatre. The rent had been increased in recent years. Negotiations between Associated Theatre Properties, Limited, and the L.C.C. are continuing.

In April another announcement said:

> The Gaiety Theatre has been purchased by Crompton Parkinson, Limited, manufacturers of electrical equipment, who propose to erect a block of offices in place of the theatre. Mr. Frank Parkinson, chairman of the company, said yesterday: 'We realize that we have acquired one of the most prominent positions in London, and mean to erect a building in every way in keeping with the site.'

In September the theatre was stripped of its fittings and all that remained was the empty shell.

The war came and put a stop to all their schemes; the Lyceum
became a dance hall and the Gaiety remained derelict—during the
blitz the roof was severely damaged. After the war the L.C.C.
decided on different traffic plans for the area which included the
continuation of the old Kingsway tram tunnel under Wellington
Street. There were hopes that the old theatre might re-open.

In 1946 Lupino Lane was reported to have purchased the
theatre for £200,000, and in 1949, though building restrictions
were still tight, *The Daily Telegraph* reported:

> Mr. Lupino Lane, the actor and owner of the disused Gaiety
> Theatre, Strand, has been told by the Ministry of Works that
> he can spend £10,000 on weather-proofing the building. He is
> to approach the Government for sanction to spend a further
> £10,000 to enable him to reopen the theatre.
>
> Mr. Lane stated yesterday: 'For the past three years I have
> spent £7,600 annually on the ground rent of this building. I
> am anxious to re-open the theatre, not only as a musical
> comedy house, but to institute there a school of art, teaching
> ballet, singing and spoken word.'
>
> Mr. Leslie Henson, the comedian, whose early triumphs
> were at the Gaiety, said yesterday: 'I am prepared to find
> backing for Mr. Lupino Lane up to £250,000 if this famous
> theatre can be re-opened.'

If ever the theatre had a lost cause this was the biggest, and
Lupino Lane, its champion, was doomed from the start. In July
1950, defeated by high finance and building permits, *The Daily
Telegraph* again carried on the tale:

> London's old Gaiety Theatre, in the Strand, is to become a
> building of offices. It was sold yesterday by Mr. Lupino Lane
> for 'round about' £190,000 to a solicitor on behalf of a business
> man.
>
> Mr. Lane bought the theatre in 1945 for about £200,000.
> Since then, he has been hoping to re-open the theatre on its
> old traditional lines. He has spent over £25,000 in rebuilding,
> repairs and taxes.
>
> He said last night: 'I lost a lot of money over the last four
> years and nobody came forward to help me. I was on the
> verge of bankruptcy, so there was nothing I could do but to

sell, for the sake of my family. I put all my life's savings in it. I got so disappointed that I just took the highest offer. I postponed selling it for offices for a long time, but had to give in in the end. So my dream of making it into a theatre again has gone.'

Poor Lupino Lane died a broken hearted man in 1959.

The plans for a new building, to be the head office of the English Electric Company, were passed in March 1957, and demolition commenced. The trumpeting angel on the dome wa: to be preserved and placed surmounting a fountain in the garden of the central court of the building. The new building, designed by Dr. Charles Holden, with the giant statues of 'Power' and 'Speed' by Sir Charles Wheeler, was completed in August 1960.

All that is left to remind passers-by is a large metal plaque on the Strand side of the building commemorating the Gaiety Theatre. It says:

> On this site stood the Gaiety Theatre built in 1903 from designs by Richard Norman Shaw for impressario George Edwardes. The theatre opened with the performance of 'The Orchid Girl' and until it was closed in 1938 remained the home of musical comedy and one of London's most famous playhouses.'

This contains firstly one definite error, *The Orchid* not *The Orchid Girl* was the opening production, and secondly a rather misleading statement as to the architect of the theatre. Though an L.C.C. Improvements Committee Report of 17 June 1902 stated:

> The Council has given its approval to a design submitted by Mr. Ernest Rüntz and based upon Mr. Norman Shaw's sketch design for the elevation of the new theatre and restaurant. Mr. Norman Shaw very kindly made suggestions for the architectural treatment of the buildings in question and produced a sketch design in illustration of his suggestions.

It is well known that Shaw was engaged in an advisory capacity to judge the Strand-Aldwych Improvements Competition, and that he gave his services voluntarily to see that a good job was done.

A contemporary architect's perspective, signed G.W.E. 1902, of the new theatre as finally built, was published in *The Sketch*

30 September 1903, and is stated as 'from the original design by Ernest Rüntz and Co., the Architects.' A photo of the model of the theatre published at the same time was similarly credited.

The present architect to the Greater London Council, Hubert Bennett says:

> While the existence of drawings by Rüntz in the library of the Royal Institute of British Architects which show the building as executed, there is still doubt as to whether Shaw or Rüntz had the deciding hand in the exterior. In view of the ambiguous part played by Shaw, I consider that it is impossible to state categorically that Ernest Rüntz was the designer of the Gaiety Theatre.'

This would also, it seems, apply to the claims of Norman Shaw. The closing of the theatre was in 1939, not 1938 as stated on the plaque. Since writing the above a letter pointing out these mistakes appeared in *The Daily Telegraph*, in consequence of which a new plaque was placed in position in January 1968. It now reads:

> 'On this site stood the Gaiety Theatre built in 1903 for impresario George Edwardes. The theatre opened with the performance of "The Orchid" and until it was closed in 1938 it remained the home of musical comedy and one of London's most famous playhouses.'

It is to be hoped that the remaining error, that of the closing year, will soon be revised.

5
The Gate Theatre Studio

FIRST THEATRE

The Gate Theatre Salon
28 Floral Street, Covent Garden
Top floor of a warehouse

Opened 30 October 1925 with *Bernice*, a play by Susan Glaspell.
Produced by Peter Godfrey.
Under the management of Peter Godfrey and Molly Veness.
Closed March 1926

SECOND THEATRE

The Gate Theatre Studio
16A Villiers Street, Strand

Opened 22 November 1927 with *Maya*, a play by Simon Gantillon.
Produced by Peter Godfrey.
Under the management of Peter Godfrey and Velona Pilcher.
Closed June 1940.
Damaged in the blitz 16 June 1941.
Premises re-built over the period 1946-1966 but not yet occupied.

THE HISTORY OF small theatres not under the jurisdiction of the
Lord Chamberlain can be divided into two eras. The first, before
the Licensing Act of 1843, which broke the monopoly of the drama
which had been held since the Restoration under the Royal
Patents by the two Theatres Royal (Drury Lane and Covent

Garden) and from 1766, by the Haymarket, during the summer months when the other Patent houses were closed.

In the early years of the nineteenth century, when minor theatres in central London and the outer suburbs were opening, they could only operate on what became known as a Burletta Licence. This allowed music and dancing and only plays which included five musical pieces in each act or a musical accompaniment. The production of classical and legitimate drama (Shakespeare etc.) was forbidden, but ways round the situation were found. Songs or a chord struck on a pianoforte in the orchestra pit at intervals during the performance of a Drama, for instance, was held by some to be within the limits of the Licence: but any management contravening the law was open to prosecution on information laid before the Magistrates by a Common Informer, usually at the instigation of one of the Patent theatres if a minor theatre manager was too bold or flagrant in his defiance of the situation.

Small theatres were opened from time to time and Assembly Halls were adapted for theatrical use, calling themselves Subscription Theatres. This meant no money was taken at the doors, and many were the subterfuges designed to sell tickets—the purchase of sweets or a cup of coffee at adjoining premises allowing free admission to the place of entertainment, was a favourite device.

But at best many of the lesser managers led a precarious existence at the mercy of the Law. The Olympic (number 13), the Royal Strand (number 19), the St. James's (number 22), the Royalty (number 20), were all operated in this way and survived into the new era after 1843. (See also the Adelphi, the Scala, the Lyceum, the Old Vic and Sadlers' Wells in *The Theatres of London*.)

Other buildings in and around London used for theatrical performances led a hand to mouth existence and mostly vanished after short careers. The Pantheon (number 16), the Sans Souci (number 23), and the predecessors of the Trocadero (number 28), the Little Catherine Street Theatre (see number 4), and the earlier Argyll Rooms in Argyll Street, off Regent Street, among them. The need for these had gone with the new found freedom, and only the few places used by amateurs and occasional professional entertainments remained in central London during the mid-

Victorian era. (See the Polygraphic Hall, number 27, the St. George's Hall, number 21.)

The second era commenced with the advent of the new drama in the late eighteen-eighties and early nineties. The actor managers, in what we would now call the commercial theatre, were not interested in the work of Ibsen and his followers. Censorship, in the hands of the Lord Chamberlain since 1737, was vigorous in preventing the performance of anything that would disturb Victorian prudery.

As early as 1886 a private society had been formed for the performance of Shelley's banned play *The Cenci*. This led the way to the formation of the many play producing societies which sprang up and flourished for the next fifty years.

Most of these, either dedicated to the presentation of 'modern' drama, which often meant banned plays, or the revival of classics denied a place in the commercial theatre, did not appear in their own premises but performed in the regular theatres on Sundays and for matinées.

As the new century advanced so a few small halls and converted rooms also became the home of advanced plays. Among those were the Rehearsal Theatre, Maiden Lane (next to the stage door of the Adelphi, now an empty bombed site), and the King's Hall, 43 King Street, Covent Garden, (the National Sporting Club), which later housed the Players' Theatre on its top floor.

Before the Copyright Act of 1911 these little theatres, and those in the outer ring like the Bijou, Archer Street, Bayswater (later re-named the Twentieth Century and still in existence), and the Ladbrook Hall (later a cinema and now a recording studio), were continually being used for the single copyright performance necessary to protect the author's rights.

Between the wars most of the little theatres which achieved fame were outside the West End where rents were cheaper and premises more easily available. The Everyman, Hampstead, the Barnes Theatre, the Mercury, Notting Hill Gate, the 'Q' Theatre, the Embassy, Swiss Cottage, of the twenties and thirties, though the days of the Lindsay, Notting Hill Gate, the Boltons, Kensington and many others, mark a definite phase in theatre going and dramatic history. Their story has been told by Norman Marshall in *The Other Theatre* (1947).

Post war economies forced all the 'other' theatres out of business, anyway their work was done: the West End had accepted the new drama and the classics. Theatres like the Old Vic (for the classics), the Royal Court, the Royal Shakespeare Company at the Aldwych (for modern plays), had achieved a regular place in the theatre lists. Also the Censor had become more liberal minded: little was left to be said or performed only in private or in an attic theatre. The Lord Chamberlain's jurisdiction still remains to prevent the unspeakable (which every year grows less and less!) It is a needed managerial self-protection preventing lapses into bad taste in presentation of the living or the recently deceased, blasphemy and the exploitation of pornography for its own sake; also as a salutory reminder that the theatre is for entertainment and not a political or documentary lecture hall.

In the West End only the Arts Theatre, opened 1927, the Players' Theatre, founded 1936, and the Little Theatre Club, (the Hovenden) founded 1950, still exist (see *Theatres of London*).

Most of the premises used in the earlier years of the century were licensed by the L.C.C., and money could be taken at the doors, provided it was not a society or club performance of a banned play. Later the club theatre itself came into existence. The Gate, which opened in its first premises in Floral Street, Covent Garden, in 1925, can claim to be the first club theatre.

The first Gate 'The Gate to Better Things' was on the top floor of a ramshackle warehouse and held ninety-six people. A critic reporting at the opening said:

The theatre was a bare room which had served as a wine loft. It was hung with canvas and coloured cloth, and lamps hung from the rafters. The stage was without scenery, merely plain cloth being used, and brown canvas was made to serve as a curtain.

But in this frugal setting a performance was given of which a West End theatre might have been proud. A psychological play of profound conflict and intricate character studies, it could not have had a more appropriate presentation.

Like Clemence Dane's novel, *Legend*, *Bernice* concerns a dead woman who lives spiritually in many characters.

Molly Veness gave a deeply convincing study of Margaret, the searcher for truth. Edmund Kennedy, the father; Peter Godfrey, the husband, and Caroline Keith, the house-

woman, all of whom are implicated in Bernice's tragedy, were
particularly good.

Norman Marshall adds:

The stage of those Floral Street premises could hardly have
been smaller, and the dressing-room accommodation was so
limited that several of the cast used to have to make their
changes on the stage itself during the intervals. The front
curtain . . . more than anything else made me suspect that the
Gate smelt of artiness. But I was wrong. It smelt of dirt and
size and coffee and greasepaint and sweating humanity, but it
was not arty. Peter Godfrey, its founder, was thoroughly
professional in the best sense of the word. Although he was
still in his early twenties he was widely experienced in the
theatre. He had begun as a boy conjuror 'on the halls': he
toured Ireland with a fit-up; he had been a member of Ben
Greet's Shakespearian company, travelled with a circus as one
of the clowns, worked as a film extra, and acted and produced
with repertory companies at Southend, Wakefield and
Plymouth. It was while he was at Plymouth that he began
reading the new 'expressionist drama' that was being
produced in Germany and America. These plays, which at
that time seemed so excitingly unorthodox in their technique
and choice of subject, made Godfrey more than ever dis-
contented with the succession of stale West End successes
which were all that the repertory theatres would allow him to
produce or act in. So he and his wife, Molly Veness, conceived
the fantastic idea of founding in London a theatre of their own.
It was a fantastic idea because they had no money. Week by
week they saved on their tiny salaries, and at last they had
enough to rent that top floor in Covent Garden.

Molly Veness herself says the Gate was started on savings of
twenty pounds to which her mother, an artist, added a further
two hundred and she was also responsible for the decoration
on the curtain and her pictures were sold from the little
gallery in the coffee bar at the back of the auditorium.

It was not originally Godfrey's intention to run the Gate
as a private theatre. Later it became labelled as a theatre to
which people went to see banned plays, so it is interesting to
note that in the first season of eighteen plays only one of these

could possibly have been refused a licence by the Lord Chamberlain. The Gate was opened as a private theatre not to escape from the jurisdiction of the Lord Chamberlain, but because the London County Council not unnaturally refused to license as a public theatre a loft in Floral Street to which the only entrance and exit was a rickety wooden staircase.

The decision to run the theatre as a private club was a bold one and entirely new . . . this was the first time that anyone had conceived the idea of using the privileges of a theatrical club not merely for one or two performances but for a nightly run of two or three weeks.

The Gate opened on October 30 1925, with Susan Glaspell's *Bernice*. The opening production ran for a fortnight and was followed by a double bill consisting of *The End of the Trail* by Ernest Howard Culbertson and Copeau's *The House Into Which We Are Born*. Then came Strindberg's *The Dance of Death* and another double bill consisting of Schnitzler's *The Wedding Morning* and de Musset's *A Door Must Be Either Open or Shut*. The Christmas production was Molière's *George Dandin*.

Up to now the theatre had been struggling along without attracting any particular notice. The tiny capital had long ago been eaten up. There were some weeks when the salaries of the cast amounted to only a few shillings each. Even a char-woman was a luxury which the theatre could not afford. The two directors used to come down each morning an hour or so before rehearsals and clean the theatre themselves.

Had it not been for James Agate, it is very unlikely that the Gate would have been able to exist long enough even to finish its first season. It was Agate's notice of the next production, *From Morn to Midnight*, which was the turning point in the early history of the Gate. Up to then Agate, in common with most of the dramatic critics, had paid very little attention to the Gate, but in his notice of *From Morn to Midnight* he more than made amends. He did more than just write an enthusiastic notice of the play and production and urge his readers to go to the Gate. He gave full details of how to join, and even included the theatre's telephone number in his notice. 'Breathes there a serious playgoer', he wrote, 'with soul so dead that he will neglect to support a theatre of such aim and achievement as I have outlined? I refuse to think so. If I may add a further recommendation', he continued, 'it is that people who intend to be interested should be interested now; it is no use bringing the tube of oxygen after the patient is dead. What is wanted is practical sympathy now and not the *beau geste* when it is too late.'

On the Sunday evening of the day this article appeared the Gate was packed. By Monday morning applications for membership were pouring in by telephone and by post. By Monday evening every performance for the rest of the run of the play was sold out.

The run could easily have been extended for several weeks, but Godfrey had promised his members a long programme for the season and he very wisely refused to break faith with them for the sake of making as much money as possible out of a single production. At the end of its three weeks run at the Gate the production was transferred to the Regent, King's Cross where Claude Rains took over the part played by Peter Godfrey, who refused to leave the Gate . . .

During the first season there were eighteen changes of programme, comprising twenty-three plays (sixteen full-length and seven one-acters), making altogether a total of two hundred and fifty-two performances. In addition to the plays already mentioned, the season's programme included Ibsen's *Hedda Gabler*, Hauptmann's *Rosa Berndt*, Toller's *Hinkemann* Masefield's *The Tragedy of Nan*, Capek's *The Land of Many Names*, Evreinoff's *The Theatre of the Soul*, Dostoievsky's *The Brothers Karamazov*, and *The Race with the Shadow* by Wilhelm von Scholz . . .

The next season was a little less hectic, as this time there were only fourteen changes of programme (comprising thirteen full-length plays and five one-act plays). These included Gorki's *The Lower Depths*, Maeterlinck's *Monna Vanna*, Jules Romains' *Dr. Knock*, Elmer Rice's *The Adding Machine*, Wedekind's *Erdgeist*, and Erekmann Chatrian's *The Polish Jew*. The programme was shorter than the previous one because in March the Floral Street premises were closed. New premises had been obtained in Villiers Street.

There were the usual difficulties and delays over the reconstruction. The first two productions of the third season had to be given at the Rudolf Steiner Hall. The new theatre was not opened until November 22, 1927. The play was Simon Gantillon's *Maya* . . ."

The new Gate Theatre Studio was constructed in part of the large complex premises which had been acquired by the Gattis over the years since 1867. These consisted of the Arches under Charing Cross Station and the forecourt area between the steps up to Hungerford Bridge and the open archway which gave a way through to Craven Street, beside the side entrance to the station. One of these arches (Gatti's Arches Music Hall) is now the Players' Theatre (see *The Theatres of London*).

In part of the forecourt area, in Villiers Street, Gatti's had a restaurant and billiard saloon, the back part of this, siding on the arches and entered from the open court facing the Music Hall, had been converted into a skittle alley, under changing ownership since the Gattis had left in the early years of the century.

The adaptation (says Norman Marshall) of this ramshackle building, measuring only fifty-five feet by thirty feet, was done with extraordinary skill and ingenuity at the minimum of cost. Godfrey's wisest step was to plan the stage first and the auditorium afterwards. As a result the Gate possessed a well-proportioned stage, which in size was out of all normal proportion to the auditorium. It occupied, in fact, over one-third of the floor space of the entire building. It must have required considerable determination to resist the temptation to sacrifice a few feet of stage-space for the sake of that extra row of stalls which would have made all the difference to the finances of the theatre.

Godfrey showed further originality and courage in completely ignoring all the usual principles of theatre design. As the roof of the building was, for the purposes of a theatre, comparatively low, he built the stage only eighteen inches high so as to obtain the greatest possible height for his settings. He compensated for this by steeply raking the auditorium. The stage was so close to the audience that those sitting in the front row could—and sometimes did—sit with their feet resting on the edge of the stage . . . The Gate mercilessly revealed any sort of trickery or staginess. Yet although over-acting was so relentlessly magnified, it was possible for the

actor to let himself go as full out at the Gate as at any other
theatre, providing that he was acting with absolute sincerity
and never overstraining . . .

New theatres are seldom successful when they first open.
The new Gate proved to be an exception. *Maya*, with Gwen
Ffrangcon-Davies in the lead, was easily the Gate's greatest
success up to date. It ran for fifty-three performances, and was
followed by another success, O'Neill's *The Hairy Ape*, which
ran for thirty-three performances. Other successes of this
season were a revival of *From Morn to Midnight*, Cocteau's
Orphée, and *20 Below* by Robert Nichols and Jim Tully. In all,
two hundred and forty performances were given this season,
with nine changes of programme.

But the fourth season was less successful (he was now joined
in partnership by Charles Spencer as business manager). The
most notable feature of this season was that at Christmas
Peter Godfrey inaugurated the series of musical burlesques
which he produced so brilliantly. The first was Mrs. Mowatt's
Fashion; or, High Life in New York, which was afterwards
transferred to the Kingsway. Subsequent Christmas shows
included *Ten Nights in a Bar Room; or, Ruined by Drink*, *The
Red Rover's Revenge*, *Uncle Tom's Cabin*, *Little Lord
Fauntleroy* (with Elsa Lanchester in the title role) and two
revues under the title of *Peter's Parade*, in which Hermione
Gingold, who was afterwards to be the star of many Gate
revues, made her first appearance at the theatre.

From now on many notable plays were produced and many
reputations were made by their casts, but by 1932 Godfrey, a tired
man shouldering the responsibility of the theatre by himself (his
associates were no longer with him), tried an amalgamation with
the Cambridge Festival Theatre which failed, and in 1934 he
handed over to a new company formed by Norman Marshall. The
full story of these years and the successful plays produced are
part of between-the-wars theatrical history, and is fully told by
Norman Marshall himself in *The Other Theatre*.

The most remembered plays, some of which transferred into the
West End after battling with the Censor, are *Victoria Regina,
Parnell, Oscar Wilde, The Children's Hour, Of Mice and Men* and
Boys in Brown.

The annual Gate revues brought intimate revue back into favour and became an institution both at the Gate and later in the West End.

The same air raid which destroyed the Little Theatre in the Adelphi (see number 12) blew the roof off the Gate, and it remained derelict until after the war was over. The lease of the Gate and surrounding premises was acquired by William Box and since that time re-building has been slowly carried on. The building now stands ready for a new tenant to take over, and equips for use either as a small theatre or a night club.

Following the lead of the Gate Theatre other West End club theatres achieved some measure of success during the next thirty years. There were, apart from the Arts and the Players' already mentioned, Play Room Six, opened by Reginald Price and Hilda Maude in January 1927 at 6 New Compton Street, (moved to 43 King Street, Covent Garden in 1934—its later history as the Players' is told in *The Theatres of London*); the Portfolio Playhouse, opened by Fay Compton at 6A Rodmarston Mews, Baker Street in January 1937 and destroyed in the blitz; and the Watergate Theatre, 29 Buckingham Street, Strand opened by Elizabeth Denby, Velona Pilcher and Elizabeth Sprigg in November 1949 and closed in 1956 when the new block, Villiers House at the corner of Villiers Street, was built—Shaw's *Far Fetched Fables* was produced here in 1950 and *Cranks* in 1956.

The Club name was continued at the Comedy Theatre as a cloak to produce, under club conditions, *Tea and Sympathy*, *View from the Bridge* and *Cat on a Hot Tin Roof*—three plays then banned by the Censor.

The Watergate Theatre itself was the home of many successful late night revues during its short career, as was the Irving Theatre opened by D. P. Chaudhuri at 17 Irving Street, Leicester Square in September 1951. It closed in 1964 and became a restaurant.

Other small theatres, licensed for public performance, now lost were the Childrens Theatre, 81 Endell Street run by Joan Luxton and Agnes Lowson from 1927 to 1931 (the building still remains, used as a warehouse), the Torch Theatre, 37 Wilton Place, Knightsbridge opened in 1938 by Gerald Cooper and closed in 1954, now a restaurant, and the Grafton Theatre, Tottenham Court Road opened by Judith Wogan in May 1930. It eventually became a B.B.C. studio during the war.

E

6

The Globe Theatre

Newcastle Street, Strand
With entrances and stage door in Wych Street

Opened 28 November 1868, with a revival of *Good for Nothing* by
J. B. Buckstone, followed by an address by Sefton Parry and
Cyril's Success; An Every Day Story by Henry J. Byron.
Under the management of Sefton Parry.
Closed March 1902 and demolished for the Strand (Aldwych and
Kingsway) development scheme.

IN THE MAZE OF STREETS at the eastern end of the Strand during the
nineteenth century there were three theatres, the Olympic (the
oldest, see number 12), the Globe and the Opera Comique (see
number 13). These were swept away at the turn of the century,
along with the first Gaiety Theatre (see number 4) in the Strand
(Aldwych-Kingsway) development scheme. The neighbourhood
had acquired a disreputable reputation and had long been awaiting
clearance.

The scheme for a new road was reported in *The Era*
18 November 1882:

> No less than three places of amusement are directly affected
> by the schemes for improving the present means of com-
> munication between Holborn and the Strand, while the
> theatres situated in the district must all materially benefit
> by the carrying out of an efficient plan. The precise details of
> the schemes under the consideration of the Metropolitan
> Board of Works cannot yet be given to the public, but the
> principal points will be of interest to our readers. The first

plan proposes the widening of the street north of St. Mary's Church from New Church Court to Newcastle Street; which street will be widened to 70ft. leading northwards, to a new street to be formed across Houghton Street and Clare Market to the west side of Lincoln's Inn Fields, thence by Gate Street to Holborn, where the width proposed is 100ft. This plan further provides for the demolition of both blocks of houses on the south of Wych Street, and south of Holywell Street, and the formation of one building site with a frontage to the Strand, which would be widened to 85ft.; and a frontage to Wych Street, which would be widened to 60ft. The second plan provides the widening of the street north of St. Mary's Church at its junction with Newcastle Street, which would be widened to 60ft.; and a new street formed north-wards, as in the first scheme, leading to the west side of Lincoln's Inn Fields, then into Holborn, but avoiding the destruction of the Royal Music Hall. It also provides for the demolition of the block of buildings south of Holywell Street, with two suggestions, the throwing the space thus obtained into the Strand roadway, making the width of 120ft., or retaining one half for a building site, with a frontage of the original line in Holywell Street and a frontage to the Strand. A third plan proposes the widening of Little Queen Street, making a direct communication northwards by Southampton Row and the formation of a new street across the gardens at the back of Lincoln's Inn Fields to a 'circus' near Clare Market, from which point would lead two streets south-ward, one to Newcastle Street and one to the Law Courts. By a fourth plan the line from Holborn to the Law Courts is followed to Carey Street and the Strand. Among the recom-mendations from outside the Board is one from Mr. A. Ventriss, the surveyor to the Strand Board of Works, that in dealing with the two blocks of houses between Wych Street and the Strand the east-end of Wych Street should be widened, and the houses on the north-side of Holywell Street and those between that street and the Strand should be demolished, a block of buildings with an arcade (similar to the Opera Arcade in Pall Mall, to be closed at night) being placed on the site thus obtained, whereby the foot traffic of Holywell Street would be preserved. It is urged that this site would have a frontage to the widened Strand, in which commanding entrances could be obtained for the Globe and Opera Comique Theatres. An eminent valuer has given his opinion that the site occupied by the theatres, if in the hands of the Board of Works, and cleared, would offer great advantages as very valuable property for the building of Law Chambers; and, therefore, form a recoupment to the Board.

The whole plan in yet another form did not take shape until the late nineties, and spread over into the first decade of the new century.

Eventually the Strand was widened, Wellington Street shortened at its eastern end, the arc of Aldwych driven through shortening Catherine Street, which had originally ended in the Strand itself. Wych Street, Holywell Street, Newcastle Street and the accompanying courts and alleys in the area between St. Mary le Strand and St. Clement Danes, vanished. Their location is now buried somewhere under the vast block of Bush House and its neighbours. The old Gaiety (which had stood in a spot now in the middle of the road), was re-sited on the corner of the new Aldwych and the widened Strand (see number 4).

The road connecting Aldwych and Holborn called Kingsway brought the theatre in Great Queen Street, which was re-named the Kingsway in 1907, near to the new thoroughfare (see number 11). In this road was also built the London Opera House (later the Stoll Theatre) in 1911 and pulled down in 1958. Its site is now partly covered by the Royalty Theatre (Cinema) (see *The Theatres of London*). The new roads were officially opened with due ceremony by King Edward VII on 18 October 1905.

The Globe and the Opera Comique, which were back to back, becoming known familiarly as 'the Rickety Twins', were both speculative ventures. The Opera Comique also acquired the nickname of 'Theatre Royal Tunnels'.

In the sixteenth century Lyon's Inn, one of the Inns of Court, stood in Newcastle Street between Wych Street and Holywell Street (on the site of a hostelry with the sign of 'The Lyon'). This fell into disuse by the end of the eighteenth century and was converted into dwellings of a dubious nature. Part of this area was cleared for a building speculator, the Strand Hotel Company, in 1864, which ended in failure. On the ground covered by Lyon's

Inn was built the Globe Theatre in 1868 and the Opera Comique in 1870. The whole scheme was a gamble on the eventual clearance of this area for reconstruction and street widening for which a large compensation would have to be paid for buildings of a jerry built nature hastily put up. This was before the powers of the Board of Works were consolidated in 1878, to give safety to places of public entertainment.

Sefton Parry, who built the Globe, was a notorious speculator who had already opened a theatre in Holborn in 1866 (see Number 8), the first new theatre to be built in central London since the Princess's in 1840. Among his other later ventures was the building of the Avenue Theatre (now the Playhouse, see *The Theatres of London*) in 1882, in the hopes of the ground being required for an extension to Charing Cross Station, which never materialised.

Sefton Parry designed the new Globe theatre himself, which was built by G. Simpson, to hold some 1,800 people. It opened on 28 November and *The Era* of the following day described the evening:

The opening of a new theatrical establishment is an event, the importance of which will be especially estimated by those whose welfare it is our particular province to study, and the interest attached to the first night of the New Globe Theatre was demonstrated in the most emphatic manner by the numerous and fashionable throng which took possession of the building directly the portals were unclosed. The principal entrance, in Newcastle Street, Strand, leads direct into the boxes. The approaches to the pit and gallery are in Wych Street, and the very first glimpse of the interior sufficed to assure the visitors to each portion of the house that their comfort and accommodation had been most scrupulously studied in all the arrangements. The form of the new Theatre, which revives the title of the old Bankside building, two centuries and a half ago the summer house of Shakespeare and his fellows, is characteristically circular. [The Rotunda in Blackfriars Road was also called the Globe from 1833 for a few years.] In size it most nearly approaches the Olympic, and affords space for about eighteen hundred spectators. The pit and stalls are at least a dozen feet beneath the level of the roadway, but the perfect ventilation of the 'auditorium' is secured by the lofty ceiling, illuminated by a brilliant sunlight, and which may be roughly estimated as some fifty feet from the floor. The spacious gallery lies directly above the dress circle, and is furnished with a row of amphitheatre stalls. The stage, which has considerable width, and quite sufficient depth for any purpose likely to be required, is well supplied with all needful mechanical appliances, and commodious dressing-rooms are provided on each side. Of the general appearance of the Theatre it will be sufficient to say that a most favourable impression is produced on the spectator from every point of view, and the eight private boxes are singularly commodious, and are most luxuriously appointed. We may comprehensively record in this place that the *Carton Pierre* decorations have been designed and executed by White and Co., of Great Marylebone Street; the seating by Messrs. Jeffrey, of Liverpool; the gas-fittings by Jones and Co., of Bow-Street; the stage and machinery by Mr. F. Stripling; and the gildings, decorations, and upholstery by the well-known Mr. B. Hurwitz, of Southampton Street, Strand.

The audience portion of the house consists of ninety orchestra stalls, five hundred and sixty pit seats, one hundred and thirty dress circle, one hundred and thirty amphitheatre stalls, six hundred seats in gallery and eight private boxes. There is a very commodious and elegant saloon and refreshment room, attached to which is a large room set apart exclusively for ladies. There are also refreshment rooms for pit and gallery. The approach to the dress circle, stalls, and private boxes is from Newcastle Street, and only five doors from the Strand. The entrance is without any steps at either end, and the audience reach the dress circle and private boxes without either ascending or descending. This is the only Theatre in London which can boast of such an approach. The entrance to the pit and gallery is in Wych Street. In this street there is a private entrance for members of the Royal family. In form the new Globe is perfectly circular, being, as we believe, the only Theatre in London in which that construction is rigidly adhered to. The gallery, as is usual in houses of this size, comes immediately above the dress circle, beneath which the pit runs back to the outer wall of the building. The pit is, of course, much below the ground, which, as we have said, is on the level of the dress circle, and a still deeper excavation has been made for the stage. The stage itself is, we need hardly say, one of those complicated arrangements of wood and iron which all stages now-a-days are bound to be, every plank, post, and tie being constructed to shift from its place at a moment's notice. The height, also, is very great, being no less than sixty feet from the floor to the gridiron roof. The act-drop, was to have represented a view of Stratford-on-Avon, the birthplace of the great dramatist after whose own Globe Theatre the present edifice is named. The decoration of the audience portion is in white and gold, the box fronts, &c., being moulded in *papier maché*. A small amount of colour is introduced here and there to heighten the effect; but the judicious application of gilding, relieved by the crimson curtains of the private boxes, has been relied upon for the principal effect. The ceiling is of a form not hitherto adopted in any London Theatre, being a perfect dome, decorated, like the remainder of the house, in gold and low relief, and lit by a sunlight or novel arrangement and great illuminating power. The somewhat ghastly glare of this peculiar method of lighting is, however, modified by enclosing the sunlight in a sort of basket of cut glass, of very rich and handsome design. There is not a seat in the house but has a good view of the stage.

Following the modern fashion of prefacing the principal entertainment of the night with a short piece, which shall enable all comers to be comfortably seated before their attention is particularly claimed, the Proprietor of the new Theatre last evening inaugurated his spirited undertaking by a performance of Mr. Buckstone's comic drama of *Good for Nothing*. The favourite piece, obviously chosen for the purpose of introducing to the London stage Miss Clara Thorne, a very youthful actress, who made a most promising *début* as Nan, went off as merrily as could be desired. The *débutante* quickly won favour of the auditory. Mr. E. Marshall was amusingly characteristic as the generous-hearted gardener, Tom Dibbles; and Mr. C. Warner as the carpenter, Charles Dormer; Mr. John Newbound as the railway stoker, Harry

Johnstone; and Mr. H. Andrews and Mr. Paulo as Mr. Simpson and Buttons, completed the cast. At the fall of the curtain Miss Clara Thorne was personally greeted with warm congratulations. The original act-drop curtain painted by Mr. Telbin and Mr. W. Telbin, was unfortunately destroyed a few days ago by the calamitous fire in the Charles Street painting-room; but these artists speedily supplied the loss by a new one, representing Ann Hathaway's cottage at Shottery, near Stratford-on-Avon, which, with a striking group of figures in the foreground, proved a most effective substitute.

After a brief interval Mr. Sefton Parry, hailed with repeated rounds of applause immediately he appeared, came before the footlights and delivered a short address, in which he welcomed the audience to the Globe Theatre with the same heartiness, he declared, as he had greeted their presence in his new Holborn Theatre two years before. In referring to the loss he had sustained by the destruction of the painting-room in Drury Lane, Mr. Sefton Parry alluded to the generous offer of assistance he had received from his friend John Baldwin Buckstone, a name no sooner mentioned than it was recognised amidst the heartiest acclamations. With every kind of good wish, and an assurance that he would do all in his power to merit their support, Mr. Parry bade the public welcome to the Globe. The applause, which frequently interrupted the short speech, was even more emphatic at the conclusion, and Mr. Sefton Parry then withdrew amidst renewed expressions of encouragement. Then came the prominent feature of the playbill, a new and original five-act comedy by Mr. Henry J. Byron, entitled *Cyril's Success*.

As the literary hack, Matthew Pincher, Mr. J. Clarke, most effectively 'made up,' gave the fullest point to his caustic speeches, and perfectly succeeded in ingratiating himself with with the exceedingly appreciative audience assembled in the new Theatre. The discovery of his matrimonial relationship with the starched schoolmistress, Miss Pamela Grannet, most characteristically portrayed by Mrs. Stephens, kept the house in roars of laughter. The popular author, Cyril Cuthbert, entitled rather by his connection with the title than by his prominence in the performance, to be considered the hero of the comedy, introduced to the London stage Mr. W. H.

Vernon, a young actor who bids fair to attain a good position on the Metropolitan boards. He is easy in his deportment, and delivers his lines with an earnestness that demonstrates the fullest appreciation of the due significance to be imparted to every word. As an important accession to the Theatrical ranks as a *jeune premier* he may be cordially welcomed, but it may be reasonably suspected that his strength lies in the delineation of eccentric character. As Cyril's wife, Kate Cuthbert, Miss Henrade acted with a vast amount of animation, and gave the more sentimental passages of the dialogue the advantage of an interpretation thoroughly in accordance with the author's intentions. Mr. David Fisher, as Major Treherne, was warmly welcomed back to the London stage, and by his natural performance of the thoughtless but not irreclaimable libertine, sustained the high repute he had formerly enjoyed. Miss Hughes, another excellent performer too often missed of late among the familiar faces with which playgoers are familiar, gracefully personated the young widow, Mrs. Singleton Bliss, and the minor parts of Perkins, Mrs. Cuthbert's maid, by Miss Behrend, the valet Pepper, by Mr. W. J. Hurlstone, the Viscount Glycerine, by Mr. C. Warner; the calculating Manager of the Royal Polygon Theatre, Mr. Fitzpelham, and the religious publisher of Paternoster-row, Jones Grimley, acted by Mr. John Newbound and Mr. H. Andrews, and suggestive of portraits drawn from living personages, were all most efficiently depicted. Mr. J. Tyndale and Mr. Younge, as Colonel Rawker, Unattached; and Paul Bingo, the Royal Academician, effectively appeared among the members of the Grantley Club. A special welcome must be given to Miss Maggie Brennan, who, as the musical amateur, the Hon. Frederick Titeboy, captivated the audience by her manners, and fascinated them by the grace and intelligence with which she rendered a character apt to betray young actresses into affectation and extravagance. The applause which accompanied the performance of the comedy enforced a reappearance of the principal representatives at the end of the third act, and on the fall of the curtain general acclamations testified to the complete success of the comedy, brought on all the performers before the curtain, and evoked another speech from Mr. Sefton Parry, who, in explanation of the

E*

absence of the author, from professional engagements at Manchester, stated that a telegram should at once communicate the satisfactory result. Without any great pretension to brilliance of decoration the new scenery, presenting a succession of interiors, reflects great credit on Mr. John O'Connor, who has pictorially illustrated the Grantley Club, St. James's, and Mr. T. W. Hall, who has depicted the other apartments in which the personages of the play assemble. The National Anthem was played by the orchestra before the comedy commenced. Mr. Sefton Parry has given the London public a very comfortable Theatre, and from the result of the first night a most favourable augury may be drawn of the ultimate success which will attend the speculation.

The reporter was quite right, the new play was a success and ran for 100 performances, a very good run for those days. But Parry's management did not continue with this luck and Fanny Joseph took over for a while, with as little success, and the theatre was closed in June 1870. It was taken over by Bessie Alleyne and drastic re-construction took place. When she re-opened as actress-manageress on Saturday, 8 October *The Era*, the following day, gave details of the changes:

Thoroughly redecorated, and partly reconstructed, this now very elegant and commodious Theatre opened last night for the season under the Management of Miss Alleyne, who for the first time occupies the important post of Theatrical Directress. The improvements made in the interior are considerable, and are to be at once recognised. The closing in of the dress circle not only enables the front of the house to assume a more elegant aspect, but removes that objectionable current of cold air which used to sweep round the corridor with the entrance of every box visitor. The stalls are furnished with large lobbies, the seats in the pit have been advantageously re-arranged, and the ten new private boxes, which have been added, afford the most luxurious comfort to the occupants. The ceiling has been raised, the 'sunlight' placed in a much more desirable position, and new staircases constructed to lead to the upper boxes, which command an excellent view of the stage. The plans, remarkable for their ingenuity, have been carried out under the entire direction of

Mr. Walter Emden, architect; and with the elegant decorations by Mr. E. W. Bradwell, of Great Portland Street, most
brilliantly and tastefully executed, the general effect is
admirable, redounding greatly to the credit of both the
gentlemen thus associated. A most encouraging sign of the
judgment of the new Manageress is the selection of Mr.
Walter Lacy for the important post of Stage-Manager, and of
Mr. W. S. Emden for the equally responsible position of
Acting-Manager. Their long experience, and the high esteem
in which they are respectively held by the public, will be of
direct value to the new undertaking.

The new management was also short lived, but did contribute to
theatrical history. On 3 December a play by Lord Newry, called
Ecarté, was produced. Clement Scott, the critic, in his book
The Drama of Yesterday and To-Day, (1899), tells the story:

It is a very rare occurrence for a play to be acted for 'one
night only.' This was however the unhappy fate of the maiden
effort years ago of an able young man, always an enthusiast in
the cause of the drama, a very brilliant amateur actor, and who
has since proved himself to be an expert and clever dramatist.

His first dramatic child was, alas! stillborn, or got strangled
at its birth; and it gave rise to one of the most remarkable
scenes I have ever witnessed.

The play was called 'Ecarté,' and it was written, I think,
in the interests of the star—Miss 'Nita Nicotina'—[Bessie
Alleyne], who began life in a tobacconist's shop in the Strand,
and was the idol of the smart young clerks at Somerset
House, many of whom were my intimate friends, and most of
us had been schoolfellows together at Marlborough, where
our attachments were most sincere. So they took me behind
the scenes of the tobacconist's shop to flirt with the beautiful
girl long before she dreamed of going on the stage, in order to
gain notoriety as an actress. [She first appeared in burlesque
at the St. James's in 1864.]

In the course of the play, which might in other circumstances have been a very good one, there was a picnic scene;
and the enthusiast, anxious to be liberal as well as artistic and
realistic at the same time, provided a sumptuous repast from
Fortnum and Mason in Piccadilly. So good were the Perigord

pies, the truffles, the seductive chickens, and the etceteras—
particularly the champagne, 'which flowed like water' as the
reporters say, that the action of the comedy was considerably
delayed, and tried the patience of the Saturday night audience,
which has always one eye on the stage and the other on the
clock, since to go home unrefreshed must ever be a serious
personal inconvenience.

At any rate there have been more first-night 'rows' on
Saturday than on any other night of the week. It seemed as if
that stage picnic in *Ecarté* would never end. The laughter,
the jokes, the repartees of the picnic party were no doubt very
amusing to the artists, but they were irritatingly inaudible to
the audience. Besides, was it not adding insult to injury when
the poor occupants of the pit and gallery seats saw their
chances of a stirrup cup on a Saturday night disappearing
altogether, whilst those on the stage were tasting the dainties
they could not touch, and drinking the Pommery that would
never delight their parched throats?

Unfortunately, unlimited champagne does not agree with
the sober art of acting. It is apt to obfuscate the intelligence,
and make the actor or actress, as the phrase used to be, 'thick
in the clear.' That fate befell poor 'Nita Nicotina,' [Miss
Alleyne], a remarkably handsome woman, but I fear an
indifferent actress. She forgot her words, and in endeavouring
to recover them, gave a ghastly and silly grin. This tickled the
'gods' immensely, who in those days used to chaff much more
than they do at present. They didn't wait until the end of the
play to applaud or 'boo' as they do now, but accompanied the
dialogue with a running fire of chaff. Once that spirit had set
in seriously, the play was usually doomed. Nothing could
stand against it. No human effort could pull the play out of
the fire of failure.

The dimmed star got worse and worse. She managed to
save herself through a scene or two, and at last appeared
hopelessly dazed and demoralised, in boots of different
colour, one green, one red! Whereupon there was a wild yell of
derisive laughter, which evidently annoyed the fair actress,
who came forward to the footlights and said, in a well wadded
voice, 'Now, you stupid fools, when you have done laughing
and making idiots of yourselves, I will go on with this

(hiccup) beastly play.' This of course was a somewhat serious affront to the poor author.

From that moment the game of *Ecarté* was played out. She had trumped her partner's best card, and the sad author did not win on this particular speculation.

Since consecutive runs had commenced in the theatre in the sixties this was the first play to be acted only for one night, a record which has not often been repeated in theatrical history.

After the season of opera bouffe in April 1871 (for which the theatre added the title 'Royal'), the management passed into the hands of H. J. Montague who, with David James and Thomas Thorne, had built the Vaudeville Theatre in 1870 (see *The Theatres of London*). Harry Montague did not agree with his partners' policies and seceded from the management. He took the Globe and opened with a strong company including Henry Compton and Carlotta Addison, but the theatre could not be made to pay its way and Montague gave up in 1874 and went to America where he died a few years later when only thirty-five. He was a handsome leading man and the matinée idol of his day.

The next management of importance was that of Alexander Henderson who, in 1875, presented his wife Lydia Thompson in the burlesque *Blue Beard*, transferring it from the Charing Cross Theatre (see Number 25). In all it ran 251 performances.

Jo, adapted from Dickens's *Bleak House*, produced under the management of Edgar Bruce in 1876, made the name of Jennie Lee, who played the little Crossing Sweeper, famous on both sides of the Atlantic.

Edward Righton managed the theatre with varying success for the next two years, but little of note was produced.

Henderson returned in 1878 bringing *Les Cloches de Corneville*, again from the Charing Cross Theatre, (by now the Folly Theatre), to carry on its run of 705 performances. He continued his run of light operas with *Les Mousquetaires* by Louis Varney in 1880 and *La Boulangère* by Offenbach, 1881, among others, and the Globe enjoyed a period of unwonted prosperity.

From December 1881 melodramas held the stage under the management of F. Maitland. During his regime an adaptation by Thomas Hardy and Comyns Carr of the former's novel *Far from the Maddening Crowd* caused a storm in a teacup, with the Kendal's at the St. James's Theatre, over the resemblance of their production of Pinero's *The Squire* to Hardy's novel. Much ink was spilt on both sides; nevertheless the St. James's play succeeded and the Globe's failed.

After an English comic opera *The Vicar of Bray* by Sydney Grundy and Edward Solomon, which was later to be revived by D'Oyly Carte at the Savoy, Mrs. Bernard Beer became Manageress. Her first production was *The Promise of May*, 'A new and original Rustic Drama in Prose' by Alfred Tennyson, produced in November 1882. It had a stormy passage with a rowdy first night audience. Even though it was revised it did not escape a second night protest from the stalls by the Marquis of Queensbury, who denounced the poet, proclaiming himself an agnostic and objecting to what he called a misrepresentation of free-thinkers and secularists as expressed by Herman Vezin in the character of Edgar. The play only lasted a few nights, needless to say, and later Mrs. Beer tried a version of *Jane Eyre* with little more success.

From 1882 to 1888 once again the theatre became the Royal Globe, but this did nothing at first to add to its dramatic prestige. Success did not come till 1884 when *The Private Secretary* by Charles Hawtrey transferred from the Prince of Wales' Theatre where it had failed, with Beerbohm Tree as the Rev. Spalding, earlier in the year. Hawtrey became his own manager and cast W. S. Penley in the part and the play became a hit: and ran in all 785 performances. It was revived twelve times up to 1930 for Christmas seasons. Hawtrey tried other plays at the Globe with varying success, and revived *The Private Secretary* in 1887 and followed it with *The Arabian Nights*, a farce by Sidney Grundy, again with Penley.

In 1888 Wilson Barrett became the lessee and manager, opening with *The Golden Ladder*, which he followed with a revival of *The Silver King*, one of his most famous parts.

From May 1888 an adaptation by Hugh Moss of John Strange Winter's *Bootles' Baby* ran 121 performances, and made the name of Ellen Terry's young niece, Minnie Terry.

Two seasons of interest, firstly in 1888-1889, are those of Richard Mansfield, who made a big personal success as Richard III, but whose other plays were not well received, and secondly the first London season of Frank Benson's Shakespearean

Company who played *A Midsummer Night's Dream* with great acclaim, at Christmas 1889, and followed this with *Hamlet* and *Othello* among other plays, until the following May.

There is nothing of note to record in the next few years, except to remember Master Leo Byrne, 'The Wonderful Australian Boy Actor' in *Ned's Chum* in 1891, and *Ma Mie Rosette*, a romantic opera by Paul Lacome in 1892.

Success returned to the theatre when W. S. Penley returned in January 1893, with *Charley's Aunt*, which he had produced at the Royalty Theatre the previous December and transferred after only a few weeks. It was to stay at the Globe to run in all 1,466 performances, and to remain in one form or another current coinage of the theatre for generations to come.

After Penley, John Hare took over the theatre in 1898 and, with an excellent company, produced a number of new plays and revivals. *The Master*, brought Kate Terry back to the stage, after a long retirement since 1867, to assist at her daughter, Mabel Terry Lewis's debut. He revived Robertson's *Caste*, *School* and *Ours* and produced Pinero's *The Gay Lord Quex* with Irene Vanbrugh and himself in 1899 which ran for 300 performances.

The life of the Globe was drawing to its close. The Strand improvements were under way. The Opera Comique and the Olympic closed in 1899 and, after Hare left the Globe in 1900, there were few managers who wanted to be in at the death of the remaining theatre.

A few 'end of run' transfers; *Sweet Nell of Old Drury*, January 1901; *H.M.S. Irresponsible*, September 1901; among them. Then Fred Terry and Julia Neilson returned in February 1902 and produced *The Heel of Achilles* 'a languid melodrama of Anglo-Russian politics,' by Louis N. Parker and Boyle Lawrence. It failed completely and at the end of the month they revived *Sweet Nell of Old Drury*.

The theatre finally closed in April and the housebreakers moved in. Somewhere beneath Bush House and its surrounding roadways lies the site of long forgotten theatres, 'The Rickety Twins.'

Another Globe was to figure in the Theatre List in June 1909 when the Hicks Theatre in Shaftesbury Avenue, which opened in 1906, (see *The Theatres of London*), changed its name.

7
The Royal Amphitheatre

The Holborn Amphitheatre, The National Theatre, The Grand Central Rink, The Royal Connaught Theatre, The Alcazar, The International Theatre, The Holborn Theatre, The Holborn Central Hall, The Holborn Stadium

High Holborn
In a block bounded by Dane Street and Red Lion Street, with Eagle Street (and stage door) at the rear

Opened as the New Royal Amphitheatre 25 May 1867 with a mixed programme of equestrian entertainment and *Grim Griffin Hotel; or The Best Room in the House*, a farce by John Oxenford and Professor Pepper.
Under the management of Thomas M'Collum and William Charmon.
(Usually called the Holborn Amphitheatre after 1870.)
Converted into a theatre and re-opened as the National Theatre 11 October 1873 with a miscellaneous entertainment and a revival of *Middy Ashore*, a farce by Bayle Bernard and *Eurydice! or Orphée aux Enfers*, a new version by W. F. Vandervell of Offenbach's opera bouffe.
Under the management of Frederick Strange.
Became the Royal Amphitheatre and National Theatre of Novelties in December 1873 and reverted to the name of the Holborn Amphitheatre December 1874.
Under the management of John Hollingshead.
September 1874 called Newsome's Circus (late Amphitheatre), but after November again called the Holborn Amphitheatre.
Became the Grand Central Skating Rink March 1876 for over a year.
Re-opened as the Royal Amphitheatre October 1877 with a comedy drama *Simon*.

Under the management of James Taylor.
Called Hamilton's Royal Amphitheatre November 1878 to June
1879.
Re-opened as the Royal Connaught Theatre 1 November 1879
with *Alcanara*, a comic opera by B. E. Woolf and Julius Eichberg,
preceded by *Bachelor's Hall*, a farce by G. L. Gordon, and
followed by *Lotus Land*, a ballet written and composed by Mons
Camille and produced by John Lauri.
Under the management of J. W. Currans.
Re-named the Alcazar and re-opened 26 December 1882 with
Cinderella, a pantomime by Frank Hall.
Under the management of John Baum.
Re-named the Holborn Theatre and re-opened 12 April 1884 with
Callender's American Coloured Minstrels, preceded by *A Silent
Woman*, a one act farce.
Under the management of George Rignold.
Closed as a theatre April 1886, subsequently becoming in turn the
Holborn Central Hall; the National Sporting Club; a Y.M.C.A.;
the Holborn Stadium and lastly the Stadium Club.
Damaged in the blitz February 1941 and demolished.
An office block, Templar House, (81 to 87) now covers the site.

IN THE EIGHTEEN-SIXTIES behind High Holborn, on the north side
between Dane Street and Red Lion Street, there was a large horse
and carriage repository called the Metropolitan Horse Bazaar. It
was a circular building and had been erected on land owned by the
St. Clement Danes since the sixteenth century. The building was
bought by a company formed for the purpose, and arrangements
made to erect an Amphitheatre for Circus performances on the
site with its entrance at 85 High Holborn, under the direction of
William Charmon and Thomas M'Collum. *The Era* 5 May 1867
says:

It must be a matter of considerable surprise to many persons
that the equestrian interest should have, to all appearance,
died out in the world of public amusement. London once had
its regular equestrian theatre (Astley's), which was one of the
most prosperous under the Lord Chamberlain's control; and
it is with pleasure we announce to our readers that a most

spirited attempt will shortly be made to revive the glories of
the peaceful sawdust ring. On the site of the Holborn Horse
Bazaar is now rapidly progressing towards completion an
Amphitheatre which will vie with any building in London in
the beauty and elegance of its decorations, and its admirable
arrangements for the safety and comfort of the public. The
Royal Amphitheatre, under the Management of Mr. Thomas
M'Collum, a gentleman of great practical experience and
excellent judgment in such matters, will soon be thrown open
to the public on the evening of the 18th inst., when the
Directors may feel sure of seeing their commodious Theatre
filled from ground floor to roof. We now proceed to give our
readers some particulars of the building and its exceedingly
satisfactory arrangement. The plan of Mr. Thomas Smith,
the architect, of Bloomsbury Square, is remarkably ingenious
in detail, and in the employment of the space at command he
has most carefully studied the interests of the Proprietors, the
performers, and the public. The building has three entrances.
The 'Grand' is wide and roomy, and arches are to support
the ceiling. Decorations in the Pompeian style are to be used
here, and an extremely handsome stone staircase (carved
balustrades) leads to the boxes. The corridor at the back is
entered through an aperture, which can be closed with steel
shutters, and the Amphitheatre will contain twenty-four
private boxes. A balcony follows the circle in front of the boxes,
and in it will be placed 200 damask-covered spring seats
(numbered and reserved). The pit, which is entered from the
west side, is intended to accommodate 500 persons, and here
again stuffed seats will be supplied. The gallery, access to
which will be made from the east, is arranged to seat 550
persons. The front row will be cushioned and reserved, and,
like those lower in the building, will turn back. The curve of
the Amphitheatre is extremely imposing, and the ceiling will
be constructed of stretched and illuminated canvas, with a
large centre flower radiating from the sunlight. The mouldings
are by Jackson, of Rathbone Place, and the decorations by
Green and King, of Baker Street. To mention these well-
known names is at once to suggest that a cultivated and
correct taste will regulate the embellishments of the Amphitheatre. All the entrances are fire-proof, and all the staircases

of stone; and especial care has been taken to provide facilities for clearing the building in a few minutes, should that necessity ever arise. Ventilation is promoted by an immense air-shaft, which runs through the entire structure, and the lighting has been entrusted to the well-known firm of Defries and Sons. A crystal sunlight, nine feet in diameter, and containing nine hundred and sixty burners, will illuminate the whole of the auditorium. The supply of water will be copious, hydrants being fixed on every floor. Refreshments will be procurable in the theatre. The Box-office and Saloons will be under the supervision of Mr. Nugent, who is decidedly the right man in the right place. At the back of the Pit will be found an enclosed Promenade fifteen feet in width. Iron doors and steel shutters are the rule throughout the establishment. There are two separate sets of stables, and sixteen dressing-rooms, replete with comfort, for the use of the double company of equestrians and dramatic artists.

When the new Amphitheatre did open, a little later than it was hoped, *The Era* 26 May, after repeating the description given earlier, says:

We may, however, venture a little more into the statistics, for the sake of supplying such of our readers as are curious in those matters with a record for future reference. The entire span of the Theatre, which has a very elegant appearance, is seventy-six feet in the clear—the whole length being 130 feet. From box to box the width is sixty feet, and the length from proscenium to box is sixty-eight feet. In the centre of the house, and facing the stage, is the Royal box, with an ante-chamber immediately behind. The dress circle is arranged at the side, where the private boxes are usually placed, and the private boxes (twenty-six in number) are in the front of the house. In front of these boxes is a row of stalls, calculated to hold two hundred occupants, with folding seats, so as to gain additional space of one foot six inches. The pit is divided into 550 seats, all numbered, with standing room for about 200 persons more. The amphitheatre stalls amount to 700, with 500 ordinary sittings, so that, when full, about 2,000 spectators can be accommodated. The arena is 120 feet in circumference. A drop curtain, effectively painted by Mr.

Julian Hicks, and of a classical design, tastefully sets off the proscenium; and the stage, though not very deep, is commodious enough for the light dramatic entertainments which are to be given in conjunction with equestrianism. Let us add that the builder intrusted with the carrying out of Messrs. Smith and Son's architectural designs is Mr. Thomas Ennor, of Hardinge-street, Commercial-road; that the 'seating' is by Mr. Henry Chandler, of Horse-Shoe Court, Clement's Inn; the stage machinery, by Mr. Burkett, of the City of London Theatre; and the costumes, by Mr. May, of the well-known establishment in Bow Street.

The Amphitheatre thus efficiently prepared for the reception of the public was last night filled by a fashionable audience, whose satisfaction with the arrangements made for their reception was expressed in the most unreserved manner. The performances were likewise of a character which indicated the intention of the management to take high ground in this form of amusement, and the equestrian company collected must certainly be regarded as the best for many a year seen in the Metropolis. Continental travellers well know the attractions in this way offered at the Cirque de l'Impératrice of the Champs Elysées, Paris; and there, as well as at Vienna, Berlin, St. Petersburgh, Moscow, and Constantinople, several of the equestrian, acrobatic, and grotesque *artistes* who last night made their *début* in the New Holborn Amphitheatre have already gathered several of the greenest laurels in their respective wreaths of fame. The seats were all filled at eight o'clock, when the performance commenced, and the occupants, as they rose in recognition of the usual loyal compliment of the National Anthem, which had the double signification on this night of inaugurating the new season of a new Theatre, and celebrating the anniversary of her Majesty's birthday, obtained a yet more commanding view of the building. The survey from every portion of the house was most satisfactory, and the early experience gained in this way of the facilities afforded the visitors for moving from their places without inconveniencing their neighbours elicited remarks which might have been listened to with profit by the Managers of some of the older Theatres of the Metropolis. The band, which is a very good one, under the direction of Mr. Clemments, then played the overture to *Zampa*, and from that time the scenes in the circle were continued for three hours with only an interval of ten minutes between the two parts. The amusement of the audience was ensured by some quaint quips supplied by 'Charlie' Keith, who, besides being distinguished through his extended professional career in all countries as the 'Roving English Clown,' enjoys the special distinction of being 'Clown to the Prince Imperial of France.' His *entrée comique* and a clever performance with two chairs gained for him peals of acclamation, whilst a leap through a paper hoop, in the course of which he became mysteriously possessed of a long night-gown, displayed equal ingenuity and dexterity. His continental travelling was illustrated copiously by a free use of foreign phrases. The gymnasts, John, Joseph, and Henri Delevanti, with other members of the 'family,' exhibited some extraordinary somersault throwing, and the juggling act on horseback of Joseph Delevanti, with which the programme commenced, was executed with singular neatness and quickness. Balls, cups and balls, and daggers are thrown and caught with marvellous precision. Mr. Charles Abbott, the whimsical grotesque, is remarkable for a great deal of fun, in words as well as action, and his hand-springs and somer- saults are very cleverly performed. The feat of throwing somersaults round the circus through a succession of hoops especially excited the admiration of the spectators. Mr. Thomas Fillis, the Jester, who is enriched with the reputation of being 'world-renowned,' is of the class known as 'the Shakespearian Clown.' A speech, in which he introduced with tact and taste the names of the various newspapers and periodicals, was very heartily applauded, and his 'orations' generally were full of humour. Madame Rose Gerard Goudschmidt, who is the *première equestrienne* of the Cirque Napoleon, performed gracefully a 'trick act' in the first part, which included some astonishing flights over flags and through paper balloons, about twenty of which were dashed through without a single misadventure. Another agile *equestrienne* is Madame Anne Bradbury (*nee* Montero), from the Cirque du Prince Impérial, who with her husband executed on horseback a *pas de deux*, in which some surprising combinations were formed with equal facility and elegance. Mdlle. Virginie Lambert, also of the Cirque Impérial, a graceful rider in the style characteristic of the *haute école*, commenced the second part with a pleasing illustration of the various movements to which she had trained her docile steed. The lady, as with the rest we have named, had to reappear, to respond to the plaudits of the delighted spectators. From the Oriental Cirque, Constantinople, comes Mdlle. Juliette Latunia, whose 'trick acts' are, with those of Mdlle. Rochez, reserved for another occasion to minister to the entertainment of the patrons of the New Amphitheatre, but they claim mention as members of the company. Mr. Alfred Bradbury, an equestrian of great skill and daring, afterwards performed a wonderful 'jockey act,' which is announced as being seen for the first time in England. The performer leaps on his horse careering at full speed, and maintains his footing at an acute angle. The achievement provoked enthusiastic plaudits from every part of the house. Mons. Gerard Goudschmidt, of the Cirque Napoleon, takes a very extraordinary 'tunnel flight,' through a series of connected hoops, eight feet long, passing through them with a somersault and alighting on the back of his horse whilst galloping round the circle. This is another of the peculiar feats which will render these performances talked of for their daring and dexterity. The eccentricity called 'Les Nains,' by Messrs. J. Delevanti and F. Felix, who go through a 'Lord Dundreary' kind of entertainment, with two admirably executed masks for their respective figures, excited roars of laughter. Mr. J. Powel and his four children are members of the company, and on another occasion will vary the already excellent pro-gramme provided. The Brothers Daniel, the well-known 'musical Clowns,' proved most efficient supporters of the entertainment, and their violin performances in the most difficult of positions, their imitations of Christy's minstrels, and their simulated 'voluntary' on a church organ, with only their fiddles to produce the deep sounds, excited general admiration. They were thrice recalled to give fresh proofs of their talents. The 'fire' horse, Zamor, was introduced by Mr. James Fillis, professor of the *haute école*, and exhibited the effects of the patient training he had received by mounting a lofty pedestal on the stage, and coolly obeying the word of command amidst the distracting influences of a blaze of fire-works. This impressive *tableau* terminated the first part, and the applause given to this extraordinary evidence of perfect control over the animal was equally emphatic and deserved. A promising feature of the entertainment is the 'Lightning Zouave Drill' of Captain Austin, a distinguished American officer, who has never before appeared in England. The rapidity with which he went through a series of military evolutions with his rifle, both with and without the bayonet, testified to the vast amount of practice which had rendered the weapon so easy to his hand. The feat he accomplishes is not to be described in any terms which could convey an idea of Captain Austin's marvellous dexterity, but the plaudits he gained were proofs how thoroughly it surprised and delighted the spectators. Mr. C. Bradbury's changeable act of 'The Three Nations,' England, Ireland and Scotland, when he appears at last as a young Highlander, must not be forgotten as among the principal attractions of the programme. A new farce, called *Grim Griffin Hotel; or, The Best Room in the House*, the joint production of Professor Pepper and Mr. John Oxenford, wound up the evening, and brought the new stage into requisition. Mr. Richard J. Sheridan is a traveller, named Jeremiah Mum, who has to encounter the adventures in the 'Best Room,' prepared for him by the landlord, Bustler (Mr. Henry Lynn,) and who is waited upon by Seraphine, the landlord's daughter (Miss Jeannette Macgregor); Pertzer, the chambermaid (Miss Sallie Turner), who sings 'The Bailiff's Daughter of Islington;' and Handzur, the boots (Mr. James Francis). The scene represents the Bed-room of a Country Inn, with a huge four-poster occupying the centre of the stage, from which a gorilla, and a succession of different personages, emerge after a fashion well known to those who have seen any of the various adaptations of the Polytechnic Cabinet of Proteus. It was eleven o'clock when the farce commenced, and it is so evidently only intended to be a vehicle for optical effects, that it would be impertinent to criticise it from a literary point of view. The dramatic portion of the programme will, doubtless, receive fuller development in time. The whole of the equestrian entertainments afforded

the highest satisfaction to the spectators, who liberally distributed their applause among the performers appearing in the
arena, and there can be no doubt a very attractive place of
amusement is added in the 'New Amphitheatre' to those
already existing in the Metropolis.

Despite the auspicious opening and the expectation that
Londoners were anxious for a new home for circus, the project
did not succeed and the building was put to various other uses.
Promenade concerts and Minstrel entertainments were tried;
other attractions included the American 'Ethescope, an illusory
olio entertainment, embracing almost every variety of optical
illusion, on a much larger, pleasing and effective scale than any
heretofore witnessed.'
    The opera of *Faust and Marguerite* was presented on 30 May
1870. This would seem to be an ingenious combination of the
magic lantern, 'Pepper's Ghost' and singers.
    Circus was tried again in 1870, under the management of
William Charmon, for the Christmas season, after which it was
mostly closed until another circus season opened in 1871.
    An advertisement offering the Holborn Amphitheatre to be let
or sold stated invitingly it 'could be converted into a theatre if
necessary' and that Sunday evening services were among its
regular bookings.
    It re-opened as a circus, the Grand Cirque and Amphitheatre, in
December 1872, under the management of C. Weldon, but was up
again to let in April and only some concerts were held in May 1873.
    A new lessee, Frederick Strange, was found in October. He
took the hint and converted the building into a theatre, calling
it the National Theatre, (the first of this name, later to be
used again when the Queen's, Long Acre was called the National
Theatre for a short time in 1877).
    Holborn now had two legitimate theatres (as well as the Royal
Music Hall), and the many changes of name in the next few years
of both these theatres has led to much confusion among theatrical
writers. The Holborn Theatre Royal opened in 1866 (also called
the Mirror and the Duke's), was burnt down in 1880 and vanished
for ever from the Theatre List (see Number 8), while the re-
named Amphitheatre was to have many other names after it
became the National, before it too ceased to be a theatre in 1886

the Royal Connaught, the Alcazar, the International and ending
s the Holborn Theatre after its near neighbour had been burnt
down).

An advertisement in *The Era* 5 October 1873 announced the
change of status of the Amphitheatre and said 'the auditorium had
been re-modelled and re-decorated, a new stage constructed and
very arrangement made in order to enhance the comfort of the
visitors.' The new National Theatre duly opened on 11 October
and *The Era* reported the following day:

Lest any of our readers start at the above ambitious title and
ask where is located the establishment which bears it, we
hasten to satisfy their curiosity by telling them that the
Holborn Amphitheatre, metamorphosed by Mr. F. Strange,
is henceforth to be thus designated. The place which knew
sawdust shall know it no more. The daring bare-back rider,
the graceful *equestrienne*, the performing elephant, the
educated mules, the horses skilled in the saltatory art, tightrope dancers, slack-wire walkers, 'aerial wonders,' Lu-Lus,
and a host of other phenomena more or less wonderful, must
now seek fresh fields and sawdust new; while Clowns, if
Clowns at all are permitted to play their fantastic tricks within
these walls, must wait until Christmas, when high jinks
everywhere hold sway, permits them to leave the ring and
mount the boards legitimate. Certainly it seems somewhat
anomalous that a Theatre taking to itself the title of 'National'
should inaugurate its career with opera bouffe, essentially the
offspring of Gallic soil. But then what's in a name? The
'National' as any other name will, we hope, smell as sweet,
and the house itself, we feel sure, will smell even sweeter.
Alterations have not brought about much in the way of
decorations, and when things have been got into something
like working order we shall expect to find many improvements,
especially in front of the curtain. The bill of last night
contained not one item that was new. Yet did it suffice to
attract an audience which filled the house from floor to
ceiling, and although there were two or three hitches in the
course of the evening, and an escape of gas threatened at one
time to clear the house, the initiatory performance may be
regarded as giving no little promise of future success. The

entertainments were commenced by the Brothers Elliot and
Kellino, proficient in the art of ground and lofty tumbling,
their agile movements and daring tricks eliciting much
applause. Bayle Bernard's farce *Middy Ashore* followed. In
this we are unable to give anything like commendation to more
than two of those engaged in the cast. These two are Miss
Bella Goodall and Mr. Plumpton. The lady made a very lively
representative of Harry Halcyon. She entered heart and soul
into the fun of the piece, and, whether talking or dancing, or
engaged in some mad prank, 'Middy' in this instance supplied
abundant amusement, and gained well-merited admiration. A
better Tom Cringle than Mr. Plumpton we have no desire
to see, but seeing him shall wonder. Mr. Plumpton, in the
role of a Jack Tar thoroughly salted, is to the manner born,
and the success of this part of the performance was due in a
great measure to his efforts. Of the rest of the cast, including
Mr. J. E. Everard as Lieutenant Norton, Mr. Crofton as
Limberback, Mr. F. Vernon as Mr. Tonnish (the swell), Mr.
Roffey as Stubbs, Miss K. Hudson as Lady Starchington, and
Miss Vokins as Emily, we can only say that they afforded
another illustration of the unadvisability of putting square
pegs in round holes, the Lady Starchington being conspicuously inefficient both in make-up and acting. The great
attraction of the evening was Mr. W. F. Vandervell's version
of Offenbach's *Orphée aux Enfers* with the title of *Eurydice!*
This, we need hardly remind our readers, was produced at the
Surrey Gardens in May last under Mr. Strange's management.
The most important feature to note in the reproduction of the
work is the discovery and introduction to a London audience
of a new *prima donna* in the person of Signora Inez Arco,
announced as from the 'Teatro della Scala.' If this lady has
never before appeared before an English audience she may be
complimented on her thorough acquaintance with the English
language. She has a good voice, and this was heard to
advantage in the role of Eurydice; and although it seemed to us
totally unnecessary and somewhat inconsistent to interpolate
an air from an Italian opera (*Ernani*, if we mistake not,) in
order to show her ability in the best possible light, her efforts
as a vocalist were none the less acceptable, and she was
deservedly the recipient of considerable applause. Her acting

was hardly up to the mark, but then good singing and good acting do not too often go together, and we must be content to get something to our taste without being greedy. Miss Annie Beauclere made an energetic Orpheus. Miss Lizzie Marshall looked very handsome, and rendered good service as Mercury. Mr. Rosenthal was Pluto, and in the disguise of Aristaeus his imitation of an amatory country bumpkin was excellent. It is not necessary to insist here on Mr. Rosenthal's skill as a vocalist. It will readily be believed by all who have heard him that in his hands—or shall we say in his mouth— the music received full justice. Mr. Charles Heywood was Styx, and, as on 't'other side of the vater,' he was loudly applauded for his rendering of 'If I were King of Boetia.' Mr. Plumpton again distinguished himself as Charon. The ferryman has, as Mr. Vandervell would say, one of the ferry best songs in the piece, and this, called, we imagine, 'Off to Pandemonium,' he chants prior to taking his customers across the Styx. In response to a vociferous encore. Mr. Plumpton introduced the following verse:

> Here you are, here you are,
> Your presence means a good round sum,
> And proves that you to Strange prove true
> In this our Pandemonium.

This allusion elicited loud calls for the Manager, and Mr. Strange, on making his bow at the footlights, was hailed with tremendous cheering. The Celestials were represented by a host of pretty girls in picturesque and appropriate attire, and only the exigencies of space prevent our chronicling the surnames of a swarm of Lizzies, and Berties, and Jessies, and Nellies, and Maggies. In the splendid scene representative of Pluto's Palace the now famous Sisters Vaughan appeared in a 'grand ballet of Furies,' invented and arranged by Mr. J. Milano. Miss Kate Vaughen heads the *troupe*, and she startled the spectators not only by her graceful and really marvellous movements, but by appearing in black skirts and black 'tights,' relieved by gilt trimming. This was, indeed, an innovation in the ballet. But novelty is rare now-a-days, and everybody seemed delighted. We must not forget to mention that with the introduction of Jupiter and the Celestials we had also the introduction of political, social, and domestic allusions to recent events, and some of us will find comfort in the assurance that those who rob the poor in the matter of coals in this world will themselves have a rare flare-up in the next. The 'National' boasts a large and fully efficient band; the entire stage arrangements have been entrusted to the able care of Mr. J. Milano, and Mr. J. Reeves has once more under his direction a corps of giants, whose stalwart proportions offer sufficient guarantee for the maintenance of order throughout the house.

The new regime was not a success and by December the name Royal Amphitheatre and National Theatre of Novelties was being used for a miscellaneous Christmas entertainment of 'Comedy burlesque, ballet, Pantomime, etc.', at very cheap prices.

When this ended once again the 'To Let' advertisement made a regular appearance in *The Era*. Still calling itself the Royal Amphitheatre and Theatre of Novelties, the only novelty would have been a tenant during most of 1874!

At last John Hollingshead from the Gaiety took over the theatre made improvements and re-opened as the Holborn Amphitheatre on 19 December 1874 with *Cinderella; or, the Fairy Queen and the Glass Slipper*, 'a Comic Musical Drama and Opera with a new Christmas Pantomime ending'. It was a loose version of Rossini's *La Cenerentola* with additional music by Donizetti and Bellini among others. *The Era*, the following day, commented:

During the seven years of its existence the Holborn Amphitheatre has undergone many changes, but to Mr. Hollingshead is due the last and best, that of converting the Equestrian Temple into a home for light comic opera and extravaganza. The alterations made have been most judicious, and the central space, formerly devoted to scenes of the circle, now forms a capacious pit. Ample stall accommodation is furnished, and attached to the balcony is a smoking-room, and the gallery is not only very large, but affords the spectators a view of the stage, such as they do not usually obtain from that portion of the house. The terrible draughts which of old made the Amphitheatre a Temple of the Winds as much as a Temple of the Drama have been shut out completely, and the pit and stalls are thus rendered thoroughly comfortable. These advantages, combined with an attractive programme, filled the house last night to overflowing by the time the curtain rose upon *Cinderella*, which charming fairy story supplied the entertainment of the evening.

ven Hollingshead, whose magic touch had made the Gaiety amous, failed to put the Amphitheatre on the map. He tried to ransport whole productions from the Gaiety repertoire including *a Fille de Madame Angot*, *The Beggar's Opera* and William reswick in Shakespeare and Beaumont and Fletcher, but he had give up in March in the face of defeat. He had been running ree theatres at the same time; the Gaiety, the Opera Comique nd the Holborn Amphitheatre, which may have had something do with this failure.

Once again 'To Let', it re-opened as Newsome's Circus (late mphitheatre) in September 1875. James Newsome remained control till November. Now advertised as re-fitted up with 47 foot ring it was offered to let as a Circus and was leased y Rizareli's Grand Cirque and again called the Holborn mphitheatre. After their Christmas season ended the Amphi-heatre became the Grand Central Rink for over a year. This was the beginning of the craze for skating. It re-opened as the Royal mphitheatre with a play, *Simon*, in October 1877 which ran till anuary 1878. Then once again a pathetic advertisement for a nant was put in by H. Vernon, who could be applied to on he premises at 85 High Holborn.

It is not till 16 November 1878 that it re-opened as Hamilton's oyal Amphitheatre. The manager, Harry H. Hamilton, nnounced the interior had been re-embellished and a new stage onstructed. *Hamilton's Excursions*, a popular entertainment which ad been shown on tour and at Halls around London for some ears, was a mixture of Panorama, Magic Lantern and live ntertainment which foreshadowed the cinema. *The Era*, 17 November, described the performance:

Under the above title Mr. Harry H. Hamilton re-opened the Holborn Amphitheatre last night, being encouraged in his enterprise by the presence of a large and certainly an enthusiastic audience. Indeed, there were times when we could have wished the enthusiasm to have been of a less boisterous character, but indulgence on an opening night may well be accorded, while on the stage happily no indulgence was necessary, although Mr. Winter Haigh apologised for the gas, which persisted in burning dimly as if ashamed of itself and sulky at the superior brightness of the electric light. This, however, did not interfere with the scenic effects, for, by keeping all the strength—or rather weakness—of the gas for the stage and preserving a faint glimmer for the audience, all went well. We have so frequently praised the Excursions of Mr. Hamilton that to a great extent we should travel over familiar ground if we described in detail all the excellent features of an entertainment which could not be surpassed of its kind. We must remark, however, that, while giving in substance the same entertainment we have seen before, it is varied and enlivened by so much that is new, and the scenic effects are upon so elaborate a scale, owing to the increased space now at Mr. Hamilton's command, that it is far and away superior to what it was before. The 'Excursion to America' is a most comprehensive one, since no peculiarity of American life is omitted. There are glimpses of natural scenery such as cannot be found elsewhere on the face of the earth, and the singular varieties of character and costume which may be found in the vast territory under the control of the President of the United States affords brilliant opportunities to the artist. Some of the eccentricities of American life arising from the mingling of races, and the presence of settlers who have in many cases left England and Germany in a state of poverty to win a rapid fortune in the new world, give many chances for the clever lecturer to indulge in a bit of quiet fun. Starting from Euston Square we are speedily at Liverpool, where we embark on board the magnificent steamer Germania, and speedily find ourselves on the open sea. The vessel, seen by moonlight, makes an exquisite picture, and the bustle and kaleidoscopic variety of New York life is presented in a representation of the Broadway in the open day, and again at night, illuminated by thousands of lamps. While beautiful scenes are being shifted before our eyes in the smoothest and most effective manner a host of performers are seen and heard in front, with songs and dances, all of which were extremely successful. Mr. Andy M'Kee was one of the greatest favourites, his humour being of the most comic and whimsical kind. The applause he won was vociferous. Next a charming young lady, Miss Beaumont, sang 'The Nightingale's Trill,' and later in the evening Clay's ballad 'She wandered down the mountain side,' being received with great favour by the audience. The night and day effects at St. Patrick's Cathedral were greeted with great enthusiasm, as they deserved to be, being extremely well managed. The champion skaters, Messrs. Ashley, Smith and Hess, gave a couple of very amusing scenes; and Mr. Winter Haigh, besides his valuable aid in describing the various scenes, was also very successful in his songs, 'The Mocking Bird' being loudly encored; but Mr. Hamilton, with great wisdom, sets his face against encores, which, while a number of beautiful scenes are in progress, would, if permitted, soon become a bore. Mr. Charles Heywood, the tenor, sang several times, and joined Mr. Haigh in the duet 'All's Well,' which was greatly appreciated. Mrs. Haigh in a quaint American song met with plenty of admirers. Mr. Andy M'Kee, Mr. W. Gant, Mr. Diamond, and Mr. Gulliver appeared in a comic Negro sketch called *The Sleepwalker*, and Mr. Gulliver introduced a banjo solo and song which pleased greatly. Mr. W. Harrison gave a passing sketch of public events; and several other admirable sketches and songs were given during the scenes illustrating the return home. An excellent band rendered efficient aid, and the entertainment altogether was thoroughly worthy of the applause constantly bestowed upon it. We may add that some of the finest scenery is from the pencil of Mr. W. Telbin, and does him infinite credit.

Hamilton remained in possession until 7 June 1879. The next change was more drastic. In September it was announced that the theatre had been acquired by James Wylie Currans, and he would re-open on 1 November, as the Royal Connaught Theatre, by special permission, in honour of the Duke of Connaught, a son of Queen Victoria, who had just been married. The theatre was once again re-furbished, the programme noted:

The Manager begs to inform his patrons that no expense has been spared to make the 'Royal Connaught' one of the most Elegant and Comfortable Theatres of the West

End. Thoroughly and luxuriously furnished throughout, by Lyons, of Holborn, who has supplied the new Fauteuils, upholstered in Blue Satin, the rich velvet hangings, and the Brussels Carpets of a pattern specially designed for this Theatre. The Body or Pit of the Theatre has been boarded over, carpeted and boxed in all round, so as to exclude all possibility of draught. A new Stage has been built, a splendid Promenade, Foyer, and Tier of Private Boxes have also been added, the whole of which work and decorations have been carried out under the superintendence of Mr. Littlejohns, Contractor of the Globe, Folly, &c. The new Gas arrangements, Chandeliers and Devices, by the firm of Messrs. Defries and Sons. Messrs. Watts & Fowler, Refreshment Contractors, of Holborn, will have charge of the new Saloons.

The triple bill of fare, comic opera and ballet with which the new manager opened was received with reserve, and soon the opera was changed to *La Fille de Madame Angot* which ran ti December. A new drama, *London Pride*, was announced o Boxing Day. The management had changed during earl December: according to the programme E. G. Osborne becam Director and John Vale Manager. The internal strife this repre sents was the subject of a court action the following April, and th promised drama did not appear. Instead, George Rignold wa engaged to appear in *Alone* and *Black Eyed Susan*, two of hi established successes. He remained playing other roles in hi repertoire until February 1880. This was followed by stoc melodramas with little success, and in April a panorama *The Par Exhibition of 1878* was exhibited.

After the supposed settlement of the litigation, with John Vale a licensee, the theatre was 'To Let' till May, when it re-opened wit a comic opera under May Blumer's management called *Th Obstinate Bretons*. This ran for over one hundred and sixt performances (it should have opened at the Duke's but did no owing to legal difficulties). She followed this with other attractions but had to close in September as the litigation over the ownershi of the lease started up again. This kept the theatre closed until i was announced in December that Charles Morton, the famou music hall manager, had taken a long lease to produce comi opera and ballet. He re-opened with Offenbach's *La Fille d*

Tambour Major, in an 'entirely re-decorated and upholstered' theatre, on 1 January 1881 with a good company. But the following month he let the theatre to Harriett Jay, the novelist, who had stage aspirations to appear as Lady Jane Grey in *The Nine Days' Queen*, a romantic drama by Robert Buchanan. Its run was terminated in March by the Board of Works and the Lord Chamberlain who demanded that a fireproof wall be erected between the stage and auditorium.

The theatre was again advertised 'To Let', and it was to be assumed the required work had been carried out. No tenant was found and eventually the theatre was put up for sale in February 1882:

Valuable Pieces of Leasehold Land with the Theatre and buildings thereon, situate in High Holborn, in the County of Middlesex, and known as the 'Royal Connaught Theatre,' And also the Plant, Fixtures, Machinery, Properties, Scenery, and other effects now being in and belonging to the said Theatre, to be sold by private treaty, subject to the sanction of the Court of Chancery of the County Palatine of Lancaster. The Premises are held under several leases of the St. Clement Danes Charity, for the residue of several terms expiring in September, 1921, at the Annual Aggregate Ground Rent of £315. The Theatre is a modern building, and has all the latest improvements and requirements, and has three approaches from High Holborn, and has also three other entrances. The property is now vacant, and possession will be given upon completion. The said buildings might easily be adapted for the purposes of a depot for goods or a post-office. Apply to Messrs. W. W. Wynne & Sons, Solicitors, 40, Chancery Lane, London; and to Messrs. Simpson & North, Solicitors, 3, Water Street, Liverpool.

The results of this announcement are not immediately obvious for it is not till December that the theatre, now re-named the Alcazar (the name of the abortive theatre in Leicester Square in 1878) is announced as re-opening on Boxing Day, 1882, under the full management of John Baum. Again re-decorated and re-furnished, and according to the advertisement 'almost re-built entirely'. A pantomime was given called *Cinderella and the Little Glass Slipper; or, Harlequin Prince Peerless and his Pretty Sisters and*

F

the Three Young Kings of Sicely, a title longer than its run! This only lasted a few nights, as the Board of Works stepped in and informed the Lord Chamberlain that the theatre had re-opened without a licence, and the required alterations ordered earlier had not been carried out. The new manager had opened in defiance of this order. He was brought before the Bow Street Magistrate and fined.

By May the agreed repairs were in hand, and the theatre soon ready for occupation, but no tenant came upon the scene till December when Marguerite Dinorben became the Lessee. She opened on 22 December 1883 with *Mizpah; A Story of To-day* and once again the name of the theatre was changed, this time to the International. *The Era* 29 December, commented:

> The old Holborn Amphitheatre, which, under various changes of name, has never been able to win fortune, re-opened its doors last Saturday, and, with the incomprehensible title as above, once more wooed the wayward goddess. Some changes have been made in front of the house, the most important of which is found in the improved means of exit for the audience. The decorations of the auditorium have been furbished up and brightened; the ground floor of the house has been devoted to its pit patrons, having been comfortably carpeted and supplied with well-cushioned seats, which are furnished with backs; whilst the private boxes are hung with crimson satin curtains. The proscenium wears a clean exterior, and the footlights are screened by stained glass, which shields the glare of gas from the eyes, without casting any gloom on the little orchestra. On the stage Mr. Grieve has supplied some attractive scenery, aided by an artist unnamed, who has provided a charming picture for the opening prologue of the new play, and by Mr. Bigney, who has painted an uncomfortably yellow scene, which is one of the plainest interiors that we can remember. Miss M. Dinorben, the lady named as the manageress who offers hostages to fortune in undertaking the responsibilities of this unhappy theatre, has ventured her first stake with a play by an unknown dramatist. We doubt, however, if *Mizpah; A Story of To-day*, will do much to bring the name of its author, Mr. Benjamin Sykes, from the obscurity to which it has hitherto been

doomed. We say 'hitherto', for when Mr. Sykes made his appearance in front of the curtain, whither he was summoned by the good-natured, if not numerous, audience, we saw in the gentleman who came on to bow, with hat, overcoat, and umbrella, quite supplied to turn his steps in another direction, if necessary, an elderly man who must have been some years waiting for his chance if he commenced writing for the stage at the age at which most playwrights are attacked with the *cacoethes scribendi. Mizpah* is not a work that will benefit anybody, we fear. A young man in the pit provoked the attention of the gods by taking a good half hour's sleep there. Whether it was induced by the comfortable seats or the slowness of the piece we cannot say; but we should not like to assert that he had the smallest enjoyment of the evening.'

A month later *Our Boarding House*, by Frank Rogers, occupied the stage. The manageress played a small part in each production. In less than a month the management folded and the company found the theatre shut against them the 'Ghost having failed to walk' the previous week. The theatre remained closed until George Rignold returned, this time in management with J. Allison. They changed the name of the theatre once again, calling it the Holborn Theatre (the Holborn Theatre Royal had been burnt down in 1880). Rignold opened 12 April 1884 with a consolidation of Callender's and Haverley's American Coloured Minstrels, preceded and followed by a one act comedy. They were in residence for a month's season then Rignold, himself, returned as Adam Bede in June, which he acted with other plays till he went on tour in the mid summer. The theatre re-opened on 16 August with *War to the Knife*, a revival of H. J. Byron's comedy, and a new burlesque by Frederick Bowyer called *Little Lohengrin; or, The Lover and the Bird*. Though the new manager, Rex Pierson, did not advertise sufficiently in the Press he received quite good notices. Money must have been short as the actors were not paid and the ensuing riot was described in *The Era* 30 August:

On Saturday night last a disgraceful riot occurred at the Holborn Theatre, under circumstances that might have been attended with fatal results to individuals owing to the unjustifiable and cowardly conduct of the occupants of the gallery. A new burlesque, entitled *Little Lohengrin*, was announced as the principal item of the evening's entertainment, to be preceded by a farce. At the time of opening the house was fairly well filled, apparently by a very orderly audience, who listened to the overture with every sign of appreciation. Some time elapsed, and as there was no signs of the curtain rising, expressions of impatience were indulged in by a portion of those assembled. It has since transpired that the delay was caused by the action of an actor who was engaged to play in the farce, but refused to do so until the other half of his salary had been paid. The dissension extended to other members of the company, and Mr. Charles Coote and Miss Lizzie Coote eventually refused to sustain their parts in the burlesque. Owing to the protracted delay the audience, which had been considerably augmented, vented their displeasure by hooting and hissing. In this dilemma Mr. Rex Pierson, the manager of the theatre, was compelled to go in front of the curtain and announce that there would be no performance that night, but the money taken at the doors would be refunded. A scene of indescribable confusion ensued, the audience rushing bodily to the pay-box in front of the theatre. It was with the greatest difficulty that Mr. Pierson succeeded in reaching there with the alleged intention of returning the money taken. But there a fresh difficulty presented itself, for it was discovered that two of the money-takers for the pit and gallery were not forthcoming with the amount taken by them. All the money taken at the box-office was refunded to the first comers, and in order to satisfy the demands made upon him, Mr. Pierson says that he paid upwards of £2 out of his own pocket. Not having sufficient to pay the multitudinous demands he was compelled to make an announcement to that effect. This appears to have exasperated those assembled to such a degree that a rush was made on the pay-box, and in a very few seconds it was completely demolished, Mr. Pierson and a Mr. Vincent and a young lady of the company being very roughly handled, the lady in question being seized by the hair and dragged away, while Mr. Vincent's clothes were literally torn into shreds. He was seized, and everything in his pockets was taken from him, his pockets being turned inside out. While he was subjected to this treatment, Mr. Pierson had lifted the lady on to his right arm, while with his left he was compelled to literally fight his way back inside the theatre. There a most disgraceful scene was being enacted. The occupants of the gallery had commenced to tear up the seats, and had thrown several into the pit, where a large number of people had assembled, and were trying to prevent Mr. Pierson from reaching a place of safety behind the scenes. Fortunately no one was hurt. The disorders in the gallery were extended to the refreshment bar at the back, considerable damage being done to this department, one of the beer engines being literally torn from its fittings. Similar disorders occurred in the pit, some of the seats being torn up, and a large and valuable mirror in the refreshment bar was smashed. While this work of destruction was proceeding, Mr. Pierson was surrounded by an angry mob, who, in addition to demanding money paid for admission, insisted upon money being returned that had been paid for cloakroom fees, and for programmes of the evening's entertainment. This department had been sub-let to Mr. Scrutton, the refreshment contractor, and Mr. Pierson consequently explained that he was entirely powerless in the matter, as the persons responsible had left the theatre. Upon this announcement being made those assembled became still more infuriated, and again attacked Mr. Pierson. Blows were freely exchanged, and two or three of the employees, while defending their manager, sustained severe contusions, Madame François, the housekeeper, particularly being roughly handled, her arm being so severely injured that she was unable to raise it. At one time fears were entertained that the limb was broken, but happily this proved to be incorrect. By the aid of Booth, the carpenter, assisted by the under gasman, Mr. Pierson and the lady above mentioned succeeded in reaching the stage, and with great difficulty secured the iron doors. This was not effected until some of the mob had forced their way through. To evade them Mr. Pierson, with his lady companion, was compelled to take refuge in the 'flies' and even here they were not secure. By this time Mr. Vincent had escaped from the front of the house and endeavoured to rejoin Mr. Pierson. The iron door leading to the 'flies' was opened to admit him, but no sooner had this been done than three men who had followed him unperceived rushed through and demanded their money. They were paid, and were shown out of the theatre by the stage-door. While this was transpiring the disorders in the auditorium had increased. The windows in the gallery were smashed, and some of the occupants of the pit had scrambled over the stalls and made an attempt to raise the curtain. The ropes, however, had been secured by Booth, but despite his efforts to prevent it, several people got on to the stage. By some means access was obtained to a portion of the wardrobe, and eventually, it is said, some children were seen wearing it in the neighbouring streets. Every effort was made to find Mr. Pierson, and the rumour having spread as to the place where he was concealed, loud yells and hoots were given vent to. Several shouted out, 'Let's set fire to the theatre and burn him out.' A body of constables eventually arrived on the scene, and with great difficulty succeeded in clearing the theatre. For a considerable time afterwards a crowd collected in front of the theatre, threatening vengeance on Mr. Pierson, and it was only by means of a subterfuge that he and his companions eventually succeeded in getting out of the theatre at all. A rumour was current that it was intended to make an attack on the theatre on Monday, but proper precautions had been taken to prevent a recurrence of one of the most disorderly scenes witnessed in a theatre for some years.

Messrs. Scrutton and Co. write as follows:—'The notice of the riot at the above theatre conveys the impression that the cloak-room fees were not returned. This is not the case. The money was given back in every instance, and the mob helped themselves to the programme money, the men who had been selling them coming in for some very rough treatment from the rioters, who not only took the few shillings they had taken for bills, but what little money they had in their pockets also. We and our assistants were the last to leave the building after assisting the police to make a clearance.'

Later it was said that a large part of the audience had come in on free passes and had tried to get money back on these!

The 'To Let' advertisement was in *The Era* for the rest of the year. One week said hopefully 'To let from to-night for one week or thirty-eight years' (evidently the remainder of the lease!) No-one ook advantage of this opportunity till Mat Robson became 'sole lessee' and re-opened 12 September 1885 with a melodrama at 'popular prices' called *Woman of the People*. He followed this with *East Lynne*, but the season ended after a month.

The next proprietor, W. T. Purkis (of the Royal Music Hall), tried comedy and comic opera. The first production *The Pet of Newmarket* on 12 December closed after a week. The following year it was opened for twelve nights in January 1886 with *Not Alone*, and though once again advertised in February as 're-decorated and re-seated,' the last tenant was T. A. Kennedy 'The World's Greatest Mesmerist' with a variety entertainment in the last week of April, then this much named theatre closed its doors.

There was still trouble about its safety for the next four years: even when it eventually became the Holborn Central Hall it was refused a music licence for some time.

At the turn of the century, with an extended frontage (Nos. 86 and 87) it became the National Sporting Club and a boxing stadium and was handed over to the Y.M.C.A. for a centre during the first World War. In 1919 it was once again a boxing stadium, the Holborn Stadium, and it was put on the map by Charles B. Cochran. It was here that Bombadier Billy Wells met Joe Beckett on 27 February 1919, and the legendary Georges Carpentier and Joe Beckett fought the following December. It remained in use as the Stadium Club until it was severely damaged in the blitz in February 1941. What was left was cleared and the empty site remained until a new office block called Templar House was built on the site of the theatre and adjoining premises; it was completed in 1959.

Dean Street was re-named Dane Street in 1907 to avoid confusion with the similarly named street in Soho.

8
The Holborn Empire

Weston's Music Hall, The Royal Music Hall, The Royal Holborn
Theatre of Varieties.

High Holborn
In a block of buildings at the top of Little Turnstile, backing on
buildings in Whetstone Park, Lincoln's Inn Fields, Stage door and
exits in Little Turnstile.

FIRST BUILDING

Opened as Weston's Music Hall 16 November 1857
A conversion of the Six Cans and Punch Bowl Tavern and the
adjoining Holborn National Hall Schools.
Under the management of Henry Weston.
Became the Royal Music Hall 30 November 1868.
Closed 18 July 1887.

SECOND BUILDING

Opened as the New Royal Music Hall 12 September 1887
Under the management of W. T. Purkiss
Called the Royal Holborn Theatre of Varieties in 1892.
Closed June 1905.

THIRD BUILDING

Opened as the Holborn Empire 29 January 1906.
Under the management of Walter Gibbons.

Damaged in the blitz 10-11 May 1941.
Pulled down 1960.
An extension to the Pearl Assurance Company's Head Office now
covers the site.

IN HOLBORN DURING the seventeenth century there were two
turnstiles. These were to prevent cattle straying from Lincoln's
Inn Fields. Their existence became perpetuated in the names
Great Turnstile and Little Turnstile, at the western end of High
Holborn before it joins New Oxford Street.

At the top of Little Turnstile stood a Tavern, the Six Cans
and Punch Bowl, and in the early years of the nineteenth
century sing-songs and harmonic meetings were held in the bar
parlour.

By the late eighteen-forties Music Halls began to evolve, and
following the pattern set by Richard Preece and Charles Morton
south of the river, Henry Weston the Licensed Victualler of the
Holborn Tavern since 1835, acquired the adjoining premises,
which had been a Nonconformist chapel, and subsequently the
Holborn National Hall Schools. He converted them into an
elegant hall which opened as Weston's Music Hall, on
16 November 1857. Charles Morton had just re-built the Canterbury on a grand scale, and the immediate success of Weston's,
nearer to the West End, was to inspire him to build the Oxford
in 1861 (see Number 14).

The Era 17 November records:

The inauguration of the Weston Music Hall, at 242, High
Holborn, was celebrated with considerable *éclat* on Friday
(yesterday) evening. Upwards of 300 visitors sat down to an
elegant repast consisting of all the delicacies of the season;
and the supply of wines was an excellent vintage.

Edward Huggins, Esq., of the well-known Brewery firm
had kindly consented to take the chair, and took his seat in the
hall at a few minutes past five o'clock. At his right hand were
seated Messrs. Henry Weston and Thos. Wm. Flavel,
solicitors to Messrs. Reid and Co. On the immediate left was
Mr. Alderman Wire and several other friends.

The interior of the building is well worthy the inspection of

F*

every inhabitant and visitor to London. It is so far advanced that it is intended to open it next Monday. It has been designed by Messrs. Finch, Hill, and Paraire, architects, of No. 1, St. Swithin's Lane, City. The length of the hall is 103 feet, and the width, forty; in height we have thirty-five feet. Longitudinally the building is divided into ten compartments by highly-decorated beams, with shields in the centres, and bunches of flowers. Due ventilation is afforded by a variety of trellissed panels and coffers in ceiling and wall. There is a commodious gallery, projecting six feet from the side walls, and on the northern end of the room, on the same level as the gallery, there is a supper-room. The front of this gallery stands out in bold relief, and is remarkably conspicuous. It is highly embellished with ornamental work in relief, representing natural foliage, and at intervals emblazoned shields, with monograms on their fronts, and surrounded by scroll-work relieved by gilding. The gallery is supported by twelve iron columns. The walls throughout are decorated by panel painting, admirably executed in imitation of fresco, by Messrs. Homann and Beensen, of Charrington Street, Camden Town. At the orchestra end of the hall, beyond the proscenium, a large amount of decoration is bestowed on the wall. In its centre is a large semi-circular arch, the pilasters and spandrels of which are painted with subjects in colour, and over it is a tasteful representation, in *alto-relievo*, of Tragedy and Comedy. The hall is lighted with five magnificent glass chandeliers, furnished by Messrs. Defries, the well known firm of Houndsditch. The central one weighs nearly one ton, and is eleven feet in diameter. Messrs. Patrick and Sons, of Westminster Road, were the general contractors for the work, which, we are bound to say, has been brought to so successful a termination.

The musical arrangements were entrusted to the full members of the company, but under the arrangement of Mr. John Caulfield, late of the Canterbury Hall. Misses Eva Brett, Pearce, and Mrs. Caulfield, with Messrs. G. Allen (who was deservedly encored in 'The Merry Men of England'), Parkinson, Corri, S. Heartley, and Matz, all united efficiently to produce sufficient entertainment, in this respect, during the entire evening. When the cloth was withdrawn, the National Anthem was sung, and the usual loyal and patriotic toasts were given and responded to.

Mr. Weston shortly afterwards came forward, and replied to the toast. His appearance upon the platform, or stage proscenium, was the signal for loud and long-continued applause, in return for which he bowed repeatedly. When silence had been sufficiently restored, he stated that he had been highly complimented by the worthy chairman who had proposed his health, and as equally gratified at the heartfelt response which the public had made to it. As regards his feelings upon the present occasion, when he saw himself surrounded as so young a man, he most certainly ought to feel proud. They had rallied round him in the most handsome manner, and he should never forget it. Whenever they chose to repeat the visit, he should feel highly delighted to see them, and he would do all in his power to make them comfortable and happy.

Mr. Alderman Wire mentioned that he took the opportunity of proposing a toast, which was as agreeable for him so to do, as for the company to receive, viz. 'The health of their worthy chairman, Mr. Huggins.' But before he remarked further upon that topic he (the speaker) might be allowed to give his countenance and approval of the step taken by his friend Mr. Weston. They were met there to inaugurate a magnificent building, which was intended to be devoted to the amusement of the people, with a strict regard to the decencies of life; and thus realize and participate in the high mental enjoyment of the higher classes. If such means of opportunity for rational enjoyment were afforded they ought eagerly to be embraced, as the free right of the public. From all he anticipated of the future, he might be allowed to prophesy that none would come within the compass of these walls but what would depart gratified. As to proper conductorship, when the fact became known throughout London that Mr. Weston had invested between £8,000 and £9,000 in the speculation, that would surely be received as an indubitable guarantee that such would be the case. He (Mr. Alderman Wire) would now recur to the toast which it was his present duty to propose, viz. 'The Health of Mr. Huggins, their worthy and respected Chairman.' All knew his sterling commercial integrity—his high vindication of all that was good, useful, and talented; and in saying this it was surely his best recommendation to their notice. (Loud cheers).

It duly opened its doors to the public on 16 November. Weston was later joined and followed in the management by his son Edward, who sold out to John Samuel Sweasey and William Holland in April 1866 for £16,000. (The following year Sweasey became sole proprietor.) It was then calling itself Weston's Grand Music Hall, but in April 1868 it changed to Weston's Royal Music Hall. The following November Weston's name was dropped and it became the Royal Music Hall. At this time the proprietor was W. T. Purkiss, with Sam Adams as his manager. The hall which had remained almost unchanged since it opened, was completely re-built in 1887 from designs by Messrs. Lander and Bedells. The re-opening of the New Royal Music Hall (the 'New' was soon lost from the name) which held 2,500 people is reported in *The Era* for 17 September 1887:

> It is quite unnecessary to describe the architectural beauties of the New Royal, which now rears its head on the site, with added space, of the building long known as Weston's; suffice it to say that the handsome and well-proportioned new temple of variety built under the practical directions of Mr. W. T. Purkiss will compare favourably with any in the metropolitan area, and is but another instance that the taste for a music hall or vaudeville entertainment spreads, in spite of the grand-motherly restrictions that hedge round caterers and do much to prevent that further improvement in the staple known as 'variety' which is equally desired by managers, artistes, and the public. Mr. Purkiss has contrived the new hall so that all within can both see and hear. A wide and spacious balcony, supported by pillars, overhangs a comfortable pit; the stalls, elegantly upholstered in blue velvet, as of old, slope down to the orchestra, stained glass is largely used at the exits and entrances, which are plentiful; and the building is constructed of fire-proof material as far as possible. An essential difference has been made in the size of the stage, which is extensive enough, and with every facility for producing ballet or spectacle. The new grand ballet divertissement which marks the renewed career of the 'Royal' is entitled *Civilisation*,

one of the scenes of this, an exquisite mountain bit by Calcott, with real waterfall, proving the possibilities of the enlarged stage and increased mechanical facilities. The principal strength of the entertainment lies in the favourite serio and comic singers interspersed throughout the programme. Mr. Tom Bass makes an early commencement with humorous songs and patter. He is an old Royal favourite, and his engagement under the new condition of things seems to give a good deal of satisfaction. Miss Katie Seymour once again elicited the warm admiration of her rapidly increasing legion of admirers for her very delightful exhibition of step-dancing. Most fascinatingly dressed, the Sisters Williams asserted their claim to the favouritism which will surely be theirs with such pretty faces and agreeable style of singing. Mr. Frank Travis's very interesting old gentleman of ninety sings rather vigorously considering his age; but *The Colonel's Evening Party*, at which he arrives in due course without any legs, has other guests, who voiced by the clever ventriloquist, entertain the audience with conversation, witticisms, and songs that are always in good taste. Some who follow Mr. Travis's line of entertainment display, unhappily, much anxiety to pander to the tastes of the more vulgar in an audience. As given at the Royal, his show is happily free from this grave fault, and the hearty laughter and applause heard during the 'conversations' of his figures abundantly testified to the fact that success can be won by legitimate means, provided always that sufficient ability be displayed. As a step-dancer Miss Lottie Collins occupies a prominent position on the music hall stage. Mr. Sam Adams has wisely secured her services here, and she is already a great favourite. Mr. Sam Torr, besides his Salvation Army skit, has other songs in his budget that are highly relished; and we again listened with the greatest pleasure to Mr. and Mrs. Watson, in their truly refined entertainment. The audience showed their good taste by encoring Mrs. Watson in her Tyrolean melody, which she sings charmingly. Miss Topsy Venn returns to revive memories of the old Strand some fourteen or fifteen years since. Time has amplified her figure, but has otherwise dealt gently with her. Her voice still preserves its freshness, and she is as active and agile as of yore. She sang on Tuesday, the night of our visit, 'A Matter of Taste,' and also gave a contribution of the American song and dance order which merited the applause it received. Messrs. De Voy, Le Clercq, and company contribute their funny sketch *Down goes the Lever*, little Le Clercq's comicalities being, as a matter of course, heartily laughed at; Mr. G. H. Macdermott, the favourite actor-vocalist, sings 'The Wild, Wild West,' 'Jubilation,' and 'I'd have done it;' the Sisters St. Felix have reduced step-dancing to a fine art, and give an entertainment that has rightly met with the appreciation of the British public; and the programme closes with the duets of the Sisters Collins. The courteous Mr. Sam Adams, assisted by Mr. Tom Carlton, looks after the general manage-ment of the front of the house, whilst a good chairman has been found in Mr. W. B. Fair. To give éclat to the opening night (Monday) the Covent Garden choir of boys and girls sang the National Anthem, after which Mr. Gwyllym Crowe conducted his latest and prettiest waltz, with an increased orchestra, and the chorus in tasteful costumes. The new Royal, with its roomy staircases, its plentiful outlets, and its set of sprinklers over the stage, seems built for safety. Its comfort is luxurious, and good ventilation—that vexed question of sanitation—would seem to be secured by a sliding roof, and by two air-propellers, each of which will remove 30,000 cubic feet of air per minute.

The programme followed the general pattern of the Music Halls of the period: though artists were employed, generally each hall had its special favourites who would remain for long engagements, or re-appear regularly. This hall in particular seems to have culti-vated artists throughout its whole existence, and to have had its own particular public.

Following the prevailing fashion it became the Royal, Theatre of Varieties, when it changed hands in 1892. Purkiss had disposed of his interest to a Public Company which subsequently went into liquidation and a new Company formed by whom it was re-constructed and re-decorated. *The Era* 17 September 1892 tells:

The completion of the alterations and re-decorations which Messrs. Brill and Ellis have had in hand for some months at the Royal, was inaugurated on Monday (12 September) evening at the Holborn establishment with much éclat and congratulations all round. The numerous volunteers for the special entertainment, which has come to be regarded as a very necessary accompaniment to the festivities rampant in front on such occasions, enabled the manager, Mr. Arthur Swanborough, to present a programme of gigantic proportions, and kaleidoscopic in its character. From an early hour in the evening until the chimes of midnight the stage was occupied by the élite of the variety profession, and the evidences given of the heartiest satisfaction were frequent and enthusiastic. The stallites, when they had finished admiring the new carpet, could gaze with delight at the new act-drop painted by that master of his art Mr. T. E. Ryan. Mr. Ryan has not gone to 'furrin parts' in order to find a subject for his brush. He has taken a bit from our beautiful Thames, and has given us a view of it from Richmond. The curtains round the scene are very happily treated, the whole effect being rich and artistic without being garish. On the arched roof just over the proscenium are painted figures of goddesses and cupids. The general scheme of decoration is pale amber and gold, and the appearance of the house has been very much lightened and improved thereby. The old boxes were formerly in a line with the balcony. They have now been thrown back and the side balcony seats brought to within a foot or two of the proscenium, the greatest ingenuity having been exercised in order that every occupant of a seat in the upper part of the house should have an uninterrupted view of the stage. The electric light has yet to come to the Royal; but the new proprietors may be felicitated on the vast improvement they have made in their property. The evening's entertainment, as we have pointed out, was laid down on very liberal lines. Among the fairer favourites who appeared during the evening were Miss Florrie Robina with a song anent the foibles of the young men of the day; Miss Ada Reeve, who went 'over' in her 'romp' and song, for the special delectation of the gentlemen seated aloft; Miss Billie Barlow, looking very pretty in a canary-coloured tunic and tights in which she sang 'Tol-lol-lol;' Mdlle. Adelina a graceful trapeze performer; and Miss Florrie Gallimore, in a Tyrolean song. A roar of welcome greeted Mr. Dan Leno, who, pressed for time, gave but one verse of his 'waiter' song; and then the band struck up that favourite coster ditty 'Eliza,' indicating, of course, the arrival of Mr. Albert Chevalier. But that popular comedian did not occupy the stage. Little Chip came on to sing a Dutch song, which he followed up with his well-known impersonation of the 'Little Nipper.' The audience evidently felt some disappointment at the non-appearance of this youngster's 'stage' father, and did not hesitate to express it in emphatic terms. The excitement, however, soon subsided, and the entertainment proceeded merrily with the clever 'Silence and Fun' entertainment of Ardel and West, who give a really wonderful exhibition of neat and unpretentious tumbling; with the quips and songs of Mr. Eugene Stratton, with the practical fooling of the M'Naughtons, and with well-varied and clever turns by the following: Brown, Newland, and Le Clereq, black burlesque team; the Jackleys, society marvels; Miss Marie Collins, serio-comic; Charles Bignell, comic; Miss Pearl Penrose, serio-comic; George Leyton, comic; Newham and Latimar, variety duettists, appearing respectively as General Booth and a serpentine dancer; Virto, a player on the clarionet, cornet, and saxophone; Mr. Fred Harvey, comedian; Mr. Jolly John Nash, the laughing man; Fred. Herbert, Rosie Vernon, Connie Courtney, Edgar Romaine, Nellie Navette, Ethel Buchanan, Sisters Belfrey, Albert Christian, Arthur Albert, A. Ling, and Major Newell. A crowd of proprietors and agents honoured the occasion with their presence. We noticed Messrs. Charles Morton, J. H. Jennings, J. L. Graydon, Vernon Dowsett, Edward Swanborough, Adolf Tressider, H. J. Didcott, Richard Warner, Fred. Higham, Tom Holmes, and Tom Heath. Good wishes were prevalent during the celebration supper which was given after the entertainment.

In 1896 the Royal came up for sale. *The Era* 7 March reported:

The Royal, one of the most popular variety houses in the metropolis, was sold by auction on Monday afternoon by Mr. Ernest Tabernacle at Masons' Hall, Masons' Avenue, Basinghall Street. Built in 1887 and capable of accommodating 2,500 people, the sale of the hall in August, 1891, to Messrs. Brill and Ellis for £35,000 is well within the recollection of the music hall world, strongly represented at the auction-room on Monday. The auctioneer in offering the property, stated that he had been instructed by the proprietors of the Royal who are dissolving partnership, to offer that partly freehold and partly leasehold property, together with the goodwill and possession, as a going concern. Included in the property offered for sale was the adjoining public-house, The Royal, with fifteen residential rooms over it. The purchaser would have to take over a contract which had been entered into for a building lease of the adjoining property, 243, High Holborn, for a term of seventy-one years from Michaelmas, 1895, at a ground rent of £150. This lease provided that the present building (243) should be pulled down and rebuilt within two years at a cost of £1,500, the elevation to be in accordance with that of the Royal Music Hall. On the west side of the hall the freehold of No. 2, Little Turnstile, had been offered to the vendors for £800, and no doubt the offer would be open to the purchaser of the hall. The ground-rent of the latter was ridiculously low, being only £300 per annum, and the lease had seventy-one years to run. The Royal Music Hall had borne an unblemished reputation (remarked Mr. Tabernacle) from the time when it was known as Weston's Coffee House to the present day. From his knowledge of the income that had been taken out of it by successive proprietors he could say that it was a sterling and genuine property, and if it succeeded in the past there was no earthly reason why it should not be even more successful in the future, especially now that arrangements had been made for providing the much-needed additional accommodation. They knew that all licensed property, and music halls in particular, had been severely attacked during the last few years, but their enemies had now been defeated and disgraced, and the class of property referred to stood on a firmer foundation than it had done for a long time. The reason for the sale was that Messrs. Ellis and Brill had so many irons in the fire that they could not give proper attention to this particular business, and therefore wished to dissolve the partnership and take their money out. The auctioneer having answered questions as to the contracts to be taken over, &c., the sale was proceeded with, the first

bid being £35,000 from Mr. Jacobs for Mr. Freeman Thomas.
Messrs. Jacobs, Thomas, Langton, and one or two others
competed for some time at £500 advances. When £40,000
had been reached the auctioneer accepted bids of £100, and
finally, amid cheers, the property was knocked down at
£40,500 to Mr. John Brill, one of the vendors, who topped
Mr. Jacob's last bid for Mr. Thomas by a hundred. After the
sale Mr. Brill received the congratulations of a large number
of his friends.

The frontage was duly re-built in 1897 to the designs of Ernest
Rüntz combining the two buildings into one new façade.

In 1905 the Royal was bought by Walter Gibbons. It was
closed in June and completely re-built at the cost of £30,000, to seat
nearly 2,000 people. *The Era* 27 January 1906 gives full details:

> The old Royal Music Hall has been closed since June, and,
> during that period, the whole of the building, with the
> exception of the frontage to Holborn, has been pulled down
> and rebuilt, from the designs of Messrs. Frank Matcham and
> Co., architects. [It now had exits in Little Turnstile.]
>
> Mr. Gibbons, the proprietor, has shown great enterprise
> in such a venture, and he has given his architects instructions
> practically carte blanche to make the Royal the handsomest
> and most comfortable hall in London, and it will be seen
> from a visit how well his wishes have been carried out.
>
> The old building was approached practically level from the
> street, and was a one-tier house, containing a balcony only
> over the ground-floor.
>
> The architects were met with most unusual difficulties in
> the planning of the hall, as, among other troubles, rights of
> ancient lights prevented the raising of the new building above
> the old level, and to obtain the usual number of tiers required
> it was necessary to lower the building to the basement, and to
> utilise the old cellars that existed, and were practically useless.
> This has enabled them to erect a much larger hall than could
> have been anticipated, considering the room that has to be
> given up for the number of exits and staircases required to
> carry on successfully two performances a night, as it is Mr.
> Gibbons' intention not only to do this, but to give matinées
> every day during the week.

The striking difference between the new and the old Royal will engage the attention of those who had a knowledge of the old building immediately they enter, for the stage, which was originally on the left-hand side, is now immediately facing the entrance.

The levels of the hall have been so altered that the visitor now enters direct from the street into the grand circle, and descends to the stalls on both sides; but owing to the level of Whetstone Park (at the rear) being considerably lower than Holborn, the occupants of the stalls can make their exit on the same level as their seats, in a similar manner to the patrons of the grand circle, who exit practically on a level with Holborn.

Although the frontages of the Empire remain the same as before, the alteration of the position of the stage and the absorption of the oyster-bar in Holborn into the music hall scheme has enabled the architects to more than double the number of exits, which of course was necessary in consequence of the increased accommodation.

The principal entrance is from Holborn through the existing outer vestibule, the walls of which remain in Faience, but with artistic Mosaic panels introduced, representing music, singing, &c. The floor is covered with cube Mosaic, and the ceiling is panelled out and decorated with an art panel in the centre.

Entering the inner vestibule through pairs of polished mahogany doors, we find the commencement of the new order of things, the walls being formed with white and green marble, in bands, with a deep panelled frieze over a beautifully-designed and decorated ceiling. The floors again are Mosaic. Six wide white marble steps divide this vestibule, and on the higher level is the pay and booking office, and from here pairs of polished doors open into the foyer. This is most ingeniously contrived in the construction of the grand circle. It is 40ft. in length, and is divided up with curved panelled beams and arches, the walls being panelled and filled with silk. Between the pilasters and columns are luxurious settees, upholstered in cloth, with embroidery border and the crown in the centre. The floor is laid with super Saxony carpet, and the electric light has been introduced with good effect. The decorations are simple but very effective, in green and white.

From this foyer a wide staircase leads direct to the stalls and corridors on each side, conducting the visitor to the grand circle seats, on the lower level. A separate staircase from the outer vestibule is provided to the upper seats of this circle, at the rear of which is a raised promenade, with balustrading dividing this from the seating, and from this promenade entrance is obtained to one of the finest lounge bars in London. This is obtained by utilising the old disused rooms over the entrances, the windows of which overlook Holborn. It is divided into two parts by a large opening, flanked by pedestals and columns, between which three wide steps conduct the visitor to the lower level of this saloon. This is fitted with a counter and fittings, and the room is furnished with lounge chairs, settees, and tables, the floor being covered with thick velvet pile carpet and the windows draped with rich silk-brocaded curtains, the walls and ceilings being artistically decorated, and the whole lighted with five polished brass electroliers.

The pit entrance is from Holborn, through a tiled corridor to the lounge at the back of the pit, and from here the pit saloon is approached. This is situated under the entrance vestibule, and is well lighted and ventilated. The whole of the walls are in Faience work, and the floor is Mosaic. The fittings are of polished oak, and the whole room is tastefully decorated and brilliantly lighted.

The gallery, which is formed over the grand circle, is approached from Holborn by a wide staircase, carried up to the promenade, from which access to the gangways dividing the seats is obtained. A large saloon is at the rear of the gallery, well ventilated and decorated, the walls, as well as those of the gallery itself, being lined with Faience.

The auditorium is of fine proportions, and designed on somewhat novel lines, the circle having wide, sweeping curves, and good heights between them, giving fine sight-lines and free circulation of air.

The ground floor is divided up into stalls and pit, the former containing nine rows of polished wood armchairs, covered with Angora goat-hair satin, the floor being of wood-block, and covered with super Wilton carpet.

The pit is also furnished with sixteen rows of velvet-covered tip-up chairs, and the floor of wood-block flooring and cork carpet.

The walls of the stalls are formed of polished marble, in panels, and the walls of the pit are tiled, the ceilings being richly decorated. Staircases on each side of the stalls lead up to the grand circle, and to a very unique stalls saloon, designed in old English. The floor is of polished parquet, and the room is furnished with a counter and fittings, and with leather-covered settees and quaint tables and rugs. The room is decorated in subdued tints, the electric fittings corresponding in style, the whole being very effective.

The grand circle contains twelve rows of seats, and is furnished with chairs, and carpeted similar to the stalls. There are four boxes on the lower level of this circle, two on each side of the proscenium, and two boxes are provided in the top corners at the rear of the circle, and are particularly well placed for seeing the stage.

The gallery is furnished in a comfortable manner, the seats being covered with a leather material, and the whole of the floor covered with a thick, warm cork carpet.

The decorations are artistic in the extreme. They are designed in a free treatment of French renaissance, the colours chosen being white, cream, and gold, relieved by beautifully-painted panel subjects by Italian artists. The ceiling has an opened designed dome, with a sunlight arrangement in the centre, forming the ventilation scheme. The flat ceiling is set out with curved ribs, forming panels, and the sides are covered down to the walls with pilasters, and coffers, and caryatides. The box façades are well conceived, and the single boxes over those on the dress circle level take the form of balconies, with a panelled coved ceiling, and the walls are ornamented and treated with the general decorations, no draperies being used here. The gallery and grand circle fronts are of fibrous plaster, and contain shields, &c., with the electric lights designed to correspond.

The whole of the furnishing of the auditorium is in two shades of *Rose du Barry*, the carpets, seats, and draperies all being in the same colouring. The tableau curtains and box curtains, being of a watered silk material, are very handsome and effective, and when the whole is brilliantly illuminated with the electric light from the handsome brass fittings a very charming effect is obtained; in fact, it is no exaggeration to say that the new Royal will vie for elegance, comfort, and artistic design with any theatre or music hall in London.

The safety of the public has received every consideration, the usual fireproof curtain and iron doors separate the stage from the auditorium, hydrants fully equipped are provided at all important positions, and the exits are numerous.

The comfort provided for the audience cannot fail to be appreciated as, apart from the handsome auditorium, with its uninterrupted sight-lines and its luxurious seating, there are foyers and lounges, and retiring rooms for all parts of the house. The lavatory and sanitary arrangements are built with the latest improvements. The whole of the building is heated by hot-water pipes and radiators, and everything that skill and experience can suggest has been provided to make the audience comfortable and happy in their surroundings.

The stage is of goodly proportions, and large enough to comfortably stage any music hall productions. It has a hard-wood floor, and the upper part contains the usual flies, grids, bridges, &c., and an up-to-date system of electric lighting.

At the rear of the stage is the dressing-room block, containing the manager's office, property and wardrobe rooms, ballet and supers' rooms, and sets of dressing-rooms, the whole well lighted and ventilated, and comfortably furnished with lavatories and dressing-tables, the floors carpeted, and every convenience and comfort is provided for the artist.

The first night is described the following week:

On Monday evening the re-opening was marked by excellent business in both houses; but the joyous nature of the occasion was specially signalised in the second, for which most of the stalls and dress circle had been booked. There was practically no hitch in the arrangements, for, besides his well-disciplined staff, Mr. Walter Gibbons found excellent volunteer helpers in Mr. Hales, Mr. Harry Lundy, Mr. Emanuel Warner, and other friends, and by the time 'God Save the King' had been played by the orchestra, under Mr. James Sale, an eager throng —many of them evidently frequenters of the old Royal—

in stalls, pit and dress circle, had expressed admiration for the beauty of the new house, and had settled themselves down to enjoy the excellent entertainment provided. As soon as the pretty tableau curtains had been lifted behind the magnificent marble-pillared proscenium, Silent Tait, the well-known conjurer, made his appearance. Quite a cockney garden surrounds the 'speechless' magician, and a peculiar specimen of horticulture is the 'deciduous' shrub on which billiard balls are seen to be growing in profusion. Tait pretends to gather these, and makes them disappear in a way that is at once amusing and mysterious. He changes the colour of a handkerchief while passing it through a paper cone, from which he afterwards produces flags; and his duplication of cards is also particularly neat. Silent Tait has a decided sense of humour, as one discovers when he indulges in an odd little dance at the conclusion of each of his tricks.

Satan, the sentimental sketch of the bill, enables us once more to admire Mr. Edward Sillward's realistic impersonation of the faithful gorilla. The Simian is heroic, and saves the young wife of a settler, George Golding, from the clutches of the villain Silas, whom he throttles. The poor animal's bravery and timely help are misunderstood, and he is unfortunately shot by Golding, who imagines his wife is in danger. An incident that adds to the pathos of this pretty little sketch is that the monkey, who has been educated to count up to five—a thing that has been proved to be quite possible—is supposed to think that he has been shot because he couldn't accomplish the feat previously, and in his last moments performs the simple trick with straws. Mr. Sillward contributes a wonderful sketch of the ape. He literally and metaphorically gets into the skin of the part. The animal's rage is expressed with terrible emphasis towards the villain, and the struggle between the two is exciting in the extreme. The other parts are well played, but the cast is not given.

A lively and entertaining interlude in the programme is filled out by the romantic absurdity, entitled *A Trip to the Isle of Man*. Ever since the production of *Fun on the Bristol and Morocco Bound*, 'trips,' both on the variety and theatrical stage, have been quite too numerous to mention. There is always a welcome, however, for anything so frankly hilarious and frivolous as Mr. Arthur Breton's work. Much of it certainly revivifies footlight echoes of musical comedy; but that doesn't really matter. The jolly old boy, Joshua Bacon, a retired merchant, when he sings to his six charming daughters, reminds us of Mr. Rutland Barrington chortling to his six stage-wives in *San Toy*; and the lunatic Count—but we need not draw further comparisons. The fun is fast and furious, especially in the hotel scene, where Mr. Arthur Breton plays fantastic tricks while carving a 'bird'. Other incidentals in the piece—which was fully described in our columns last week— include a chic bathing costume dance by the Sisters MacGovern, and Misses Lorne and Rene, in a musical duo, 'Capital and Labour,' both well-appreciated numbers. Miss Kitty Terris, who sacrifices her personal appearance to the exigencies of low comedy, plays with complete success the part of Matilda Pickles—a quaint delineation that contributes much to the success. Some pierrots, among them we recognise that veteran performer Fred Harrington, sing a stirring military song; and fun and frolic mark the progress of the whole sketch, which is well illustrated and tastefully dressed.

The Two Bees (Harry and Flora Blake), in their comedy scene, 'Pictorial Post-Cards,' plunge the audience into the throes of excitement by the exhibition of portraits of party leaders; but the duettists touch a more sympathetic chord when they deliver lyrical tributes to—and honour the memory of—Sir Henry Irving and Dan Leno. Some of the political portraits might be better, and it would be difficult for the friends of John Burns to recognise the stalwart of Battersea in the counterfeit presentment displayed on the Bees' pictorial easel. Though some of the applause is cheaply obtained, they score a great popular success. Hill and Hull repeat their success in the lady dummy business, the complete inertia of one of the performers being cleverly simulated; Lee and Kingston combine in some amusing nonsense, the shower of missiles on the head of the male performer who burlesques Tommy Atkins, being a bit of drollery that is well appreciated; and the Australian Lady Meister Singers make a great hit. They contribute 'The Lost Chord,' and, responding to a very pronounced encore, sing 'Dinah Dee,' an American comic catch. An attractive quartette, indeed; but why *meister* singers? Ruffell's Bioscope presents a very fine picture on the Bioscope, which may be called 'The Train Wreckers,' and the programme has other contributors in Frazer and Haley, Zaro and Arno, and J. W. Rickaby.

The Hall's success continued, through the waning days of the music hall, and did, in fact, under the management of Charles Gulliver, and later George Black (running in conjunction with the London Palladium), keep the old traditions alive in the West End longer than anywhere else. Only in its last years did it succumb to revue and abandon its weekly change of variety bill. In 1928 it was given a face lift with re-decoration and re-seating.

One interesting piece of history connected with the Holborn Empire was the disappearance of Maud Tiffany. She was due to appear on 4 August 1914—the day of the outbreak of war—and having played the first two houses she left the theatre and has never been seen or heard of since. Her theatrical basket and props were left in her dressing-room and have never been collected —they remained in store at the theatre until the end.

Every well-known variety artist appeared here from time to time and at one period it was the acknowledged 'home' of Gracie Fields and Max Miller.

The Holborn Empire is particularly connected with the children's patriotic play *Where the Rainbow Ends*, which made this theatre its annual Christmastide home from 1922 to 1938.

Another distinction possessed by the Holborn Empire is that it is the only variety theatre at which full-length Greek tragedy was performed. *Medea* with Sybil Thorndike was performed when Lewis Casson and Bruce Winston presented a matinée season of Greek tragedy, Shaw and other plays in 1920.

The Holborn Empire was closed as a result of enemy action during the night of 11-12 May 1941 and stood empty and forlorn until 1960 when it was demolished. Moss Empires, who, up to 1951 hoped to re-build and re-open, sold the site to the Pearl Assurance Company and an extension to their large premises, on the other side of Little Turnstile, now covers the area.

9

The Holborn Theatre Royal

The Theatre Royal Holborn, Royal Holborn Theatre, The Mirror Theatre, The Duke's Theatre

High Holborn
Behind the corner of Brownlow Street in which were the pit and gallery entrances, with stage door in Jockeys' Fields (now the continuation of Bedford Row) at the rear.

Opened 6 October 1866 with *The Flying Scud; or, A Four-Legged Fortune*, a drama by Dion Boucicault. Preceded by *Larkin's Love Letter*, a one act farce by T. J. Williams.
Under the management of Sefton Parry.
Variously known as the Theatre Royal Holborn 1869, and the Royal Holborn Theatre, 1870.
Name changed to the Mirror Theatre Royal 24 April 1875 and re-opened with a revival of *The Hidden Hand*, a romantic drama by Tom Taylor. Preceded by *Maids of Honour*, a comedietta by Charles Lamb Kenney, and followed by *Make Yourself at Home*, a one act farce by Alfred Maltby.
Under the management of Horace Wigan.
Name changed to the Duke's Theatre and re-opened 8 January 1880 with a transfer from the Opera Comique of *Meg's Diversion*, a comic drama by H. T. Craven, followed by *Black Eyed Susan; or, The Little Bill That was Taken up*, a burlesque by F. C. Burnand, concluding with *A Tempting Bait*, a farce by W. J. Austin.
Under the management of F. C. Burnand.
Destroyed by fire 4 July 1880.
Site covered by the First Avenue Hotel, opened 1882, which was destroyed in the blitz in September 1940.

'irst Avenue House, a Government-Office block, completed in 952 now covers the site.

ᴀFTER THE CONVERSION of the Queen's Bazaar into the Princess's Theatre, which opened eventually in 1840 (see Number 17), no ᴉew theatres were opened in central London for the next twenty-ᴉx years. There was complete stagnation in theatrical speculation, ᴉnd even some existing theatres were often hard put to find a tenant.

Erroll Sherson, who had been a theatre-goer since the sixties, ᴉays (in 1925) of the situation:

It is an emphatic comment on the low ebb to which dramatic art had been reduced at the beginning of the second half of the nineteenth century that there should have been no demand for a new theatre for twenty-six years.

It is stated to have been essentially a 'proper' Age, though there are not wanting those who say that its propriety was merely veiled impropriety. The repeated veto of the Lord Chamberlain on all entertainments which he thought savoured in the least degree of either 'impiety' or 'impropriety' had been carried to a ridiculous excess. The expression 'Oh God!' was invariably altered to 'O Heaven' up to about the year 1860, and in earlier days, that is in the first years of Queen Victoria's reign, such expressions as 'Oh la!' or 'Oh lud!' were deemed profane. La Dame aux Camélias was forbidden as a play (under that title at any rate) for many years, though it was licensed as Camille and again as Heartsease and was always allowed on the operatic stage as La Traviata. Perhaps the licenser knew well that no one knew or cared for the meaning of what the operatic singers sang as long as they sang it well. In short, all entertainments which might be said to have been in the least risqué were taboo. It was an Age when England qualified for her degree of First Hypocrite of Europe! when all scandal was hidden away, shoved into corners to flourish, as such things will, better in the darkness than in the light. I can remember when it was the height of impropriety to mention 'Legs' at all, and I knew one house in Weston-super-Mare where the 'Legs' of the piano were concealed in chintz pants! I have heard that they are still so clothed in some of the smaller towns in the United States. We have certainly progressed since those days. Nowadays subjects are openly discussed and limbs openly displayed that would have been carefully avoided and covered up in the days of our grandmothers.

It was Sefton Parry, the theatrical speculator, who was responsible for the first new theatre to be built after so long. Parry, who came of a theatrical family, began his career in Cape Town. On his return to this country he became engaged in the construction and management of theatres. He built, and sometimes designed, the theatres which he usually managed himself for a short period, and then disposed of the lease. Often, it must be said, he looked for big returns on the outlay in compensation should the land be needed. His first speculation at Greenwich led him to London and the Holborn Theatre Royal in 1866. He followed this with the Globe in 1868. The Avenue was also his in 1882, among the other suburban and provincial ventures which he undertook before he died in December 1887. *The Era* 7 October 1866 tells us:

The Holborn Theatre Royal at 43 High Holborn is built on the site of the old Post Office, Stable Yard, and has the advantage of three distinct entrances—one from Holborn, one from Brownlow Street, and the other from Jockeys' Fields. The buildings forming the stables and coach-houses of the old mail carts were pulled down some five years ago. The site thus opened for building purposes offered an area of 15,000 ft., which for a period of upwards of three years remained vacant. The probable difficulties likely to arise from the claims of the adjoining tenants to the free enjoyment of light and air, taken in conjunction with the facilities afforded by the unsettled state of the law respecting this point, deterred many from venturing on any building speculation likely to bring upon them numerous expensive lawsuits. Mr. Sefton Parry, however, selected the site as one suitable for the erection of a Theatre, and with the view to overcome the difficulties the building was sunk some 11 ft. in the ground. This arrangement afforded many facilities, as it rendered the entrance to the pit and boxes more convenient—inasmuch as the pit is reached by a passage on a level with Brownlow Street, where also is the gallery entrance, while the access to the boxes is but a little above the level of Holborn, the stage entrance being from the rear of Jockeys' Fields.

Long before the walls of the building had attained the height of the enclosing wall, and before any opinion could be formed by the adjoining owners whether the structure would in any way interfere with the easement of light and air over the old stable-yard, injunctions poured forth on all sides for redress of probable or imaginary wrong about to be experienced by the parties enjoying the privilege of obtaining light and air from their neighbours' premises. These proceedings to an extent delayed the building. After considerable difficulties in law proceedings, terms were ultimately arrived at which restricted the building being carried up beyond a certain limit. These restrictions to a great extent precluded Mr. Parry carrying out his original intentions. The building is now of the following dimensions:—From foot-lights to the back of pit, 70 ft.; width of pit between walls, 52 ft.; from foot-lights to back of stage, 67 ft.; width of stage, 52 ft.; proscenium, 26 ft. by 23 ft.; the height from floor of pit to ceiling, 35 ft.

The internal arrangement of the Theatre consists in four rows of stalls, 3 ft. 6 in. from back to back; pit seats, 2 ft. 10 in. from back to back. It was originally intended that the first tier should be devoted to the dress circle, in the manner of the Haymarket Theatre. The idea was afterwards modified by Mr. Parry, and four boxes were formed on either side; the dress circle, consisting of six rows of seats 3 ft. apart, facing the stage. The second tier has four slip boxes on either side, two rows of amphitheatre stalls, and at the back is a spacious gallery.

There are no proscenium boxes as in ordinary Theatres, the space having been taken up by additional staircases; by this arrangement there is greater facility of exit in case of panic or from other causes.

At the rear of the dress circle there is a convenient saloon for refreshments and a ladies' cloak room. In the pit there is also a refreshment saloon, and throughout the building are conveniences generally so deficiently provided in our Metropolitan Theatres. The building is in the usual horse-shoe form, but such has been carefully studied so as to enable the audience, from any part of the house, to command a full and uninterrupted view of the stage; from the back seat in the gallery the foot-lights and orchestra are visible. In this point the building is very successful.

The ventilation has formed a matter of serious study. There are numerous openings left in the most convenient positions to avoid draughts, which admit the cold air, while the heated atmosphere is allowed to escape into the roof by perforations left in the ceiling, the area of which amounts to upwards of 300 superficial feet; from the roof the vitiated atmosphere escaped into the open air by louvre openings. Doubting the sufficiency of such an ample provision, a sun burner has been introduced, which is usually of itself considered sufficient for ventilating any public building. The gallery, generally the warmest and closest place in the house, has the advantage of a through draught, there being opening all round, as well as ventilators in the ceiling. Taking into consideration the ample accommodation between the seats, and the provisions made for ventilation, there is little doubt that the present Theatre will prove the most comfortable of our Metropolitan houses.

The style of decoration consists in bulged box front with projecting ornaments, and at intervals shields, containing allegorical figures; the ceiling is panelled out by projecting ribs, at the intersections of which are small pendants. The proscenium decorations consist in a dipha ground with circular ribs running round same; the tinted decorations are pale salmon, and white relieved with gold. The general effect is elegant and chaste, and the colouring judiciously applied.

To carry out the works, Mr. Parry selected Messrs. Finch Hill and Paraire, who are the architects to several of our most important Metropolitan buildings of this character. The building was carried out from their design, and under their superintendence, by Mr. Simpson; the composition works were executed by Messrs. Kettel and Battiscombe, of Marylebone Street; the tinted decorations by Mr. Honmann; the gas fittings of the house and stage were entrusted to Mr. Jones, of Bow Street; and Mr. Lyon, the experienced upholsterer, of Southampton Row, Bloomsbury, has provided the furniture of the Theatre, which is of the most elegant and commodious description.

The *carton pierre* and *papier maché* decorations comprise ceiling pendentifs, proscenium, box fronts, gallery fronts, and enriched caps and trusses. The ceiling is divided into sixteen panels, separated by enriched mouldings, terminating against the sun light, and the intersections stopped by ornamental pendants. These panels are bounded by eight triangular-shaped scroll panels, manufactured in *carton pierre*, and are of a bold and effective character. Outside these are two perforated ribs running entirely round the ceiling, and one of which finished on the pendentif. The sun light is also surrounded by a very rich perforated ornament, ten feet in diameter, in *carton pierre* and of the same character as the scroll panels, and, with the perforated triangular panels, will materially assist in ventilating the house. The appearance of the whole is exceedingly elegant and chaste. The admirable manner in which the architects, Messrs. Hill and Paraire, have arranged these perforations should be particularly noticed, as they tend to increase rather than to mar the beauty of the design. The proscenium is splayed and enriched with an ornamental trellised ground, which runs between shafts. These shafts spring from base, and run quite round the proscenium. The lower part of the same is fluted and panelled, and surmounted on each side by allegorical bas relief.

The box fronts are curved, and project slightly, and the ornamentation is exceedingly light and chaste, and is relieved at intervals by bas reliefs containing appropriate subjects.

As regards the style of ornamentation, it is somewhat of a mediaeval character, but all quaintness and stiffness have been judiciously avoided.

At half-past six, when the various approaches to the new Theatre were for the first time made accessible to the public, an enormous crowd was waiting to obtain admission. The gallery entrance, in Brownlow Street, was completely besieged, and the elegant vestibule leading to the boxes, and which presents from the Holborn side the aspect of a tasteful conservatory, was early filled with a very anxious but extremely orderly crowd. It was very quickly intimated that no more money could be taken to any part of the house, and at the same time it became evident that had the Theatre been twice as capacious as the largest structure existing there would have been a very great number of persons who, desirous of being present on the first night, would have been unavoidably doomed to disappointment. Directly the fortunate possessors of places, which had been secured long beforehand, found themselves comfortably seated a general buzz of admiration attested the delight of the spectators at the light and cheerful look of the house, and the completeness of the arrangements made for the perfect comfort of the occupants of the pit, the boxes, and the stalls. This feeling broke out into a stronger expression when the new act-drop, so charmingly painted by Mr. Charles S. James, gave the utmost effect to the picture framed by the proscenium. This act-drop, it should be stated, is a very pleasing composition of the Watteau school, and shows the highly-finished and chaste style of the artist in the most favourable point of view. There was a loud demand for Mr. Charles James, but he diffidently declined to respond.

The performances commenced at seven o'clock with a new farce, by Mr. T. J. Williams, called *Larkin's Love Letters* which derived apparently from the same French original on which the recent Strand piece of *Waiting for the Underground* was founded, is full of verbal fun and absurd situations of broad practical humour. As soon as the curtain had fallen on the farce, there was a general desire to congratulate the Manager, and when Mr. Sefton Parry came forward in the midst of a storm of congratulations, he earnestly delivered the following brief address:

'Ladies and Gentlemen,—I come to bid you welcome to my house. (Great cheering.) The welcome is warm, but I hope you will find the house cool, and, although I have endeavoured to make it roomy, I trust I shall never see any room in it. I have spared nothing to make it convenient and comfortable, and I honestly think I have succeeded indifferently well. (Applause.) If you feel a little closely packed in some parts now—if, in fact, you feel like figs in a box—it is not the fault of the box, it is the fault of the figs. (Cheers and laughter.)

'Some cheerful friends of mine encouraged me with the remark that I had lodged my Theatre too far East. I replied that the people of London will go to a good entertainment wherever it is, and I mean to give the best. (Cries of 'Bravo.')

With this resolve I addressed myself to the dramatist who really seems to wield a charmed pen and he gave me his cordial adhesion, and what was better, a new drama.

'The company contains the very best artists that I could procure, and I believe I have left no endeavours untried to win that public support on which my fortune now depends. (Acclamations.)

'Ladies and Gentlemen,—In this enterprise is embarked the savings of my Professional life, and I regard with gratified pride my ship, the only one that has been launched in London for upwards of a quarter of a century. Here I stand alone at the tiller, looking out for the breeze of public favour. I am engaged in a more perilous voyage than the Red, White, and Blue. That little wonder put to sea with two men and a dog. I am alone in my venture. Will you please to take me in tow? (Immense cheering.)

(Prompter's bell.) 'Eh! what, ho! it is the prompter! He is in a hurry to begin the drama. I told him I would allow no long waits between the acts, and he is trying the guillotine on the inventor. (Roars of laughter.)

'I was about to add—(Prompter's bell). It is no use, he won't let me add more than this:—I hereby declare and pronounce that on this, the 6th day of October 1866, and in the thirtieth year of the reign of Victoria the Good, there is opened for public entertainment and recreation a new Theatre, to be called the Holborn Theatre Royal. God save the Queen!'

Mr. Parry then retired, amidst renewed rounds of applause, and the band, which is a very efficient one, played the National Anthem, the whole audience immediately rising, and the effect of the Theatre at this moment being strikingly impressive.

At eight o'clock commenced the drama which had been written to inaugurate the new Theatre, and with that remarkable success which is no more than the well-earned result of that combination of inventive ingenuity, with a practical knowledge of the stage, possessed by very few who have written for it, Mr. Dion Boucicault's latest work, written in four acts, and entitled *Flying Scud; or, A Four-Legged Fortune*, was brought before a deeply-interested audience. Breaking

G

entirely fresh ground, this admirable dramatist has here shown a remarkable power of turning the most difficult subject to a strikingly-effective account. The 'Turf' has never been so characteristically illustrated on the stage as in this piece, and the strong dramatic interest which perfaces it will not fail to secure the sympathies of the lovers of English sport, and, at the same time, highly gratify those who care nothing for the incidents which excite the attention of the 'Sporting World.' We are hurried on through this justly-named 'racing' drama without the least slackening of the reins of imagination, and the scenes pass so rapidly that it seems the shortest interval of time between our first start with the characters and our arrival at the place where we leave the owner of 'Flying Scud' to tell anew the strange and exciting story of his career.

The plot of this drama is so full of incident, and the action so rapid that it is quite impossible to detail the story in all its parts.

Thus brilliantly has been inaugurated the first season of the new Theatre Royal, Holborn; and when the Snow Hill viaduct is finished and the Thames embankment completed, both being events which will have a direct influence on the increased traffic through the thoroughfare in which this Theatre stands, we may have to repeatedly refer to this establishment, not merely as being one of the best situated Theatres in the Metropolis, but also as one of the most decidedly prosperous.'

The Company included George Belmore, George Neville, Charlotte Saunders and Fanny Joseph. (The two ladies playing male parts!) It was a big success and ran for 207 performances. It was immediately followed by another drama: *The Antipodes; or, The Ups and Downs of Life*. The cast included 'Mrs. Watts *née* Miss Ellen Terry as Madeline a child of nature.' This was not a success, and during the summer the theatre housed 'distinguished amateurs, assisted by other noblemen and gentlemen, and ladies of high professional position'. It did not re-open professionally till October with T. W. Robertson's *For Love*, which lasted till a pantomime was produced for the Christmas season. This was joined by a revival of *The Flying Scud* in January 1867. After this

finished the theatre was used for occasional Benefits and did not
re-open until September, when it came under the management of
Fanny Joseph, who staged H. J. Byron's *Blow for Blow*, which ran
till Christmas and pantomime time came around. She remained in
control till March, then the theatre was taken by Barry Sullivan, an
actor of the 'Old School' who had a large provincial reputation.
He is remembered to-day in the writings of Bernard Shaw, who
greatly admired his work, and by the name of Barry Jackson, who
was christened after the actor.

Barry Sullivan announced 'Performances of the Highest Class of
Dramatic Literature' and opened with Lytton's *Money*. He
followed this with *A School for Scandal* which continued for his
second season in September 1869. *The Era* said 'His new campaign
is undertaken with vigour' and continued:

> During the recess various alterations have been made,
> which the visitors were not slow to recognise as decided
> improvements. The entrance from Holborn has been enlarged,
> and the vestibule rendered a convenient and handsome
> lounge. The rows of stalls have been entirely reconstructed,
> and are now arranged in a circular form, so that whilst the
> occupants command a fuller view of the stage, they are at
> the same time more in sight of each other. The orchestra is
> concentrated in a kind of parterre, so that the seats are
> curved round it in a semi-circular border, and the effect is at
> once novel and pleasing. A new Royal Box has been con-
> structed with a sumptuously-furnished ante-room, and
> throughout the whole of the auditorium increased care has
> been taken that visitors to box, pit, and gallery shall be
> comfortably seated.

The Gamester and *The Lady of Lyons* were among other plays
produced before he gave up his tenancy in January 1870.

The Royal Holborn Theatre had its most famous 'galaxy of
talent,' on 4 April 1870 for a Benefit in aid of the 'Sleigh Fund'.
A silver fringed satin bill, perfumed by Rimmel, announced:

> The Committee conducting the Benefit, make this appeal
> on behalf of Adderley, Annie and Louisa Sleigh, aged respec-
> tively four, six and eight years, who have been left in a totally
> destitute condition without any means of support whatever,

either directly or indirectly; they have been deserted by their Father, formerly Treasurer of the Princess's and Holborn Theatres, for upwards of two-years-and-a-half no tidings or assistance having been received from him during that period. Their mother, Louisa Sleigh, died in the Consumption Hospital, Brompton, on the 25th May last; many sorrows and privations consequent on her husband's desertion had reduced her to the condition of a permanent invalid, for more than a year prior to her death. Endeavours are being actively made towards placing one, perhaps two, of these unfortunate Children in the Royal Asylum of St. Anne's Society, in the furtherance of which object, the proceeds of this Benefit, it is hoped, will materially assist; and any Donations for the purpose will be most thankfully received by F. Ledger, Esq., Treasurer of the Fund, 'Era' Office, Catherine Street, Strand.

The company included: J. B. Buckstone, Henry Compton, in *Box and Cox*; Irving and Toole together in *The Spitalfield Weaver;* besides E. A. Sothern, Charles Warner, Marie Litton, Amy Sedgwick and Amy Roselle in other pieces, with Blanche Cole and Rebecca Isaacs to sing. A moment of glory for the theatre.

For the rest of the year managements came and went. A back-stage drama, *Behind the Curtain*, had a short run, but the theatre was often closed. Sefton Parry himself tried management again, but in March 1871 it was announced that the original lease was up for sale. The sale took place on 4 May:

This well-known and elegantly-appointed Establishment, situated in the very best part of the now principal thoroughfare of the Metropolis, and enjoying the extraordinary advantage of Omnibuses passing to and from every part of London, will be sold by Auction, by order of the Proprietor, by Mr. Marsh, 54, Cannon Street, E.C., at the Guildhall Coffee-House, Gresham Street, City, on Thursday, the Fourth Day of May, 1871, at Twelve, for One-o'clock precisely, in one lot, unless previously disposed of by Private Contract. The Theatre was erected in 1866, from the designs, and under the superintendence of the Architects, Messrs. Finch, Hill and Paraire, and no expense was spared to render it as perfect as possible. It is estimated to hold an Audience of 2,150 people. The Elegant and Extensive Scenery (painted by Telbin, James, Craven, &c.), Machinery, Mirrors, Gas Fixtures, valuable Furniture, Carpets, Properties, &c., will be included in the Sale. The whole of the property is held for a long term at a nominal ground rent, and is Let for Twelve Months from the 1st day of May at a Rental of £2,200. May be viewed by orders only, and full particulars obtained of R. Pearpoint, Esq., 50 Leicester Square; Messrs. Hughes, Hooker and Buttanshaw, St. Antholm's Chambers, Budge Row, Cannon Street; and of the Auctioneer.

The result of the sale is not reported, so the announced 'Let' for a drama *Silence* seems appropriate! This opened on 6 May and quickly closed.

Nothing more is heard till the theatre re-opened under the management of Richard Mansell for drama and opera bouffe in October. He was taken to task by *The Era* 1 October:

This establishment once more opened its doors to the public on Monday evening last, Mr. Richard Mansell being determined to try his hand where so many of his predecessors have failed. His first bid for public favour in his new home can hardly be said to have been judicious. Is it the mission of the Holborn Theatre to hold up the actor's art to scorn and to villify its professors; to exhibit the dramatic world under its worst aspect; to initiate the curious into the supposed mysteries of the Green-room, and to afford further opportunity to the enemies of the Stage to pour out the vials of their wrath on an honourable profession? It was on these boards not long ago that we were introduced to a dramatic agent, who occupied his spare moments in swindling and seduction; to a clown getting helplessly drunk in the middle of a performance; to an actress making assignations with the swells of the boxes; and to actors, who were the boon companions of swindlers and blacklegs; while the dressing-rooms of our Theatres were represented as no better than so many tap-rooms, where the principal occupation was smoking short pipes and drinking pots of 'cooper.' All this was bad enough, but it was impersonal. Now, however, on these same boards, on which so degrading a view of the Profession was presented to the public,

we have the illustrious actor of whom we are all so proud—
the actor whose fame was world-wide—and whose name will
never die while dramatic art lives; we have our great Edmund
Kean held up to our astonished gaze as a sot, a liar, a vulgar
brawler, and an intriguer with fair women, and, although the
reverse side of the picture shows us his many nobler impulses,
we like it none the better. The 'romance of the stage,' entitled
Edmund Kean, is a stupid translation of Alexandre Dumas'
stupid play, and although by the excellence of the acting of
several of the cast the interest of the story was maintained
almost to the end of four acts, and the applause at times was
vigorous, we must take leave to doubt whether such a travestie,
of not only the English Stage but of the manners of English
Society, will attain any lasting popularity.

Thomas Swinbourne played Kean for the two weeks that the
play was on. The theatre was closed the rest of the year, and
remained so until the following March when Joseph Fell put on
the Offenbach *La Vie Parisienne*, which ran till Hervé's *Doctor
Faust*, in which the composer appeared. This opened on 20 May
and ran till mid July. Fell was still in control when the theatre
re-opened in October with a drama *Miss Chester*, which ran till
the end of the year, but its successor terminated the management
early in January 1873.

In March W. H. C. Nation took the theatre for a season. This
wealthy eccentric whose fad was to take a theatre, pay a company
good salaries, produce old-fashioned adaptations by himself, with
music of his own composition interspersed at random, attended
every performance and sat in a stage box with both hands firmly
grasping a large umbrella. Very few people ever paid to come in,
so the hobby must have been expensive, but as his will was proved
at over £300,000, hardly ruinous.

Between 1866 and his death at the age of seventy-one, in 1914, he
managed seasons at Sadler's Wells, Astley's, the Holborn, Toole's,
the Scala, Terry's and the Royalty.

In May the theatre was to let, and remained so while its equally
unlucky neighbour, the Royal Amphitheatre, changed its name
to the National Theatre.

The Royal became the home of French plays for a fourteen week
season between October and April 1874, under the management of

M. M. Valnay and Pitron. For this season the stalls were re-arranged and new boxes built in the circle.

The next managers, Walter Joyce and W. R. Field, engaged the American comedian John S. Clarke for a month's season, and after five months' closure, except for a one night Benefit, another manager tried his luck. Morris James Guiver put on *Newmarket*: *a Legend of the Turf*. This ran until a pantomime, and was announced for revival in February, but after January the theatre remained closed.

On 24 April 1875 a change of name was tried on the theatre and it re-opened as the Mirror Theatre Royal, under the management of Horace Wigan. Needless to say the theatre had been 'embellished and re-decorated where needed'. The revival of *The Hidden Hand* was well received. *The Detective* by Clement Scott and E. Manuel, *The Dogs of St. Bernard* and other pieces kept the theatre occupied. In October was produced *All for Her* by Palgrave Simpson and Herman C. Merivale which, with *The Flying Scud*, was one of the biggest successes this theatre had yet had. This play, with a central character admittedly derived from Sidney Carton in Dickens' *A Tale of Two Cities*, was to give John Clayton one of his greatest successes. It ran for 152 performances. After it ended on 5 January, the name of the theatre was changed yet again by its new manager F. C. Burnand to the Duke's Theatre.

There had not been a theatre of this name in London since the days of the Restoration. The first Duke's Theatre was the con-version of Lisle's Tennis Court, Portugal Street, Lincolns Inn Fields by Sir William Davenant in 1660. He took the name with him to his new Playhouse, designed by Sir Christopher Wren, opened in 1671 in Dorset Garden, between the River and Fleet Street. This later fell into disrepair and was not used after 1706.

Burnand opened with his company transferred direct from the Opera Comique on 8 January with *Black Eyed Susan* (its 578th performance), which he had written, and two other plays: *Meg's Diversion* and *A Tempting Bait*, to make up the evening. He remained till April when the theatre was taken by Charles Morton for an Easter season of Sam Hague's Minstrels.

After this, amateurs and Benefits, for odd nights, were the only attractions until Promenade Concerts were advertised for a Sum-mer season and Broekman's Circus from September to March 1876. London was inundated with 'Grand Cirque' at this period. Lord

George Sanger was at his Amphitheatre in the Westminster Bridge Road (he had taken over the declining Astley's in 1871 which he ran till it was pulled down in 1893), and Frederick Hengler was at his Circus in Argyll Street, which opened in 1871 and was used as such till 1895. The neighbouring Holborn Amphitheatre, after a return to circus during the winter of 1875-76, was at this time a skating rink.

The Duke's did not open its doors again till 31 March 1877, when it was taken by M. L. Mayer and a 'Grand Sensational Drama' *The Two Mothers*, a much censored play on the Tichbourne case was produced. This only lasted a few nights and the theatre was empty till November when Violet Dacre presented Byron's *Sardanapalus*, with its spectacular climax of the destruction of Ninevah. A critic remarked:

> There were several calls in the course of the evening, and after a special summons Mr. Thomas W. Charles (Sardanapalus) was seen through the asphyxiating fog caused by the final explosion. The gallery was unusually noisy, and at times inclined to be foolishly personal, but the merit of the scenery tamed the 'gods' down to the propriety expected from civilised beings, and all appearances of storm at the outset faded into the calm of a distinct success.

It lasted till the new year. Soon a new manager, Thomas W. Charles, opened with a revival of Sydney Grundy's comedy-drama *Mammon*, which was succeeded in April by the ever popular *East Lynne* for '12 nights only'. Other similar melodramatic revivals followed, and the next management in June was forced to print a warning in the programme:

> As this Theatre has been frequently utilised for dramatic representations of an accentuated type, it is deemed expedient to announce (without disparagement to any reputable form of theatrical entertainment) that the Drama now performed at the Duke's Theatre, is not of a melodramatic nor sensational character, *Little Cricket* is a simple picture of French peasant life, transferred from the pages of the late Madame Sand to mimic action on the stage. *Little Cricket* is founded upon *La Petite Fadette*, one of the most pure, delicate and pathetic pastoral romances, writen by the gifted lady whose numerous

masterpeices of exquisite fancy and tender sentiment are justly admired by the gentle-minded and refined throughout the civilised world. It would be idle to expect that a play, inspired from such a source, and in design and construction deviating but slightly from the chaste original, could please the taste of those who visit the Theatre to revel in sound and fury, and who enjoy the smell of stage gunpowder. These—if any come to see *Little Cricket*—may find scant entertainment in the story of a poor friendless girl and her village love; her humiliation, sacrifices, and final happiness. Still it remains to be seen if a tale so modest and unpretentious in its homely simplicity cannot evoke one sympathetic echo in the hearts even of those who are less impressionable than the mass of humanity, vulnerable to the touch of Nature which 'makes the whole world kin.'

It ran till July.

As if to counter the last management's announcement, when Clarence Holt and Charles Wilmot opened their management in September 1878 with *The Barricade*, founded on Victor Hugo's *Les Misérables*, they told the public:

> The new management have fully determined to make this the People's Theatre, by giving the best Entertainment in London at Popular Prices. No Stalls, Reserved Pit, or Amphitheatre. The entire area of this commodious and comfortable Theatre, converted into one spacious Pit, seating 1,400 persons, at 1s.: the whole of Gallery, 6d.; Dress Circle reduced to 3s. (Bonnets allowed); Boxes, 2s. None but the best Dramatic Works produced. Private Boxes and Dress Circle Seats can be secured in advance at the Box Office, open daily from 11 to 5, and at all the Libraries. No charge for Booking.'

Their faith was 'pinned to low prices and stirring pieces.' They followed with Boucicault's *The Octoroon* and *The Colleen Bawn*, Jerrold's *Black Eyed Susan*, and *The New Babylon*, a drama of modern life by Paul Meritt, which was produced in February 1879 and proved a great success. It ran to the end of January 1880, in all 330 performances, and it was followed by W. G. Wills' 'New and powerful' drama *Forced from Home*.

The policy of strong meat was at last, it seemed, keeping the

G*

theatre open. Other revivals and new dramas followed, with Wilmot in sole charge. Then May Blumer announced the production of *The Obstinate Bretons*, a comic opera, on Whit Monday, but the following week there were legal difficulties. The piece running at the Duke's, *Conrad and Lizette*, was still drawing and its manager, who had leased the theatre from Charles Wilmot, would not vacate. Miss Blumer took her production down the road to the Royal Clarence Theatre (as the Amphitheatre was now called). Whatever transpired behind managerial doors, Wilmot advertised a return of *The New Babylon*, which had been on tour, for Whit Monday, and preceded it by a farce, appropriately called *Turn Him Out!* The 410th night and last week of *The New Babylon* was advertised in *The Era* 4 July 1880, and a new production to open on Bank Holiday, 2 August:

> Mr. and Mrs. Hubert O'Grady, the Celebrated Native Irish Comedians, and their Real Irish National Company, in Hubert's O'Grady's Great Original and Immensely Successful Modern Irish Drama, *The Eviction*.

Fate willed otherwise. On the same Sunday as this *Era* was published the theatre was destroyed by fire. This was described in *The Era* 11 July, 1880:

> At a few minutes to five o'clock a tenant of one of the houses situated in Brownlow Street, a thoroughfare in which the pit entrance was situated, was looking out of his back-room window when he saw smoke issuing from the windows of some of the dressing-rooms of the Theatre. On perceiving this he immediately gave the alarm, and within a very few minutes several steam engines arrived upon the scene. It was some time, however, before the firemen could gain an entrance to the Theatre, owing to the fact that they had to break open the doors of the box entrance in Holborn. By the time this was effected no fewer than twelve steamers were in full working order, and as there was a plentiful supply of water the whole almost simultaneously began to play upon the flames, which by this time were raging in every part of the Theatre. The fire, owing to the extremely inflammable nature of the materials with which the building was erected, took such a firm hold that it was evident from the first that the utmost efforts of the

fire brigade would be unavailing except to save the surrounding premises in this densely-populated neighbourhood.

After the fire had been raging for about twenty minutes the
roof fell in with a tremendous crash, carrying in its descent
portions of the gallery and upper boxes. This had the effect of
setting the pit on fire, notwithstanding that it was almost
submerged in water. The fire, although extremely fierce, was
not of long duration, as may be gathered from the fact
that from the first outbreak till it was virtually over it did not
occupy more than three hours. Mr. Clarence Holt, who was
on the scene, stated that he thought the fire commenced on
the stage near the green-room. This supposition would
appear to be borne out by the fact that it was from that part of
the building the smoke and flames were first seen to issue.
From thence it quickly caught the property-room and stage,
which were in an incredibly short space of time destroyed,
together with a large amount of machinery under the stage.
As may be supposed, there were immense crowds of persons
to witness the progress of the fire, but these were kept well
back by a large body of police of the E Division, under
Inspectors Clifford and Pinnock. Captain Shaw was at an early
hour on the scene, and with his usual skill and energy directed
the operations of the firemen, through whose exertions no
property in the immediate neighbourhood of the Theatre was
materially injured.

Up till eleven o'clock at night the firemen were still engaged
in playing upon the ruins. The damage is estimated to amount
to over £25,000.

No cause can be assigned for the fire. After the curtain fell
on the previous night the Theatre was left in the custody of a
watchman, and all then appeared safe. The place, however,
strange to say, was left unprotected during the day, thus
rendering the appliances about the building useless in case of a
disaster. The building is the property of Mr. James Gordon,
who, we understand, is fully insured, but Mr. Wilmot, the
Lessee, was uninsured, and is a sufferer to the extent, we
believe, of about £2,000.

The site was cleared and eventually covered by the First Avenue
Hotel, opened in 1882, which took in the buildings up to

Warwick Court. This was damaged by the blitz in September 1940 and eventually pulled down. First Avenue House, a block of Government Offices completed in 1952, now covers the site from Brownlow Street to Warwick Court.

10

The Imperial Theatre

The Royal Aquarium Theatre

Tothill Street, Westminster
At the corner of Tothill Street and Dartmouth Street with stage door

The theatre was part of the Royal Aquarium Summer and Winter Garden opened 22 January 1876.

The Royal Aquarium Theatre opened 15 April 1876 with a transfer from the Globe Theatre of *Jo*, an adaptation of Charles Dickens' *Bleak House* by J. F. Burnett, preceded by an address by Edgar Bruce and Jennie Lee.

Under the management of Edgar Bruce.

Name changed to the Imperial Theatre 21 April 1879 during the run of *She Stoops to Conquer* on the first night that a burlesque *The Lady of Lyons* by W. Young was added to the bill.

Under the management of Marie Litton.

Closed as a theatre 1889.

Re-opened after extensive structural alterations and re-decoration 11 April 1898 with a touring company of *Morocco Bound*, a musical comedy by Arthur Brascombe and F. Osmond Carr.

Under the management of Oswald Brand.

Closed February 1899.

Interior completely re-built and re-opened 22 April with *A Royal Necklace* by Pierre and Claude Breton, produced by Arthur Coe.

Under the management of Lillie Langtry.

The whole site acquired by the Wesleyan Methodists, 1902.

The Aquarium closed 2 January 1903 and subsequently demolished leaving the theatre which remained open until 16 June 1906, after which it too was demolished and the interior removed and re-built as the Royal Albert Music Hall, Canning Town.

The Central Hall, Westminster, opened 1912, now stands on the site.

In the mid eighteen-seventies, at the Westminster end of Tothill Street, on the north side, from Prince's Street (now Storey's Gate) to the corner of Dartmouth Street, (now Matthew Parker Street) backing on the houses in Queen Street, there was a large area of nearly three acres which had been cleared of old property. On this site was built the Royal Aquarium Summer and Winter Garden, which opened on 22 January 1876.

On a small part of the plot, in Tothill Street, had stood the Westminster Subscription Theatre, a long forgotten playhouse which had a very short life, even for one of the small theatres of its time, built in 1832 by an undertaker named Gale, and closed in 1835. It never had a licence so operated as a subscription theatre. Early managers were T. D. Davenport—said to be the original of Dickens' Vincent Crummles—Dibdin Pitt and John Douglas. But little was added to theatrical history.

The scheme for a large place of amusement and instruction is described in *The Era* 16 January 1876:

As will be seen from our advertising columns, the opening of the Royal Aquarium is arranged for Saturday, the 22nd inst. The Duke of Edinburgh, in the unavoidable absence of the Duchess, will open the Aquarium with an interesting ceremonial. The great advance made in the building since our last notice enables the spectator to judge of the qualifications of the Aquarium as a popular resort for the West End. Few who remembered Tothill Street in the 'bad old days' would have speculated upon such a transformation as this. Westminster bids fair to become what it was in the olden times, the residence of the aristocracy, abounding as the locality does with palaces and public buildings, to say nothing of the grand old Abbey and the Houses of Parliament. The original idea of utilising the vacant space on the north side of Tothill Street by erecting a vast building for public instruction and entertainment was due to the fertile brain of Mr. Wybrow Robertson, and an association being formed to carry out the project, Mr. Bruce Phillips being the Secretary, the public took kindly to the idea, and with Mr. A. Bedborough as architect, and Messrs. Lucas as contractors, no time was lost in erecting the Aquarium, the whole period occupied being only eleven months. The architect had no easy task in making such a design as should at once be ornamental in appearance, and yet be available for all the purposes required. The front is divided into compartments by columns, thus avoiding monotony, and the bays are ornamented with groups of sculpture, adding greatly to the artistic effect. The principal entrances are on the Tothill Street side, and the first grand effect upon the mind of the visitor will be made by the great hall, which is 340 feet in length by 160 feet wide. This fine promenade is covered with a roof of glass and iron, and the grace and freshness of a winter garden will be a great attraction, the hall being surrounded by palms and exotic trees and shrubs, the whole having the general aspect of a vast conservatory filled with splendid sculpture. Between these artificial groves fountains will play, and on the opposite side of the entrance is the grand orchestra, capable of accommodating 400 performers, with a large organ. Around the hall are the tanks for the reception of the marine and fresh water creatures. To supply the thirteen tanks lie hid under the floor of the promenade nine great reservoirs—seven for salt and two for fresh water. These are built of brickwork on a four-feet bed of concrete, and will hold 700,000 gallons of water. They are lined with asphalt, and the supply pipes and valves are made entirely of vulcanite, to preserve the salt water from the chemical action which would arise from its contact with iron. The continuous circulation system has been adopted. Towards the north-west corner of the building is a large reading room, wherein tired sight-seers will find English and foreign newspapers, magazines, and other current literature. It is also proposed to collect a complete library of books of reference, to provide convenience for letter writing and materials for the delectation of chess players. There is a telegraph office for the despatch and reception of messages— and furnished, moreover, with a division bell in direct communication with that in the House of Commons, as it is deemed possible that the Royal Aquarium will be largely patronised by both Houses of Parliament. The Aquarium will be an agreeable refuge from Dr. Kenealy for the Home Rulers. The craze of the present day—the skating rink is not overlooked, and the lovers of that form of recreation will be able to enjoy themselves at the Aquarium. The Fine Art Exhibition will, it is expected, be one of the features of the Aquarium. A good selection of pictures ought to be made considering that Mr. Millais is at the head of this department. As may be expected, a great number of daubs have been rejected, and Mr. Knight, the Secretary, is somewhat in doubt whether room can be found for all that has been accepted. Music will of course be an important attraction with Mr. Arthur Sullivan as conductor; and a charming little Theatre is also included in the building.

The new Aquarium which cost some £200,000, was duly opened by the Duke of Edinburgh. *The Era* 23 January reported:

Nature herself favoured the opening of the Royal Aquarium and Summer and Winter Garden yesterday, for rarely in the midst of an English winter do we have such a bright, clear, mild, and cheerful day as that which enlivened the ceremonial that introduced to the public another palace of pleasure, everybody took kindly to the Aquarium immediately, and prognosticated for it a prosperous career. There was a foretaste of what will eventually be done in the musical way, and exceedingly gratified all must have been to hear the really splendid band conducted by Mr. Arthur Sullivan. It was a body of *artistes* which our admirable English composer evidently felt proud to conduct, and let us here pay him a compliment justly due. Music and the Drama are twin sisters, and we are glad to remark that a Theatre constructed with every attention to the comfort and enjoyment of an audience of over 2,000 persons, will be under the control of Mr. John Hollingshead, whose good taste and experience will be a guarantee for the high quality of the dramatic entertainments. Mr. Charles Morton will undertake the arrangements of opera bouffe performances. The reading-room will, we predict, be extremely popular. It is just the refined quiet, cosy sort of place where one can spend a leisure hour with genuine enjoyment; and when, at the end of a course of mental food the visitor is ready for 'three courses and dessert' there are

Messrs. Bertram and Roberts always ready and more than willing to supply the wants of Nature. More recreation still is in store for those who visit the Aquarium, for there will be found a delightful room where the smoker can enjoy the 'soothing weed' and, after a refreshing whiff a turn into the handsome billiard-room will possibly be agreeable to many. That some portions of the building are still unfinished is only what might have been expected when we remember the short period that has elapsed since the site of the Aquarium was a promenade for the cabs of Westminster, a receptacle for broken bottles and oyster shells, surrounded by hoardings covered with flaming posters. When the hour arrived for the ceremonial there was quite enough to show what important and brilliant results will be ultimately attained. The doors were opened at half-past eleven and great numbers entered the building at once. The band of the Scots Fusilier Guards conducted by Mr. J. P. Clarke, played a selection of pieces, and at a quarter past twelve the band of the Coldstreams conducted by Mr. Fred. Godfrey, followed with an interesting programme. At a quarter-past one the Lord and Lady Mayoress arrived and at half-past His Royal Highness the Duke of Edinburgh and suite, being received by the Executive Committee, and conducted to a splendidly decorated pavilion fronting the orchestra, and embellished with choice exotics supplied by Mr. John Wills of Onslow Cresent, South Kensington, who has had the entire charge of the floral ornamentation, no less than thirty thousand varieties of plants, shrubs, and flowers being collected, from palms and tall climbing plants, which will soon cluster luxuriantly round the columns and tracery of the building, to the delicate flowers and exotics with which the beds are filled; the effect of the whole being enhanced by choice groups of sculpture rising from the midst of these beautiful beds and banks of flowers; while hanging from various portions of the building are seen baskets of trailing plants, adding their grace and beauty to the scene. The Duke of Edinburgh, having pro-ceeded to the Royal box, accompanied by the Royal Naval Artillery Volunteers as a guard of honour, the united bands struck up the Russian National Anthem, and then 'God Save the Queen.' General Cotton, the Deputy Chairman of the

Executive Committee, then read an address, to which his
Royal Highness responded in suitable terms, and concluded
by declaring the building open. The bands then played the
National Anthem, and the Lord Mayor visited the Royal box
and conversed for some time with the Duke. Then came the
chief musical event of the day, commencing with Professor
Macfarren's Festival Overture arranged for the occasion by
the composer. Madame Patey then sang Dr. Arne's song
'General Youth,' and afterwards Wallace's song 'Sweet and
low,' both exquisitely. Madame Edith Wynne, who was never
heard to greater advantage, gave Bishop's 'Bid me discourse'
and Clay's charming song 'She wandered down the mountain-
side.' The appearance of Mr. Sims Reeves was the signal
for a lusty shout. The popular tenor was in excellent voice,
and sang 'When other lips' and 'Good-bye, Sweetheart,' with
delightful expression and ample power. The minuet and trio
from Sterndale Bennett's Symphony in G minor and Mr.
Sullivan's Procession March were included in the programme. After this the guests paid a visit to the picture
galleries, in which will be found a collection of modern works
second only to the exhibition of the Royal Academy. In this
department the services of Mr. W. F. Knight have been
invaluable. The fine art galleries will, we are certain, prove
an immense attraction, especially if, as we learn, there are still
more important works to be hung. During the afternoon there
were further performances by the band of the Coldstreams
and Fusiliers, and in the evening by the Aquarium orchestra,
conducted by Mr. George Mount, the talented conductor of
the British Orchestral Society. Only Fellows and season ticket
holders were admitted to the opening ceremonial, but at five
o'clock the public were admitted upon payment of five
shillings. The admission during the forthcoming week will be
half-a-crown.

The Theatre, situated at the far end of the building, at the
corner of Dartmouth Street, was not completed until April and
was opened as the Royal Aquarium Theatre on 15 April. *The Era*
the following day tells us:

This new Theatre is situated at the west end of the Royal
Aquarium building and facing Tothill Street. The dimensions

are as follows:—Length, 75 ft.; width 62 ft.; in the clear off the walls; and height from floor of stalls to the ceiling, 48 ft. It consists of stalls, dress circle with balcony, amphitheatre, and pit, with the addition of a Royal box and five other private boxes—one on the ground floor opposite to and corresponding with the Royal box and four on the dress circle floor. The floor of pit and stalls is on the incline, having the orchestra sunk two feet below the floor of the stalls, so that the band, although performing in the body of the building, are almost entirely screened from view. The stage, which is 62 ft. in width by 40 ft. in depth, has been fitted with all the best and improved methods, and carried out in a satisfactory manner by Messrs. T. Grieve and Son.

The walls of the auditorium are divided by panelled and enriched pilasters in three heights, over the top caps of which a cornice runs, and is continued entirely round the building and carried over all the window heads and recesses. From this cornice springs a very bold cove, panelled and filled in with a trellis pattern, with star patterns at the intersections, above which runs an enriched string of olive leaf and berries around the entire upper portion of the ceiling, intersecting and breaking it up into panels of various geometric shapes, into which are introduced six painted subjects representing the Muses, and panels having in them busts of composers. The auditorium is lighted by two gas sun-burners, the ceiling being pierced in such a manner as to carry off the vitiated air.

The colours prevailing throughout the ceiling are a light canary tone for the stiles of the panels, with azure blue for the panels themselves, and the mouldings and enriched portions of the work brought out with gold, white and crimson.

The proscenium is altogether a novel and pleasing feature, being a treatment of light engaged columns supported on brackets at each side of the opening, surmounted by ornamental foliated caps and brackets, between which is a delicately-diapered cove similar in treatment to that of the ceiling, and above a cornice and cresting out of which springs a shield containing the Royal arms and motto. The balcony fronts of galleries are enriched with sculptured figures of Cupids bearing foliated swags and shields of various designs standing upon a ground in the lower gallery of pale sea green, and the upper a French grey, the enrichments picked out in gold. The Royal box and private box opposite have handsome fronts with Caryatides supporting the balcony above, and are raised considerably above the audience on the ground floor, direct access to the Royal box being gained from Dartmouth Street by a private entrance *en suite* with a private retiring-room. The entrances for the public are situated in Tothill Street, and are supplemented with extra exits, which can on an emergency be thrown open.

The works have been carried out under the able supervision of the architect, Mr. A. Bedborough.

The house was last night opened to the public, and attracted a large and enthusiastic audience. Mr. Edgar Bruce, with his company from the Globe, has been the first to take possession, and very wisely has he determined to rely upon *Jo* as the principal feature of the liberal entertainment he is prepared to offer. Miss Jennie Lee once more touched all hearts by her marvellously realistic portraiture of the poor outcast, who is so repeatedly 'moved on.' Miss Dolores Drummond again stirred her audience to enthusiasm by her wonderfully clever interpretation of the *role* of Hortense; while Miss Hibbert as Lady Deadlock, Mr. Burnett as Buckett, Mr. Wilmot as Chadband, Mr. Steyne as 'the young man by the name of Guppy,' with Messrs. E. Price, Cartwright, Edwards, Howell, and Misses Nelly Harris, Katie Lee, Harrison, and Robertson gave efficient support, and added to the complete-ness of a performance which should be seen by all. The inaugural programme also very properly embraced the National Anthem, sung by the entire company, Miss Jose Sherrington, Mr. George Perren, and Mr. Winn undertaking the solos, the Aquarium band upon the stage furnishing the accompaniment. Prior to the drama Mr. Edgar Bruce and Miss Jennie Lee delivered an address written specially for the occasion by Mr. Clement Scott, and received with great applause.

Once the whole building was open, the various entertainments provided in different departments got under way. As Erroll Sherson remarks:

The Royal Aquarium, in short, was intended to be a sort of Crystal Palace in London within easy reach of Charing Cross, a covered-in promenade for the wet weather, with the glass cases of live fish thrown in. In truth, the attractions of the place soon began to be very 'fishy' indeed. Ladies promenaded there up and down o'nights without the escort of any gentleman friend (till, maybe, they found one) and the appeal of the management to sensation-lovers was very wide indeed. Barebacked ladies dived from the roof or were shot out of a cannon, or sat in a cage covered with hair and calling themselves 'Missing Links.' Zulus, Gorillas, Fasting Humans, Boxing Humans and Boxing Kangaroos, succeeded one another in rapid changes, and failed in time to attract.

The high tone of the place set at the opening soon deteriorated and various showmen-managers like Farini and Josiah Ritchie kept the place before a popular public. Besides the side-show entertainments and band concerts, music hall artists appeared amid circus performers and acrobats. At first the theatre gave special matinées of companies from other West End houses, and a resident company performed in the evening with popular successes. At Christmas a pantomime was staged.

In 1878 Phelps made his last appearance on the stage during a season of famous plays, almost dying in the wings after speaking Wolsey's farewell.

The theatre came under the management of Marie Litton, wife of Wybrow Robertson, and her classic revivals with good casts for matinées were quite successful. A spectacular production of *Uncle Tom's Cabin* was given, and then Miss Litton took complete control and the theatre staged old comedies and burlesque both afternoon and evening. During the run of *She Stoops to Conquer* the name was changed on 21 April 1879 to the Imperial Theatre. Among her other successes were *The Beaux' Stratagem* and *As You Like It*.

After Miss Litton left in 1880 W. Edgcombe Rendel presented comic opera, burlesque and drama with varying fortune.

In 1882 Lillie Langtry tried her hand at management and appeared in Tom Taylor's *An Unequal Match* and *As You Like It*. She was followed by a Captain Disney Robuck who ran the theatre with revivals, but the house had not been able to establish itself and become consistently successful. From this time it was more often closed than open and was used as an annexe to the Aquarium for side-show entertainments.

In 1898 it had a complete overhaul, and opened as a 'Touring Date'. *The Era* 16 April reports:

> Under the management of Mr. Oswald Brand, the Imperial Theatre, Westminster, was re-opened on Easter Monday. The house has undergone extensive structural alterations, from the plans of Mr. Walter Emden, to meet the requirements of the London County Council, and the safety of the public is ensured by the provision of fireproof staircases and a fireproof curtain. The interior has also been re-decorated and brightened generally. Mr. Oswald Brand opened with that merry musical comedy *Morocco Bound*, a very attractive bill-of-fare for the Easter holiday-makers. Mr. Arthur Branscombe's No. 1 company includes a number of clever artists.

The new system was not a success either and after the pantomine at the following Christmas the theatre again closed.

In 1900 the lease at £3,000 a year was bought by Mrs. Langtry who completely re-built the interior on a grand scale. She was financed by Edgar Cohen, with whom she was living at the time. He is said to have spent some £40,000 on the building. The new Imperial opened on 22 April 1901.

The Era records the occasion:

> Mrs. Langtry's new theatre—for the Imperial has been practically rebuilt—besides being exquisitely beautiful, bears the stamp of the fair manageress's individuality. It is sumptuously real, from the marble which lines the walls even of the spacious pit to the elaborately embroidered draperies of which the curtains and hangings are composed. Much has already been written about the auditorium; but even the detailed descriptions which had been vouchsafed before the opening of the Imperial on Monday, gave but a poor idea of the magnificence of the auditorium, striking features of which are the two 'Royal boxes,' one on each side of the proscenium, each surmounted with a dome, from which are suspended curtains of buttercup yellow silk with white

powderings of *Fleur de lys*. The draperies which hang over the fronts of these boxes are of green silk, richly embroidered with gold. The other adornments of the house quite fulfil the expectations created by the accounts given before the opening. The embroideries are artistic in design and are marvellous examples of modern needlework, and the comfort of the audience has been carefully studied by the architect, Mr. Frank Verity, who has not sacrificed convenience to artistic effect, but has clearly contrived to attain both of those very desirable objects.

The opening production was in excellent harmony with the tone before the curtain. In the case of a play like *A Royal Necklace* 'atmosphere' is everything. We require to feel the languorous charm of the Trianon, to behold the grace and beauty of the dying regime and to inhale its fragrance, in order to understand the apathy which made the French Revolution what it was. Only a Turgot or a Benjamin Franklin could resist the emollient witchery of the lovely landscape which Mr. W. Telbin, at the bidding of Mrs. Langtry, has conjured up for us in his set for the second act of *A Royal Necklace*; and when we are taken to the Palace of Versailles, and are shown the *coucher du Dauphin*, the full significance of etiquette in the antc-Revolutionary period is impressed upon us. The ladies-in-waiting tower and bridle in all the glory of gowns and head-dresses as real as M. Blanchini's and M. Worth's designs and Mr. Clarkson's delicate art can make them. The furniture and the details of the surroundings assist the illusion immensely; and we realise what court life in France in the eighteenth century meant.

Mrs. Langtry has rarely acted with so much energy and intensity as in the third division of MM. Berton's piece. There was genuine force and fire in her depiction of Marie Antoinette's proud and intense indignation, and she looked, as she did throughout her performance of the part, 'every inch' a Queen. Clever, too, was her indication of the vivacious flightiness of Mdlle. Oliva, who appears on several occasions in the course of the evening with startling suddenness after the disappearance of the Queen, the necessary 'quick change' being marvellously managed. There was loud and persistent applause after the conclusion of the performance on Monday,

and Mrs. Langtry, in a brief but neat speech, thanked her
audience for the reception given the piece, apologising for the
somewhat long waits between the acts, and expressing her
determination to merit public favour in the future. What
with the interest connected with the beautiful theatre, the
magnificent mounting, and Mrs. Langtry's great popularity,
A Royal Necklace will be a decided success.

Her opening play was a complete failure and was withdrawn.
She followed this with *Mademoiselle Mars* with Lewis Waller as
Napoleon, a revival of *The Degenerates* by Sydney Grundy. She
then prepared for a tour of America with *Cross-ways* by herself
and Hartley Manners. This was given before an invited audience
for one performance only at the Imperial on 8 December 1902, by
special command of King Edward, who was present with Queen
Alexandra and the Prince and Princess of Wales (later King
George and Queen Mary). A unique royal visit to the theatre,
and an honour no doubt well earned and deserved by Mrs.
Langtry!

After this triumph she did not reappear at the theatre, though
she remained lessee until 1903. During her management Réjane
appeared for a season and *Everyman* was performed by William
Poel's Elizabethan Stage Society.

In 1902 the whole Aquarium building, including the theatre,
was acquired by the Wesleyan Methodists as a site for a new
Central Hall. The Aquarium finally closed its doors on 2 January
1903 and was demolished. The lease on the theatre had another
three years to run, and it was left standing. During its last years
Ellen Terry went into management in April 1903 and presented
her son, Gordon Craig's, production of Ibsen's *The Vikings*. This
was ahead of its time and was severely criticised and quickly
withdrawn. She followed this with another Craig production,
Much Ado About Nothing.

The remainder of the lease was then taken up by Lewis Waller
who started his tenure with a revival of his evergreen success
Monsieur Beaucaire, in November 1903. During the next three
years he produced *A Queen's Romance*, *Miss Elizabeth's Prisoner*,
A Marriage of Convenience, *His Majesty's Servant*, *Henry V*,
Romeo and Juliet, *Hawthorne U.S.A.*, *The Perfect Lover*, *The
Harlequin King* and *Brigadier Gerard*. Evelyn Millard was his

eading lady in most of these productions. Waller transferred his company to the Lyric Theatre in May 1906.

The end of the Imperial came with *Boy O'Carroll* which Martin Harvey presented from 19 May to 16 June 1906. The theatre then finally closed and was dismantled. The interior was taken down and re-built as the Imperial Palace, Canning Town (a re-building of the old Royal Albert Music Hall). It opened in 1909 and later became a cinema, the Imperial, which was destroyed by fire in 1931. The present building, also the Imperial Cinema, opened in 1934, is now used for Bingo.

The last of the Aquarium building vanished and on an island site arose the Central Hall. Dartmouth Street was continued round the back of the site (now re-named Matthew Parker Street) to join Prince's Street (now called Storey's Gate). The new Central Hall opened in 1912.

11

The Kingsway Theatre

The Novelty Theatre, the Folies Dramatiques Theatre, the Jodrell Theatre, the New Queen's Theatre, the Eden Palace of Varieties, the Great Queen Street Theatre

Great Queen Street
Stage door in Parker Street, at rear of building

Opened as the Novelty Theatre, 9 December 1882 with *Melita; or the Parsee's Daughter*, a comic opera by Juba Kennerley, music by Henry Portet.
Under the management of G. Somers Bellamy.
Name changed to the Folies Dramatique Theatre 29 March 1883 and re-opened with *Ascot*, a farcical comedy by Percy Fendall and a revival of *Les Cloches de Corneville*, an operetta by Robert Planquette, in a new version by Messrs. A. & G. Moore and Claude Templer.
Under the management of Francis Fairlie.
Name reverted to the Novelty Theatre 5 January 1884 and re-opened with a revival of *The New Magdalen*, a drama by Wilkie Collins. Preceded by a comedetta *The Wilfull Ward*.
Under the management of Nelly Harris.
Name changed to the Jodrell Theatre 22 October 1888 and re-opened with *The Demon*, an opera by Anton Rubenstein (sung by the Russian National Opera Company).
Under the management of Mrs. Churchill Jodrell.
Name reverted to the Novelty Theatre 7 June 1889 and re-opened with *A Doll's House* by Henrik Ibsen.
Under the management of L. and H. Nathan.
Name changed to the New Queen's Theatre and re-opened 4 August 1890 with a revival of *The Corsican Brothers*, a drama by Dion Boucicault (from the French).

Under the management of J. A. Cave.

Name reverted to the Novelty Theatre 30 August 1890 with *Light O'Day*, a comedy drama by Brian McCullough.

Under the management of Brian McCullough.

Name changed to the Eden Palace of Varieties and opened as a twice nightly Music Hall 26 March 1894.

Under the management of Charles Morritt.

Name reverted to the Novelty Theatre at end of season in August 1894. Open intermittently until June 1898, then closed and remained unoccupied.

Interior completely re-constructed and re-opened 24 May 1900 as the Great Queen Street Theatre, with a revival of *A Little Ray of Sunshine*, a comedy by Mark Ambient and Wilton Heriot, preceded by *The Lost Legion*, a one act play by W. J. Locke.

Under the management of W. S. Penley.

Partly re-constructed, re-decorated and re-opened as the Kingsway Theatre 9 October 1907, with *Irene Wycherley*, a play by Anthony P. Wharton, preceded by *A Maker of Men*, a one act play by Alfred Sutro.

Under the management of Lena Ashwell.

Closed 11 May 1941. Suffered war damage and remained derelict until pulled down in 1956.

An office block now covers the site through which Newton Street has been extended to join Great Queen Street.

IN *The Era* 18 June 1881 a small paragraph gave the first hint of yet another London theatre:

A space of ground on the northern side of Great Queen Street, Lincoln's Inn Fields, has been cleared for the proposed erection of a new Theatre, intended chiefly, we believe, to accommodate dramatic amateurs. The architect is Mr. Thomas Verity, and the building is to be raised on the site of No. 8, Great Queen Street, and, enclosing some ground in the rear fronting upon Parker Street, will be estimated to seat about eight hundred persons. Forty years ago Wyatt's Amateur Theatre, at the back of a tobacconist's shop on the same side of the way, was a small edifice adapted to the same purpose, but it had only a short existence.

The site had been occupied at one time by a Boys' Refuge. Th
ideas behind this scheme were both speculative; firstly the sit
might be wanted for the Metropolitan Railway, but if not, advantag
could be taken of the plan mooted to make a new road betwee
Holborn and the Strand. This did not actually take effect till th
construction of Kingsway, in the Strand (Aldwych-Kingsway
development at the turn of the century (see numbers 4 and 6). Thi
left the new theatre, when it was built, in a kind of 'no man'
land' and was the main reason for its continual failure in its earl
years.

By August 1882 plans were well under way, and a name, th
Novelty Theatre, had been chosen. *The Era* 12 August tells:

> This new building, which, as our readers are aware, is
> situate in Great Queen Street, oppostite to the famous Free-
> mason's Tavern, is to be carried on by a limited liability
> company, with Mr. G. Somers Bellamy as managing director.
> The work of construction has been carried on by Messrs. Kirk
> and Randall, the builders of several theatres, including the
> Avenue, under the experienced direction of Mr. Thomas
> Verity the architect of the Comedy and the Criterion Theatres.
> It is boasted by the directors that the plans of the theatre
> show that the house will hold at least 1,200 seated, while yet
> giving to every visitor more room than is obtainable in any
> other London theatre. They also show that the Novelty will
> have one of the largest vestibules in London. Every care will
> be taken to insure the safety of the public in case of an alarm
> of fire. There will be two exits opening outwards from every
> part of the house, and it is proposed to have iron ladders
> outside from each tier leading to within a few feet of the
> ground. It is also proposed to light the theatre with the
> electric light, and to make extensive use of fire-resisting paint.
> As a further precaution, and to guard against the possibility
> of a panic, through an accident at any time throwing the
> theatre into darkness, the directors further propose to have
> small lighted gas jets, supplied by a separate meter, placed at
> each exit. It should also be stated that the interior of the
> building is fireproof. The basement below the vestibule, and
> of the same size, will be used as a property-room and work-
> shop. The foyer above the vestibule, and of the same size, will

be open to the public on presentation of their visiting cards at the same times as the booking office and theatre, usually without charge for admission. This foyer will be utilised as an art gallery for the sale of pictures on commission. In the foyer there will also be a studio for taking photographs by the electric light. It is proposed to make the Novelty a comedy house, it being felt by the directors that there is just now a decided public reaction in favour of this class of entertainment. The directors feel that the system of paying special regard to the comfort and convenience of the theatre-goer may with advantage and profit be carried to a further point than has yet been done. They therefore propose, besides disallowing all fees of every kind, and taking additional precautions to ensure the civility of the attendants, to provide, at an estimated outlay of £100, the use of opera glasses free of charge to the occupants of the private boxes, stalls, and dress circle. It is proposed to produce new plays by new authors on certain Saturday afternoons. All plays sent to the managing director will have consideration in due course, and this fact will certainly induce more than the ordinary number of new plays to be sent to him. The directors feel therefore that, on the principle of the law of average, they will stand more chance than their competitors of occasionally securing a piece that may prove a great monetary success. It should not be forgotten, say the directors, that from time to time various plays, after having been offered to, and often never even opened by numerous managers, have been at last produced with the most satisfactory pecuniary results. It should be stated that the site of the Novelty Theatre has been scheduled by the Central Metropolitan Railway Company in the bill before Parliament, which has been thrown out for the present session. The proposed railway is from King's Cross to Charing Cross. Should the bill pass in its present form during 1883 or afterwards, the site of the Novelty Theatre would ultimately be required by the railway company, who, of course, would have to compensate the shareholders of the Novelty Theatre Company.

The theatre was ready for opening on 9 December 1882. *The Era* 6 December gave full details:

The opening of a new London theatre last Saturday night was an event of considerable interest to playgoers; and although there were many rival attractions, the Novelty Theatre was well filled. The decorations, which, of course, were displayed to greater advantage when the theatre was fully lighted, have been carried out with great taste by Mr. E. W. Bradwell. The entrances and exists of the Novelty will bear comparison with those of much larger theatres. A handsome vestibule is the first approach to the theatre, and the visitor passes through rich curtains to the stalls and boxes. It is claimed for this theatre that special precautions have been taken against fire or panic, as there are double exits from each part of the building, and the floors are constructed of concrete. The entrance to the pit is in Great Queen Street, by the side of the stall entrance; the gallery entrance being in Parker Street, at the back of the theatre. The prevailing colours employed in decorating the auditorium are peacock blue and dark crimson plush. The proscenium resembles a picture frame, and, instead of a drop curtain of the old-fashioned type, there are curtains made of embossed silk of the colour of old gold, having a rich yet harmonious effect. The dress circle projects considerably over the pit, and causes the theatre to look smaller than it really is, the number of seats being a little over one thousand, while an altogether new feature in the arrangements is the numbering of the pit seats, so that they can be secured in advance and reserved for the evening, as in more expensive portions of the house. The theatre is the property of a company, Mr. Somers Bellamy being the manager, Mr. E. E. Marriott the secretary, and Mr. Harrington Baily acting-manager. The announcement that light comic opera would form the sole entertainment of the opening night was doubtless an attraction to many, as that kind of fare is much in vogue. The opera chosen for the opening was a three-act work entitled *Melita; or, the Parsee's Daughter*, the composer being Mr. Henry Portet, and the author of the libretto Mr. Juba Kennerley. Very few persons present last Saturday night knew anything of the author or composer, and still less were they acquainted with the subject of the opera. We have regretfully to declare that we can find little to praise in the new opera. The entire production appears to be the work of novices. The libretto of Mr. Juba

Kennerley is filled with weak and feeble dialogue, half of which might be cut out without any detriment to the dramatic interest, for the plot, such as it is, could very well have been developed in a single act instead of three. The music of Mr. Portet is, at times, tuneful; and, in one instance, a gavotte, set to the words 'Sweet surprise to meet you here,' had sufficient attractiveness to gain an encore; but, as a rule, the music was entirely of the ballad kind, and it was so far from being original that echoes of Balfe, Wallace, Bellini, and Donizetti met the ear constantly. Occasionally there were agreeable phrases, but nothing that could strictly be called operatic composition; while the arrangement of the orchestral parts was thin, feeble, and commonplace to the last degree. As a proof that the instrumental portion required little attention, the conductor merely had a pianoforte score. The entire work gave the impression that the composer had, at various times, written drawing-room ballads, and that the author had concocted a sort of framework for the introduction of these ditties. With regard to the performance we have more scope for commendation. We cordially praise the manner in which the opera was placed upon the stage. Showy and brilliant dresses and some picturesque scenery gave all the requisite splendour to the stage effects. There was a good chorus and the orchestra was large and efficient. Miss Clare Leslie, as the heroine, exerted herself to make that character effective, and although most of the vocal music allotted to her was common-place, her talent and zeal gained her applause. Miss Grace Balmaine, Miss Edith Burgoyne, and Miss Evelyn May represented the three other Parsee maidens agreeably. Mr. Henry Hallam, having a good tenor voice, made the most of the music given to Captain Melville, but the ultra-sentimental character of some of his songs defeated the good intentions of the vocalist. Mr. Frederick Thorne tried his utmost to make the character of Lieut. Buzzer amusing, but the author had made the part so ridiculous that Mr. Thorne's talent was sometimes thrown away. A British officer, who is represented as being in a contant state of inebriation, sometimes only 'fresh' and at other times 'completely screwed,' becomes a wearisome and even an offensive personage in the course of three acts. Whenever Mr. Thorne could get a chance of being droll he availed himself of it most fully. Mr. Rosenthal sang the music of the chief Parsee so as to win the favour of the audience, cordial applause being bestowed even when the music had but slight merit. Mr. Fred Clifton, although he had but a few lines to speak, proved himself an *artiste*. Mr. E. D. Lyons, as Patrick Malony, the sentry, was, perhaps, the most successful *artiste*, his one song being rendered with great drollery. Miss Warner sang the solo of the Nautch girl in a pleasing manner. At the close of the opera the author and composer were called for, but the verdict of the audience was far from being entirely favourable, the 'ayes' or 'noes,' as they say in Parliament, being about equal, and it is with considerable regret we are compelled to admit that there was reason for disapprobation. An opera in three acts requires to have some character, variety, and originality in the music, and some grace, fancy, humour, and freshness in the libretto, and something like a connected plot. Much allowance was, however, made by an indulgent audience. *Melita* has all the faults and but few of the merits we expect to find in a modern comic opera.

This was not a very auspicious start for a new theatre, and it wa: empty by Christmas!

It next appeared in the theatre list under a new name, the Folie Dramatique Theatre, under the mangement of Francis Fairlie. Hi opening bill, a revival of *Les Cloches de Corneville*, received ver bad notices and he tried again with a Strauss operetta, *Princ Methusalem*, which also flopped. As one critic expressed it 'Unless great improvements can speedily be made the career o Prince Methusalem is likely to be an exceedingly short an certainly not a merry one.' This was followed by *Estrella*, anothe comic opera, but by July the theatre was closed. It reverted to it original name of the Novelty, under the management of Nelli Harris, and opened on 5 January 1884, with a revival of *The Ne Magdalen* with Ada Cavendish in her original part. Nellie Harris sister of Sir Augustus (Druriolanus) was the first of a long line o Actress Managers of this theatre.

At last the Novelty began to become established. *Nita's First*, farcical comedy, ran 139 performances from March 1884. (It wa revived in 1888.) This was followed during the year by Kat

Vaughan in a burlesque *Lalla Rookh* and *Polly* a comic opera by
Edward Soloman.

During 1885 the theatre was mostly 'dark'. It was not till
September that it re-opened, under the management of Willie
Edouin with Lionel Brough and Alice Atherton and its new
manager in a burlesque drama, *Japs; or, the Doomed Daimio*.
t was the burlesque that was 'Doomed', and it lingered for only a
short time. Other burlesques were tried: *Vanderdecken*, and *Oliver
Grumble* with even less success, and the theatre became the home
of amateurs with an occasional professional production. In 1887,
he firm of theatrical costumiers H. and L. Nathan, were ill
advised enough to enter theatrical speculation and took a lease of
he theatre. In September 1887 they sub-let to Harriet Jay who
re-decorated the theatre and put on *The Blue Bells of Scotland*,
by Robert Buchanan, but this did not run and its successor saw
the end of her regime. The theatre was only opened intermittently
until yet another change of name came in October 1888.

The theatre was taken by an American actress, Mrs. Churchill
Jodrell (a member of the famous family). She opened on 22
October as the Jodrell Theatre with Rubenstein's opera *The
Demon*, sung by the Russian National Opera Company—far too
large an organisation for such a small theatre!

After a few disasters she too retired from the scene, and the
Nathans returned and restored the name of the theatre to the
Novelty again. Their first effort was the English prèmiere of
Ibsen's *A Doll's House*, with Janet Achurch, Herbert Waring and
Charles Charrington, but little success attended the re-opening.
From 4 August 1890 J. A. Cave the veteran manager of the Old
Vic and other minor melodrama houses, changed the name to the
New Queen's Theatre, and produced *The Corsican Brothers*. This
was a dire disaster and by the end of the month Brian McCullough
was presenting a season of his own dramas at the, yet once again,
Novelty Theatre.

Yet another short change of name came in March 1894 when
Charles Morritt ran a season of twice nightly Music Hall, calling
the theatre the Eden Palace of Varieties. When he finished in
August the name reverted to the Novelty once again and was only
open intermittently for professional and amateur productions.

The theatre hit the headlines in 1896, not for its histrionic
strength but for another kind of notoriety. A provincial leading

lady, Victoria St. Lawrence (Mrs. Walter Tyrrell), had taken the
theatre in April for a stock season of melodrama, preceded by a
farce, which changed weekly. The titles themselves tell their own
story and explain the scope of her management: *Below London
Bridge, A Woman's Fault, Snatched from Death, Sealed to Silence*
She also revived old favourites including *The Lady of Lyons* and
The Two Orphans.
    It was on 10 August that the season achieved a place in theatrical
history. *The Sketch* 19 August gives the story:

Sensational realism suddenly developed into tragic reality
on the stage of the Novelty Theatre a few minutes after
midnight on Monday of last week, when a terrible accident
occurred, without parallel in the story of the London stage.
The venerable farce, *Ici on Parle Français*, had given place to
Mr. Frank Harvey's stirring melodrama, *Sins of the Night*, and
the fifth act had nearly drawn to its close. The audience had
followed the plot of the play, which was being presented
for the first time in London, with eager interest, through all its
developments, including more particularly the seduction and
supposed murder of the sister of one Pablo, a Créole, by the
villain of the piece, Manuel Ramez. Sympathy was powerfully
enlisted on the side of the injured Créole, played by Mr.
Wilfred Moritz Franks, and when, in the final scene—Squire
Thorne's drawing-room—Pablo checks the triumphant,
laughing exit of Ramez and stabs him to the heart, the excited,
emotional spectators cheered lustily, little dreaming that for
once a real tragedy had been acted before their eyes in place
of the usual sham and illusion of stageland, and that Mr.
Temple E. Crozier lay dead behind the curtain, the victim of
one of the saddest mishaps which ever cut short one young life,
full of vigour and promise, and shadowed another until Time
with merciful fingers shall dull the record of terrible disaster.
    'I have kept my oath—my sister is avenged—die, villain,
die!' cried Pablo, and in another moment Ramez lay upon the
stage with the stiletto only too surely in his heart, bravely
telling his horror-stricken comrade not to 'worry,' and that
he was 'all right', when he overheard Franks moan out in
dazed fashion, 'What is the matter—what have I done?'
Intensely pathetic is this story of the two handsome young

fellows, full of creditable ambition, excellent friends, suddenly divided for all time in this tragic fashion, and saddest of all that the accident was preventable, and due, probably, in some degree, to the not unnatural vanity of youth, which led the young actor who played Pablo to prefer a jewelled stiletto of his own—a present from his relative, the late Ada Cavendish —to the ordinary 'property' dagger provided by the management. It may even have been—for actors are notoriously superstitious—that the unfortunate young fellow regarded the stiletto as an omen of success in a new part, for to life's ironies there is no end. Be that as it may, as the audience filed out into the street, full of excitement, and with nothing but praise for the liberal programme provided for them by Miss V. St. Lawrence—the clever and charming lady under whose capable management a theatre, long under a cloud, is fast being turned into a success—a sad group had gathered round their dead comrade, and what would have been a congratulatory reunion after a successful production was changed into an occasion of mourning. Miss St. Lawrence has run the theatre with her own stock company, with Mr. Temple Crozier as one of her leading men, in which capacity he was popular with the whole company. Mr. Crozier, who was a son of the Rev. Temple Crozier, of Coston Rectory, Melton Mowbray, was only twenty-four, and had, like so many actors, been originally intended for commerce, and spent eighteen months with a well-known firm in Liverpool. But the stage fever was upon him, and after a variety of experiences in the north, he eventually got an engagement at the Novelty as 'heavy lead.' Without doubt, Mr. Crozier had a promising future when Fate cut the thread of his life so prematurely and so pitilessly, for he was good-looking, young, talented, popular, and daily gaining a varied experience which must have told strongly in his favour as the years went by. But it was not to be, and while hundreds were still talking over his latest impersonation, he lay dead, in the evening-dress *de rigueur* of the stage-villain, with his fine face made up to represent the swarthy Spaniard in whose guise he was destined to speak his last word upon the stage.

Miss St. Lawrence was in her dressing-room at the time of the accident, and when the sad news was broken to her she fainted. She has widespread sympathy, for everyone interested in stage matters has watched her experiment at the Novelty with cordial goodwill.

Death upon the stage is no unheard-of thing in the chronicles of the play, but the present case has no positive parallel in the annals, at all events, of the London theatres.

In the case at the Novelty there has never been for an instant any doubt that the unhappy occurrence was purely an accident, possibly due to the excitement of one or both of the actors. The moral of the tragedy is, without question, that dangerous weapons should be absolutely forbidden for use upon the stage. Diderot may go to extremes in declaring that the best actor is he who is devoid of sensibility, but Sir Henry Irving has pointed out that actors have their own temperaments, and cannot always avoid feeling their part. 'But,' he adds, 'it is quite possible to feel all the excitement of the situation and yet be perfectly self-possessed.' Yet, he takes care to point out, 'untrained actors, yielding to excitement on the stage, have been known to stumble against the wings in impassioned exit.' Mr. Franks is not an untrained actor, but he is young and probably acutely sensitive, and it is possible that excess of excitement may have had a good deal to do with the sad fatality at the Novelty. At any rate, be this as it may, the one obvious moral of the tragedy is that stage weapons should invariably be harmless.

Wilfred Franks was arrested, charged with manslaughter and released on bail. At the inquest the Coroner returned a verdict of misadventure and the charge was dropped.

Harold Child tells in his autobiography *A Poor Player* (1939) what happened at the theatre after the accident:

Next morning a very shaky and horrified company met to discuss what to do. They took the brave and wise course of resolving to carry on. That night (Tuesday 11 August) they acted the play, but without the final scene. I can find no record of who took the parts of the dead man and his slayer. But meanwhile I had, for once in my life, been prompt to action. The stage-manager of the Novelty Theatre was Newman Maurice, who had been with me at the Strand. I telegraphed to him that I was coming, caught the next train to London, reminded him that I was the 'quickest study' he had ever known, and offered to play the villain's part as soon as ever they liked. That night (Wednesday, 12 August) the Manager made a little speech before the play began, announcing that I should be the player of the villain for the remainder of the week.

After this publicity the manageress kept going over Christmas, when she put on a pantomime *Red Riding Hood* with herself as principal boy. Her season ended in June 1898 and the theatre became quite deserted.

A new lease of life was given to the Novelty with the new century. It was acquired by W. S. Penley out of the fortune he had made from *Charley's Aunt*.

By 1900 the Strand development was well under way and the exact route of the new road was under final discussion. It was suspected that the site would be needed and that large compensation would have to be paid, but eventually Kingsway (opened in 1905) passed some thirty yards east of the theatre!

Penley opened 24 May 1900 with a revival of *A Little Ray of Sunshine*, calling his theatre the Great Queen Street Theatre. An account of the re-construction appeared in *The Era* 26 May 1900:

The building has been reconstructed by Messrs. Murray and Foster, under the superintendence of Mr. John Murray. The lines and proportions of the auditorium are pleasing and convenient; the seating arrangements—the furniture and draperies being by Messrs. Maple and Co.—are comfortable; and the proscenium and the fronts of the tiers are agreeably ornamented with figures of youthful nymphs and satyrs modelled in high relief. The house is essentially a comfortable one, the electric lighting being excellent, and the organisation in front quite creditable.

On Thursday the early arrivals had before their eyes a khaki-coloured fireproof curtain which presently drew slowly up, revealing the act-drop, a classical subject by Mr. Arthur J. Black, representing a dance of girls to the music of a lyre played by an aged musician. The drop also ascended, and showed Mr. W. S. Penley in evening dress, supported by the members of the company; and, somewhat to the surprise of his hearers, Mr. Penley came forward and sang 'God save the Queen' quite in concert style, the company and the audience joining in enthusiastically. Then came the performance of the first piece, a one-act play by W. J. Locke, which was first performed at the Shakespeare Theatre, Liverpool, on Nov. 7th 1898, entitled *The Lost Legion*. Mr. G. Harrison Hunter played Will Ormthwaite with expressiveness and spirit, though a little more breadth might have improved the impersonations. Mr. Julius Royston was quite realistic and convincing, both in manner and appearance, as Richard Ormthwaite; and Miss Amy Lawborn was agreeably earnest and ingenuous as Marion Day, Mr. Gilbert Laye acting judiciously the little part of Perkins. After *The Lost Legion* came a revival of Messrs. Mark Ambient and Wilton Heriot's comedy *A Little Ray of Sunshine*.

This was performed for the first time in London at the Royalty Theatre on Dec. 31st, 1898, after a production at Yeovil on May 5th of the same year. The complete success of the piece has made its story sufficiently familiar to absolve us from the task of description, and we need only now allude to the acting, which was excellent all round. Mr. Penley, in his original character of Gerard, Lord Markham, once more convulsed the house with his dry, quaint, and irresistible oddity; Mr. Julius Royston resumed the character of Dick Markham, and sustained it with agreeable spirit and vivacity; Mr. G. Harrison Hunter was excellent in every way as Sir Philip Ashton; Mr. J. Sebastian Smith was comically boyish as Reggie Ashton; Mr. A. E. Raynor gave a smart and smooth embodiment of Mr. Carlton; and Mr. Fred Epitaux was fortunately available to repeat his admirable embodiment of Mr. Dobbs, Mr. Richard Blunt being a dignified and amiable old butler, and Mr. Gilbert Laye giving a careful and well-considered performance as Saunders. Miss Beatrice Selwyn's Lady Dorothy was firm, easy, and graceful; Miss Amy Lamborn made a most winning and attractive Connie Markham; and Miss Gertrude Scott was dainty and spirited in her original role of Madge Ashton, Miss Dorothy Heathcote playing Evelyn Kemp prettily; and Miss Cordelia Daubeney giving a neat and effective impersonation of Polly. The comedy was cordially received, and at its conclusion Mr.

Penley came before the curtain, and made a brief and evidently unstudied speech, first asking the audience if they liked the house, and then expressing his gratitude and his cheerful expectations of the future.

Among other productions Penley tried a revival of *The Private Secretary* and of *Charley's Aunt* in July 1901 which only ran a few months. After this he retired from the stage, but retained his interest in the theatre. He had suffered a big loss in his efforts to re-establish this unlucky theatre.

On 10 March 1902 the Purcell Society staged Handel's *Acis and Galatea* and *The Masque of Love* from Purcell's *Diocletian*, under the direction of Martin Shaw (for the music) and Gordon Craig (for the production). A critic in *The Playgoer* April 1902 commented:

Let me make this remark about Mr. Gordon Craig's *pseudo-eccentric* ideas of dressing, the persons, and the stage. The idea of a tent-like chamber seems to me quite in keeping with the mystic, far off, dreamy and visionary scenes of the works produced. He uses paper for his dresses; the effect is electrical. The use of penny air-balls among the peasants of Sicily, gambolling in very joy of delight of life, struck one as funny, but it all seemed to fit in. The joyous boy who invented it all belongs to that race—that rare and radiant race—whose 'women are heroes,' and as a dear dead friend of mine said long ago in a noble poem—

Where the women are heroes
What should the men be?

From November 1902 till 1907 the theatre was leased to Hans Anderson, who ran the German Theatre Company, which had appeared the previous season at the St. George's Hall. They played yearly seasons of classics and modern plays in German and achieved a great reputation. King Edward visited the theatre on two occasions. In between these seasons other companies came and went. In 1905 the Mermaid Society, 'for the production of old English plays' (which had performed mostly at the Royalty in Dean Street), moved in and called themselves the Mermaid Repertory Theatre, under the direction of Philip Carr.

On 10 June 1907 the Irish National Theatre Company from the

Abbey Theatre, Dublin, gave the first London performance of
Synge's *The Playboy of the Western World* during their season
At the end of June the theatre closed.

In 1907 a complete interior re-construction took place to the
designs of Frederick W. Foster for its new manager. In a manifesto
dated 23 September 1907 Lena Ashwell said:

> I have secured a long Lease of the Great Queen Street
> Theatre, which I have now re-named the 'Kingsway.' Save
> for the actual site, very little remains of the old theatre. Apart
> from great alterations to the exterior, the whole of the interior
> has been 'gutted.' The seating of all parts of the house has been
> more conveniently and comfortably arranged, every seat,
> including those in the Pit and Gallery, being numbered and
> reserved, thus avoiding the necessity for tedious waiting.
>
> I hope you will think the Theatre beautiful, for Mr.
> Frederick Foster, has re-decorated it—in the style of the
> Louis XVI period. The Entrance Hall is approached by a
> flight of white marble steps. The floor of the hall is also of
> marble, and the prevailing tone of the decorations is cream.
> The electric lighting of the Theatre has been entirely re-
> arranged and brought up-to-date, and I am assured that no
> theatre in London has a more complete and effective system.
>
> The means of access—The Kingsway Theatre is now
> peculiarly accessible. Within a few yards of the Theatre is the
> Kingsway itself, with L.C.C. trams and a fine service of
> horse and motor 'buses. Another line of 'buses running from
> Victoria to King's Cross passes the very door. The Theatre
> can be reached on foot in two minutes from the
> British Museum Station on the Central London Tube
> Railway, or in one minute from the Holborn Station of the
> Piccadilly Tube. The cab fare from nearly all the principal
> hotels and railway stations is 1s.
>
> The policy of the theatre—I propose to alternate Plays of
> serious interest with comedies, and to produce at Matinées
> pieces which, while worthy of production by reason of their
> artistic merit, would not perhaps interest a sufficient number of
> the public to warrant their being placed in the regular evening
> Bill. Thus, in course of time, I hope to form a Repertoire of
> Plays likely to appeal to the varied tastes of my Patrons.

The opening play—The Theatre will open with a Play in three acts of serious interest, entitled *Irene Wycherley*. This is the first dramatic work of a new author, Mr. A. P. Wharton. I have also arranged with some of the best known Authors to supply me with Plays, and have secured several pieces of great interest by the younger generation of dramatists.

The company—I have been fortunate enough to secure Mr. Norman McKinnell to produce the Plays. The Company will then consist of Mr. Norman McKinnell, Mr. Henry Vibart, Mr. C. M. Hallard, Mr. Dennis Eadie, Miss Frances Ivor, Miss Christine Silver, Miss Gertrude Scott, and Miss Muriel Wylford, who, I hope, will long be associated with me.

The Orchestra and Music—A distinctive feature at the Kingsway Theatre will be the Music. The Orchestra will be composed of stringed instruments only, and I hope to include in the selection the works of younger composers who are struggling to obtain a hearing. The Programme will be frequently varied, and a special slip giving details of the Music to be performed will be inserted in each programme.

Refreshments—This department will be under my own control, and everything supplied will be of the best quality. A special feature will be made of afternoon teas in the large foyer during the entr'actes and after the performance at matinées. There will be no Cloak-Room fees.

At last Kingsway and Aldwych were an established fact, and it was hoped that at last prosperity would come to this little hidden theatre.

The complete re-building inferred by the new manager was not as drastic as it would seem. It was mainly re-decoration. The exterior changes were slight, and above street level, according to pictorial evidence. The proscenium was set back a few feet improving the proportions of the house. *The Era*, 5 October, meticulous in recording such changes, only refers to those at the Kingsway under 'Theatrical Gossip':

Miss Lena Ashwell held a reception in her new theatre, the Kingsway, on Thursday afternoon, and a large number of her friends were present to view the Great Queen Street theatre under its new name, and entirely transformed and improved. The style of the decorations is Louis XVI., and the impression created is that of artistic simplicity, the prevailing tones being cream and terra-cotta. The handsome central hall is approached by a flight of white marble steps, and everything has been done in detail that can add to the comfort and convenience of Miss Ashwell's audiences.

The seating will accommodate 600. The lighting is by four electric lamps, their rays softened by ground glass. Every seat in the auditorium is numbered and reserved, and may be booked. The stage is flat, a distinct slope being given to the floor of the auditorium. The pit will be provided with 'tip-up' chairs.

Irene Wychlery opened on 9 October 1907 and ran 139 performances, it was followed by *Diana of Dobson's* by Cicely Hamilton, which ran 142 performances.

There was a strong air of militant woman suffrage about the new Kingsway with its manageress and a woman playwright! During the next two years Lena Ashwell staged *The Sway Boat, Grit, The Truants, The Earth*, with matinées of one act plays, etc.

In 1910 Herbert Trench leased the theatre for *Don*, by Rudolf Besier. Then came several transitory managers including Lawrence Irving, Lydia Yavorska, who produced matinée and charity productions till the end of 1911. It was not till Granville Barker and Lillah McCarthy took the theatre and transferred Shaw's *Fanny's First Play* from the Little on 1 January 1912, that the Kingsway became once again 'on the map.' During the run of the play (in all it gave 622 performances divided between both theatres), Barker had a brush with the Lord Chamberlain on a play, *The Secret Woman* by Eden Phillpotts. One does not associate the the author, who was to write *The Farmer's Wife* and other simple West Country stories, with 'salacious drama.' The following letter appeared in *The Times*, 14 February, 1912:

A play by Mr. Eden Phillpotts, in rehearsal at the Kingsway Theatre, has been refused a licence by the Lord Chamberlain. It is held (apparently) to contain improper passages. These have been marked by the Lord Chamberlain, and if the author would consent to strike them out, the play would be licensed after all, and no one outside the office (and Mr. Phillpotts himself) need ever know what sort of fellow he had tried to be. Thus, it seems, all would be well.

Now we, his fellow-writers, have read this play, and find it to be the conscientious work of an artist doing his best in his own way, not necessarily our way, for no two writers who have anything to express can express it identically. Not thus would we have written, though many of us would have been proud to have written thus. To our mind, then, the play is worthy work, such as a stage of high aims should ever be ready to welcome, and we feel a warm indignation over the stigma cast by the Lord Chamberlain upon an author whom his fellow-writers, and the English-speaking world generally, have for many years held in admiration and esteem. Never in all these years of novel-writing has a word been breathed by any responsible paper or person against his fair name, but the moment he has the ambition to write a play in the same spirit which inspired his novels he is at the mercy of an official who knows no better than to use him thus. We say only of the Lord Chamberlain that he knows no better. We do not doubt the kindliness of his intention when he offers to show us how to alter our work to his satisfaction; and we are sure he does not understand that these offers to save us from ourselves and hush the matter up are to authors the greatest insult of all.

If we do not come to the aid of this particular author who declines to accept this way out, he is helpless, and the public are left to presume that the Lord Chambelain was right and that Mr. Phillpotts would be an unworthy author if he was allowed.

Mr. Phillpotts is the victim to-day, but of course it may be any one of us tomorrow. Many of us have never written plays, though most of us would like to do so; there is not perhaps another field so fine in the England of to-day for a man or woman of letters, but all the other literary fields are free; this one alone has a blind bull in it. We are not referring to the man but to his office. The dramatist's indeed is the only calling on British soil that is not free. We who sign this letter may be otherwise engaged, some of us may be old and done and no longer matter, our chance has gone by, but there are men and women who are coming—are they, also, to be warned off? can we strike no blow for the young?

In this particular case there is, we find, one thing we can
do. Miss Lillah McCarthy and Mr. Granville Barker being
willing to make us a free gift of the production, we, his fellow-
authors, can present Mr. Phillpotts' play at the Theatre
for the six afternoon performances that had been
proposed. We can make no charge for admission, nor may the
author be paid one penny for the work of half a year; but we
can invite the public to come in free of charge to judge for
themselves whether with this play Mr. Phillpotts has for-
feited their regard. All arrangements for this have now been
completed, and the first performance will take place at the
Kingsway Theatre on the 22nd of this month, at 2.30. Thus
we can have the public verdict in this case.

                                       Yours faithfully,
William Archer, J. M. Barrie, R. C. Carton, Joseph Conrad,
Arthur Quiller-Couch, W. L. Courtney, Arthur Conan Doyle,
John Galsworthy, Frederick Harrison, Anthony Hope
Hawkins, Maurice Hewlett, W. H. Hudson, Henry James,
Jerome K. Jerome, George Moore, Gilbert Murray,
John Masefield, Alfred Noyes, Arthur Wing Pinero, Elizabeth
Robins, G. Bernard Shaw, Alfred Sutro, H. G. Wells,
I. Zangwill, Arnold Bennett, Cecil Raleigh.

Lena Ashwell became worried about her tenant and tried to
stop the performance. Barker wrote to *The Times*, 21 February:

Sir,—the public had been invited to six morning performances of *The Secret Woman* by Eden Phillpotts, at the
Kingsway Theatre.

Miss Lena Ashwell, apprehensive that the performance of
the play in its entirety would involve her in serious conse-
quences at the instance of the Lord Chamberlain and
jeopardise her licence, applied to-day in the High Court of
Justice for an injunction to restrain the management from
permitting the proposed performances. On the ground that
the performances are to be private the injunction was not
granted. An undertaking to this effect renders it impossible
for anyone to be admitted to the pit and gallery on the
presentation of their card as had been intended. These seats
will now be reserved and invitations to them issued in due
course. H. Granville Barker.

The matinée took place and *The Era* commented:

> Beyond being rather unhealthy in conception and broad in treatment there seems to be little in the play harmful to public morals, and one can recall others that have escaped the blue pencil much more baneful in effect. Many indeed might find a salutary lesson in the play; certainly it is loaded—really overloaded with dramatic scenes and with a good deal that is highly humorous.

The offending earthy melodramatic plot concerned a wife who murdered her husband because of his mistress and was brought to trial. The programme noted:

> No consistent attempt will be made to assume the Devonshire dialect, partly because the actors cannot, partly because very few of the audience would understand them if they did.

Matinées of Euripides' *Iphigenia in Taurus* and *The Double Game* by Maurice Baring, were given during the run of the Shaw comedy, which itself continued for matinées.

In September 1912 *The Voysey Inheritance* by Barker himself went into the evening bill. In November John Galsworthy's *The Eldest Son* was produced, and in December Shaw's *John Bull's Other Island* was revived for matinées (*Fanny's First Play* was also still in the matinée repertoire).

In March 1913 *The Great Adventure* by Arnold Bennett was produced by Granville Barker. It ran 673 performances, with Henry Ainley and Wish Wynne, and achieved the longest run in this theatre's chequered history. The McCarthy-Barker management ended with *The Dynasts*, a laudable attempt to stage Thomas Hardy's epic drama of Napoleonic days. This was a magnificent record considering Barker had, at this time, also been staging his famous Shakespearean revivals at the Savoy Theatre, *Twelfth Night* and *The Winter's Tale* in 1912, and a season of repertory and new plays at the St. James's Theatre in 1913.

The Kingsway was taken over by J. E. Vedrenne and Dennis Eadie (Lena Ashwell was still the proprietress), and after an opening flop, *Advertisements*, they invited the Liverpool Repertory Company to London for a season. 'Repertory' was fast becoming an established system in the provinces and they played a selection of plays old and new in May 1915.

The Great War years were not good for the Kingsway, and many managements came and went. New plays, which did not succeed, revues and revivals filled the bill, but not the theatre. It is only necessary to recall *The Starlight Express*, by Algernon Blackwood and Violet Pearn, because of Elgar's incidental music, and an early appearance of Lynn Fontanne, at Christmas 1915.

Lena Ashwell sold the theatre in 1916 to a syndicate; the Kingsway Theatre Ltd. The managing director, J. Herbert Jay, remained in control of the theatre until 1936.

Lillah McCarthy returned under her own management in 1919 and presented *Judith* by Arnold Bennett and *St. George and the Dragon* by Eden Phillpotts—neither with much success. Still the endless procession of productions came and went, in 1921 Bronson Albery presented a revival of *The Knight of the Burning Pestle*, directed by Nigel Playfair, with Noël Coward as Ralph, and in 1922 Ivor Novello made an early stage appearance in *Spanish Lovers*, a genuine Spanish play via the French 'done' into English!

Mrs. Patrick Campbell was again seen as Hedda Gabler in June of this year. After the phenomenal success of *The Beggar's Opera* at the Lyric Theatre, Hammersmith, under Nigel Playfair, an attempt was made to rival this with *Polly*, its sequel, in December 1922. It ran 327 performances.

In 1923-1924 Donald Calthrop was in management and produced *Twelfth Night*, *A Midsummer Night's Dream* and other plays, an operetta and a revue *Yoiks!* In the latter, Noël Coward's first lyric 'Every Little Peach' was sung by Mary Leigh.

Another regime came in 1925-1926 when Barry Jackson took over the theatre with his Birmingham Repertory Company. He presented plays by Shaw and Ibsen, the famous first 'modern dress' *Hamlet*, a revival of *The Immortal Hour* and plays by modern authors.

The Macdona Company played a season of Shaw in 1926-1927, then came *Marigold*, an arcadian comedy by Harker and Pryor, which was a big success and ran 642 performances from 21 April 1927 (it was revived in 1929). Its successors—*Thunder on the Left* by Richard Pryce and *Mrs. Moonlight* by Benn Levy—did not have so great a success. Simon Ord, who had been manager since Barry Jackson left, revived *The Rising Sun* by Heijermans, *The*

School for Scandal in 1929 and *Liberty Hall* by R. C. Carton in 1930 among other productions.

A short *succés du scandale* was caused by *Her First Affaire* later in 1930, but it soon transferred to the Duke of York's, leaving the Kingsway to be used again by transitory managements. These included the Macdona Players and the Prague Group of the Moscow Art Theatre who gave a season in December 1931, but otherwise there is little worth recording except a newly formed company, the Independent Theatre Club, which opened in the Kingsway for members only from October 1932 to produce plays which would not pass the censor. The direction of the company was by Terence de Marney and its producer Komisarjevsky. Their plays were *Versailles* by Emil Lüdwig, *The Werewolf* by Rudolf Lother and *Fräulein Elsa* by Arthur Schnitzler in which Peggy Ashcroft 'had the longest part ever written for a woman'. After this season the plays once again came thick and fast. *Young England* transferred for part of its long run in 1934-1935, *Murder in Motley* ran for a few months, *The Rivals* was presented in a musical version by Mansell and Hughes.

In July 1936 it was announced:

Kingsway Theatre, Great Queen Street, W.C., was bought privately by Mr. Mark Wolfe, the London cinema and hotel proprietor, yesterday for a sum that was not disclosed. Earlier in the day the property was offered for sale by auction, but the bidding stopped at £19,500 and the auctioneer, Mr. Warwick Daw, said he could not sell at such a low figure and would have to withdraw. He proposed to buy it in at £25,000 on behalf of his clients. Mr. Wolfe said afterwards, 'It is my intention to carry on as a theatre, and I will endeavour to maintain the traditions of the place. I hope to put on plays in the near future.'

Wolfe tried to run the theatre, unsuccessfully, during 1937, but by 1938 Herbert Jay was again in control.

The next play of note was the Farjeons' *An Elephant in Arcady*, a musical in October 1938, a season of *La Chauve Souris* at Christmas lost without its late director, Nikita Balieff.

The year before the war was a lean one for the theatre. Failure after failure, and as war broke out a revival of *Lady Precious Stream* in December 1939 at cheap prices for the troops. When the theatres had re-opened, in February-March 1940, Donald Wolfit gave his first London season with his own company and produced six Shakespearean plays, playing Hamlet, Benedict, Shylock, Othello, Malvolio and Petruchio. The next production was a revival of *While Parents Sleep*, which opened 30 April 1940, twice nightly, it was put on by Leon M. Lion. The run abruptly ended on 11 May and the theatre closed for good.

The auditorium and stage suffered considerable damage in the blitz and stood derelict until after the war. There were several schemes mooted for its re-building. The principal one was launched at a party in the foyer of the theatre on 20 July 1954 by the newly formed English Stage Company under George Devine. They took a long lease of the theatre and their aims and objects were set out in a manifesto:

> London has no theatre with a consistent policy towards contemporary drama. The English Stage Company, which was formed in the interests of the modern playwright of poetic imagination, has acquired the Kingsway Theatre for the production of plays by such dramatists. At a time when no new theatres are being built and the number for the public presentation of plays is being reduced, it is exciting to be able to announce that this historic building will shortly re-open. The stage, which was destroyed during the war, has to be reconstructed and the auditorium entirely renovated but, once completed, it is intended that it shall be a theatre where playwrights, actors and producers will find conditions for creative work which are not easily obtainable elsewhere, and where the public, both metropolitan and visiting, can enjoy the results of a consistently progressive policy.
>
> In this way, the English Stage Company hopes to fill a serious and rather shameful gap in the pattern of the London Theatre.

After much talk it was eventually announced in *The Evening News*, 19 November 1955:

> London, we were told last summer, was to have another theatre. This, at least, would be some consolation for the possible removal of others for offices. Yes, the Kingsway, damaged during the war and closed for some 15 years, was to

be re-opened after £50,000 had been spent on restoring it. The Earl of Harewood, a member of the committee of the English Stage Company, announced that it was hoped to open the Kingsway in January.

The sum of £50,000 was reported to have been put down in solid cash by a Manchester businessman, Neville Blond, venturing into show business for the first time.

The theatre is still a shell; the manager who had been engaged is there no longer. But this is not the end of the English Stage Company. Neville Blond tells me that they have bought the Royal Court; they plan to begin work there in the Spring. Costs in these days are so gigantic that it was thought it would be better to have a 'ready-made theatre with a splendid tradition' which the Royal Court certainly has. [The Royal Court opened 2 April 1956].

The Kingsway was purchased with adjoining property by a development company and was pulled down in 1959. An extension of Newton Street to join Great Queen Street was made through the site and a new office block was built on the remainder of the ground.

12

The Little Theatre

John Street, (Now John Adam Street)
Adelphi, Strand
In a block bounded by Adam Street and Durham Street (Now Durham House Street) at side and rear. Stage door in Durham Street

Opened 11 October 1910 with *Lysistrata*, an adaptation by Laurence Housman of Aristophanes' play produced by Cavendish Morton.
Under the management of Gertrude Kingston.
Balcony constructed and theatre re-decorated 1912.
Partially destroyed in an air raid on 4 September 1917.
Re-built and re-opened 24 February 1920 with *Mumsée*, a play by Edward Knoblock.
Under the management of J. E. Vedrenne and Frank Vernon.
Again heavily damaged in the blitz on 16 April 1941. Remained derelict until pulled down in 1949. A block of offices, the Little Adelphi, built on the site.

THE SITE OF THE ADELPHI, in the middle of which the Little Theatre was built, was originally covered by Durham House and its grounds. After this was pulled down, in 1650, the land was occupied by several other buildings (see the Tivoli Number 24).
   The Adam brothers commenced to build their Adelphi and its terrace on great brick arches down to the river, in 1768, creating Adam Street, Durham Street and John Street (now John Adam Street). In John Street they built premises for Thomas Coutts, the banker, (who married as his second wife the actress Harriet Mellon). The building was linked in 1799 to others in the Strand by a bridge over what was then William Street (later Durham Street and now Durham House Street). Thomas Coutts lived in

part of the premises until his death in 1822, and Coutts Bank remained in possession until early in the twentieth century when they moved to the opposite side of the Strand and built new premises on the site of the Lowther Arcade.

There was little left in the John Street premises of the original Adam brothers' structure except the actual walls and the vaulted arched foundations.

In April 1910 it was announced that 'the former banking hall of Messrs. Coutts is now in the process of being converted into a small theatre, and a portion of Number 17 John Street is being absorbed into it for the purpose of a foyer. The work is being carried out at the expense of the freeholder, Mr. George James Drummond.'

The opening Souvenir of the theatre states:

All the present decorations, including the ceiling in foyer and vestibule, are modern reproductions put up under the careful supervision of the architects and faithfully copied from existing Adelphi examples of Adam work, as seemed to be only fitting in a building situate in a locality so intimately associated with them.

Owing to the premises being formerly used as a bank they are unusually substantially built, and the walls are of great thickness and strength, and involved heavy work in making the necessary openings, etc. They are in some cases three feet in thickness. The dressing rooms beneath the stage are formed out of old strong rooms used by Messrs. Coutts, while the whole structure itself stands on arches reaching to a depth of more than thirty feet beneath the auditorium floor. These arches are of very massive and heavy construction, and were erected by the Adam brothers to bring John Street and the Adelphi generally up to the same level as the Strand. The two lamp standards on either side of the main entrance doors are exact reproductions, by the Coalbrookdale Co., of those formerly existing on the estate, and of which three still remain.

The theatre has accommodation for 250 persons, and the cloak room accommodation, both for ladies and gentlemen, has been planned on a generous scale not usually found in London theatres.

The vestibule, *foyer* and the two refreshment rooms, all

leading out of one another, form a large and roomy set of lounges, occupying an area as large as the auditorium itself, and forming a special feature.

The floor of the auditorium has a rake of 1 in 13-75, and gives, therefore, a good view of the stage to every spectator, and the range of boxes at the back have a full uninterrupted front view, there being no seats with a side view only, as in so many places of entertainment. Owing to there being no galleries or tiers there are no projecting ceilings, and as a result there is none of that sense of oppression always associated with seats under the tiers in an ordinary theatre.

The attention of visitors is directed to the four paintings (one each in the *foyer* and vestibule and over the entrance steps to the boxes). These are the old original ceiling paintings by Angelica Kauffman saved from a ceiling, unfortunately demolished many years ago. They came into the architects' possession and were carefully preserved by them for future use, and have now, it is hoped, found a permanent home.

The work of converting the premises from a bank into a theatre has been carried out according to the designs and under the superintendence of the architects, Messrs. Hayward & Maynard.

The general contractors were Messrs. Macey & Sons, Ltd.

The new theatre was leased by Gertrude Kingston, a well known actress. Her policy was stated in the same souvenier:

It is the intention of the Manageress to cater for the play-going public, particularly ladies, who require comfortable surroundings while enjoying a theatrical performance, and to this end there will not be any pit or gallery, the auditorium being entirely devoted to stalls and seven boxes.

Miss Kingston's managerial policy on the stage will be on a par with her innovations in the front of the house. Although in no sense a repertoire theatre, she hopes to produce a new play once a month, but such new productions will not interfere with the established run of a successful piece, as they will only be performed for four consecutive Tuesdays in each month, until required to take their place in the regular bill.

Another novelty will be that the authors' names will be withheld until after the first performance has been criticised.

Notwithstanding the smallness of the house and the stage, there will be no limit to the ambition of the manageress; a small theatre will not mean a small programme or a *pot-pourri* of playlets. Neither will Miss Kingston confine herself to any particular exposition of dramatic art, tragedy, comedy, farce and farcical comedy, all will be given in turn, and whichever is appreciated most by her patrons, will be continued. All her endeavours will be directed to find good plays and good players.

It is to be noted that the Little Theatre does not contain an orchestra and the stage has been freed from the conventional scene cloths, exteriors being represented by a system of 'horizon' lighting, introduced with much success by Herr Reinhardt on the German stage.

The theatre opened on 11 October 1910. *The Era* 15 October reported:

Exquisite taste is shown in the decoration of Miss Gertrude Kingston's Little Theatre, in John Street, Adelphi. The lines are of classical simplicity, and the colours soft and restful to the eye. One passes through the 'Adams' vestibule into a lovely little foyer, in the middle of which stands a bronze statue of Phryne. Round the walls are delightful specimens of German art. The smoke room is of a subdued lavender shade and Turkey carpeted. The tea room has walls of soft yellow, which form an admirable background for some choice Japanese prints. The auditorium is of Wedgwood blue, with a couple of medallions in white on the walls, while the rich red of the curtain takes away any possible suggestion of chilliness. The attendants are also gowned in Wedgwood dresses, and wear pretty ribbons to match in their hair. The stalls are square in shape and exceedingly comfortable, the back of each being provided with a large square silk bag, in which all 'portable luggage' may safely be stowed. Altogether the Little Theatre is a gem.

It opened its doors to the public on Tuesday night with an adaptation of *Lysistrata*, the famous comedy by Aristophanes, 'a political satire in favour of peace,' which was played in Athens 412 B.C. The play, in its adapted form, is a proof of the well-worn axiom that history repeats itself, for, not-

withstanding its antiquity, it stands just as much for a political
satire of the present day as it did apparently over 2,000 years
ago, though whether it be in favour of peace to-day is an open
question. Certainly it is an argument in favour of the peace
desired by the large body of militant suffragettes, for it ends
on a decisive note of victory for women. It advocates the
policy of equal political rights for the sexes, and may certainly
be called 'up to date.'

There is very little action in the play and the charac-
terisation is shadowy, but there is much poetic language,
and the colour effects of the dresses against the exquisite
background of grey marble and sky are extremely beautiful.

Miss Gertrude Kingston played Lysistrata with a
tremendous undercurrent of strength and a fine reserve power
that were immensely effective. Her Lysistrata was the woman
whose reason dominates her actions, able to foresee the
logical result of her deeds, yet with enough of her sex's
instincts in her to understand and sympathise with her more
emotional and less intelligent companions. Miss Kingston
made a wonderfully commanding figure in her flowing
Grecian draperies, and the final scene, in which—the reunited
couples having danced gaily off to their homes—the lonely
figure of Lysistrata is left standing on the city walls outlined
against the dark, star-spangled sky, is a stage picture which
will not be easily forgotten or surpassed. In admirable contrast
with the calm and stately Lysistrata of Miss Kingston is the
delightful Myrrhina of Miss Dorothy Minto, a dainty,
wayward creature, a very Puck for mischief, much in love
with her husband, yet enjoying to the full the task which has
been sent her of tantalising him to the utmost limit of
endurance by her coquetries, and, at the moment when he
imagines she is on the point of relenting, slipping from his
embracing arms and darting off with a mocking little laugh.
Another feminine type, the fond and foolish woman, following
timorously in the footsteps of her stronger sister, is excellently
portrayed by Miss Margaret Watson. Miss Watson evidently
possesses a natural gift of effective and unexaggerated acting,
her comedy being especially worthy of commendation. Miss
Isabelle Merson as Chorus declaimed a fine speech beautifully; and as Lampito, a Spartan woman, Miss Maud Cressall

was full of fire and life. Mr. Charles Danvers was good as an inefficient leader of men, and Mr. Guy Rathbone played the deserted husband Cinesias with much spirit. An extremely pretty Greek dance was done by the Misses Annie and Irene Spong, and some charming and suitable music had been arranged by Mr. Brigata Bucalossi.

The policy of anonymous plays, the authorship being withheld until the Monday following production was probably instituted because Gertrude Kingston, an ardent feminist and suffragette, was anxious that women authors should have their work presented without prejudice. However, perhaps her friend and adviser, Bernard Shaw, was behind the idea. His *Fanny's First Play* (under the management of Lillah McCarthy) was given as by Xxxxxxx Xxxx on 19 April 1911, and was his first commercial success. It moved to the Kingsway Theatre on 1 January 1912 and ran 622 performances. It is still Shaw's longest original run.

Just before the Shaw play opened, Noël Coward made his first stage appearance on 27 January as Prince Mussell in *The Goldfish*, a children's play, and received a notice in *The Stage* for his song 'My Queen'. June Tripp, later June the musical comedy star, was also in the cast.

The work of building a balcony was undertaken in the summer of 1912, 'the lessees having found that accommodation for cheaper seats is desirable.' The seven original boxes and the cinematograph box, which had been installed, were demolished. The roof was raised and four new boxes and a balcony were inserted. This work was again carried out at the expense of the freeholder to designs by the original architects. At the same time the auditorium was re-decorated, the Adam style still being preserved. The theatre re-opened with a revival of Shaw's *Captain Brassbound's Conversion* on 15 October.

From April 1913 Ethel Warwick took the theatre for a short season, opening with *The Cap and Bells* by Robert Vansittart. In November of the same year G. K. Chesterton's fantastic comedy *Magic* was first produced and ran 168 performances. In February 1914 a private performance of Brieux' *Damaged Goods* was given, later in the year Sydney Carroll became manager, reviving *Forget-Me-Not*, a drama by Herman Merivale and Frederick Fenn, which was originally seen at the Lyceum in 1879, Miriam Lewis played the part created by Geneviève Ward. The Irish Players of the Abbey Theatre, Dublin, gave a season in 1915. After their season ended on 25 May the theatre remained closed.

On the night of 4 September 1917, 'a bomb dropped by a German aircraft caused havoc in the Little Theatre.' Gertrude Kingston retired from the management (she died in 1937), and the building remained damaged and empty until after the war.

The theatre was re-built in 1919-1920 from the plans by the original architects, Hayward and Maynard, by Messrs. Bovis. The theatre was re-constructed to almost the same designs as before, only the boxes were dispensed with, giving the theatre a capacity of 377 seats.

The re-built theatre was re-opened on 24 February 1920 under the management of J. E. Vedrenne and Frank Vernon, with a war play *Mumsée* by Edward Knoblock. A Souvenir gave the intentions of the management:

The policy of Vedrenne and Vernon is to produce the best plays dealing with contemporary life by authors whose mental attitude is modern, and to fill the casts of the plays with actors and actresses qualified by temperament and experience to interpret modern authors; and in carrying out such a policy it is definitely of advantage that the Little Theatre is, in fact as in name, little.

It is an intimate theatre, and intimacy is the first considera-tion for the staging of modern drama. And, intimate though the Little Theatre is, its actual stage is, as a result of the now completed alterations, larger than those of many West End theatres. There are no reasonable demands which the dramatist can make upon its staging capacity which cannot be adequately met; while the auditorium embodies the result of many years' experience in the adaptation of means to end, the end being the perfect comfort of an audience.

The seating is arranged in such a way that every one has an uninterrupted view of all parts of the stage. In winter the theatre will be evenly heated throughout and in summer a special system of ventilation will be employed to cool the house.

The Theatre is a Service, and those who serve it at the Little Theatre in the Adelphi have as their stimulus the hope that their policy will further the great work of national re-construction which is proceeding with such energy in every walk of life in the new post-war England.

The Stage, 26 February reported:

Since the Little was wrecked by a German bomb in September, 1917, when the stage was destroyed, that has been re-constructed so skilfully as to appear to be twice or three times as large as before. In other respects the house differs from the Little as opened by Miss Gertrude Kingston some years back, the light blue, pink and primrose hues having given place to pale yellow and white used for walls, alike in the auditorium and in the vestibules and entrance hall, the last having hung up therein complete lists of the Vedrenne-Barker and Vedrenne-Eadie productions at the Court, Savoy, Royalty, and other theatres. The floor of the house is now devoted entirely to stalls, with a couple of raised rows at the back, and above there is a balcony. Close attention has been paid to the seating, lighting, heating, and ventilating arrangements, and a most artistic act-drop, showing a charming river scene, has been painted by Marc Henri.

About the play and its author the reviewer continues:

Mr. Knoblock, when engaged in the Intelligence Department, stationed in a small town in a neighbourhood located without much difficulty, is said to have written *Mumsée* in his spare moments, finishing the last act just after Armistice Day, which perhaps accounts for what now seems the rather cheap theatricality of the concluding portion of a play of which many of the incidents, we are also told, 'were suggested by events occurring on the spot.' One wonders whether these include, in the obvious tailing-off process towards ordinary war drama, that painful scene in which the French mother, on one of her sons being accused of having given valuable information with respect to a munition train to the approaching enemy for a thousand francs, vehemently denounces her beloved boy Noël as 'a traitor to France, to England, to us all,' the lad, just self-confessed, to be a 'coward through and through,' rehabilitating himself by screwing up his courage, and taking a message to a British commander, clearly an errand fraught with danger. Finely though this

scene was played by Miss Eva Moore, with a further
passionate outburst, 'They cannot touch the soul of France,'
by Mr. Arthur Pusey, commendably sincere in his playing as
the unhappy youth, and by Mr. A. Dawson Milward, as an
English Colonel to whom the mother offers to give herself
to save her boy, it goes certainly against the grain; and rather
in the nature of claptrap is the final scene, in which take part
an American sergeant, a poilu, and two Tommies in the
battered church hurriedly decorated with flags.

The new management did not find the modern plays as it hoped
and José Levy took over the theatre as manager and Joseph
Benson became lessee (he handed over completely to Levy in 1922).
A season of *Grand Guignol* was started in September 1920. Lewis
Casson produced and Sybil Thorndike appeared in three of the five
plays which made up the first programme. London's *Grand
Guignol* became a success and in all eight series of plays were produced. Lighter plays were sometimes included and, in 1922, (the
last programme), Noël Coward's *The Better Half*, an early one act
play, was included. But most of the plays were strong meat in
those days and hospital nurses were kept posted in the theatre
ready to attend to any members of the audience who might be
overcome by the horrific happenings enacted on the stage!
The Little Theatre became associated with intimate revue in
October 1922 when *The Nine O'Clock Revue* was produced. It
ran 385 performances and was followed in October 1923 by
The Little Revue Starts at Nine which ran 196 performances and
later had several new editions. Jack Hulbert, Cicely Courtneidge,
Bobby Howes, Morris Harvey and Beatrice Lillie are names
remembered in connection with these revues.
In 1925 and 1926 there was little new of importance produced
but the famous Barnes Theatre revival of *The Seagull* transferred
here with John Gielgud as Konstantin, for 56 performances.
In February 1927 *Dracula* was first produced in Hamilton
Deane's version of Bram Stoker's novel. It ran 391 performances
(but not all were at this theatre).
A Shaw season by the Macdona Players in 1927, *A Man with
Red Hair* with Charles Laughton in 1928, Lucille la Verne as
Shylock in 1929, and Hamilton Deane in *Frankenstein* 1930, are
still remembered and bring this decade to its close.

In November 1930 Maurice Browne started the London
Theatre Company with all the good intentions and aspirations
which, in theatre history, have so often proved fruitless:

The London Theatre Company has been established, at
the Little Theatre, in order to present plays and entertainments of distinction, with a West End Company, under West
End conditions.

It is hoped to build up a permanent organisation similar to
that of the New York Theatre Guild.

The performances are open, like those of any other theatre,
to the general public.

Although the seating accommodation at the Little Theatre
consists solely of stalls and balcony, prices of admission have
been so graded as to provide the maximum number of seats at
a minimum cost. Over 60% of the seats in the theatre are
available at 6/- and under. All seats are bookable in advance.

Each play will be run for a short period only and will then
be transferred to another West End theatre or taken off to
make room for a new play.

Simultaneously with the founding of the London Theatre
Company, an organisation known as the Associates of the
London Theatre Company is being formed.

Subject to acceptance by the Management and the terms
endorsed on the card of Membership, Membership in this
Association is open to all interested in the theatre.

The opening play, a revival of *The Unknown Warrior*, was
followed by a revue and later by *The Venetian* by Clifford Bax—
this transferred to the Apollo in April and the venture ended.

See Naples and Die by Elmer Rice ran 101 performances from
April 1932, later in the year Nancy Price became connected with
the theatre and made it her headquarters for the People's National
Theatre. Amongst her presentations were *Alison's House* by
Susan Glaspell, John Galsworthy's *The Silver Box*, Bernard
Shaw's *Getting Married*, and a version of *Alice in Wonderland*
(1932), John Masefield's *The Witch*, Elmer Rice and Philip
Barry's *Cock Robin*, W. E. Gunn's *Scott of Abbotsford*, Sutton
Vane's *Overture*, Galsworthy's *Strife*, Maeterlinck's *The Burgo-
master of Stilemond* (1933), Shaw's *The Village Wooing* had its
London première in 1934, *The Life That I Gave Him* by Pirandello,

translated by Clifford Bax, and *Lady Precious Stream* by S. I. Hsiung, this play also had three revivals at the Little Theatre— in January 1935 when it scored 247 performances, in September of the same year when it scored 456, and again in November 1936.

In 1935 there was a revival of *Ghosts*. Nancy Price's other big success at this theatre was Mazo de la Roche's *Whiteoaks*, produced in April 1936, which ran for two years (827 performances), being transferred during its long run to the Playhouse. June 1936 saw a revival of the Capeks' *The Insect Play*. In 1937 Nancy Price left the Little Theatre and *The Ascent of F.6* by W. H. Auden and Christopher Isherwood was transferred from the Mercury.

The theatre was closed from June to December then Herbert Farjeon took over the management and presented *Nine Sharp*, a revue he wrote himself with music by Walter Leigh. This was followed in 1939 by *The Little Revue*, also written by Farjeon and composed by Leigh. The former ran for 405 performances and the latter was as successful with 415 performances. Later a non-stop version to fit the black-out hours was given '1.15 to 6 continuous' in September 1939.

In April 1940 *The Country Wife* was produced, with Alec Clunes and Hermione Baddeley, and The Ballet Group gave lunch-time performances between October 1940 and February 1941. The air raid shelter in the old vaults of the Bank was advertised as one of the safest in London.

The theatre was heavily damaged on the night of 16 April 1941, and after remaining derelict until 1949 it was demolished and a large office block, the Little Adelphi, in traditional Adelphi architecture to fit its surroundings, arose on the site.

13
The Olympic Theatre

Olympic Pavilion, Pavilion Theatre, Olympic Saloon, Astley's Theatre, Astley's Middlesex Amphitheatre, New Pavilion Theatre, Theatre Royal Pavilion, Little Drury Lane Theatre, Olympic New Theatre, Royal Olympic Theatre, Olympic Theatre of Varieties

Newcastle Street and Wych Street, Strand

FIRST THEATRE

Opened as the Olympic Pavilion 18 September 1806 with Feats of Horsemanship and *The Indian Chief; or, British Heriosm*, a pantomime.
Under the management of Philip Astley.
Variously known in the following years as the Pavilion Theatre, Olympic Saloon, Astley's Middlesex Amphitheatre and Astley's Theatre.
Enlarged and improved as the New Pavilion Theatre 1811. (Later called Theatre Royal Pavilion [Astley's].)
Again partly re-built and re-modelled and name changed to Little Drury Lane Theatre.
Opened 19 April 1813 with an Appropriate Address by Mr. Barnard followed by *Love's Perils; or, the Hermit of St. Kilda*, a performance by Sieur Sanches on the Slack Rope and 'his almost incredible feat of walking against the ceiling with his head downwards!' concluding with a pantomime *Punch's Festival; or, Harlequin's Christmas Box* by William Barrymore.
Under the management of Robert William Elliston.
Name changed to the Olympic Theatre December 1813.
Partly re-built and opened as the Olympic New Theatre 16 November 1818 with *Rochester; or, King Charles the Second's*

Merry Days, a comedy by W. T. Moncrief and a revival of *Giovanni in London; or, the Libertine Reclaimed*, an operatic extravaganza by W. T. Moncrief.
Under the management of Robert William Elliston.
Burnt down 29 March 1849.
From 1826 this building and the two successive theatres called themselves the Royal Olympic Theatre on and off during their lifetime.

SECOND THEATRE

Opened as the Olympic Theatre 26 December 1849 with an Occasional Address by Albert Smith delivered by Anna Cora Mowatt, followed by *The Two Gentlemen of Verona* by William Shakespeare and concluding with *Laugh and Grow Fat; or, Harlequin Nutcracker*, a pantomime by Nelson Lee.
Under the management of William Watts.
Closed 25 May 1889 and demolished.

THIRD THEATRE

Opened on an enlarged site as the New Olympic Theatre 4 December 1890 with *The People's Idol* by Wilson Barrett and Victor Widnell.
Under the management of Wilson Barrett.
Closed 17 November 1899 and demolished in 1905 to make way for the Strand (Aldwych and Kingsway) development scheme.

UP TO THE SIXTEENTH CENTURY, what we now know as Drury Lane was called the Via de Aldwych. Towards the southern end, in the latter days of Elizabeth's reign, Drury House was built by Sir William Drury. This gave a new name to the upper end of the Via, the lower end becoming Wych Street, preserving part of the old name. Here, too, other courtiers built themselves country houses. The ground down the Strand was eventually to be covered with the maze of streets, passages and courts as the gentry moved westward, all of which was swept away at the turn of this century in

he Strand (Aldwych and Kingsway) development scheme, in-
luding the Globe Theatre (see number 6), the Opera Comique
see number 14) and the Olympic Theatre.

Drury House passed, in the sixteen-hundreds, into the hands
f Lord Craven. He re-built it as Craven House and lived there
ill he moved to Bayswater at the turn of the century. After 1700
art of it had become a tavern, shorn of its gardens, bearing the
ign of 'Queen of Bohemia' in memory of the Earl of Craven's
nistress, the daughter of James I and titular Queen of Bohemia,
vhom he later married privately.

By 1805 the old building was so dilapidated that it was pulled
lown and the ground cleared. Part of the site, of irregular shape,
t the corner of Newcastle Street was leased by the then Lord
Craven to Philip Astley for ten years at £100 per annum with
roviso 'that if at the expiration of that term he find his place
succeed, he will purchase the ground for £2,000'. A newspaper
utting 13 September 1805 in the British Museum Olympic
Collection says:

> Mr. Astley is very active in making preparations for a new
> theatre on the site of the old houses at the back of Wych-
> street; and the Winter Managers, it is said, are equally active
> in making legal preparations to prevent the erection of such
> an edifice, alleging that it would interfere with their patents,
> and that he has already a theatre in the metropolis.

Astley had established himself on the south side of the river
in Lambeth in 1769, and Astley's Amphitheatre, which only
had a summer licence, had become the centre of feats of horsemanship, and the owner thought he could well move across the
river and open another establishment for winter use. He obtained
a licence, through the influence of Queen Charlotte, which allowed
him 'Music, dancing, pantomime and equestrian exhibitions'.

Astley bought up an old French warship, the *Ville de Paris*, a
naval Prize which was up for sale, and with the timbers and the
help of workmen from the local public house, he set to work directing operations himself, on a building to his own design, in the form
of a tent. It seems there was little brickwork in the building. The
yards and bowsprits of the ship formed the uprights and supports,
the deck was used for the stage and floors, and the sides for the

outside walls. The whole was covered with a tin roof, canvassec over and pitched and tarred. The entire cost was only about £80c On 1 March 1806 a newspaper says:

> The Pavilion in Wych Street may, in a military point of view, be considered a very useful national edifice; it is 50 feet high and stands upon 6000 square feet of ground. The equestrian circle of the Pavilion measures upwards of 150 feet in circumference; a space quite sufficient to exercise several parties of cavalry, and every way convenient for such science, from the number of stables, &c. attached to this excellent and *nouvelle* piece of workmanship—*Vraiment un petit Bijou.*

Another contemporary comment on 22 March 1806:

> The cupola of the new Olympic and Musical Pavilion in Wych Street is the admiration of all ranks; it is entirely covered with the best blocked tin, as a security against fire; the dreadful effect of such is severely felt by the Proprietors of two places of Public Amusement. Every seam of the blocked tin is soldered in a finished style of workmanship, manifestly giving the Pavilion a great superiority in point of force and effect of musical expression. The wits say, the idea was borrowed from the Concert Spiritual in Paris (an edifice so called—Be it so).

We are told also:

> Grecian chandeliers by Messrs. Neale & Barley, St. Paul's Churchyard . . . Decorations and embellishments by Messrs. Bridges & Davenport . . . The Olympic Pavilion will be attended every day by that able Equestrian Artist, Mr. Davis, for the purpose of instructing ladies and gentlemen in the elements of Riding, as also for improving the action of horses in general.

Astley opened his Olympic Pavilion on 18 September 1806 with the usual popular feats of horsemanship and a pantomime.
The Monthly Mirror, September 1806, says:

> In Newcastle Street, Strand, by the authority of the Lord Chamberlain, Mr. Astley, Senr. on the 18th of September opened the new Olympic Pavilion, for the exhibition of

horsemanship, vaulting and pantomime. The theatre represents a spacious tent, and the arena in which the games and feats are performed is larger than that of the amphitheatre at Westminster Bridge. The boxes are elegant, but not calculated to hold many persons; the pit is larger, and in its common place, but the gallery is under the boxes, behind the pit. The whole space devoted to the spectators does not appear to be able to contain more than would produce £80. The music is situated in an elevated orchestra on the left of the curtain, and the house is principally and all-sufficiently illuminated by twelve Grecian lamps of great brilliancy, suspended gracefully from the ceiling.

The performances consist chiefly of horsemanship, in which Master Davis distinguishes himself in a surprising manner. The excellence of Mr. Smith is well known. The cavalcade with which the entertainments commence is truly grand and full of effect. Twelve horses enter with all their *ephippia*, richly caparisoned, first unmounted and then mounted, and by their evolutions form a very animating spectacle. After many varieties, which we have no room at present to enumerate, the whole concludes with a serio-comic pantomime called *The Indian Chief*, in which Mrs. Parker appeared to great advantage, and attracted, as formerly, much applause. This piece is interesting, and the scenery beautifully painted. We want however in pantomime what we shall perhaps soon have, our old friends the clown and harlequin. In consequence of being narrow in their limits, the scenes that meet are produced both on one side, and then joined, but it is managed with much skill as not to be very destructive of effect.

The bill of the night is prefaced by an appeal from Mr. Astley, Senr. to the public, in whose service he has spent much of a long life, and in the exertion of his profession, here and at Paris, experienced severe losses. We trust that this '*old veteran*' will meet with encouragement, and that the aged horse will by his masters be supported in ease and comfort, in this snug little paddock, to the end of his days.

A newspaper cutting dated 22 September 1806 tells:

On Thursday last, the public were gratified by the opening of the Olympic Pavilion in Newcastle Street, in the Strand,

with the best set of entertainments we ever remember to
have seen in their line; the powers of some of the performers in this new scene of merit and wonder are the theme
of admiration in everything they do, especially Smith,
Crossman, and Mrs. Parker, who is absolutely more agile and
fascinating than ever, the neatness and effect of the infantine
feats of Master David were loudly and universally mani-
fested; and, indeed, the whole arrangements of the novelty,
variety and whim, equestrian and pedestrian, met the most
unbounded applause, and promises to be the most favourite
lounge in London.

An announcement on 29 September 1806 adds:

D'Exercises D'Equetation . . . will continue every evening
this week. To begin at seven o'clock precisely, in the following
order: 1st Class—Grand Cavalcade. 2nd Class . . . Horsemanship on one, two, and three horses. 3rd Class . . . An Operatical
Pantomimical Ballet, called *The Hibernian Reapers*. 4th
Class . . . An uncommon trial of skill by the young Equestrian Artists. 5th Class . . . Sagacity and Docility of the horse.

Unfortunately while he succeeded on the south side of the river,
nothing could bring luck to his new venture, though his equestrian
ballet, *L'Ecole de Mars*, did have some popularity, and the music
was published in 1808. He tried boxing and changes of names:
Pavilion Theatre (1809), the Olympic Saloon, Astley's Middlesex
Amphitheatre, Astley's Theatre (1810), but nothing would draw
the public.

Pony races by Six little Forest Ponies, to be rode by infant
jockies of feather weight: N.B. four times round the race
course to be considered a heat. [racing done on] a large
platform race course, expressly prepared for the occasion,
entirely covering the whole of the stage and Equestrian
Circle.

Even improvements, and yet another change of name to the
New Pavilion Theatre (December 1811), a colonnade to the
frontages, a horse ride and a small gallery over the boxes did
nothing to help.

In February 1812 a newspaper says:

The following is a correct sketch of the present popular Dramatic Horse Stage Piece, now performing nightly at Astley's Pavilion Theatre with rapturous applause:

Baghvan-Ho, a Tartarian chief, who, by his exploits, has become the idol of the surrounding tribes, led on by the homage paid to him, and his own emulative spirit, takes upon himself the title and authority of King of Tartary, and is generally acknowledged as such. This is supposed to have taken place at a period when Blue Beard and Timour the Tartar were in the zenith of their glory. The usurpation of Timour, and the cruelties of the Bashaw, excite a spirit of jealousy and indignation in the breast of Baghvan-Ho who resolves upon establishing his own fame by the destruction of both! Accordingly, Furdoch O'Drogheda M'Gowdu, who, from a slave, has become exalted to the distinguished rank of interpreter, is despatched to Russia, China and the Tribe of Mingals, from each of whom he requests the aid of a renowned chief; upon the arrival of the parties, Baghvan-Ho regales them at a splendid banquet and proceeds on his intended scheme. From this, the observer is led to the castle of Blue Beard, where he arrives in great pomp with Fatima and here he is about to enforce her bestowing her hand upon him, when intelligence is brought that Baghvan-Ho is advancing to attack the walls of his castle, and finding himself too weak to oppose a force so much superior, he has recourse to flight at the solemn hour of midnight, forcing with him the disconsolate Fatima and her sister, with the whole of his attendants. Baghvan-Ho, upon his arrival with his friends at the castle, learning that Blue Beard has fled for safety, sets off in pursuit of the fugitives. He is next seen in his encampment, on the advance upon Blue Beard's retreat, where he is joined by Selim, the favoured lover of Fatima. Blue Beard now arrives at the castle of Timour, and claims his aid against the general enemy, which is readily assented to by Timour who, in the event, becomes enamoured of Fatima, and stealing upon her repose, is about to force her to his wishes; but the arrival of Baghvan-Ho's party prevents his purpose, and joining his forces with those of Blue Beard they ply to resist the enemy. Their united efforts cannot avail; the castle is carried by storm; a dreadful havoc of men and horse ensues, the Bashaw

and the haughty Timour are both slain, and their forces overpowered, while Fatima and Selim are made happy by the
noble and valiant Baghvan-Ho!

In October 1812, now called Theatre Royal Pavilion (Astley's):

The stage is fifty feet wide, fifty feet high, and sixty feet long;
but the scenery and machinery attained to the dramatic
performances &c., only occupies three-fifths of this space,
save and except when the new mechanical equestrian circle
appears, which is precisely forty feet in diameter, and strictly
conformable to theatrical perspective . . .

The season ended on 29 January 1813 and Astley decided to cut
his losses which, it is said, amounted to some ten thousand
pounds, and put the building up for sale. It was bought by Robert
William Elliston for three thousand guineas down and an annuity
of twenty pounds for the rest of Astley's life—not a bad bargain
as he died the following year! Elliston also bought a house in
Craven Buildings which he added to the site. The ground rent
and taxes of the whole was about two hundred pounds a year,
held on lease of fifty-three years from Lord Craven.

Elliston partly re-built and re-modelled the interior as a theatre,
making improvements to attract a superior type of audience. He
opened on 19 April 1813 with the name Little Drury Lane
Theatre on the bills. This was virtually the first minor theatre to
open in central London. The Sans Pareil in the Strand, built by
John Scott for his daughters' *Entertainments* in 1806, did not
become a theatre till it changed hands and its name to the Adelphi
in 1819 (see *Theatres of London*). Elliston's opening programme is
announced in *The Times* 19 April 1813:

Olympic and Musical Pavilion.
This Theatre, established in the year 1806, and the first of
the new establishments, will be open this evening, Easter
Monday, under the new title of the Little Drury Lane Theatre.
The first intended entertainment will be *Love's Perils; or, the
Hermit of St. Kilda*. In Act III a Strathspey by Mr. Ellar and
Miss Green. After which, Sieur Sanches will go through
his performances on the Slack Rope; assisted by Mr. Williams,
as Clown. N.B. Those persons who have hitherto been
disappointed in not witnessing the extra-ordinary effort of

this performer suspending himself from the ceiling, are reminded that after the holiday week, he may be seen at eight o'clock precisely. The pantomime for the present, will be the popularly revived production of *Punch's Festival; or, Harlequin's Christmas Box*, written by Mr. Barrymore, jun. The Theatre has been properly prepared for public patronage, and will be opened with an appropriate address, by Mr. Barnard. Boxes, 5s. Pit, 2s. 6d. Gal. 1s.

The 'embellishments and decorations' were executed by Signor Gente, Mr. Orme, Mr. Smith and Mr. Branscomb.

The new name at once caused trouble with the Patentees of the Theatre Royal up the road, and they immediately notified the Lord Chamberlain that Astley's original licence was really only for equestrian performances, and only when his Westminster Amphitheatre was closed. The result was that the licence was suspended on 11 May by the Lord Chamberlain on the grounds that the performances had exceeded the privileges which it comprehended, and the theatre was closed. Through his influence at Court Elliston obtained a new Burletta Licence, but had to change the name to the Olympic Theatre, which he re-opened in December 1813.

A cutting in the British Museum Scrap-book, hand dated 1 January, 1814, says:

This tasteful and elegant Theatre opened last night for the season . . . The house has undergone very considerable alterations in the internal department . . .

An advertisement in *The Times* of the same date announces:

The alterations of this Theatre having met with universal approbation, and the Entertainments having been received by crowded audiences with the most distinguished marks of satisfaction and applause, will be repeated this evening. According to the fixed arrangements of this Theatre, a new Piece will be produced every Monday, and the amusements of each week will vary. This present evening the Entertainments will commence with a Divertisement, by Miss Green and her Pupils. After which, an Occasional Address will be delivered by Miss Dow. To which will be added, the Grand Melo-Drama called *Blood Will Have Blood*. To conclude with the favourite Interlude, called *The Christmas Holydays, or School's Up.*

This advertisement, the first to appear, seems to imply that the theatre had already been open several nights, and some sources do give this first performance as the 27 not the 31 December.

For the next five years the Olympic gave its patrons mixed programmes of pantomime, ballet, farce and melodrama, all under the heading of Burletta, often supported by other attractions to make up the bills. He maintained a good company, and the theatre began to establish itself.

In 1818 he again partly re-built the theatre at a cost of two thousand five hundred pounds, calling it the New Olympic Theatre, Newcastle Street, the 'New' was later dropped from the bills.

Elliston's preparations for the new theatre are told in *The Life and Enterprises of Robert William Elliston, Comedian*, by George Raymond (1845), a wonderful account of 'The Great Lessee'. He says:

A few evenings previous to the opening, as Elliston was mounting a staircase in his theatre, he was seized by a severe fit; but by timely assistance was soon restored to his accustomed energies. The newspapers having announced this attack as apoplexy, and that the manager still continued in a dangerous state, Elliston addresses a letter to the *Courier*, which, being so highly characteristic, we cannot forbear inserting.

'Sir,—Although I should be reluctant to make unnecessary stir, respecting my temporary illness, you will, I trust, excuse my desire to quiet any public alarm which might arise from the perusal of the paragraphs of yesterday evening. My attack was not of an apoplectic description; but mere exhaustion, arising from the unremitting attention I have been compelled to give in the reconstruction of my theatre, which I pledge myself shall open on Monday next, the 16th, with *unrivalled attractions.*' R. W. Elliston.

Elliston's new theatre was described in a press cutting on 16 November 1818:

The talents of the architect have proved truly successful, and taste and convenience appear to have gone hand in hand to-

wards completion of one of the most brilliant little theatres
in the metropolis. The mouldings round the boxes are light
and elegant, and superbly gilt upon a pale flesh coloured
ground. Over the stage doors is the head of Apollo encircled
with rays of glory, with the lyre underneath, supported by the
tragic and comic muse. The light iron pillars throughout the
theatre have a neat pleasing effect, and are lackered over so
as to resemble the appearance of silver. The boxes are
commodious, with a good lobby behind, and have got sliding
panels to drag up and down when the house is full. The pit is
enlarged; and the gallery rendered so capacious that every
person can see the stage with the most perfect ease. The glass
chandelier in the centre of the house, which is a piece of fine
workmanship, with numerous opaque lamps, and aided by
12 other small chandeliers, renders the tout ensemble of the
house brilliant and attractive. The glare of light which is
complained of at the larger houses is here softened and
becomes more pleasant to the eye. In the centre of the ceiling
(which represents a bright blue sky) is a handsome moulding
most superbly gilt which gives a complete and elegant finish
to the chandelier. The saloon, though small, is most tastefully
fitted up to correspond, and the walls are decorated with
French paper, full of exquisite subjects, finely executed, among
which are to be seen the dancing girls of the East, tiger
hunting, &c. and some delightful picturesque scenery. This
boudoir, almost, as it might be termed, is illuminated by gas
by two splendid chandeliers suspended in the middle of it.
The whole of the building has been designed and executed
under the immediate attention of Mr. Lethebridge of Drury
Lane Theatre; the scenery is also excellent, and painted by
Mr. Greenwood.

In the opening programme, on 16 November, 1818, the manager
himself appeared in *Rochester*, by W. T. Moncrief, who was also
responsible for the operatic extravaganza which followed.

The excellence of the company and the success of the new
play brought money, and a fashionable audience, to the box
office, and with the profits Elliston was able to become the lessee
of the Theatre Royal, Drury Lane, which was on the market
at that time. In his agreement with the Committee of Manage-

ment at the Patent house he was forbidden to be concerned with the running of any other Metroplitan theatre, so he put the Olympic up for sale by auction.

From the particulars of the sale on 13 June 1820 we learn:

> The apparatus for warming the theatre was completed by the Marquis de Chabanne.—Private Boxes = 16 in number . . . Theatre possesses a very comfortable residence in Craven Buildings, communicating with the theatre, and can be used as a wardrobe room. The theatre ornamented on two sides by an Arcade . . .

It did not find a ready purchaser, so Elliston let it jointly to George Reeves, the composer, and a Captain Barlow. They re-opened on 22 October 1820. The theatre was newly embellished, 'and a superb central chandelier, constructed on a new plan, sheds a rich but judiciously tempered light over the whole theatre. A drop curtain, from an original design, has been executed by Hollogan, and presents great correctness of outline and effect of colouring.'

Although they engaged a good company, including William Dowton, Benjamin Wrench and William Oxberry, they did not succeed.

The following year Daniel Egerton tried his luck, and in 1822 Oxberry opened a season. In his hands it proved such a losing concern that one night the company, not having been paid, refused to perform, and the audience had to be dismissed.

During the next three years the names of Frampton, Vining and Cockerton appear at the top of the bills. At least four of its lessees ended in the bankruptcy court! Elliston at Drury Lane, even though he had had Edmund Kean as his chief attraction, had also lost everything he owned, and the Olympic was sold by order of the mortgagee on 27 February 1826, for £5,103. This sum included the building, scenery, wardrobe and all. It was bought by John Scott, who had sold the Sans Pareil, in 1819. At this time the theatre was said to hold 1,300 people, and to measure 50 feet from the stage to the back of the pit, and have a stage width of about 25 feet. The season allowed by the licence was from Michaelmas to Lady Day (29 September to 25 March).

During the summer closure the theatre was again re-constructed and new comforts installed, and for the first time lit by gas. When it re-opened on 6 November, the name Royal Olympic was also first used. For almost the next seventy years the title 'Royal' made its appearance on the bills of each succeeding theatre, at the whim of the then manager. Scott's policy was one of lurid melodramas, to attract quite a different public than before. *Casco Bay; or, the Mutineer of 1727* by Bayle Bernard played over one hundred nights from December 1827. Other titles: *The Wild Boy of Bohemia, Lord of the Castle, Baron French; or, the Dungeons of Magdeburg*, tell their own story. It was not until 1831, under the management of Eliza Vestris, that the theatre, the address still given as Newcastle Street with the Box Door in Wych Street, again became fashionable, and took a leading place in the theatrical world of London. Eliza Vestris was a clever actress and singer, who had established herself as a talented performer and as a vivid personality, both for her ability and her amours. She made her name singing ballads: 'Cherry Ripe' in *Paul Pry*, 1825 and 'Buy a Broom' were both her successes. She had also made a speciality of male parts with Macheath in *The Beggar's Opera* and Don Giovanni in *Giovanni in London*. In 1830 she decided the time had come to try out some of the ideas she had for the reformation of stage scenery and production and she was abetted by James Robertson Planché, the dramatist, designer and antiquarian, who had already put some of his costume reforms into practise. On 3 January 1831 she opened the Royal Olympic, and became the first woman manageress in this country. (She had as partner at the start of her venture, another established actress, Maria Foote.) In her opening address by John Reynolds, she said:

> Nobles and gentle matrons, patrons, friends,
> Before you here a 'venturous woman bends—
> A warrior woman, who in strife embarks,
> The first of all dramatic Joan-of-Arcs!
> Cheer on the enterprise thus dared by me,
> The first that ever led a company;
> What though until this very hour and age,
> A Lessee lady never owned a stage.

Her first programme included four pieces: *Mary Queen of Scots*, (with Maria Foote), *Olympic Revels*, a topical extravaganza by

I*

Planché and Charles Dance, (with Madame Vestris as Pandora, and foreshadowing what we now call revue, which was not to be 'born' till 1893). *The Little Jockey*, (again with Maria Foote), and a burletta *Clarissa Harlow* (with Julia Glover). Definitely the accent was on the female interest.

Leigh Hunt, who seems to have forgotten that the name Olympic Pavilion had not been used since 1813! reported in *The Examiner* 4 January 1831:

> What a phrase is this, the Olympic *Pavilion* and how smoothly it flows over the tongue, especially since a lady has become the *womanager* (for manager we must not call her)! It is truly a 'silken term precise;' for pavilion, besides its implication of draperies and colours, means a moveable habitation; and though the Olympic be a gay and comfortable-looking place inside, it seems, outside, just such a box as Gulliver was carried away in by the Brobdingnagian bird. You seem as if you could lift it from the street.
>
> We do not remember what the interior was, when we last saw it; nor did it appear very probable, when we got in last night, that we should be able to refresh our memory; for we beheld nothing but a crowded lobby, with a multitude of men and hats filling up the spaces over the open backs of the boxes. The house was overflowing. When we afterwards got a view of it, we found one of the prettiest interiors we are acquainted with, a perfect circle all but the stage, with the fronts of the boxes painted in medallions, and the whole presenting an aspect warm and cheerful. The lobbies are not so well. The backs of the boxes are no higher than pews; and although this be convenient for increasing the number of spectators, and perhaps for ventilating the house, yet it is bad for the hearing of those who sit farthest from the stage, and presents obstacles in the way of such as like to have everything smooth and pleasant in the way to the seats they have taken. However, we cannot but think that Madame Vestris has made a good speculation. She has pitched her tent midway (as it were) between city and west-end; will entice the one to come and look for the gaieties of the other, and the sprightly part of the town to come and see what attractions can take place so near the city. At least we hope so; for we cannot see a

woman making the attempt, and two others helping her, and all three of so good-humoured a kind, without wishing them success. If last night is to be a specimen, there is no fear; for there seemed an absolute rush from all quarters. Several noblemen were there; one of the Fitz-Clarences; and various Olympic thunders proclaimed the presence of rival gods. We heard the people complaining, that nobody had respected the box-book. The rush took place, they said, the moment the doors were opened, and those who got possession of the seats were inexorable to the after-comers.

The painted medallions were copied from the work of Francesco Bartolozzi, Vestris's grandfather (she had married Armand Vestris, in 1813 but he deserted her in Paris a few years later).

The decorations were by John Crace, who painted the ceiling to represent a silk curtain drawn tight by garlands of flowers held by flying cupids. A crystal chandelier hung from the centre. The proscenium was decorated with wreaths of flowers. Boxes were added in place of the two traditional stage doors (an earlier attempt to abolish these was made at Drury Lane in 1812 but they had to be restored at the demand of the actors).

During her eight years at the Olympic, Vestris, though always limited to burletta by the ever-watchful Patentees, continued to carry into effect her theatrical reforms, the first important movement toward modern staging, using only extravaganzas and burlesques as her medium. Her extraordinary energy and devotion to the theatre accounted in no small measure for her success. She produced her company carefully: no manager had as yet attempted anything so revolutionary as the custom of serious daily rehearsals. She was careful of every detail of her productions, and when she was not on the stage herself, she would watch the play from a box, checking up on any slovenly performance and assuring herself that the stage effects were as fresh and successful on the last as on the first night. Planché tells us with admiration and surprise that she would re-costume a whole burletta if, in the course of time, it began to look shabby.

Her desire for realism, accuracy, and perfection was so great that it led her into enormous expenditures. When she staged *The Court Beauties*, she went to the trouble of obtaining permission for her scenic artists to study the portraits at Hampton Court. For this same play she bought a certain historic tapestry which had been made by the ladies of Charles's Court, as well as the actual curtains, green with gold embroidery, which had for years covered the Lely portraits at the Palace. Now it was again used to hide her actress-beauties before they were revealed as living pictures on the stage. King Charles spaniels, real silks and laces, and furniture of the period picked up in old shops (no longer painted on the scenery or reduced to essentials) completed an effective and historically accurate stage picture. This was begun nineteen years before Charles Kean, who is often supposed to have started the movement toward realistic staging at the Princess's Theatre.

Matthew Mackintosh, who had been the stage carpenter at the Olympic, wrote in 1866: 'I believe that no more perfect sets were ever seen on any stage'. From him we learn that the stage itself was formed upon a principle then quite novel, being elaborately yet simply built of component parts. Each of these was four feet in depth from the footlights, and divided into six sections upon which were set all the properties for each scene, thus avoiding any awkward changes in sight of the audience. In 1837 Vestris also had her curtain divided in the middle and parting sideways in the graceful looped way, dispensing with the green baize rolled curtain then generally in use.

One of her most important innovations was the introduction of completely boxed-in sets for her interiors. For the first time in England a stage room was given walls and ceiling and furnished according to the standards of reality. Though she is said to have introduced them as early as 1833 there is definite pictorial evidence from *Court-Favour* produced in 1836. Her out-door scenes were equally effective. In order to reproduce Bird Cage Walk in *The Court Beauties* in 1835, she arranged to open the back part of her stage on to a long corridor which led to the adjacent Craven Buildings. This passage was one hundred feet long and she lined it with trees and decorated it with hanging lanterns and real birds in their cages—birds who were incited to sing by their masters who were hidden behind the shrubbery for the purpose. When the ingenious manageress came walking down this miniature Mall, clad as a page of Charlie's household and leading a brace of magnificent buck-hounds which her royal friends at Windsor had lent her, the effect was so lovely that with the applause Vestris forgot all about the sums spent and owed in producing so thrilling an effect.

During her years of Olympic management she produced an astonishing number of new pieces. New burletta followed burletta on her bills, as well as many extravaganzas. After seven years of classical subjects, *The Olympic Revels, The Olympic Devils, The Paphian Bower, Perseus and Andromeda*, and the rest, Planché devised his fairy-tale extravaganzas, (now thought of as pantomimes). These were adapted from the French, and many names still familiar today made their first appearance in the theatre.

In addition to her unceasing efforts as manager and stage director Vestris took the leading part in most of her more important productions. Hers was the guiding hand, the inspiration and the force that made of the Olympic the theatre of the moment. Her superhuman energy never seemed to flag; she was always hunting for new ideas, new music, new stage effects, and new production methods. Her generosity was proverbial, and though she made her actors work as they had never done before, she also paid them well. She gave them a whole week's salary as a bonus on the Saturday before the Olympic opened, a most unusual procedure at the time and probably the first occasion on which actors were paid for rehearsal.

Her company always included established favourites. John Liston, who had partnered her at the Haymarket, was with her in 1833. In December 1836 Charles James Mathews (son of Charles Mathews), made his first appearance on the stage (he was thirty-one years old) as Vestris's leading man in *The Humpedbacked Lover*. The actress (who was seven years older), had found the ideal partner, both on and off the stage, they were eventually married in 1838.

In September 1838 they went on what was to prove an unprofitable trip to New York, the reason, it is said, for their hasty marriage! While they were away the Olympic was managed by Planché for the 1838-39 season, but by 2 January Vestris and Mathews were back at the Olympic in Planché's *Blue Beard*.

They then entered into negotiations for the lease of the Theatre Royal, Covent Garden, and gave their last performance at the Olympic on 31 May 1839. This ended one of the most artistically successful and fashionable managements of its era.

Only two prices were charged latterly, the gallery had been converted to upper boxes with the highest price of admission four shillings, and with the pit at two shillings, it is difficult to see how such a company of established players could be paid and the elaborate productions mounted with the hope of any profit. Always liberal and extravagant herself, and heavily in debt, she seems to have soaked her rich admirers to finance her ambitions. The trip to New York had been planned to recoup some of the losses sustained and the move to Covent Garden was eventually to lead to bankruptcy.

The fascinating story of *Madame Vestris and her Times* is told by Charles E. Pearce (1926) where a full list of her Olympic productions is to be found.

After Vestris left, the Olympic again fell on evil days, and during the next nine years new names at the top of the play bill were frequent. Firstly in February 1840 Samuel Butler, a tragedian, tried presenting the usual comedies prescribed by his licence. He remained for two seasons but by December the theatre was let to amateurs. The theatre was now given on the bills as in Wych Street.

Next came George Wild, who tried cheap prices from April 1841. His policy of popular comedies, dramas of London life and pantomime lasted through to May 1844, when T. D. Davenport (the original of Dickens' Vincent Crummels) took over to star his daughter, Jean. He did not last long, and in October 1845 Kate Howard was trying a 'local' drama, *The Queen of Bohemia*.

In 1846-47 George Bolton became manager for a very unsuccessful regime which came to a sudden end although he had engaged a good company. December 1847 saw Davidson as 'Sole lessee and manager' and 'Henry Spicer as responsible proprietor'. Though the theatre had been freed since 1843 from the restrictions previously imposed, little use had been made of this until now. A strong company was engaged, comprising Isabella Glynn (her first appearance in London), Benjamin Conquest, William Davidge and G. V. Brooke. Brooke was making his first appearance in London as a leading tragedian. His Othello on 2 January 1848 was a brilliant triumph and was repeated for 30 nights. He played Richard III, Hamlet, and in *The Hunchback* and *A New Way to Pay Old Debts*, establishing himself as a popular favourite. But his career was marred by his intemperance and he lost his public before he was drowned on his way to Australia in 1866.

The Olympic at last again enjoyed a modest success. In April Anna Cora Mowatt and E. L. Davenport, the Americans, were here and later Fanny Stirling (who had made her début at the Olympic in 1840) and Alfred Wigan appeared in several light comedies. After a pantomime at Christmas, Davidson's tenancy was drawing to a close when the theatre was burnt to the ground on 29 March 1849.

The Illustrated London News, 31 March 1849 reported:

One of the most rapidly destructive conflagrations that has occurred in the metropolis for some years broke out on Thursday evening, about half-past five o'clock, and resulted in the entire demolition of the Olympic Theatre, and the partial destruction of upwards of a dozen other buildings.

The flames were first seen from the outside of the Theatre by a constable, who lodged at a house in Wych Street, the back windows of which overlooked the theatre. As he was passing upstairs he noticed a dense body of smoke pouring from the roof.

Messengers were instantly dispatched in all directions for the engines, but before sufficient time had elapsed for one engine to reach the scene, the whole of the roof, gallery, and boxes, were in a general body of flames; and so intense did the heat become that six or seven houses in Craven Buildings, with the Pavilion Tavern, in Newcastle Street, and several other houses, caught fire simultaneously.

Numerous engines soon arrived, and not a moment was lost in setting them to work; but, notwithstanding that the supply of water was most abundant, and nearly a dozen engines were in full operation, the flames continued to spread most fiercely in various directions. The firemen mounted the roofs of the houses not on fire, and by that means were enabled to extinguish the flames in the Pavilion Tavern, and also to keep them from spreading further in the direction of Craven Buildings, although it was several hours before the fire in those last-named premises was wholly extinguished. The main body of fire in the theatre continued to blaze until a fearful crash was heard, caused by the falling of the gallery and boxes. This had hardly subsided when the roof fell in.

By eight o'clock the fire was so far got under as to allay all

fear of extension. The following particulars connected with
the origin of the fire were stated to our reporter by a gentleman connected with the theatre. Mr. Sterling, the stage
manager, whilst standing on the stage, had his attention
directed to the curtain, and saw flames running up the lining.
He immediately called the carpenters together, and told them
to cut the leech lines. The men mounted the wings, and having
divided the cords, the curtain partially fell, but the lines still
remaining on the other side of the curtain the flames mounted
upwards into the machinery, and very soon they extended to
the lawn coverings of the boxes and gallery, so that in less than
five minutes every part of the theatre was fired.

The fire is said to have been occasioned by the carelessness
of a boy in lighting the gas at the first wing. The lamps at that
time being turned towards the stage, and the curtain at the
same time being withdrawn, and overhanging the lamps, the
curtain took fire, and instantly communicated it to the wing.
The theatre was insured in the County Fire-office; but nothing
belonging to Mr. Davidson, the lessee, or any of the actors
was insured.

To give an idea of the rapidity of the catastrophe, a Correspondent states that he was passing the Theatre at twenty
minutes after five o'clock, at which time there was, externally,
no appearance of fire; and within half an hour he witnessed,
from the parapet of a house in the Strand, the falling in of the
Theatre roof. The exertions of the Fire Brigade were un-
wearied; but their efforts to save the property were unavailing.

The lesseeship and management of Mr. Davidson have, it
is understood, been successful. His tenancy was fast drawing to
a close, and the performances advertised for Thursday (the
evening of the fire) were 'for the Benefit of Mr. Charles
Bender, and the Last Night but One of the Season'.

The exterior of the theatre was the least sightly of all the
London theatres, and for inconvenience of situation it was
unmatched. The interior was circular in plan, with one entire
circle of boxes, and half-tiers level with the gallery, and the
usual private and stage boxes; and the pit was spacious. Out
of the timbers of the Ville de Paris that this theatre was
erected, the masts of the vessel formed the flies, and they

withstood the fire on Thursday evening until after the roof fell in.

Though an explanation for the fire was given, there was a strong suspicion of incendiarism current at the time.

Plans for a new theatre were soon put in hand to designs by F. W. Bushill and, with the speed accustomed in those days, the theatre was ready for opening on an enlarged site by December of the same year. The new proprietor, Walter Watts, was to become notorious in the annals of fraud. Meantime, *The Illustrated London News*, 12 January 1849 gave a description of the theatre:

The new Theatre has the form of an elongated horse-shoe, with but few projections, so as not to present any interruptions to sight or sound.

The Pit Seats are circular in plan, so that each person looks directly to the centre of the stage. The ceiling and proscenium are *match boarded*, and canvassed for decorations. The height from the Pit floor to the highest part of the ceiling is about 36 feet. The Stalls contain 38 sittings; the Pit will hold from 800 to 850 persons, the Boxes about 200, and the Gallery 700 to 750. The decorations were entrusted to Mr. Aglio, and executed conjointly by him and his son. The ceiling is divided into four compartments, representing the Seasons—each compartment being separated by ornamental designs in the Arabesque style, connected in the centre in an ornament, giving apparent support to the chandelier. The front of the gallery and box tiers is divided into seven compartments, by the gilded and bronzed columns supporting the boxes and gallery. Each compartment in the gallery tier is decorated with arabesque ornaments, within which are introduced masks, musical instruments, and cameos, in *chiaroscuro*, on gold ground. The proscenium is intended simply to form a frame to the decorations of the stage. The decorations were designed and painted in the short space of seven weeks. The stage and machinery were designed and executed by R. J. Strachan, the well-known stage-machinist, who, as he tells us, has designed and constructed the machinery of eight of the principal London theatres. The front of the house is lighted by a large chandelier, manufactured by Mr. Apsley Pellatt. The gas-fittings were put up by Mr. J. Palmer, jun., and present several useful precautionary measures. The exact cost of the theatre has not been arrived at, but it is stated by the architect, Mr. F. W. Bushill, as under £10,000, including the cost of purchasing some adjoining property. The act drop representing an 'Italian loggia opening on a cortille,' was painted by Messrs. Dayes and Gordon, and is a very creditable work.

We quote these details from the *Builder*, wherein also are given some instances of construction peculiarly adapted to secure the safety and comfort of the audience. Among these are two fire-proof (stone) staircases to the gallery, one for entrance and *both for exit*. There are also two ways out of the pit, and a separate way from stalls and boxes—so that the house may be cleared in a few minutes. The whole of the entrances, passages, &c., including staircases (slate) to the private boxes and slips, are fire-proof.

Among the commendable points of management before the curtain of this theatre is the abolition of all fees to attendants, who present gratuitously to each visitor to the boxes, stalls, and pit, a bill of the night's performances. The gratuity system, at the best, insures but an *ad valorem* degree of civility; and we hope soon to see it forbidden in all our places of amusement.

The opening on 26 December had been covered in the same Journal three days later:

This theatre commences the season in gallant style. Mrs. Mowatt opened the house with an appropriate address, which was admirably delivered; after which, the National Anthem was sung; and then *The Two Gentlemen of Verona* acted. The selection of this play may be accepted as an example of the elegant taste which is likely to preside over this management. Mr. E. L. Davenport made an excellent Valentine; Proteus was by Mr. John Ryder; and Miss Fanny Vining (Mrs. E. L. Davenport) appeared as Julia.

Then came the pantomime, *Laugh and Grow Fat; or, Harlequin Nutcracker*—a highly whimsical *mélange*, contrived by Mr. Nelson Lee, in which the fun begins even before the piece—a special drop-curtain having been provided for the occasion, pictured over with 'Nuts to Crack' in abundance. The whole getting-up is excellent; the scenery being, in fact, nothing less than superb. We must not omit, in our great

admiration of Mr. T. Matthews (the clown), to record that
Mr. Cormack was the Harlequin, Miss Malcolm the Columbine, and Mr. Morris the Pantaloon. All did their spiriting
with precision, force, and grace.

The house was crowded with a highly fashionable audience;
and the whole performance testified to the liberality of the
management, giving an earnest assurance of success, as well
as of determination to deserve it.

The next attraction to draw the public was Anna Cora Mowatt's
own play, *Fashion; or, Life in New York*, in January 1850. It was
the first American play to present contemporary life, and had been
produced in New York in 1845. G. V. Brooke joined the company
but the theatre suddenly closed in March and the whole tragic
story of Walter Watts was exposed. He had been arrested for
fraud. E. L. Blanchard writing in *The Era Almanack* in 1879 says:

On Saturday, July 13th, 1850, the public learned that Walter
Watts, lessee of the Marylebone and Olympic Theatres, had
hanged himself that morning in Newgate Prison. After a
protracted prosecution he had been sentenced to ten years'
transportation for defrauding the Globe Insurance Company.
A long time before Mr. Watts became mixed up with theatrical
speculations, he was regarded as a singular and somewhat
extravagant person. He kept his town house, and also a country
establishment near Brighton; and when he came to town he
had his carriage and servants in readiness to take him where
he wished. Although he had a good salary, it was a matter of
astonishment to many how he could keep up such establishments. His defalcations in the Globe Insurance Company
reached, it is said, to nearly £80,000.

The theatre re-opened for a short season in August under the
management of George Bolton with *The Malcontents* by John
Marston and Fielding's *Pasquin*. But by September the new
manager was William Farren. His tenancy was to last till September
1853 and during that period G. V. Brooke and Helena Faucit
appeared in *Philip of France* by Westland Marston (November
1850). Laura Keene made her first London appearance in October
1851. But the seasons, though given with a strong company, were
not strikingly successful until Farren introduced Frederick

Robson to the West End stage. He first appeared at the Olympic in March 1853 in *Catching an Heiress* but it was when he played in Talford's burlesque of *Macbeth* in April that his true worth was first seen. His tragi-comic style took the town by storm. He followed with a burlesque, *Shylock; or, the Merchant of Venice Preserved*, 'a Jerusalem Hearty Joke' and on 24 May he played Jem Baggs in *The Wandering Minstrel*, a farce in which he sang 'Villikins and his Dinah'. He drew all fashionable London for the rest of the season and set the town singing the nonsense chorus of what has now almost become a 'Folk' song.

Alfred Wigan succeeded Farren as manager, retaining Robson in the company. In October a new play by Tom Taylor, *Plot and Passion* was a big success with Fanny Stirling, Sam Emery, Robson and Wigan himself. Robson continued to be the main attraction in various plays and burlesques, including *The Yellow Dwarf* (1854), *Medea* (1856) and *Daddy Hardacre* (1857). The biggest successes of the management apart from Robson were *Still Waters Run Deep*, produced in May 1855, and *A Sheep in Wolf's Clothing* in February 1857: both by Tom Taylor.

Alfred Wigan handed over the management to Robson and W. S. Emden in August 1857. The same policy of dramas and burlesque was continued with varying success for the next seven years. The most remembered play of the era is Tom Taylor's *The Ticket of Leave Man*, produced in May 1863, which ran for 406 nights, the longest run of a play at that date. The success of this was damped by the death of 'The Great Little Robson' in February 1864 at the age of forty-three. Barton Baker says of him:

Robson was a great genius; who that saw him when in the full possession of his powers can ever forget the strange-looking little man with the small body and the big head, who played upon his audience as though they had been the keys of a piano, now convulsing them with laughter as he perpetrated some outrageous drollery, now hushing them into awe-struck silence by an electrical burst of passion or pathos, or holding them midway between terror and laughter as he performed some weirdly grotesque dance? The impression he conveyed in those moments of extreme tension was that of a man over-wrought by excitement to the verge of madness; the wild, gleaming eyes, the nervous twitchings of the marvellously plastic features, the utter abandon to the feeling of the moment, whether it were tragic or grotesque, the instantaneous transition from the tragedian to the clown, were no stage-tricks, but an inspiration, an irrepressible impulse. He was morbidly timid and nervous; he could never realise the great position he had attained, and was ever haunted by a fear that his fall would be as sudden as had been his rise; success had a delirious effect upon him, and to deaden the stage-fright, which he could never overcome, he resorted to stimulants—with the usual result.

Poor Robson, his career was brief as it was brilliant, and its brilliancy was dulled long before the end. He had been famous scarcely seven years when his powers began to fail, and his terror of facing the audience became so great that while waiting for his cue he would gnaw his arms until they bled, and cry out piteously, 'I dare not go on, I dare not!' until the prompter had at times absolutely to thrust him before the footlights.

Emden carried on as manager to the end of the season but in November 1864 Horace Wigan took over 'After extensive alterations and improvements' till 1868. He established a style of play called at the time 'The Olympic Drama', mostly with Henry Neville and Kate Terry in the leads. These included *The Serf* (1865), *Henry Dunbar* (1865) and *Love's Martyrdom* (1866). He also revived *Twelfth Night* with Kate Terry as both Viola and Sebastian (1865). She also played Julia to her sister Ellen's Helen in *The Hunchback* (1860).

Offenbach's *Blue Beard* was first given in English in 1866, the same year Charles Mathew returned to the Olympic in a revival of *London Assurance* with his second wife Lizzie Weston (Mrs. Davenport) in the cast (Vestris had died in 1856). Nellie Farren, later of the Gaiety, was in the company from 1865 to 1868.

Benjamin Webster took over from Wigan in 1868 for one season and revived *The Ticket of Leave Man* among other plays. The next manager was W. H. Liston who, till 1873, presented a mixed number of plays, old and new, which included *Little Emily*, a version of Dickens' *David Copperfield*, *The Princess*, a burlesque by W. S. Gilbert (later to become the libretto for *Princess Ida*), both in 1870. Another version of Dickens' *Nell, or The Old*

Curiosity Shop was produced in 1870 and *The Woman in White* by Wilkie Collins in 1871.

It was not till Liston had left and Ada Cavendish took over in December 1872 that the Olympic had another big success. She played Mercy Merrick in *The New Magdalen* by Wilkie Collins, which ran for 112 performances from May 1873. She was succeeded in September by Henry Neville who was in charge for the next six years. During this period the following were produced: *Clancarty* (164 performances, 1874), *The Two Orphans* (214 performances, 1874 and revived 1878 for another 154 performances), *The Scuttled Ship* and *The Moonstone* (1877). Neville also revived old successes and some classics during his management, which ended in 1879.

For the next few years managements came and went season by season leaving little of note to record. They include Fanny Josephs (1879-1880) during whose time *Brighton* by Bronson Howard was produced with Charles Wyndham in the lead. *Moths* from Ouida's novel was given in 1882. Ada Cavendish was back for a spell till Geneviève Ward played *Meg Merrilees, Medea* and *Forget-me-not* under her own management in 1883 and Mlle. Beatrice and her comedy-drama company were continual visitors. It seemed a 'Woman's' theatre.

Under a Mrs. Anna Conover in December 1883 the programme for a revival of *She Stoops to Conquer* stated the theatre had been:

Entirely re-constructed, improved entrances, &c., from plans, approved by the Metropolitan Board of Works, Designed by C. J. Phipps, Esq., F.S.A. carried out by Messrs. Patman and Fotheringham, Builders. The Decorations (from Designs by Mrs. Conover), and Upholstery by Messrs. Druce and Co., of Baker St. Stage Furniture by Lyon and Son. New Act Drop painted by Mr. W. Telbin.

This manageress remained at the helm till 1886. She presented herself as Lady Macbeth to terminate her regime, but little of interest was produced, except during an interim management by Edgar Bruce when *The Great Pink Pearl* was produced in May 1885. *Alone in London; or, A Woman Against the World* is the title of one of Mrs. Conover's last productions, and tells its own story!

In March 1886 Grace Hawthorne was presenting herself in

A Ring of Iron. Edward Terry leased the theatre from her while his new theatre was being built in the Strand (see number 25), and produced *The Churchwarden* in December 1886. The next lady in charge was Agnes Hewitt in 1887. *The Pointsman* was quite a success and ran 105 performances. She followed this with revivals of old melodramas and let the theatre for a while to Yorke Stephens who tried a play by Rutland Barrington called *Mr. Barnes of New York* in 1888. Fire prevention was uppermost in the minds of both public and management and the programme gave the special precautions available:

This Theatre is the SAFEST in LONDON. Every part has at least two separate exits. There are no tortuous corridors or long passages in which a block could take place; and the Theatre is surrounded on all four sides by open streets.

Each of the Special Exits is kept open and guarded by a Constable ready for use in case of emergency:

Stalls. Special—On the right side into Maypole Alley. Special—On the left into Wych Street. Usual entrance through Grand Entrance.

Dress Circle. Special—On the left side, separate entrance into Wych Street. Special—On the right into Maypole Alley. Special—At the back into Gallery Exit. Usual Grand Entrance.

Gallery. Usual Entrance. Special—At the left into Wych Street.

Upper Boxes. Right into Wych Street. Left into Maypole Alley. Special—Right into Wych Street.

Pit. Usual Pit Entrances. Special—Right into Maypole Alley.

All Parts of the House across Stage into Maypole Alley and Craven Buildings.

Modern science has so far invented only one absolute safeguard against the possibility of an audience being left in darkness. Gas may be turned out and electric currents can be broken. The only final protection of an audience is the provision of lamps totally disconnected from any general supply, and each having its separate lighting power within itself—namely, oil lamps. The Olympic Theatre will be provided with these safeguards in every part of the house, and Miss

Hewitt invites practical scientists to suggest a better means if such be possible, of absolute protection.

In the Olympic Theatre every special exit door will be kept open during the whole of the performance, ready for use in case of emergency, and will be guarded by a constable of the E. Division of the Metropolitan Police specially detailed for that express purpose.

Incidentally this gave an accurate location of the theatre and its surroundings at this time.

Just before it was demolished, in the spring of 1889, John Coleman presented a season at 'Popular prices'. He opened with *East Lynne* and on 18 May presented his own play *A Silent Witness*, which well and truly 'got the bird'. It was off by the end of the week and the theatre closed for good.

It was acquired by Charles Wilmot, speedily demolished, and re-built almost completely. Only part of the main outside wall of the 1849 theatre was used in the new building.

There were rumours of the imminence of the long mooted East Strand improvements, and there is little doubt that the theatre was re-built on a grand scale as a speculation in the hope of substantial compensation should the ground be required.

Meantime *The Era* 25 October 1890 reported:

Some time during November there will be restored to the list of London playhouses the New Olympic Theatre, which, as an example of modern scientific theatre-building, will form a more than ordinarily notable example of what can be done in the way of providing for the comfort and safety of the public in the erection of places of amusement.

The site of the old Theatre has been dealt with by two very rising young architects, Messrs. Crewe and Sprague, who have caused a large modern theatre to be erected by the builders, Messrs. Holliday and Greenwood, who are now quite experts in theatrical building. The result of their joint labours, assisted by other firms in various departments, which will receive due recognition later on, is such as to lead to the belief that the new theatre will be as creditable to themselves as the projectors as it will be satisfactory to Mr. Charles Wilmot, the proprietor, and profitable to Mr. Wilson Barrett, who has become its tenant for a long term. The exterior of the building has been entirely altered; indeed, the greater part of it is absolutely new, only portions of two of the old flank walls now remaining, and these are scarcely recognisable, having been so completely worked in to the new design. The principal front has a decidedly classic character; but what will first strike the visitor is the tremendous array of exit doors, there being no less than seven of these facing Wych Street, in addition to the duplicated exits from the pit and gallery, making seventeen in all. These extend right along the classic front, and are continued throughout the ground level of the added portions which adjoin the entrance. This notable feature is a source of congratulation to all concerned, for, by the special arrangements which have been carried out, the entire auditorium will be able to leave their seats and gain the street in the short space of from two to three minutes, and this is saying much when it is borne in mind that the new house is a very large one, capable of accommodating an audience of thousands. Each level will have exits on both sides of the theatre, and all the staircases are very 'easy going', dangerous curves having been very adroitly avoided. This would render anything like an ugly crush very improbable, if not absolutely impossible. No-one can legislate for a panic-stricken audience; everything in such a case must of necessity be left to chance; designers of large buildings can only take the greatest possible care, and this condition has apparently been more than fulfilled by Messrs. Bertie Crewe and W. G. R. Sprague. Again, the building is fireproof as far as modern science can make it so. The construction of the building is entirely of fireproof materials—concrete and iron being the principal employed; the iron has been reduced to a minimum, and it has been thoroughly encased, so that fire cannot easily attack it. The box-fronts have been constructed of steel girders, from which radiate the iron-work supports, upon which rests the concrete forming the steps which make the gradual rise to the back; this rake is so graduated that the feeling which oftentimes comes to audiences of being perched up so that they fancy they are falling forward is quite avoided; again, in the entire interior there is not a single beam, column, or stanchion to be seen, the view of the stage is, therefore, quite uninterrupted, and the seating arrangements have been so laid out that an excellent view of the stage is obtained by those seated in the remotest parts of the house. The sight line has been most carefully studied, the same remark applying to all parts of the theatre, the gallery being as satisfactorily looked after as the dress circle and upper boxes. The main building has been subdivided into sections, so that it really consists of several buildings in one, these being effectually isolated by fireproof walls between. Thus there is the theatre proper, the dressing-room blocks on either side, and the electric light block. The roofs, with one exception, are constructed of concrete; but that of the stage is timber, it being thought well to construct it in that material, so that, should a fire occur on the stage, the 'devouring element' would have a natural vent, and thus there would be more likelihood of saving the auditorium in such a case. The approach Wych Street is by the semi-circular box-office or through the grand entrance lobby, a splendid hall, measuring 30 ft. by 18 ft., from whence the staircases lead to the stalls, dress circle, upper boxes, and grand saloon. This is the same size as the entrance hall, and like it, it is to be very handsomely decorated, a particularly pleasing effect being produced by the raised decorations in the cove under the ceiling. On this level are the managerial offices, while ladies' and gentlemen's retiring-rooms and lavatories are to be found on every floor, and are all admirably fitted up. Refreshment buffets are equally well placed, and the arrangements for serving and for stores are really admirable. The dress circle itself is on a very graceful curve, and at the back are nine very comfortable private boxes, while the passage-way all around is 4 ft. 6 in. in width. On this level is 'the Prince's' box, with its pretty suite of retiring-rooms, decorated in Oriental style; and this is approached from Wych Street by a special entrance door and staircase. On the dress circle tier there are two proscenium boxes on either side, and these are continued on the next level. The curves of the circles are so schemed that each sets a little back from the other; that is to say, the segment is in each case slightly flattened. This not only adds to the effect, but it also makes the sight line so much better. There is a good promenade at the back of the upper boxes, and even the gallery level has the same provision. The seating capacity is nearly 3,000—viz., gallery, 1,000; upper boxes, 300; dress circle, 230; pit, 1,200; stalls and private boxes, of which there are nineteen in all, about 270. This means a money-holding capacity of about £275 to £300, at ordinary prices. There is safe standing room for 500 more persons. The auditorium is about 55 ft. wide, the depth from the footlights to back of the pit is about 95 ft., and the height from floor to under side of ceiling is about 60 ft. The decorations are entirely in the Louis XVI style; all the ornamentation is in raised *carton pierre* or plasterwork, which is very well modelled, and which will be richly decorated. Electric lights are made to peep out through all points of the design. The ceiling will be a very important item of the decorative scheme, as it should be. It is shaped like an inverted saucer, a huge sun-burner occupying the centre, and electric lights in festoons at intervals all around; the decoration is a tracery of colour, through which will be seen the semblance of a rich blue sky. The four spandrels at the corners are used for decorative groups, and to afford the means of introducing the electric lights, which will also be found studded about the circle and box fronts and depending from the boldly decorated panel in the ceiling over the footlights. The prevailing tints are the shade of rose known as *Rose du Barry* and various shadings of gold, at times bright and at times dull, thus obtaining a brilliant effect of light and shade. The proscenium opening is 30 ft. wide. This is a massively decorated, bold feature formed of columns on double raised plinths in panels enriched, while heavy wreaths of flowers and variegated leaves encircle the columns, which are terminated with very handsome capitals supporting the frieze. The colouring of all this will be principally decorated gold. The stage is a very excellent piece of work. The dimensions of this are: Depth from footlights to back wall, 50 ft.; width from wing to wing, 60 ft., but this width is increased to about 130 ft. by supplemental buildings on either side; the height to under part of gridiron is 65 ft.; thus those elaborate sets and complete changes of scene, for which managers must now provide, can easily be effected here. Rolled-up scenes are done away with, everything going straight up. The stage has two full bridges, one half-bridge, and all necessary cuts. A fire-escape has been specially arranged so that exit can be made through the roof of the stage, and thence over the other roofs to the lower levels in Wych Street. There are more than twenty dressing-rooms, large and small, some very large, but none too small for three or four persons. These are all fitted with lavatories and there are three exits from the stage to the street on two sides of the buildings. The question as to whether the artistes have been looked after may safely be answered in the affirmative, as the ventilation, sanitary arrangements, and other accommodation appear to be excellent. The stage and dressing-rooms will be lighted by electricity; and this has been arranged by Mr. Harry South on a triplicate system which makes failure well nigh impossible. The stage has been laid by Mr. Wood; the curtains, upholstery, and stall lounges or divans, which will be a special luxury, have been made by Messrs. Oetzmann and Co.; Messrs. Vaughan and Brown are responsible for the gas and heating arrangements; while the hydrants, of which there will be plenty, are by Messrs. Shand, Mason, and Co.; and the decorations, which promise to be very attractive, have been executed by Messrs. Allard and Co., of Paris.

Nine adjacent houses and gardens were absorbed into the site to form the stage, which began where the back wall of the old theatre stood. The stage was second only in size, at that time, to Drury Lane. The stage door was in Maypole Court.

The opening of the theatre, under the management of Wilson Barrett, is noted in *The Era* 6 December 1890:

The audience which awaited the raising of the terra-cotta curtains at Mr. Wilson Barrett's New Olympic Theatre on Thursday evening was, for two reasons, favourably disposed towards the forthcoming entertainment. In the first place, the interior was found to satisfy, if not even to exceed, expectations. The occupants of the pit had special reason for the gratitude which they expressed through their spokesman later on. The steep 'rake' of that part of the house, and the excellent seating arrangements in this and other parts of the house, did great credit to Mr. Charles Wilmot's ideas and Messrs. Crewe and Sprague's powers of contrivance. The general effect of the interior somewhat reminded us of that of the Grand Theatre, the bosses of ground glass through which

the rays of the electric light shone with softened radiance
being similar to those in Mr. Wilmot's Islington house. The
fact that the arrangements for exit, both in ordinary and
extraordinary circumstances, had been carefully attended to
was emphasised by prominent labels of direction in all parts
of the house, and it was also agreeable to notice the absence of
any pillars to obstruct the view. When the luxurious plush
curtains divided, and showed the 'set' of the first scene of
The People's Idol, it was easy to believe, as was actually the
case, that the proscenium possessed a width of over thirty-four
feet, and the stage a depth of over fifty. Mr. Barrett's new
theatre is in every way well adapted to the purposes for which
it was constructed, and Mr. Wilmot's ripe experience and
sound judgment have been exercised with excellent and
admirable results.

The audience were eager to welcome back to London an
actor whose services to the native drama have been very valuable, whose personal character is high and unblemished, and
whose elevated rank in his profession has never been in
dispute.

The play which Mr. Barrett and his young collaborator,
Mr. Victor Widnell, have concocted for the opening of the
new house, is not deficient either in variety of incident, excitement, or interest. *The People's Idol* contains many proved
elements of popularity; and when the necessary curtailments
have been made, and, perhaps, some other solution of the
dénouement difficulty have been discovered, Messrs. Barrett
and Widnell's drama may win a very large amount of public
favour. With such excellent acting as that bestowed upon the
play all-round on Thursday, failure would, indeed, have been
almost impossible. Mr. Wilson Barrett, whose toils and travels
have not in the least abated his moral energy, or subdued his
physical vigour, enacted Lawrence St. Aubrey with all his old
earnestness, elevation of style, and histrionic ability. The
manly self-control of some parts of his performance was
advantageously contrasted with that intensity and power
which he at other times displayed; and whether haranguing
riotous workmen, engaging in a wrestling bout with the excit-
able demagogue, or breathing love into the ear of Grace
Duncan, Mr. Barrett's Lawrence St. Aubrey was quite worthy

of this fine actor's well-established reputation. At the close of
the performance Mr. Barrett was called before the curtains
amidst intense enthusiasm, and, in an evidently unstudied
speech, stated that his adoption of lower prices would not
affect the high standard of his entertainments, as he believed
that he could make the theatre pay at the rates upon which
he had decided. He then introduced his young collaborator,
Mr. Victor Widnell, and finally, in obedience to a hearty call,
led out Mr. Charles Wilmot, whose appearance was the signal
for a fresh outburst of applause. The warm friendliness of the
audience, both throughout the performance and at its
conclusion, was unmistakable, and Mr. Wilson Barrett may
be assured that absence has but served to ripen his popularity,
and that by his spirited bid for patronage at the New Olympic
he will secure cordial support from the public of which he is
so popular an 'idol'.

The new play was not an unqualified success and Barrett fell back
on revivals of old favourites: *The Silver King*, *The Lights o' London*,
and a new version of *Belphegor* called *The Acrobat* and *The
Stranger*. He gave up his tenancy in May 1891.

It is significant that, owing to the westward trend of the centre
of theatrical life to Shaftesbury Avenue, the Olympic should
become a white elephant; and that Barrett, after some years in
the wilderness, should have his greatest success in 1896 at the
Lyric Theatre on his return to the West End with *The Sign of the
Cross*.

Murray Carson became sole lessee in August 1891. Grace
Hawthorn who had been associated with Barrett at the Princess's,
revived *Theodora*, and first produced *A Royal Divorce* by W. G.
Wills in September, with Murray Carson as Napoleon and
she playing Josephine. The play was to become the property of the
company manager, W. W. Kelly, who toured it for years after
as a vehicle for his wife, Edith Cole. The next few years are
filled with dismal failures. An opera season run by Signor Largo
in September 1892 ended abruptly, but did give London the first
opportunity of seeing Tchaikovsky's *Eugène Onegin*. The pantomime *Dick Whittington* at Christmas did bring full houses, but
everything else was tried and failed. During August and September
1893 Farini tried Music Hall and the house became the Olympic

Theatre of Varieties. At the end of 1895 the complete Drury Lane 'Autumn Melodrama' *Cheer, Boys! Cheer!* was transferred to make way for the traditional pantomime. This brought a flood of melodramas, mostly naval: *True Blue* (1896), *The Free Pardon* 1897), *Mariners of England* (1897).

In December 1896 Grace Hawthorne had come back with an American version of *Pilgrim's Progress* which seems to have been a mixture of pantomime, scenic tricks and ballet. The manageress herself played Christian, 'The Principal Boy'. It failed, was revised and revived to no effect.

During the spring of 1897 Ben Greet took the theatre for a season of Shakespeare; Nutcombe Gould played Hamlet and Shylock, Louis Calvert and Janet Achurch Anthony and Cleopatra. Calvert was also seen as Macbeth.

'The last scene of all that ends this strange eventful history' was *A Trip to Midget Town;* 'Carl and Theodor Rosenfeld of New York; the theatre entirely redecorated throughout [presents] the Lilliputian Burlesque Company in a grand spectacular and musical play in four acts and eleven Tableaux.' This strange entertainment ran for 90 performances, coming off on 17 November, when the theatre closed for ever. It was not stripped of its fittings until May 1905 but remained derelict and boarded up. It was finally cleared away with its near companions, the Globe (closed April 1902), the Opera Comique (closed April 1899), and the Gaiety (closed July 1903), to make way for the widening of the Strand and re-construction of the whole district, into what we now know as Aldwych and Kingsway.

14
The Opera Comique

Strand
With entrances in Holywell Street and stage door in Wych Street

Opened as the Royal Opera Comique 29 October 1870 with
Les Prés St. Gervais, a play by Victorien Sardou. Preceded by
Un Soir Qu'il Neigeait, a comedy in one act by M. Joltrois and
followed by *Les Forfaits de Pipermans*, a farce in one act by
A. Durv and H. Chivot.
Under the management of Messrs. Leslie, Steele and Norton.
The title Royal was dropped in 1876.
Closed 30 April 1899 and later demolished for the Strand (Aldwych
and Kingsway) development scheme.

THE HISTORY OF THE SITE on which the theatre was built has
already been told in connection with its companion, the Globe
(see Number 5), and does not need repetition here. The remainder
of the ground cleared in 1864, on the half of which the Globe was
built in 1868, was used two years later for the Opera Comique,
another speculative venture.

The theatre's main entrance was at 299 Strand but its frontage
there was in reality the beginning of a passage under Holywell
Street. The theatre, which was built on ground between Holywell
Street and Wych Street (in which it also had entrances), backed
on the Globe Theatre. This led to the nickname 'Theatre Royal
Tunnels' which became associated with the theatre.

The theatre itself was mainly underground—a long flight of
stairs from the Wych Street stage door led to stage level.

The Era duly recorded its opening as The Royal Opera Comique
on 29 October 1870:

It is hardly possible to speak too highly of the new Theatre opened last night under the above title by Messrs. Leslie, Steele, and Norton. For elegance of design and perfect adaptability to the requirements of dramatic art it is not surpassed, if indeed it be equalled, by any existing Theatre. Considering the number of our Metropolitan temples of the Drama it would at first seem that anything approaching to originality of design was simply impossible, yet, upon entering the new Theatre, we are at once struck with an agreeable sense of novelty. Without being a large area, such admirable art has been employed in the architectural plan, and in the elaborate decorations, that the spectator is impressed with a feeling of space and airiness which has hitherto been associated only with our largest Opera Houses and similar establishments. The combination of really high art with the convenience, comfort, and luxuries necessary for a cultivated audience, is so completely carried out in every detail, that we may, without flattery, unhesitatingly pronounce the New Opera Comique—perfection. A brief description will give our readers some idea of the internal arrangements. There is no pit in the ordinary sense, the ground floor being entirely appropriated to stalls, but frequenters of the pit will find admirable accommodation in the extensive amphitheatre, which not only commands a perfect view of the stage, but is so airy and well lighted that the ordinary stuffiness of that portion of the house is entirely avoided. An enclosure running round the pit stalls at an elevation of four feet only, forms a most attractive balcony, which we prophesy will be largely patronised by the fair sex, as a better situation for the display of an elegant toilette could nowhere be found. Above the balcony is the dress circle proper, and there are twelve private boxes, four on each tier, magnificently furnished. The ceiling, slightly arched, has a small dome in the centre for ventilation, and contains a very handsome sun-burner, which alone is sufficient to impart a brilliant light to every part of the house. The proscenium is gracefully supported by winged figures, admirably modelled by Mr. Woodington, above them being a large painting of the story of Sappho, with allegorical representations of Morning, Noon, Evening, and Night. Emblematical panels also enliven the lunettes of the upper

K

circle, the general character of the decorations being of the Genoese-Italian school, a style of art admirably adapted for vivid ornamentation. The prevailing colours are white and gold, chastened by graceful paintings, and by the rich draperies of blue and gold that decorate the boxes. The facilities for exit in case of emergency are very great, there being several entrances from Wych Street and Holywell Street, the principal entrance being from the Strand, exactly opposite the Royal Strand Theatre. The carrying out of this tasteful design reflects the highest credit upon all concerned. The architect, F. H. Fowler, Esq. adopting Mr. Ruskin's famous theory, that the construction of a public building should not be concealed, has produced a Theatre of which he may well be proud; and that the builder, Mr. Reed, of Hammersmith, understands his duties perfectly, may be seen in the solidity and finish of the whole work. Mr. E. W. Bradwell has had the entire management of the decorative department, in which the *carton pierre* and *papier maché* work of Messrs. White and Co., of Great Marylebone Street, forms a most conspicuous feature. Admirable examples of this class of work have been executed by the same firm at many of our principal Theatres; and the ornamental ceiling, proscenium, balcony front, and the whole of the elegant embossed work of the Opera Comique is another triumph for them, and merits our heartiest commendation. The figure painting of Mr. Ballard is elegant and finished in execution and striking in design, and the subdued colouring he has adopted forms an admirable contrast to the richness of the general decorations and to the magnificent upholstery work of Messrs. Villars. The position of the Theatre will puzzle many readers when we write of the principal entrance being from the Strand. In fact, by means of a clever contrivance on the part of the architect and builder, a subterranean passage under the south side of Holywell Street has been made, and forms the communication with the main thoroughfare, passing in its course the famous Holy Well which gave its original name to the street above. Another singular fact connected with the Opera Comique is that the wall which encloses the back of the stage actually adjoins the back wall of the Globe Theatre also. With regard to the entertainments given in the new

Theatre, we may remark that, in addition to comic opera, light and sparkling comedies of the French school will be performed, and the engagement of the celebrated *artiste*, Mlle. Déjazet, from the Theatre Déjazet, Paris, indicates one class of the pieces likely to be produced. It is also, we understand, the intention of the Lessees to vary the entertainments with English musical and dramatic pieces of a sprightly and amusing character. A mixed performance, consisting of a French comedy, followed by a musical extravaganza, or a comic operetta, in English, would be likely, we think, to make a very popular bill of fare, and would have the advantage of not competing with the programme of any other Theatre. This, however, is for the consideration of the Lessees themselves, and we proceed to speak of the present performance.

The entertainments commenced appropriately with the National Anthem, sung with considerable effect by an excellent choir, in which the rich deep notes of one or two bass voices of fine quality told remarkably well. The solos were given by Mlle. Du Maurice and Mr. Heywood. Then came the overture to *Masaniello*, a capital one for the occasion, and well played by the band, after which the curtain rose upon the *petite* comedy in one act by M. Joltrois, entitled *Un soir qu'il Neigeait*. This pretty trifle may be termed a drawing-room comedy, as it is performed with three characters merely. Mlle. Legrand, as the young wife, played with the utmost possible grace and delicacy, and towards the conclusion, when the truant husband, unable to withstand the dullness, is on the point of bolting, her assumed sadness was most cleverly depicted, and was fascinating enough to win back any man, who was not, as Mrs. Brown says, 'a orrid brute.' M. Georges was excellent as Lucien Delcourt, representing most effectively the character of a man of affectionate disposition, who is yet thoroughly bored. Mlle. Davenay, as Suzette, had little to do, but contrived, as a French actress always will, to make one or two effective points, which the audience amply recognised. But the piece upon which the company appeared most to depend for public appreciation was *Les Prés St. Gervais*, by the now-celebrated author Victorien Sardou. In this we cannot help remarking that the audience seemed slightly dis-

appointed. The fame of the author is so great in consequence
of his recent powerful and original dramas that they evidently
expected too much. Beyond a somewhat peculiar part which
gives Mlle. Déjazet scope for her undoubtedly great
abilities the comedy is not very interesting. It was one of the
author's earliest works. Mlle. Déjazet gave ample proof,
however, notwithstanding the cruel march of Time, that she
is still a remarkable and original actress, and by her singing
satisfied the audience that she must once have been a very
perfect *artiste*. Little now remains of the voice that once
delighted overflowing Parisian audiences; but Mlle. Déjazet
makes such skilful use of what voice she has that the effect
was really most agreeable, and justified the hearty encores
which were given. The most amusing piece, and the one
which seemed to please the audience best, was the farce in
one act which concluded the entertainments, entitled *Les
Forfaits de Pipermans*. The house was very full, and was
honoured by the attendance of H.R.H. the Prince of Wales
and other fashionable and distinguished visitors. Altogether
we may congratulate Messrs. Leslie, Steele and Norton,
and we trust the success of the opening night will long
continue.

The presence of Royalty at a première is uncommon. Later, as
King Edward, he graced the new Gaiety Theatre on its opening
night.

The opening season was not a success, but in May 1871 the
Comèdie Française Company made its first appearance outside
France, and naturally their visit caused great excitement in
theatrical circles and with a section of the public.

Later in the year a musical adaptation of Molière's *La Medecin
Malgre Lui* by Richard D'Oyly Carte, under the title of *The Doctor
in Spite of Himself*, brought a name to the theatre which was soon
to become closely associated with its fortunes. The Opera Comique
became the London home of visiting foreign companies, but was
closed for long periods between seasons. Ristori made a re-
appearance here after a long absence in 1873. A series of musical
productions followed and Emily Soldene appeared in opera bouffe
during 1874. Later in the year Richard D'Oyly Carte became
manager of the theatre and he made an abortive attempt to

.tablish English comic opera. One of his later to become famous
mouncements 'To the Public' stated:

> In announcing the re-opening of this elegant Theatre, I wish
> to address to you a few words. It is my desire to establish in
> London a permanent abode for Light Opera, played with all
> the completeness and attention to detail which is recognised
> in the representations given at even mediocre Continental
> Theatres. The difficulties of this task will be appreciated by
> all those who have compared the performances given by
> French and English Companies, and I have no doubt that, at
> first, I shall have to claim a measure of indulgence from you.
> Confident, however, in ultimately arriving at the desired
> result, I beg to submit a programme worthy of your patronage.

'he season was unsuccessful and for a while he returned to the
\toyalty Theatre (see Number 19), where his 'discovery' of Gilbert
md Sullivan, with *Trial by Jury* in March 1875 was to bring him
ack to the Opera Comique in 1877.

Meantime F. C. Burnand (with burlesques) and Charles Morton
with opera bouffe) tried their luck in managing the theatre.

In March 1876, coupled with Offenbach's *Génèvieve de Brabant*,
rial by Jury was revived with several of the original company.

It is strange that D'Oyly Carte and Gilbert and Sullivan should
>e at this theatre independently before they were to bring it
ame and fortune together, but in the year before this was to
appen John Hollingshead transferred his company from the
jaiety Theatre with the burlesque *The Bohemian G-Yurl* and
ther productions. Also in 1876 the title Royal was dropped from
he name of the theatre.

A record of the Gilbert, Sullivan and D'Oyly Carte regime was
iven in *The Era* 15 October 1898 (when the theatre was closing),
nd summarised the story which is to be found, in detail, in all the
nany books on the famous partnership:

> . . . and then in November 1877 Mr. R. D'Oyly Carte took
> possession as manager of the 'Comedy Opera Company,
> Limited,' when the Gilbert-Sullivan series of pieces were
> started the theatre was licensed to Mr. Richard Barker, who
> has been associated with Mr. Carte ever since. The first
> Gilbert and Sullivan opera produced was *The Sorcerer*,

Nov. 17th 1877. In the cast were Messrs. Richard Temple,
G. Bentham, Rutland Barrington, F. Clifton, and George
Grossmith, jun., as he was then; Mrs. Howard Paul, Miss
Alice May, Miss Everard, and Miss Giulia Warwick, from the
Carl Rosa company. On the same evening was put on a new
operetta by Arthur Cecil called *Dora's Dream*. *The Sorcerer*
ran till the middle of May 1878, when on the 25th one of the
greatest successes of all was produced—*H.M.S. Pinafore*,
which filled the theatre till April 1880. In the meantime,
however, *The Spectre Knight*, an operetta, by James Albery,
with music by Alfred Cellier, was done on Feb. 9th 1878, and
Cups and Saucers, by George Grossmith, Aug. 5th. Miss
Emma Howson was the first Josephine, Miss Everard the
Buttercup, and Miss Jessie Bond the Hebe. The gentlemen
were the same, with the addition of Mr. George Power. After
a while Mr. Grossmith gave his drawing-room entertainment
every night at ten called *Beauties on the Beach*. In August,
1879, there was a split in the camp of the Comedy Opera
Company, and certain shareholders, wanting more than
Messrs. Barker, Carte, Sullivan, and Gilbert cared to give,
left the theatre to those gentlemen, who wisely took possession, and produced *H.M.S. Pinafore* on their own account
at the Imperial Theatre, Westminster. But the Imperial
vessel soon sprang a leak, while the Opera Comique ship
sailed merrily along, and at Christmas a juvenile crew was
organised, and every morning, except Friday, the same opera
was represented by children players, Mr. Grossmith giving an
entertainment each afternoon after the opera called *A Juvenile
Party*. On Dec. 16th *After All*, a vaudeville by Frank Desprez
and Alfred Cellier, was added to the programme. Another
piece, *In the Sulks*, by the same writers, replaced this on
Feb. 21st, 1880, and on April 3rd *The Pirates of Penzance; or,
the Slave of Duty*, a melodramatic opera, in two acts, was
produced. There were several additions to the company for
this, including Miss Marion Hood, Miss Julia Gwynne, and
Miss Emily Cross—the latter being replaced by Miss Alice
Barnett during the run. No new piece of any kind was needed
until April 23rd, 1881, when *Patience; or, Bunthornes' Bride*,
took possession of the bills, and Miss Fortescue and Miss
Leonora Braham figured in the company for the first time.

Uncle Samuel, by George Grossmith, preceded the opera, in which also, by-the-way, Mr. Durward Lely and Mr. Frank Thornton played. On Oct. 10th, 1881, the Savoy Theatre was opened, and thence was at once transferred in its entirety *Patience* and company, and Mr. Carte's interest in the Opera Comique ceased.

Vhen D'Oyly Carte left, Richard Barker was joined by John Iollingshead, who again returned to the theatre. In October 1881 hey revived *Princess Toto*, by Gilbert and Frederick Clay, which ad originally been produced at the Royal Strand in 1876. At this ime the theatre was partially re-constructed and re-decorated. A note in the programme states:

A New Exit has been constructed for the Stalls and Balcony Stalls, leading into Wych Street. For Stalls and Balcony Stalls, principal entrance in the Strand, exit by Strand and Wych Street. For Upper Circle, entrances by Strand, Holywell Street, and Wych Street, exits Holywell Street and Wych Street. Gallery and Amphitheatre entrances and exits— Holywell Street and Wych Street.

In May 1882 a 'continuation' of *H.M.S. Pinafore* by Horace Lingard and Luscombe Searelle was produced. A contemporary notice says:

Why, when Messrs. Lingard and Searelle made up their minds to produce a new comic opera, they should have deliberately handicapped themselves by giving us, under the title of *The Wreck of the Pinafore*, a kind of sequel to Messrs. Gilbert and Sullivan's famous work is not very clear. Under other conditions they might have scored a success, but when we see Sir Joseph Porter, and Captain Corcoran, and Ralph Rackstraw, and Little Buttercup, and the rest pacing the deck as of old, without the peculiar fun or the sparkling music, we feel that something has gone wrong; and though Mr. Lingard's lines are not without merit, and Mr. Searelle's melodies are often decidedly pleasing, we grow dissatisfied, and the dissatisfiction increases as we note the hard matter-of-fact way in which the story is finished up. Mr. Gerald Moore as the First Lord of the Admiralty, suffering from love and the *mal-de-mer* is as amusing as the circumstances will allow him to be. Miss Madge Stavart makes an excellent Little Buttercup, and displays considerable feeling in the rendering of her principal song, 'My Heart is Very Sad.' Mr. Arnold as Captain Corcoran, Mr. Breeden as Ralph, and Miss Leo as Josephine, strive heartily to bring about the desired result, and frequent encores somewhat readily taken testify to their success. The piece is prettily mounted, and is given under the direction of the composer.

This strange piece had two acts: 'At Sea.—The Wreck' and 'On Tropical Island.—The Rescue'. It had a very short voyage.

In October 1882 Lila Clay's 'Musical and Dramatic Company composed entirely of Ladies performed evenings of very miscel laneous entertainments which included an all woman orchestr and an operetta *An Adamless Eden*, unfortunately written by tw men! (Saville Clarke and Walter Slaughter).

Various actor and actress managers tried their luck through th eighties with little success. Hilda Hilton, John S. Clarke and th famous American comedienne, Lotta (Carlotta Crabtree) amon them.

By the end of 1884 the theatre was closed and up to let. The proprietors decided on a complete overhaul to attract nev tenants.

The Era, 4 April 1885 tells that:

During the last few months a series of alterations and re-decorations have taken place at this theatre that are calculated to make it one of the most convenient, handsome, and acceptable places of amusement in the metropolis. Approaching the main entrance in the Strand, attention is at once directed to the handsome new pair of lamps in front, and to the magnificent illumination surmounting the doorway. Here a new departure has been made from the ordinary style of exterior theatrical illumination, leaded coloured glass with various emblematical figures painted thereon, being largely employed, and giving an effect at once rich and harmonious. Descending the steps from the main, or Strand entrance, the approach to the reserved portions of the house is through an extensive foyer, which, furnished as it is with comfortable lounges and settees, will form an agreeable resting place during the *entr'actes*. In the old theatre this room was disfigured with a bar counter running its whole length. Under the new management this, to many, objectionable feature has been entirely removed. On the right of the foyer, but entirely separated from it, is the refreshment-room, and on the opposite side a commodious, well ventilated, and spacious smoking-room has been constructed, space having been obtained by the purchase of premises in Holywell Street. The foyer, refreshment rooms, and the passage leading to the stalls have been entirely re-furnished, re-carpeted, and re-decorated. Arriving at the theatre proper the first innovation that strikes the eye is the presence of a pit capable of accommodating 500 people. Those who remember the theatre as originally planned will find that virtually the present pit takes the place of the old balcony. Though the pit has been brought forward considerably into the space originally occupied by the stalls, yet room has been found for 100 *fauteuils d'orchestre*. On the first tier there are two rows of dress circle seats, and immediately behind these are two rows of upper boxes. The tier above is devoted entirely to gallery, the former division of this part of the house into amphitheatre and gallery having been dispensed with. There are twelve commodious private boxes. It should be stated that the entrance to the pit is in Wych Street, and that a new staircase has been constructed to give, in case of panic, an extra exit to Holywell Street. On the ceiling of the theatre will be found four large paintings representing the seasons, while the whole of the auditorium has been re-upholstered, re-seated, and re-gilt. The decorations have been carried out by Mr. Boekbinder. New carpets have been laid, and every effort has been made to promote the comfort of the audience.

The new manager, when the theatre re-opened on 6 April, was David James, but the farce, *The Excursion Train*, 'failed to attract' and by June the theatre was again closed and on offer to any aspiring manager.

Marie Tempest made her stage debut in *The Fay O'Fire* on 14 November 1885, but the following years brought little luck to the theatre. Mrs. Bernard Beer had a season (1887-1888) with *As in a Looking-Glass*, *Ariane* and *Masks and Faces*, but the theatre,

K*

though open most of the time, had no long runs or productions o importance.

In 1891 George Edwardes took the theatre and tried a 'Gaiety burlesque, *Joan of Arc* with Arthur Roberts and Marion Hood which had a good run.

In 1893 the 'New Drama' invaded the theatre with Ibsen' *Brand* (the 4th act only) and *The Master Builder* and the followin; year Mrs. Langtry was not lucky with *A Society Butterfly*. Th theatre by now was mainly used for special matinées and try-outs but in April 1896 comic opera returned with Villiers Stanford' *Shamus O'Brien*. It ran until May but the rest of the year wa dismal in the extreme.

At Christmas 1898 a version of *Alice in Wonderland* was pro duced and on 27 April 1899 *A Good Time; or, Skipped by the Ligh of the Moon* by George R. Sims received the shortest of all firs night notices: 'No!' It opened on Thursday and on the Saturda; it came off.

The theatre which had once again used for this production th title Royal on its programme closed for all time. It awaite demolition for a while, then passed, with its 'Rickety Twin, into limbo under the new Aldwych.

15
The Oxford

The Oxford Theatre, The New Oxford Theatre

Oxford Street
Side entrance in Tottenham Court Road, stage door in Hanway
Street at rear of building.

FIRST BUILDING

Opened as a Music Hall 26 March 1861 with a Grand Inaugural
Concert.
Under the management of Charles Morton.
Partially destroyed by fire 11 February 1868.
Repaired, restored and re-opened 9 August 1869 with a Music Hall
bill.
Under the management of Messrs. Maurice R. Syers and
W. Taylor.
Partially destroyed by fire 1 November 1872.
Repaired, restored and partially re-built on an enlarged site with an
additional frontage in Tottenham Court Road.
Re-opened 17 March 1873 with a Music Hall bill.
Under the management of Maurice R. Syers.
Closed 4 June 1892 and demolished.

SECOND BUILDING

Opened 31 January 1893 with a Music Hall bill.
Under the management of the Oxford Limited (the Newsom-
Smith Syndicate).
Began to present revue and musical plays from 1913 and during the
run of *The Better 'Ole* in 1918 started to call itself the Oxford
Theatre.

Closed 25 September 1920.

Partially re-built, re-decorated and opened as the New Oxfor
Theatre 17 January 1921 with *The League of Notions*, a revu
devised and staged by John Murray Anderson with music b
Augustus Barrett.

Under the management of Charles B. Cochran.

Closed May 1926 and demolished.

Lyons Oxford Corner House built on the site. Closed 196
for conversion by Mecca Limited into a restaurant and plac
of entertainment.

CHARLES MORTON, originally a licensed victualler, ran severa
taverns around London before he settled at the Canterbury Arm
in Upper Marsh, Lambeth, in December 1849. At this momen
the birth of Music Hall was taking place. Edward Winder openec
the Mogul Saloon (later the Middlesex) in Drury Lane ir
December 1847 and Richard Preece at The Grapes, Southwarl
Bridge Road, opened the Surrey Music Hall in November 1848

Morton, though he lived to become known as 'the Father of the
Halls,' dying in 1904 at the age of eighty-five, was not the true
parent, though he was the first to build a hall especially for the
new kind of entertainment—at the Canterbury in 1852 which he
re-built on a grand scale in 1856. The success of Henry Weston ir
Holborn from 1857 (see Number 7), made Morton realise that a
new West End bohemian audience could be attracted from the
Song and Supper Rooms to the Music Hall.

Stuart and Park, in the first history of Music Hall, *The Variety
Stage* (1895) tell the story of how Morton:

> . . . began, metaphorically speaking, to cast his eye around in
> different directions for a suitable site whereon to erect yet
> another temple of variety. While thus prospecting, his
> attention was directed to the old Boar and Castle Inn, which
> stood near the junction of the Tottenham Court Road and
> Oxford Street, and with the adaptability of which to his
> requirements Mr. Morton appears to have been immediately
> smitten. The inn formed one of those old roadside taverns
> which belonged essentially to the days of stage-coaches and
> post-chaises, and which the advent of the steam monarch
> had already begun to wipe out of existence. It dated back to a

period prior to the Great Fire of London, when its spacious yard, around which ran the picturesque gallery peculiar to these old inns, doubtless afforded an excellent opportunity for the presentment of the theatrical and other entertainments which it was usual to give in these places. Down to the reign of Queen Anne, the inn retained all the characteristics of a genuine village hostelry and posting-house. Stage-coach drivers, postboys and carriers thronged its roomy yards, while the traveller found refreshment and accommodation after his twelve hours' tedious and rather hazardous journey from Oxford by the lumbering stage-waggon. Here nightly assembled the wit and wisdom of the rapidly growing district, with perhaps a 'gentleman of Oxford,' or a Tony Lumpkin of the period come up from his paternal acres in some Buckinghamshire hamlet to 'see the town'. At this period the 'village' pound and gibbet of St. Gilas' stood nearly opposite the Boar and Castle, on the south side of the Oxford road; and even at the end of the last century there might yet be seen from the back windows of the old hostelry such vestiges of rural scenery as an orchard, a pond, and a rustic windmill.

The long room on one side of the inn yard was used in the manner of the day for nightly entertainments in the eighteen-forties and fifties. Morton acquired the Boar and Castle and on the ground mainly afforded by the old inn yard built a Music Hall on a grand scale, which he opened with an inaugural concert on 26 March 861. *The Era* 31 March tells of this:

The new building, No. 6, Oxford Street, which has for some time past been in course of erection, was opened to the public on Tuesday evening last, with a grand inaugurative Concert, as a Music Hall and Supper Room. The official description of the hall is as follows:

The entrance from Oxford Street, is through a bold Corinthian portico, thence by a passage, 12 feet wide, 38 feet long, and 16 feet high; the architectural treatment of which consists in detached Doric columns, supporting the entablature, over which spring semi-circular arches. These divide the entrance into so many bays, seen in perspective from the street. The floor is laid with coloured tiles, the pattern following the leading architectural lines. At the end of the entrance-passage, is the grand staircase. The stairs are of stone, with moulded faces, and start on either side, by which access is given to the gallery. The Music Hall is a large lofty room, measuring 91 feet in length, 44 feet in width, and 41 feet high. The width of 44 feet only represents the dimensions between the columns which support the roof; beyond these, there is a promenade 6 feet wide, making the total width 56 feet. The ceiling is coved on to the walls, and springs from the top of an ornamental entablature, supported on Corinthian columns. These columns are not placed at an equal distance from each other but are arranged in pairs, leaving a larger opening between each pair, thereby affording more seeing room. The lines of the columns are carried across the ceiling by ribs, the centre portion of which is enriched by projecting ornaments of elegant design; these ribs are further connected together by large centre flowers fixed in a deep recess. The ceiling ornaments are generally perforated to allow an easy escape for the heated air, through which perforations it is admitted into the roof, and escapes from thence to the open air by means of louvre boarding fixed on the upper part of the roof. To supply the necessary cold air, numerous windows have been left in the outer walls, by which means the supply can be readily regulated. The character we have mentioned respecting the columns, is carried to the gallery points, which is divided by blocks into large and smaller bays. The large bays are decorated with relievo ornaments, while the smaller bays have a projecting shield surrounded by laurel leaves, the whole supported by two small figures. The execution of the works were intrusted to Messrs. White and Palby.

The Corinthian columns of the proscenium appear, by contrast with the Ionic columns, much larger than if isolated. On the right there is a promenade, the whole of which is visible from the Hall. There is also a large cut-glass chandelier over the staircase. In the Hall the lighting is effected by means of twenty eight elegant crystal stars. This character of fittings has been carried out throughout the building by Messrs. Weston and Corel.

The contractors are Messrs. Holland and Hannen, who carried out the works from the drawing, and under the super-intendence of Messrs. Finch, Hill, and Paraire, the architects.

The lighting of the Hall is upon the same principle as that adopted at St. James's Hall viz., by a number of stars—only, in the present case, these stars, instead of being of metal, are handsomely decorated with cut glass. The chandelier over the staircase is an extremely magnificent one of frosted and cut glass, the effect when lighted up being superb to a degree. The Hall appears to be well adapted for sound, and when the various decorations are completed, which, at present, are in a very unfinished state, it will, no doubt, be as fine an edifice of the kind as can be found in London. The Concert which inaugurated the opening, was supported by Miss [Elizabeth] Poole, Mdlle. Parepa [later Mrs. Carl Rosa], Mr. G. Kelly, Mr. [Charles] Santley, Mr. Swift, Mr. George Genge, and many other ladies and gentlemen, who sang several pieces of a popular character, and were received with the highest demonstration of applause. The only novelty in the programme of the evening was a ballad. 'Upon the wide wide sea,' written by Mr. C. Mackay, and composed by Mr. Frank Mori, and sung, for the first time in public, on this occasion, by Mdlle. Parepa, who was warmly cheered. Miss Poole gave 'Wapping Old Stairs,' for the sweet and artless singing of which she stands alone, and Messrs. Swift, Santley, and George Genge also did much to enhance the enjoyment of the audience. Miss Rosina Collins, the violinist, played the 'Carnival de Venise' with her usual skill. The conductor was Mr. Jonghmans, and Mr. E. L. Hime officiated as accompanyist.

The cement covering the walls, which is of a peculiar kind, is remarkable for its great hardness, adding materially thereby to the acoustic properties of the building and was supplied by Mr. J. Cumberland Part.

Stuart and Park add:

Sims Reeves was offered his own terms to come and sing on that occasion, but although at first the celebrated tenor appeared to entertain Morton's liberal proposal, he subsequently thought fit to decline it, expressing, however, at the same time, the greatest interest in the undertaking.

The first Oxford hall, in point of architectural beauty, was one of the finest then existing. One of its chief features the system of lighting employed, the twenty-eight brilliant 'crystal' stars,

were thought very charming and effective but were shortly afterwards superseded by four large chandeliers suspended from the
roof, with smaller ones in the galleries. To the Oxford belongs the
unenviable distinction of being the first London Music Hall to be
destroyed by fire. Early in the morning of 11 February 1868 as
The Era 16 February reported:

A fire occurred at the Oxford Music Hall, in Oxford Street,
by which a great part of the building, one of the finest of its
class in London, has been destroyed. About three o'clock in
the morning a fireman employed to watch the premises found
the stuffed seats in the corner of the gallery opposite the stage
on fire, and the flames rapidly spreading through the cocoa-
nut fibre with which the cushions were stuffed. About the same
time the police saw smoke rising from the building, and
while they were endeavouring to ascertain the cause flames
burst from the roof, showing that the fire had already spread
through the whole interior of the building. The inmates of the
houses adjoining the Hall were at once aroused, and information of the outbreak was sent to the station of the Metropolitan Fire Brigade in Crown Street, and within a quarter
of an hour or twenty minutes after receipt of the call Captain
Shaw and Mr. Bridges, the senior foreman, arrived with the
engines and between forty and fifty firemen. The flames,
however, had made rapid progress. In less than an hour from
the time when the fire was first noticed the greater part of the
roof fell, and with it the great glass chandelier which lighted
the Hall. The stage and balcony boxes were then in flames,
and it seemed that no part of the building would be saved from
destruction. Immediately beneath the Hall are cellars, in
which a large quantity of wines and spirits is stored, and had
the flames reached these the danger to the neighbouring
buildings would have been much increased. But although the
immense roof fell on to the floor immediately over the cellars,
there is no opening made into the vaults. On the arrival of the
firemen fifteen steam and manual engines were at once set to
work, and brought to bear on every part of the burning
building. Several of the engines were conveyed up the main
entrance, and made to play on the interior, in spite of the heat
and smoke which nearly suffocated the firemen. After working

for about three hours, however, they finally extinguished the flames. Of the roof nothing now remains in position but a few charred beams, which sway to the slightest wind, and threaten to fall and add to the ruinous pile beneath. One end of the gallery is completely destroyed. Several of the colossal stone pillars which ascend from the gallery upwards were much damaged, long and deep pieces having been split from them, presumably by the falling roof. The floor is covered with a mass of glass, plaster, burnt wood, and the inflammable cocoa-nut fibre, all saturated with water. Surprise is excited at the fact that the private boxes, immediately adjoining the portion of the gallery most completely destroyed, are comparatively uninjured, the discolouration of the crimson curtains by the smoke at their entrance being the only perceptible damage done to them, and that in recesses of the walls bottles and glasses of every description stand in many cases intact, although some were seen to have been cracked and starred in all directions by the heat. The mirrors at the back of the stage were split and cracked, and the stage itself was heaped up with the rubbish that had desended from the roof. Among it were the remains of two bass instruments, which in consequence of their size and weight had not been stored away with the other instruments on the previous night. The grand piano still stood upright, though charred and blackened, and rendered useless as a musical instrument. With the exceptions mentioned, the whole of the instruments remain uninjured, having been stored in a room not touched by the fire.

As soon as the ruins were sufficiently cool to allow an examination to be made, the surveyors and assessors of losses from the fire insurance-offices met in the Hall for the purpose of ascertaining the value of property destroyed, and, if possible, how the fire occurred. Mr. Morton, the Proprietor of the Hall, stated that he was awoke by the fireman, employed in the Hall, crying out 'Fire.' He at once jumped out of bed, proceeded to the grand balcony just over the principal entrance, when he found smoke in dense bodies issuing from behind the stuffed seats in that part of the building. He at first thought that a bucket or two of water would extinguish the fire, but before sufficient time had elapsed to procure a single bucket the fire seized the cocoa-nut fibre in the balcony, and also the hair and fibre stuffing in the chairs and lounges behind and passed through the back of the ornamental work, which allowed it to extend along the open apertures near the main outer brick walls. It thus gained the south end of the roof, and spread with wonderful rapidity. Mr. Morton stated that the Hall would comfortably seat about 1,800 persons, and that, with the decorations, the building cost £23,000. He believed that if the rebuilding of the Hall was left to him, he could have it fit for opening in a month or five weeks, for the outer walls being so strongly cemented together, he believed that there was no necessity to take any portion of the brickwork down. He believed that some one had left a partially-burnt fusee on one of the seats just under the private boxes, and after smouldering for some two or three hours, it burst forth in flames. The building and its contents were insured for £16,000.

The following is Captain Shaw's estimate of the damage done:

Called at 3.30 a.m. to the Oxford Music Hall, 6, Oxford Street, in the occupation of the Oxford and Canterbury Hall Company (Limited); roof burnt off; balcony and stage severly damaged by fire, rest of building and contents by fire, water, and breakage. 8, Oxford Street, G. Bean, hosier; shop and contents damaged by water and removal. No. 11, Messrs. Lightfoot and Co. brewers; beer cellars under Music Hall and contents damaged by water. 9, Hanway Street, Moses Cohen, china dealer; contents damaged by removal. No. 17, G. Greenwood, jeweller; contents and building damaged by water and removal; insured in the North British and Mercantile, London and Lancashire, Sun, London and Southwark, Northern, and Royal Exchange offices.

If it had not been for the timely arrival of the Fire Brigade, it is very probable that the Music Hall and the buildings in communication with it would have been totally destroyed.

A 'Grand Day and Night Fete for the Benefit of the sufferers by the late Fire at The Oxford' was held at the Crystal Palace on 2 March at which all the famous stars of the period appeared.

Morton gave up the Oxford after the fire, and transferred his

attention to the Philharmonic Theatre, Islington. It was re-built
by its new proprietors Messrs. M. R. Syers and W. Taylor and
re-opened on 9 August 1869. *The Era* 15 August said:

The Oxford Music Hall, incomparably the handsomest in
London, has, of late years, had a chequered existence. It seems
but a short time ago that the line in the contents bill of the
daily papers, 'Destruction of the Oxford Music Hall by fire,'
came with a certain shock upon those who had known the
far-famed establishment in its best days. The Oxford was
not destroyed, as the public were glad to hear, but it was
seriously injured, and ceased to be included among the
places of amusement in London. At one time it was reported
that the Oxford was to be converted into a Theatre, and
rumour had even fixed upon the names of the probable
Managers. But it was reserved for Messrs. Syers and Taylor
to set the question at rest, and to restore the Oxford to the
proud distinction it has always held among the Music Halls of
London. In making the attempt to resuscitate the Hall they
have shown a courage and determination for which they may
fairly claim high credit; and the performance of Monday night
must have assured the public of the new Proprietors' firm
resolve to provide a first-class entertainment for their patrons.
In the first place they have spared no expense to make the
Hall a model of brilliant and elegant decoration. All the
modelling, colouring, and gilding is in excellent taste, and the
lighting is perfect as anything can possibly be. The entrance
hall is, in its new dress, exceedingly pretty, and the accommodation on the ground floor of the building is everything
that could be desired. We perceive the new Lessees have not
provided carpet or matting for the floor in any part of the
building, and we can but think they are in the right, as the
occupants of the stalls and area do not, as a rule, show
themselves sensible of this attention to their comforts. The
privilege is more frequently coarsely abused than valued as it
should be. A sanded floor is more in the style of most Music
Hall audiences than one luxuriously carpeted. The regular
orthodox class of entertainment is given, and, as a foundation,
a good and thoroughly efficient band, under the direction of
Mr. Jennings, is engaged. This liberal arrangement is wisely

made by the Proprietors, and the instrumentalists now at the Oxford are thoroughly competent to undertake any duty. Mr. Jennings is a careful and, at the same time, an energetic conductor, as any one could discover during the performance of a new cantatina, smartly written by Mr. Albert Grey, and entitled *The Apple of Discord*. The subject is, of course, the mythological legend of Paris (Miss Rivers), and the three goddesses, Venus (Mlle. Trebelli), Juno (Miss Gould), and Minerva (Miss Dalato). These ladies are superbly costumed, and are all clever vocalists. Another character, Mercury (Mlle. Anato) has very little to do. The scene is suggested according to the olden custom; and by placards hung up at the back of the stage 'Mount Ida,' 'Sheep Grazing,' and 'A Grove of Orange Trees,' were indicated in this way. To the absence of scenery as enjoined by law Paris neatly referred before proceeding to pronounce who was fairest of the celestials. A few bars of the chorus 'The flocks shall leave,' from *Acis and Galatea*, precedes the appearance of Miss Rivers, who sings charmingly, and makes a captivating and piquant Paris. Her first solo is to the melody of the famous barcarole in *Fra Diavolo*, and throughout the cantatina the music is very well arranged by Mr. Jennings. A duet for Mlle. Trebelli and Miss Rivers was encored, and the *Finale*, led by Miss Gould, as Juno, was likewise redemanded. Raslus, the Roman gyrist, is new to London, and gives a performance of a somewhat novel character. He swings on a rope extended from one side of the Hall to the other, and while in full career hangs therefrom suspended by two loops round his ankles. Raslus was vociferously applauded and recalled for his final exploit, which consists in his leaving the rope when in mid-air and turning a somersault on to the stage. The spectacle of a supple gymnast swinging about over the heads of the visitors is something novel after all. Mr. Leslie, an American *artiste*, and a dry, humourous exponent of Negro eccentricities, came before the English public for the first time on Monday night, and was cordially received. His 'stump oration' produced hearty laughter, and contained an allusion to the false charge made by the police against the three young men in the Haymarket. A candle stuck in a champagne bottle, a huge white jug of water, and the indispensible baggy umbrella, heightened the ludicrous effect of this part of the entertainment. Mr. Leslie is a good dancer and clever performer on that primitive contrivance the bones, and also appears as a singer of Nigger songs. Mr. Raynor is another comedian engaged, and richly merits the honourable title. His grimaces, while playing a solo which may be regarded as a burlesque on the violoncello players of the Concert Rooms, are the perfection of the amusingly grotesque, and his odd appearance in black tights is all in his favour. Mr. Raynor is really funny, and we cannot pay him a higher compliment. Miss Hetty Tracy, a serio-comic vocalist far more feminine in manner and ladylike than the majority of the sisterhood, and second to none in personal attractions, gives, in costume, a vocal medley, and previous to doing so sings two songs in ordinary evening dress. Miss Louie Sherrington, Miss Davies, and Miss Kate Bella appear in the same department. The latter young lady dances with a skipping-rope accompaniment. Mr. St. Albyn, one of the most genuine vocalists ever connected with Music Hall life, is a member of the new *troupe*. Forrest and Sons, the musical Clowns, gave their clever entertainment, and to the great delight of the audience exhibit their remarkable skill in hand-bell ringing. The name of Mr. C. Sydney, a comic singer, also appears in the list of engagements. 'God save the Queen,' solos and chorus, created quite a *furore*, and the last verse was encored. This demonstration was made in favour of Miss Rivers, who sang with wonderful spirit. We are sure the young lady will forgive our cautioning her against the too common error of neglecting the pure and strict pronunciation of the words. After the National Anthem had been sung, Mr. Syers and Mr. Taylor were called forward. Both gentlemen addressed the audience, the latter very briefly. We much regret not having been able to hear a word, from the uninterrupted conversation at the side bar. The Hall was specially licensed to keep open till three o'clock, and as the evening wore on the attendance was numerous. The Acting and Stage-Management is in the hands of Mr. Huxley.

The Hall continued its success (later under the sole proprietorship of Syers), but was once more the victim of fire in 1872, when it was again partially destroyed on 1 November. *The Era* reported on 3 November:

'The Oxford'—certainly the most magnificent Music Hall in London—was yesterday (Friday) morning almost totally destroyed by fire. On Thursday evening the performance by the admirable company engaged took place as usual, but by six o'clock on the following morning nothing remained but the handsome vestibule, the two saloons which flank the Hall, and a mass of charred and blackened ruins. The fire, we understand, was first discovered at 3.55 a.m. by a cabman, who was passing through Hanway Street, and who at once gave the alarm. The situation of the Hall, hidden as it is from the street, favours the probability that some time must have elapsed between the first outbreak and the discovery, so that when the engines arrived the flames had secured a hold which it seemed almost impossible to overcome. Captain Shaw, Superintendents Bridges, Palmer, and others, were among the first on the spot, and as happily plenty of water was forthcoming, the firemen and the salvage corps went to work with a will, and in about a couple of hours succeeded in arresting the progress of the flames. In the afternoon we visited the scene of the disaster, and this is what we saw. The floor of the noble Hall was one confused heap of charred timber, broken glass, iron rods, twisted gaspipes, battered sun burners, fractured slabs of marble, shattered musical instruments, half-burnt chairs, fallen plaster, disfigured ornaments and debris which it is impossible to describe. The stage, the balcony, the private boxes, the massive pillars which formed such prominent features in the architectural beauties of the Oxford, all presented a scene of desolation and disfigurement. Above, nothing stood between us and the sky but the blackened rafters, from which dangled the iron rods used as supports for the trapeze apparatus, generally brought into use in the course of an Oxford entertainment. In the saloons, which, as we have stated, have suffered but little, we were glad to notice that the statues and valuable pictures are almost entirely uninjured. Some valuable music scores, kept underneath the stage, have also beeen preserved, and although several instruments (including the identical frames of the drums which suffered by the fire which took place here during Mr. Morton's Management, about four years ago) have been totally destroyed, the majority have happily been secured. Two servants, who slept in close proximity to the stage, had a narrow escape. The fire had made considerable progress ere they became alarmed, as they attributed the noise of falling rafters to the bustle usually going on in an adjacent brewery. They made their escape eventually by climbing through a window, and by crawling over the tiles of a neighbouring house into the brewery-yard, where they alighted, suffering only from the fright they had experienced. During the day the ruins were visited by the surveyors and assessors of the different Insurance Offices, but no satisfactory conclusion was arrived at as to the cause of the fire.

The following is Captain Shaw's official report:

November 1st 1872, 3.55 a.m.
Called to fire at the Oxford Music Hall, No. 6 Oxford Street, W., Proprietors, Messrs. Syers and Co. The contents and building insured in the Liverpool and London and Globe Fire Offices, and also in the Town and Country Fire Office.

Damage—Body and balcony of Hall nearly burned out, the roof destroyed, rest of building and contents, consisting of refreshment-rooms, dining-bars, the entrance halls, and dwelling houses, damaged by heat, smoke, and water.

Nos. 9 and 10, Hanway Street, Mr. Sampson, jeweller; No. 13, do., Mr. King, perfumer; No. 17, Mr. P. Greenwood, jeweller, buildings damaged by heat and water. Insured in the Westminster and Sun Offices.

We are pleased to be able to add that Mr. Syers, in order to prevent loss to his large and efficient staff, has made arrangements to transfer them to the Canterbury Hall, which he will open on Monday evening. Mr. Jennings, the Manager, commands our sympathy, as arrangements had been made for his annual benefit on the 13th inst., and he will consequently be a sufferer to a considerable extent.

Phoenix-like the third Oxford arose from the ashes, on an enlarged site. A side entrance was made in Tottenham Court Road, leaving a block of buildings on the corner of Oxford Street and Tottenham Court Road around which the Oxford nestled.

The new building was opened on 17 March 1873. *The Era* reported on 23 March:

> The first glimpse of the interior reveals that some important changes have been made, and that without in any degree altering the graceful outlines which in their classic beauty always satisfied the most fastidious eyes. Among the changes and improvements may be mentioned a splendid promenade in place of the boxes, at the back of the balcony. This makes a most agreeable lounge for those who prefer freedom of action and wish to gossip with their friends between the pauses of the entertainment, and from this spot the best view of the stage and the performances can be obtained, while the appearance of the Hall from this point is quite dazzling. A new stage of much larger proportions than the old, with a handsome proscenium, an elegant scene in the back-ground, and a charming drop-scene, painted by Mr. G. A. Gordon, attracts especial notice. The footlights are sunk to the level of the stage, and the orchestra placed somewhat beneath it. The stage altogether is fitted for entertainments of the highest class, and by its increased width displays the performers to much greater advantage than hitherto. Private boxes are made at each end of the balcony, and fixed appliances are let into the ceiling, so as to avoid the unsightly appearance which is caused by making holes in the roof for gymnastic performances. In point of colour and decoration the Oxford may vie with any building in the kingdom. The prevailing tint is light blue, the relievo ornaments white, with stencilled decorations upon the walls, and choice salmon tints filling up the spaces. Mr. Homann, the accomplished decorator of the Mausoleum of the late Prince Consort, has executed this portion with exquisite skill. Considering the short time Mr. Homann has had for the work the effect is remarkable. The building operations have been conducted by Messrs. Holland and Hannen, under the superintendence of Mr. E. L. Paraire, one of the original architects. The Hall was densely crowded, when the band, under the able conduct of Mr. Jennings, played Auber's overture to *The Crown Diamonds*,

after which the National Anthem was given, Mr. J. W. Turner
and Mlle. Du Maurier taking the solos with admirable effect.
Mr. W. Bint then sang a couple of comic songs, which were
received with great favour, and Miss Alice Gillie with 'I want
a handsome Beau,' 'Good-bye, Robin, dear,' and a lively
dance, delighted her admirers. Messrs. Holmes and Gant
in their eccentric photographic scene, as usual, evoked infinite
merriment and applause. Mr. Mark Alberts in his comic
ditties, 'Keep off the Grass,' 'Puss, Puss,' and the song of the
Soldier, 'won golden opinions from all sorts of men'—and
women, for Mr. Alberts is evidently a favourite with the
fair sex. Mlle. Du Maurier was extremely successful in the
scene 'Tacea la notte,' from *Il Trovatore*, and in Levy's
song 'Esmeralda.' Mr. Ryley and Miss Barnum were greeted
with enthusiasm in a comic duet, and their never-tiring
Quaker's duet was heartily encored. During the evening there
had been occasional calls for Mr. Syers, but now there
swelled such a chorus that it was impossible to resist, and
Mr. Syers, coming forward, attempted to speak a few words,
which were, however, drowned by the continuous cheering.
Under great disadvantages Mr. Syers read an address. Owing
to the exuberant enthusiasm of his friends, much of the
address was inaudible; but he could not complain of any lack
of enthusiasm, for the applause was deafening. Mr. Jennings,
the esteemed musical director, was then called for, and
appeared to thank his friends for their reception, although
anything like a speech was quite out of the question. When
this ebullition of feeling had subsided the performances
continued merrily. Miss Jenny Hill came next, and in her
song 'Good-bye at the Door' gained immense applause; as
also in the lively ditty 'The Chap what I calls mine.' The
graceful young lady *artistes* the four Sisters Vaughan appeared
with great success; also Moe Brothers and Miss Emma
Wilson, whose dancing has already made her famous. It will
be seen, therefore, that nothing was wanting to make the
enjoyment of the visitors complete. The band, besides their
admirable rendering of the overture and other selections, was
most efficient throughout, Mr. Jennings proving himself
an able conductor as of old, Mr. W. Bint as the chairman
satisfied all requirements, and with regard to all minor

arrangements for the comfort of the visitors the Oxford has scarcely been equalled in this respect, combining the ease and freedom of a private assembly room with the attraction of a modern and musical temple of the highest class. That the Oxford will enter upon a new career of popularity, eclipsing all previous achievements, seems absolutely certain.

Performances were still once nightly. (The twice nightly system did not become established until the turn of the century.) During the seventies theatres began to give matinées—then called morning performances—the Music Halls followed suit only to find the legality of these challenged under their music and dancing licence combined with that of being licensed premises for the sale of intoxicants. Syers seems to have found a way round the law; a programme announcement in December 1874 said:

> At the desire of many Friends and Patrons of the Oxford, I have willingly undertaken to resume the Saturday Morning Performances, as this can Legally be done by opening the Hall at Five o'clock, and continuing the Entertainment until Seven. During these two hours all the *élite* of the Oxford Company will appear, assisted occasionally by aspirants of ascertained ability only.
>
> The doors will be opened precisely at five o'clock, and the Overture will Play the Audience in; the Artistes following in rapid succession. The Oxford Morning Performances have hitherto occupied only Two Hours and a Half, therefore there will be little diminution in the actual duration of the Entertainment. I trust this arrangement will be favourably received, until an alteration is made in the Act of Parliament under which I hold my Licence.

The success of the Hall continued into what we now look on as the golden age of Music Hall, although still a Hall in the original meaning of the word. It was not till its next metamorphosis that it became a fully fledged theatrical auditorium. By the nineties most of the other Halls had either vanished under the weight of the safety restrictions demanded by the Board of Works in 1878, or were re-built in a more theatre like form.

In the course of time J. H. Jennings, the musical director, became acting manager and finally the proprietor. He sold out to

James Kirk for £27,100 in October 1891, but the following year he too sold his interest. The purchasers this time were a syndicate formed by H. Newsom-Smith to run other London Halls, including the Tivoli and the London Pavilion.

The new proprietors felt the time had come to re-build the Oxford on more modern lines, and it was closed on 4 June 1892 and demolished.

The fires of 1868 and 1872 did not totally destroy the old Oxford and were not as completely disastrous as many historians would have one believe. From the pictures of the first Hall in 1861 up to 1892, and the end of the 'third' building, the interior retains familiar characteristics—in fact the same wood-cut illustrations of the building were used on programmes before and after the fire of 1872!

The fourth building, designed by Messrs. Wylson and Long, and built by Frank Kirk, arose, not from the ashes, for the first time.

Charles Morton laid the foundation stone on 15 August 1892. The new building was opened on 31 January 1893. *The Era* reported:

Music hall entertainment has never been enshrined in a more beautiful interior than that which the public saw for the first time on Tuesday evening, when the new Oxford opened amidst much éclat, after a closure which commenced on June 6th last year. The opening of the doors was eagerly awaited by a large crowd both at the new Tottenham Court Road entrance and in front of the iron-gated vestibules in Oxford Street, and soon after seven o'clock the house was packed. The survey of the chaste decorations of gold, electric blue, and pale pink; of the plush-covered stalls—in a pretty shade of green to match with the handsome tableau curtains—and of the graceful outlines of the dress circle proved at once that the new building was aesthetically perfect. What is of even more consequence, however, to the public and to the directorate is the fact that there is a splendid view to be obtained from every part of the house, which is built on the cantilever principle, entirely doing away with the necessity for supporting pillars. Palms, exotics, and bouquets added to the beauty and brilliancy of the scene, and when Mr. W. G. Eaton's orchestra

of eighteen good men and true began to play the first bars of
'God Save the Queen,' and the curtains parted disclosing the
company on the stage, grouped round an immense floral
horseshoe, the deafening shouts from the gallery for some
minutes prevented Miss Ethel M'Alpine, the well-known
operatic vocalist, commencing her solo. Quiet was soon
restored, however, and the whole of the vast audience stood
while the National Anthem was sung. 'The Queen,' we should
add, had a mixed reception. The programme, of course, on
such an occasion reached festival proportions. Though many
of the higher lights of the music hall are still enlivening
pantomime, enough, and more than enough, stars were
anxious to lend importance to the first programme by
appearing. We missed Albert Chevalier, Herbert Campbell,
and Dan Leno, the former, unfortunately, too indisposed to
appear, and the two latter being prevented from appearing
by their engagements at Drury Lane. They will, however,
seek the suffrages of audiences here later on. Miss Marie
Lloyd for a short time doffed the red cloak of Miss Riding
Hood to sing 'Oh, Mr. Porter,' and to take the earliest
opportunity of reviving in the new building the triumphs
won in the old. Miss Lucy Clarke, too, whose excellent
singing was such a feature of the Oxford entertainments
last year, made her re-entrée to the London variety boards,
and sang with her wonted charm and expression 'You and I.'
Mr. Charles Godfrey celebrated the occasion by introducing
for the first time a scena which tells with eloquent force a tale
of filial devotion. An aged and suffering Siberian captive wins
his liberty by the exertions of his daughter, who throws herself
at the feet of the Tsar, and obtains her father's pardon. The
selection was welcomed with much cordiality. Another
novelty was Miss Fannie Leslie's song which skits the
threatened invasion of the hooped skirt, which was such a
familiar feature of John Leech's sketches in *Punch* some thirty
years ago. Miss Leslie wore the dreaded addition to feminine
costume, the skirt being of pink silk, and a green jacket fitting
close to the figure. Perhaps the good-natured satire of the song
will do more to help John Strange Winter's crusade against
crinoline than hundreds of protests in newspapers. Let us
hope so. There were comedians in galore. Mr. James Fawn

sang his well-known patent medicine ditty, Mr. G. W. Hunter roused the house to laughter in 'All the comforts of a home,' Mr. Tom Leamore repeated his song concerning 'Mary Ann,' Sam Redfern contented himself with a short excerpt from his budget, which fetched the house; Brown, Newland, and Le Clercq played once again their funny and extravagant travestie *Black Justice*, and the Brothers Horne put plenty of bustle into their boxing business, which is supposed to illustrate street life. Harry Pleon, who came late, and who appeared in all the sober respectability of evening dress, treated the audience to a burlesque of the Dagonet ballad; Mr. J. C. Rich contributed his 'Vinder man,' and Mr. Edwin Boyde, who sang a medley, proved once again that he gets more like his father, Mr. J. W. Rowley, every day. Mr. Tom White created a genuine diversion with his 'School up to Date,' and the ventriloquial entertainment of Mr. F. W. Millis was much appreciated. Among the ladies Miss Nellie Navette scored with a plantation song and dance. Another Nellie—Miss Richards—sang 'Where are you going to, my pretty maid?' with piquancy and spirit; Miss Kate James, droll, demure, and dainty, had a big recall for 'Simple Maiden,' a similar honour being paid to Miss Millie Hylton for her 'Rowdy-Dowdy Boys;' Miss Peggy Pryde exhibited her inherited gifts for comedy; the Three Sisters Levey, three fine specimens of womanhood, were heartily welcomed; the Sisters Tilley created something of a sensation by their vigorous dancing and high kicking in skirts; Miss Flo. Bilton looked pretty in an elegant black costume; Miss Florrie Robina appeared as an extra turn; Miss Lily Burnand entertained in lively fashion; Miss Minnie Cunningham danced prettily; and Miss Bessie Bellwood set the house in a roar with 'Good Old Boss.' The specialities included the Ethardos, in their posturing enter-tainment entitled 'Bric-à-Brac;' Mr. Evans and Miss Luxmore, in musical selections on the bells; the Two Macs, in a knockabout show; and the Mitsutas, Japanese acrobats, in an extraordinary and daring exhibition of tumbling. The principal musical attractions of the programme were Mr. Howard Reynolds, who played a cornet solo; Seeley and West, who play several instruments; and the Stavordales, with a selection on banjos. Other entertainers were Harry

Champion and the Sisters Belffrey. At the conclusion of the
entertainment loud calls for 'Brighton' were heard; and that
gentleman speedily came to the footlights. He said that their
kind reception had robbed him of the power to express his
thoughts as he would wish to do. Speaking on behalf of the
directorate of the Oxford, Limited, he assured them that the
programmes presented would be the best possible. Talent
would roll up on that stage like waves upon the seashore. He
ventured to hope from the enthusiasm exhibited that night
that the Oxford had entered upon a successful career, and
concluded his speech by calling for thrcc chccrs for the
directors, an invitation that was heartily responded to. Mr.
Adolph Tressider came from the Pavilion to stage-manage,
and kept up the supply of artists at lightning speed. Some
excellent 'cloths' have been furnished by Mr. Ryan, the view
of Dover and the Horse Guards especially being truthful
reproductions of well-known scenes.

As the 'Gay Nineties' drew to a close so the Music Halls found a
new family respectability. In 1904 Oswald Stoll, with his London
Coliseum, made Variety a new form of entertainment. But
lacking the robust vulgarity of the older Halls, the Oxford was
to remain truer to the old traditions. However, by the time of the
Royal Command Performance at the Palace in 1912, the downhill
slide of the Halls was under way.

In 1913 the Oxford had to let in touring revues and musicals.
In 1917 C. B. Cochran took over and presented Bruce Bairns-
father's war time extravaganza *The Better 'Ole* which ran for
811 performances. During the run in 1918 the name the Oxford
Theatre began to be used but after a few uneventful productions
it closed on 25 September 1920 for conversion into a real theatre.

It returned to the Theatre Lists as the New Oxford Theatre on
17 January 1921 with a spectacular revue staged by John Murray
Anderson, starring the Dolly Sisters, called *The League of Notions*.
The Stage on 13 January reported a preview of the theatre:

at the private view given on Friday afternoon, January 7, to
enable one to take in the details of the changes which have
turned the Old Oxford Music Hall into the New Oxford
Theatre. Before reaching the auditorium of the house, now

radically altered, the visitor has to pass through the successor to the former Oxford saloon, a tastefully adorned lounge or drawing-room, reached by a short passage with walnut panelling, and ornamented with old furniture, with china displayed in cabinets, and with carefully chosen pictures, amongst which one notices works by François Boucher and Jean Baptiste Huet. This charming lounge is but the first of the many novelties to be found at Mr. Cochran's beautiful playhouse.

The dominant note of the decorations carried out so artistically by White, Allom, and Company, may be described as being of dove grey, with gold, with regard to the fronts of the two circles and of the boxes, to which have been added four, with canopies of stretched silk. In these and elsewhere the draperies are of material which might be termed rose-tinted, as well as deep cerise or crimson. Along the dress-circle are hung eight crystal lights, with floral screens or shields, and there are others, of pattern somewhat different, in front of and behind the upper circle. The Oxford pit has disappeared, and with it any coign of vantage for standing room, for the whole of the floor of the house, or parterre, has been converted into comfortable stalls, priced as much as 24s. (tax included) for the evening performance of *The League of Notions*. From these and from the front rows of the dress circle (with charge the same), may be had the best view of the proscenium and of the beautiful dome, which will form the chief glory of the auditorium, of the New Oxford. With the apt elimination of almost every trace of plaster, the proscenium has been skilfully caused to form a single line virtually with that of the boxes and the circles, and if one looks beyond or above any section of the rose-and-white tableau curtain may be observed a globe placed above two medallions of classical design, with, beneath them, the masks of Comedy and Tragedy.

We have reserved for final consideration the blue dome, adorned with golden rays and lighted by some eight or nine silvery and seemingly bewinged stars of varying sizes, from which comes the main illumination of the interior of the house. Some of these glass stars, of butterfly shape, were being hoisted into their allotted positions on Friday, when one was enabled to form the opinion that when their installation is complete and in full working order few more beautiful sights will be presented to playgoers here than that formed by this star-irradiated Oxford dome, the hue of which approximates more nearly to turquoise than to sea-green. To glance at this dome alone thousands are likely to visit Mr. Cochran's new local habitation at the corner of Oxford Street.

The League of Notions ran for 360 performances.

At Christmas 1921 Cochran presented his first pantomime: *Babes in the Wood*, with the Dollys as the Babes, Nellie Taylor and Joyce Barbour as the principal boy and girl, and A. W. Baskcomb as Dame.

A new revue, *Mayfair and Montmartre*, followed starring Alice Delysia. The next success was a musical comedy, *Battling Butler*, in which Jack Buchanan starred and also presented. It ran 238 performances from December 1922.

By this time Cochran had become established with revue at the London Pavilion (which he christened The Centre of the World). He found that the New Oxford was not the success he had hoped; changes of policy at old established places of entertainment, even though new surroundings are created, have never proved spectacularly successful throughout theatrical history.

The New Oxford went over to films for a while in 1922, and the following year Cochran presented a season of French plays, with the Guitrys and Yvonne Printemps, and an Italian season with Elenora Duse. After this an American song and dance show, *Little Nelly Kelly*, ran for 265 performances from July 1923. Then once again came a season of films.

1924 was the first year of the British Empire Exhibition at Wembley, and Cochran thought the many visitors to London should see the work of Lilian Baylis's Old Vic Shakespeare Company in central London. He presented their first West End season from 16 June for four weeks: *The Taming of the Shrew*, *As You Like It*, *Hamlet* and *Twelfth Night*, all produced by Robert Atkins. The company included Ernest Milton and Ion Swinley (who shared *Hamlet*), John Laurie, Florence Saunders, Jane Bacon and Hay Petrie.

After this several productions came and went. In 1925 an Italian company appeared with Ruggero Ruggeri in plays by Pirandello

1. The Royal Panopticon of Science and Art. A watercolour dated 1855, by Thomas Hosmer Shepherd, in the British Museum.

2. *Below*. The Royal Panopticon of Science and Art. A wood engraving from *The Builder*, 1854.

3. The Alhambra Palace. Converted into a Music Hall, complete with proscenium a:
1860. A coloured poster in the Enthoven Collection advertising the exploits of Léot;
immortalised by George Leybourne in his song:

> *He'd fly through the air with the greatest of ease,*
> *A daring young man on the flying trapeze,*
> *His movements were graceful,*
> *All girls he could please*
> *And my love he purloin'd away!*

The Royal Alhambra
Palace. A photograph
showing the re-construc-
tion of Leicester
Square. Taken when
the gardens were
opened on 4 July, 1874.

5. *Below*. The Alhambra Theatre of Varieties. A photograph taken in 1895 showing the restoration of the original frontage remaining after the fire of 1882.

6. The Alhambra Theatre. A photograph of the interior taken in 1897.

7. The Alhambra Theatre. Charing Cross Road entrance built in 1897. A photograph taken in 1904.

8. Daly's Theatre. A photograph taken in 1904.

9. Daly's Theatre. A drawing by Spencer Chadwick, the architect, from *The Builder*, 1893.

10. The Parisian Hall, Saville House. A wood engraving from *Paul Pry*, 1857.

11. *Below*. The Empire Theatre. A photograph taken in 1895.

12. The Empire Theatre. The foyer, the promenade, the grand staircase and the auditorium. A wood engraving from *The Illustrated Sporting and Dramatic News*, 1884.

13. The Strand Musick Hall, 1864. The architect's sectional view of the interior.

14. *Below.* The Gaiety Theatre. Centre of the block between Wellington Street and Catherine Street. A photograph *circa* 1880.

15. The Gaiety Theatre. A wood engraving from *The Illustrated London News*, 1868.

. *Below*. The Strand. A photograph taken in the early 1890s showing the Gaiety
Theatre and Restaurant at the corner of Catherine Street.

L*

17. The Gaiety Theatre with the new Aldwych and widened Strand. A photograph tak
in 1909.

18. *Below*. The Gaiety Theatre. A photograph taken in 1903.

. The Gate Theatre Salon, Floral Street, 1925. A watercolour by A. Campbell in the possession of Molly Veness.

20. *Below*. The Gate Theatre Studio, Villiers Street. A drawing by Hutson from *The Magazine Programme*, 1930.

21. The Globe Theatre. A photograph taken in 1902.

22. The Globe Theatre. A wood engraving from *The Illustrated London News*, 1869.

23. The Royal Amphitheatre, Holborn. Remains of the original frontage next to the Stadium Club. A photograph taken in 1955.

24. *Below.* The Royal Amphitheatre. A wood engraving from *The Illustrated Times*, 1867.

25. Weston's Music Hall. A lithograph published in 1860.

26. The Royal Music Hall, 1892.

27. The Royal Music Hall, 1892.

28. The Royal Music Hall. The new frontage, 1897, from a programme front.

29. The Holborn Empire, 1906. From a programme front.

30. The Holborn Empire. A photograph taken in 1941.

he Holborn Theatre Royal, when the Duke's Theatre (centre). Part of a drawing by
Henry Hodge, 1881. In the Holborn Central Library.

'he Holborn Theatre.
wood engraving from
'he Illustrated London
News, 1866.

33. The Royal Aquarium Theatre, with the entrance to the Imperial Theatre at the end of the building in Tothill Street. A photograph taken in 1895.

34. The Imperial Theatre. A photograph taken *circa* 190

THE LITTLE THEATRE

). The Little Theatre. A drawing by Hutson from *The Magazine Programme*, 1929.

40. *Below*. The Little Theatre. A photograph taken in 1910.

41. The Olympic Pavilion, Newcastle Street, 1806. A watercolour by James Winston, in the British Museum.

42. *Below*. The Olympic Pavilion, Newcastle Street, 1808. The music front to the dances in *L'Ecole de Mars*.

43. The Olympic Theatre, Newcastle Street, as altered, 1813. A coloured aquatint by Daniel Havell from Edward Brayley's *Historical and Descriptive Accounts of the Theatres of London*, 1826.

44. The Olympic Theatre, Wych Street, frontage. An engraving of a drawing made by R. B. Schnebbelie on 20 March, 1816.

45. The Olympic Theatre. As re-constructed 1813. An engraving after R. B. Schnebbelie dated 1816, from Robert Wilkinson's *Theatrum Illustrata*.

46. *Below*. The Olympic Theatre, Wych Street frontage, 1830. An engraving aft Thomas Hosmer Shepherd.

47. The Olympic Theatre, 1849. As re-built in Wych Street after the fire. A contemporary lithograph.

48. The Olympic Theatre, 1849. A contemporary wood engraving.

49. The Olympic Theatre. The saloon, the vestibule, the proscenium and boxes from the dress circle and the façade to Wych Street. A drawing in *The Illustrated Sporting Dramatic News*, 1890.

The Opera Comique, 1870. With the Lock scene from *Found Drowned* (*Our Mutual Friend*). A watercolour by A. Boycott, in Harvard Theatre Collection.

Below, The Strand at St. Mary le Strand with the frontage of the Opera Comique (right). A photograph *circa* 1890.

52. The Oxford. A wood engraving from *The Illustrated Sporting and Theatrical News*, 1861.

53. The Oxford. From a programme front, 1870.

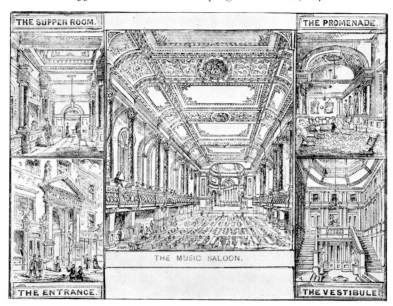

THE SUPPER ROOM.

THE PROMENADE.

THE MUSIC SALOON.

THE ENTRANCE.

THE VESTIBULE.

54. The Oxford. A drawing by Tom Pennell from *Harper's New Monthly Magazine*, 1890.

. The Oxford, before its demolition in 1892. A painting by Walter Sickert in *The Yellow Book*, 1894.

56. The Oxford. A photograph taken in 1904.

57. The Oxford. A photograph taken in 1893.

58. The Pantheon. An engraving dated 1795.

59. *Below*. The Pantheon, 1772. A painting by William Hodges and John Zoffany in the collections of the Leeds City Art Gallery and Temple Newsam House.

60. The King's Theatre Pantheon on the opening night, 17 February, 1791. A watercolour by Thomas Rowlandson, in the collection of N. Q. Radcliffe-Platt.

61. *Below*. The Pantheon, 1830. An engraving after Thomas Hosmer Shepherd.

62. Pantheon Masquerade, 1809. From an aquatint by Rowlandson and Pugin in *The Microcosm of London*.

63. *Below.* The Pantheon Theatre, as re-built, 1813. An engraving from Robert Wilkinson's *Theatrum Illustrata*.

64. The Pantheon Theatre, derelict. A lithograph *circa* 1830.

65. The Pantheon Bazaar. A lithograph published in 1834.

66. The Princess's Theatre. An aquatint published in 1851.

67. The Princess's Theatre, as opened for promenade concerts. A wood engraving from *The Mirror*, 1841.

68. The Princess's Theatre *circa* 1865. A watercolour by A. Boycott in Harvard Thea
Collection.

69. *Below.* The Princess's Theatre. A photograph taken in 1890.

70. The Princess's Theatre. The vestibule, the small foyer, the auditorium, the saloon and the smoking-saloon. A wood engraving in *The Illustrated Sporting and Dramatic News*, 1880.

71. St. Martin's Hall. A wood engraving from *The Illustrated London News*, 1847.

72. *Below*. The opening of St. Martin's Hall. A wood engraving from *The Illustrated London News*, 1850.

73. The Queen's Theatre. A wood engraving from *The London Journal*, 1867.

74. *Below.* The Queen's Theatre. The original entrance remaining as part of Odhams Press. A photograph taken in 1927.

75. The Royal Strand Theatre. A lithograph by J. W. Gear *"Taken from the stage as it appeared on the night of its opening on 26th of January 1832, and the view of the proscenium taken from the pit."*

76. *Below*. The Royal Strand Theatre *circa* 1865. A watercolour by A. Boycott, Harvard Theatre Collection.

77. The Royal Strand Theatre. A Box-office plan, 1885.

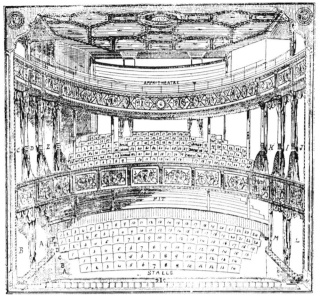

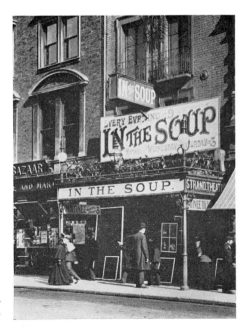

78. The Royal Strand Theatre. A photograph taken in 1900.

79. Miss Kelly's Theatre, 1840. A
contemporary engraving.
80. *Below*. Miss Kelly's Theatre.
A watercolour in the London Museum.
81. *Right*. The Royalty Theatre, 1882
A watercolour by John Crowther in
the Guildhall Library.

. The Royalty Theatre *circa* 1865. A watercolour by A. Boycott in Harvard Theatre Collection.

83. *Below.* The Royalty Theatre. A Box-office plan, 1885.

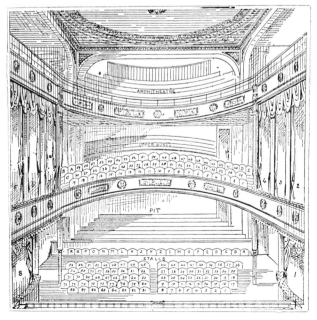

84. The Royalty Theatre. A photograph taken in 1906.

85. The Royalty Theatre. A phot
graph taken in 1913.

. St. George's Hall. A photograph
taken in 1933.

87. St. George's Hall. A wood engraving from *The Illustrated London News*, 1867.

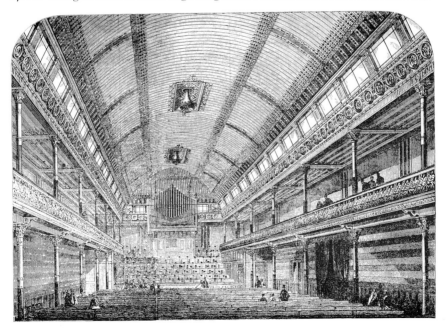

88. St. George's Hall. From a programme of Maskelyne and Devant's Mysteries, 1911.

89. *Below*. St. George's Hall. Converted into a B.B.C. Studio. A photograph taken 1938.

90. The St. James's Theatre. A drawing by W. H. Prior, engraved in *Old and New London*, 1878-80.

1. *Below*. The St. James's Theatre. A watercolour by A. Boycott *circa* 1865, in Harvard Theatre Collection.

92. The St. James's Theatre. A photograph taken in 1902.

93. *Below.* The St. James's Theatre. A photograph taken in 1957.

94. The Sans Souci Theatre, Leicester Place. With colonnade added in 1797. A watercolour in the Guildhall Library.

95. *Below.* The Sans Souci Theatre, Leicester Place. Charles Dibdin's 'Entertainment,' 1796. An engraving after Van Assen.

96. The Shaftesbury Theatre. A wood engraving from *The Penny Illustrated Paper*, 1888.

97. The Shaftesbury Theatre. A photograph taken in 1939.

. Terry's Theatre. A wood
graving from *The Pictorial
World*, 1887.

). Terry's Theatre. The architect's
drawing from *The Builder*, 1886.

100. The Tivoli Beer Garden and Restaurant (left), and the premises to the corner
Durham Street. A photograph taken just before demolition in 1888.

101. The Tivoli. A photograph taken in
1890.

. The Tivoli. A photograph taken
after its re-modelling, 1891.

3. The Polygraphic Hall. Woodin's entertainment *The Olio of Oddities*. A wood
engraving from *The Illustrated London News*, 1856.

104. Toole's Theatre. Entrance, staircase, auditorium, foyer and vestibule. A wood engraving from *The Illustrated Sporting and Dramatic News*, 1882.

The New Queen's Theatre, 1837. A watercolour by R. B. Schnebbelie in the
tminster Public Library. The act drop represents one of the pair of paintings by
ry Dawe on which the play *The Sea* was founded, and produced by Elliott in 1837.

106. *Below*. The Argyll Rooms between 1863-1878. A watercolour by
J. P. Emslie in the Westminster Public Library.

107. The Argyll Rooms between 1863-1878. A watercolour by J. P. Emslie in the
Westminster Public Library.

108. *Below.* The Trocadero Palace of Varieties. A sketch by Oliver Paque
from *The Sketch*, 1893.

and *The Gorilla*, 'a thrilling-chilling-killing mystery, the merriest, maddest mystery play' had a short run. W. A. Darlington's *Alf's Button* was given its second Christmas season, but the end was in sight after a flop musical *Turned Up*, an attempt to show London 'The Famous Denville Stock Company' twice nightly in melo-dramas, finally closed the theatre in May 1926.

The building had been sold to J. Lyons for a new Corner House, which was opened the following year. The Oxford Corner House covered the whole site and in a small way perpetuated the name.

In January 1967 it was announced that Lyons had sold a ninety-nine year lease of the property, from 1 June, to the Mecca organisa-tion, who had applied for planning permission to convert the premises 'for catering and entertainment'. They intend to run them on similar lines to those which they had found successful in their transformation of the Trocadero into Tiffany's (see Number 28).

16
The Pantheon

The King's Theatre, Pantheon, The Pantheon Theatre, The Pantheon Bazaar

Oxford Street
With exits in Poland Street at the side and in Great Marlborough Street at the rear

FIRST BUILDING

Opened as a place of Assembly for Masquerades and Concerts 27 January 1772.
Under the management of Philip Elias Turst.
Converted into an Opera House, the King's Theatre, Pantheon.
Opened 17 February 1791 with *Armida*, an opera by Antonio Sacchini and *Amphion et Thalie ou L'Élève des Muses*, a ballet by D'Auberval.
Under the management of Richard O'Reilly.
Destroyed by fire 14 January 1792.

SECOND BUILDING

Opened as a place of Assembly with a Masquerade 9 April 1795.
Converted into a theatre, opened as the Pantheon Theatre 27 February 1812 with *I Venditore D'Aceto*, a burletta by Johann Mayer and *I Giardinieri*, a ballet by Rossi, followed by *Il Diavolo a Quattro ou Le Donne Cambiate* a burletta by Marcos Portogallo and by *Il Monte Parnasso*, a ballet by Rossi with music by Vittoria Tranto.

Under the management of Joas Caldas.

Closed May 1812 and partially destroyed by fire 12 November 1812.

Re-opened 22 July 1813 as an English Opera House (The Pantheon Theatre), with *The Cabinet*, a comic opera by Thomas Dibdin, followed by *The Deserter of Naples*, a pantomime.

Under the management of James Hill. Finally closed as a place of public entertainment 14 January 1814 and allowed to fall into decay.

THIRD BUILDING

Re-built as the Pantheon Bazaar, opened 27 May 1834.

From 1867 became the offices of W. & A. Gilbey, wine merchants, until 1937 when it was demolished.

A Marks and Spencer's Store now occupies the site.

THE GROUND ON WHICH the Pantheon was built was originally covered by two houses facing Oxford Street, their gardens, and a large piece of waste ground behind, which was enclosed by these gardens and those of houses in Great Marlborough Street and Poland Street. The freehold of this site passed into the hands of Elizabeth Turst in 1732, and descended by 1769 to her nephew, Philip Elias Turst.

In the early seventeen-sixties 'several Noblemen and persons of Fashion' had intimated 'that a place of public entertainment was wanted for the Winter Season similar to that of Ranelagh for the Summer'. Via mutual acquaintances, Turst and 'Persons of Fashion' were brought together, and later in the decade Turst and Mrs. Cornelys (of the famous Carlisle House in Soho Square) were negotiating for such a scheme as was envisaged, but these preliminaries came to naught.

A Miss Ellice 'said to be a person of fortune' and a friend of Turst and his family 'took divers Opportunities in conversations she had with some of the Nobility and other Persons of Rank and Fortune to learn from them whether the Erection or Structure of a Dome, Building or Pantheon for Winter's Evening

Entertainments would be agreeable and likely to meet with the Approbation of the Nobility in General'.

She received a favourable response, which she passed on to Turst and his wife, and 'hinted to him the great Advantage that might probably accrue to them from such a Place of Entertainment'. Turst was 'much pleased', and repeatedly importuned her 'to become a joint sharer or partner with him', to which she agreed.

The first estimated cost of the building was £15,000. This sum to be raised by the sale of shares. The subsequent negotiations and legal proceedings are fully described in the *Survey of London*, Volume 31 Chapter XVIII. Suffice it to say that Miss Ellice eventually withdrew from the agreement. Building commenced in June 1769 to designs by James Wyatt, at a then estimated cost of £28,000. There was a formidable list of shareholders and members of the Committee who Turst found at times rather intractable. At last, after many difficulties during the next two and a half years while the building was in course of construction, the Pantheon opened on 27 January 1772. The building as described in contemporary accounts seems to have been a splendid edifice— the *Survey of London* summarises them and says:

> The large south quadrangle was given over to the great assembly room, or rotunda, and a sequence of vestibules, card-rooms, etc., filled the smaller quadrangle fronting Oxford Street. There, the main doorway, sheltered by a portico, and the two side doorways opened to a vestibule, beyond which were three ranges of rooms, wide between narrow, extending southwards. The vestibule, 50 feet wide and 15 feet deep, was divided by screen-colonnades into three compartments, the middle one having an apse with a door opening to the first card-room. This was circular, some 25 feet in diameter, with three doorways and a fireplace on the cardinal axes, and four apses on the diagonals. On the east and west sides of this card-room were corridors or galleries, each 42 feet by 10 feet, the east one leading to an apse-sided ante-room, forming the axially placed main entrance to the great assembly room. The west corridor led south to the grand staircase, rising in a D-shaped compartment, and thence into the northwest angle of the great room. Between the two corridors

was a smaller card-room, a square with east and west apses, lit by a Venetian window from an oblong area, 10 feet wide, between the two card-rooms.

There is general agreement that the scheme of the great room, or rotunda, was derived from Santa Sophia at Constantinople. This is particularly true of the plan, which was, nevertheless, most skilfully contrived for its purpose and for architectural effect. The great central space was contained in a square of 60 feet, with triangular piers splaying off the corners. On the east and west sides were superimposed colonnades of seven bays, screening the aisles and galleries. The north and south sides opened to short arms, 40 feet wide, terminating in shallow segmental apses. The triangular piers were linked by segmental arches, framing the spreading pendentives of the central dome. The north and south arms had segmental-arched ceilings and saucer semi-domes to the apses, and the ceilings of the aisles and galleries were flat.

However Byzantine the plan, the forms and decorations of the Pantheon were as truly Roman as eighteenth-century taste could achieve. Two superimposed orders were employed throughout the great room, Ionic below Corinthian, the latter being raised on a pedestal with balustrades between the columns. The entablatures of both orders were continued all round the room. The columns forming the screens to the aisles and galleries, and the pilasters flanking the piers, had plain shafts of scagliola imitating 'giallo antico' marble. The walls behind the colonnades were simply treated, with statues placed in niches. Alternately semi-circular and straight-headed, and this treatment was repeated in the upper stage of the large north and south apses. The piers supporting the dome had apses containing stoves in the lower stage, and statues framed in tabernacles above. The soffits of the great segmental arches were coffered in squares alternating with oblongs, the tympana over the east and west screens were decorated with figure subjects in large panels, and each of the pendentives to the dome was adorned with a large oval medallion amid scrolling arabesques. The dome was copied, almost exactly, from that of the Roman Pantheon, albeit in plaster on a flimsy wooden framing, with five graduated rings of twenty-eight quadrangular coffers, each with four sinkings and a central flower, and a wide band of fan or velarium ornament surrounding the glazed oculus.

Below the great room was the tea and supper room, of the same form but divided into five aisles by the piers supporting the floor of the great room. No records appear to exist of the decorations in this room, or in the entrance and card-rooms, other than Horace Walpole's observation that 'the ceilings, even in the passages, are of the most beautiful stuccos in the best taste of grotesque'.

The front to Oxford Street originally designed by James Wyatt, was a charming composition of two storeys, with a central feature of three bays, wide between narrow, slightly recessed between attic crowned pavilions. A Doric portico of three bays, with plain-shafted columns and a simple entablature with a low-pitched pediment, projected from the ground storey. This last had a rusticated face, with a round-arched doorway between two rectangular windows behind the portico, and a round-arched doorway in each pavilion. The upper storey was underlined by a pedestal, with a blind balustrade below the window in each pavilion. These windows were each dressed with an architrave and a triangular pediment resting on scroll-consoles, and set against a face of smooth ashlar. The three bays of the central feature were divided by plain-shafted columns and antae of an engaged Ionic order. In the wide middle bay was a Venetian window, also Ionic, the frieze and cornice of its entablature-impost being continued across each narrow side bay, above a niche with a statue and below an oblong panel modelled with an urn between griffins. There was a full entablature across the central feature, surmounted by an open balustrade, but the pavilions had only the frieze and cornice, and, above the blocking-course, a low attic stage with an oblong window and a pyramid roof.

The site had been extended, during building, to include a house in Poland Street which provided extra entrances and exits to the original design. A second house was added shortly after the opening:

When the Pantheon 'which for some time past had raised the expectations and engrossed the conversation of the polite world' opened:

There were present upwards of seventeen hundred of the first people of this Kingdom; among whom were all the Foreign Ambassadors, the Lord Chancellor, Lord North, Lord Mansfield, Lord and Lady Clive and eight dukes and duchesses. A foreign Nobleman observed, that it brought to his mind the enchanted Palaces described in the French Romances, which are said to have been raised by the potent wand of some Fairy; and, that, indeed, so much were his senses capitivated, he could scarcely persuade himself but that he trod on fairy ground.

Fanny Burney was not quite so enthusiastic, and she was not alone in comparing the Pantheon unfavourably with Ranelagh. She makes her heroine Evelina relate how:

About eight o'clock we went to the Pantheon. I was extremely struck with the beauty of the building, which greatly surpassed whatever I could have expected or imagined. Yet, it has more the appearance of a chapel, than of a place of diversion; and, though I was quite charmed with the magnificence of the room, I felt that I could not be as gay and thoughtless there as at Ranelagh, for there is something in it which rather inspires awe and solemnity, than mirth and pleasure.

The visit which Boswell and Dr. Johnson made to the Pantheon on 31 March 1772, when the subscribers were holding their fifth 'Meeting' or assembly, was later described by Boswell:

The first view of it did not strike us so much as Ranelagh, of which he said, the *'coup d'oeil* was the finest thing he had ever seen.' The truth is, Ranelagh is of a more beautiful form; more of it, or rather indeed the whole *rotunda*, appears at once, and it is better lighted. However, as Johnson observed, we saw the Pantheon in time of mourning, when there was a dull uniformity; whereas we had seen Ranelagh when the view was enlivened with a gay profusion of colours . . .

I said there was not half a guinea's worth of pleasure in seeing this place. JOHNSON. 'But, Sir, there is half a guinea's worth of inferiority to other people in not having seen it.' BOSWELL. 'I doubt, Sir, whether there are many happy people here.' JOHNSON. 'Yes, Sir, there are many happy people here. There are many people here who are watching hundreds, and who think hundreds are watching them.'

For the next few years the Masquerades and Concerts were the haunt of fashionable London. The seasons, during the winter, usually consisted of twelve Assemblies, two Masquerades and twelve concerts all by subscription. Fanny Burney's Evelina relates that:

> There was an exceeding good concert, but too much talking to hear it well. Indeed I am quite astonished to find how little music is attended to in silence; for though everybody seems to admire, hardly anybody listens.

After 1777 the building was also used out of season for exhibitions: Lightning Conductors, Stained Glass and Lunardi's Balloon among them.

The centenary of the birth of Handel was celebrated in great style at the Pantheon in 1784 the concert being attended by over 1,600 people.

Various alterations were carried out to improve the acoustics from time to time, but it is not till 1791 that the story of the Pantheon enters the realm of theatrical history.

The opera house in the Haymarket, the King's Theatre, was burned down on 17 June 1789 (see *The Theatres of London*) and two rival schemes arose for a new opera house, namely a re-building on the old site, which was supported by the Prince of Wales, The Lord Chancellor, Richard Brinsley Sheridan, and the proprietor of the old House, William Taylor, and the building of a completely new theatre on the north side of Leicester Square (see the Empire, Number 3.)

This scheme, the aim of Richard O'Reilly, had the support of the King, the Lord Chamberlain and the Duke of Bedford. O'Reilly had been legal adviser to the mortgagee of the King's Theatre and was deeply involved in the provision of a new opera house. His plans for Leicester Square went awry, but as he held a patent for a theatre from the Lord Chamberlain he had to look for an existing building. His approach to the shareholders of the Pantheon was received with open arms and it was arranged for him to lease the building for three thousand guineas a year and convert it into an opera house. His licence was for four years, to present

Italian Opera. Some £34,000 was spent on conversion to the design
of James Wyatt. The gardens of the houses behind the Pantheon
were bought to enlarge the stage, and a royal entrance in Great
Marlborough Street was planned.

Edward Wyatt, 'a very eminent artist', was paid £685 'for
carving, gilding and ornamenting the inside of the Pantheon'.
Henry Tresham painted the ceiling and the curtain—the latter
representing 'The Apotheosis of Metastasio'. The frontispiece
over the proscenium arch was designed by William Hodges, R.A.,
who was described in a prospectus as 'Inventor and Painter of the
Decorations'.

The Times said that though small in scale 'we may reckon it
among one of the prettiest (theatres) in Europe', while Dr. Burney
considered that 'though many of its internal beauties were hidden
and annihilated, it still was a perfect model of a complete theatre
in its new form'. After a life-time of theatre-going the Earl of
Mount Edgecumbe wrote that 'Mr. Wyatt by this conversion
produced one of the prettiest, and by far the most genteel and
comfortable theatres I ever saw, of a moderate size and excellent
shape, and admirably adapted both for seeing and hearing . . .
On the whole I never enjoyed the opera so well as at this theatre.'

While this conversion was being carried out a new building was
arising on the site of the burnt out theatre in the Haymarket.
Unsuccessful attempts were made to reconcile the two rival
establishments when they were both nearing completion in
January 1791. The Lord Chamberlain's licence being held by
O'Reilly, the King granted the title of King's Theatre to the
Pantheon. With this advantage it opened as the King's Theatre,
Pantheon, on 17 February 1791, with a new opera *Armida* by
Antonio Sacchini and a ballet to make up the evening's entertain-
ment. A contemporary newspaper tells:

> The late hour at which this entertainment concluded last
> night, necessarily renders us very brief in our report of the
> performance. This theatre opened yesterday evening to a
> large and very elegant audience with the charming opera of
> *Armida*, which, besides the original music of Sacchini,
> contains some very fine additional airs of Mazzinghi.
>
> Mara was delightfully in voice, and sung with vast impres-
> sion. Pacchierotti, in his best days, hardly exceeded his

N*

performance of last night. Several of his *cadences* were new and skilfully managed. The new tenor singer Lazzerini is already become a great favourite with the *cognoscenti*; his voice is strong, clear, and melodious, his taste is correct, and his execution remarkably neat. He was vehemently *encored* in one air.

The opera was altogether surprisingly correct for a first night. Of the band, stored with such performers, and with such a leader as Cramer, it is unnecessary to speak with commendation as its merits are so conspicuous.

The printed book is dedicated to Lady Salisbury, by the Manager Mr. O'Reilly, who is the translator, and the version is highly creditable to his poetical conceptions and literary character.

The dances of which we have hardly room to speak, are well composed and were admirably performed. Little Theodore received a fervent plaudit at her entrance. She is increased in bulk but as light and elegant as ever. Madamoiselle Deligny, the new serious dancer, possesses a beautiful person and an expressive face. She is a very excellent performer. Didelot is very much improved and now may rank with the first in his profession.

The dance of *furies* introduced in the Opera had a very striking effect, though some of them were very *clumsy devils* in the management of the torches.

The scenery is peculiarly grand and beautiful and worthy of the pencil of Hodges. The curtain of Tresham appears to be rather softened in some of its stronger tints. It is a noble effort of imagination.

The Dukes of York and Clarence and a long list of Nobility were present.

The Theatre exhibits a beautiful and splendid *coup d'oeil*.

The season ran until 19 July. A complete list of operas and ballet performed is to be found in *The Italian Opera and Contemporary Ballet in London 1789-1820* by William C. Smith [1955].

Meantime the Haymarket opera house was completed, but could only be opened privately to subscribers on 10 March 1791. Only public 'concert' performances of opera were allowed, but this state of affairs was not to last for long.

The second season at the Pantheon opened on 17 December
1791, and on 14 January 1792 the building was almost completely
destroyed by fire:

> About half past one o'clock on Saturday morning, the inside
> of this beautiful building was discovered to be on fire by the
> patroles, who were employed to watch the inner part of it.
> It broke out in a new building, adjoining the Pantheon, which
> had been erected for a Scene-Painter's room. To this part of
> the building, the patroles had no access, so that it is supposed
> the fire had been kindling some time before it was discovered.

An inhabitant of one of the houses in Great Marlborough Street
which backed on to the Pantheon relates:

> I was awoke by the shrieks of females, and the appalling
> accompaniments of watchmen's rattles. I threw open the
> window, and heard the cry of fire. The watchmen and patrol
> were thundering at all the neighbours' doors, and people were
> rushing to their windows, not knowing where the calamity
> was seated. Mr. and Mrs. Siddons, who resided opposite, had,
> *en chemise*, thrown up the sashes of their bedroom, on the
> second floor, and called to us, that the Pantheon was in
> flames.

The fire appears to have started at the north end of the building,
and he and the firemen therefore entered from the south and
gained access to the stage, where they:

> beheld a sight such as few ever witnessed . . . In consequence
> of the cold temperature, the rush of air into the theatre was
> furious. The very large and magnificent glass chandeliers,
> that were suspended from the roof of the building, were
> whirled round; and the vast damask curtains, with which the
> upper parts of the house were enriched, majestically waved,
> like the spacious flags of a first-rate ship of war. Now the
> leathern hose from several engines in Marlborough-street,
> were brought through the passages of the houses, and the
> firemen directed the stream from the branch pipes to the
> boxes nearest the spreading flames . . . But, vain were the
> efforts of these powerful machines. The fire proceeded from
> north to south, and, bursting through the boxes and gallery,

I distinctly saw this finest of modern temples, with its scaglioli columns and gorgeous embellishments, enveloped in flame, which, whirling to the centre of the roof, bursting a passage exposed the interior of the lofty dome. This vast column of fire now finding vent, raged with such irresistible violence, that the firemen, finding their efforts to save the building vain, thought it prudent to retire. No language can describe the awful sublimity of this scene.

O'Reilly was ruined and fled the country. There were rumours that the rival management in the Haymarket had been the cause of the fire, but nothing was ever proved.

Needless to say the licence passed to the other theatre and by an arrangement with the two Patent theatres (Drury Lane and Covent Garden) opera was finally settled in at the King's Theatre and drama at the other two houses as long as their monopoly lasted.

The Pantheon remained a ruin and the shareholders advertised the site to be let on a building lease. At the end of 1792 Crispus Claggett took up the lease and began to clear the ruins.

Claggett, who owned the Apollo Gardens in Lambeth, re-built the Pantheon to his own design, using what he could of the old building. His intention was to provide masquerades and concerts in the principal large room. He re-opened on 9 April 1795 but he met with little success and disappeared leaving a trail of debts.

The shareholders resumed control of the new building and from 1798 to 1810 continued the original policy of concerts and masquerades interspersed with lectures and exhibitions.

In 1810 the building was leased for a projected 'National Institution for improving the Manufactures of the United Kingdom, and the Arts connected therewith'. Although well intentioned the scheme failed to mature and one of its directors sold the lease to Henry Francis Greville, who was proprietor of the Argyll Rooms in Argyll Street, Regent Street. He held an annual licence from the Lord Chamberlain for music, dancing and the performance of burlettas, and occasionally dramatic performances by children under seventeen. He found the Argyll too small for his need and obtained permission to transfer his licence to the Pantheon in July 1811. (He had used the San Souci in Leicester Place for children's performances in 1806.)

Plans were drawn up by Nicholas Cundy to adapt the Pantheon for theatrical performances. Greville found the costs too high for his means and he sold his interest in the Pantheon and his licence to Cundy who, in partnership with Joas Caldas, raised the necessary finance to convert the building into a theatre. Caldas, a Portuguese wine merchant who had been director of the Lisbon Opera, was to manage the theatre.

The conversion, which added more garden ground to the site, made a large theatre and stage, later described as a 'colossal theatre too large for any rational purpose of dramatic representation'.

It opened as the Pantheon Theatre on 27 February 1812 with a mixed bill of burletta and ballet. Difficulties began to appear on all sides. There was a question as to the regularity of the licence even before the theatre opened, and as soon as it did the Lord Chamberlain ordered its closure on the grounds that it was unsafe. Caldas went bankrupt. John Nash, the architect was called in to supervise repairs, as was James Wyatt. Eventually in May the season was resumed; then the manager of the King's Theatre claimed infringement of their licence and in June, Cundy also went bankrupt.

The Lord Chamberlain would only allow a music and dancing licence to Greville, refusing permission for comic opera, allowing only public balls and assemblies and theatrical entertainment by subscription. Greville refused on these terms and the theatre remained closed.

On 17 November 1812 another fire destroyed passages and the lobbies and the vestibule from the Oxford Street entrance.

Repeated requests for a licence were met with refusal. In February 1813 Greville was even refused the terms which he had been offered in 1812. At last Cundy re-opened the theatre as an 'English Opera House' without a full licence—only the original music and dancing one held by the building. The old trick of striking an occasional chord on a piano during a dramatic piece was tried, thus technically making it a musical piece. Continual summonses and appeals kept the theatre alternately open and closed until the Autumn. A pantomime was tried at Christmas 1813 which ended after three weeks.

The musical and dramatic fare presented during this turbulent period was of little import, it was mostly revivals, and the company consisted mainly of little known actors. Once again closed it never re-opened as a theatre although attempts to get a licence were made. Eventually the building was stripped of its fittings in October 1814 and the theatre stood a dismal and empty shell until the end of the lease of the original shareholders expired in 1831.

The freehold now passed to the descendents of Turst's sister and attempts were made on several occasions to sell the building by auction. The last attempt was made in April 1833, and when this also failed to find a purchaser the Trustees leased the building, now in a very bad state of dilapidation, to 'a few gentlemen' who 'decided to erect a bazaar at their joint expense'. Once again extra land was acquired to enlarge the site.

The new building, designed by Sydney Smirke, incorporated the existing Oxford Street and Poland Street entrances and certain rooms connected with them. The Pantheon Bazaar opened on 27 May 1834. Admission was free, the proprietors taking a commission on all sales.

In 1867 the Bazaar was bought by W. and A. Gilbey, the wine and spirit merchants, and converted into their head office. They remained in possession until 1937, when they sold the property to Marks and Spencer. The building was then completely demolished and the present store erected.

It was hoped to save the Oxford Street façade which had survived since 1772 (with alterations by Claggett and Smirke). It was dismantled and the stones numbered for future re-erection, but unfortunately the plan came to nothing; the war intervened and the stones disappeared into oblivion.

Four volumes of newspaper cuttings, manuscript notes, playbills, auction particulars and prints covering the whole history of the Pantheon, which appear to have been compiled by successive owners through the ages, remained in the possession of Messrs. Gilbey until 1960 when they were handed over to the Authors' Collection.

17

The Princess's Theatre

The Royal Bazaar, the Queen's Bazaar, the Court Theatre

Oxford Street

Entrance in a block of buildings between Winsley Street (Pit and Gallery Entrances) and Adam and Eve Court, with the Stage Door in Castle Street (later re-named Eastcastle Street), at the rear of the building

FIRST BUILDING

Opened spring 1828 as the Royal Bazaar, British Diorama and Exhibition of Works of Art.
Burnt down 28 May 1829

SECOND BUILDING

Re-built 1830 and known from 1831 as the Queen's Bazaar.
Conversion into a theatre began in 1836. This to be known as the Court Theatre, but not completed and licensed until 1840, when it opened as the Princess's Theatre, 30 September 1840 with a season of promenade concerts.
Under the management of Thomas Hamlet.
Re-modelled and opened as an Opera House, the Princess' Theatre, 26 December 1842 with an address by Henry Wallack, followed by *La Sonnambula*, an opera by Vincenzio Bellini, concluding with *The Yellow Dwarf*, a burletta by Gilbert à'Beckett
Under the management of J. M. Maddox.
(The apostrophe 's was added again to the name later in the year.)

Became the Royal Princess's Theatre, under the management of
Charles Kean and Robert Keeley, 28 September 1850.
Closed 19 May 1880 and demolished.

SECOND THEATRE

Opened as the Royal Princess's Theatre 6 November 1880 with
Hamlet (Edwin Booth Season) preceded by *An Old Master*, a
one act comedy by Henry Arthur Jones.
Under the management of Walter Gooch.
Closed October 1902. After remaining empty until 1905, the front
and vestibule converted into shop premises, and the auditorium,
etc. used for storage.
Demolished in 1931.
Woolworth's Stores with an enlarged frontage in Oxford Street,
now covers the site. The offices above, entered from Eastcastle
Street, are called Princess House, perpetuating the name.

THE ROYAL BAZAAR, British Diorama and Exhibition of Works of
Art, was built on ground at the rear of Number 73 (later re-
numbered 152), Oxford Street, called White Lion Yard. The
entrance in Oxford Street was in a block bounded by Winsley
Street and Adam and Eve Court with Castle Street (now re-
named Eastcastle Street) at the rear.

It was opened in the spring of 1828 'Under the special patronage of His Majesty George IV'. It was the first attempt ever made
to combine, with other attractions, stalls for the disposal of fancy
articles which had been considered a novelty at the Bazaar in
Soho Square when opened in 1816. The undertaking was the
speculation of Thames Hamlet, a well known silversmith and
jeweller in Princes Street, Piccadilly. The Diorama originally
consisted of four large pictures by Clarkson Stanfield and David
Roberts, and represented the 'Lake of Maggiore in Italy', the
'Interior of St. George's Chapel, Windsor', the 'Wreck of an
Indiaman and Storm on the Coast', and the 'Ruins of Tintern
Abbey by Moonlight'. The speculation was not immediately
successful but after the first year the attendance largely increased.
On the 27 May 1829 the Bazaar was unfortunately almost entirely

burned to the ground, with all its valuable pictures. The fire originated in the Diorama gallery, and was supposed to have been caused by the flame of some turpentine communicating with a transparency near which it was placed. The loss was estimated at fifty thousand pounds.

With a speed surprising in these days, two rooms which had escaped damage were re-opened by July and according to an advertisement, the completely re-built Bazaar was ready by 1830.

Ramsey Richard Reinagle occupied the Rooms for a while. Then once again a Diorama was installed. In 1831 the name was changed, in honour of Queen Adelaide, to the Queen's Bazaar. It was here that the famous Charles Mathews Collection of Theatrical Paintings (now in the Garrick Club), were exhibited in 1833.

Unfortunately the Bazaar was not a complete success. The original Soho Bazaar and the newly re-built Pantheon, opened as a Bazaar in 1834, were formidable opposition.

The property was put up for sale in March 1836, but failed to find a buyer and 'At length' *The Mirror of Literature, Amusement and Instruction,* 16 January 1841 tells us:

> the spirited owner, resolved to erect on its site one of the most beautiful theatres in the metropolis; towards the accomplishment of which he spared no expense; many annoying difficulties met him at the outset; but, by dint of great perseverance and unwearying application, they were surmounted.
>
> Mr. Hamlet, after having obtained a license for these premises, declined opening any part of them, on account of the alterations and contemplated improvements not being completed. Having applied at the Middlesex Sessions (October 1837), for a renewal of the license,—the theatre being previously let to Mr. Wade,—it was refused; but on the next application, the license was granted. It remained, however, unemployed as a place of entertainment, until the autumn of last year, when it was opened, for the first time, on Wednesday, the 30th of September, under the title of 'The Princess's Theatre,' with promenade concerts, on an extensive and magnificent scale.
>
> The theatre was completed from the designs of T. M. Nelson, Esq., the architect, and the decorations principally

in the Louis Quatorze style—than which, for richness and boldness of relief, none is better adapted to the embellishment of theatres—were executed by Messrs. Crace and Sons, and the joint labours of these justly-admired artists have produced a most splendid theatre. There are four tiers of boxes, the first and third private, the second and fourth public. The decorations of all the tiers are different. The front of the first is adorned with a rich gold moulding, crimson paint, hanging with tassels from the top of the box. The second tier is painted with Arabesque ornaments, a series of nymphs terminating in those vegetative implications which are common to this style, while a gilt Cupid in relief, parts every two boxes. The fronts of the third and fourth rows are painted with different scrolls, and the tops of these boxes are beautifully ornamented with golden points. The lining of the boxes is crimson and fancy chintz. The chandelier is superb; a circle of children playing musical instruments is placed one over each lamp. A profusion of gold adorns the proscenium; rendering the *tout ensemble* the most brilliant scene imaginable.

The size of the theatre is somewhere between the English Opera House (Lyceum), and the Haymarket (880); and the accommodations and facilities are as ample as can be required. The pit forms an extensive saloon for promenades; and the new and splendid orchestra was erected expressly for these performances. The leader of the band, which consists of upwards of sixty first-rate instrumentalists, is the eminent Mr. Willy, whose solos on the violin are too well-known and appreciated, to be here commented upon. The second leaders, are Messrs. Dando and J. Bannister. With such pre-eminent talent, it is impossible but what the Princess's Theatre must always be a place of the greatest attraction, and command the patronage of the public.

It was originally intended to call the new theatre the Court, but during the prolonged difficulties between 1836 and 1840, the name the Princess's was decided upon. On the bills in 1842 and on the façade of the theatre, it was given as the Princess'; this was changed on the bills in 1843, but remained on the building for many years.

The original architectural design by Duncan was carried out, with subsequent improvements, by T. Marsh Nelson, it was said to have cost some £47,000 to build.

The promenade concerts, under the conductorship of John Willy, did not last long and Hamlet became bankrupt. He had lent money, on the security of bonds, to both the Duke of York and the Prince Regent, and these were repudiated. The theatre was sold to Montague for £14,500.

In 1842 a lease was taken by J. M. Maddox, and after suitable alterations the premises became a theatre. It had a burletta licence for music and dancing and opened on 26 December 1842 with opera. The stage manager, Henry Wallack, delivered the inaugural address and Bellini's *La Sonnambula*, with Eugénie Gardeia as Amina, was produced. The usual burlesque made up the evening.

The first season, during which *Fra Diavolo, Lucia di Lammermoor, Il Puritani* and a new opera by Balfe *Geraldine; or, The Lover's Well*, were produced, ended in September 1843, and was pronounced a success financially.

The second season started the following month. The passing of the new Licensing Act in 1843 now allowed drama to be produced without hindrance. A dramatic company was engaged and a mixture of opera, ballet and plays held the stage, with pantomime at Christmas and extravaganza at Easter. In February 1845 the American tragedian, Edwin Forrest, played Macbeth with Charlotte Cushman as Lady Macbeth, and created a sensation. She also played Rosalind and Mrs. Haller in *The Stranger*. Later in the year Macready acted a round of his famous parts. He was back the following year, after pantomime, and appeared in a new play *The King of the Commons*, by the Rev. James White.

All the famous names of the contemporary theatre were seen during these early years at the Princess's, and new operas produced include Loder's *The Night Dancers*, an operatic *Giselle* (October 1846). Fanny Kemble made a reappearance in 1847, Macready again tried a new play *Philip van Arteveld*, by Henry Taylor, which only ran 5 performances and Charlotte Cushman joined by her sister, Susan, acted *Romeo and Juliet*. In 1848 the American actress, Anna Cora Mowatt, appeared with E. L. Davenport in *Much Ado About Nothing*. But the play and operas heard during the year did not bring much in at the box office, and Maddox terminated his management in April 1850.

The theatre re-opened under new management in September

1850. A partnership was formed by Robert Keeley and Charles Kean, and they took the theatre for two years. Robert Keeley and his wife Mary (Goward), were a famous partnership in the early Victorian theatre, popular for their performances primarily in comedy and domestic drama. Charles Kean and his wife Ellen (Tree), were also famous for their work together in Shakespeare and the higher drama. The partnership of Mr. and Mrs. Keeley and Mr. and Mrs. Kean was of a domestic nature, dear to the mid-Victorians.

They opened on 28 September with *Twelfth Night* and a farce by Bayle Bernard, *Platonic Attachments*, and a ballet divertissement by Flexmore. Keeley retired from the management after the first season.

During the first season, which ended in October 1851, a profit of seven thousand pounds was made, due, no doubt, partly to the influx of visitors to London for the Great Exhibition. Twenty-seven pieces were acted, of which twelve were new.

The theatre re-opened under the sole direction of Charles Kean, on 22 November 1851 and one of the most brilliant periods of mid-Victorian theatre commenced. His regime was to last until 29 August 1859. In his farewell speech he was able to boast:

> In this little Theatre, where £200 is considered a large receipt, and £250 an extraordinary one, I expended in one season alone a sum little short of £50,000. I have given employment, and consequently weekly payment, to nearly 550 persons, and if you take into calculation the families dependent on them, the number thus supported may be multiplied by four. Ten thousand pounds has been besides expended in improvements and enlargements of the building.

The story of this management is told in full in *The Life and Theatrical Times of Charles Kean, F.S.A.* by John William Cole (1859), and need not be recounted in full here; sufficient to say the magnificent, archaeologically correct revivals of Shakespeare became a byword, and set a pattern for several generations to come.

The following are the main events of the eight years' management.

The first play under the sole direction of Charles Kean was *The Merry Wives of Windsor*, George Bartley being Falstaff;

Charles Kean, Ford; Robert Keeley, Sir Hugh Evans; Alfred Wigan, Dr. Caius; John Ryder, Pistol; John Harley, Slender; Drinkwater Meadows, Shallow; Mrs. Charles Kean, Mistress Ford; Mrs. Keeley, Mistress Page; Miss Mary Keeley, Anne Page; and Eliza Winstanley, Mistress Quickly. Many of these names were to become the backbone of the resident company. The Christmas pantomime was *Harlequin and Billy Taylor*.

An elaborate revival of *King John* in February 1852 was the first of the series of brilliant Shakespearian productions. Kate Terry, then a child of ten, was Prince Arthur. On the 24 February *The Corsican Brothers* was first produced and obtained a run of 66 nights during the first season. In June George Lovell's *The Trial of Love* was produced, and this was followed by Boucicault's melodrama, *The Vampire*. The season closed in July. It re-opened on 18 September 1852 with Boucicault's *The Prima Donna*, in which Caroline Heath made her stage debut (she was to be closely associated with this theatre for many years), and Walter Lacy succeeded to the position vacated by Alfred Wigan. This was followed in a short time by Bayle Bernard's *Mont St. Michel; or, the Fairy of the Sands*, then Westland Marston's *Anne Blake* was played 42 nights from October. On 18 December, the fiftieth anniversary of his appearance in London, the veteran George Bartley took his leave of the stage as Falstaff in *Henry IV, Part I*.

The pantomime for 1852, *Cherry and Fair Star*, ran ten weeks. On 22 January 1853 Douglas Jerrold's *St. Cupid; or, Dorothy's Fortune* was produced. This had been acted at Windsor Castle on the preceding evening (many of Kean's productions were taken by Royal Command to Windsor), however, although it was played 37 nights it was not a commercial success. In February an elaborate revival of *Macbeth* opened and ran for ten weeks at the rate of 3 performances a week.

The Easter spectacle was *Marco Spada*, adapted by Palgrave Simpson from the libretto supplied by Scribe to Auber's opera. In June Lord Byron's tragedy of *Sardanapalus* was produced with magnificent scenic splendour, with which, after 61 performances, the season closed in September.

The fourth season began on 10 October 1853, with *Sardanapalus* again and in November *The Lancers* was produced, adapted by Leicester Vernon from the *Fils de Famille*.

The Christmas pantomime was *The Miller and his Men*.

In February 1854 Colley Cibber's version of Shakespeare's *Richard III* was revived and presented with the usual attention to detail, but it ran only 19 nights. *Faust and Marguerite*, played in Easter week was, on the contrary, an extraordinary success, with Charles Kean as Mephistopheles.

At the end of June the drama of *The Courier of Lyons* (better known under its later title *The Lyons Mail*), adapted from the French by Charles Reade, was acted 26 nights, till the theatre closed in August 1854.

Douglas Jerrold's *A Heart of Gold* opened the next season in October, but had a brief career and early in November it was succeeded by Palgrave Simpson's adaptation of *Schamyl*, a costly spectacle, which ran only 23 nights.

The Christmas pantomime was *Blue Beard*. In February 1885 Charles Kean made one of his greatest triumphs in *Louis XI*. The play by Boucicault, from the French of Casmir Delavigne, was acted this season for 62 nights. On 16 May a splendid revival of *King Henry VIII* was seen, in which Mrs. Charles Kean made her re-appearance after a long absence from the stage through illness. The play remained in the bills for 100 consecutive nights and carried the management triumphantly through till September when the season, prolonged to 11 months, terminated.

The house re-opened on 27 October with *Henry VIII*, which ran 50 more nights. *The Maid and The Magpie* was the title of the Christmas pantomime. In March 1856 a drama by Charles Reade and Tom Taylor called *The First Printer* failed and was only played for 9 nights. On 28 April *The Winter's Tale* was brought out 'with great attention to every department'. Mrs. Charles Kean giving a powerful reading of Hermione, Charles Kean as Leontes, Caroline Heath and Carlotta Leclercq as Florizel and Perdita. Ellen Terry made her first appearance on the stage as Mamillius. This brilliant Shakespearean revival ran till the end of the season in August, when it had reached 102 nights.

The new season commenced 1 September with a spectacular revival of *Pizzarro* (Sheridan's adaptation of a German original), which ran till the second week of October, when *A Midsummer Night's Dream* was produced. Fanny Ternan made her first appearance here as Oberon; Carlotta Leclercq was Titania, and Ellen Terry a youthful Puck. The pantomime was *Aladdin and the Wonderful Lamp*.

The first notable event of 1857 was the production of *Richard II* on 12 March. This achieved a great success, and was followed by *The Tempest*, brought out with equal care, judgment, and spectacle. Charles Kean was, of course, Prospero; and Ariel was played by Kate Terry. The season, which had included 242 nights devoted to Shakespeare, closed in August.

When the theatre re-opened on 12 October 1857, the run of *The Tempest* was resumed, and completed a run of 87 nights, when *Richard II* was restored to the programme. The pantomime produced at Christmas was *The White Cat*.

Various Shakespearean and other plays from the repertoire were given during the spring, while Kean prepared for his next revival, *King Lear*, which was produced in April. The play was performed 32 consecutive nights, and was withdrawn in June to make way for *The Merchant of Venice*, which ran to the end of the season. The season ended on 3 September, when *The Merchant of Venice* was represented for 72 consecutive times. In a brief address Kean announced that the house would be re-opened on 2 October and that he intended to resign the management on 29 August the following year. Notwithstanding the brilliant success attending these revivals, the expenditure incurred was so great that the loss on the season was estimated at four thousand pounds. The Princess's began the new season with *The Merchant of Venice*, followed in a fortnight by *King John*, and in November by *Macbeth*, which was succeeded by *Much Ado About Nothing*, with Mr. and Mrs. Charles Kean as Benedick and Beatrice.

The pantomime was *The King of the Castle*. The last Shakespearean revival was *Henry V* on 28 March 1859, which ran 84 nights, being withdrawn in July to make way for a return of *Henry VIII* to the bills. The remaining period of the season was devoted to a repetition of the popular plays associated with the greatest triumphs of the preceding years, and on Monday 29 August, Charles Kean closed his managerial career at the Princess's and his eighth season. The play selected for the last night was *Henry VIII*, thus ending one of the most remarkable epochs in theatrical history.

The premises re-opened under the management of Augustus Harris (father of the famous manager of Drury Lane), on 24 September 1859, with a drama by John Oxenford (Drama Critic of *The Times*), called *Ivy Hall*.

The play bill stated in large print:

Re-decorated, under the superintendence of Mr. E. W. Bradwell. The Medallions painted by M. Thiele. The gilding by M. Perocchy. The Upholstery by Messrs. Hampton and Russell. The Chandelier by Messrs. Defries and Sons. The Refreshment Saloon has been re-embellished and a new Staircase erected to connect it with the Dress Circle.

In this play Henry Irving made his first London appearance. The new management kept up the policy of good revivals with important actors. Samuel Phelps appeared in some of his famous parts in April 1860, as did James Anderson later in the year. In October Charles Fechter made his first English speaking appearance in London. Though always considered a French actor, he was, in fact, born in London of mixed parentage. He made his name originally in France (he created Armand in *La Dame aux Camélias* and the two brothers in *Les Frères Corses*). His first appearance in *Ruy Blas* in October was a great success. He played Hamlet the following March, and brought a new interpretation to the part which was to make him famous on both sides of the Atlantic. He shared the season with Phelps during the summer, and in the autumn played Othello. After the usual pantomime season Fechter played Iago to the Othello of John Ryder and they later alternated the parts during the season.

In May 1862 Mr. and Mrs. Charles Kean returned to play some of their famous parts until the season ended in October and the management of Harris finished.

The Keans were back in May 1862 for farewell performances prior to a disastrous trip to Australia, and in the same month the management passed to George Vining. During his regime were seen Stella Colas, who created a sensation as Juliet, the Brothers Webb as the two Dromios in *The Comedy of Errors*, and the first performance, on 1 August 1864 of *The Streets of London* by Dion Boucicault, a melodrama (naturally stolen from the French), which was to be revived for the next hundred years in one country or another. It originally ran until March 1865, a consecutive 209 nights, a length unusual for those times. The same writer's *Arrah na Pogue*, which followed, ran till September, then came *It's Never Too Late to Mend* by Charles Reade. This caused a first night sensation on 4 October, when there were protests at the realistic treatment of the prison scene. The story is told first hand in *The Era*, 8 October 1865:

The realisation of the gloomy aspect of prison life is vividly depicted in the second part. The treadmill, with the prisoners at work upon it, a gang of convicts picking oakum, a convict weaving at the loom with which he has been supplied, and all the details of penal punishment, are here exhibited with appalling minuteness. The great scene, however, in this part is that which represents the corridors of the model prison, a singularly effective stage arrangement, evidently copied from the Pentonville establishment, though the locality is not identified. The receding passages, with the cells ranged along them on each side, and illumined by jets of gas, whilst huge iron winding staircases communicate with the different stories, produces a marvellous appearance of depth, and excites some wonder even in the minds of those most familiar with the devices of theatrical mechanism, how so complicated a 'set' can be presented in so short a time. The object of the novelist, it will be remembered, was to reform the abuses of the 'solitary' and the 'silent' system, which, under the sanction of ignorant and unfeeling officials, had at last grown to a height that called forth the interference of the Home Secretary. The atrocities perpetrated in the Birmingham Borough Gaol, as recorded in the 'Blue Book,' which published the facts elicited during the Parliamentary investigation, have long since ceased to exist, and it seemed therefore felt by the audience, who saw them re-enacted on the stage, that an unnecessary shock was given to their feelings by forcing upon their notice the sight of brutalities which made the heart sicken and the mind shudder to contemplate, even with the knowledge that the barbarity was only assumed and the writhing of the tortured victims merely simulated. Whether from the feeling that these thrilling examples of bygone cruelty were simply brought forward to no more profitable purpose than that of creating a 'stage sensation,' or that a strong objection to the degradation of supernumeraries by compelling them to wear the felon's garb, provoked remonstrances from playgoers of acute sensibility, may be left to conjecture. Certain it is that a storm of indignation broke forth during the last scene of the act, after some ominous premonitory mutterings that threatened to bring the piece to a premature conclusion. Voices were heard from the stalls loudly protesting against the representation as 'revolting,' and one of the dissentients, whose excitement was stronger than his discretion, made himself so conspicuous at the moment that he was readily identified as a well-known dramatic critic [Guest Tomlins of *The Morning Advertiser*] who, with other modes of expressing his opinion, might perhaps have more judiciously reserved his utterances for the morning newspaper he represented. The clamour thus raised compelled Mr. Vining to drop for a time his assumed character of Tom Robinson and address the audience as follows:

'Ladies and Gentlemen,—With all due submission to public opinion, permit me to call your attention to one fact, which appears to have been overlooked. It has been acknowledged that the work from which this piece is taken has done a great deal of good. We are not here representing a system as it is, but the abuses of a system, and I may refer to the Blue Book— here a voice from the pit shouted out 'we want no Blue Books on the stage'—for the truthfulness of these things. This question can be discussed elsewhere, and I believe that I am not wrong in supposing that most of the dissentient persons have not'—Here the Manager paused significantly—'Come in Free.'

The words had the effect, in some measure, of allaying the turbulent spirit that had been aroused, and the act-drop soon after fell amidst applause. Several ladies in the stalls were much distressed during the representation of some of the sterner examples of the 'Governor's' brutality and the vindictive conduct of the hardened warders acting under his instructions, and when the poor boy, Josephs, so pathetically personated by Miss Louisa Moore, was seen on the point of committing suicide by hanging, to escape the infliction of further tortures, there was an indescribable thrill of horror running through the whole body of spectators. It may be seriously doubted, however, whether the retention of such a painful exhibition as that of convicts undergoing severe punishment is in accordance with managerial policy, and notwithstanding the excessive outlay on this portion of the piece, there is every reason to believe it might be omitted with every advantage to the Theatre and the public.

Despite the controversy, or perhaps because of it, the play ran some 140 nights till March 1866, though the prison scene was toned down after the first night.

The Keans once again appeared on their return from Australia in May 1866, and in July London first saw the Can Can, introduced by the Parisian Grotesque Dancers into a play *The Huguenot Captain*, but the rest of the year and the next was not memorable. Revivals of past successes, given by established performers in the classics, were the main attractions.

Early in 1868 Boucicault, himself, and his wife (Agnes Robertson), appeared in revivals of his own plays: *The Octoroon* and *Arrah na Pogue*. But Vining was finding it hard to keep things going, and the theatre was closed from April, except for a short uneventful summer season, till the winter season opened in August, with *After Dark*, a new play by Boucicault, which proved a draw till pantomime time. In 1869, after a failure, *After Dark* returned for a while, but things were generally at a low ebb, and after several more failures the theatre abruptly closed. The following notice was posted on the Bill for the evening's performance on 18 October:

> The Theatre is closed. All claims on Mr. Vining to be sent in forthwith to Mr. E. T. Smale, Treasurer. N.B.—For all places secured the money will be returned, per Post-office Order, on application by letter.

The theatre did not re-open till Christmas, and then under the management of Benjamin Webster, who tried the established success of the theatre *After Dark* and *The Streets of London*. These and other Boucicault plays ran till the season ended in April 1870. In the summer a French season run by Raphael Felix was presented. In the autumn Webster was joined by F. B. Chatterton in the management. Two melodramas: *Peep o' Day* and *The Great City* were produced. The next year saw the first success for some time, an Irish melodrama by Edmond Falconer *Eileen Oge; or, Dark's the Hour before the Dawn*, in which the author appeared. This ran 118 nights during 1872. Fechter again played *Ruy Blas* in July, and a round of his characters

on his return from an American tour, and in the autumn Phelps
and Creswick appeared together in *Macbeth* and other classics, bu'
the theatre had now become the home of many changing managements; James Guiver presented Mr. and Mrs. Rousby in some o:
their famous parts in turgid historical dramas in 1873-74. In 187:
M. L. Mayer presented *Round the World in Eighty Days*, the Car
Rosa Opera Company gave a season, and Joseph Jefferson with
Rip Van Winkle made a re-appearance in November. All showing
the uncertain state of the theatre at this period.

The following year Caroline Heath returned with a play by
W. G. Wills called *Jane Shore* in September. This was an immediate success and ran 116 performances. During this time the
management of the theatre passed from Chatterton to Walter
Gooch. He was responsible for H. J. Byron's *Guinea Gold*, which
ran in 1877. In 1878 melodramas like *Queen's Evidence, Uncle
Tom's Cabin* and a revival of *It's Never too late to Mend* were the
staple fare.

One of the big successes associated with this theatre in later
Victorian days is *Drink*, a version by Charles Reade of Zola's
L'Assommoir. This provided a vehicle for Charles Warner as
Coupeau, who gave an unforgettable performance of *Delirium
Tremens*. He was still playing the part on tour in 1902. It originally
ran 222 performances.

After this Warner appeared in a revival of *The Streets of London*,
from February till May 1880.

The days of the old Princess's were numbered. On Wednesday
19 May the last performance within its walls was given. Scenes
from *It's Never too Late to Mend, Queen's Evidence, Drink* and
The Streets of London, with William Rignold and Charles Warner,
and a farce *Mr. and Mrs. White* with Fanny Leslie (Mrs. Walter
Gooch), and Harry Jackson, made up a gala last night. In a farewell
speech Walter Gooch said:

> Ladies and gentlemen—Looking forward to this occasion, it
> seemed one of the easiest of matters to say good-bye; but now,
> when at length I stand before you for the last time in the old
> house, I realise what it is to part from generous and kindly
> friends, though it may only be for a while. This Theatre is
> forty years old. It has a good character—I may say a high
> character. It has had its troubles and its trials; and not even

my illustrious predecessor, Mr. Charles Kean—a scholar, an artist, and a gentleman—found the task an easy one. Personally, ladies and gentlemen, I have been more fortunate in that respect; you have been my steadfast friends, and it is owing to your generous patronage that I shall be able to build—with the help of the architect, of course—a better house upon this site. The new Theatre will be more commodious, brighter—may I go so far as to say cleaner—than this one, fitted with all modern appliances; but I am not sure we shall be happier than we have been within these walls, never more dear to me than to-night; and now I have to say good-bye to you, though only for a while. For three years we have been friendly together—the audience, the company, and the Manager—and we have had our triumphs, too—our legitimate triumphs of art. We have seen some good acting of the best plays upon this stage, before and since my time. Why, Shakespeare himself used to be made quite at home in Oxford Street! It would take too long just now to mention all the good actors who have graced this stage. Perhaps you may not know them all even by name; for many a good actor never gets a chance of showing the public all that he is capable of doing. It is, however, no secret—not even a stage secret—that a great reputation has been gained in this Theatre, and if I were offering you wine instead of words, I would ask you to pledge Mr. Charles Warner in *Drink*. (Cheers) I know that those cheers will make him happy to-night, for the children of the footlights love applause; and, please, don't forget the Stage-Manager, Mr. Harry Jackson, who literally has an eye like an eagle for the best interests of the Princess's Theatre. Ladies and gentlemen, it is not often that a Manager finds an opportunity of addressing the public by word of mouth, and, maybe, I try your forbearance? ('No, no!') Well, I am glad you are so patient—I shall soon be finished. Thank you, ladies and gentlemen, for your kindness to me and mine. May I ask you to join with me in thanking the ladies and gentlemen of the company of this Theatre—one and all, from the highest to the lowest—for their zeal in our service; my part will be to make the new Princess's comfortable from floor to ceiling—theirs to entertain you with good plays well acted. And now, kind friends, I feel something rising in my throat—something tells me it is time to say good-night, not good-bye. Please come and see us in the new house, you will be heartily welcomed.

Plans by C. J. Phipps, the architect, were made for the new theatre (out of the profits of *Drink*) and its opening was announced for October. *The Era* 17 October said:

In twenty-three weeks, the whole of the old Theatre has been pulled down, the materials removed, and the new buildings erected; and when it is considered that they occupy an area of 21,000 superficial feet, it must be acknowledged that the best use has been made of the time.

The Theatre proper, that is to say the auditory, will not occupy a larger area than originally, but the stage, and all the approaches and dressing-rooms entirely external to the auditory, are increased in area fourfold.

The disposition of the buildings may be thus classified, as they really form distinct blocks, separated one from the other by solid walls, and arranged with a view to lessen the risk of fire spreading in case such an event should ever occur:—1. The Theatre proper, including auditory, stage, scene-docks; 2. the approaches from Oxford Street, with saloons and staircases; 3. the approaches from Winsley Street, for pit and gallery; 4. the dressing-room block in Castle Street.

The entrance in Oxford Street is now by a spacious and handsome vestibule 20 feet wide. This will be for the audience to the stalls, the dress circle, private boxes, and upper circle.

The frequenters of the stalls on entering the inner vestibule or crush-room pass to the auditory on the level through a small *foyer* without a single step from the street. The audience to the dress and upper circles pass to the several levels by a staircase 14 feet wide, divided by a brass rail in the centre. On the first landing (where will be found a picturesque arrangement of rockwork and ferns) the staircase divides, the dress circle audience passing to the right and the upper-circle to the left up distinct and spacious staircases. The entrance in Winsley Street is for the audience to the pit, who pass to the auditory from the street on the level. Adjoining is the entrcane to the amphitheatre and gallery by a staircase

6 feet wide, ascending by short flights of not more than six
steps to each flight round an inner newel wall. All staircases
have handrails on both sides, and there are no winding stairs
in any part.

Entering the Theatre, the auditory presents a very striking
appearance. The stage opening is 30 feet wide, and is flanked
on either side by three tiers of private boxes, three on each
tier. On the left side facing the stage is the Royal box, with its
ante-room and private entrance from Castle Street adjoining.
There are five rows of stalls, giving sitting room for 100
persons. These stalls, as well as those in the dress circle, are
Mr. Phipps's registered seats, which turn up to allow facility
in passing, and the width of each platform, i.e., from back to
back of seats, is greater than we have noticed in any Theatre,
and will satisfy the most fastidious. Behind the orchestra
stalls is a spacious pit, which will hold from 800 to 1,000
persons. Both these divisions are approached, as before stated,
from different streets, on a level with the street, without a
single step. Adjoining both stalls and pit will be found cloak-
rooms and refreshment-rooms.

On the first tier, the balcony or dress circle has five rows of
seats to hold 140, and behind these nine private boxes, as at the
Gaiety and Haymarket (also constructed by Mr. Phipps).
The balcony advances nearer the stage than we have ever
noticed in so large a Theatre, and the curves of the front are
so designed that there is not a single side seat. Every seat in
the five rows faces the stage. On this level will be found a
spacious and lofty *foyer* or saloon, decorated with Corinthian
pilasters and columns. This will be available for the audience
to the stalls and the two circles. Attached to this saloon, and
approached by a bridge over the entrance vestibule, is a
smoking-saloon on the first floor over the entrance, having an
open loggia, 8 feet wide, facing into Oxford Street. Every
convenience in the way of retiring and cloak rooms is on this
level also.

The upper circle, or second tier, has six rows of seats, and
will hold 400 persons. The front of this tier recedes 7 feet
6 inches farther from the stage than the dress circle; while the
amphitheatre, or third tier, recedes 2 feet more. The total
area of ground covered by the various blocks of buildings is

21,000 feet superficial, or only 1,000 feet less than the area of the Royal Italian Opera, Covent Garden.

A special feature of the arrangements is a separate transfer staircase from the highest level of the gallery to the ground level of the pit. So that on crowded nights the overflow from the gallery can transfer down to the pit without mingling with the persons still ascending by the main entrance staircase; also from the pit, a passage at the back affords a means of transferring to the front entrance vestibule, where access is at once obtained by the several higher tiers of the auditory. A third staircase, which may be called an escape stairs, is constructed on the opposite side of the gallery, and will admit of the audience being dismissed into another exit way (formerly the old pit entrance) in Oxford Street.

On every floor, however, the audience have available access to at least three distinct staircases, all fireproof, and leading directly into the streets. The very best arrangements, therefore, are made for the safety of the audience. The auditory is also separated from the stage by a solid brick wall nearly two feet thick, and this is carried up above the roof; and there are numerous fire hydrants in the various corridors all charged from the high pressure mains in the streets. The general ornamentation of the Theatre is French Renaissance, the fronts to the several tiers being richly moulded and gilded, the proscenium boxes being specially rich both in design and ornamentation.

The general arrangement of colour is a cream ground, light on the ceiling, on which the decorative ornament is painted in colours, and gradually deepening towards the lower parts of the auditory. The walls are covered with a rich crimson flock-paper, while the walls of the private boxes are of green and gold, the hangings and curtains being of a rich silk tapestry of deep crimson. The general colour of the seats is a dark maroon. Over the proscenium, and in the groined spandrils on either side, is an allegorical figure subject representing the Arts allied to the Drama, painted by Ballard.

The traditional green curtain will be adopted, and Mr. Beverly is painting, as an act-drop, a tapestry curtain. The large block of buildings known as the Princess's Concert Rooms, in Castle Street, has been attached to the Theatre, and utilised entirely for dressing-rooms. The gentlemen and ladies have distinct staircases, and the rooms are, without exception, the best we have ever seen in any Theatre.

The frontage in Oxford Street, 21 feet wide, is of Portland stone. It has wide pilasters on the ground floor, the entrance between being 17 feet wide. Over this is an illumination, supported by massive stone corbels, and surmounted by a balustrade in front of the loggia of the smoking-room. From the level of this balustrade there are two fluted and carved pilasters on either side, over which a semi-circular arch is turned, richly moulded and carved, this being crowned by a bold projecting cornice and balustrade. The works of this frontage are now being continued night and day without intermission, so that when the Theatre opens it may be completely finished in every part.

Mr. Mark Manley has been the general contractor, Messrs. Drake have erected the concrete staircases, Messrs. Jackson have prepared the box fronts, proscenium, and ceiling in their fibrous plaster; Mr. Edward Hill has executed the painted decorations and gilding, Messrs. Strode have constructed the limelight, which illuminates the Theatre from the centre of the ceiling; Mr. Wharton has constructed the stage, and Mr. D. Jones has laid on the gas and water mains. Messrs. Campbell and Smith have executed the painted and stained glass for the entrance vestibule screens, and the smoking-rooms and various other places, and the entrance vestibule and crush-room are laid with marble mosaic by Burke and Co. The fernery is constructed by Willis and Co., the ornamental gates by Cotton and Co., and the upholstery and carpets have been supplied by Gregory and Co. Mr. Edward Nightingale has been the clerk of the works for the architect.

The theatre duly opened on 6 November, 'Only one week after the date originally announced'. *The Era* the following morning continued:

The new and beautiful Theatre, which at an enormous outlay Mr. Gooch has provided for the accommodation of playgoers, was last night opened, the public—or as many of the public as could be admitted—walking in as the workmen walked out.

o

Those whose privilege it was to be present must, indeed, have been as much astonished as delighted at the transformation which has been effected within the old walls, and the signs of lavish expenditure, good taste, and a determination to promote comfort, which everywhere met the eye. There were some who were content to remain for a time in Oxford Street to admire the remarkably handsome frontage to the building, and to regard with envy the more fortunate ones who between the acts were tempted to stroll on to that open-air smoking balcony, to which allusion has already been made. Much might be said of the luxury which is characteristic of the higher priced parts of the house; of the elegant surroundings of the saloons; of trees and flowers and rippling fountains; of inviting lounges; and of glorious etchings embellishing the walls of the *foyer*. But our business now is rather with the stage, and so, staying only to chronicle the fact that the house was filled almost from footlights to ceiling, and that the audience numbered a host of the shining lights of the worlds of art, literature, and fashion, we pass at once to a consideration of the programme with which Mr. Gooch inaugurated a 'new departure,' attended by the best wishes of everybody for that success which pluck and energy and liberality and enterprise fairly deserve. *An Old Master*, though not of merit equal to that of the same author's *Clerical Error*, still being presented at another establishment, tells a simple and interesting, if somewhat improbable, story, and was received with considerable favour.

The most important event of the evening was, of course, the appearance upon the English stage, after an absence of nearly twenty years, of Mr. Edwin Booth, the eminent American tragedian.

It was as the melancholy, philosophic Prince of Denmark that Mr. Booth last night stepped upon the stage of the new Princess's Theatre to receive at the hands of the audience an enthusiastic welcome. Mr. Booth's personation of Hamlet is certainly good, but it cannot be called great, and although it in many passages called forth the enthusiastic plaudits of the pit and gallery, and, indeed, of many in the more fashionable sections of the house, we felt there was something wanting, and that something we take it was inspiration.

The other plays in the season, which lasted till March 1881, were *Richelieu*, *Othello*, (he alternated Othello, and Iago, with Henry Forrester), *The Fool's Revenge* and *King Lear*.

After a sensational drama *Branded*, which had one act set in a cemetery chapel and only lasted a few weeks Gooch handed over the management to Wilson Barrett. At this time Barrett (who had married Caroline Heath) was leading man to Helena Modjeska at the Royal Court, of which he was also manager. He brought her to the Princess's on 4 June in *Frou Frou*. After she finished her engagement he revived several of his own past successes. It was *The Lights O'London* by George R. Sims, produced on 10 September, that gave Barrett one of his first big commercial successes. It ran for 226 performances and became a stock melodrama for years to come.

Barrett and his new leading lady, Mary Eastlake, were to remain together for the rest of his stay at this theatre, during which many plays which became household names were first seen: *Romany Rye* (George R. Sims, June 1882), *The Silver King* (Henry Arthur Jones and Henry Herman, November 1882), *Claudian* (Henry Herman, December 1883).

In October 1884 he produced *Hamlet*, giving a chance to E. W. Godwin (father of Gordon Craig), to contribute his archaeological researches to the decoration of the play. Barrett, who delighted in the most décolleté of costumes, appeared as a romantic Germanic Prince hot foot from Wittenberg. After this the next plays were *Junius* (Lytton, February 1885), *Hoodman Blind* (Henry Arthur Jones and Wilson Barrett, August 1885), *The Lord Harry* (Jones and Barrett, February 1886), and *Clito* (Sydney Grundy and Barrett, May 1886). When this failed Barrett sub-let the Princess's and went on a tour of America. He gave a series of farewell performances of *Clito*, *Claudian* and *Hamlet* before he finished on 22 July 1886.

His tenant, in September, was Charles Hawtrey, who presented himself in *Harvest* with little success. Then Charles Warner returned with *The Noble Vagabond* in December and *Held by the Enemy*, in April 1887. In July, Grace Hawthorne, an American actress, took over the theatre entirely and produced a series of melodramas: *Shadows of a Great City*, *Uncle Tom's Cabin*, *The Mystery of a Hansom Cab*, *The Still Alarm* and *Hands Across the Sea*. In May 1888 she presented Wilson Barrett and his Company, newly returned from the States, in *Ben-My-Chree* by Hall Caine and Barrett. He also revived *Hamlet* and *The Lady of Lyons*, *The Silver King* and *Claudian*. Grace Hawthorne herself joined him in a new play *Now-a-Days* in March 1889. His season ended in May.

Grace Hawthorne was now faced with a series of failures, her management, never at any time particularly successful, ended in May 1890.

In November 1890 Lillie Langtry put on *Antony and Cleopatra*. *Lady Barter* followed in February 1891 and *Linda Grey* in April, which ended her tenancy.

The last years of the Princess's are the story of one dismal failure after another put on by transitory managements. *The Swiss Express* played a Christmas season in 1890-91. Drury Lane 'Autumn Melodramas' were revived by Augustus Harris during 1894-95. The theatre was often closed for long periods, 'renovated and re-opened' only to quickly close again. Mostly melodramas both old and new were the stock fare.

There was a last blaze of glory in September 1896, when Albert Gilmer (who had come to the theatre earlier in the year), presented *Two Little Vagabonds* by George R. Sims and Arthur Shirley. The title roles were played by Sydney Fairbrother and Kate Tyndall, with such pathetic appeal that the play ran 275 performances and toured for many years. Unfortunately for the poor Princess's there was no 'follow up' to consolidate this, and series of topical melodramas of the South African War which followed did not last long. Revivals, Charles Warner back again in *Drink*, in 1900, and Van Bien in *The Broken Melody* in 1902, bring the theatre to its last year. The last production, on 25 August 1902, was *The Fatal Wedding* by Theo Kremer, presented by Bert Coote. 'A play of great heart interest. A play of New York Life.' This was a near success and ran just over 50 performances, closing in October.

There was talk of re-opening as a Music Hall (with non-stop Vaudeville), under the management of Benjamin Keith (the American Music Hall pioneer who had bought the theatre), but the L.C.C. were on the war path. They demanded drastic and costly alterations before they would allow him to put his ideas into operation, and he backed out with the theatre left on his hands.

Another manager, T. C. Dagnall, contemplated re-opening in 1905, but did not do so and the theatre remained empty and abandoned. It eventually became a furniture warehouse; the vestibule was given a front and turned into a shop and the arched façade above was glazed in and became a display window for the furriers who later took over the premises. The old theatre remained behind forgotten until demolition began in June 1931. The ground had been bought by Woolworth's for a new store.

This firm and other similar multiple stores have a liking for theatre sites for their new premises as they give access to at least two other streets, besides the principal entrance in the main thoroughfare. The Pantheon became a Marks and Spencers', Terry's Theatre became a Woolworth's, and at one time this firm bought the Adelphi Theatre for eventual re-development. This was before the L.C.C. ruled that a place of entertainment must be included in any new building on the site of a demolished theatre.

18
The Queen's Theatre

St. Martin's Hall, the National Theatre

Long Acre
In the block bounded by Endell Street and Charles Street (now Arne Street), with Wilson Street (now Dryden Street) at the rear, with pit and gallery entrances in Wilson Street and the stage door in Charles Street

FIRST BUILDING

St. Martin's Hall opened 11 February 1850 as a concert hall for the development of choral singing.
Under the management of John Hullah.
Partially destroyed by fire 26 August 1860.

SECOND BUILDING

St. Martin's Hall re-built and opened 6 January 1862 with Rumsey and Newcombe's *Ethiopian Minstrels*.
Closed May 1867, interior gutted and converted into a theatre.
The New Queen's Theatre opened 24 October 1867 with *The Double Marriage* a new and romantic drama by Charles Reade (adapted from his novel *White Lies*), preceded by *He's a Lunatic* a one act farce by Felix Dale.
Under the management of Alfred Wigan.
(The 'New' was dropped from the name the following year.)
Re-named the National Theatre, opened 27 October 1877 with *Russia; or, the Exiles of the Angara*, a melodrama by H. B. Farnie and Robert Reece.
Under the management of Alexander Henderson.

Resumed its old name in January 1878 closed in the following July and dismantled January 1879.

Converted into the stores of the University Co-operative Association and in 1911 absorbed into the buildings of Odhams Press. The frontage remained until 1938 when it was re-built. Parts of the outside walls in Long Acre and Arne Street still remain, incorporated in the present building.

IN 1847 A SITE on the north side of Long Acre, near the corner of Endell Street, was presented to John Hullah by a city company on which to build a hall for his singing classes. These had started at the Exeter Hall in the Strand in February 1841. Originally intended for school teachers, they were later extended to the public. His 'System of Choral Harmony' was a great success. He moved to the Apollonicon Room in St. Martin's Lane in 1844 for a time. In 1847 his pupils provided the chorus for a series of concerts which he gave at the Exeter Hall, in aid of funds to build himself a permanent home. With the money raised, and the new site acquired, designs were drawn by Richard Westmacott (the younger), for a magnificent hall.

The foundation stone of St. Martin's Hall was laid in 1847, and a concert given at the Crown and Anchor Tavern in the Strand to celebrate the occasion. Later in the year part of the building was completed and brought into use. The whole hall was not even completed when opened officially on 11 February 1850. *The Illustrated London News* 16 February described the occasion:

> The opening of the great hall took place on Monday night: it is, however, not yet its intended length—fifty feet more are to be added, when the leases of some houses fall in at the west side; galleries are also to be added, and the decorators as yet have done little or nothing. There is, consequently, a naked aspect at present, which is little tempting to induce us to dwell on its architectural pretensions. There is no organ, and we do not think the disposition of the orchestra judicious; the façade is much too elevated for a good distribution of sound. The Hall is well lighted with elegant chandeliers, and there was animation in the general appearance when completely filled with amateurs; and the orchestra presented its band of some seventy players and nearly 500 singers, the

latter principally selected from Mr. Hullah's upper singing
schools. His presence in the conductor's seat was the signal
for a general burst of applause. By his perseverance he has
gained great estimation, whatever may be the opinions as to
the merits of his system of tuition. The programme opened
with Mendelssohn's cantata, *Praise Jehovah*, the Latin
version of which, *Lauda Sion*, was performed at the
Liverpool Philharmonic Festival. The solos were sung by
Miss Birch, Mrs. Noble, and Messrs. Benson and Whitworth.
After which Miss Dolby sang *Mea tormenta*, from Hasse's
oratorio *Magdalena*, which was followed by Dr. Crotch's
motet 'Methinks I hear the full celestial choir,' by Mr. W. H.
Seguin and chorus; and Handel's air, 'The smiling dawn,'
from *Jephtha*, sung by Miss Rainforth. The first part then
terminated with Mr. Henry Leslie's festival anthem, 'Let
God arise,' the words selected from the 68th Psalm. It was
praiseworthy to inaugurate the Hall with the performance of
a work by a native composer. The second part was appropriated to secular music, comprising gleanings from Mozart's
Idomeneo; the two grand scenas from Weber's *Der Freischütz*
and *Oberon* for tenor and soprano, sung by Mr. Sims Reeves
and Miss Luscombe—the latter admirably executed her air;
Beethoven's Sonata in C minor, exquisitely played by Ernst
and Sterndale Bennett; Purcell's air, 'I attempt from love's
sickness to fly,' in which Mr. Lockey was deservedly encored;
Spohr's trio, 'Night's lingering shades,' sung by Misses
Luscombe, Rainforth, and Dolby, &c.; terminating with
the National Anthem!

The building was finally completed and opened with a concert on
1 December 1853. It had a domed iron roof and was conceived in
the Elizabethan style. A contemporary Guide to London says:

> The roof reminds one of the town halls in Belgium. It has
> three entrances, from three different sides of the building;
> from Long Acre; in the east part in Charles Street; and in the
> north part in Wilson Street. The great concert hall will
> accommodate three thousand persons; in addition to which,
> there is a smaller concert hall, used for the purpose of
> rehearsals and quartette concerts. There are also several
> committee rooms attached to this Hall.

Hullah ran his singing school at moderate fees—fifty lessons for twelve shillings—and at the concerts given by the students with professional soloists, many oratorios and new choral works popular at that period were first performed.

The hall was used for political and social meetings, for lectures and entertainments. It was here that Mr. and Mrs. German Reed started on their successful London career in 1855 (see Number 21).

In 1858 Charles Dickens gave a reading from his works on behalf of the Great Ormond Street Children's Hospital, and a few weeks later launched himself professionally with his readings. He used St. Martin's Hall again on numerous later occasions.

Here also Henry Mayhew gave character readings of his London types, later embodied in his book *London Labour and The London Poor* (1862).

In the early hours of the morning of 26 August 1860 a fire broke out in the coachmaker's premises next door at the corner of Endell Street. The flames soon spread to the adjoining hall and the building was burnt out. The organ and all the contents were completely destroyed.

The corner premises were re-built as a coachmakers (which they remained till taken over by Odhams in 1907), and the re-building of the hall itself, on the original plans, was eventually put in hand. The lease was sold in June 1861 and Hullah gave up his licence. A new licence was granted to Anne Dumergue in September and by January 1862 the large hall was ready for re-opening. During the preparations *The Era*, 5 January, tells us of an accident that occurred:

which has already resulted in the loss of three lives, and has caused most serious injuries to three other persons, occurred on Friday afternoon in St. Martin's Hall. It appears that the Hall had been taken by Rumsey and Newcombe's Minstrels (known as the 'Twelve Stars') and for the purpose of their performance a gas chandelier had to be affixed to the ceiling. The work was entrusted to Mr. Defries, gas-fitter, of Houndsditch, and was carried on under the superintendence of Mr. E. Stevens, his foreman. With a view to the affixing of the chandelier, a stage was erected, forty feet from the ground, composed of planks placed across two poles, supported by four ropes from the roof. Every precaution was taken to ensure the stability of the stage, and the tieings were thoroughly tested before they began their labours. Seven men, including the foreman, were engaged in their work when suddenly one of the poles snapped asunder; the planking, of course, gave way, and six of the persons were precipitated to the ground. Mr. Stevens had a most miraculous escape. By a sudden impulse he seized one of the ropes, and there hung suspended for full five minutes. His position was most perilous, for he could not hold out much longer, and there were apparently no means of extricating him from the fate which had befallen the others. Happily at this critical juncture, a workman on the roof had the presence of mind to cut the rope which tied one of the ladders, and to pass it down through an opening, when it was grasped by Mr. Stevens with one hand, and he kept swaying to and fro, seemingly in no better position than before. One of the workmen, however, steadied the ladder, on which Mr. Stevens managed by the greatest exertion to obtain a footing, when, climbing up, he was dragged through the roof perfectly uninjured.

J. Defries and Sons, in a letter in the same issue, stated they were responsible for the lighting and ventilation of the hall only, not the erection of the scaffolding.

Rumsey and Newcombe's *Ethiopian Minstrels* opened on 6 January for a short season (the Minor Hall was still to let until the following month), by 2 February the hall was announced as 'closed to complete alterations and decorations.' It re-opened later in the month but was not a success. Spasmodic lettings for meetings, odd concerts and lectures were all that occupied the bills for the next few years. Typical is the advertisement in *The Era*, 26 April 1863:

ST. MARTIN'S HALL, LONG ACRE,

To be let—These valuable Premises, admirably adapted for any purpose requiring great space, and consisting of large Hall 122 feet long by 55 wide, minor Hall 52 by 40, with Class and Refreshment Rooms, an excellent Dwelling House and extensive Cellars to be Let for a long term or by the Month or Week as a place of entertainment, or for business purposes; or the lease will be sold. Entrance in Long Acre and in

Wilson Street. For particulars apply to Messrs. Dangerfield and Fraser, 26, Craven Street, Charing Cross.

And in October 1864 attempts to establish a theatre in the Minor Hall were made:

To Artists, Amateurs, Vocalists, Lecturers, &c., &c.,
SAINT MARTIN'S HALL,
Long Acre.

The Minor Hall of this splendid and centrally-situated Establishment is now newly Decorated and fitted-up as an Elegant Amateur Theatre, for Private Theatrical or Operatic Performances, Concerts, Lectures, Entertainments, &c., &c., A capacious and well-arranged Stage has been erected, with a handsome Proscenium and Scenery. There are spacious and comfortable Dressing-rooms with every requisite comfort and convenience. Artistes, Amateurs, and Dramatic Tutors are invited to examine this establishment, which in respect to situation, accommodation, completeness, and comfort will be found equal to any in London. It is now TO LET on moderate terms. Apply to or address Mr. W. Corbyn, Secretary, St. Martin's Hall, Long Acre, London, W.C.

This issue of *The Era* also carried the following advertisement:

Dancing for the Stage or Ball Room.—St. Martin's Hall, Long Acre.
Mr. Cormack, of the Theatre Royal, Drury Lane, is now forming Classes for Instruction in Dancing at the above spacious and central Hall. Lessons will also be given to Private Pupils, who may here rapidly acquire a perfect knowledge of the most Fashionable Dances of Good Society.
    Professionals will find unusual advantages, and a Special Class is organised for the *Corps de Ballet* on moderate terms, for which and all particulars apply to Mr. W. Corbyn, Secretary, at the Hall, from Twelve till Three daily.

Promenade concerts were tried early in 1867. Eventually in April: 'Mr. Harrison's convenient and elegant portable Theatre' set up in the Minor hall was for hire, and plans for converting the whole building into a theatre were passed. This was announced in *The Era* on 19 May 1867, and the Hall was closed. It had been bought by Lionel Lawson, part proprietor of the *Daily Telegraph*, as a speculation. He gutted the building and built a theatre within the shell, the Queen's. This he leased to another journalist and politician, Henry Labouchere (the editor of *Truth*), though the nominal lessee, whose name appeared on the programmes, was the actor Alfred Wigan.

The new theatre was larger than any in London at that time except Drury Lane and the two opera houses. The opening on 24 October is recorded in the *Morning Advertiser* the following day:

St. Martin's Hall, Long Acre, for many years one of the largest school-rooms, and one of the least successful concert-rooms in London—'everything by turns, and nothing long'—the trysting-ground, we are told, of questionable speculators in political gatherings, promenade concerts, nigger entertainments, Japanese exhibitions, and amateur performances, no longer exists. Through the plucky enterprise of a cool-headed capitalist, who ungrudgingly expended some fifty thousand pounds on acquiring the property and completing the transformation, there now stands on the old site in this eminently theatrical region, facing the leading approach to the Royal Italian Opera House, a commodious and elegant structure, where the drama will find an appropriate home, and the play-going public secure the most perfect enjoyment. 'The New Queen's Theatre' such is the title of this addition to our West End places of amusement—was opened last night under the management of Mr. Alfred Wigan, and looking to all the attractions which surrounded the event, it is hardly necessary to state that there was assembled on the occasion an audience fairly filling every part of the building before the curtain. Orchestra and balcony stalls were tenanted to repletion. The dress circle had not many vacant seats, while the pit and gallery, though by no means overflowing, presented in the treasury point of view what must have been considered a satisfactory appearance. Many of the ablest professors of the histrionic art were present, and literature put forward quite a phalanx of her most gifted sons to assist in bidding 'God speed' to Mr. Wigan at the recommencement of his managerial career in the very heart of a district identified with dramatic associations.

It required but the most cursory glance, after entering, to feel convinced that 'The New Queen's Theatre' is a gem of theatrical architecture, enriched by remarkable elegance of decoration, having an auditorium so arranged that the maximum of comfort is secured for all classes of visitors, and with a capacity of accommodation rivalling that of the Princess's Theatre. There was ample evidence that the workmen had not ceased their labours many minutes before the doors were punctually thrown open at the appointed hour. Here and there unfinished patches met the eye, and more especially in the upper region of the building, where the ventilation, though aided 'by the height of the tiers and a thorough system of extracting flues,' was far from effective. These little short-comings will, however, no doubt be speedily remedied. The architect, Mr. C. J. Phipps, F.S.A., has already won his spurs as the constructor of no less than six theatres—Bath, Nottingham, South Shields, Brighton, Swansea, and Bristol. Had he a clear open space on which to have worked out his idea of what an English metropolitan theatre ought to be, there is very little doubt that with his provincial experience some details in the construction of the Long Acre temple of the Muses would not have found favour in his plan of operations. The four main walls, the roof, and the original vestibule of St. Martin's Hall presented such a substantial appearance that they were ordered to stand, and within this casing the theatre is built. Under these circumstances and conditions the only wonder is that Mr. Phipps has presented such a successful solution of the difficulty. In its general form the house does not greatly differ from that of other theatres. Availing ourselves of information supplied in the official description of the structure, we may state that the upper tier forms with the top of the proscenium a complete circle. There are two tiers of boxes, each receding, so that a double balcony is formed. The dress circle tier is distinguished by seven rows of commodiously-arranged chairs, and the upper box tier, with six rows of seats, is similar in form, but larger in radius. The two front rows of the gallery tier are appropriated to those amphitheatre stalls which have of late years been so much in favour, and behind ranges a gallery affording space for upwards of 600 spectators. The pit, which accommodates rather more than this number, is so arranged as to give every individual an unimpeded view of the stage. There are five rows of stalls, where luxurious armchairs enable the occupants to combine with the amusement of the evening the enjoyment of the utmost personal ease, and eighteen private boxes, fitted up in the same costly style, similarly invite the presence of those who desire to unite the gratification of their dramatic tastes with the preservation of all drawing-room comforts. In the decorations hardly any ornament is in relief; there are none, or next to none, of the solid plaster cornices, mouldings, and scrolls which have hitherto formed the stock material of theatrical house decoration. It has been found that such things become convenient resting places for every stray atom of dust, so whatever has been done in the way of ornamentation is the work of the painter alone. Very artistically has that work, mainly Raphaelesque, been executed by Messrs. Green and King, and by Mr. Albert Moore, who has painted the more important pieces, in particular a fine scene from the *Antigone* —a group of life-size Greek figures in various attitudes, listening to and watching the representation of a play. The ceiling consists of a semicircle, prolonged horizontally over the greater part of the auditorium, and beyond this a flat portion raking up over the gallery. The latter is panelled out into squares, lozenges, and circles, which are treated in such a manner as to enhance the brilliancy of the former, which is divided by radiating ornaments into ten compartments, enriched with brilliant arabesques, and with medallions, containing musical instruments and other devices, upon a soft neutral ground. Beneath the proscenium frieze is an entablature, which, continued in a circle round the whole house, forms the gallery front, and is enriched with a bold anthelion, and other ornaments. The lower box fronts are painted with brilliant arabesques and borders, and are further embellished with gold mouldings and delicate amber satin curtains, resters, and Vandyke valances, which contrast admirably both with the pale sage green and gold box linings, and with the ebony seats and cerise-coloured cushions. The proscenium itself is richly decorated with gold and colours harmonising with the other portion; and the drop curtain, by Mr. W. Telbin, in general harmony with the decoration of the house, represents a Greek temple, very beautifully painted in a medallion, set in a frame of lace and fringed with amber drapery. It is almost needless to say that the ceiling is conspicuous by the absence of the ancient and now exploded chandelier. In place of that costly folly the lighting is effected by a powerful sun-burner. The footlights on the stage, too, are so arranged that they emit neither heat, smell, nor vapour. Behind the scenes great advantage has been taken of the height of the old hall, and beams of the roof may still be seen beneath the gridiron. The 'flats' in the upper flies are so constructed that they work without rollers, and a piece of canvas 30 feet in height may be hidden without being folded.

So much for the general arrangement and appearance of the house, which last night looked in every respect one of our most elegant and comfortable theatres when the curtain rose, with the full force of Mr. Wigan's well-selected company assembled on the stage for 'The National Anthem.' A new comedietta, *He's a Lunatic*, by Mr. Felix Dale, afforded some twenty minutes' amusement, and enabled Mr. Sanger, amid considerable merriment, to display both agility and versatility in his conception of an assumed mad baronet, Sir March Hare; but the one-act trifle can hardly be said to have achieved success. There is far too much clap-trap in its dialogue, and some of those which, no doubt, the author considered 'telling points' had better been altogether omitted.

The plot of Mr. Charles Reade's five-act romantic play, *The Double Marriage*, which followed, and constituted the *pièce de résistance* of the entertainment, need not be told. Founded on the well-known novel of *White Lies*, a story suggested by, if not based upon, the French drama *Le Château Grand*, the incidents are pretty closely adhered to, and the *dénoument* results in an unexpected appearance of Colonel Dugardin (Charles Wyndham), just at the moment when Captain Raynal is about to become really allied to Josephine Beaurepaire. Everything that taste or ingenuity, combined with lavish expenditure, could devise, evidently has been done to place the drama before the public to the utmost possible advantage, and with the greatest chance of securing success. The scenery, including the garden of the old Château de Beaurepaire, and the camp before Philipsburgh, as well, indeed, as the old Château itself, is really very beautiful, and reflects high credit on the artist. Every one of the actors engaged in the piece, from Mr. Alfred Wigan, who naturally delineates Captain Raynal, to Mr. Seyton, the sturdy representative of the not over sober Sergeant Lacroix, and from Miss Fanny Addison, with her exquisite portraiture of Josephine, to Miss Henrietta Hodson as the garrulous but tender-hearted maid of all-work, Jacintha—the entire *dramatis personae* sustain their respective parts with an amount of power and ability one would have supposed almost sufficient to carry any tolerably-constructed and moderately well-written romantic play through the ordeal of a first night's representation to the complete approval of an indulgent audience. The *Double Marriage*, however, had no such luck. It hung fire almost at every stage. Excellent acting failed to secure for the piece, or any sections of the piece, either genuine or even apparently hearty applause, and until the pruning-knife is applied, and some of the ridiculously improbable situations are completely excised, Mr. Wigan need not hope to find the leading feature in his opening enterprise running smoothly in the groove. Mr. Reade writes capital novels; but taking the *Double Marriage* as a sample of his adaptive power, he is more successful as a novelist than a dramatist or romantic play constructor. His latest effort requires considerable reconstruction, cutting down, and 'closing in,' and the sooner he sets about the task the greater is the chance that the *Double Marriage* will remain for many nights at the Long Acre theatre. Mr. Lionel Brough, who made his first appearance before a London audience as Dand, fully justified the 'good words' which heralded his approach from the provinces. He has all the material for an excellent actor of the low comic school, and he went through his probationary course last night in such a manner as to leave no doubt that the provinces will see him no more, except, indeed, it may be as an occasional 'star.' Miss Fanny Addison, too, has made her mark. No success could be more complete than hers, and no applause more deserved than that which the audience, throughout the play and at the conclusion of each act, when she was called before the curtain, so freely accorded her. Miss Ellen Terry showed occasional carelessness in her

realisation of a character which might have been made more
prominent and *prononcé;* but this could easily have been
avoided had she taken even one leaf out of the book so
artistically held and read by Rose's mother, the Baroness de
Beaurepaire, truthfully played by Mrs. E. F. Saville.

The strong company engaged did not make the play a success,
and was succeeded by a revival of Tom Taylor's *Still Waters Run
Deep.* The theatre's first success was with H. J. Byron's *Dearer than
Life* on 8 January 1868. In the cast were: J. L. Toole, John Clayton,
Lionel Brough, Henry Irving and Charles Wyndham. Among the
ladies were: Henrietta Hodson (Mrs. Henry Labouchere) and
Fanny Addison.

Burlesque, as always at this date, completed the evening's
entertainment and W. S. Gilbert's *La Vivandière; or, True to the
Corps,* was added to the bill. It satirised Donizetti's opera *The
Daughter of the Regiment.* Irving remained in the company to play
in *The Lancashire Lass,* a melodrama; *The Rivals* (as Falkland)
and to act with Ellen Terry for the first time; they played Katherine
and Petruchio in Garrick's perversion of *The Taming of the Shrew*
in 1868, Ellen Terry then left the stage for the second time.
Irving also played Bill Sykes in a version of *Oliver Twist* with
Henrietta Hodson, Nelly Moore, J. L. Toole, John Ryder, Lionel
Brough and John Clayton: but even with this great cast it failed
and vanished after only a month's run.

F. C. Burnand's *Turn of the Tide* in 1869 was a moderate success
and the company was strengthened, if this were possible, with
Mr. and Mrs. Frank Matthews, Hermann Vezin and George
Rignold.

In 1869-70 Mrs. Wybert Rousby (Clara Dowse), took the
theatre for a season and appeared, with her husband, in an
adaptation of Victor Hugo's *Le Roi S'Amuse* called *The Fool's
Revenge* (known to-day only for the operatic version, *Rigoletto*).
She then appeared in a drama by Tom Taylor, *'Twixt Axe and
Crown.* She had a great success; Erroll Sherson remembers her
as:

> 'the beautiful Mrs. Rousby', for whom Tom Taylor had a
> mania for writing historical plays. She had been a Miss Dowse,
> daughter of an army officer whom Rousby, lessee and manager
> of the Jersey theatre, had met there and married when she

was but sixteen. Beautiful she certainly was, if not a great actress, and scored a very popular success in a play called *'Twixt Axe and Crown* dealing with episodes in the life of the Princess Elizabeth before she became Queen. It was the usual type of historical play setting all history at naught. In one scene of this, as the Princess Elizabeth, she is discovered in a dungeon of the Tower awaiting execution by order of her sister, so elegantly called in our English history books, 'Bloody Mary.' The scene is very dark; Mrs. Rousby with her beautiful hair hanging down her back is shivering with dread; we hear the hammering of the scaffold as it is erected outside; she delivers a long speech on the iniquity of her sister and her own situation and then, uttering a blood-curdling shriek, falls fainting to the ground. Playgoers would go again and again on purpose to hear this shriek, as they did many years later to hear Haidée Wright shriek in *The Sign of the Cross*. Such were the means by which Mrs. Rousby made her name as an actress—great beauty and a loud shriek—and she was doubtless much helped by the confirmed belief of Tom Taylor that his mission in life was to write historical plays for her to act in.

She returned to this theatre in 1871 in *Joan of Arc*, another Tom Taylor play.

Labouchere came out of the background and bought the theatre after a dispute over the position of his wife in the company. His main aim in entering the theatrical world was to exploit Henrietta Hodson, and for the next few years he ran the theatre himself, more or less successfully. With John Ryder as his producer, he revived *A Midsummer Night's Dream*, with Samuel Phelps as Bottom, *The Tempest*, with Henrietta Hodson as Ariel, *Cymbeline*, in which she played Imogen and *Virginius*, for the same lady to play Virginia, but he had his failures as well as his successes. Labouchere tells in *Truth* 16 August 1877:

> The piece on which I lost most was an adaptation of *The Last Days of Pompeii* [January 1872]. Everything went wrong in this piece. I wanted to have—after the manner of the ancients— acrobats dancing on the tight rope over the heads of the guests at the feast. The guests, however, absolutely declined to be danced over. Only one acrobat made his appearance. A

rope was stretched for him behind the revellers, and I trusted to stage illusion for the rest. The acrobat was a stout negro. Instead of lightly tripping it upon his rope, he moved about like an elephant and finally fell off his rope like a stricken buffalo. In the second act, the head of a statue was to fall off and to crush Mr. Ryder who was a magician. There was a man inside the statue whose mission was to push over the head. With folded arms and stern air Mr. Ryder gazed at the statue awaiting the portentous event that was to crush him to the earth, notwithstanding the mystic power that he wielded. The head remained firm on its neck. The man inside had solaced himself with so much beer that he was drunk and incapable, and Mr. Ryder had, much to the amazement of the audience, to knock down the head that was to crush him. In the third act, the stage represented a Roman amphitheatre. In the midst of the gorgeously dressed crowd, sat Mr. Ryder. 'Bring forth the lion,' he said. The audience thrilled at the idea of a real lion being marched on to the stage. Now I had no lion, and I had discarded the idea of putting a lion's skin on a donkey. An attendant therefore walked in and said, 'Sir, the lion will not come.' Those of the audience who were not hissing roared with laughter. The last act was to represent the eruption of Vesuvius and the destruction of Pompeii. The mountain had only been painted in time for the first night. I had never seen it. What was my horror when the curtain rose upon a temple with a sort of large sugar loaf behind it. At first I could not imagine what was the meaning of this sugar loaf. But when it proceeded to emit crackers, I found that it was Vesuvius.

Henrietta Hodson was Nydia, the blind girl, showing what she could do in pathetic parts as well as in the role of 'principal boy' in burlesque or any other kind of 'breeches' part.

After Labouchere got tired of running the theatre solely for the gratification of his wife, at great personal expense, the Queen's was let to various managements. Ryder remained to play in several plays while the theatre was managed by E. Clifton. *Amos Clark* by Watts Phillips was quite a success in October 1872.

Marie Litton from the Royal Court, Daniel Bandman and his wife, Millie, (Mrs. Bandman Palmer), were both there for seasons.

In 1873 Charles Reade's *The Wandering Heir* was revived an
he persuaded Ellen Terry to return to the stage (for the thir
time) to take up the part of Phillipa, vacated by Mrs. John Wood

Among other managers, John Coleman presented himself a
Henry V in 1876 and Phelps made one of his last appearances a
Henry IV in an interpolated scene from the earlier play, used as
prologue. Salvini played Othello and Hamlet (both in Italian)
the same year, and was only prevented by illness from adding
Macbeth to the characters he portrayed during the season.

The theatre had fallen on bad times, it lacked a guiding hand
no actor-manager was in complete control.

In July 1877 Promenade concerts were tried under Jules
Rivière. He tells the story of this season in his reminiscences *My
Musical Life and Recollections* (1893):

> . . . it was altogether a disastrous affair for me in Long Acre.
> And yet the names of the four promoters of the scheme
> looked well on paper. They were Mr. N., a City banker,
> Mr. S., a brewer, Count d'A., and Mr. B., [J. C. Bennett]
> who was spoken of as the manager. There was nothing to
> complain of for the first fortnight, seeing that the salaries were
> paid on Saturday at the regular time; but, at the end of the
> third week, only part of the money was forthcoming, and I
> was put off with a positive promise for the payment of the
> balance. The over-due account, however, was not paid at the
> beginning of the fourth week, and, yet, for my own sake, I
> did not like to break faith with the public by stopping the
> concerts, so we went on. The last night, by arrangement, was
> set apart for my benefit, and with the kind assistance of several
> leading and favourite artists, I was able to advertise a most
> attractive programme. With a view, as I thought, of taking all
> necessary precautions, I had our book-keeper from Leicester
> Square to look after the receipts, and my old friend D'Oyly
> Carte volunteered to come and survey matters for me in front
> of the house. Disaster, therefore, seemed to be impossible,
> but it nevertheless came. I found the house quite full on my
> arrival for the concert, and I was, moreover, put in good
> temper by the garlands of flowers I found ornamenting my
> conductor's desk, not to mention a handsome bouquet that
> was placed in front of my wife's box. The first part of the

concert over, I naturally hastened round to the front to learn something about the figures, and was horrified to learn that the four worthy directors and managers had cleared out, taking care before their departure to pocket every shilling of the receipts. Nor was this all, for the brokers were in the building for rent, and among the things seized was an Erard's grand piano. I felt considerably discouraged, I own, but I made an appointment for all the musicians and vocalists who had taken part in the concerts to meet me on the following Monday afternoon. Meanwhile I got together the necessary sum to pay everybody, and this amounted to nearly £600. I have never seen any of these four directors since, and all I have ever learnt of them was that the 'city banker' was soon afterwards in the bankruptcy court for £40,000.

At these concerts a touch of novelty was introduced by the exhibition of The Wonderful Electrical Instrument the Telephone

THE TELEPHONE

Invented by Mr. Cromwell F. Varley

By means of which Musical Sounds are transmitted over long distances. The following Melodies will be Played at the Canterbury Hall, in the Westminster Bridge Road, and rendered audible at this Theatre:

1. *The Blue Bells of Scotland.* 3. *Home, Sweet Home.*
2. *The Last Rose of Summer.* 4. *See, the Conquering Hero Comes.*

An Explanatory Address will be spoken by Professor Field. [This was printed in the programme.]
The Telephone, or Musical Telegraph, is an apparatus by which sounds of variable pitch can be conveyed from one place to another by means of electricity. To such perfection has this invention, which undoubtedly ranks with the most wonderful ever evolved from the mind of man, already been brought, that the component notes of a melody can be sent along a wire and re-produced in proper order, distinctly and loudly, at the distant end.

Sound of any kind is produced by agitation of the atmosphere, the pitch or tone of the sound being determined by the amount, or rate per second, of this agitation or vibration. When the pulsations follow one another slowly, however violent they may be, the resulting note is of low pitch: as they increase in rapidity the pitch ascends, each note of the scale having its own peculiar rate of vibration, the slightest divergence from which causes it to sound sharp or flat.

To transmit sound by the Telephone, these atmospheric vibrations have to be collected and transformed into electricity, which must then be sent along a wire in waves or impulses corresponding in their number per second to the atmospheric vibrations which are proper to the particular note to be reproduced. At the distant end, these electrical impulses have to be re-converted into sound, and in this process lies the most novel part of the invention, Mr. Cromwell F. Varley having found means to produce what is nothing more nor less than musical thunder.

Lightning, that is, electricity of very high tension, in passing, forces the air away on all sides, leaving a vacuum in its trail. The motion of the air rushing to fill this vacuum produces the sound called thunder. In the Telephone, by means of an instrument, technically known as a condenser, of very special construction, each electrical wave or impulse received from the wire is made to establish a vacuum which the air immediately rushes to fill. It does this, and is re-expelled as many times per second as impulses arrive from the wire, causing a sound sufficiently loud to be heard in every part of a large theatre, and of any desired pitch.

A singer's voice may thus be transmitted along a wire, and heard afar off in the shape of miniature thunder.

The melody issuing from the Telephone can be accompanied on the pianoforte or by a full orchestra in the same way as a vocalist can. It is also capable of many amusing modifications. For instance if two Telephones are placed side by side on a platform in London, the ends of the wires in connection with them terminating, one at Brighton and the other at Liverpool they will sing a duet in good style; and in the same way Brighton, Edinburgh, Bristol, and Ipswich, if the necessary arrangements could be carried out, would perform a quartet, the four artistes being guided by a conductor in London beating time by telegraph simultaneously to all four places.

In 1877 a change of name was tried. Alexander Henderson took over and re-christened it the National Theatre. (This name had been used before when Frederick Strange converted the Royal Amphitheatre Holborn into a Theatre in 1873.) Henderson opened on 27 October with the 'Production of a Melo-Drama, in a Prologue and Three Acts, founded on a Novel by Prince Lubomirski, and entitled *Russia; or, The Exiles of the Angara*,' it was by H. B. Farnie and Robert Reece.

The Programme notes . . .

Scenery by Julian Hicks, H. P. Hall and Numerous Assistants. The Characteristic Russian and Siberian Dresses executed by Mrs. May, Mrs. Corgan and Assistants, after Original Drawings. Arms and Accoutrements from proper authorities. Properties and Accessories by Brunton. Machinery and Effects by George Banting and Assistants. Groupings and Incidental Dance by Mr. John Lauri.

Herman Vezin, John Billington and once again Henrietta Hodson were in the cast. The programme describes the action, scene by scene:

PROLOGUE
Scene 1.

Reception Room, Ball, and Illuminated Garden Scene at the

Winter Palace, St. Petersburg.

How Madame Dugarey, wife of the French Ambassador at St. Petersburg, forms a Ladies' Club, and how Tatiana, Countess Lanine becomes a member—How Olga, sister of Count Vladimir Lanine is wooed, but not won by Schelm, of the Diplomatic Bureau—How finding himself snubbed by the Czar, and ousted in Olga's affections by L'Estrange of the English Guards, Schelm intrigues with his creature Muller for a deadly vengeance—The Sham Plot The Letters—The rendezvous for No. 17, Square Tcherbakoff—How Vladimir vows to seek his wife, and how L'Estrange swears to go with him—The faithful Flannigan, and the triumph of Schelm over his rival, Palkine, Colonel of the Gendarmerie.

Scene 2.

The Old House on the Neva, by Moonlight.

The Patrol—The Police Agents—The meeting of Schelm and Muller—Arrival Vladimir and L'Estrange—Into the trap!

Scene 3.

The Conspiracy

The address of Muller to the Gambling Club—Treason— Arrival of Vladimir and L'Estrange. The vengeance of Schelm bursts—Attack of the Military on the Conspirator's haunt—Arrest of Schelm's rivals and his victims—Siberia!

ACT I

Scene 1.

Hut of the Exiles in the Snow-Wastes of Siberia.

How Tatiana and Olga by permission of the Czar, share the fortunes of the Exiles, Vladimir and L'Estrange, in the snow-wilds of Siberia—How they arrive from Irchutsk and the welcome surprise they bring—A little supper in slavery, and the intrusion of the Cossack Patrol—Arrival in the village of the Pilgrims, who are to minister to the poor exiles—One Pilgrim—and a welcome one—comes to the fireside, (rather stove-side) of Vladimir—Preparations for escape—The new Governor arrives on a visit of inspection—Schelm!—Olga is obdurate—and the Exiles, taking for once the law into their own hands, imprison Schelm, and escape into the deserts of Siberia!

Scene 2.

Outskirts of the Pine Forest.

The remnant of the conspiracy of No. 17, Square Tcherbakoff —How Muller, once a creature, now a victim of Schelm, forms against his old tyrant, the brotherhood of the Lake.

Scene 3.

Virgin Snow Forest.

The Exiles lost in the forest—The sledge overturned—and reindeer dead—How the soldiers track down the fugitives, and Schelm again renews his visit to Olga—The compact over the inanimate body of Tatiana—A love for a life!— Return of Vladimir and L'Estrange, and meeting with the Brotherhood of the Lake—Vengeance!—Down with Schelm!

ACT II

Scene 1.

The Governor's House.—The Conflagration.

The Bridal of Schelm and Olga—How Tatiana gleans the truth from the Cossack Officer—A marriage scene between husband and wife, and the midnight attack of the Brethren of the Lake—Muller settles account with Schelm—The torture by fire—Conflagration of the Governor's Chalet.

Scene 2.

Rocky Ravine leading to the River.

The fugitives on their way to the frontier, near the banks of the Angara—The farewell Muller.

Scene 3.

Block House and Ford on the Angara River.

How the boatman of the Angara ferries Tatiana, Olga, and Vladimir across; and how L'Estrange and Flannigan held the Block house against the pursuing Cossacks—How plank by plank the boat house falls, and the brave defenders of the Ford are overpowered—How in that bitter moment, they see also Olga and Tatiana captured on the further side of the river —Schelm again triumphant.

ACT III

Scene

The Commandant's Quarters on the Upper
Fortifications of Irchutsk.

How Schelm, scorched and wounded almost to death, gloats over the last vengeance, he is about to exact from his victims—How he tries to delay the arrival of the Czar, by a letter, and the letter fortunately falls into the wrong hands—How the exiles are ordered out for death, and how the arrival of the Czar cuts the Gordian knot, restores our heroes and heroines to liberty, and hastens the disgrace and death of Schelm—
Denouement.

The production was a complete failure and in January 1878 the theatre resumed its old name.

The end was in sight. More or less the same company acted in *Fatherland*, an adaptation of Sardou's 'Great Historical Drama' *Patrie*. This too only ran a few weeks.

Mrs. Rousby returned with a revival of *'Twixt Axe and Crown* in February 1878. Neville Moritz, a Hungarian tragedian, appeared as Shylock and Othello to storms of derision from the press, and Mrs. Rousby returned yet again in April and May. She evidently had a difficult time as she made the following statement in *The Era:*

> At the conclusion of my Management of the Queen's Theatre I beg to offer my sincere thanks to the Ladies and Gentlemen who have so ably assisted me, and to acknowledge the kindness with which they have, in addition to Miss Henrietta Hodson, Mr. Arthur Wood, and Mr. John Ryder, tendered their services on the occasion of my Benefit this Evening.
>
> To the Public, I owe a deep debt of gratitude for their support, and more especially for the generous expression of sympathy which greeted an appeal I was compelled to make for their protection and assistance to put down what appeared to be an organised and cowardly attempt on the part of a well-trained clique to interrupt the performances generally and make me the special object of their malicious persecutions.
> May 18th 1878
>
> CLARA ROUSBY

The Theatre is advertised as 'To be Let' in the following issue. The next mention is for 'A Grand Amateur Performance' under very distinguished Royal Patronage, and with a company of 'Society Ladies and Gentlemen.' They performed *New Men and Old Acres* on 13 July 'For the Benefit of Mrs. Beaumont, lately Lady Housekeeper at Drury Lane and the Adelphi Theatres, who has met with a sad accident at Drury Lane Theatre, and has sustained such severe injuries that she is now lying at St. Thomas's Hospital, and will be unable to move for some weeks, and it is improbable that she will ever be able to resume her duties. She is quite destitute owing to the desertion of her husband and there are three children to be supported.'

That night the theatre held its last audience and it went up to let once again, but the advertisements soon vanished. The building was sold by the end of the year, the auditorium demolished and converted into the stores of The Universities Co-operative Association, which opened 1 September 1879. *The Illustrated Sporting and Dramatic News* 20 September explained the conversion:

> The Clergy Co-operative Association, which started in November last year, and subsequently by a vote of the shareholders changed the title to the Universities Co-operative Association, purchased the premises, and early in January sold all the fittings of the theatre and commenced its entire demolition, the bare walls only being left standing. The building has now been transformed into a very handsome store. The entrance hall and the staircases, which are remnants of the old building, form prominent features in the new one. The entrance hall is 50 by 23 ft., and is ornamented in the upper part with busts of Chaucer, Shakespeare, Milton, and other celebrities.

Eventually the premises were taken over in 1911 by Odhams Press who were gradually extending their vast buildings all across Endell Street to Arne Street, and over Wilson Street (re-named Dryden Street). Parts of the old Theatre and Stores remained incorporated in the Odhams buildings. In 1938 the frontage of the Theatre which had remained throughout, facing down Bow Street at Number 92 Long Acre, was re-built as Odhams main entrance. External walls of the long forgotten Theatre still remain beyond this entrance and in Arne Street.

The name 'Queen's' has been recurrent throughout theatre history.

The first theatre in the Haymarket was called the Queen's when it was built in 1705. (It became the King's on the death of Queen Anne. See *The Theatres of London*, Her Majesty's Theatre.) Later the Little Tottenham Street Theatre was called the Queen's on and off between 1831 and 1865 when it became the Prince of Wales's (see *The Theatres of London*, the Scala Theatre). The Royal Albion became the New Queen's in 1833 (see number 28) and the Novelty was called, among its many names, the New Queen's Theatre in 1890, but only for a few weeks (see number 11). The name was to be revived again in 1907 when another Queen's Theatre, in Shaftesbury Avenue, was opened (see *The Theatres of London*).

19
The Royal Strand Theatre

Reinagle and Barker's New Panorama, Burford's Panorama, The New Strand (Subscription) Theatre, Punch's Playhouse

Strand
In a block bounded by Surrey Street and Strand Lane, backed by Surrey Lane (now Surrey Steps)

FIRST BUILDING

Opened as a Panorama, Reinagle and Barker's *New Panorama; a Picturesque View of Rome, and The Surrounding Country*, 1803. Under the management of Ramsey Richard Reinagle and Thomas Edward Barker.

Became a dissenting chapel 1830, converted into a theatre 1831.

Opened as the New Strand (Subscription) Theatre, 26 January 1832 with an address delivered by Miss Cleaver, and *Professionals Puzzled; or, Struggles at Starting*, a burletta, followed by a revival of *Mystification*, a comedy in one act, and a revival of *Love's Frailties; or, Passion and Repentance*, a domestic drama.

Under the management of Benjamin Lionel Rayner.

The title Subscription was dropped by 1833 but New remained until 1850.

Enlarged and gallery added 1839.

Known as Punch's Playhouse (Strand Theatre), 28 April 1851.

Under the management of William Copeland.

Name reverted to the Strand Theatre 1852.

Re-decorated and partly re-constructed and re-opened as the Royal Strand Theatre 5 April 1858 with *Nothing Venture Nothing Win*, a comedy by Sterling Coyne, followed by an occasional address by Albert Smith, delivered by Ada Swanborough, and *Fra Diavalo*, a burlesque by H. J. Byron.

Under the management of Ada Swanborough.
Partly re-built and enlarged, re-opened 18 November 1865.
Closed 29 July 1882. Completely re-built on an enlarged site,
giving exits and entrances in Surrey Street and Strand Lane,
with stage door in Surrey Street.

SECOND THEATRE

Opened as the Royal Strand Theatre 18 November 1882 with a
revival of *The Heir-at-Law* by George Colman the younger,
followed by *Frolique!* a new musical comedy in one act by H. J.
Byron and H. B. Farnie.
Under the management of Mrs. Edward Swanborough.
Closed 13 May 1905 and demolished.
Aldwych Tube Station and an office block now covers the site.

THE LITTLE THEATRE on the south side of the Strand, between
Surrey Street (which led directly down to the river bank), and
Strand Lane, began its life as a Panorama.

    The inventor of this form of exhibition was Robert Barker, who
obtained a royal licence in 1787 for the exclusive use of his
invention for fourteen years. The *Survey of London* volume 34
explains:

> The Patent stated that 'after much Study, Labour and Expence
> he hath Invented an entire new contrivance or Apparatus
> which he calls La Nature a coup d'oeil for the purpose of
> displaying views of Nature at large by Oil painting . . . or
> drawing, [and] that he is the first and true Inventor thereof.'
>   The principal problem which he had to overcome was that the
> drawings being made on flat surfaces, when placed together
> in a circle the horizontal lines appeared curved instead of
> straight, unless on the exact eye level of the eye; and to meet
> this difficulty Barker had to invent a system of curved lines
> peculiarly adapted to the concave surface of this picture, which
> should appear straight when viewed from a platform at a
> certain level in the centre. After exhibiting views of Edinburgh
> and London in various large rooms, he built himself a circular

building especially for his purpose, on a plot of ground on the east side of the new Leicester Place, with its main entrance at 14 Leicester Square, in the extreme corner. He opened in 1793.

The rotunda, which was 90 feet in diameter and 57 feet high, was divided into two compartments, which are concentric circles: this contrivance gives a double exhibition, by presenting for view two distinct pictures, an invention that happily has produced the most beneficial effects, not merely in pecuniary advantage, but in having at all times a picture to exhibit whilst the other is in painting.

The upper picture was suspended from the roof, and as the circle of the upper picture is much less than the under, an advantage is attained, that the under picture without interruption can occupy if requisite, almost the whole height of the sides of the building.

It is said that a joint stock company (in which Lord Elcho took a prominent part) was formed to help Barker to pay for the new building, but that the profits of the exhibition soon enabled him to buy all the shares.

This Panorama, under the Barker family and their successors the Burfords, existed until 1865 when it was closed. The building was then adapted as a French Church, the main entrance reconstructed in Leicester Place, the Leicester Square entrance remaining as the entrance to a school, part of the Church property. After war damage in 1940 the Church was re-built, still retaining its old rotunda shape from the original Panorama. Part of the old Panorama entrance in Leicester Square still remains as an entrance to a French Social Club and a snack bar.

Robert Barker was assisted by his sons, Henry Aston Barker and Thomas Edward Barker. When the original patent expired in 1801, Edward, who had quarrelled with his father, and one of his father's assistant painters, Ramsay Richard Reinagle, joined together and made plans to build themselves a rival Panorama on ground between Numbers 168 and 169 Strand, two doors west of Surrey Street. 'Reinagle and Barker's New Panorama, near the New Church in the Strand,' eventually opened in 1803.

The Picture of London for 1804 (published December 1803), after noting the Leicester Square Panorama, gives:

Reinagle and Barker's New Panorama; being a Picturesque View of Rome, and the surrounding Country, now exhibiting near the New Church, in the Strand.

This view is taken from the Villa Lodovici, on the brow of the Pincian Hill, by R. R. Reinagle. The building for exhibiting it was erected under the immediate direction of Thomas Edward Barker, eldest son of Mr. Barker, of the Panorama, Leicester Square. This picture is to be succeeded by a second View of Rome, from the Tower of the Capitol, which embraces all the well known antiquities of the Forum, now the Campo Vacino; the most part of the old walls and aqueducts, &c. and every object that can interest the public, in a view of that celebrated city.

Among the great number of similar exhibitions which we have had, and have, this when taken in every point of view, claims a decided pre-eminence. The aerial part of the painting is admirably conceived, and wonderfully delineated; without hardness of outline, or observing the other parts of the picture, it gives that misty hue which we often see in Nature, but which Art had not often succeeded in imitating.

Robert Barker when he died in 1806 left the Leicester Square Panorama to his son Henry, with no mention of Thomas in his Will. Henry continued the family business, and took John Burford into partnership, they bought out their rival in the Strand in 1816 and continued to run it together till 1826. From this date John Burford (who died the following year), and his brother Robert who succeeded him, showed Panoramas here till 1830. He then devoted his energies entirely to the Leicester Square business, and the Strand building was converted into a dissenting chapel and used for a short time by some 'wandering sectarians'. In 1831 it was taken over by Benjamin Lionel Rayner, an actor famous for his Yorkshire characters. He had as his partners in the venture, a 'Captain Bell and a Mr. Galbraith who performed as a conjuror under the name of Henry'. The work of re-construction was done in the short time of seven weeks, with Charles Broad as architect.

The theatre was opened as the New Strand (Subscription) Theatre on 26 January 1832. A play bill announcing the opening stated:

New Strand (Subscription) Theatre. Late Burford's
Panorama, two doors from Surrey Street. Under the direction
of Mr. Rayner.

The Proprietors of this establishment having built, within
the walls of these Premises, an entirely new Interior, substantial and complete in all its parts, with the closest care and
attention to convenience, comfort and elegance—where seeing,
hearing, and respiration, have formed the leading features
of the design—under the superintendence of an Architect of
experience and ability, consisting of a Dress Circle, First
Circle, Twelve Private Boxes, and Pit: And having selected,
in addition to many well-known Favourites from the Metropolitan Theatres, such available Talent of established reputation, as could be procured from the Provinces, without
arrogating to themselves more than an anxious desire to
render the combination as effective as possible, respectfully
submit the whole to the approbation of the already numerous
list of Subscribers, and whose who hereafter may think proper
to honor them with their commands, fully assured that they
will support where they are satisfied, and patronize only where
they are pleased.

The critic of The Tatler, 25 January 1832, went to a preview of the
theatre:

We were much pleased on entering here last night, to partake
of the private view, to see a display of taste and elegance
which whatever may have been the case in former times, may
now in this and other instances, be fairly associated with our
ideas of a minor theatre. The house itself is more commodious
than we expected, and the seats, generally speaking, seem
arranged with proper regard to the visual organs of the
visitors. There is one exception however: and as we are not
unlikely to be personal sufferers by it, we will be patriotic
enough to mention it beforehand. The partitions of the two
private boxes in the upper circle (on each side) ought to be
slanting, the same as those in the dress circle; straight as they
are at present, the persons who may have the ill fate to sit by
them, will not have the least sight of the stage. This is an
inconvenience felt more or less at all the houses, particularly
at the small ones, owing to their narrowness; but here the

house being wide, rather than deep, the remedy may easily
be applied. The panels of the boxes are of a pale colour, the
lower tier ornamented, but not too profusely with gold,
relieved in the centre and between each, with a little crimson;
those of the upper tier are of the same ground, with somewhat
more of the gold, and without the crimson: six handsome
glass chandeliers are suspended round the boxes. There is a
new drop scene, and a handsome crimson curtain, or rather
curtains, which withdraw on each side like those at the
Olympic. The *ensemble* strikes the eye pleasingly. How deep
the stage may be we know not; but from what we saw of it,
we should expect to find it sufficiently roomy for all its purposes. There can be no doubt that everybody (after our corner
friends are accommodated) will be able to see and hear. We
must not forget a peculiarity,—there is no gallery. The
division of the house is into boxes, dress and upper tier at
different prices, and pit; the prices 4s., 3s., and 2s. We offer no
opinion on the expediency of this policy; if not found to
answer, there will, we conceive, be no insurmountable difficulty in erecting one, considering the space still left between
the present roof and the sky. There is, moreover, in addition
to all we have mentioned, a small saloon, with a handsome
chandelier, the expense of which, with the other fittings,
must have been no trifle. The company present were amused
with a few songs during the evening, including 'God save the
King' and 'Rule Britannia,' sung by a part of the audience,
and the whole concluded with three cheers for the success of
the proprietors. In this we beg to join, in the qualified words
of our friend Sir Oliver, though with a happier presage,
'May they have all the success they deserve.'

The first night was described by another critic:

Struggles at Starting concludes with the exhibition of a transparency representing an unlikeness of William IV, with
the motto, 'Reform it altogether.' In *Mystification*, a Mr.
Parker, as a jealous, furious Spanish Don, made so fierce an exit
through two folding-doors in the back of a scene, that he
fairly knocked them both off their hinges. The audience
only laughed at this, but anon roared at the sight of the once
more displayed transparency, with the advice staring the

P

violent jealous gentleman in the face to 'reform it altogether!'
I have just read the fourth edition of Macnish's *Anatomy of
Drunkenness;* but in the part that treats on the various effects
of this failing, I do not remember seeing any mention of the
one represented by Mr. Dodd when enacting drunkenness to
the life. He not only lost his hair, but lost it *en masse*; while,
to complete the strangeness of the phenomenon, a fresh crop
of a totally different colour immediately appeared in the place
of the fugitive scalp! I, moreover, always read the published
lists of new inventions and new patents; but among the
former, though so richly deserving the latter, I have yet seen
no mention of a door fixed at the side that bears the handle,
bolts, and latch, and opening at the hinges! yet such a door
did I, and all assembled, observe in frequent action in a
cottage scene, on the Thursday afore-named. The curtain,
which opens and closes *à la Vestris*, was sadly refractory,
stubbornly refusing to vanish when we were anxious to see
what was behind it; and when we were not wishing for it nor
dreaming of it, slipping its moorings and rushing im-
petuously together. It meets, moreover, with such force
that it invariably opens again, just soon and far enough to
betray the scampering off the stage of fixed groups of fainted
ladies.

Another said:

A comic opening address was delivered by Miss Cleaver, a
débutante, and two new burlettas were produced, one—
founded on the *fracas* between the majors and minors—
called *Professionals Puzzled; or, Struggles at Starting*, and the
other entitled *Mystification*, in which Mrs. Waylett was to
have appeared, but being suddenly indisposed, Miss Cleaver
became her substitute at a short notice. The last piece was
Love's Frailties; or, Passion and Repentance to introduce
Rayner as Lubin Greenwell.

The house was estimated to hold 1,501. At this time in theatrical
history a concerted effort was being made by the minor theatres
to break the monopoly of the Patent Houses (see Number 13),
and vindicate their own rights. E. L. Blanchard says:

For a long time the theatre had to contend with legal difficulties arising from the want of a Lord Chamberlain's licence, and money was taken by the sale of tickets anywhere but at the theatre 'Tickets and boxes to be had of Mr. Dickson, next door to the Theatre: and of Mr. Goodwin, opposite the Theatre; Also at the Box-office, No. 3 Surrey Street; Ebers' Library, Bond Street; C. Wright, Wine Merchant; H. Wray, Music-seller, Haymarket; and of Mr. Sams, Bookseller to His Majesty, St. James' Street.' A few weeks after opening Harriet Waylett was in control as manager, and was the chief star, and her charming ballads were everywhere on the lips of the lovers of song, but they would not come to the new theatre to hear her sing them. Bayle Bernard brought out for her his capital piece of *The Four Sisters; or, Woman's Worth and Woman's Wrongs*, but the first month was not encouraging to the management. In March, Madame Celeste appeared here in a drama called *Alp the Brigand*, and Captain Bell, who had a pecuniary interest in the undertaking, came out as an actor, and very soon went in again. In vain did that highly-gifted and versatile writer, William Leman Rede, besides taking an active part in the direction, ply a busy pen to provide a constant succession of novelties. Though excellently supported by a capital company, then including Miss M. Glover, Selby, and Oxberry, and on the second Saturday in November the Strand closed for want of patronage. Rayner was to have had a 'complimentary' benefit on the Monday night, but the doors were not opened to the few who came with their tickets, and then people remembered that the musicians had been frequently seen for some nights previously to take up their hats and walk out of the orchestra, and how they had often left the vocalist to sing to a solitary violin, whilst rumbling sounds of deep voices in angry dispute were frequently heard beneath the stage as a discordant accompaniment.

In January 1833 Fanny Kelly re-opened the theatre and gave her one woman entertainment 'in which she embodied some twenty distinct characters'. She was a success and the theatre filled. She also started her Dramatic School here at this time, (see the Royalty Theatre Number 20). In October Benjamin Wrench and James

Russell took over and a farce, *His First Champagne*, by W. L. Rede, was produced with great success, but the management put on the playbill: 'The public are respectfully informed that Money will be taken at the doors.' The Lord Chamberlain, acting, as usual, on information laid by one of the Patent managers, closed the theatre after a week. Later, in December, Russell re-opened with an entertainment written for him by Tom Dibdin, calling himself 'the Stranded Actor'. Farces, burlesques, and burlettas, were the main attraction, but all kinds of expedients were now resorted to in order to evade the strict letter of the law. It was declared illegal to take money at the doors, and to escape the penalty the money was taken at a *window*! Then an adjoining sweetmeat establishment was annexed to the premises, and visitors paid four shillings an ounce for rose lozenges, and had an admission to the Strand given them, or bought half an ounce of peppermint drops for two shillings, and had a gratuitous check for the pit thrown into the bargain. In 1834 Miss Waylett was back again in management. She opened on 24 March 1834. By an arrangement with Glossop, who ran the Royal Victoria Theatre across the river, the bill announced:

Admission Gratis

The Purchaser of a Ticket for the Dress Boxes, 4s., for the Royal Victoria Theatre, may receive an Admission Gratis to the Boxes of the Strand Theatre; The Purchaser of a Ticket for the Upper Boxes, 2s., for the Royal Victoria Theatre, may receive an Admission Gratis to the Pit of the Strand Theatre. Purchasers of Half Price Tickets for the Royal Victoria, may receive an Admission Gratis at half-past 8 to the Strand Theatre.

Purchasers of Private Box Tickets for the Royal Victoria Theatre, may be admitted to a Private Box Gratis at the Strand Theatre.

The above Tickets will be admitted on separate Evenings at either Theatre. Box-Office of the Royal Victoria Theatre, next door to the Strand Theatre, under the direction of Mr. Wardell, where Tickets may be purchased, and Places and Private Boxes taken.

The company, besides Harriet Waylett, contained Louisa Nisbett, and Pricilla Horton. Its playwrights included Gilbert à Beckett and other well-known burlesque writers of the period. In the midst of success and probably because of it, the theatre was again closed by the Lord Chamberlain in March 1835, and the company summonsed to Bow Street and fined. It was said that 'By order of the Lord Chamberlain eighty-six families were suddenly thrown out of a comfortable subsistence'. It was not till a year later that, Blanchard says:

> An act of justice too long delayed was performed. The inter-dict hitherto imposed by the Lord Chamberlain was removed, and the Strand was then allowed to be opened for entertainments similar to those of the Olympic and the Adelphi. A public meeting had been called, at which Thomas Duncombe, M.P., had consented to preside, but the matter having been in the meantime amicably arranged, it was considered unnecessary to discuss the question. Rayner had a month before this opened the theatre, with a magistrate's licence, and with a series of 'non-dramatic' entertainments, which were regulated in strict accordance with the terms of his privilege. The manager took occasion, however, in his opening speech, to draw attention to the great absurdity of the whole proceeding. His licence for the Strand was, he explained, exactly the same as that for Astley's, the Surrey, and the Victoria; yet he could not exhibit dramatic pieces as they did on the other side of the Thames because those theatres were 'out of the Lord Chamberlain's jurisdiction.' This glaring anomaly had never been so clearly illustrated before. The force of public opinion helped to show the errors of the whole system, and soon after to bring about the passing of the Act which came into operation in 1843, and broke the monopoly of the Patent theatres.

The theatre re-opened on 25 April 1836 with *The Painter of Ghent* by Douglas Jerrold, in which the playwright made his stage debut in the title role. Under the joint management of Douglas Jerrold himself, and his father-in-law, W. J. Hammond.

The theatre was enlarged and a gallery added to hold 800 people at one shilling, half price at 8.45. Boxes were three shillings and the pit one and six. The new management achieved an outstanding success with *Othello* (*According to Act of Parliament*), 'a dramatic burlesque burletta which satisfied the prevailing restrictions on the drama at the minors.' It set the pattern of burlesques at the theatre which was to persist for many years. Jerrold went on from strength to strength as a playwright and Hammond made enough money to take Drury Lane in 1839, but lost at the Patent house what he had made at the Strand.

The luck of the Strand did not hold and for a time managements came and went, till Henry Hall, a burlesque comedian who had been in Hammond's company, remained from 1842 to 1845. The theatre then became a show place for General Tom Thumb and the Bosjesmans Family of South African natives.

The colourful Victorian playwright, journalist and manager, Fox Cooper took the theatre and reduced the prices to stalls, three shillings; boxes, one and six; pit, one shilling and gallery, fourpence. The lowest was reached in 1847 when it was converted into a dance hall, with the pit floor raised to the stage level. A contemporary account says:

We were passing through the Strand the other evening, when our eyes were suddenly arrested by a placard, on which was printed, in large characters, the immortal name of *Frascati*. *Frascati!* thought we, can he have again entered into the land of the living, and taken up his abode in the *Strand Theatre?* he whom kings, nobles, and the loveliest dames of *la belle France* were in the habit of assembling, to win or lose their thousands of a night, whose magnificent *salons* were fitted so gorgeously as to excite the admiration of the world? We will enter. The thought had no sooner passed through our cranium, than we found ourself paying our twelvepenny profile of Victoria, and in we went.

'Heavens! what a sight burst on our enraptured gaze!'

Yes, we, who remember Frascati in its palmiest days, when we thought its splendours could never be equalled, saw them eclipsed! yes, in the small area of the *Strand Theatre!* It is indeed, what the poet Bunn would call a 'blaze of triumph.' The boxes are entirely covered with looking-glass, magnificent chandeliers, Cupids, Mercurys, nymphs, and satyrs; figures bearing flaming torches in their hands, are suspended from the ceiling; splendid works of art, placed upon pedestals, meet you at every corner, the whole forming a *coup d'oeil* that must be seen to be believed. The orchestra, in which we counted forty of the first musicians of the day, led by Mr. Sedgwick, is one sheet of glass. Under the Orchestra, more glass, and the rarest exotics; if we were to describe it poetically, we could not do justice to the scene; 'tis, in fact, a perfect enchantment—a realization of fairy land! Go, pay your shilling, look for and at yourself.

It was not till 1848, five years after the monopoly had been broken, that the Strand became a recognised home of 'the British Drama'. William Farren (the second of that name), with his son Henry, took the theatre and put on *The Clandestine Marriage, The Road to Ruin, The Love Chase* and other stock 'old comedies'. In his company were Julia Glover, Fanny Stirling, Mr. and Mrs. Leigh Murray and Henry Compton. This regime was the first to raise the reputation of the Strand to that of a major London house. Farren left to take over the Olympic in 1850 and the hard won prestige soon was lost.

It was called Punch's Playhouse from April 1851 for a year, under the management of William Copeland, a provincial manager from Liverpool. The theatre reached again its lowest fortunes in the next six years. Managements were many and runs short and the programmes varied: operas (Rebecca Isaacs); Shakespeare (Barry Sullivan). Pantomime and adaptations from Dickens were a strong feature at this theatre in the fifties. The Strand became the most hopeless speculation in London theatres.

In 1858 William Swanborough defied all the auguries and took the theatre, completely overhauled it to the designs of S. Reynolds, and put it in his daughter's name, 'for pecuniary reasons' on the bills as manager. Ada Swanborough, a popular actress, was surrounded by her parents with a strong company of burlesque actors. With H. J. Byron as their chief writer they entered on to the second great era of burlesque at the Strand. Barton Baker says:

The hour had struck for something new, and the man was there to supply it, a struggling young author just rising into fame, who boldly carved out a path for himself. He took the transpontine drama—of the ludicrous exaggeration of which the north side of the Thames was far from being free—as the butt at which to shoot his shafts of ridicule; the brigand in six-tab tunic and buckled belt stuck all round with daggers and pistols, and basket-hilted swords, with combats to music, the heavy father always invoking his grey hairs, and given alternately to cursing and blessing, the village maiden walking through frost and snow in silk stockings and sandalled shoes, of which playgoers were beginning to tire, here were splendid materials for burlesque. A capital company entered heart and soul into Byron's fun—'little Johnny Clarke,' James Rogers, James Bland, who, until the appearance of Robson, was the king of burlesque, Charlotte Saunders, Patty Oliver, and Marie Wilton. Nothing more delightfully *piquante* than Marie Wilton in burlesque can be conceived; her style was not that of Vestris or of Waylett, it was her own and nobody else's. As far as it can be described, Dickens admirably hit it off in a letter to Forster:

'I really wish you would go, between this and next Thursday, to see *The Maid and the Magpie* burlesque,' he writes. 'There is the strangest thing in it that ever I have seen on the stage—the boy Pippo, by Miss Wilton. While it is astonishingly impudent (must be, or it couldn't be done at all), it is so stupendously like a boy, and unlike a woman, that it is perfectly free from offence. I never have seen such a thing. She does an imitation of the dancing of the Christy Minstrels —wonderfully clever—which, in the audacity of its thoroughgoing, is surprising. A thing that you cannot imagine a woman doing at all; and yet the manner, the appearance, the levity, impulse, and spirits of it are so exactly like a boy that you cannot think of anything like her sex in association with it. It begins at eight, and is over by a quarter-past nine. I never have seen such a curious thing, and the girl's talent is unchallengeable. I call her the cleverest girl I have ever seen on the stage in my time, and the most singularly original.'

A series of burlesques of opera, drama, even ballet, kept the theatre busy and prosperous, so much so that Swanborough who now appeared as manager on the bills, decided to drastically reconstruct the theatre in 1865.

The Era, 12 November gave particulars of the changes:

Alterations of the most comprehensive nature have been for some time past in progress, under the direction of Mr. John

Ellis, of Austin Friars, an architect of great practical knowledge, as will be seen by the subjoined detail of the important
changes effected in the interior and front of the house. The
builder is Mr. C. Foster, of Whitefriars, and the Theatre has
been, in effect, almost reconstructed. Mr. Ellis's design has
included new stone and brick staircases both to pit and gallery,
and the box entrance will be found redecorated in a very tasteful manner. That most important requisition—safety in the
event of fire—is, as far as possible, secured, and the means of
exit materially increased. The seats throughout the house
have been renewed, the old ones having given place to others
far more comfortably arranged. Special care has also been
taken in the fitting and ornamenting the box set apart for His
Royal Highness the Prince of Wales. A new roof, of fifty-two
feet in span, and ten feet higher than the former one, is
certainly not the least of the improvements for which the
public will be indebted to Mr. Ellis's skill in his vocation.
It is supported upon iron Stauncheons, resting on concrete
and brick piers, springing from the absolute foundation, and
above are to be found a new property room and dressing
rooms, which are well ventilated and comfortable. The
ceiling over the pit is arranged in panels and elaborately
ornamented with gilt mouldings. A new proscenium, designed
by Mr. Ellis, is part of the general plan. The light is to be
supplied, according to well-tried modern custom, from a
sunlight three feet six inches in diameter, and from this centre
of heat a ventilating tube of wrought iron rises into the open
air. New scene docks, flies, and loft are constructed, with a
separate ventilator thereto, and from the lower cellar into the
roof chambers an iron staircase passes, close by the prompt
side. The architect, the Management, and the public, are
equally to be congratulated on a plan which must result in the
striking improvement of this popular Theatre.

The re-opening on 18 November is reported the following
day:

A brilliant illumination outside announced to the public the
re-opening of their favourite Theatre, and the plentiful
employment of Rimmel's 'vaporisor' within, completely
dispersed any lingering odour of paint which might have

P*

deterred the old patrons of the Theatre from paying thus early a visit to the Theatre under its new aspect.

The entrance hall has been redecorated in pale green and fawn colour, and handsomely gilt; the other walls of box passages, stairs, &c., being in pale green scagliola marble. A new act drop has been ably designed and cleverly painted by Mr. Frederick Fenton. The gallery is greatly enlarged, and will now accommodate, it is said, a thousand persons. The boxes, which have a row of stalls in front to be retained the entire evening, are very comfortable and commodious, and the ventilation of the Theatre is perfect. Though the house was last evening crowded to excess, everybody could breathe freely, and the arrangements for entrance and egress were so complete as to give rise to general expressions of admiration. The principal attraction of the opening night was a new and original opera burlesque, by Mr. F. C. Burnand, founded on Meyerbeer's last grand lyric work, and entitled *L'Africaine; or, The Queen of the Cannibal Islands*. The music of the extravaganza is entirely original and shows Mr. Frank Musgrave once more as a clever composer well entitled to be considered the 'Offenbach' of the Metropolis.

The burlesque, which is carefully got up, was preceded by the popular Strand comedietta of *Short and Sweet*, in which Mr. Parselle, Mr. H. J. Turner, Miss E. Johnstone, and Miss Fanny Hughes appeared, and was followed by the farce of *An Alarming Sacrifice*, in which Mr. Thomas Thorne, as Bob Ticket, represented the chief comic character. The audience evidently appreciated the greater comfort they derived from the alterations made, and, thus invested with fresh attractions, the Strand may be said to commence a new career, which, it is to be hoped, will prove permanently prosperous.

The note of the 'special care' for the comfort of the Prince of Wales recalls a drawing by that most observant of cartoonists, Alfred Bryan, showing the back of a familiar royal figure gazing in a pastrycook's shop window, which displays a bill for the 'Best Burlesque in London' and directly above proclaims itself a 'Noted shop for tarts'!

The Swanborough family all appeared in turn at the top of the

bills as manager. Mrs. Swanborough followed her husband, late
in the sixties, and remained lessee till 1887 (Edward Swanborough
died in 1886). The policy of burlesque at the new theatre was to
continue until 1872. Barton Baker says:

> There certainly was a 'go', an excitement about burlesque at
> the Strand in those days that was never approached by any
> other house. The enjoyment of the performers was really, or
> apparently, so intense that the wild ecstatic breakdown into
> which they broke at the end of almost every scene seemed
> perfectly spontaneous; it was a frantic outburst of irrepressible
> animal spirits, and they seemed to have no more control over
> their legs than the audience had over their applause. You
> might call it rubbish, buffoonery, vulgarity, anything you
> liked, but your temperament must have been abnormally
> phlegmatic if you could resist the influence of that riotous
> mirth and not be carried away by it.
>
> Every vein, however rich, must be exhausted at last, and the
> same situations and the same word-twistings at length grew
> monotonous, more especially as the company became more
> and more mediocre, and the old spirit gradually evaporated.
> The acme of dreariness perhaps was attained in a burlesque
> called *The Vampire*, the last, or one of the last, of the long
> procession of Swanborough burlesques iu 1872.

Burlesque continued actually until 1879 but sharing public favour
with comedy and opera bouffe. Several works by Gilbert were
given and *Trial by Jury* was revived in 1877.

The Strand was also associated for many years with the
American comedian, John Sleeper Clarke, who appeared in
comedies from 1868, when he paid annual visits to London. As
burlesque finally waned at the Strand, so the newer trend for
comic opera gained a complete foothold. *Madame Favart*, by
Offenbach, ran from April 1879 for 502 performances, this was
followed by *Olivette*, by Audran, in 1880, and Lecocq's *Manola*
in 1882. Finally *La Mascotte*, by Audran, was transferred from
the Comedy Theatre. All these operettes were presented under the
direction of Alexander Henderson.

There had been a number of theatre fires at this period, both
in this country and on the continent, and the Board of Works
had become very strict over safety conditions in old theatres. The

Strand was condemned and closed for re-building on 29 July 1882. The new theatre was described in *The Era*, 18 November 1882:

Since the 29 July the whole of the old theatre has been pulled down, with the exception of a part of the side walls and a portion of the roof; but long before that works were in active operation on the newly acquired land at the back of the theatre. In the new theatre what was formerly the back wall and the whole extent of the stage are now added to the auditory, the present proscenium and curtain being in the exact position of the former back wall. Behind this, and extending as far as the Strand Lane, have been built the stage and dressing rooms. The width of the principal entrance in the Strand has been more than doubled by the acquisition of some adjoining property, so that now the theatre, which in former times was, perhaps, the worst off in London in respect of entrance and exit, will be one of the best. The theatre has been built from the designs and under the personal supervision of Mr. C. J. Phipps, F.S.A., architect of the Gaiety, the Haymarket, the Savoy, and other theatres. The plans were approved by the Lord Chamberlain and by the Metropolitan Board of Works under the Act of Parliament, and all the latest improvements and suggestions have been carried out.

The principal approach will be from the Strand, the entrance opening into a spacious vestibule. The visitors for the stalls then pass to the left, and those to the balcony or dress circle to the right, each having a separate corridor and staircase. The stalls corridor has two staircases, giving access to the auditory both right and left of the stage; and out of this corridor is another exit to Surrey Street, which will be always open. This will also form the entrance for the Royal family when visiting the theatre, and adjacent is a small retiring room conveniently placed. The pit entrance is in Surrey Street, and has a staircase 5 ft. wide leading up to the back of the pit. The gallery has two staircases, one on either side, and both in Surrey Street. Both these staircases will be always open and available at all times. The usual stage entrance is, also, in Surrey Street, by a fireproof corridor under the south side of the pit; but there are doors leading off the Mezzanine stage directly into Strand Lane, which can be used whenever necessary. The auditory of the theatre, though enlarged, still retains the same divisions as before. On the floor are six rows of orchestra stalls, affording seats for 107 persons in arm-chairs, and behind these is a spacious and convenient pit, three times as large as in the old theatre. On the first tier the balcony has six rows of arm-chairs holding 170, divided into two prices, but without any division or railing. On the second tier is the gallery, holding about 400 persons. There are six private boxes on each side of the proscenium. All the entrances, passages, and staircases are of brick and stone, the flights of stairs are supported at each end by solid brick walls, having handrails on either side; and there is no part of the theatre which has not two distinct means of egress in case of necessity, all of which will be kept open during time of performance. The stage is separated from the auditory by a solid brick wall, carried up so as to divide the two roofs completely. Water is laid on from the high pressure mains, and hydrants are placed in various parts of the building. The refreshment saloon is adjoining the staircase to the dress circle, and it is intended to construct a smoking-room on the ground floor off the stalls corridor.

The ornamentation of the theatre is Italian Renaissance in character, the box fronts being decorated in white and gold, and this treatment is continued on the ceiling, which is flat and divided by moulded ribs into panels. The whole of the proscenium frame and ceiling is of gold. The walls of the auditory are covered with paper of a dark turquoise and peacock blue tone, with flowers of a brighter colour; and the hangings and curtains are in figured plush of a claret-red colour. The seats are all upholstered in old gold-coloured plush with carpets of a deep red. The whole interior presents a rich, bright, and comfortable appearance.

The contractors who have been engaged upon the works are as follows:—Messrs. Patman and Fotheringham for the whole of the builder's work; Mr. Wood for the stage; Messrs. Jackson and Sons for the ornamental plaster work in box fronts and proscenium; Mr. E. Bell for the painting, papering, gilding and decorating; Messrs. Strode and Co. for the sun-light and the special gas work for the lighting the stage; Mr. Hinkley for the ordinary gas fittings; Messrs. Lyon and

Son for the upholstery and seating, the armchairs being the architect's registered design; Messrs. Merryweathers have supplied the hydrants and fire appliances; the act drop and scenery have been painted by Mr. T. E. Ryan; Mr. J. E. Walker has been the architect's clerk of the works.

The opening night, a rather stormy evening, was described the following week:

The action of the Board of Works, if sometimes it involves managers in serious and unexpected outlays, undoubtedly confers benefits upon the playgoing public, and as the patronage of a theatre generally increases in proportion to its enhanced comfort and convenience, we may hope that in the long run the lessees who have been put to the greatest cost will reap the most abundant harvest. There was every sign that the crowded audience of Saturday night at the Strand Theatre appreciated the change in this popular establishment. We gave last week full particulars of the elaborate transformation of the theatre with figures, enabling the reader to judge of the important enlargements of the house. But 'seeing is believing,' and it was only when old frequenters of the Strand were actually seated in the house that the improvements could be fully understood. Even at the entrance, however, the change had a pleasant influence upon the audience, for, instead of a cramped and narrow staircase leading to the auditorium, wide, handsome approaches, well lighted and beautifully decorated, gave the visitors a luxurious sense of enjoyment which was realised to a still greater extent when they had taken their seats in the mellow old gold-coloured stalls. The house is now infinitely better lighted than before, and the stage is so well planned that from all parts of the theatre the performances are distinctly visible. There is also an improvement in the acoustic qualities of the theatre, owing to the change in its form, and partly perhaps to the flat roof. In the course of the evening the audience expressed satisfaction in the various changes by an emphatic compliment to Mrs. Swanborough and Miss Ada Swanborough. Seeing these ladies in a private box, there was a tremendous cheer for Mrs. Swanborough, and as it died away a cry was heard of 'One more for Miss Swanborough,' which was responded to by the entire house with the utmost cordiality. The performance of the National Anthem and 'God Bless the Prince of Wales' also evoked great enthusiasm. The first item on the present occasion was the comedy of *The Heir-at-Law*, and we need hardly say that the remarkable impersonation of Doctor Pangloss by Mr. John S. Clarke was an attraction of the most welcome kind. Mr. Clarke has made this character so completely his own, and has so finished every detail, that it stands forth one of the most remarkable examples of which the modern stage can boast.

Following the comedy came a so-called new musical comedy, by Henry J. Byron and H. B. Farnie, in one act and three *tableaux*, from the French, entitled *Frolique!* It was hardly wise to call the sketch a 'new musical comedy,' and it was somewhat pointedly resented by the audience when the piece was discovered to be a rearrangement of some scenes from Mr. Planché's two-act comedy *The Follies of a Night*, produced at Drury Lane Theatre forty years ago, with Mr. Charles Mathews in the character played by Mr. John S. Clarke last Saturday. Madame Vestris and Mr. Compton were in the original cast of Mr. Planché's piece, which was founded on the French vaudeville *Charlot*. Messrs. Byron and Farnie have reduced the piece to one act and three scenes; and, to be frank, they have sacrificed much of the liveliness and spirit of the original. The amusing acting of Mr. John S. Clarke gave the most satisfaction to the audience. *Frolique!*, as the authors have chosen to call the extravaganza, was well placed upon the stage, with brilliant scenery and elegant dresses, and some bright pieces of music were skilfully arranged by Mr. Fitzgerald. But there was a certain disappointment with the piece when it was found to be an old friend with a new face, and when the curtain fell this disappointment was rather angrily expressed. Nevertheless, the extravaganza, slight as it is, may serve until something really entitled to be called 'new' is forthcoming. Meanwhile, we are justified in predicting that the reconstructed Strand Theatre will not only retain, but increase, the popularity it has so long enjoyed.

The calling of *Frolique!* a 'Musical Comedy' is probably the earliest use of this term. The true Musical Comedy, a musical in contemporary dress, was not to come into existence for another decade.

J. S. Clarke had virtually become the manager of the theatre, and in 1887 two years before Mrs. Swanborough, who was in bankruptcy, died at the age of eighty-five, he took over completely as lessee. The early years of the new Royal Strand were not conspicuously successful. *Vice-Versa* ran from June to December in 1883, with a burlesque, *Silver Guilt*, in the same bill. The theatre was then let for a season by the Compton Comedy Company, with Edward Compton and his wife, Virginia Bateman, in old English comedies.

The irrepressible American, Minnie Palmer, opened in *My Sweetheart* in January 1884, a part she had played, and was to continue to play, all over the world for many years. (She returned to the Strand with the same play in December 1885.) In 1884 the long running farce *Our Boys* was revived, and ran 263 performances.

After this came a period of rapid changes during which the theatre was let to several managers, including the second visit to London of Augustin Daly's Company from New York (1886) and seasons of the Compton Comedy Company (1886-1887). A comic opera *The Sultan of Mocha*, by Alfred Cellier, ran for a while in 1887-1888.

In 1888 Willie Edouin took over the management and presented a series of farces which included *Our Flat* (transferred from the Prince of Wales') to run 645 performances, *The Late Lamented* 228 performances 1891-1892, *Niobe* (*All Smiles*) 550 performances 1892-1893.

By this time Edouin was sole lessee of the theatre (with Clarke still as proprietor), but in 1895 he handed over to Harry Paulton, another comedian, who continued the farce tradition. (He had been in and part author of *Niobe* which he revived.) J. S. Clarke gave his last season of personal management in 1897—he died two years later. His last success was *What Happened to Jones*, the inevitable farce, in 1898 (383 performances).

The theatre passed to the American Broadhurst Brothers as lessee and manager (George Broadhurst had written the current running farce), they followed with *Why Smith left Home*, *The Wrong Mr. Wright* and other similar farces. The theatre was much used for special matinées and experiments in the new Drama of this time. At the turn of the century the theatre came under the control of Frank Curzon who continued with farces and musicals.

But though the days of the theatre were numbered, at the last it had its biggest success: *A Chinese Honeymoon*, a musical play by George Dance and Howard Talbot. This opened 5 October 1901 and ran for 1,075 performances. It made the name of the comedienne Louie Freear, and introduced Lily Elsie to London. Its successor *Sergeant Brue* opened in June 1904 with Ethel Irving and Zena Dare in the cast. It ran 280 performances.

The Strand redevelopment scheme was now almost accomplished. On the north side, opposite the theatre, the new Aldwych and Kingsway had come into being. The theatre was sold to an Underground Railway Company (the Great Northern, Piccadilly and Brompton Railway) to become the terminus of their new Strand-Holborn line and offices.

The Royal Strand closed 13 May 1905. The last play was *Miss Wingrove*, a musical by Howard Talbot, which only ran a few performances from 4 May.

The theatre was demolished and the new tube Station then called Strand opened on 30 November 1907. It was re-named Aldwych in May 1915. It still remains, though little used, with its entrance in the Strand and its side in Surrey Street, awaiting the long proposed extension of the line to Waterloo.

20

The Royalty Theatre

Miss Kelly's Theatre and Dramatic School, the Royal Soho Theatre, the New English Opera House, Théâtre Français, the New Royalty Theatre, the New Royalty Operetta House

Dean Street, Soho. In a block bounded by Meard Street and Richmond Buildings partly backed by Richmond Mews (with stage door)

Opened 25 May 1840 as Miss Kelly's Theatre and Dramatic School with an Appropriate Address by Fanny Kelly, *Summer and Winter*, a new piece in one act by Morris Barnett, followed by *The Serjeant's Wife*, a drama by John Banim, concluding with a revival of *The Midnight Hour* by Eliza Inchbald.
Under the management of Fanny Kelly.
Re-decorated and re-opened as the Royal Soho Theatre 30 January 1850, with an amateur performance by the Vanbrugh Club of *Rent Day* by Douglas Jerrold, *Not a Bad Judge* by J. R. Planché and *John Dobby* by John Maddison Morton.
Under the management of Charles Gilbert.
Called the New English Opera House for a short season from 5 November 1850. Portico added 1851 to number 73.
Called the Théâtre Français for a season 1861.
Interior re-constructed and re-decorated and re-opened as the New Royalty Theatre 12 November 1861 with *Atar Gull*, a melodrama by George Almar (founded on a romance by Eugène Sue), followed by *Camelia*, a vaudeville.
Under the management of Albina di Rhona.
Called the New Royalty Operetta House for a season May 1862.
Under the management of Elliot Galer.
By 1872 the 'New' had been dropped, but it returned in 1878-9.
Interior re-constructed and re-decorated and re-opened as the

Royalty Theatre 23 April 1883, with *The Merry Duchess*, a comic opera by George R. Sims and Frederic Clay.
Under the management of Kate Santley.
Interior re-constructed and re-decorated and re-opened 7 September 1895 with *The Chili Widow*, a play, (adapted from *M. Le Directeur* by Alexander Bisson and Fabrice Carré), by Arthur Bourchier and Alfred Sutro.
Under the management of Arthur Bourchier.
Interior re-constructed and re-decorated, the frontage re-modelled and re-opened as the New Royalty Theatre, 4 January 1906 with *Le Souris*, by Edouard Pailleron, preceded by *La Sauvegarde*, a one act play by Karl des Fontaines, in a season of Théâtre Français.
Under the management of Gaston Meyer.
Became again the Royalty Theatre 12 April 1911.
Under the management of J. E. Vedrenne and Dennis Eadie.
Closed 25 November 1938 on the withdrawal of its licence by the Lord Chamberlain on the advice of the London County Council. While awaiting several abortive re-building plans, before and during the war, the theatre became derelict and received blitz damage. It was eventually demolished 1953.
An office block, Royalty House, completed in 1959, now covers the site.

THE LITTLE THEATRE which opened in Dean Street in 1840 owed its existence to the actress, Frances Maria Kelly. Born in 1790, a niece of Michael Kelly, she made her debut at Drury Lane at the age of ten. Fanny Kelly grew up to become a popular favourite and was immortalised by Charles Lamb in his essay *Barbara S—*. The full story of her career is told in *Fanny Kelly of Drury Lane* by Basil Francis (1950) and need not be recounted here; suffice it to say that she had strong ideas on the need for a dramatic school for young actors and actresses, and having saved some sixteen thousand pounds during her career, in 1832 set about putting her schemes into practice. The first attempt to provide tuition for students of dramatic art was planned on similar lines to the Royal Academy of Music which had recently come into existence. Firstly she took the new Strand Subscription Theatre and went into management, presenting herself, in January 1833, in a one woman entertainment which ran till March. While there she conducted classes and made announcements of the formation of a 'Modern and up-to-date School for the teaching of the Drama'.

Though she had the direct patronage of the Duke of Devonshire, she was not able to consolidate her position at the new and unlucky little theatre which was being strongly opposed by the Patent theatres (see Number 19). The strain of her season taxed her strength, and though she abandoned her own entertainment she continued to use the theatre for her school, under her own super-vision and with additional tutors. She still kept in mind her need for a compact modern little theatre built to her own requirements, and decided to build one for herself, behind her house, number 73 Dean Street, Soho, where she had moved in 1834. At the rear of the house there was a large mews and coach-house, and on this ground and that behind the next door house, number 74, Fanny Kelly made plans to build her theatre, to the designs of Samuel Beazley. Her manifesto, set out on paper embossed with the Royal Arms, stated:

Royal Dramatic School and Theatre, Under the Patronage of His Grace the Duke of Devonshire. Miss Kelly has the Honour to announce to the Nobility, Gentry, her Friends, and the Public, that she has at length matured the Plan, some time since submitted to their approval, for the establishment of a Dramatic School.

A License has been granted for a Winter Season, and the patronage and protection of some of the first rank and talent in the Country accorded to the undertaking.

Thus encouraged, Miss Kelly has embarked a considerable capital in the purchase of property, and in erecting a small but commodious theatre, attached to her own residence, in which talent may be cultivated and practical knowledge advanced, by Courses of Lectures, daily readings, and stage studies.

Those who have it in intention to adopt the Theatrical Profession will be directed in that line of Art to which their talents may incline them; and it is proposed that in the gradual introduction of Candidates for Public notice, merit alone shall take the lead: the best adapted powers being brought to bear upon the best productions of our established Dramatists.

There is one point to which Miss Kelly has directed the most anxious consideration, and in the accomplishment of which she still is, and must continue to be, most actively engaged; namely, the necessity of providing resources for those who, whilst preparing for the Profession, are without the means of subsistence.

Too many possessing considerable talent, urged by necessity, rush into humble and even disreputable positions in the Profession, from which they never rise, for want of those advantages which time and cultivation would have afforded them. Others, through some channel which commands a temporary footing, monopolize a station they have not talent to adorn; and, in either case, the result to *Female Candidates* is at least dangerous, if not pernicious, in their after course through life.

To avoid this evil, Miss Kelly has devoted a branch of the Establishment to the intellectual improvement, and the industrious occupation of the youthful pupils of both sexes; affording to each a fair proportion of the funds arising from their own exertions. Thus every one will possess a power to provide against the chance of failure in the Dramatic Art, by the exercise of some ability, which, in another walk of life, may be esteemed both useful and respectable.

Thus far Miss Kelly has, by her own unaided exertion, and with no other funds than the thrifty savings of her professional life, surmounted every difficulty, and prepared for the public operation of her Plans; and willing to abide the test of an honest intention and earnest activity, ventures once again before the Public as an humble, but faithful, labourer in the Dramatic Art, with those who would recall the stage from a state of degradation to all its intellectual and moral usefulness.

An Annual Subscriber of Two Guineas will be entitled to admission on Six occasions, reserved for the Patrons during the Spring Season; and as the Subscription Nights are fixed for the first Monday in every month, Subscribers all have the privilege, by giving timely notice, to fix their own time for the admission of their Tickets.

The Plan and Drawings of the Theatre, with the more minute details of the undertaking, will be open to Subscribers from Three o'Clock till Five daily, at Miss Kelly's Residence. 73, Dean Street, Soho Square.

Through her influence in high places she had, in August 1834, obtained a Lord Chamberlain's licence for 'a series of daily dramatic readings and twice weekly theatrical performances' from Michaelmas to the following Easter, for the specific purpose of 'preparing, under her own immediate surveillance, pupils for the metropolitan stage without their being necessarily compelled to pass through the usual ordeal of a provincial career or apprenticeship.' For this mark of favour she sent a duly grateful letter of thanks to the Duke of Devonshire, the Lord Chamberlain!

She took a formal leave of the stage at Drury Lane on 8 June 1835, and set about the building of the theatre, which continued until 1837. By now she had moved herself into number 74, leaving next door as an entrance to the theatre.

Though no longer Lord Chamberlain, the Duke of Devonshire, still her patron, was to be honoured in the name of the new theatre, to be called the Duke's Theatre and Royal Dramatic School. An announcement submitted for approval to the Duke read:

> The Duke's Theatre and Royal Dramatic School. Miss Kelly has the honour to announce to her pupils and Subscribers that she will commence a course of Private Lectures on the Dramatic Art preparatory to opening her Theatre to the Public in September next. The Teachers of the Establishment will be in attendance on Mondays and Thursdays for Elocution, Tuesdays and Fridays for Vocal and Instrumental Music, and on Wednesdays and Saturdays for Dancing, Fencing, and Gymnastic Exercises.

The Duke declined the honour of having the theatre named after him, but remained as patron and subscribed two hundred guineas. Many others also became annual subscribers. The Duke of Wellington, however, declined to support the venture, writing 'I have kept myself clear of all theatrical matters purposely because I saw that they were coming to the state of confusion in which they now are. The manners of the people and the habits of Society will not allow of good theatrical representations in the Town.'

The opening of the theatre to the public was delayed from the Spring of 1838 for two years while a new type of stage machinery of all metal construction was being installed. The inventor, Rowland Macdonald Stephenson, a civil engineer who was later knighted and became Deputy Chairman of the East Indian

Railway Company, exhibited a model of his contrivance in the autumn of 1838. It was patented in February 1840, and received considerable publicity.

Stephenson's ideas looked well on paper but were impossible to work in practise. Though ambitious, they were unnecessarily ingenious in their attempt to change scenes rapidly and on the whole cumbersome and particularly noisy in use. A series of cog-wheels placed beneath the stage, moved by leverage power, formed the mechanism by which 'the wings could be shifted, the borders changed, the scenery raised or lowered, and even the stage sunk, cleared of whatever might be on it, re-set, and wound up again.'

This apparatus, which it was predicted would revolutionise stage art, required, it has been said, only the services of a horse to set the cog-wheels in motion!

Fanny Kelly, headstrong and zealous in her pioneering efforts, achieved what is probably the most monumental failure in the long history of the British theatre. Her little theatre, scarcely holding two hundred, but more elegant and comfortable than any before, had swallowed up most of her private fortune when the public were allowed in to see it in May 1840.

Her first blow came when the hoped for presence of the Queen and Prince Albert, at the opening on 25 May 1840, was prevented owing to a previous engagement, which later turned out to be a visit to Astley's, the Circus in Westminster Bridge Road! Nevertheless a distinguished audience assembled in Dean Street to hear Fanny Kelly formally open her own theatre as Miss Kelly's Theatre and Dramatic School. After her opening address a short comedy, *Summer and Winter*, with the author, Morris Barnett, supporting Mrs. Franks and Miss Cooper, and a promising pupil of seventeen, Lee Morton, who later became famous under his own name of Dion Boucicault as an actor and dramatist.

Miss Kelly herself then appeared in her old success *The Sergeant's Wife*, and the evening concluded with the drama *The Midnight Hour* in which she again appeared. *The Era*, 30 May, kindly reported:

Miss Kelly's.—This little theatre opened on Monday evening with a new piece, by Mr. Morris Barnett, called *Summer and Winter*, in which that gentleman most ably sustained the

principal character with his usual ability. It is a piece replete
with that interest which the contrast of age and youth can give.
Mr. Barnett seems to understand the true light and shade, the
real *chiari obscuro* of the drama—and his piece was received
with unanimous applause. Miss Kelly, in the *Sergeant's Wife*,
and the *Midnight Hour*, was quite herself, and herself in her
best days—and this is saying every thing that can be said.
The mixture of the dramatic school with her performances
gives Miss Kelly a claim which no other theatrical proprietor
can get up for the patronage of the public—and as she deserves
it, we trust she will receive it. The ingenious machinery invented by Mr. Macdonald Stephenson, and which is about to
be adopted, we understand, in several foreign theatres, was
exhibited for the first time on this occasion.

The Times described the theatre as 'most elegantly fitted up and
appointed, and painted in a light tasteful manner. The pit is half
occupied by chairs and half by benches; the part corresponding
to a gallery is considered as a tier of upper boxes, and the lower
tier has a distinguishing price.' The theatre was designed as 'a
bijou for a fashionable audience.' A box was taken by Queen
Adelaide, and most of the others, according to a newspaper puff,
by 'the heads of our old aristocratic houses, for themselves, and
the youthful members of their families, who, of course, can come
and go as they would to an apartment beneath the paternal
roof.'

The fiasco of the opening performances is vividly described by
Basil Francis in his biography of Fanny Kelly:

> Stephenson's elaborate machinery had ruined the entire
> performance. What should have been the peak of smooth
> professional excellence was reduced to the level of clumsy
> amateur fumbling.
>
> The machinery *worked* all right; no one in the entire
> building—even the whole street—had any doubt of that! But
> it worked so noisily, with such a clank of chains and rattle of
> block and tackle, that the actors were all but inaudible. The
> monstrous crank housed beneath the stage which was the
> motive power for the entire complicated arrangement revolved
> with such a clatter as to turn the drama being enacted on the
> boards above into a pantomimic farce.

Barton Baker says:

> Stephenson had represented that the whole arrangement
> could be worked by one man, but when it came to the test a
> horse had to be employed. The theatre was a mere bandbox,
> and the trampling of the horse beneath the stage and the
> working of the cog-wheels shook every plank in the house and
> gave the audience St. Vitus's dance.

Basil Francis comments:

> It is a good story and possibly true, though a study of the
> drawing does not reveal any provision for an attachment in
> the form of a treadmill or similar apparatus, but no doubt the
> ingenious Stephenson would have had little difficulty in
> designing it!
> The high prices charged, seven shillings each seat for the
> first tier of boxes and stalls and five shillings each seat for
> public seats and family boxes, coupled with a lack of names
> in the company to support the manageress, may also have
> helped to undermine the confidence of the Town, and though
> she tried a second night with the same disastrous scenic results,
> by Friday, the fifth night, she had to dismiss the company
> and announced the closure of the theatre to the public for 'an
> indefinite period.'

Undaunted, she spent what remained of her savings in having the
offending stage machinery removed from the theatre. Having
been built solidly into the fabric it took time and money to make
good the damage. By the end of the year she was able to announce
her re-opening 'notwithstanding some difficulties in the scenic
department,' for 22 February 1841. Though she continued the
school during this period her health had suffered considerably
through her disasters. She seems to have been a highly strung
woman with great determination and a strict moral code. She
never married, having refused Charles Lamb's offer, and remained to the end a militant feminist in the masculine world of the
theatre.

For the re-opening she returned to her one woman show, *Miss
Kelly's Dramatic Recollections and Studies of Character*, given at
reduced prices. After a successful season she toured the provinces,

leaving her school in other capable hands, and letting the theatre for 'Private Theatricals' and amateur performances.

By the end of 1841 she was forced to retire completely, her health broken and her money lost. She had to apply for financial assistance from the Duke of Devonshire in 1845, the year in which the theatre was used by Charles Dickens and his company 'The Amateurs' for a performance of *Every Man in his Humour*, on 20 September. The production of which seems to have worried the manageress, in case of any unseemly dialogue! The same company performed for Miss Kelly's Benefit on 3 January 1846, and she herself spoke a prologue. The receipts and subscriptions did much to alleviate her pressing needs and creditors. She continued her school and gave Shakespeare readings, but by the end of 1849 the crash came. Writs were issued, the bailiffs were put in possession of the little theatre, and she was evicted. She moved to Bayswater to eke out her existence with her private pupils.

A proposed farewell Benefit in 1853 failed to materialise, but the substantial subscription helped her to live quitely, still teaching, until she finally left London, when nearly eighty, to live at Feltham where she died on 6 December 1882 at the age of ninety-two.

After Miss Kelly left, the theatre was taken by Charles Gilbert. The name was changed to the Royal Soho Theatre, and it was completely re-decorated by William W. Deane and S. J. Nicholl. The first occupants were the Vanbrugh Club, a company of young architect and engineer amateurs, who presented three plays on 30 January 'for one night only'. The theatre was mainly used for Benefit performances and amateurs during the next few months.

In November another change of name was to bring no luck at all. *The Illustrated London News*, 9 November 1850, said:

> It would be a matter of deep regret if any foreign musician or amateur of note had been present at the opening, last Tuesday night, at the Soho Theatre, formerly belonging to Miss Kelly, of what is called 'The New English Opera House.' What a notion would have been formed by the foreigner of our musical resources! Could he have believed that London, with a population of two millions—with the finest choral singers in the world—with a body of most accomplished instrumentalists—with a number of really eminent English com-

posers, and a very fair sprinkling of principal vocalists, could have produced such an exhibition of incompetency and puerility? The only relief to the annoyance caused by the melancholy display, being that it presented itself nearly throughout a three-act opera—*The Last Crusade*, by Mr. Mitchell, the blind composer—as a burlesque; and as such was laughed at by those amateurs who could not feel how much injury was done to 'native talent' by the disastrous performance; whilst, on the other hand, the 'friends' of the establishment, by a series of parodies on great lyric triumphs, in the shape of encores, re-calls, and ovations, were adding fuel to the flame of disgust and discontent. Criticism on Mr. Mitchell's pretensions is utterly disarmed by the glaring deficiency of the executieon. For th future foundation, on a permanent basis, of a really National Opera House, nothing could be more fatal to art and artists than Tuesday's *Last Crusade*.

The season obviously terminated forthwith!

The following year an entrance portico was added to number 73 (number 74 had become a separate property) and amateurs were again in possession most of the time, with the occasional Benefit. The lease was taken over in 1852 by Thomas Mowbray, who managed the theatre, and advertised 'Pupils prepared for the Stage', an echo of Miss Kelly's school.

A notice in November 1856 tells us:

A Miss Percy Knowles has been acting at this theatre in the masculine characters of tragedy—such as *Othello*, *Shylock*, and *Hamlet*—and with some success; the novelty of the attempt attracting the curious to an exhibition not to be commended. The débutante has been stated to have become celebrated in America, and this sort of prestige has, it seems, been injudiciously encouraged; but we are requested, on authority, to state that Miss Knowles is comparatively a novice, and claims the usual indulgence accorded to un-practised Candidates.

In 1860 the Soho became the Théâtre Français, with plays to attract the cosmopolitan residents of the district.

In 1861 yet another transformation and change of name took

place when the theatre was taken over by Albina di Rhona, a Servian dancer and actress. She had the theatre re-decorated and partly re-constructed to the designs of M. Boulet of Paris, calling it the New Royalty Theatre. (There had been an East End Royalty Theatre, in Wellclose Square, from 1787 till it was re-named the East London in 1810.) She opened on 12 November. *The Era*, 17 November 1861 says:

New Royalty—Under this title the little Theatre in Dean Street, hitherto known as the Soho, was opened on Tuesday last under the Management of Mdlle. Albina di Rhona. The embellishments of the new Theatre are of a costly and tasteful character, the cut-glass lustres, painted panels, blue satin draperies, gold mouldings give a very elegant aspect to the interior. It would seem the object of the new Management to unite with Vaudeville and Ballet, Dramatic Entertainments of a more substantial kind; but, for the success of the specula-tion, the lighter piece should most assuredly form the staple of the bill of fare. The occasion inaugurated by the following Address, spoken in a very pleasing manner by Mdlle. di Rhona, and received with general plaudits:

Ladies and Gentlemen,—When ambition grows from gratitude surely its error if error there be, should claim indulgence; so, my kind patrons, if this venture of mine in erecting a little Temple for the worship of your favour is presumptuous, I can only reply it is your past kindness, and the hope of proving myself worthy of permanent patronage, which have inspired the deed. My ambition has been to create a home where I have found my welcome, and while promising to devote my heart and strength to your service, let me express my pride and sincerest thanks for the encouragement you have already awarded in your generous reception of me as a stranger. That my name, associated with the little Royalty, should be with you a household word, is the mark at which I aim. I will not tire you with a Programme of intentions. My promises will be my efforts, and I feel assured that while according your usual indulgence to my beginnings, you will soon, by your patronage, give me the glad tidings that I have hit the mark, and give the prize of success.

The opening piece was a new Melodrama, in three Acts

and five tableaux, called *Atar Gull*, and founded on one of Eugène Sue's earliest romances bearing the same name. The plot is closely followed, with some changes as to locality, and few novel-readers need to be reminded how the leading feature of the story is the persevering ferocity of a Negro, who, in revenge for his father having been hanged by a Jamaican planter, devotes himself to the task of exterminating all members of the planter's family. Firing houses, poisoning his victims, and encircling a young girl with a poisonous snake, with which coiled round her body, she rushes through a verandah shrieking upon the Stage, the slave accomplishes his ends, and keeps the spectators thrilled with every kind of atrocity. The piece has been carefully got up, the scenery and appointments are excellent, and the acting, especially that of Miss Ellen Terry, Mr. Graham, and Mr. James, all that could be required to give effect to their personations. The Low Comedian, Mr. Worboys, also contrives to produce a re-markable amount of fun out of a very slight part, but the piece is not of that class which will prove of the most advantage to the establishment. Mr. R. Hall, who was the Leader of the Boston Brass Band in America, made his first appearance in this country afterwards, and skilfully performed some airs, with variations, on the bugle, which obtained great applause. The Vaudeville called *Camelia* followed, and presented Mdlle. Rhona as a lady's maid, in which she not only played with great vivacity, but went through a variety of dances with an exuberance of gaiety, and a combination of grace and agility, that quite enraptured the audience. A peculiar attraction might be given to the Theatre if the programme was thus organised to blend the Vaudeville and the Ballet, and the taste of the visitors on the opening night was decidedly shown to run in this direction.

Even though the company included the fourteen-year-old Ellen Terry and the young David James, success did not follow. By mid-January creditors were asked, in *The Era*, to get in touch with a firm of Solicitors!

Amateurs and a burlesque company preceded another change of name to the New Royalty Operetta House, under a short-lived régime by Henry Gayler. During this time Ellen and Kate Terry were together on 30 July 1862 in an evening of three short plays supported by amateurs 'For the Benefit of Miss Kate Terry'. The famous stage children were undergoing the difficult transition to adult stars.

After a closure and return to its name of the New Royalty Mowbray let the theatre to any manager who came along with a pressing need for a Benefit, or to present a débutante for stage honours 'at a price' with, of course, the usual amateurs and pupils

In August Mrs. Charles Selby took the theatre and in September had a success with a burlesque *Ixion; or, the Man at the Wheel* by F. C. Burnand, which introduced Ada Cavendish to London. The theatre seating had to be reorganised to cope with the rush for places—at least the advertisements said so! It ran for 153 performances. Mrs. Selby followed with other burlesques and extravaganzas till the end of the season in June 1864.

After 'a recess during which extensive alterations and improvements for the convenience of its patrons' including a new box entrance were carried out, the Misses Pelham (Harriet and Rose) re-opened as proprietors and sole managers in September. They revived *Ixion* (by November it had been performed in all 300 times), and produced another extravaganza by Burnand, *Snowdrop, or, the Seven Mannikins and the Magic Mirror*, which ran 173 performances.

The unlucky little playhouse was at last gaining a foothold in the London Theatre List. The season ended in June, and when it re-opened in September it was under the direction of Fanny Reeves, who continued with a similar policy, but early in March 1866 the theatre closed. It re-opened at the end of the month with Martha 'Patty' Oliver in management.

It is strange how this theatre, from its inception, had attracted female managers, and was to go on doing so for many years to come. The policy of burlesque was still carried on by the new manageress. She let the theatre during the summer for Benefit and amateur performances, resuming herself in September after a re-decoration by the ubiquitous E. W. Bradwell. This management was quite a success as Patty Oliver had been at the Strand and brought the burlesques from that theatre with her, even members of the Swanborough family itself were to be found assisting in various departments of the theatre.

In October a play, *Meg's Diversions* by H. T. Craven, started on a run of 330 performances, with the manageress acting, with the support of the author himself, and Charles Wyndham, who had produced the play. Coupled with a burlesque of *Black Eyed Susan*, by Burnand, produced in November (400 performances), they filled the theatre all through the next year. New editions of the burlesque, and other plays, ran on until March 1868. To follow W. S. Gilbert provided Patty Oliver with a burlesque *The Merry Zingara*, which lasted out the season.

In the autumn Burnand's *The Rise and Fall of Richard the Third; or, a New Front to an old Dickey* which, with its attendant pieces, ran till the following year. After the usual August holiday the season continued with similar burlesques of popular subjects; *The Flying Dutchman* by William Brough being the most successful, and lasting till February 1870. A revival of *Black Eyed Susan* followed till Patty Oliver gave up her lesseeship in May.

In September Henrietta Hodson opened a season in management with the usual burlesque, this time *F. M. Julius Caesar* by Burnand, then *Whittington, Junior and his Sensational Cat*, by Robert Reece tided over till February 1871. The season ended in June with *Little Robin Hood; or, Quite a New Beau*.

W. H. C. Nation took the theatre for his regular strange assortment of productions during the summer. His burletta, *The Gay City* was 'nightly greeted with rapturous applause by the warmhearted and intelligent pit and gallery'—presumably the unintelligent stalls and boxes either remained away or were, as usual, laughing up their sleeves at Mr. Nation!

After this a series of amateurs once again held the stage till opera bouffe came, under the management of J. E. Mallandaine, who revived and conducted *Chilperic* on 18 September 1871. This ran until his own composition *Paquita* was produced in October, but it closed the following month, and the 'To Let' sign was outside the theatre till Nation returned in February with another mixed programme of his own concoction, with the usual interpolated songs, at prices from sixpence upwards. He remained until May. The following month Edith Bertram tried her luck as manageress with some light comedies and revivals. She ended her season in July. W. H. Swanborough ran the theatre with burlesque from September to November and was followed by a French season from December.

After a long closure, Henrietta Hodson returned in October

1873. She held the theatre for the next three years, at first acting herself in new plays and revivals of little historical worth. By the following July she was offering the theatre to let—'Amateur Societies treated with'.

It was on 30 January that Selina Dalaro a 'Queen of Opera Bouffe', produced Offenbach's *La Périchole*, with herself in the title role. Richard D'Oyly Carte was her manager and history was in the making. The opera was short, and Carte, who had been an agent and had his finger in many theatrical pies, was called upon to think of an idea to fill up the bill. He had known both Gilbert and Sullivan separately and had noted their first, but rather abortive, collaboration at the Gaiety with *Thespis* in December 1871. He asked Gilbert if he had anything to suggest as a libretto for a short curtain raiser. The eventual result, *Trial by Jury*, was offered to Sullivan who agreed to set it to music. The Programme at the Royalty on the first night of *La Périchole* noted:

> In preparation a New Comic Opera, composed expressly for this Theatre, by Mr. Arthur Sullivan, in which Madame Dolaro and Miss Nelly Bromley will appear.

Meantime 'fill in' curtain raisers were used until 25 March 1875 when *Trial by Jury* was produced. *The Era*, 28 March, reported:

> We live in an age of dramatic novelties, but we venture to say there are few who would have expected to hear of a Trial by Jury treated as a dramatic cantata. We have had the incidents of a trial arranged for the stage many a time, and the famous case of Bardell versus Pickwick furnished Mr. Toole with one of his happiest and most amusing impersonations. But to hear Mr. Toole haranguing the Jury as Sergeant Buzfuz can hardly be compared as a novelty to the present production. At the Royalty *Trial by Jury* is actually set to music, Mr. Arthur Sullivan having composed airs and recitatives to the verses of Mr. W. S. Gilbert. Everybody could guess beforehand when they saw the title what the subject-matter of the trial would be, especially when they perceived also from the bills that Miss Nelly Bromley would be Plaintiff, Mr. Walter Fisher Defendant, and Mr. Fred Sullivan the Learned Judge. A musical Counsel for the Plaintiff is also provided in Mr. Hollingsworth. Even the Usher of the Court is musical, and

the Jury deliver themselves of the verdict in a chorus. Great curiosity was naturally felt as to the manner in which Mr. Gilbert would deal with this unprecedented libretto, and a large audience was present on Thursday evening, when the dramatic cantata was produced for the first time. Shouts of laughter accompanied the fall of the curtain, and Mr. Sullivan and Mr. Gilbert, with the chief performers, were called for and greeted with hearty applause. *Trial by Jury* is but a trifle— it pretends to be nothing more—but it is one of those merry bits of extravagance which a great many will go to see and hear, which they will laugh at, and which they will advise their friends to go and see. Therefore its success cannot be doubtful. Mr. Sullivan's music serves its purpose exactly, and it is in many instances extremely clever, particularly in the mock-heroic strains when the Judge first makes his appearance.

On this foundation D'Oyly Carte built the successful triumvirate, which was to blossom at the Opera Comique (see number 14), and mature at the Savoy Theatre, built expressly for the operas in 1881 (see *The Theatres of London*). *Trial by Jury* remained in the Royalty bill while the main opera bouffe was changed several times before the season ended in December.

A short regime in January under D'Oyly Carte and George Dolby was followed by Mrs. W. H. Liston. Both continued the comic opera fashion. But from April the theatre was on offer once again to the amateurs.

In December 1876 Kate Santley was in a revival of Offenbach's *Orphée aux Enfers*, but the next year was a quiet one for the theatre. On 11 October 1877 Kate Santley re-opened under her own management. She had secured a long lease of the theatre, and on the programme it said:

During the recess the Theatre has been entirely Re-Decorated and Re-Furnished; New Stage laid; New Private Boxes added; the beautiful New Act Drop from Frost's Celebrated Picture 'Nymphs disarming Cupid,' by Messrs. Gordon & Harford; the whole of the entirely New Scenery, together with Designs and Decorations, by the same artists; Machinist, Mr. Rhodes; Gas department by Mr. Pepell; New and Elegant Crystal Chandelier by Messrs. Defries; New and Gorgeous Dresses,

Q

from Designs by Grevin, by Mr. Reddish, Miss Dolman, and
Mons. Alias.

The Era 14 October 1877 reported:

> There have been various alterations in the structure and
> decoration of the theatre. The architects have not been able to
> give two entrances to the stalls, or to add to the convenience
> of the visitors who do not care to be glued to a seat for many
> hours, and the auditorium has been done up in a style which
> shows that 'imitation is the sincerest form of flattery.' At
> present the place does not seem finished. The stalls are not
> screwed together, and the carpets are missing. When all is
> ready no doubt the Theatre will be pretty enough.

After a series of revivals from farce to comic opera, Kate Santley
let the theatre to other managements when they could be found
to take the little theatre. In May 1878 Emily Fowler presented
herself in W. G. Wills' *Nell Gwynne*. Kate Santley was back again
in October until the new year. Later in the year she sub-let to
Edgar Bruce who put on *Crutch and Toothpick* by George R.
Sims with great success—it ran for 234 performances. He also
revived *The Zoo*, an early 'musical folly' by Arthur Sullivan, as
an after piece for part of the run. In 1880, before Bruce's sub-
lease ran out, he let the theatre to Jennie Lee of *Jo* fame, this time
for a play called *Midge*, and to Kate Lawler for a series of burlesques.
In 1881-1882 Alexander Henderson was presenting farces and
opera bouffe in a re-decorated theatre with his wife, Lydia
Thompson. He was followed by Hilda Hilton in a revival of *Meg's
Diversion*.

The theatre was attracting the attention of the fire authorities,
and in 1882 they recommended the Metropolitan Board of Works
to close it. Kate Santley closed the theatre, then said to hold 645
people, and had it completely re-constructed to the designs of
Thomas Verity. She acquired a right-of-way through number 74,
at ground level, to the theatre. It re-opened on 23 April 1883.

The Era, 28 April, reported:

> The Royalty Theatre opened on Monday night with the new
> comic opera, by Messrs. G. R. Sims and Frederick Clay,
> entitled *The Merry Duchess*, and the audience evidently
> regarded with great satisfaction the improvements made for

their comfort and enjoyment in the auditorium and the approaches thereto. Few London theatres in past days were more uncomfortable in their arrangements or more objectionable in their exits and entrances than the Royalty; but Miss Kate Santley has totally reformed all these drawbacks, and now the visitor who does not appreciate the new Royalty must be hard to please. The appearance of the auditorium is extremely elegant, and the first thing that strikes the eye is the picturesque act-drop, painted by Mr. Henry Emden, who has availed himself of certain features of Japanese art to produce an elegant and appropriate effect. Glancing round the house we are reminded in many portions of the admirable workmanship and artistic skill of Mr. E. W. Bradwell, who has carried out the designs of Mr. Verity, the architect, in the most satisfactory manner, so as to combine comfort, utility, and elegance; while the taste of Miss Santley herself has been employed with graceful effect in the medallions decorating the front of the boxes; another novelty being the pearl decorations of Messrs. Macallum and Hodson, of Birmingham, which prettily contrast with the rich hues of the velvet background and satin hangings. The fact that visitors now enter the stalls almost upon a level with the street must be a consideration of importance to those who have any fear of fire or panic, but Miss Santley assures her audience that the new theatre is fire-proof. Increased space is given everywhere, and in all respects there is a complete transformation in front of the curtain. The production of a new comic opera by an English author, English composer, and English artistes indicated an enterprising spirit in the management which will not lack appreciation on the part of the public, and a crowded and enthusiastic audience eagerly welcomed the work of Messrs. Clay and Sims. *The Merry Duchess* is a sporting comic opera. It is full of laughable allusions to the turf. The author and composer were loudly called for at the end of the first act, but Miss Santley said they preferred to await the verdict of the audience at the close, when they were again summoned and greeted with a round of applause that must have convinced them that in *The Merry Duchess* they had completely won the favour of the audience, nor have we any doubt that the opera will be received with cheers and merriment for many

a night to come, as it possesses ample qualifications to secure
the approval of lovers of light opera, and it is besides commendably free from those features of opera bouffe which
offend playgoers of the better class. Mr. R. Barker, who has
done much in the stage-management to add to the success,
was also honoured with a call. *The Merry Duchess* is as
harmless as she is amusing, and will gain, we believe, a large
circle of admirers during her sportive career at the
Royalty.

After the summer another comic opera, *Gillete* by Audran, was
produced, followed by *The Three Hats* at Christmas. From April
1884 the theatre became the home of French companies brought
over by the impresario, M. L. Mayer, who had introduced the
Comédie Française to London. He raised the prices and brought
success to the little theatre during its winter seasons. During the
summer months English managements tried for theatrical glory
with the usual comic operas and comedies, without achieving
much of lasting value, though Willie Edouin had some success in
1887.

Between French seasons, in 1888, Forbes-Robertson was seen
in an adaptation of *The Scarlet Letter*, under the management of
Edgar Bruce, and in the summer of 1889 *Mignonette*, an English
comic opera, was given. The following year Arthur Roberts tried
his luck in management, with disastrous results, producing a
burlesque *Tra La La Tosca!*

In December 1891 the Independent Stage Society, founded by
J. T. Grein, produced *Ghosts*. This unleashed the great controversy which raged around Ibsen and his plays: even the withdrawal of Kate Santley's licence was demanded by some critics!
They produced Shaw's first play, *Widowers' Houses*, in December
1892. Penley immediately followed with the first London production of *Charley's Aunt*. It was only on at the Royalty from 21
December till 30 January, 1893, then it moved to the Globe. It
ran, in all, for 1,446 performances.

During 1893 and 1894 the New Drama had its home on and off
at the Royalty. *A Doll's House* with Janet Achurch was seen in
March and *The Wild Duck* the following year. William Poel used
this stage for his experiment in the Elizabethan staging of Shakespeare with *Measure for Measure* in November 1893 (and on

later occasions), but the itinerent managements quickly came and went.

It is not till 1895 that a settled regime came, and Arthur Bourchier became lessee and manager (Kate Santley still holding the Lord Chamberlain's Licence). Before he opened on 7 September the theatre received yet another drastic re-construction and was lit for the first time by electricity. *The Era* critic reported on 14 September 1895:

> The Royalty Theatre dazzled and delighted those who visited it on Saturday to see the adaptation by Arthur Bourchier and Alfred Sutro from MM. Alexandre Bisson and Fabrice Carré called *The Chili Widow*. The general effect of the passages and the auditorium of the altered house is really brilliant. The seating accommodation has been increased by a third. There is a very pretty drop curtain, and the scheme of colour being cream and white, the electric light is reflected from the decorations and mirrors in a manner which makes the interior seem much larger than before. We hardly recognised, indeed, in the dainty little playhouse the rather *rococo* Royalty Theatre of old days. The entertainment is certainly judiciously adapted so as to be in keeping with the ornamentation.

The second play, *The Queen's Proctor*, established Bourchier and his wife, Violet Vanbrugh, in management and they moved on to the Garrick Theatre.

In October 1896 George Alexander, of the St. James's, took the theatre for a second company producing *His Little Dodge*. After this for a time there is little to record. A farcical comedy, *Oh! Susannah* with Louie Freear ran 161 performances in 1897-1898, and W. S. Penley put on *A Little Ray of Sunshine* in December 1898, which he revived at his new Great Queen Street Theatre in 1900. It ran 195 performances. The Independent Stage Society used the theatre for the first performance of Shaw's *You Never Can Tell* on 26 November 1899.

In February 1900 Mrs. Patrick Campbell took the theatre for a season and revived *Magda* which ran 164 performances. This was followed by *Mr. and Mrs. Daventry*, Frank Harris' play on Oscar Wilde's scenario, *Pelléas and Mélisande* (with Martin Harvey), *The Fantasticks* by Rostand, revivals of *The Second Mrs. Tanqueray* and *The Notorious Mrs. Ebbsmith*. Björnson's *Beyond Human*

Power was also among the plays of this management, which ended in December 1901.

After some transfers Mrs. Lewis Waller appeared in *Zaza* in 1902 and scored a big success. Charles B. Cochran made an early essay into management, in partnership with George Giddens, in October 1902 but with little luck, and Martin Harvey appeared unexpectedly as Napoleon in *The Exile* in May 1903. A play called *The Money Makers* in 1904 did little to live up to its title for the management. After numerous special performances including the first visit to London by the Abbey Theatre Dublin Company in April, the theatre closed in 1905 for yet further extensive alterations which had been demanded by the London County Council since 1903. Kate Santley had meantime acquired all of number 74, now at last the whole of the two buildings were again made one and suitable reorganisation could be carried out. The souvenir of the re-opening on 4 January 1906 said:

By the incorporation of adjoining premises the theatre has been considerably enlarged, the interior entirely remodelled and new exits provided. The entrance vestibule and the grand saloon have been extended to better proportions, and separate bars have been arranged for the pit, the upper circle and the gallery. There is now a third more seating accommodation in the stalls than before, and the popular pit has been made more than double its original size. All the seats have been so arranged that an excellent view of the stage may be obtained from every part of the house (capacity 657).

A very needful and ingenious alteration has also been made in the stage, where the roof has been raised fifteen feet. By means of this improvement the scene shifting is facilitated during the progress of the play, thus reducing the time of waiting between the acts. All the upholstery and curtain materials throughout the theatre are absolutely fireproof. The sanitary arrangements are remodelled on the latest system, and careful consideration has been given to the important matters of warming and ventilation. Thus the new Royalty Theatre may be said to rank as one of the most secure and comfortable houses in the kingdom.

The entire work of enlarging, redecorating, lighting, heating, and furnishing, was entrusted to Messrs. Smee & Cobay of 139, New Bond Street, W., and we have pleasure in congratulating them upon the ingenuity and taste they have displayed, and also upon the rapidity with which the work has been done. Taking into consideration the nature and difficulties of the work, we believe it constitutes a record in theatre reconstruction.

The scheme of decoration employed is characteristically French. Indeed it was a happy inspiration that prompted Messrs. Smee & Cobay to adopt the delicate 'Regency' style which, with its exquisite soft colourings and restrainedly fanciful decorations, make it the *mode de rigueur* for high-class theatre embellishment.

The walls throughout are treated in very pale cream, with the raised ornaments daintily touched with gold. The main entrance has a fine marble floor laid with Swedish green and Sicilian white, and the balustrade of the staircase has been executed in wrought iron, with a handrail of Derbyshire alabaster. This staircase leads to the foyer and grand saloon, where the decorations are of a soft tint of Celadon green, with raised decorations and mouldings in cream. This comfortably furnished lounge and saloon will form a pleasant promenade and *rendezvous* for the guests of the New Royalty Theatre.

The royal box is appropriately decorated with Gobelin blue and gold walls, and gilt furniture covered with Aubusson tapestries in delicate colourings.

The carpeting throughout is cerise with a cream border of ribands, and is in the style of the 'Regency'.

The *pièce de résistance* of the scheme of colour, however, is the proscenium drapery. This, we believe, to be unsurpassed in the theatrical world for its delightful colouring and sumptuous embroidery. The valance and tableaux curtains are of rich colours of an exquisite tint of cerise, with an elaborate appliqué of scroll work and floral sprays of shaded silver satin upon a trellis of pale Gobelin blue. The effect is a lovely construction of most delicate tints, unique in its result, being at once elaborate and yet in excellent taste.

The exterior was re-modelled, the upper part of 74 re-faced and the difference in window level camouflaged. A new canopy and entrances united the whole façade.

The New Royalty Theatre re-opened with a French season
under Gaston Mayer, the son of M. L. Mayer, and the old
tradition was carried on. On 4 January 1906 Réjane appeared
before a fashionable audience in *La Souris* to inaugurate the
season, which lasted till March. A comic opera, with May de
Sousa and Harry Fragson, was produced in April and failed dismally, and the French season re-opened at the end of May.

By the end of the year the ownership of the theatre was vested
in a company, The Royalty Theatre Ltd., with Gaston Mayer as
managing director, and the theatre was let out between the French
seasons year by year, but little of note was seen. *The Follies* gave
a season in 1907, and later in the year Sarah Bernhardt appeared
with her own company in *Phèdre, La Tosca, La Dame aux
Camélias,* and also other plays. Tom B. Davis was now the lessee
of the theatre and French companies ceased. Charles Hawtrey
presented Arnold Bennett's *What the Public Wants* in May 1909,
but it belied its title as in March 1910 did *The Way the Money
Goes*—certainly not into the Box Office!

That all was not well can be judged by the fact that W. H. C.
Nation, still up to his old tricks, was in occupation in October (he
died in 1914 aged seventy-one).

In 1911 yet another transformation took place. The theatre
was taken by J. E. Vedrenne (fresh from his partnership with
Granville Barker), and Dennis Eadie, the actor. They announced:

The Theatre has been entirely re-modelled, renovated and
re-decorated.

The seating of the Stalls has been rearranged; the Dress
Circle and Upper Circle have been entirely re-constructed
from the plans of Mr. Herbert H. Gissing, Architect and
Surveyor, and the line of sight has been materially
improved.

The decorations have been carried out by Messrs. F. de
Jong & Co. The re-construction work by Mr. John Brunskill.

The new Act Drop painted by Mr. Joseph Harker.

By a special arrangement made with the Commissioner of
Police a cab-rank in the immediate neighbourhood provides
the Theatre with a continuous supply of motor cabs, hansoms
and four wheelers without interfering with the engaged rank
for private carriages and Motor Cars. Patrons of this Theatre

will find the conveyances can be obtained after the performances without delay.

They opened on 26 April with Jerome K. Jerome's *The Master of Mrs. Chilvers*, with Dennis Eadie and Lena Ashwell in the cast. This was not a big success and they let the theatre during the summer to Lydia Yavorska, and by October Marie Tempest was in *The Honeymoon*, by Arnold Bennett, with Dennis Eadie in the cast. This ran for 126 performances.

Vedrenne and Eadie were back in January 1912 with Galsworthy's *The Pigeon*, with Gladys Cooper in the company. A season of matinées presented 'new worth-while plays to discerning audiences', and on 5 March *Milestones* was first produced. This play, often to be revived later, was by Arnold Bennett and Edward Knoblock. It ran for 607 performances, with the matinées continuing during the run. Nothing new was needed in the evening till September 1913 when *Interlopers* by H. M. Harwood opened. The programme contained a slip which told the audience:

The strike of London painters and decorators has greatly interfered with the re-decoration of the Theatre, which it was proposed to carry out during the short time it has been closed.

Everything has been done to put the Auditorium into as finished a condition as possible, but the difficulties have been great, and the very kind indulgence of the audience is claimed for the incomplete state of parts of the house.

The work is being carried out by Messrs. Townsends, of Dean St., W.

The Auditorium has been re-upholstered.

An iron safety curtain of the latest type authorised by the London County Council has been fixed by Messrs. T. W. Vaughan & Co.

There is now an entirely new Electric Lighting Installation, carried out by Mr. W. Saunders, under the direction of Mr. J. W. Barber, A.M.I.E.E., Consulting Engineer.

A new system of ventilation has been provided by Messrs. J. Keith & Blackman Co., who have also brought the heating apparatus up to date.

In November *The Pursuit of Pamela* by C. B. Fernald was produced with Gladys Cooper in the title role. She followed this, still playing

Q*

opposite Dennis Eadie, with *Peggy and her Husband* and *My Lady's Dress*, both in 1914. In the latter a small part was played by Lynn Fontanne.

A revival of *Milestones* in October 1914 filled in till a wartime spy play, *The Man who Stayed at Home*, was produced in December, it ran 584 performances. In April 1915 Dennis Eadie appeared in the title role in *Disraeli* by Louis N. Parker, for 128 performances. The next few plays were not such successes, but luck returned with *The Man From Toronto*, with Iris Hoey, in May 1918. This achieved 486 performances. In 1919 Maugham's *Caesar's Wife*, with Fay Compton, ran 241 performances. When the run ended Frank Curzon replaced Vedrenne as Eadie's partner. They revived Barrie's *Admirable Crichton*, *My Lady's Dress* and *Milestones* (a further 104 performances), and produced *The Romantic Young Lady*, by Sierra, in 1920.

As a fill-in in the hot summer of 1921 'a Pierrotic Entertainment' *The Co-optimists*, *In a Midsummer Night's Scream* was staged with the savings of Laddie Cliff and his wife Phyllis Monkman. It caught the Town and was launched on an initial run of 500 performances as *The Co-optimists*. (It transferred to the Palace in October.) It ran almost continuously at various London theatres till disbanded in 1927. It was re-formed in 1929 and 1935.

Subsequent successes were *If Four Walls Told*, 'a village tale' by Edward Percy (1922) and *At Mrs. Beam's*, a comedy by C. K. Munro (1923). In December 1924 Noël Coward's *The Vortex*, originally presented at the Everyman, Hampstead, was transferred here for a run of 224 performances. In August 1925 the Oxford Playhouse production of *The Cherry Orchard* had John Gielgud as Trophimoff.

The records of the theatre in the next years contain some outstanding productions but few long runs. Sean O'Casey's *Juno and the Paycock* was produced here in 1925 and was O'Casey's first big success. Dennis Eadie returned as an actor after a long absence in *Docter Knock*, by Jules Romain, in 1926.

A policy of transfers from the smaller outlying theatres gave the West End some exciting evenings. In 1927 came Noël Scott's *The Joker*, with Eadie in the cast, and Dion Titheradge's *The Crooked Billet;* in 1928 John Drinkwater's *Bird in Hand*, which ran for 364 performances, (this came from Barry Jackson's Birmingham

Repertory Theatre). In 1929 G. B. Stern's *The Matriarch* brought Mrs. Patrick Campbell back to London.

The policy of interesting transfers was resumed with Edith Evans in Nigel Playfair's Hammersmith production of *The Beaux' Stratagem* in 1930, followed by *Mariage à La Mode*.

In December 1930 the theatre came under the management of Leon M. Lion, among the plays he presented were *The King's Messenger* with Martin Harvey (April 1931), and *While Parents Sleep!* which ran 826 performances and caused many raised eyebrows. As a contemporary magazine said 'This entertaining comedy is written by Anthony Kimmins, who is an officer in the Royal Navy, and the breeziness of the dialogue, which contains many, many naughty words, proves somewhat strong meat for the more delicate constitutions of some landlubbers.'

This play eventually transferred to the Garrick Theatre and Eden Philpotts' *A Cup of Happiness* took its place at the Royalty in December 1932. Since Dennis Eadie had died in 1928 the theatre had been licensed to Arthur Gibbons, who now assumed full control and presented *The Brontës*, which ran 238 performances from April 1933. The following year Norman Macdermott presented O'Casey's *Within the Gates* and Pirandello's *As You Desire Me*, with Jean Forbes-Robertson, an artistic success, as was *Frolic Wind*, by Richard Pryce, in 1935.

Further changes in ownership and management brought little luck to the theatre, though Anmer Hall's production of *Storm in a Teacup*, February 1936, ran in all 432 performances, but not at this theatre as it transferred almost immediately to the Haymarket, leaving the Royalty to have a number of short runs. *Marigold* was revived in October and Priestley's *I Have Been Here Before* ran 210 performances from September 1937. This was the last success the theatre was to have. *The Survey of London*, Volume 33, records:

> By 1936 the danger of fire from celluloid-stores and other adjacent properties was thought to override the consideration, strongly pressed on the Lord Chamberlain by the licensee, that the theatre had been on the site before the development of inflammatory trades nearby, and finally it was decided not to renew the licence after November 1938.

An air of gloom hung over the last year of the theatre, and plays

quickly came and went. The last run was *So English!* which
opened on 8 November 1938 and quickly closed. The final
performance in the theatre was a matinée by the Southern Cross
Players of *The Milkman's Round* on 25 November. *The Survey of
London* says:

> Abortive plans for complete rebuilding had already been made
> in 1928-9 by Robert Cromie. Others, for conversion to a
> cinema, were now prepared by Charles Brett. Proposals for
> rebuilding as a theatre were renewed in 1943 when Cecil
> Masey submitted designs.

The Royalty was announced for re-opening, by Lawrence Leslie,
on 26 December 1944 as a Night Club: Lou Praeger's Royalty
Orchestra with Edna Kaye and Francesco and his Rhumba Band
were to play from 10.30 onwards, but the blitz seems to have
finished this project.

After the war, in 1954, plans were submitted to the London
County Council for a theatre to seat 1,000, by T., P. H., and E.
Braddock. All these plans were basically similar, aiming to provide
the maximum accommodation in a cinema-like auditorium with
stalls and a single deep circle. Cromie's scheme was for re-building
on the site of Nos. 73 and 74, but the designs by Masey and
Messrs. Braddock made use of No. 72 for side exit passages and
other accommodation.

By this time the theatre was almost derelict. Blitz damage had
destroyed the stage and the roof, time and the weather had also
contributed to the decay. The ruins were finally cleared away in
1953, and on the site of the theatre, with the addition of number 72,
arose a block of offices, designed by Messrs. Braddock, called
Royalty House and completed in 1955.

Over the years there were several stories of the reputed haunting
of the Royalty Theatre. The ghost of a lady of the Queen Anne
period, who had been murdered and found in the basement of one
of the original houses, was said to descend the stairs and disappear
in the middle of the vestibule.

A similar story involved the ghost of a gipsy girl with a
tambourine, who appeared only when the orchestra was playing.
Her presence was explained by the reputed discovery of a body
entombed in a hollow wall at the time of one or other of the
re-constructions of the theatre.

These stories have had long currency in the annals of haunted theatres, but they are insignificant compared with the definite first hand evidence of the appearance of Fanny Kelly herself, as late as 1934, when a lady in Victorian costume was seen by one of the present authors, (Joe Mitchenson), seated in the prompt side box at a rehearsal of *Murder in Motley*. This was but one of her many reputed appearances, wandering gently and happily, in daylight around the theatre, observed by attendants, actors and playgoers alike.

As yet there have been no reports of a transference of any of these happenings to the new building. The demolition man and the bulldozer may have laid these ghosts for ever.

Another Royalty Theatre was built on part of the site of the London Opera House (the Stoll Theatre), Kingsway, and opened 23 June 1960 (see *Theatres of London*). It is now a cinema.

21

St. George's Hall

St. George's Theatre, St. George's Opera House, Matinée Theatre, Maskelyne's Theatre of Mystery, Maskelyne's Mysterys, Maskelyne's Theatre

Langham Place, Regent Street
In a block bounded by Riding House Street and Mortimer Street, with Great Portland Street and the stage door at the rear

Opened 24 April 1867 as a concert hall for the New Philharmonic Society with an inaugural address by H. T. Braithwaite, delivered by Fanny Stirling, followed by a miscellaneous concert.
Under the management of Dr. Henry Wylde.
The hall could be fitted up and used as a theatre, St. George's Theatre, and was first used as such by amateurs, the Wandering Thespians, on 3 December 1867, presenting *A Woman's Whim*, by Walter Stephens.
Name changed to St. George's Opera House 18 December 1867 and opened with *The Contrabandista*, a comic opera by F. C. Burnand and Arthur Sullivan, preceded by a revival of *Puss in Petticoats*, an operetta by Jacques Offenbach and followed by a revival of *Ching-Chow-Hi*, an extravaganza by Jacques Offenbach.
Under the management of Thomas German Reed.
It reverted to its original name at the end of the season March 1868.
Name changed to Matinée Theatre 17 April 1897 and 'A series of High Class Vaudeville Entertainments' presented, including *La Revanche des Cigales*, a wordless play by Jules Oudot and Leon Schlesinger and *A Royal Roundhead*, an operetta by Hugh Seton and Denham Harris. It reverted to its original name by the following year.
Taken over by John Nevil Maskelyne for his magical entertain-

ment, opened 2 January 1905 with *The Coming Race*, a drama with magical effects (founded on Lord Lytton's novel) by David Christie Murray and Nevil Maskelyne. The hall became known as Maskelyne's Theatre of Mystery from 1922 (Soon shortened to Maskelyne's Mysterys and Maskelyne's Theatre). Premises acquired by the BBC for a studio concert hall October 1933. Destroyed by enemy action 10 May 1941.

The site is now covered by the St. George's Hotel, and Henry Wood House (BBC), opened in 1963.

WHEN REGENT STREET was constructed in 1820 land was acquired by the Crown from the Duke of Portland in the area which we now know as Langham Place. Part of the ground on the east side was subject to a lease held by John Marks, a coachmaker, who had his premises there in Riding House Lane. When the new street was finished and Langham Place formed, the coachmaker repository and stables were re-sited on the right hand side at the corner of Riding House Street (as it became) facing the new All Soul's Church, through to Great Portland Street and siding on private houses in Mortimer Street. The Langham Place frontage beside the entrance to the repository consisted of three houses: 18, 19 and 20, Langham Place. In 1851 the southern half of Mark's Carriage Repository was converted into the Portland Bazaar, entered from Great Portland Street and siding on the Mortimer Street houses.

In 1862 there was a scheme to convert the Bazaar into a concert hall and exhibition gallery, the Prince of Wales' Hall, but this was opposed by the residents. The following year a fire destroyed part of the Bazaar, but it was quickly re-built.

In 1866 a lease of part of the Bazaar (often called the German Bazaar) and 19 Langham Place (later re-numbered 4) was acquired by James Ferguson and Dr. Henry Wylde for the purpose of re-building as a concert hall, to be called the St. George's Hall.

The rest of the building up to Riding House Street remained in various uses until they were pulled down in 1891 and Queen's Hall was built on the site. (Opened 25 November 1893.) The remaining house Number 18 (later numbered 3) Langham Place became part of St. George's Hall in 1905. Dr. Wylde, Gresham lecturer on Music, had been the inspiration behind the building of the new hall, which was opened on St. George's Day, 23 April 1867. *The Era* 28 April reported:

> On Wednesday night the new Hall, built for the New Philharmonic Society, was formally opened with a *Conversazione*. Dr. Wylde, the President, will conduct the first concert in the room on Wednesday next. The Council had issued a large number of invitations, and the Hall, with its galleries, will accommodate from twelve to fifteen hundred persons. The *salon* to be henceforth occupied by the Society is 110 feet in length, 50 in breadth, and 45 in height. The elliptical roof is of wood, the lighting is managed by sunlights, and proper ventilation is secured by double windows and a perforated frieze in communication with the lanterns in the roof. The balcony runs round three sides of the room, and is very shallow, space for two rows of seats only being allowed. Facilities for exit are provided, and occupants of seats on the ground floor will find no steps to ascend or descend. Colour is extensively made use of in the decorations, and the architect is Mr. John Taylor, of Whitehall. A combined entertainment was submitted to the visitors, the proceedings commencing with a poetical address, written by Mr. H. T. Braithwaite. This was read by Mrs. Stirling, and formed the prelude to a concert, in which Mdlle. Poellnitz, Miss Abbott (London Academy of Music), Miss Madeline Schiller, Miss Rose Hersee, Herr Ganz, Herr Reichardt, the Brothers Thern, and Messrs. T. H. Wright, Chipp, Paque, and Ould, appeared Works of art, comprising water-colour drawings, portraits, &c., were open for the inspection of visitors. St. George's Hall has three separate entrances, from Langham Place, Regent Street; Mortimer Street, and Great Portland Street.

The Illustrated London News added:

> The orchestra may easily be removed to give place to a handsome proscenium and stage for operatic performances, the hall being licensed by the Lord Chamberlain for the purpose. There is a smaller hall for private concerts, with several class-rooms and other apartments.

The first use as a theatre (St. George's Theatre) was by an amateur dramatic company, the Wandering Thespians, who presented *A Woman's Whim*, a new play by Walter Stephens, on 3 December 1867.

The first professional use was for a Christmas season under the management of Thomas German Reed, a name which was later to figure largely in the history of the hall. They called the building St. George's Opera House, and presented a triple bill, noteworthy for the production of an early Sullivan comic opera, written with F. C. Burnand, *The Contrabandista*, which Reed commissioned after seeing the charity performance of Sullivan and Bernand's first effort *Cox and Box*, earlier in the year. (It was later revised as *The Chieftain* at the Savoy Theatre in 1894.)

The Era 22 December 1867 reported the first performance:

English Opera appears to be an irrepressible Institution. The results that too often follow well-meant efforts in its behalf are, to say the least, discouraging, but faith is strong, and at the eleventh hour some energetic Manager invariably comes to the rescue, and risks much in what has frequently proved a somewhat precarious undertaking. This time it is Mr. German Reed who determines to uphold the cause of native art, and his resolve in this particular is emphatically proclaimed in the production of a new opera by that exceedingly talented young musician, Mr. Arthur Sullivan. This is certainly a good beginning, and all who make acquaintance with Mr. Sullivan's *Contrabandista*, or any such fresh, original, and charming work, will thank Mr. Reed for the opportunity offered, and wish him every possible success in his undertaking. Any Manager who may decide upon the production of English Opera speedily finds himself surrounded, or rather confronted, by many serious difficulties. It is very well for the indignant advocate of native talent to complain that little or nothing is done to cultivate that comparatively rare plant, but where are the artists able to sing and act to equal perfection? There is no abundant supply of these doubly-gifted personages, and it thus happens that a Manager is, to a great extent, compelled to rely upon the merest amateurs in acting, though they may be even above reproach as singers. Mr. German Reed, subject to this hard and inevitable condition, has, no doubt, done his best to collect a good company, but it would be simply absurd to say that, as at present constituted, the St. George's *troupe* is perfect. On the contrary, there are certain lamentable weaknesses which, to 'speak by the card,' can escape neither the eye nor the ear of so competent a judge as Mr. German Reed. Judging from this gentleman's evident earnestness in his work, he will, doubtless, strengthen his company at the earliest opportunity, and thus secure the sympathy and support of the public. The Opera House, as the Hall is now called, has had a more distinctive character imparted to it by the introduction of four private boxes, and on Wednesday night last, the date of the first performance, the audience included many literary, musical, and artistic celebrities. Mr. German Reed himself conducted the orchestra during the first and last pieces, and Mr. Sullivan presided during the progress of *The Contrabandista*. Offenbach's *Puss in Petticoats* a facetious illustration of the transmigration of soul doctrine, commenced the entertainments, and introduced Mdlle. Anna as Minette, the human kitten; Mr. Edgar Osborne as Guido, a student; Mrs. Aynsley Cook as Marianne, the nurse (who expresses a very natural surprise when the charming Minette begins to lap milk on the feline principle); and Mr. Neilson as Dig-dig, an individual in the disguise of an Indian juggler. A piece of absurdity of the *Puss in Petticoats* order requires the best of acting to render it welcome. The music Offenbach has composed on this theme is pretty and melodious enough to find enthusiastic recognition among amateurs. Mr. Arthur Sullivan, on entering the orchestra to conduct his comic opera, *The Contrabandista*, was greeted most cordially. He has enjoyed the co-operation of Mr. F. C. Burnand as librettist, and this gentleman's talent for inventing amusing situations and writing humorous dialogue is once more proved beyond dispute. The plot of the opera is slight indeed, as will be seen from the following sketch:—Inez de Roxas (Miss Lucy Franklein), the young widow of a defunct brigand chief, holds in captivity a forlorn Spanish damsel named Rita. The prisoner's rescue is determined upon by her lover, Count Vasquez (Mr. Edgar Hargrave)—wonderfully like the Mr. Edgar Osborne of the first piece. His efforts are for some time foiled, and the persecuted Rita is constantly watched by San José and Sancho (Messrs. Aynsley Cook and Neilson). These two amiable Iberian thieves are nicknamed respectively the

Wolf and the Lion. They are deadly enemies, and candidates
for the hand of Inez de Roxas. Any one fortunate enough to
captivate this dusky Queen of banditti immediately becomes
the captain of the band. 'Such is the law of the Ladrones,'
and the Wolf and the Lion being equally unsuccessful, compel
a tourist photographer, one Mr. Grigg (Mr. Shaw), to sue to
the robber's widow. He is condemned to be married in four
days, and is forthwith invested with the 'sacred Hat,' worn by
the successive leaders of the Ladrones. The game of cross
purposes is still industriously played by the Wolf and the
Lion, and they both terrify poor Grigg in the most cruel
manner. The Lion at last turns traitor, and leads a party of
Spanish soldiers to the rescue of Rita and the photographer,
and to the very camp of the Ladrones. Such is the plot, which
is elaborated and worked out by the aid of wild absurdities
too numerous to recount. Mr. Arthur Sullivan's music is
melodious and captivating to a degree. The orchestration is
smooth and varied, besides being technically clever. In the
whole treatment of the subject supplied by Mr. Burnand
the composer proclaims his true musical instinct. In the
concerted music especially Mr. Sullivan displays a light,
graceful fancy, and a facility of writing nothing less than
admirable, and *The Contrabandista*, taken on its own merits,
is a triumphant vindication of the fact that musical talent is
not denied to the English. In every instance the music is in
perfect keeping with the spirit of the words, and, while a
necessary richness of harmony and orchestral colouring is
preserved, that tendency to excessive modulation, which
cloys rather than enchants, is most successfully avoided. Mr.
Sullivan knows as well as any one the above failing is common
to young composers, though it is a fault after all on the right
side. The opening duet, 'Hush! hush!' for Sancho and José,
with chorus, and the trio in the first act, for the two brigands
and Grigg, are models of composition that would lose but
little by any comparisons which could be made. A capital
buffo song, 'From rock to rock,' is given by the photographer,
and the melody is worked into the *finale* of act the first. There
is no overture, and one phrase for brass instruments in the
short introduction is heard again when the Queen bids them
bring forth 'the sacred Hat,' a situation slightly recalling the

investiture of Fritz with the 'sabre of my sire' in *The Grand Duchess*. Grigg's song was encored, and the *finale* was similarly complimented. The serenade sung by Vasquez in the second act had no chance whatever of making an impression. A song interpolated for Rita was unaffectedly sung by Miss Arabella Smyth, and in the course of this scene, occurs another excellent trio, 'Of that man we all require.' The *finale*, formed on a *valse*-like subject, brought down the curtain with loud applause. The principals were called forward, and a most enthusiastic greeting was very justly awarded to Mr. Sullivan, who led on Mr. Burnand. Mr. German Reed was afterwards brought before the curtain. Mr. Aynsley Cook worked hard as usual, as the Wolf, and was fairly seconded by Mr. Neilson. Miss Lucy Franklein bids fair to be an undoubted acquisition to the English lyric stage. Mr. Shaw was irresistibly comic as the timorous Grigg. The opera is well mounted as regards scenery and dresses. Offenbach's operatic extravaganza, *Ching-Chow-Hi*, that was so popular at the Royal Gallery of Illustration, concluded the evening's amusements. Madame D'Este Finlayson played her original character of Pet-Ping-Sing, Mr. Shaw, resumed the part of the Chinese 'Emperor of a Province,' Mr. Gayner performed the Mandarin Tee-To-Tum, and Mr. Morelli, Ba-Ba-Wang.

For the next few years a pattern of concerts, amateur dramatic performances and solo readings kept the hall busy. The Rev. J. M. Bellew the famous reciter and Mark Lemon, sometime editor of *Punch*, giving readings as Falstaff, are typical examples.

The first professional use as a theatre was for a season at Christmas 1868 when H. S. Granville presented his drama *Saved* and his burlesque of Byron's *Sardanapalus*. The following year the original Christy Minstrels were in occupation and a season of Italian opera was given in December 1872.

St. George's Hall was really to come into regular public favour from the time when *Mr. and Mrs. German Reed's Entertainment* appeared regularly for annual seasons from 20 April 1874. It was to remain in occupation until 9 March 1895.

Thomas German Reed and Priscilla Horton were married in 1844. He was the conductor of the Haymarket Theatre orchestra and she an actress and singer at Covent Garden Theatre and the Haymarket with Macready. They carried on their independent careers until 1854 when they toured the provinces in a programme of songs and parodies, this proved so successful that they took St. Martin's Hall, Long Acre, (see Number 17) in 1855 for a season and *Mr. and Mrs. German Reed's Entertainment* became established in London.

It provided a polite entertainment for the Victorian middle class family audience who would not patronise the theatre, much less the new music halls.

From St. Martin's Hall they moved to the Gallery of Illustration, a hall in Waterloo Place, in 1856, where they established themselves till 1873. They were joined by their son, Alfred Reed, who took over management with his mother when his father retired in 1871 (he died in 1877). Mrs. German Reed continued to take an active part in the company until she too retired in 1879. The Christmas season at St. George's Hall in 1867 was a prelude to a long association with this Hall. Corney Grain a piano entertainer, joined the company in 1870, and was eventually, in 1877, to become partner with Alfred Reed. Together they took a long lease of the hall which they let to amateurs, when not playing themselves, at fifteen guineas for dramatic performances, ten guineas for evening concerts and seven guineas for morning concerts (1883).

The *Entertainment* was given four nights and two matinées a week, for specified seasons. *The Era* 26 April 1874 reviews the opening performance and gives a good idea of the entertainment:

Mrs. German Reed and her small but talented company have now taken possession of St. George's Hall, where during the season they propose to reintroduce to those in search of merriment a series of those charming little sketches with which they have already delighted thousands at the Gallery of Illustration. Two special favourites have seceded—Mr. Arthur Cecil going to the Globe and Miss Fanny Holland to the Criterion; but their places have been judiciously filled, and still everything goes 'merry as a marriage bell.' Mr. W. S. Gilbert's romantic legend *Ages Ago*, enlivened by Mr. F. Clay's lively and tasteful music, has been revived, and the applause with which it was greeted on the opening night fully testified to the

fact that its popularity is far from being exhausted. Mrs.
Reed is equally amusing as Mistress Maggie McMotherly, the
superstitious old Scotchwoman, and as Dame Cherry Maybud,
the vivified portrait painted by Sir Godfrey Kneller; and we
need hardly say that to her artistic skill both as vocalist and
actress much of the success attending the performance is still
due. Miss Leonora Braham, who succeeds Miss Fanny
Holland, is a charming singer and a pleasing actress, and she
met with much favour as Rose and the vivified Lady Maud de
Bohun, her rendering of 'So please you, sir, 'tis I' narrowly
escaping an encore. Mr. Alfred Reed displayed considerable
versatility as Sir Ebenezer Tare, the pompous alderman and
tallow-chandler, and as Lord Carnaby Poppytop, Maud's
great-great-great-great grandson. Mr. Stanley Betjeman's
excellent voice was heard to advantage in the *rôles* of Mr.
Columbus Hebblethwaite and Sir Aubrey de Beaupre; and
Mr. Corney Grain as usual proved thoroughly efficient as
Angus MacTavish. The last-named gentleman furnished the
only novelty of the evening. This was a musical sketch
entitled *A Day in Town in Fifteen Minutes.* He introduced us
to 'Ma,' up from the country with the girls; described to us
in amusing fashion how they shopped; how they walked in
the 'Row;' how they visited the Royal Academy, the Soho
Bazaar, and the Panorama; and then took us with them to
Signor Scracci's annual concert, and showed us how easy it
is to turn a comic song into a classical air; imitated the
Italian gentleman whose object it is to get through the music
allotted to him at railway speed; the French singer, whose
mission it is to cry himself, and to make his hearers cry with
him; the ballad vocalist, whose conundrums are always
answered by the man with the trombone; the Spanish singer;
and his sisters Georgie and Porgie in their duet. He introduced us to sundry specimens of the genus swell at Lord's,
and illustrated the music and the 'fiery steeds,' at the Circus.
Whether talking, singing, or playing Mr. Corney Grain was
always in his element, and the fifteen minutes which were
comprised in his *Day in Town* afforded fifteen minutes of
irresistible mirth, followed by a double call to the footlights
for himself. This sketch is certainly one of his happiest efforts,
and is sure of protracted popularity. The concluding item was

Charity Begins at Home, and once more, in the persons of
Mrs. Reed, Miss Braham, and Mr. Corney Grain, Mr. Alfred
Reed, and Mr. W. A. Law, did we make the acquaintance
respectively of Mrs. Bumpus, the fisherwoman of the old
school; of Rebecca Giles, with her awkward questions; of
Susan Bumpus, with her pretty song of the pump, and
Betsy Clark, taking a prominent share in the arithmetical duet;
of Mr. Gorringe, the wandering photographer, anxious to
take the village pump and 'make a *carte* of it'; of the parish
beadle, horrified at the thought; and of the charity boy,
'dressed up such a guy'. The whole entertainment has lost
none of its freshness, and the large and fashionable audience
present sufficiently indicated that in their new home the clever
little company will find a renewal of the patronage they so well
deserve, and which hitherto they have never failed to
command.

The years passed, divided between the *Entertainment* and amateurs,
until 1895, with little to record except the bursting of William
Poel on to an unsuspecting public. This eccentric amateur
Shakespearean scholar and producer, and founder of the Elizabethan Stage Society, was to prove the inspiration of Granville
Barker and his followers, and through them to revize the whole
outlook of Shakespearean production in the next half century.
Poel first used St. George's Hall in 1881 and was to return
there many times later. His first exploit was to stage the first
quarto of *Hamlet*. Joseph Knight, the famous critic, wrote in
The Theatre May 1881:

> Any attempt to cast a light upon remote and arduous points of
> Shakespearean criticism deserves to meet with recognition.
> Such an attempt was made under peculiarly honourable
> circumstances, on Saturday afternoon, the 16th of April, at
> St. George's Hall, when a company of amateurs gave the first
> recorded performance of what is known as the first quarto
> *Hamlet*. So general ignorance concerning the value and
> significance of the quarto editions of Shakespeare's plays
> prevails among the most conscientious students of the stage,
> that it is pardonable and even desirable to state what is the
> point at issue. Until the year 1823 the quarto edition of
> *Hamlet* of 1604, now described as the second quarto,

supplied the earliest known text of the play. In that year (1823) a quarto differing in many important respects from that of 1604 and dated a year earlier, was discovered by Sir Henry Bunbury, among some books collected, as is supposed, by his father. This copy formed a portion of a volume which came ultimately into the possession of the Duke of Devonshire. It has since its discovery been often reprinted and facsimiled, and is known as the Devonshire quarto. Unfortunately it was deficient of the last leaf.

In 1856 a second copy, possessing the missing leaf, though wanting a title page, was bought from a student of Trinity College, Dublin, for a shilling by a Dublin bookseller, by whom it was sold for £70. Mr. J. O. Halliwell-Phillips subsequently acquired it for £120, and it is now in the British Museum. For the purpose of reproduction, the first quarto was now complete. Since that period it has given rise to no small amount of controversy.

From the second quarto, in which is found a text that with comparatively unimportant variations has been maintained, the first quarto widely differs. It is in the first place not much more than half the size, containing two thousand one hundred and forty-three lines, against three thousand seven hundred and nineteen. For the name of Polonius appears that of Corambis, while the character now known as Reynaldo is called Montano. The order of the scenes is other, the language differs widely, and much of what is most poetical, and almost all of what is most philosophical in the later text, is wanting. A discussion which has since been maintained, and is likely to be interminable, at once arose. According to one class of thinkers, the *Hamlet* of 1603 is an early draft of the tragedy which Shakespeare subsequently remodelled; in the opinion of others it is a maimed and distorted version, obtained by piracy, whether by being taken down in shorthand during representation, or 'cribbed' by some one with access to the stage copy, or by a combination of the two methods, is not clear. Of the latter view, Mr. John Payne Collier was the earliest champion, and he has been doughtily supported by W. W. Lloyd (a critical essay on *Hamlet*, contributed to Singers' second edition), Tycho Mommsen in *The Athenaeum*, the editors of the Cambridge Shakespeare (W. G.

Clark and W. Aldis Wright), and Mr. Moy Thomas. Charles Knight was the first to espouse the opposite view, and he has had with him, in the main, Staunton, Dyce, Gervinus, Herr Delius, Herr Elze, and Mr. F. J. Furnivall, the founder and director of the new Shakespeare Society, under whose direction the histrionic experiment now chronicled was carried out. To this opinion leans also, if we may judge from expressions in his edition of *Hamlet*, Dr. Howard Furness, the well-known editor, so far as it has extended, of the American Variorum Shakespeare.

Into a controversy like this it is needless to enter. Upon a question that will never be settled it is worse than useless to be dogmatic, and less than wise to seek an opinion if one does not force itself upon you. Göethe says that speculations to which no answer is possible are amusing occupations for the dilettante, but a man with serious work to do will do well to eschew them. Whether Shakespeare's *Hamlet* took at first the shape it assumes in the 1603 quarto and was afterwards expanded, or whether a dishonest publisher took advantage of the popularity of the play upon the stage to dish up a mutilated and imperfect version, is a matter which doctors disagree, and upon which no fresh light is likely to be thrown.

Fresh light is at least not likely to come from the representation that has been given. A certain amount of illumination is cast upon the text of Shakespeare by the most incompetent performance. It may accordingly be maintained that those who watched the presentation of the first quarto 'Hamlet' gained at least a clearer idea of its meaning. The question of its authenticity has, however, to be settled by means wholly different. Very lively arguments on both sides are deducible from the text, but no addition to their cogency can be obtained from a performance. This indeed, in the present instance, scarcely went beyond the average of amateur acting. Miss Helen Maude was a competent Ophelia, and Miss Zoe Bland a satisfactory Queen. Mr. W. L. Hallward's Horatio was a manly piece of acting, and something may be advanced in favour of the King of Mr. H. Stacke, and the Corambis (Polonius) of Mr. F. J. Lowe. Mr. Wm. Poel, however, who played Hamlet, failed to assign any distinct individuality to the role. The text was spoken with a cultivated delivery which is not common upon our stage, and to which accordingly it is pleasant to listen. As a whole, however, the exposition was languid, emphasis was rarely adopted, and when adopted was injudicious, and the presentation was inadequate in all respects.

The customs supposed to be in vogue in Shakespeare's days were rigorously observed. No scenery or decoration beyond a raised platform—on which the dumb show was presented or the like—was employed, and the costumes were all Elizabethan. Not even an intimation in writing was affixed to indicate the scene of the action. In the case of a play with which the audience is so familiar as it is with *Hamlet* no great inconvenience attends this sytem; it would probably work less satisfactorily were the drama produced an entire novelty.

Before the curtain was raised Mr. Furnivall delivered a short explanatory address or conference. The amateurs are to be congratulated upon their zeal and enterprise. No slight trouble is involved in acquiring the text of a play like this, and the lines were, as a rule, spoken with commendable accuracy. If we are unable to attach any great value to the performance, we are at least glad to have seen it. To students of *Hamlet* it is pleasant to recommend Mr. Grigg's photo-lithographic reprint of the text of the quartos, which of course reproduces with minutest accuracy every feature of the original, and brings at slight cost the rarest of Shakespearean volumes within the reach of all.

Helen Maude (Maud Holt) was to become the wife of Beerbohm Tree in 1883.

The German Reed Entertainment finished their winter season 9 March 1895 and were due to re-open again after Easter, but on 10 March Alfred Reed died. Corney Grain followed him on 16 March and the double shock proved fatal to old Mrs. German Reed who died on the 18th at the age of seventy-seven. This was virtually the end of *The Entertainment* though an attempt to revive it was made here in 1902 without success.

For the next few years St. George's Hall again languished. An attempt at a Matinée Theatre in 1897 was unsuccessful.

In 1899 it was proposed to completely re-construct the hall as a restaurant and concert hall and join it to Queen's Hall. Plans and drawings were made but the idea came to nothing.

A season of German plays, Deutsche Theater in London, in 1900-1901 introduced some little known classics to London, including Hauptman's *The Beaver Coat*. In 1902 a French company from the Théâtre des Capucines appeared with Charlotte Wiehe and Max Dearly.

In 1904 the hall was closed but a new era dawned when J. N. Maskelyne took over the lease. He made many improvements in the hall, adding in the other house in Langham Place, and re-opened on 2 January 1905. *The Era* 7 January says:

The hall has been wonderfully improved, and now presents more the appearance of an immense drawing-room than of a theatre. The stage has been brought forward, and its capacity thereby much increased. There are no wings, their place being taken by an inner and outer proscenium. The curtain of the inner is a clever painting of the exterior of the Egyptian Hall in Piccadilly, and what may be called the act-drop represents a pretty classic landscape. As the Messrs. Maskelyne contemplate producing a series of important magical pieces, the machinery and lighting of the stage have become naturally matters of the first importance. Framing the outer proscenium are no less than 300 electric bulbs. This arrangement entirely disposes of unnecessary shadows, which are so difficult to get rid of. When the actor walks to the footlights he is surrounded by a ring of unseen lamps of which there are no less than two thousand on the stage, and the power can be lowered to the merest glimmer, or by insensible gradation increased to a potential glare. Thus all sorts of effects, from the feeble light of the breaking dawn to the blaze of noonday sunshine can be readily simulated. These results are obtained by the employment of Wirt dimmers, of which twenty-seven are required for the eight hundred lamps affixed to the battens, besides the movable lamps which will be used at special points.

In their new scheme of amusement the Maskelyne management come into line with the theatres, and in their production challenge criticism in serious drama with magical effects. For this purpose Lord Lytton's novel, *The Coming Race* has been fashioned into a play by Mr. David Christie Murray and Mr. Nevil Maskelyne.

Before the curtain rose on the drama, Mr. J. B. Hansard came through the inner proscenium, and in the dress of an ancient Crier, addressed the audience as follows:—'Oyez, Oyez, Oyez! It having been decreed that the ancient, and at one time refined thoroughfare, known as Piccadilly, shall henceforth be devoted to the consumption of grub—where you may upset your little Marys from the modest sum of one and six—science and art are constrained to seek a pure atmosphere. We have therefore turned our backs upon the old and dingy Egyptian Hall—we have left Isis and Osiris to the flesh pots, and have turned to St. George, purity, and truth. Be it known, therefore, that this hall, dedicated to our patron saint, shall henceforth receive the sub-title, 'England's New Home of Mystery.' The lessee and his sons will continue to emulate St. George by giving death-thrusts to the dragon of superstition and imposture, in whatever guise he may appear, and by providing high-class, interesting, and wholesome amusement at reasonable prices they hope for a continuance of that patronage so liberally bestowed upon them for thirty-one years at the old home of mystery. Oyez, Oyez, Oyez! As loyal and dutiful subjects of his Majesty King Edward the Seventh, it is meet we inaugurate these proceedings by singing the National Anthem. Miss Iris Lincoln and Mr. Leslie Burgess will therefore appear upon the auxiliary stage and sing, 'God save the King.' Let us all join in the refrain with heart and voice, for our Teddy's a good one, and don't you forget it!' Miss Lincoln and Mr. Leslie Burgess then sang the soli, and the audience assisted with impressive cordiality. The small orchestra is under the direction of Mr. Cramer, and the accomplished 'cellist, Mr. Ivimey, and the clever violinist, Mr. Denti, played some capital solos during the entr'actes.

As Maskelyne and Devants', Maskelyne's Theatre of Mysteries, or simply Maskelyne's Theatre, it was to become the home of Magic until October 1933. A spokesman for the family tells their story:

In 1873, John Nevil Maskelyne 'the Grand Old Man of Magic' came to London. Prior to this step, which was destined to alter the whole course of his life, he had been appearing in the provinces with his friend George A. Cooke.

Everything must have a beginning, and the beginning of Maskelyne's Mysteries has assumed an atmosphere of romance to which it is justly entitled. In 1865 Maskelyne witnessed the 'performance' of two so-called Spirit Mediums, the Davenport Brothers, and during the supposed séance he, in a fleeting moment, discovered that they were resorting entirely to trickery for their manifestations. To Maskelyne this was an irresistible chance for showing them up, and this he proceeded to do by reproducing the entire performance! It may be added that the Davenport Brothers came from America and, so far as is known, they returned there, after their exposure with all possible speed, little more being ever heard of them.

During the next eight years, Maskelyne continued to develop the type of entertainment for which his name is now a household word in every corner of the world. It was his idea that a season of three months in London would greatly enhance his reputation in the provinces, and on April 1st, 1873, after a preliminary five weeks' engagement at the Crystal Palace, he produced his entertainment at St. James's Hall, Piccadilly. At the end of a month he found that he was winning the support of the public; but, as St. James's Hall was no longer available to him, he had to change the scene of his operations. Just over the way, on the opposite side of Piccadilly, stood the Egyptian Hall; Maskelyne negotiated a three months' lease of the hall and transferred his entertainment there on May 26th, 1873.

The opening programme, which had begun to be one of the chief topics of conversation in London, included some of the best known effects that were ever associated with 'Maskelyne and Cookes,' namely: 'Chinese Plate Dancing,' 'Decapitation Extraordinary,' 'The Floating Lady,' 'The Box Trick' and 'Will, the Witch and the Watchman,' the last, perhaps, the best known magical sketch ever written.

All these things at that time made the Public 'gasp and wonder'; the consensus of Public opinion was that 'such marvels have never before been seen.' But Maskelyne was not content to let matters rest at that, for, within the following eighteen months he produced his famous card-playing automaton 'Psycho,' which created one of the biggest sensations of the time.

But Maskelyne by no means relied entirely upon automata and mechanical illusions for his programme. That he was a juggler of considerable dexterity is plain from his 'Japanese Top-spinning' and his 'Plate Dancing' acts, the latter, as performed by Maskelyne, probably stands alone as an example of pure physical dexterity. He would begin with two ordinary plates and with clever fingering set them spinning on a table; he would then add to their number, one by one, first with one hand and then with the other, until he had as many as ten plates, or more, and one large pudding-basin all spinning merrily at once!

For many years, the magical sketch was a leading feature of Maskelyne's programme. 'Will, the Witch and the Watchman' has already been mentioned; but others, almost equally famous, included 'Mrs. Daffodil Downey's Light and Dark Séance,' 'My Twin Spirit,' 'The Bloomsbury Proper-Ganders,' 'Arcanc,' 'The Entranced Fakir,' 'The Philosopher's Stone,' 'The Scarab,' and several others. Nearly all burlesqued the Occult in some way or other, and in most of them the magical effects were produced in a setting of fun and frolic.

Throughout the long period at the Egyptian Hall, many world-famous magicians were, from time to time, associated with the entertainment: Charles Bertram, Bautier de Kolta, Charles Morritt, David Devant and Paul Valadon, to mention a few. In 1904 the Egyptian Hall was condemned to be pulled down to make way for shops and offices; so Maskelyne was compelled once more to seek a new home. He found one in St. George's Hall.

On February 5th, 1904, George Cooke died, thus ending an association that had existed ever since Maskelyne's entertainment had begun, though Cooke had never been actually a partner in the business.

St. George's Hall was opened with *The Coming Race*. But it did not appeal to Maskelyne's audience, so it was withdrawn, after about two months, and the programme reverted to magical variety with occasional special matinées.

In collaboration with David Devant, who became a partner later in 1905, a very long series of famous illusions were produced, as well as many magical sketches. The name of Devant will ever be associated with 'The Magic Kettle,' the 'Burmese Gong,' 'Vice-Versa,' 'The Sylph' and, perhaps above all, 'Mental Magnetism' or Silent Thought Transmission.

In November, 1906, came a magical presentation of the Witches' Scene from 'Macbeth' with all its appropriately uncanny mystery.

In 1910 'Psycho' reappeared in public after a retirement of nearly thirty years, and thereafter Maskelyne's appearances on the stage of his theatre began to be somewhat fewer, his place being taken by his sons, Nevil and 'Archie' (E. A.) Maskelyne. In 1915 Devant retired from the business, leaving Maskelyne and his two sons in complete control. It was on Tuesday, May 2nd, 1917, that Maskelyne made his last public appearance—oddly enough in a revival of one of his earliest and most popular successes, 'Will, the Witch and the Watchman'—and that night his first and last illness seized him. He died on May 18th, 1917, aged 77.

It was now left for Nevil and 'Archie' Maskelyne to carry on the business which they did until September, 1920, when 'Archie' died. Towards the end of 1920 Captain E. Clive Maskelyne, M.C., Nevil Maskelyne's second son, joined his father in the business.

In 1924, Jasper, Nevil's youngest son, also went into the business. In September of the same year, Nevil Maskelyne, whose health had been poor for some while, died suddenly, leaving the business to be equally divided among his four sons. Clive and Jasper continued to carry on the entertainment while their eldest brother, John Nevil, was appointed Chairman of the Company.

In 1926 Clive retired to undertake an extensive tour of India and the Far East; but unfortunately, he was taken ill and died at sea on the outward journey. It was after Clives' death that Noel, third son of Nevil Maskelyne, joined his brothers John and Jasper in active association with the business.

To Mary Maskelyne who often appeared with the company her brothers owed a debt of gratitude for her loyalty and encouragement and never-ending cheerfulness in times of anxiety.

Times and tastes were changing and in 1933 the lease of St. George's Hall was acquired by the B.B.C. and Maskelyne's Theatre closed in October. The building was immediately transformed into a B.B.C. Concert studio. *The Radio Times* reported:

We walked through the stalls, of which the first four rows, representing sixty-one seats, had been taken up to make room for an enlarged orchestra pit. We clambered gingerly on to the stage, and looking rather forlornly for traces of magic nearly tumbled twelve feet down through a gap. It is a magnificent stage, with the floor laid in small sections which could be removed to meet the demands of every trick in the Maskelyne repertoire. We asked Mr. Noel Maskelyne to explain the plan of the stage, but he wasn't giving much away. We searched for tell-tale evidence of how the lady had floated, of how the box had vanished. But there was nothing. Maskelyne's stage had kept its secrets to the end. All traces of magic had gone from the hall. We admired the very efficient lighting system, wandered through the dressing-rooms—one of them now equipped with listening gear for the Balance and Control men—clambered up a very dirty iron spiral staircase, tried, at Mr. Maskelyne's invitation, the weight of one of the thirty drop battens, crawled out on to the part of the roof adjoining the Queen's Hall—realised, with something of a shock, that the two buildings actually touched each other—but still found no magic.

So we determine to make the most of the new brand of magic that has invaded the place, and called again on the morning of October 28. It was the last rehearsal for the first 'Music Hall' programme to be relayed from St. George's Hall. Beauty had come back in the guise of the Eight Step Sisters. There were the Houston Sisters, Jack Payne and his new band, Stainless Stephen, and other 'top-liners'.

Miracles of renovation had been performed since our last visit. Brand new microphones had been slung across the proscenium opening, and from the dust and chaos of two days earlier a spick-and-span theatre had re-emerged, a shining new home for 'Music Hall'.

That night, afflicted by an insatiable curiosity about a theatre in action, we arrived early. We had sampled the intimate joys of the show in rehearsal, and we wanted now to see it put over, to the accompaniment of a crowded house, lively orchestra, curtains, lights and all. We went first to the stage door, to see the artists arrive, and were nearly swept by enthusiastic autograph hunters into the pictures that the photographers were taking by flashlight of the artists as they arrived. We slipped in by the stage entrance, and noted, with satisfaction, that all the artists in the bill had a dressing-room to themselves; trespassed on to the stage, and found Miss Marie Burke at a last-minute rehearsal. Curiosity satisfied for the moment, we went round to the front of the house, and waited impatiently for eight o'clock.

There was no escaping the air of expectancy, the almost intolerable excitement of that 'first night' atmosphere. The house was packed. A few minutes before eight o'clock, the Theatre Orchestra stilled conversation with a brisk overture, and then, on the hour, No. 1 flashed up in red on the indicator. St. George's Hall was on the air for the first time in its sixty-six years of life. It was a grand show. Everybody seemed keyed up to the occasion. From the genial opening gambit of Hazell and Day to Jack Payne's brilliant finale, it was an hour of variety of which any music hall could be proud. In a sound-proof cubicle at the side of the stage Christopher Stone was explaining the scene to listeners. But there was no need for him to explain the thunderous applause, the warm ripple of appreciation, the sense everywhere that here was unbuttoned joy, stuff with the real 'Music Hall' tang.

There could be no doubt that 'Music Halls' had found a congenial home again, and had started brilliantly on their new tenancy. Will they be as lucky with their next home, whatever that may be?

The end came in the early hours of 24 September 1940 when fire bombs fell through the glass roof on to the back of the stage, and the Hall was gutted. Queen's Hall, its neighbour, was reduced to an empty shell in the raid on 11 May 1941, and an era came to a close.

Schemes to re-build Queen's Hall as a memorial to Sir Henry

R

Wood, taking in the St. George's Hall site, fell through and the ground was sold for re-development. The St. George's Hotel and Henry Wood House (B.B.C. offices) opened in 1963, now cover the site. The staff entrance to the B.B.C. and the southern end of the gound floor showrooms of Ryman Edgleys marks the position of the entrance to St. George's Hall.

22

The St. James's Theatre

The Prince's Theatre, The Theatre Royal, St. James's, The Royal St. James's Theatre

King Street, St. James's
In a block bounded by Angel Court (with stage door) and Crown Passage, backing on buildings in Pall Mall.

Opened 14 December 1835 with an opening address by James Smith, spoken by Clara Selby, followed by *Agnes Sorel*, a new grand original operatic burletta by Mrs. Gilbert à Beckett (Mary Ann Glossop), followed by *A Clear Case*, a farce by Gilbert à Beckett and *The French Company*, a farce by Gilbert à Beckett.
Under the management of John Braham.
Re-named the Prince's Theatre, opened 27 April 1840 with *Der Freischütz*, by Carl Maria von Weber, in a season of German opera by the Mayence Company. Directed by Herr Schumann.
Under the management of Alfred Bunn.
Name reverted to the St. James's, 7 February 1842.
Under the management of John Mitchell.
Interior remodelled and re-decorated and opened 16 October 1869 with *Treasure Trove*, an operetta by Jacques Offenbach, followed by *She Stoops to Conquer*, by Oliver Goldsmith. Concluding with *The Magic Waltz*, a ballet by Mme. Collier, with music by W. H. Montgomery.
Under the management of Mrs. John Wood.
The names, the Theatre Royal, St. James's and the Royal St. James's Theatre were sometimes used during the period up to 1879.
Interior re-constructed and re-decorated and opened 4 October 1879 with *Monsieur le Duc*, a play in one act by Val Princep,

followed by a revival of *The Queen's Shilling*, a comedy in three acts (from the French), by G. W. Godfrey.

Under the management of John Hare and W. H. Kendal.

Interior re-constructed and the adjoining building, up to and over Angel Court, refaced and partly re-built and added on to the theatre with the stage door in Angel Court.

Re-opened 1 February 1900 with *Rupert of Hentzau*, a play by Anthony Hope.

Under the management of George Alexander.

Closed 27 July 1957 and demolished.

An office block, St. James's House, completed in 1959 now stands on the site.

THE ST. JAMES'S THEATRE was built by John Braham, the famous tenor, who had been the idol of London for over thirty years. Born in 1774, originally named Abram, he had made his debut in 1787 at the Royalty Theatre in the East End and risen to be one of the most powerful and popular of English singers. By the eighteen thirties, having amassed quite a considerable fortune, and with his retirement in mind, to say nothing of the encouragement of his extravagant wife who wished to keep up her lavish state of living when the great voice should have ceased to be a commercial asset; Braham decided to build a new theatre.

Already, early in 1835, he had tried management. In partnership with Frederick Yates, at the Colosseum in Regent's Park, a place of varied entertainments. He was persuaded to buy the freehold of property in King Street, St. James's. Nerot's Hotel at numbers 23 and 24 had been opened in 1776 in one of the principal houses in King Street, which from 1695 had been the town house of the Earl of Ranelagh, and had had later owners before conversion. While an hotel its patrons had included Edmund Burke and Lord Nelson. By 1811 the hotel had removed to Clifford Street and the old house gradually descended to being a warehouse and was fast becoming derelict when Braham bought and demolished it in 1835. He paid £8,000 for the property and spent over £18,000 on the new theatre he built to the designs of Samuel Beazley.

As usual, at this date, the proprietors of the Patent theatres objected to any granting of a licence to another theatre, but eventually, through the influence of King William, a seasonal

(Michaelmas to Easter) burletta licence was granted in July 1835, and was renewed yearly until the end of the monopoly in 1843. This was the height of the trouble over the Strand Theatre (see number 19). Owing to building difficulties and local opposition the construction was delayed but eventually accomplished in the 'almost incredibly short space of thirteen weeks, six days of which were so wet as to cause the work to be suspended'. The builders, Messrs. Grissell and Peto, worked hard, but though the theatre opened on 14 December 1835, the exterior of the building was not completed until the summer of 1836. The building is described in *The Times* 15 December:

This house, the offspring of Mr. Braham's enterprise, was last night open with great *éclat*. Long before the public could gain admission, King Street, St. James's, presented a long line of carriages, and the theatre was surrounded by an impatient multitude. At length, about 7 o'clock, the box doors were thrown open; a rush immediately took place, and many coats, which were unfortunately thrust against the newly distempered walls, suffered a very considerable change of colour. This precipitancy was unnecessary; for, though the house was extremely well attended, it was not uncomfortably crowded. Much has been said in approbation of the form, and in praise of the decoration, of the theatre. These laudatory *avant-courriers* are rarely to be depended on as the heralds of truth; but in this instance they have rather fallen short of than gone beyond the fact. This theatre is indeed a beautiful structure, and as unique as it is beautiful. The audience part of the house inclines very slightly, almost imperceptibly, to the horse-shoe form. The prevailing colour is a delicate French white. A series of arches, supporting the roof, and sustained by Caryatides, runs entirely round the upper part of the theatre. The effect is novel and very pleasing. The chandelier is a most striking object. It is formed of gilt copper, and is elaborately carved. It is for splendour of appearance, and curious elegance of design, the handsomest thing of the kind that we have ever seen. It throws forth an immense flood of light, and, aided by the girandoles which are placed round the dress circle, creates a mimic day. To the architect, Mr. Beazley, much praise is due; and the decorator (Frederick Crace and

Son of Wigmore Street), who has, to a nicety in every point, imitated the gay yet splendid style of the age of Louis Quatorze, must not be passed by without high eulogium. He has executed his task with extraordinary ability, and he deserves the highest commendation. The *tout ensemble* of the house is light and brilliant. It looks like a fairy palace. Then, the two great points which are most important to the comfort of an audience—hearing and seeing—have been sedulously consulted; and, with reference to them, we think that the new theatre takes the lead of all its brethren.

The Morning Herald added:

The *façade*, which immediately faces Duke Street, is of the pure Roman architecture of the middle ages; and, though not very extensive, will present, when completed, an extremely chaste and elegant appearance. The portico is composed of six Ionic columns, with angular volutes fully enriched, supporting a stone balustrade; behind which, and sustaining the main cornice of the front, is a range of Corinthian columns, with richly-embellished entablature of the same order. The centre of the building is appropriated to the box-entrance, whilst at the extremities, right and left are commodious approaches to the pit and gallery. The box visitors are admitted through the portico into a small entrance-hall, leading by a handsome flight of stone steps into a compact vestibule adjoining the dress circle, from whence two circular stone staircases ascend to the upper boxes and saloon, which is in front of the building, looking into King Street. Owing to the lateness of the season, the front will not be stuccoed, nor will the various entrances be finished off, until the approaching spring—till when they will be temporarily fitted up with draperies. When completed, it is intended that the entrance-hall, the ceiling of which is coved, shall be supported on either side by four imitative marble columns, between which, in niches, are to be placed six figures from the antique.

The interior, which is something less in size than the English Opera House, comprises two tiers of boxes under the gallery, with what are known as 'slips' on each side of it. The dress circle, consisting of sixteen boxes, is kept considerably lower than in any other theatre, so as to place the spectator as

near with the level of the stage as possible. On each side of the
pit nearest the stage, are two compact, private boxes, which
command a perfect view of the performances. The gallery is
so constructed as to admit of the stage being seen from every
part—a *desideratum* not obtained in other theatres.

The lobbies running entirely round the theatre, are formed
of stone landings and brick walls, so as to prevent the possibility of danger from fire; and the staircases, every where in
the public department, are of stone. The walls and timber
would 'laugh a siege to scorn,' being of unusual strength and
thickness, further secured by iron chain-ties, which have been
worked in the centre of all the walls, at intervals, from the
bottom upwards, so as to strengthen them during the harden-
ing of the mortar.

The ceiling, encircled by a carved cornice, on which rest
six groups of children in bas-relief, is composed of rich,
spreading foliage, branching from the centre into six, enriched
panels, from which are suspended carved swags and drops of
fruit and flowers. The ceiling is supported by Caryatides on
gilded plinths, and terminates in a cove formed into twelve
arches, in the spandrels of which are paintings of sylph-like
figures, emblematical of music.

The gallery front is arranged in panels, in a form peculiar
to the style adopted, intersected by circular ones, formed of
twining palm, in which are paintings of children, playing on
various instruments.

The first circle is also arranged in panels, but varying much
in their form from the above. These contain paintings after
the manner of Watteau, relating to the origin of the Italian
drama and pantomime, and between them are smaller panels
of gilt trellis-work. Over this circle is a carved canopy,
supported by eight pilasters.

The front of the dress circle, which is formed with a bold
swell, is embellished with a carved foliage in high relief, and
of most tasteful design, on which the light, owing to its
peculiar form, strikes with great splendour. This circle has
also its canopy and pilasters, but more splendid; from the
latter spring handsome girandoles, each bearing three wax
lights, in addition to a magnificent, central chandelier.

The proscenium is quite novel in its decoration, having no

drapery at top, but a richly carved, undulating line instead. In the three arches above the stage, which form part of the twelve we have described as belonging to the ceiling, are introduced three beautifully executed paintings. That in the centre represents a medallion of the royal arms, from which children surrounding it are raising a crimson drapery; whilst those on its left and right are symbolical of Comedy and Music, also personated by children; these are inclosed in rich framework. The lower part of the proscenium consists of a rich entablature, ornamented with trusses and swags of flowers, supported by fluted columns, with intersecting enrichments, and splendid, gilt capitals resting on carved pedestals. A foliage of palm, terminating against the entablature, is the decoration of the upper box; the lower one is formed by a curved canopy. The box front is a trellis panel, containing a mask surrounded by foliage, with frill and shell-work in burnished gold. The whole of these splendid ornaments on a white ground, which is the prevailing colour of the interior, have a most chaste and pleasing effect. The interior of the boxes is a rich crimson.

Complete as is the audience part of the St. James's Theatre, no less so are the arrangements for the stage and scenic departments. Besides a very extensive stage, which possesses every modern improvement, are excellent painting rooms, with an adjoining building, six stories in height, containing dressing and green rooms, at the top of which is a tank of water for fire services.

Some of this was partly existing buildings incorporated into the theatre for the dressing room wing and as private living accommodation for the Braham family, entered through Angel Court.

The theatre opened with a mixed programme of opera and two farces. After 'An Opening Address' delivered by Clara Selby, the new operatic burletta, *Agnes Sorel*, was performed with Braham himself, supported by Miss Glossop, who was making her début, in the title role. Her sister, who had composed the music, was the wife of Gilbert à Beckett, the resident dramatist, who provided the two farces which followed the opera, as it was unashamedly billed after a few nights in spite of the authorities!

A full description of the opening night and the Address is in

The St. James's Theatre. Its Strange and Complete History, 1835-1857, by Barry Duncan (1964), which is a source for most data on this theatre. There is also *A Chronicle of the St. James's Theatre,* a short anonymous history (1900) and *St. James's Theatre of Distinction* by W. Macqueen Pope (1958).

After the opening production, which was not in itself conspicuously successful, there was added to the bill a Christmas burletta, *Rasselas; or, the Happy Valley* founded on Dr. Johnson. It was not till January that a really successful new piece, *Monsieur Jacques* by Morris Barnett, was produced, but on the whole the first season was a failure. The out of the way position of the theatre was blamed among other things.

During the summer closure Braham changed his producer from William Mitchell to John Pritt Harley, as well as quite a few members of the company. The second season opened with Charles Dickens' first play (inevitably billed as a burletta!), *The Strange Gentleman.* Braham had commissioned an opera from Dickens and John Hullah, but as this was not ready in time Dickens adapted one of his short tales instead for the opening bill. Later this coupled with *Artaxerxes,* Arne's opera, with Elizabeth Rainforth supporting Braham as Mandane, achieved a mild success.

The promised 'opera' *The Village Coquette,* was produced on 6 December, and was well received by the press. An extension of the season to the end of May 1837, by permission of the Lord Chamberlain, did not help financially. Braham was not doing particularly well with the concerts at the Colosseum, his other enterprise. The third season from September contained the usual light pieces, mostly by à Beckett, spiced with revivals. A garbled dramatisation of *Oliver Twist* (the first) was produced and withdrawn after one performance!

Harley continued to produce operatic adaptations and farces till he was succeeded by John Hooper in April 1838, but things were no better and Braham's last season closed in June and the company disbanded. Braham was forced back to Drury Lane the following season and the St. James's was up for sale or to let. Fanny Braham tried to run the theatre for a while, until John Hooper could raise the money to take over, as he had decided to go into management himself.

His lesseeship lasted only four months; and his attractions included performing animals supporting the usual burlettas. In

R*

458 THE ST. JAMES'S THEATRE

November the notorious Alfred Bunn turned up from Drury Lane with a ballet company presenting *La Fille mal Gardée*, which was followed by a revival of *Masaniello*, with Braham back at his own theatre, but the season closed before Christmas.

From April to June 1840 Bunn brought a German opera company to London and to celebrate the marriage of Victoria and Prince Albert asked permission to re-name the theatre the Prince's. Royal patronage extended to a visit to *Faust* (Spohr's opera) in May. In the autumn a French dramatic company took the theatre for a time and even amateurs were welcomed to keep the house open.

The impoverished Braham looked to America as had many actors before him and many to come would do, as the Eldorado where they could re-establish their declining fortunes. He left his elder son in charge and an attempt to form an English opera company in November, failed as usual after a few nights. All through 1841 the theatre was closed except for occasional concerts and amateurs.

A new era opened in 1842 when John Mitchell, bookseller and founder of the Bond Street Ticket Agency, took charge of the theatre, again re-named the St. James's. He established a Théâtre Français in London with Eliza Forgeot as his director of a permanent supporting company, importing the stars from Paris. They performed three nights a week with diverse attractions on the other evenings.

The first season opened with *Le Bourgeois Gentilhomme* and *L'Ambassadeur*, with Adrien Perlet, the comedian, as the star attraction.

Mitchell at last brought success to the St. James's and for the next twelve years London saw many of the great stars of the French stage, including Déjazet, Lemaître, Rachel and Fechter, besides names which, though famous in their day, are now forgotten.

The 'off nights' of the French company were filled by Louis Dobler (a famous German conjurer), 1843 and 1844. In the latter year Charles Kemble gave Shakespeare readings and Phillipe, a French conjurer, appeared in 1845; these were among other attractions, including concerts, at which Braham made a re-appearance at this theatre.

In February 1846 the Ethiopian Serenaders, who had first appeared in London at the Hanover Square Rooms in January moved in and stayed till August and London fell to the American craze of the 'Nigger Minstrel', a form of entertainment which was to last until the turn of the century, and even now is enjoying a renewed popularity with *The Black and White Minstrels*. The Ethiopian Serenaders were back again at the St. James's in December. Robert-Houdin, the French conjurer, gave *Soirées Fantastiques* in 1848 and in 1850 Alfred Bunn, down on his luck as a manager, gave lantern lectures on the History of the Stage!

In 1850 Fanny Kemble gave her famous Shakespearean readings and the following year Great Exhibition visitors to London had a chance to see besides the French plays: William Love the ventriloquist; the Tyrolean Singers, Fanny Kemble and John Anderson, 'The Wizard of the North', and the Bateman Children. The famous showman, Phineas T. Barnum, brought Kate and Ellen, children of Hezekiah Bateman, to London in scenes from *Richard III*, *The Merchant of Venice*, *Macbeth* and some one-act plays. This season established in England what was to become one of the most distinguished of stage families, with its intermarriage with the Comptons among many others.

In 1852 marionettes were added to the list of varied attractions which held the stage at the St. James's and a German company, with Emil Devrient as Hamlet and in other famous parts, made a change from the usual French language. He was back again in 1853 and a short lived English Opera Company lasted only a week!

All through Mitchell's regime amateurs came and went on the 'off nights' and in 1854 they held the stage until April when the French season started, and London first saw *Sullivan, Comédien de Drury Lane*, a fictitious eighteenth century story which, as *David Garrick* in Tom Robertson's adaptation, was to become a famous 'vehicle' for Edward Sothern and Charles Wyndham.

At the end of the season, which finished in August with a light opera company, Mitchell gave up his tenancy. He had made the theatre fashionable, Royalty had been constant visitors, the Queen herself had been fourteen times in the last season alone and the greatest French stars had been seen by London. Since Braham's financial difficulties the theatre had been mortgaged twice, the second mortgagee put the freehold up for sale in 1844, but it was bought in at £9,400. The building was said then to be mortgaged for a sum of £14,500, but the architect Beazley valued it at between £28,000 and £30,000; Mitchell paid a rent of £1,200 per annum. Braham died in 1856 but his interest in the theatre had long passed out of his hands.

After Mitchell left a season was given by Laura Seymour, who had been in Braham's original company, before she married, as Laura Allison. She was in association with Charles Reade but their burlesques and dramas failed to attract and only lasted from October 1854 to March 1855. The theatre had been renovated and enlarged, the first tier of boxes giving way to a now more fashionable dress circle. For the rest of the year the theatre was mostly dark though Rachel made her last appearance in London during her season in August.

In 1856 only Alfred Mellon's concerts and a German company were billed in the spring and winter. A short regime in 1857 for March and April, by Sam Emery and Sir William Dodd, was the prelude to a brilliant season from May when a company under Offenbach brought a number of his brilliant opera bouffe to London, and once again Queen Victoria visited the St. James's. Minstrels were back in the autumn and an Italian comic opera company did bad business at the end of the year. For Christmas a conjurer, German this time, named Erikell, did the silver bullet trick which later was to be fatal to Chung-Ling-Soo. He ran till May 1858 and was followed by yet another magician, Carlo Andreoletti. In June Adelaide Ristori, who had taken the place of Rachel as the most famous tragedienne in Europe, appeared in a 'round of parts'. The year finished with amateurs and a French lyric company which lasted in to the new year and was followed by a similar dramatic troupe.

Braham's son Augustus with his brother Hamilton formed an English Opera Company and opened in June, but only lasted a month. A season of 'Cheap Prices', always an indication of the state of affairs, was tried by F. B. Chatterton and lasted from October 1859 to April 1860. He put on comedies and burlesques, and a pantomime at Christmas, but added nothing to 'Dramatic Literature', though F. C. Burnand had his first big chance with a burlesque *Dido* during this time. After a French season in the early summer Chatterton returned to present Barry Sullivan in some of his famous parts, and other attractions.

The next new management was Alfred Wigan who started in October with a Tom Taylor drama *Up at the Hills*, other Taylor plays were produced and the usual burlesques and comedies were tried. Kate Terry and her father Ben were in the company as was Louisa Herbert, who was later to take over the theatre herself. With the regular summer break in 1861 for a French company, Wigan continued until he gave way to George Vining at Christmas. The mixed bills consisted of the farces and extravaganzas so popular at this date. Vining remained in control till September 1862. He was succeeded by Frank Matthews, whose programmes followed the familiar lines using the Theatre Royal St. James's as the name of the theatre. His big success was *Lady Audley's Secret*, adapted from Miss Braddon's 'best seller' by George Roberts, with Louisa Herbert as the villainous leading lady. It ran 104 nights, the longest run the theatre had so far had!

Matthews finished his tenancy in July 1863 and after a refurbishing the theatre was opened under Ben Webster at the end of the year, with Webster himself, Frank Matthews and his wife, J. L. Toole, Paul Bedford, Fanny Stirling in a company, mostly from the Adelphi, as were most of the plays, though new burlesques and extravaganzas were seen. The company remained for a second season from September until Miss Herbert herself took over the theatre, opening with a Brough burlesque, *Hercules and Omphale; or, the Power of Love*, with herself as Omphale and Charlotte Saunders as Hercules. Similar titles were on the bills with other Miss Braddon adaptations, *Eleanor's Victory* and *Caught in the Toils*, and a revival of *Lady Audley's Secret*.

At the end of the year Miss Herbert tried a classic revival, *The School for Scandal*, and the following year added *She Stoops to Conquer*, *Much Ado About Nothing* and *The Rivals* to her repertoire.

In the next season Henry Irving made his first big success in London as Rawdon Scudamore in *Hunted Down; or, The Two Lives of Mary Leigh*, by Dion Boucicault (November 1866), and in December, W. S. Gilbert had his first burlesque produced, *Dulcamara; or, the Little Duck and the Great Quack*, satirising *L'Elisia d'Amore*—this ran till Easter. At this period Irving also played in Holcroft's *Road to Ruin* and other plays. A drama adapted from Ouida's *Idalia* was a big success from April, with Louisa Herbert and Charles Wyndham who had joined the company. The season ended in June with the inevitable revivals and benefits, and once again a French company, under Raphael Felix (Rachel's brother), took over for the summer. For a benefit,

Charles J. Matthews played, in the original French, the farce *Cool as a Cucumber*, on the same evening as he had acted it in English at the Olympic.

Louisa Herbert's last season opened in October, her main attraction was the first London appearance of J. S. Clark, the American comedian, in *A Widow Hunt*. In the new year William Farren and Madame Celeste appeared for special engagements and Louisa Herbert had her final benefit as Lady Teazle in April.

In June 1868 Hortense Schneider headed the Offenbach Company and London saw *La Grande Duchesse de Gérolstein* and *La Belle Hélène* for the first time in their original language, and the theatre was filled by brilliant audiences, headed by the Prince of Wales. The rest of the year was uneventful, a management by W. S. Emden from the Olympic, over Christmas, to star Mlle de la Ferté, lasted only till the holiday season was over. After another French season Schneider returned in June with *La Grande Duchesse*, *Barbe Bleu* and *Orphée aux Enfers*, and repeated the success of the previous year.

In the *Building News* 14 May, 1869, in a gossip column under the heading 'Chips', appeared the following: 'The St. James's Theatre is to be pulled down and re-built with an entrance from Pall Mall.' No further information on this scheme has been forthcoming.

In the summer of 1869 the theatre was taken by Mrs. John Wood who had the theatre completely renovated, partly re-constructed and re-decorated by James Macintosh. An advance notice in *The Era* 10 October says:

For a long time past Mrs. Wood's forthcoming campaign at the St. James's has been the subject of conversation in theatrical circles. The preliminary arrangements have been made in an unusually liberal spirit; in point of fact, the re-modelling and embellishment of the Theatre has necessitated the expenditure of large sums. Under the direction of Mr. Macintosh the building has been completely restored, and is once more a *fac-simile* of the Court Theatre at Versailles. An entirely new entrance to the stalls has been made, and the comfort of one important section of the audience is thus effectually secured. Everything is new, including the act-drop, designed and painted by Mr. John O'Connor, of the

Haymarket Theatre. The subject has an immediate and local interest, and is treated with consummate skill by this clever artist. The incident represented is King Charles the Second leaving St. James's Palace for the play. The left of this historical picture, as it may well be called, is occupied by the Palace itself, and just emerging from the archway is the King's state coach with its antique carvings and rich decorations. An escort of Life Guards follows the coach, which is turning into the Mall, at that time shaded with trees. In the foreground is a group of figures—Samuel Pepys, his wife, and the handsome Rochester, hat in hand, bowing to the lady. The whole group is full of expression, and, both as regards the drawing, composition, and colour, is a proof of Mr. Daniel Whyte's exceptional talent in this particular branch of art. Two very judicious appointments have been made, namely, Mr. W. H. Montgomery as musical director, and Madame Collier as ballet mistress; and Mr. J. R. Planché's refined taste will regulate the *mise-en-scène*. Messrs. Grieve, O'Connor, and Lloyds will paint the scenery used on the opening night, and the entertainments will include an operetta—*Treasure Trove* —by Offenbach, the comedy *She Stoops to Conquer*, and a ballet entitled *The Magic Waltz*.

The Era, reporting the opening on 16 October, held the improvements to have lived up to their preliminary 'puff':

The prevailing colours are rose pink and light blue, and the ceiling represents a clear sky studded with silver stars. Around the front of the gallery tier are panelled wreaths of raised and coloured flowers alternating with smaller panels of gilded Cupids. The walls are coloured in distemper with rose-pink, and the 'family circle' tier, as the upper boxes are now called, is decorated in blue, with panels of gilded Cupids; whilst the back of the boxes is painted in dark oak, so as to throw up the pink walls beyond. On the dress circle tier the original ornaments remain, but they have been entirely regilded, and supplemented with festoons of raised and coloured flowers. The dress circle is fitted with chairs, upholstered in blue damask, and the hanging of all the private boxes are blue satin valences and white lace curtains. The stall chairs are upholstered in blue Sardinian cloth. Two wide passages

surround the stalls, and a broad isle is opened down the
centre, so that the seats are attainable with the greatest ease.
There is no pit, the whole of the area being occupied by stalls.
The orchestra remains in its former position. When it is
added that Messrs. Spiers and Pond have charge of the
refreshments in the Theatre, that a bell rings in the saloon
when the curtain is about to rise, and that a neat playbill,
with much useful information, is gratuitously supplied the
visitors, it will be seen that the comfort of the frequenters
has been duly studied.

Matilda Wood (*née* Vining) always known as Mrs. John Wood,
surrounded herself with a good company, including Louise
Herbert and Lionel Brough. *She Stoops to Conquer* had its longest
run, of 160 performances, to that date. A burlesque, *La Belle
Sauvage*, with Mrs. Wood as the leading lady, introduced the
song whose question 'Oh where, oh where, has my little dog
gone?' would be asked for generations to come. Originally it was
sung 152 times.

It seemed settled success had come once more to the St.
James's. Mrs. Wood revived old favourites and produced new
dramas, including *Frou-Frou* (April 1870), Sardou's *Fernande*
(October 1870) in which Fanny Brough (sister of Lionel) made a
big success. T. W. Robertson's last play *War* was produced in
January 1871, he died the following month, aged only forty-two,
leaving behind, besides his plays, the reputation of being the
father of modern stage management and production.

The season ended in July and Mrs. Wood sub-let the theatre
in the autumn to yet another English opera venture, the Royal
National Opera Company, with Rose Hersee as its leading
soprano. They were followed by the annual French season which
lasted until July 1872. This disastrous season, under Richard
Mansell, for which salaries were not paid, let down the raised
tone of the theatre, and 1873 was heralded in with closed doors.

A Belgian light opera company held the stage in May, but
amateurs were in charge during the winter.

The following year Francis Fairlie opened with Offenbach's
Vert-Vert in May, with Mansell as producer. It was a disastrous
first night—under rehearsed, with a boisterous audience in
front—and it ended in chaos. Even a troupe of French dancers

with *La Riperelle* 'a scandalous dance in scanty clothes', failed to stem the débâcle. Their dance and dresses, later when the show was somehow pulled together, caused trouble with the Lord Chamberlain who ordered the costumes to be lengthened. He was tricked into saying what should be done to them and the manager announced the new costumes as, 'designed by the Lord Chamberlain!' The dance was said to be 'uncalled for and indecent' and 'one of the most indecent dances on the stage'. Because of the publicity, in spite of the original fiasco, *Vert-Vert* became a big success and ran till July. After a tour it returned to the Globe Theatre later in the year. In December a libel case helped to keep the name in the news.

From October to December Stephen Fiske tried with comic opera on his own (he had been associated with Mansell the year before), but failed dismally and amateurs were again in possession till Marie Litton, from the Royal Court, opened a season in March 1875. The bills contained the usual comedies and burlesques, and her biggest success was *Tom Cobb; or, Fortune's Toy*, a comedy by W. S. Gilbert, produced on 24 April. She also produced as a curtain raiser on 5 June *The Zoo*, 'a musical folly' by Arthur Sullivan.

Horace Wigan transferred *All For Her* from the Mirror Theatre, Holborn, in January 1876, staying till April, when Mrs. John Wood returned to her theatre. She still held the lease from the new owner, Viscount Newry (later Earl of Kilmorey), who began to take an active interest in the theatre. After Mrs. Wood's own season the original French company brought the Paris success *Les Danicheff*, by Pierre Newsky, to London for a month. During the winter Mrs. Wood played a season of comedies and dramas until the English version, *The Danicheffs*, by Lord Newry himself, was ready for production in January 1877. With Mrs. Wood, Charles Warner, John Clayton and Herman Vezin in the cast, it ran till April. After a series of revivals Mrs. Wood gave up the St. James's in May.

In December Ada Cavendish started a five month season under Sam Hayes, a ticket agent. She was seen in old comedies and *As You Like It*, with a good supporting company. She left for America in May and Hayes tried other attractions including *The Little Duke*, an operetta, but the ubiquitous amateurs were in residence later in the year until it became known that an entirely

new regime was to be instituted and the theatre closed for
alterations.

Lord Newry had been looking for an actor manager of repute
to take over the theatre and had asked the Bancrofts, who were
leaving their Prince of Wales's Theatre in Tottenham Street,
but they chose to go to the Haymarket instead and his offer was
accepted by John Hare who had been at the Royal Court for some
years with great success. In his company were Madge Robertson
and her husband, W. H. Kendal, and together they agreed to take
the St. James's.

The theatre was re-constructed and re-decorated. *The Era*,
5 October 1879, gave details:

Messrs. Hare and Kendal are now in possession of a house
which, for taste, elegance, and comfort, is far in advance of
anything the Metropolis has yet been able to boast. For them
the old St. James's has been transformed into a Temple of the
Drama complete and beautiful in all its details, and likely,
we should say, to become one of the sights of London. The
visitor, on entering, will imagine that he has passed the portals
of some Parisian mansion, for the very ticket office has all
the appearance of an antechamber sumptuously furnished.
The fancy of Mr. Walter Crane has been brought to bear upon
the designs for the decoration of the walls, which are covered
with embossed paper of green and gold. On the one side is to
be seen a curiously carved mantelpiece in walnut, surmounted
by a picture of Venus emerging from a shell, painted by
Mr. J. Macbeth, while on the other is the ticket box, having
all the appearance of an elegant cabinet, with antique clock
and choice 'blue and white' as ornaments. On the floor are
spread rich and costly rugs and Indian carpets. A flight of
stairs made of Siena marble, covered with Indian carpet, and
having brass standards on either side of the bannisters, con-
ducts to the crush-room, which is fancifully furnished, draped
with printed tapestry, and resplendent with mirrors. The
walls are tapestried, and each doorway leading to the dress
circle is draped with the simplest and most elegant formation
of *portière* curtains, by a mere looping back of the plain-cut
hanging on either side. A large oblong perpendicular Venetian
mirror, inclining forward, faces the stairs; and beneath it is a

magnificent console-table, with a grey marble slab supported on gilt carvings of an appropriate character. The apartment is furnished with superb Venetian stools; and another figure-painting, by the artist whose design decorates the mantel-piece in the hall, will attract attention here, the allegorical subject being 'Dawn', and the colour harmonising admirably with the general tone in all save the flat blue on the girders or beams which support the ceiling, which are a little out of key. The doors behind the *portière* hangings are covered with warmly toned embossed leather, and containing panels of bevelled glass in the upper division. A side passage branching from the main entrance affords access to the room which is fitted up for the Prince of Wales. Ascending again the visitor will find himself in the *foyer* or picture gallery. Ferns and cool trickling fountains may tempt him to linger, but attention will speedily be arrested by the specimens of art which cover the walls, and which convey the idea of a Royal Academy on a small scale. Among those whose works may be inspected we find such artists as Messrs. Goodall, Watts, Tadema, T. Faed, Erskine Nicol, Fildes, and Marcus Stone. Outside the gallery is a 'Black and White' exhibition. Recent labours of note by Mr. R. W. Macbeth and Mr. Du Maurier are among these attractions for connoisseurs of the first rank; the first mentioned etcher's latest triumph, 'Phillis on the New-made Hay,' and his 'Road to Ives' Market' being prominently displayed. Both the picture gallery and the collection of etchings are lit most effectively, the former on a principle which the experience of Mr. Deschamps has dictated as the best. His plan is greatly assisted by an ingenious and practically scientific appliance, which has been adopted universally by the management throughout the house, and which is the invention of Messrs. James Barwell, Son, and Fisher, of the Worcester Works, Birmingham, a firm that has inspired great confidence in these matters by its work in connection with the Holte Theatre, Aston, and elsewhere. Coming to the auditorium we find that it is elegant and commodious, and of horseshoe form, permitting a good view of the stage from all points. There is a pit, and, though a small one, it is convenient and easy of access, the well-padded seats being divided so that all comers may have their fair share of space.

The stalls, of which there is a great number, are covered with
red silk. They are sufficiently commodious, and there is plenty
of room between the rows. The dress circle contains 160 seats,
the cushioned edge of the front being of crimson plush instead
of velvet, and the seats commodious instead of cramped, as of
old. There are fourteen private boxes with outer curtains of
figured cherry red silk, and inner curtains of Madras muslin.
The panels of the boxes are in gold, pale green, and cream
colour. It is satisfactory to find that the musicians, instead of
being banished beneath the stage, will have an orchestra in
front according to the good old fashion. This orchestra,
separated from the stalls by only a festooned crimson cord
running on gilt standards, is of pretty and novel design, and is
adorned with pictures in panel by Mr. J. Macbeth. The drop-
curtain is a copy by Mr. J. O'Connor of Turner's celebrated
landscape 'Crossing the Brook.' Round both circles, at the
back, are ranged sconces for lighting these portions of the
auditory, the burners branching from *repoussé* brass-work, in
burnished plaques, mounted on crimson plush, while the
opalescent glass shades and overhanging bells of the same
material, from the Whitefriars factory, are of a peculiarly
light and fanciful design. From the street to pit and stalls there
are direct entrances, and abundant means of exit should
remove all thought of danger in case of panic. The upholster-
ing of the house has been carried out by Messrs. Hampton
and Sons, of Pall Mall, and the decorations and alterations of
the auditorium by Mr. E. W. Bradwell, of Great Portland
Street, from the designs and plans of Mr. Thomas Verity,
F.S.A., the architect.

The story of the partnership from which the following is adapted
was told by Cecil Howard in *The Theatre*, September 1888:

During the whole of the term they have done their utmost to
provide plays that would not only amuse but would elevate
the public taste, and their efforts have been so far successful
that they have experienced but few failures, and those works
that have been adapted from the French stage have invariably
been made pure and wholesome. A retrospect, therefore, of
the pieces produced by them in the nine years during which
they held their sway at the St. James's will be, perhaps, of

some value as a record. Those who attended the opening night of October 4, 1879, experienced a foretaste, from the manner in which the house itself had been redecorated and improved in appearance, of the elegance and lavish perfection with which the plays would be put upon the stage. After the singing of the National Anthem by Charles Santley, the curtain drew up on the comedietta *Monsieur le Duc*, written by Val Prinsep, A.R.A., in which John Hare was the libertine Duc de Richelieu, who discovers his own daughter in Marguerite (Cissy Grahame), a young girl whom he meant to betray. William Terriss was the Count de la Roque. The *pièce de résistance* was *The Queen's Shilling*, by G. W. Godfrey, founded on *Le Fils de Famille* of Bayard, of which there had been other adaptations. In this Madge Kendal, Mrs. Gaston Murray, Kate Phillips, John Hare, W. H. Kendal, William Terriss, William Mackintosh and T. E. Wenman appeared. This piece, first produced in London at the Court, April 19 of the same year, proved so successful as to be several times revived. December 18, 1879, saw the production of *The Falcon*, founded by Lord (then Mr. Alfred) Tennyson on a story in the *Decameron* of Boccaccio. Kendal was the Count Alberighi and his wife Lady Giovanna. Marcus Stone, R.A., painted some exquisite scenery, and the costumes were extremely rich and archaeologically correct. Kendal gained much credit for his singing of 'Dead Mountain Flowers.' This ran till March 6, 1880, when *Old Cronies*, comedietta by Theyre Smith, took its place with William Mackintosh and Wenman. From March 13 till May 22, 1880, Tom Taylor's *Still Waters Run Deep* held the boards, with Hare, Kendal, Terriss, Cissy Grahame and Madge Kendal as Mrs. Sternhold (by many thought one of her greatest assumptions). On the latter date *The Queen's Shilling* was revived, and ran till June 17, when the *Ladies' Battle* was revived, with Madge Kendal as the Countess D'Autreval; Hare, Kendal, Terriss, Albert Chevalier and Cissy Grahame; with this was given *A Regular Fix*, with Kendal as Sir Hugh de Brass. These two pieces were played till the close of the first season on July 10.

The theatre re-opened on October 9, 1880, with *Old Cronies* and *William and Susan*. The author, W. G. Wills, had written two new acts, but retained Douglas Jerrold's last act of *Black*

Eyed Susan in its entirety, merely eliminating from the play the comic element. Hare was the Admiral; J. H. Barnes, Captain Crosstree; Kendal, William (and sang 'The Old Ship,' by Walter Maynard); T. E. Wenman, Truck; Madge Kendal, Susan; and Kate Phillips, Polly. These constituted the bill till December 4, 1880, when *Good Fortune*, adapted by C. F. Coghlan from Octave Feuillet's *Roman d'un jeune homme pauvre*, was played, with Kendal, John Clayton, Mrs. Gaston Murray, Madge Kendal, but the play only ran till January 7, 1881.

Then followed, on January 8, 1881, *The Money Spinner*, by A. W. Pinero. The principals in the cast were as follows: Kendal, Lord Kingussie; Hare, Baron Croodle (one of his most famous impersonations); Clayton, Harold Boycott; William Mackintosh, in the cleverly acted but unsympathetic *rôle* of Detective Jules Faubert; Madge Kendal, Millicent Boycott; Kate Phillips, Dorinda Croodle; Mrs. Gaston Murray, Margot. With this was played Tom Taylor's *A Sheep in Wolf's Clothing*, when Mrs. Kendal appeared for the first time in London as Ann Carew, and Kendal as Jasper Carew. From April 18 till nearly the end of the following month *The Money Spinner* was alternated with *The Lady of Lyons*, with the Kendals in the leads.

Coralie, a four act play, adapted by G. W. Godfrey from M. Delpit's *Le Fils de Coralie*, was played for the first time on May 28, 1881, and ran till the end of the season, Friday, July 15.

It was originally intended to re-open on October 15, but in consequence of the indisposition of Mrs. Kendal the revival of T. W. Robertson's comedy, *Home*, was postponed till the 27th (taken from Emile Augier's *Aventurière*. This, with *The Cape Mail*, adapted from the French *Jeanne qui pleure et Jeanne qui rit*, made up the programme till December 27, except that on the 26th and 27th *Cousin Dick* was played.

The Squire, by A. W. Pinero, and one of the most admired plays, was produced on Thursday, December 29, 1881. In it Hare made a wonderful impression as the Rev. Paul Dormer, the part of Lieutenant Thorndyke was exactly suited to Mr. Kendal, and Kate Verity fitted Mrs. Kendal like a glove. With this *Cousin Dick* made up the bill till March, when *Medusa*, a one act comedietta, written by Fred W. Hayes, replaced it. This and *The Squire* drew full houses till July 15, when the company started on their annual provincial tour. During this season a matinée was given in aid of 'the persecuted Jews in Russia,' when A. W. Pinero's *Daisy's Escape*, *Good for Nothing*, with Mrs. Bancroft as Nan, and *A Quiet Rubber*, in which Jessie Millward played Mary Sullivan at a few hours' notice, Mrs. Kendal's recital of Will Carleton's 'Betsy and I are out,' and J. L. Toole's *Trying a Magistrate*, formed the programme.

The next production of note was B. C. Stephenson's five act play *Impulse* (founded on *La Maison du Mari*, of Xavier de Montepin), on Saturday, December 9, 1882, which ran uninterruptedly till July 20, 1883, when it was withdrawn in the full tide of success on account of the company's provincial engagements. Here Madge Kendal had a character in Mrs. Beresford in which she struck the happiest vein of comedy; nor was Kendal's Captain Crichton much inferior—his indescribable 'Now you are, you know, you really are,' to the handsome widow will ever be remembered. *Impulse* was resumed on September 17, 1883, with some changes of cast and Herbert Waring and George Alexander joined the company. According to promise, the management produced on Saturday, October 20, 1883, *Young Folks' Ways*, a four act comedy founded by W. H. Gillette and Mrs. Burnett on the latter's story of *Esmeralda*, under which title it was played in America, and by which name it was originally intended it should be known here. After a long absence, for Hare had only given his aid in the production of *Impulse*, the public were delighted to again welcome him, when he appeared as Old Rogers, Madge Kendal played Nora Desmond, and Kendal Estabrook, and as Esmeralda, Annie Webster, a granddaughter of Benjamin Webster, made a most promising *début*.

The piece played fifty nights, and was succeeded by a revival on December 20, 1883, of Palgrave Simpson's *Scrap of Paper* (an English version of Sardou's *Pattes de Mouche*). It was originally played at the St. James's, but was revived under Hare's management at the Court, March 11, 1876, and again on January 4, 1879, when the manager played Archie

Hamilton, and William Mackintosh Dr. Penguin. Now Hare may be said to have created a new Dr. Penguin, that for originality and artistic treatment was a triumph. The Kendals resumed their former characters of Colonel Blake and Susan Hartley.

As a first piece on the same night was played the amusing comedietta entitled *A Case for Eviction*, by Theyre Smith, in which George Alexander appeared as Frank, Linda Dietz as Dora, and May Whitty as Mary. These were of sufficient interest to draw till April 16, 1884.

The Ironmaster, play in four acts, adapted from Georges Ohnet's drama *Le Maître de Forges*, by A. W. Pinero, was produced on April 17, 1884. There was originally some idea of calling it *The Midnight Marriage*. Unfortunately for the public there was no part in it for Hare, but the piece had the great benefit of his superintendence in its production. On July 19 the theatre had to be closed for structural alterations, but re-opened on October 2, having been redecorated throughout. *The Ironmaster* still proved an attraction, and after a run of 200 nights was withdrawn on January 20, 1885.

As You Like It was produced on January 24, 1885, and was specially noticeable for the magnificence of the dresses of the Charles VII period, designed by the Hon. Lewis Wingfield, and the beauty of the scenery—that in the Forest of Arden, with its real water, was specially commended. The principals in the cast were: Hermann Vezin, Jacques; Kendal, Orlando; Hare, Touchstone; Madge Kendal, Rosalind; Shakespeare did not prove as acceptable as modern comedy to a St. James's audience, and thus *As You Like It* came to an end on March 28, and on April 6, 1885, *A Quiet Rubber* and *The Queen's Shilling* were revived. On Thursday, June 11, *The Castaways*, a duologue comedietta by Theyre Smith, with the Kendals was produced for the first time, followed by the revival of *The Money Spinner*. With these was played *The Goose with the Golden Eggs*. The theatre closed on July 11. On October 31, 1885, A. W. Pinero's five act comedy *Mayfair* was produced, which was an adaptation by him of Sardou's *Maison Neuve*. *Mayfair* proved too French in sentiment, and only ran two months, and was succeeded on January 4, 1886, by a revival of *Impulse*, with this was played *A Bed of Roses*.

Antoinette Rigaud, three act play, adapted by Ernest Warren from the French of Raymond Desclaudes, was produced for the first time on February 13, and played till May 21, 1886. Madge Kendal assumed the title *rôle* to perfection, John Hare gave one of his masterly sketches as the General de Prefond, and Kendal as Henri de Tourvel won the entire sympathies of his audience.

The Wife's Sacrifice, an adaptation in five acts of the drama *Martyre*, of MM. D'Ennery and Tarbe, by Sydney Grundy and Sutherland Edwards, was first played on May 25, 1886, but only ran six weeks, till the theatre closed on July 9th.

The re-opening on October 23, 1886, saw the first performance of *The Hobby Horse*, a clever three act comedy, by A. W. Pinero, in which Hare appeared as Spencer Jermyn, and Madge Kendal as the wife of that gentleman. Excellent representations were given by Herbert Waring and Mrs. Beerbohm-Tree. *A Case for Eviction* made up the bill for 110 nights.

Lady Clancarty, the drama by Tom Taylor, was revived on March 3, 1887, with an attention to dress and mounting that was perhaps never equalled. The assistance of Marcus Stone, R.A., was invoked to ensure the accuracy of the costumes of William III and Mary, and an exact reproduction of existing old tapestries, mantelpieces, and bureaux was given. Hare again gave up the opportunity of distinguishing himself as an actor, which he surely would have done as the King (though a better could have scarcely been found than in William Mackintosh), and devoted all his time to the stage management, and with excellent results. The Kendals were respectively Lord and Lady Clancarty. This piece ran until the summer vacation, and was again put in the bill on December 8, 1887.

This year 1888 has been one of revivals of old favourites. On January 16 we had *A Scrap of Paper* and *Old Cronies*, with more or less the same casts. Monday April 9, saw the somewhat unaccountable revival of George W. Lovell's dull four act play *The Wife's Secret*, first played in New York by Mr. and Mrs. Charles Kean, and subsequently by them at the Haymarket in 1848. At the St. James's of course Kendal played Sir Walter Amyott, and Madge Kendal his wife Lady

Eveline. Mackintosh worthily succeeded Benjamin Webster who had played Jabez Sneed, Lewis Waller was excellent as Lord Arden, and Fanny Brough piquant as Maud. Should the Kendals visit America, the piece may be a valuable addition to their *répertoire*, as it was liked there, but, though splendidly mounted, it did not prove a success, and on April 28 gave way to *The Ironmaster*. June 16 saw the last of the revivals—that of *The Squire*. The Kendals and Hare resumed their former characters. During their tenancy of the St. James's, Hare and Kendal produced twenty-one plays. Seven were accepted as purely from English sources, eight were taken from the French, and five were revivals.

The Hare and Kendal management was specially distinguished for the exquisite taste and judgment bestowed on the interiors, and the perfection of the dresses and scenery. It really became a question whether there was not almost too much thought devoted to the mounting of a play, which frequently formed so attractive a picture as to detract from the attention that should have been bestowed upon the acting.

As among the annals of the St. James's Theatre, it should be mentioned that the Kendals were summoned to Osborne, and gave a performance before Her Majesty. They played in *Uncle's Will* and *Sweethearts*, supported by Rowley Cathcart. In recognition of her talent, and the esteem in which she is held, Madge Kendal was presented by Her Majesty with a valuable ruby and diamond ornament.

The last performance of *The Squire*, on July 21, 1888, was a brilliant one before a brilliant audience, the cheers that greeted Hare and the Kendals were enthusiastic. It was only natural that a few words should be expected from the lessees, and these were well chosen and appropriate. Kendal concluded—'And now, ladies and gentlemen, the time has come to say, in this place, Farewell. We separate from our recent associations with no inconsiderable pain. Ties such as we have maintained with the St. James's Theatre through all these years are not broken without regret. We go each our way, with no shadow of rivalry save the worthy rivalry of striving each for himself and herself to earn a continuance of your favour, and to sustain the honour of our profession. (Loud cheers.)'

The Kendals went on a tour of America and Hare joined Mrs. John Wood at the re-built Royal Court Theatre, while awaiting the completion of his own Garrick Theatre.

After the Hare-Kendal era the theatre was taken by Rutland Barrington, from the Savoy Theatre and the D'Oyly Carte company. He wished to try his luck as an actor manager and opened on 13 October with *The Dean's Daughter*, by Sydney Grundy and F. C. Phillips, but it failed and Gilbert came to his rescue with a play, *Brantinghame Hall*, in November. Even though Barrington himself, Lewis Waller and Julia Neilson were in the cast this too was a dismal failure. After five weeks Barrington was bankrupt and only too ready to return to his old home.

The St. James's had a lean time for a while till Lillie Langtry took over in February 1890, presenting *As You Like It* and Grundy's *Esther Sandraz*. She was taken ill in June and her commitments were taken over by Arthur Bourchier, who was in the company. This was his first London engagement, and his début as a manager, and through inexperience only did he fail and the theatre closed in July. After the usual stand-by, a French company in the summer with Cécil Chaumont, Mrs. Langtry who was still lessee, moved over to the Princess's, and the St. James's was taken over by George Alexander at the end of 1890. With his wife, Florence, behind him as artistic director and adviser, he set about making the theatre into a smart society rendevouz, the very heart of 'Our Parish of St. James'. He opened with a transfer of *Sunlight and Shadow* on 31 January 1891, a play by R. C. Carton, which he had presented during his successful tyro management at the Avenue Theatre the previous year.

Alexander was to remain in charge of the St. James's for the rest of his life. He last acted there the year before he died on 16 March 1918, aged fifty-nine. The whole story of this wonderful regime, which added lustre to the British Theatre, and to this day remains to old playgoers the criterion for well staged, well dressed and well bred theatre on both sides of the curtain, is told by A. E. W. Mason in *Sir George Alexander and the St. James's Theatre* (1935). This contains a complete list of his productions, which include: *Lady Windermere's Fan*, by Oscar Wilde (1892); *The Second Mrs. Tanqueray*, by Pinero (1893); *The Importance of Being Ernest*, by Wilde (1895); *The Prisoner of Zenda*, by Anthony Hope (1896);

As You Like It (1896); *Much Ado About Nothing* (1898); *Paolo and Francesca*, by Stephen Phillips (1902); *If I were King*, by Justin Huntly McCarthy (1902); *Old Heidelberg*, by Meyer-Forster and Bleichmann (1903) and *His House in Order*, by Pinero (1906), to name only a few of the plays still remembered. Other playwrights included R. C. Carton, A. E. W. Mason, Alfred Sutro and Henry Arthur Jones.

During Alexander's tenancy the theatre was occupied by other managements while he was on tour, including Mr. and Mrs. Kendal (1898, 1901 and 1905), E. S. Willard (1903), Edward Compton (1907), and Forbes-Robertson (1908). In 1913 a repertory season was run by Granville Barker and Lillah McCarthy, during which Shaw's *Androcles and the Lion* was first produced, among other notable plays.

The theatre received a complete interior re-construction and re-decoration in 1899. After the play *In Days of Old* ended its run on 23 June the theatre closed and did not re-open until 1 February 1900, with *Rupert of Hentzau*, a sequel to *The Prisoner of Zenda*.

Meantime the adjoining house up to and over Angel Court was added into the theatre for offices and re-faced to bring it in line with the existing original façade, which was unfortunately spoilt by a glass and iron canopy which cut across the columns of the entrance and destroyed the beauty of Beazley's design. *The Era*, 13 January 1900 gives details of the changes:

Since the St. James's Theatre was closed at the conclusion of the season, some six months ago, a surprising alteration has been effected in the appearance of the interior of the house. It is practically a new theatre, for only the four walls of the old building remain; and the work of alteration and reconstruction, which has been carried out under the direction of Mr. Arthur Blomfield Jackson, is in such an advanced state that Mr. George Alexander hopes to be able to open the greatly improved house at the end of the present month. His aim has been, not only to increase the holding capacity of the theatre, but materially to add to the comfort of the audience; not merely to obtain a substantial increase in the size of the stage, but, in addition, to provide the members of his company with commodious dressing rooms, fitted with all the needful modern appliances. Naturally, alterations of so drastic a character have involved an exceedingly heavy expenditure, but, in return, Mr. Alexander finds himself in possession of what is practically a new theatre, bright, roomy, most comfortable, and having the great additional advantage of containing in money value £50 more than the one it replaces. And where a successful play is concerned this is a gain not lightly to be esteemed. Although the scaffolding has not yet been removed from the interior of the building, a very fair idea can even now be formed regarding its ultimate appearance. By lowering the stage and the stall flooring some 3 ft. it has been possible to provide both with a 'Rake' of so pronounced a description that no difficulty can be experienced in obtaining a clear view of the former, even from the backmost row in the pit. Having come to the conclusion, moreover, that there is no longer the demand for boxes which once existed, he has swept away all, save two, and there now remain only the Royal box and its companion on the other side of the proscenium. To the former is attached a large retiring room, with separate entrance from the street. Starting from the top of the building, it is observable that the size of the gallery has been greatly increased by the addition of some dozen rows of seats. Yet, although the most remote of these is some eighty fee distant from the stage, neither as regards seeing or hearing it is confidently expected, will the spectator placed upon it have any grounds for complaint. The same careful attention has been bestowed upon the upper circle, at the back of which runs a convenient promenade. Stalls and dress circle have also been extended and greatly improved, while the pit, which, with its added slope, should constitute one of the best points from which to witness the performance, has been considerably enlarged. A very important factor to the comfort and the safety of the audience is, further, to be found in the numerous new exits, which admit of the theatre being emptied in an exceptionally short time, if necessary. Behind the curtain the improvements are no less noticeable than in front of it. For the convenience of the artists eighteen capital dressing-rooms have been furnished, while there are new business offices and a new private room for Mr. Alexander. But the most marked alteration is in the stage itself, which now boasts a depth of 60 ft., a circumstance of great value when it is desired to create an effect by the introduction of a lengthy procession or a large concourse of people. The roof has been raised to a height of 74 ft., the distance from stage to grid-iron being 52 ft., so that the scenery can be easily and expeditiously manipulated. By the clearing away of certain old buildings a spacious 'dock' for furniture, properties, and scenery has been obtained, thus ensuring a considerable economy in time and trouble in the dressing of the stage. Another feature of the front of the house is that separate cloak-room and bar accommodation is provided for every part of the theatre. Mr. Alexander has had a brilliant idea. He is fitting up a room with every convenience for gentlemen to don evening dress. This should prove a very great convenience to City men, who cannot get home to change, and who will now be able to bring a portmanteau to town and dress at the theatre. The old dress circle and stall saloon has, meanwhile, been vastly enlarged, and with its dainty decorations in green and gold presents a wonderfully bright and gay appearance. The system of heating and ventilation is singularly complete. By means of it the temperature can be regulated at all times of the year, while fresh air is driven into the building and the vitiated air extracted by fans worked by electric motors.

Along the entire frontage of the house a new glass awning will be erected for the protection of those waiting outside in wet weather. Nor is the indispensable fireproof curtain wanting, while it is almost superfluous to say that throughout the entire building the electric light is employed. The general scheme of the decorations, designed by Mr. Percy Macquoid, is based upon that of the transitional period between the reigns of Louis XII and François I of France. Red, green, and gold are the colours chiefly in evidence, and particularly prominent on the proscenium, upon the arch of which figure, in striking relief, the coats of arms respectively of Shakespeare and Arden on the right, and St. James and Dante on the left. For the occasion of the re-opening a new act-drop, representing a picture in old tapestry, is being painted by Mr. William Telbin, and, as is generally known, *Rupert of Hentzau*, adapted by Mr. Anthony Hope from his novel of that name, is to form the first attraction which Mr. Alexander will offer to the public in his new, graceful, and essentially cosy theatre.

But for simplification of Macquoid's ornate wall decorations at a later re-furbishing, this general interior layout remained till the theatre was pulled down.

After Alexander died the lease was taken over by Gilbert Miller, the American impresario, from the new Earl of Kilmorey, (the old Earl had died in 1915). In 1943 Miller, in association with Prince Littler, acquired the theatre outright. Miller sub-let the theatre many times, but was virtually in control up to its eventual sale for re-development in 1954 and demolition three years later.

The first play of the new era was *The Eyes of Youth*, presented by Gertrude Elliott, this ran 383 performances and was followed, in September, by a season under the joint management of Miller and Henry Ainley. They presented *Reparation* from Tolstoy's *The Living Corpse*, and *Julius Caesar* which ran 83 performances from January to March 1920.

A series of sub-lets did not provide any lengthy runs, only mild successes which included *The Mystery of the Yellow Room*, with Sybil Thorndike and Lewis Casson and *His Lady Friends* with Charles Hawtrey and *Peter Pan* with Edna Best at Christmas (she was also here again in 1922). In 1921 Claude Rains was seen in *Daniel* and Edna Best, Edith Evans, Noël Coward and Henry Kendall in *Polly with a Past*, (110 performances), along with other plays. The success of 1922 was an American thriller *The Bat*, which ran most of the year and in 1923 A. S. M. Hutchinson's best seller, *If Winter Comes*, was dramatised for Owen Nares and presented by Frank Curzon from January to March. *The Outsider* with 109 performances followed and *The Green Goddess*, by William Archer, started on its run of 417 performances in September, with George Arliss as the Raja of Rukh.

It is not till Gerald du Maurier and Gladys Cooper joined to present themselves in *The Last of Mrs. Cheyney*, in September 1925, that the St. James's had another long run, when Frederick Lonsdale's play ran for 514 performances. After a Christmas season of *Charley's Aunt*, Miller and du Maurier put on *Interference*, by Ronald Pertwee and Harold Dearden, which was another big success and ran from January 1927 for 412 performances. Its successor *S.O.S.* in which Gracie Fields played her first straight part opposite du Maurier, opened in February

1928 but did not run; this, with the failure also of the next three of du Maurier's productions, gave the theatre a lean time for the next eighteen months.

Cochran brought the Lunts to London for the first time in June 1928 in *Caprice*, but nothing else of note was seen till A. A. Milne's *Michael and Mary* was presented by Miller, with Edna Best and Herbert Marshall, in February 1930. It ran five months till June when *The Swan* was produced with the same leading actors. At the end of the year an early play by Emlyn Williams, *A Murder has been Arranged*, was produced but did not have a long run, lasting only over the new year.

The rest of 1931 was uneventful, at least at the box office, though *Payment Deferred*, from C. S. Forester's novel, in May and Sheridan's *A Trip to Scarborough*, in September, were produced. It was not till April 1932 that the theatre re-opened for a of Shakespeare under Ernest Milton; his Othello was a disaster but his Shylock a success. It is not till August that Van Druten's *Behold We Live* started a run of 158 performances and audiences again filled the theatre for du Maurier and Gertrude Lawrence.

The year 1933 was completely filled from May with *The Late Christopher Bean*, an Emlyn Williams' adaptation from the French, with Edith Evans, Louise Hampton and Cedric Hardwicke. A new production was not needed till September 1934, when Gladys Cooper and Raymond Massey were seen in *The Shining Hour*, by Keith Winter. This too was a success and ran for 213 performances.

1935 was not so good, the same author's *Worse Things Happen at Sea* only had a short run. At the end of the year *The Two Mrs. Carrolls* (transferred from the St. Martin's), was running when the St. James's celebrated its centenary. Miller installed a revolving stage and presented *Pride and Prejudice*, an adaptation by Helen Jerome of Jane Austen's story. The sets by Rex Whistler are classics of their kind and still remembered. The play ran for most of the year. *Black Limelight* opened in April 1937 but soon transferred to the Duke of York's to run in all 414 performances, leaving the St. James's to have four flops in a row during the rest of the year, and 1938 was little better, though London saw Clifford Odets' play *Golden Boy*, with the original American company, in June for 109 performances.

The 'September Scare' over, the uneasy months before the war

saw Terence Rattigan's *After the Dance*, a topical play, which ran
from June 1939 until the theatre closed at the outbreak of hostilities.
The St. James's re-opened with *Ladies in Retirement*, a play by
Edward Percy and Reginald Denham, which ran 174 performances,
with Mary Clare, from December till the blitz shut the theatre in
1940. The building suffered slight damage and it did not re-open
till March 1941, when *The Nutmeg Tree* came from the Lyric for
the end of its run.

The Anglo-Polish Ballet gave a season over Christmas and
Donald Wolfit followed for a while. *Blithe Spirit* transferred to
finish its long run and Coward himself played the lead in its final
weeks.

The theatre was taken by Linnit and Dunfee in October and
The Duke in Darkness by Patrick Hamilton, opened and ran till
nearly the end of the year. Wolfit was back at Christmas (after a
few nights' run of Beverley Baxter's *It Happened in September*). In
February 1943 *A Month in the Country*, adapted by Emlyn
Williams, started a run of 313 performances and was followed in
November by Agatha Christie's *Ten Little Niggers*, which ran
260 performances in all, though its run was broken when a flying
bomb, in the last week of February 1944, severely damaged the
roof and the ceiling over the proscenium arch fell. The play moved
to the Cambridge Theatre while the damage was repaired and
the ceiling replaced in a much less elaborate form. The run of the
thriller was resumed on 9 May at the St. James's.

September 1944 saw the opening and closing of *Felicity Jasmine*
and *Residents Only* was on for ten days in November, but at
Christmas *The Glass Slipper*, by the Farjeons, was a success for
the festive season. An ill-fated version of Jane Austen's *Emma* only
ran a month at the beginning of 1945, but Emlyn Williams' *The
Wind of Heaven* ran for 268 performances and *The Glass Slipper*
was back for a Christmas season.

Gilbert Miller returned to active management when the war
was over but scored two successive 'flops' at the beginning of 1946.
It was John Clements, with his own company, who brought an
individual touch again to the St. James's with *The Kingmaker*
(May), *Marriage à la Mode* (July). All went well until Kay
Hammond's illness in August which put an end to the season.
Lonsdale returned as a dramatist with *But for the Grace of God* in
September, and it ran for 201 performances. But after this plays

S

came and went with a far too regular precision. 1947 had six new plays on the bills and 1948 was little better, in spite of a brave venture by Basil Dean which included a season of visiting provincial repertory companies. It was in September that *Don't Listen Ladies!* by Sacha Guitry opened for a run which lasted till the spring of 1949. In this both Francis Lister and Ada Reeve made their last stage appearances, though the latter was to reappear many times at the Players' and on television before she died in 1966 at the age of 92.

Terence Rattigan returned as dramatist in March 1949 with *Adventure Story* in which Paul Scofield played Alexander the Great, but not for long, as it only ran till June. Then transfers from the Lyric, Hammersmith, *Love in Albania* (142 performances) and *The Seagull* kept the theatre busy till the new year.

It was in January that the new management of Laurence Olivier and his wife Vivien Leigh opened with great hopes that the partnership of Miller and the Oliviers would bring a new stability to the St. James's. The season opened with Christopher Fry's *Venus Observed*, which ran till *Captain Carvallo* was produced in August. Tyrone Guthrie's play *Top of the Ladder* followed in October. After a sub-let to Bernard Delfont for *The Madwoman of Chaillot* in February 1951, the Oliviers appeared together alternately in Shaw's *Caesar and Cleopatra* and Shakespeare's *Antony and Cleopatra*. A brilliant supporting company helped to make these plays the big attraction of the Festival of Britain year. They ran till September when Jean-Louis Barrault and his wife, Madeleine Renaud, with Edwige Feuillère, revived the old tradition of French plays at this theatre. In October Orson Wells appeared as Othello, but after so much brilliance the nadir was reached with the Christmas production—*Snow White and the Seven Dwarfs*!

A better start to the new year, 1952, was made in January with *The Happy Time* and Clifford Odets' *Winter Journey* in April, this ran till November. The next January saw the production of *Escapade*, by Roger Macdougall, under the management of Henry Sherek. This transferred to the Strand in April to allow Olivier to present an Italian company, headed by Ruggero Ruggeri, who appeared in plays by Pirandello and the Comédie Française to follow with a short season.

The next success was *Anastasia*, which ran from August 1953 till *Pygmalion* was revived by John Clements and Kay Hammond in November. Another husband and wife team, John McCallum and Googie Withers, appeared in *Waiting for Gillian* in April 1954 for 101 performances. A Pirandello play, this time in English, followed, but *Six Characters in Search of an Author* ran for only a month. It was in September that another Terence Rattigan play, *Separate Tables*, opened and commenced a run of 726 performances, a record for this theatre. In this play Margaret Leighton and Eric Portman each played two contrasting parts in the two related plays which made up the evening and no new attraction was needed till July 1956.

It was during the run of *Separate Tables* that it became known that permission had been sought by a building speculator and granted by the London County Council to demolish the theatre and replace it with an office block. The freeholder had sold out and only the remainder of the lease was left to run out before demolition. Despite denials and protests the fate of the theatre became inevitable in June 1957.

Meanwhile, plays came and went in a half-hearted fashion. *The Long Echo*, August 1956; *Towards Zero*, September 1956-March 1957; *Double Image* (from the Savoy), March-April; *The Restless Heart*, May and *It's the Geography That Counts*, June-July. On the night of 27 July the curtain of the St. James's Theatre fell for the last time before the public.

There seems to have been some confusion in the minds of previous writers on the last night date: Macqueen-Pope (1958) gives 20 July, *The Survey of London* (1960) follows suit, but Duncan (1964) gives 29 July! *The Stage Year Book* (1958) and the entertainment columns of *The Times* prove conclusively Saturday 27 July, to be the correct date.

During the last months a nation-wide campaign, led by Vivien Leigh, had done all that could be done to save the theatre, even to the length of street marches and a protest in the House of Lords. Though this led to a motion, which was carried against the Government in the Lords, it was of no avail, except that in future the London County Council would see to it that no living theatre would be demolished in central London without a replacement being included in any new development plans.

Whilst awaiting demolition the theatre was used by a visiting Italian Opera company for rehearsals during August and in

October the interior was stripped. In November the contents of the theatre were sold by auction, and by December the newspapers were publishing melancholy photographs of the theatre being torn down.

The design for the new office block, by Robin Seifert, had already been published in June 1957, and work on the building, called St. James's House, (numbers 23 and 24), was completed in 1959. It opened in September partly occupied by the Dunlop Company Ltd. As a gesture the new owners incorporated sculptured balcony fronts on each floor above the entrance. The four bas-relief panels by Edward Bainbridge Copnall depict the heads of Gilbert Miller, George Alexander, Oscar Wilde and the Oliviers, each supported on either side by appropriate figures. A marble bas-relief portrait to the memory of Sir George Alexander and his management was in the vestibule of the theatre, this has completely disappeared since the demolition.

23
The Sans Souci Theatre

FIRST THEATRE

Strand
Between Fairfax Court and Marygold Court, near Southampton
Street

Opened 31 October 1791 with *Private Theatricals or Nature in Nubibus*, written, composed, spoken, sung and accompanied by Charles Dibdin. Preceded by a Poetic Address.
Under the management of Charles Dibdin.
Closed March 1796.

SECOND THEATRE

The Academic Theatre, The Vauderville Subscription Theatre
Leicester Place, Leicester Square

Opened 8 October 1796 with *The General Election*, a one-man entertainment by Charles Dibdin.
Under the management of Charles Dibdin.
Closed as a theatre 1835, became a warehouse and eventually the Hôtel de Versailles.
Demolished 1898, the ground absorbed into the site of Victory House, built on the corner of Leicester Place and Leicester Square. The part of Victory House which covers the site of the Sans Souci, and Number 3, the only remaining original house are now occupied at street level by a restaurant.

THERE HAS BEEN immense confusion among theatrical writers, and in text books, over the whereabouts and dates of a Sans Souci

Theatre. There were, in fact, two theatres of this name built by Charles Dibdin and the name was also used yet again for the room in Saville House. The first Sans Souci was a converted room in the Strand near Southampton Street, opposite Beaufort Buildings, opened on 31 October 1791 and closed in March 1796; the second, a new building in Leicester Place, Leicester Square (a transference, lock, stock and barrel, of the previous interior) opened 8 October 1796.

Charles Dibdin was born in Southampton in 1745, the son of a silversmith and Parish clerk, whose wife was nearly fifty when this, her eighteenth child, was born. As a boy he had little musical training, but had a pleasant voice and sang at concerts. Though destined for the Church he tried to become a church organist without success. He was a turbulent youth, always at war with the world, blaming his setbacks on others rather than his own inadequacy, though he must have been a talented natural musician. He came to London, helped by an elder brother, and became a tuner of harpsichords, starting to compose in his leisure hours. He sold these songs for a few guineas and came to the notice of John Rich, the manager of the Theatre Royal, Covent Garden. It was Rich's son-in-law, John Beard, the tenor and successor as manager of Covent Garden, who gave him his first chance with *The Shepherd's Artifice*, a musical pastoral produced in 1764.

In 1762 he had made his début as an actor and singer at Richmond, arriving via the provinces at Covent Garden as Strephon in his own piece. He later created Ralph in *The Maid of the Mill* by Bickerstaff and Arnold. He went over to Drury Lane, for which theatre he composed *The Padlock*, creating the part of Mungo, in 1768.

After this he gave up acting and devoted himself to writing and composing. He turned out piece after piece and song after song. Of the ballad operas, *The Waterman* (1774), *The Quaker* (1775) which he wrote entirely himself, and *Lionel and Clarissa* and *The Padlock* written in collaboration with Isaac Bickerstaff, are the most famous.

He had a capacity for quarrelling with managements and never getting the best of the bargain. As every London theatre became closed to him he tried management on his own account at Sadler's Wells and the Royal Circus. Eventually in 1787, after losing most of his money in various ventures, he tried a provincial tour with a one-man entertainment of his songs, interspersed with monologues and topical sketches, which became *The Musical Tour of Mr. Dibdin*. This proved a great success; as his own master and on his own he found his true place in the theatre.

He came to London and took Hutching's Auction Rooms in King Street, Covent Garden, and presented one of his programmes, *The Whim of the Moment; or, Nature in Little* in 1789. He migrated to the Grand Saloon of the Lyceum, in the Strand, (later the Lyceum Theatre), in 1790, opening on 18 October, with *The Wags; or, the Camp of Pleasure*, 'An entirely new, and perfectly original entertainment, in three parts, with an Exordium . . . the whole written, and composed, and will be spoken, sung and accompanied by Mr. Dibdin.'

He also opened a 'warehouse' at 411 Strand, opposite the Adelphi, for the sale of his music and piano-fortes. In these entertainments he first sang 'Tom Bowling' and the nautical songs by which his name is remembered today. In all he wrote some fifty plays, fourteen hundred songs, besides novels and a history of the stage.

He remained at the Lyceum, giving seasons of different entertainments, until he moved to a little theatre he had constructed in existing rooms in the Strand. These rooms (which are difficult to locate exactly) had been used by the Polygraphic Society, and were situated, according to the rate books, between Fairfax Court and Marygold Court (between numbers 371 and 395). His advertisements gave the location as 'opposite Beaufort Buildings' *not* at the back of his shop in the Strand, or in Southampton Street, as often stated. The confusion of location has arisen because Dibdin retained his shop at 411 Strand after he had opened his own theatre. The lease of 411 'opposite the Adelphi' passed to John Fry in 1797 (when Dibdin moved to Leicester Place), and with the adjoining 412 later became the site of the Sans Pareil Theatre, opened in 1806, and was later re-named the Adelphi Theatre (see *The Theatres of London*).

Dibdin called his converted room the Sans Souci, and he obtained a Licence for four years from the Lord Chamberlain, to give entertainments of recitative singing and music 'by himself only,' three times a week except Christmas Eve, Christmas Day, 30 January and Ash Wednesday. He opened on Monday, 31

October 1791 with his one-man entertainment *Private Theatricals; or, Nature in Nubibus*, preceded by a Poetic Address.

An advertisement in *The Oracle*, 31 October 1791 says:

This Amusement will embrace a large field of objects, impossible to be enumerated in an advertisement or handbill. Among a variety of other subjects, Matrimony—Lady-writing —Theatricals—Opera Speculation—Tippling—The Perversion of Epithets—Punning—Curiosity—Man Hunting—Queering—The Rights of Man—Charity—Alliteration—Perfumery—Philanthropy—and Gratitude, will not escape observation. The songs will come in the following succession.
Part I. True Wisdom—The Rara Avis—Conjugal Comfort—Poor Peg—Nothing but Drunk—The Sailor's Consolation—A Mock Recitative and Duetto.
Part II. Tack and Tack—Virtue—Tantivy—The Sailor's Return—The Waggoner—The Soldier's Last Retreat—Life's a Pun—Bill Bobstay.
Part III. The Drummer—The Beggar—Roses and Lilies—The Lucky Escape—Meum and Tuum—Jack's Gratitude, or the Royal Tar—the Sultan and the Wag.
The whole is written and composed, and will be spoken, sung, and accompanied by Mr. Dibdin.
These Rooms, now, for the first time, called Sans Souci, are disposed in a style of great beauty and peculiar novelty. Artists of the first eminence have been employed to give this undertaking every possible advantage; nor have any pains, however arduous, or preparation, however expensive, been neglected to manifest the zeal which shall ever mark Mr. Dibdin's conduct in soliciting a continuance of public favour.
Royal Pavillion and Cabins 5s. Area 3s. Gallery 2s.
Places to be taken at Mr. Dibdin's Warehouse, No. 411, Strand.
The Doors will be opened at Seven o'Clock, and the performance begin exactly at Eight.
∵ Several of the songs are already preparing for publication.
It is respectfully requested, that carriages may be set down with the horses' heads towards the City, and take up with the horses' heads towards Charing Cross.

Dibdin was extremely successful with his entertainments and

made more money from these and his songs than he had ever done before. Flushed with success he began to look for new premises when his licence from the Lord Chamberlain expired on 19 March 1796.

London was moving fast westwards, and development was taking place on the land which had been occupied by large houses and their gardens. The site of Leicester House had been acquired by Thomas Wright, a builder, early in the 1790's and through this ground he built a new road, Leicester Place, joining Leicester Square to Lisle Street (which he continued across his ground to join Little Newport Street).

On either side of the new street he built houses which he let on long leases between 1792 and 1795. Plans to make a little cul-de-sac below number 3 on the east side (the only one of the original buildings now still existing) fell through and the plot of land between the two houses was left vacant.

In his autobiography *The Professional Life of Mr. Dibdin, written by Himself* (1803) he states that 'By the time I proposed leaving the Strand, the whole of Leicester Place had been built up and finished, except a chasm which seemed to answer my purpose perfectly well.' By 1796 houses had been erected on either side of this plot, and Dibdin therefore 'had no walls to erect, except one in front of the house, another at the back and to give a greater altitude to that at the back of the theatre, for every other part of the brick work had been dry and seasoned for more than three years.' Dibdin also relates that when he 'came to measure the ground, its dimensions were to an inch, as far as it regarded the theatre, exactly the same as those of the premises I was about to quit, so I had nothing to do but remove my materials as a frame, and refix them.'

The *Survey of London*, Volume 33, says:

The lease of the site was granted by Thomas Wright to William Brooks of Castle Street, St. George's, Bloomsbury, builder. The land was leased 'with the Messuage or Dwelling house thereon newly erected and built with the Exhibition Room or Place of Public Entertainment at the back of the same called the New Sans Souci.' The plot had a street frontage of 46 feet and on its north side a depth of 64 feet; the east end measured 37 feet, and the south side (which was not straight)

S*

62 feet. The lease was to run for ninety-four years from 29 September, 1796, and the rent was £40. On 16 December, 1797, Brooks assigned the lease for an unspecified price to Dibdin at a rent of £98.

Dibdin says that 'Only twelve weeks passed between the period of laying the first stone' of the new theatre and the opening night. A colonnade was added a year later. The building, which seems to have included a shop for the sale of Dibdin's music, with living quarters above 'was executed entirely under the direction of Mr. Dibdin, at the total expense of little less than £6,000. It is calculated to hold 500 persons.'

A newspaper of the time stated that:

> The Sans Souci is fitted up in a shewy style, but with very humble pretensions to what may be called classical taste. Mr. Dibdin, however, if not a man of genius, is a man of much ingenuity. He writes ballads, sets them to musick, plays and sings them himself; and he now even engrosses the painters' art, and has embellished the Sans Souci with pictures from his own pencil.

For his opening on 8 October 1796 Dibdin chose *The General Election*, a topical entertainment. He then gave three performances a week during the winter months in his new theatre, till April 1804. (The Theatre was used for miscellaneous recitals in between.) His first season he says 'Upon the whole was very productive; but I soon found I had removed too far from the city, whence I had ever drawn my most substantial support.'

He thought about retiring in 1802, but did not get a suitable offer for the theatre, which he put up to let. He eventually mortgaged the theatre in 1804 and retired. He sold his stock of songs and their copyrights. The Government gave him a pension of £200, in recognition of his influence as an anti-Jacobin, but a new Government withdrew it! After a bankruptcy, friends gathered round and bought him an annuity. He had a paralytic stroke in 1813 and died at his home in Camden Town the following year.

Meantime the theatre was used spasmodically. A licence was granted to Frederick Schirmer for plays in German, which featured his son Albert, a talented child actor. He was followed in

1806 by Henry Greville of the Argyll Rooms, who obtained a Licence for 'Plays and Entertainments performed by Children, and for Music and Dancing.' He re-named the theatre the Academical Theatre (late Dibdin's).

Dibdin leased the premises in 1807 to Thomas Cane, a hosier, for sixty-three years, and from then theatrical performances ceased for many years; later the premises became a warehouse for B. Calder and Co., Army Clothiers and Tailors. It is mentioned by 'Chief Baron' Nicholson in his memoirs as a Gambling House, the Sans Souci Saloon, about 1820.

In 1832 the shop and theatre were occupied by a Dramatic Agent named Smithson, and he used the theatre for benefit performances, foreign companies and for amateurs, sometimes calling the theatre by its old name of the Sans Souci or the Vaudeville Subscription Theatre.

To add to the confusion of names, in January 1852 the room in Saville House was calling itself the Sans Souci; or Theatre of Variety. (See Number 3).

In 1836 the whole Leicester Place premises were occupied by a linen draper, Isaac Newton, who used it as an annexe to his adjoining premises in Leicester Square. It however became a restaurant in 1841 and eventually the Hôtel de Versailles.

It was demolished in 1898 when the whole corner site was cleared and Victory House, a block of shops and offices, was built. It is the return front of this building, which faces the square. It is the entrance in Leicester Place beyond the doorway up to the next building (the last original house—Number 3) which covers the site of the theatre. At street level this portion of Victory House has been joined to the ground level of number 3 and houses a restaurant.

24
The Shaftesbury Theatre

Shaftesbury Avenue
An island site bounded by Greek Street (now Newport Place),
Nassau Street (now Gerrard Place) and Gerrard Street
Stage door in Nassau Street

Opened 20 October 1888 with *As You Like It* by William
Shakespeare.
Produced by J. C. Smith.
Under the management of John Lancaster.
Last performance 7 September 1940.
Destroyed by enemy action 17 April 1941.
Part of the outer walls still remain round a derelict site used as a
car park.

SHAFTESBURY AVENUE was constructed through the heart of Soho,
linking an enlarged Piccadilly Circus with New Oxford Street and
was opened in 1887. It was to become the new theatrical centre
of the West End of London.

The gradual move westward of theatre-land had been going on
slowly for many years. From the traditional heart in Drury Lane
and Covent Garden, arteries spread down the Strand drawing in
the two fashionable Haymarket houses. The first theatre in the
new Avenue, the Shaftesbury Theatre built in 1888, and the
latest, the Saville Theatre built in 1931, cover the era of the
greatest change—the Lyric, December, 1888, the Palace, 1891,
the Apollo 1901, the Globe, 1906, the Queens, 1907, the Princes,
1911. (See *The Theatres of London*.)

By the end of the last century nearly all the theatres of the
eastern Strand had gone, and though some new theatres were to

arise, the heart itself had moved. Victorian theatre-land centred on the Strand yielded place and 'Shaftesbury Avenue' became synonymous with bright lights and commercial entertainment as much as 'Broadway' implies the New York equivalent.

The Shaftesbury Theatre was built on a plot of municipal ground for which John Lancaster, a wealthy Manchester Cotton Manufacturer, had obtained an 80 year lease. Designed by C. J. Phipps and built by Messrs. Patman and Fotheringham, it cost some £17,000 to construct and was meant to exploit Lancaster's wife, Ellen Wallis, a well known provincial leading lady who wished to enhance her London reputation.

Much was made, after the recent theatre fires and fatal accidents, of the safety arrangements (nearly 200 people had died in the fire of the Theatre Royal, Exeter in September 1887). The programme on the opening night noted:

> The Public is respectfully informed that the Shaftesbury Theatre is one of the safest in the world; standing entirely isolated, with Exits into four Street, viz.: Shaftesbury Avenue, Greek Street, Nassau Street, and Gerrard Street, with no impediments whatever for the free egress of an audience; also in construction being entirely fireproof, and fitted with the new hydraulic fire-resisting curtain entirely separating the Auditorium from the Stage. The Proprietor ventures to hope that he has done all that is possible for the safety of his employees and the public generally.

The Theatre, September 1888, says:

> The designs of the theatre have been prepared by Mr. C. J. Phipps, F.S.A., and received the approval of the Metropolitan Board of Works at the end of November last, since which time active building operations have been going on. The theatre stands entirely isolated, has a frontage towards Shaftesbury Avenue of 77 feet, and frontages to Greek Street and Nassau Street of 133 feet. Gerrard Street bounds the site towards the south. It will be a theatre of three tiers, the dress circle, or first tier, being only a few steps above the entrance vestibule in the frontage. The façade towards Shaftesbury Avenue has three doorways leading to the dress circle and two to the stalls. In Greek Street and Nassau Street are entrances to pit,

upper circle, and gallery duplicated, three entrances and exits in either street. The Royal entrance is in Greek Street, and the proprietor's entrance in Nassau Street, forming two additional exits, from the dress circle level just behind the private boxes. It will be thus seen that the audience have thirteen exits into three streets. The frontage, which is Italian in style, has a covered loggia on the first floor (upper-circle level) with a wide balcony opening out from the refreshment room and forming a promenade and an additional escape into the open air, only about 10 feet above the street. Above this loggia, on the gallery level, is another balcony, with means of egress from the top platform of the gallery. There are also in each side street iron balconies, with means of exit from each upper floor above them.

Every division of the audience is surrounded by a brick enclosing wall opening out into corridor 6 feet wide. All the corridors, staircases, and the framework of the several tiers are constructed of Portland cement concrete and iron; the vestibules and principal corridors being finished in marble mosaic. The several tiers will have wood floors fixed down tight into the cement concrete, it being quite as fire-resisting, and much more comfortable to persons sitting than on the cold concrete floors, however much they may be covered with carpet or matting. The mezzanine floor, the fly floors, and the dressing-room floors are all also of concrete. The number of seats provided is 1,708. The ornamentation of the interior will be Italian Renaissance in style.

The prices of admission at that date are of interest:

Orchestra Stalls, 10s.; Balcony Stalls, 6s.; Upper Circle (Numbered and Reserved), 3s.; Pit, 2s.; Amphitheatre, 1s. 6d.; Gallery, 1s. Private Boxes, from One to Four Guineas.

From *The Era*, 20 October we learn:

The hangings are of plush, a rich brown colour, lined with salmon-colour silk and reflects the highest credit on the eminent firm Messrs. Marshall and Snelgrove. A beautiful drop-curtain with view of Stratford upon Avon and statue of Shakespeare has been painted by Mr. William Telbin. The

colour of the decoration is light French grey and gold, and the
walls of the theatre are covered with a dark terra-cotta paper.
The stage is separated from the auditory by Max Clarke's
patent protected iron curtain, covered on the audience side
with green baize, and worked by hydraulic power supplied
from the mains of the Hydraulic Power Company, which run
up in the subway underneath Shaftesbury Avenue. The
auditory is at present lighted by a gas sunlight, but it is
proposed very shortly to install the electric-light all over the
building. It seems a pity though that the electric-light is not
to be used from the beginning. The acting-management
of the house will be in the able hands of Mr. W. Griffiths.

Electric light had been first used to light stage and auditorium
of the Savoy in 1881.

Though the theatre itself seems to have received general
acclaim the same cannot be said for the production of *As You Like
It*, which was chosen as a vehicle for Ellen Wallis who hoped to
repeat her provincial success. Cecil Howard in *The Theatre*
October 1888 records:

Miss Wallis, besides creating a very favourable impression as
Rosalind a few years ago in London, has established herself
as such a favourite in the character throughout the provinces
that it was no matter of surprise that she should elect to make
her first appearance at her husband's theatre in *As You Like It*.
The actress may be commended for her choice, for her
performance was more than merely intelligent and engaging,
it exhibited conscientious study and a delicate conception of
the character. In her bantering of Orlando Miss Wallis was
inimitable, and was excellent in her chiding of Phoebe, and the
more tender attributes of Rosalind were delicate if not always
as poetical as they might have been; but it was a bright and
charming performance. Mr. Forbes Robertson was excellent
as Orlando, more particularly where he consents to woo
Ganymede; this was played in a true spirit of comedy. The
Jacques of Mr. Arthur Stirling was disappointing; even in the
close of the great speech he betrayed the cynicism of his idea
of the disappointed courtier rather than the kindly
philosopher. Mr. William Farren made, as he should
have done, a noble old man of Adam. The Touchstone of

Mr. Mackintosh was a trifle too sententious, and lacked that enjoyment of his own wit which the clown should revel in; and, sad to say, he had in Mrs. Edward Saker, as Audrey, an actress who rendered him no assistance whatever. One of the best played parts was that of Sylvius by Mr. Matthew Brodie, whose acting was full of poetic fervour, and whose delivery of the lines was admirable. Miss Annie Rose was also good as Celia. Among others who may be favourably mentioned were Mr. J. R. Crauford, who looked the banished duke and was polished if not very strong; Mr. Charles Cooper, as Oliver, whose first dress was perhaps the handsomest worn during the evening, and who, besides doing it credit, made a favourable impression by the consistency of his acting; and Mr. Seymour Jackson, who sang Amiens' songs with such taste as to command encores. The costumes, from designs by H. G. Glindoni, carried out by J. A. Harrison, were most costly, accurate, and beautiful, the forest scenery exquisite, and Mr. G. W. Byng conducted the incidental and other music with skill; the only real fault in the production of the comedy was that it was taken at too slow a measure; this will, no doubt, be remedied after a night or two, and then Mr. Lancaster and Miss Wallis, who were specially called before the curtain and warmly received, may find that they have catered satisfactorily for a public for whose comfort they have undoubtedly done their utmost in the new theatre over which they reign.

Owing to the indifferent notices hasty preparations were made for a replacement and Lytton's *Lady of Lyons* was put into rehearsal and announced for 17 November, but misfortune was now to hit the theatre itself and bad luck dog the management.

The Era 24 November reported:

On Saturday last, when *The Lady of Lyons* was announced to be substituted for *As You Like It* at The Shaftesbury Theatre, an incident occurred which, it is to be hoped, will not be a common one when an iron curtain has become an indispensable adjunct to every theatre. The performance was announced to commence at a quarter past eight; but by that time the orchestra had scarcely commenced the overture. After this had been played another 'awkward pause' took place; and at half past eight Mr. Charles Arnold, in the dress of M. Deschappelles, stepped from the private box on to the stage and explained that the iron curtain would not go up, but that the inventor had been sent for, and was momentarily expected to the rescue. Mr. Max Clarke, however, when he did arrive, did not succeed in removing the obstacle to the commencement of the performance, and during his endeavours behind the scenes the 'gods' good-humouredly whistled the Marseillaise. Presently the band returned to their seats, and played a second selection. A looped rope which was dangled from the top of the proscenium evoked ironical applause, and as the time went on, and the music ceased, the gallery whistled 'We won't go home till morning'. About nine o'clock, Mr. Arnold again appeared, and stated that the curtain was still 'stubborn', and that, it would now be impossible to get through the performance in reasonable time, the management would be obliged if those present would leave the theatre and take tickets for another evening. During the whole of the delay the audience behaved remarkably well, and they showed their sympathy for the mishap, which had, after all, arisen from the efforts of the management to secure their safety from fire or panic, by departing without any expression of disapprobation. It was reported that the cause of the obstruction was want of water-power; but, according to Messrs. Clark, Bunnett, and Co. the manufacturers of the curtain, there was no defect in their machinery, the valve of the curtain having simply become jammed through want of proper oiling and attention. On Monday the iron curtain rose 'to time' amidst roars of laughter and applause, and was triumphantly let down and raised again between the first and second acts of Bulwer Lytton's well worn play, the revival of which at this date certainly presents very great difficulties to its principal representatives. Between the one alternative of the 'regulation' Claude and Pauline, speaking the bold blank-verse in the good old bumptious and 'flamboyant' style, and the other of new modern and 'finicking' readings of the two leading parts, it may be dangerous to choose. The golden mean was judiciously selected on Monday by Mr. Forbes Robertson as Claude Melnotte and Miss Wallis as Pauline. Mr. Robertson displayed great tact in the way in which he slurred over the clap-trap sentiments, avoided even a suspicion of bombast, and yet played the part of Claude with all the necessary energy and enthusiasm. Tastes, too often biased by old associations, may differ as to the virtues of some of Mr. Robertson's amendments of the recognised business; but, in many cases, he lighted up the text by the introduction of by-play which was both original and ingenious. Miss Wallis's ripe and thorough acquaintance with the *technique* of her art was of great value to her in her portrayal of the exacting role of Pauline. She did not spare herself in a depiction of hysterical emotion and violent passion, and carried the audience completely with her by the vigorous intensity of her acting in those portions of the play which more particularly demanded earnestness and force. She was scarcely less successful in her depiction of the tenderer and more distinctively feminine feelings of the much-harassed heroine, and in her development of the affectionate side of Pauline's nature. Mr. Mackintosh's Damas was not the rough-and-ready Republican veteran which has usually been the reading given to the character; but the embodiment was as humourous and as finished as it was probable and well founded. Mr. Bassett Roe, a promising young actor, who has only to acquire a perfectly finished pronounciation and more weight and presence to fully fit him for parts of this kind, was an acceptable, though not a very striking, Beauseant; and Mr. Allen Thomas gave a slightly novel reading of the role of Glavis. Mr. Charles Arnold's M. Deschappelles was an unimpeachable performance; Mr. Matthew Brodie suggested with reserved force the indignation of Gaspar; Miss Robertha Erskine's Madame Deschappelles was funny without being vulgar; Mrs. H. Leigh was an excellent Widow Melnotte; and various small parts were neatly played by Messrs. Arthur Fenwicke, S. Herberte-Basing, George Seldon, Phillips, Cowis, and Miss Lamballe. Scenery and dresses, the latter by L. and H. Nathan, were well provided, the picture at the rising of the curtain on the second act evoking a burst of applause. Whether there is money in any revival of *The Lady of Lyons* just now it would be rash to prophesy; but Miss Wallis has done much to deserve that success which is often, if not invariably, the reward of merit.

Unfortunately again the production did not meet with great success, bad luck often hits a new theatre in its early days. In June 1889 E. S. Willard and John Lart became joint managers. Their tenancy opened with a successful revival of *Jim the Penman*, a popular drama, and this was followed by the original production of Henry Arthur Jones' *The Middleman*, in which Willard drew all London to see his performance as Cyrus Blenkarn, the potter in 'The New and Original Play of Modern English Life'. It also caused great interest amongst American managers, particularly A. M. Palmer, who arranged that Willard should visit America. *The Middleman* was followed however, before his departure, by *Dick Venables* which was not a success, and *Judah*, also by Henry Arthur Jones, in May 1890. This play attracted much attention by a special matinée which was given for clergy only, it aroused one of those controversies which frequently raged around this playwright's work, when he ran counter to the middle class conscience, touching the false testimony of a clergyman and the ethics thereof. One commentator said: 'No doubt this dispute drew larger audiences than the cleverness of the play; people like to say they have been shocked, it testifies to their morality.' It ran 123 performances.

Ellen Wallis returned to the theatre in October 1890 in an adaptation of *Crime and Punishment* by Robert Buchanan, called *The Sixth Commandment*, which was unmercifully slated by the press on the first night, and Miss Wallis did the unforgivable thing of questioning her critics, and after revising the play she distributed an 'Address to the Public' at a subsequent performance ten days later.

The Era 25 October says:

A notice circulated in the theatre stating that 'the generous but all-powerful voice of the public' would that evening decide whether *The Sixth Commandment* should in its altered form be retained in the programme or at once withdrawn. The address continued:—Guided by the advice of the Press, which, whilst most kind to the artists, unanimously condemned the play, another piece would instantly have been put in rehearsal, but for one consideration—viz. the applause nightly, and what seems very like appreciation of the play on the part of the public. Therefore, when I put my question personally to you at the close of the performance, if the 'ayes' are in the ascendent I shall hopefully continue the run of the piece; if the 'noes' carry the day, then, in deference to a publicly expressed opinion, I must withdraw it, and shall cheerfully make another effort to please you and our critics. In conclusion, I have nothing but thanks to give to the latter gentlemen, whose kind consideration, and forbearance I am sure were severely taxed in an unusually long performance on the opening night. The play having since been shortened by forty minutes, and their suggestions as to alterations and excisions having been cordially accepted and adopted, I trust that, whether your verdict tonight be favourable or not, I may be allowed to acknowledge my obligations to the gentlemen of the Press for their valuable hints and kind praise where they were able to bestow it.

A reporter in *The Illustrated London News* takes up the story:

A quaint performance was gone through at the Shaftesbury Theatre last Saturday night, October 25th 1890, when, at the close of *The Sixth Commandment*, Miss Wallis, still in the dress of Anna Ivanovna, came forward to ask of the audience her mysteriously announced 'question'. What this question was to be had been indicated by an address to the public, copies of which had been distributed in the theatre. In the course of this address the voice of Miss Lancaster-Wallis, in words which may have been those of Mr. Buchanan, asked formally whether the play was to be kept in the bills or was to be withdrawn in accordance with the verdict of the press. According to the fair speaker's own showing, the play-going public had endorsed the opinion of the critics by staying away from the production in large numbers. The houses, she said, had been poor, but they they were so enthusiastic that she did not like to take the play off without giving it a further trial. 'Shall we go on with it?' she asked; and she asked it with such pretty nervousness that the chivalry of pit and gallery naturally displayed itself in a hoarse shout of 'Yes!' to which one enthusiastic gentleman appended a rider, to the effect that 'Critics are no good'. This proposition, however, could not be entertained by the astute manageress, at any rate in public; and amidst the confused shouts which brought the silly episode to a close, she was heard urging that even critics had their useful function, inasmuch as they chastened the spirit of their victims. But why drag the critics into the question at all? The proper place for Miss Lancaster-Wallis's inquiry was her own box-office, and if the answer was not satisfactory she may rely upon it she will not mend matters by sensational appeals to a small section of the great play-going public, which alone distributes the award of popular appreciation.

The play only lasted three weeks after this dramatic appeal.

In 1891 there was a season of Italian Opera, given by Antonio Lago, during which Mascagini's *Cavalleria Rusticana* had its first London performance. In April 1893 one of the earliest musical comedies was produced; this was *Morocco Bound*, which was described as 'A New Musical Farcical Comedy' by Arthur Branscombe, with music by F. Osmond Carr. In it Letty Lind made a great success as a 'Society Skirt Dancer'. This ran for 295 performances. After this, numerous productions came and went, *The Little Genius* (1896) was said to have lost £15,000 (a bad period for light opera; some £32,000 was lost in six months on various productions of this time). January 1897 saw a dramatisation of Marie Corelli's sensational book *The Sorrows of Satan*, with Lewis Waller.

The first real event of outstanding importance at this theatre was the production of the often revived *The Belle of New York*, on 12 April 1898. This was the introduction of American musical comedy to this country, and it scored 697 performances. Williamson and Musgrove were in control of the theatre at the time as 'Representatives of the late John Lancaster' who died in 1896. They were responsible for securing the play, which was by Hugh Morton (C. M. S. McLellan) with music by Gustav Kerker. This was a theatrical event of historical importance. It was the first imported company to bring a musical comedy to London. George W. Lederer's Casino Theatre Company of New York began the American invasion which has continued to the present day. With all the now accepted American self assurance, the programme stated: 'In Extenuation— the Author and Composer beg to say that whatever their play may be, it is all that is claimed for it'. *The Belle of New York* made a London Star of Edna May and she did not return to New York.

This success was followed by *An American Beauty* (1900) by the same authors and *The Casino Girl* (1900), a musical farce by Harry B. Smith, with music by Ludwig Englander, both played by the Casino Company. *Are You a Mason?* a farcical comedy which ran for 234 performances from 1901 was among the successes of this period. *In Dahomey* (1903) introduced the American coloured comedians Bert Williams and George Walker in the first all-black musical comedy seen in London. *The Prince of Pilsen*, another American musical comedy with music by Gustave Lauders (1904) ran for 160 performances and brought Camille Clifford, the 'Gibson Girl' to London.

Between 1907 and 1908 Norman J. Norman was manager and he presented several foreign companies including The Sicilian Players; and there was a season of *Grand Guignol*. Reviewing the London season Sidney Dark in *The Green Room Book*, said:

> The visit of the Sicilian Players to the Shaftesbury was one of the most interesting events of the past few months. Perhaps never before in England has one seen such virile, abandoned, and yet artistic playing. In an age when namby-pambyism has certainly established itself in the theatre, it was refreshing to watch the magnificent forcefulness of Giovanni Grasso and his colleagues.

In 1908 H. B. Irving leased the theatre and played a round of his father's successes, including *The Lyons Mail*, with which the season commenced in October.

It is strange that a theatre destined for the legitimate drama should become established in the Theatre List as a musical house, firstly with the original American invasion then with the regime of Robert Courtneidge, which commenced his management with *The Arcadians* on 28 April 1909. A 'fantastic musical play' by Mark Ambient and A. M. Thompson, with music by Lionel Monckton and Howard Talbot, ran for over two years—809 performances in all. It was in this production that Alfred Lester made such a great hit in his part of Peter Doody. Also in the cast were Harry Welchman, Phyllis Dare and Florence Smithson, and during the run Cicely Courtneidge joined the company for her London début.

Subsequently successes were scored by *The Mousmé* (1911) by Robert Courtneidge and A. M. Thompson, with music by the same composers as *The Arcadians* (209 performances); and *Princess Caprice* (1912) by A. M. Thompson from the Viennese, with music by Leo Fall (265 performances). Fall was the principal conductor at theatres in Berlin, Cologne and Hamburg. By this time Courtneidge had established an almost regular company to which he added as occasion demanded. In 1913 came *Oh! Oh!! Delphine!!!* with music by Ivan Caryll and *The Pearl Girl* with music by Hugo Felix and Howard Talbot, with Iris Hoey; and in 1914 *The Cinema Star*, by Jack Hulbert (from the German), with music by Jean Gilbert, was produced with Dorothy Ward and Fay Compton in the cast.

By way of contrast there were seasons of English Opera in 1915 and 1916 (under Sir Thomas Beecham), and then the musical comedy returned with *My Lady Frayle* by Arthur Wimperis and Max Pemberton, with music by Howard Talbot and Herman Finck, and *The Light Blues* (1916), an early grown-up appearance by Noël Coward, and a Harry Grattan revue called *Three Cheers* in which Harry Lauder and Ethel Levy appeared (1916).

In 1917 the lease of the theatre was sold by the executors of John Lancaster to Joseph Benson, who remained the owner for the rest of the theatre's life. George Grossmith and Edward Laurillard became the lessees and managers continuing the musical tradition. Their first venture on 6 September 1917 was *Arlette* which numbered Ivor Novello amongst its three composers and ran for 260 performances; followed by *Baby Bunting* (1919) and *Oh! Julie!* (1920).

For the next ten years the Shaftesbury provided varied fare, no longer did this theatre specialise in any particular style of entertainment, and managements came and went, but there were many outstanding successes, including *The Great Lover* (1920), the cast of which included Maurice Moscovitch; Clemence Dane's *Will Shakespeare* (1921); *Tons of Money* (1922) which ran for 737 performances and brought together Ralph Lynn, Robertson Hare, Tom Walls, Mary Brough and Yvonne Arnaud who transferred with the play to found the Aldwych farce team. Later hits were *The Cat and the Canary*, an American thriller (1922); *Stop Flirting* (1923), which introduced Fred and Adèle Astaire to the London stage; *Katinka* (1923), a musical with Binnie Hale and Joe Coyne; *The Rising Generation* (1923); *Toni* (1924) with Jack Buchanan; *Lightnin'* and *Clo Clo* a Franz Lehar score (1925); *Wildflower* and

My Son John (1926); Frederick Lonsdale's *The High Road* (1927); *Lucky Girl* (1928) and *Persons Unknown* (1929) by Edgar Wallace.

In August 1929 a new regime was inaugurated, prompted by the success of the farce team now firmly established at the Aldwych.

A series of light comedies under the management of Basil Foster and Tom Miller began with *The Middle Watch* by Ian Hay and Stephen King-Hall. The company, headed by Basil Foster, included Olive Blakeney, Jane Baxter, Clive Currie, Aubrey Mather and Reginald Gerdner, most of whom were to remain as a team. It ran 387 performances and was followed by *Leave it to Psmith* by Ian Hay and P. G. Wodehouse a year later. This was not so successful and before a new production was ready two musicals were produced; a complete failure (*My Sister and I*) and a revival of *The Chocolate Soldier* with Annie Croft. Basil Foster and Company returned in April, 1931, with *Mr. Faint-Heart* again by Ian Hay. This was followed in August by *The Midshipmaid* by the same writers as *The Middle Watch*, it ran 227 performances. The last of the Basil Foster series was *Orders are Orders* by Ian Hay and Anthony Armstrong, produced in August 1932. The following year he retired from the management of the theatre.

After a number of transitory managements and little success, in January 1934 John Gielgud and Richard Clowes presented Emlyn Williams' *Spring 1600*, but it, too, was a failure; Gielgud has written a graphic account of this excursion into management in his autobiography, *Early Stage*. After five flops in a row Basil Foster's partner, Tom Miller, got together some of the old team, and with the authors, Ian Hay and Stephen King-Hall, again tried his luck in August with *Admirals All* which ran 192 performances.

Although *The Dominant Sex* moved more than once during its long run, it was at the Shaftesbury that it was first produced in January 1935. Later thirties medium successes were *The Black Eye* by James Bridie (1935) which brought Stephen Haggard to the fore; *Laughter in Court* and *Heart's Content* (1936); *Thank You, Mr. Pepys* (1937); *Poison Pen*, 174 performances, *Good Bye Mr. Chips*, 132 performances, (1938); *They Walk Alone*, 156 performances, which starred Beatrix Lehmann and *Behold the Bride* which brought Louise Rainer to London (1939).

After the war broke out in September 1939 the first production at the Shaftesbury, when the theatre re-opened, was *His Majesty's Guest*, with Tom Walls, in November. During this period of opening and shutting at a moment's notice, *Behind the Schemes!* and *Good Men Sleep at Home* came and went. The prices of seats for the latter play, performed twice daily, are interesting in comparison with those of 1888: Orchestra stalls, 10s. 6d. and 8s. 6d., Dress circle, 7s. 6d. and 6s. od., upper circle, 4s. od., pit, 2s. 6d., gallery, 1s. od.

In August 1940 another revival of *The Chocolate Soldier* was produced, but the blitz put an end to the run on 7 September, and to the theatre itself which was reduced to a ruin on 17 April 1941. The outer walls covered by hoardings remain about 24 ft. high while a gap in the back wall admits motor cars on to the flattened ground, now a car park.

It awaits the fulfilment of a re-construction scheme covering the whole of this area.

The name was to return to the Theatre List in March 1963 when the re-decorated Princes Theatre (opened at the northern end of Shaftesbury Avenue in 1911, see *The Theatres of London* No. 26), was re-christened the Shaftesbury Theatre.

25
Terry's Theatre

Strand
Side exits and stage door in Savoy Buildings, backed by buildings in
Savoy Hill

Opened 17 October 1887 with *The Churchwarden*, a farce in three
acts by Rudolf Kneisel, translated by H. Cassell and C. Ogden
and adapted by Edward Terry. (Transferred from the Olympic
Theatre.) Preceded by *Meddle and Muddle*, a new comedietta by
Henry Bellingham and William Best.
Under the management of Edward Terry.
Closed 8 October 1910 and became a cinema until 1923.
Demolished 1923 as part of a Strand widening scheme.
Woolworth's Stores covers the site in a block of shops and offices
called Norman House (105-109 Strand).

AT THE TIME WHEN the movement westwards of London's theatrical
centre was gaining momentum, it is strange to find a new theatre
being built at the eastern end of the Strand. Shaftesbury Avenue
opened in 1887 and, with its new theatres being planned, was
pointing the way ahead.

The beginnings of what was to become the Strand (Aldwych
Kingsway) development scheme was in the official mind, and
speculation was in the air (see Number 6), and one theatre at
least was re-built on a grand scale in the hope of an eventual
large compensation. (The Olympic, 1890. See number 12.) The
south side of the Strand was not then due to be touched; that
did not happen till many years later.

Edward O'Connor Terry (1844-1912), the proprietor and

manager of the new theatre, was a Londoner. He had started in a City office but came to acting before he was twenty, first as an amateur, and later with a fit-up company. Years in provincial stock seasons brought him eventually to London and the Surrey Theatre in 1867. He soon moved into the West End and played the First Grave-digger in *Hamlet* at the Lyceum in 1868. From 1869 for seven years he was with the Swanborough Company at the Royal Strand, mainly playing in burlesque: 'his eccentric humour, his clever singing and dancing, and his unique powers of facial expression soon carried him to the front.' (*The Dramatic Peerage* 1892.)

He then joined John Hollingshead's Gaiety Company in 1876 and with Nellie Farren, Kate Vaughan and Edward Royce formed the famous and long remembered 'Gaiety Quartette' which provided the light musical burlesque humour which was the fashion of the day. This was another long engagement, he was with the Company until May 1885.

He then had aspirations to become a theatre owner and appear under his own management. While plans for his new venture were in hand he took the Olympic Theatre and produced *The Church-warden* on 16 December 1886. It was with this play he was to inaugurate his own theatre the following year.

Terry, who was married first to Ellen Deitz, then the widow of Sir Augustus Harris, was no relation to the famous Terry family. To quote *The Dramatic Peerage:*

He was a good citizen who has proved himself mindful of the responsibilities of real life by the energy with which he carries out the duties of a Guardian of the Richmond Board, and also those of Churchwarden. In 1889 he was elected Grand Treasurer of Freemasons, of which body he is an old and distinguished member. In the same year he was invited to read before the Church Congress a paper on the relations of Church to Stage, and the broad and lofty view he took of the subject created a great amount of serious public discussion, and without doubt elevated the actor's calling in the minds of those many prejudiced people who never grasp more than one side of a question. Mr. Terry is a Tory, and will perhaps be found among the combatants when the next General Election comes. Some little time ago he was offered a Con-

servative candidature in Ireland, but refused, as his great
desire is to be an M.P. for an English Constituency.

The new theatre was built at 105 and 106 Strand, on the site of
The Fountain (later the Occidental) Tavern, which had housed
the notorious Coal Hole where 'Baron' Renton Nicholson held
the Judge and Jury Club, early in the century.

Charles Wilmot, an Australian who had been managing the
Occidental Tavern, a resort of 'Pros', had also owned the Grand
Theatre, Islington and financed the building of the theatre to
which Terry was to give his name and have a twenty-one year
lease. The architect was Walter Emden.

In *The Era* 20 August 1887 Edward Terry, interviewed about
the new theatre, said:

I shall endeavour to make Terry's Theatre what the Strand
Theatre was in the days of John Clarke and James Rodgers—
a place in which to spend a jolly evening. This theatre will be
my home for twenty-one years. After my first season, however, I will vacate it for three or four months each year. In
the first place, I wish to, and must, carry out my provincial
engagements; and in the second, I don't want to give my
London patrons a chance of getting surfeited with too much
Terry. Terry's Theatre will be, as far as I can make it, not only
fire but panic proof. The latter is, of course, a much more
difficult matter than the former. In addition to the 'rose sprinklers', of which there are forty-five—at the trial, I may
mention, five were sufficient to flood the stage—and hydrants,
there will be a fire-proof curtain; and if arrangements can be
made in time the whole house will be lighted by electricity.
People go to the theatre to be amused, most decidedly; and
farce seems at present to serve that purpose. Whether it will
last is another matter. I do not think it will. On the principle,
however, that 'those who live to please must please to live,'
when the public taste changes I shall change my programme
with it. I am the president of at least a dozen amateur
societies. The following were in their time amateurs: Messrs.
Irving, Toole, Bancroft, Hare, Terriss, Willard, Beerbohm-
Tree, and your humble servant. To this list might be added
many more, but I think it is a tolerably representative one.
In the absence of provincial stock seasons, a school of dramatic

art is sadly wanted. But there are many difficulties in the way. The dramatic students are, I think, doing some admirable work, not only in reviving works of the old playwrights, but in bringing dramatic talent to the front. Many years ago I was concerned in a movement to establish a National Theatre, á la Comédie Français; but we differed as to the method. Some gentlemen wished a theatre the size of Drury Lane, whereas, on the principle that we must creep before we run, I suggested one the size of the Royalty, which could at that time have been rented very cheaply. After several meetings, however, the matter died out. I have, I think, read more new plays than any modern manager, and out of the hundreds I have gone through I have only discovered four good ones, my judgment being verified in every instance except one. Still, I am looking out. There is, in my opinion, plenty of room for new men's work.

Further details are given on the First Night Programme:

The Theatre is built with special precautions against fire. It will hold about 800 persons. The Main Entrances to the Dress Circle, Stalls, and Boxes, also the Extra Gallery Exit, are in the Strand. The Extra Exit to the Dress Circle is in Savoy Buildings, as are both the Pit Entrances, Extra Exit, and the Gallery Entrance. There are Three Tiers; Pit and Stalls, Balcony and Dress Circle, and Gallery and Upper Boxes. Each part of the house has two or more exits, fitted with Messrs. Chubb's patent Panic Door Lock and apparatus. The total exit accommodation is, according to the regulations of the Board of Works, equal to 3,500 persons, while, as before stated, the holding capacity of the theatre is only 800 persons. The whole, including the roof, is constructed of concrete and iron, no wood being used in the auditorium, except for doors and windows; while all the necessary woodwork, before and behind the curtain, is coated with Sir Seymour Blane's Fireproof Paint. A thorough system of Hydrants, in the best available position, is placed before and behind the scenes, a Hydrant being in each circle, one on each side, while the whole of the Stage and Flies, both above and below, are dominated with a system of Sprinklers, which Sprinklers are commanded by valves at the Stage Door, and are always

ready. Thus, while the Auditorium is entirely Fireproof, the
Stage can be deluged at a few moments' notice with a perfect
sheet of water, entirely preventing the spread of fire. The
stage woodwork is all coated with Fireproof Paint. The iron-
work is so arranged that it stands alone, the whole being tied
together with steel anchorages and bars; it is then cased with
concrete, this being again topped with the patent eureka
concrete, while the under portion, or any part which still
remains exposed, is cased in plaster. The Auditorium and
Stage are both separately ventilated by direct exhausts in the
roof of each. The Stage is divided from the Auditorium by
the Proscenium Wall, which wall passes some twenty feet
above the outside of the Auditorium Roof, the opening in the
Proscenium being closed by a Fireproof Curtain. The whole
of the building is lighted by Electricity, which is supplied by
the Sir Coutts Lindsay Co., of Grosvenor Gallery. No
Engines, Dynamos, &c. being in the Building.

The Theatre, both in exterior or interior, is in the Flemish
style. The interior colouring being a deep brown pink and
apple-green and gold; all the silk curtains and hangings being
of the same colours. The seats, which are made with enamelled
iron frames, are covered in the same colours, plush and
brocade.

The Architect is Mr. Walter Emden, who has for many
years made a study of the construction of Theatres and Fireproof Public Buildings, assisted by Mr. George Harrison,
C.E., as to the Hydrants and Water arrangements. The Con-
tractors are Messrs. Holliday & Greenwood, who have taken
especial care in the execution of the work. The Ironwork is
by Messrs. M. T. Shaw, and the Water Apparatus by Messrs.
Rose. The Carton Pierre has been executed by Messrs.
Battiscombe & Harriss, and the Furnishing by Messrs.
Atkinson, while the Tile Decorations have been executed by
Messrs. Doulton. Mr. E. Bell has executed the Painted
Decorations.

The Era 22 October reported the opening night:

The visitors could not fail to remark the excellent accommodation provided, the comfort of the patrons having been made
an especial study. Even in pit and gallery there was 'ample

room and verge enough' for all, so that the programme could be sat through with a sense of personal ease as well as intellectual enjoyment. The electric lighting arrangements, unfortunately, had gone wrong, but this was the only serious drawback to the complete success of the inaugural performance. The arrangements in front of the house, under the careful supervision of Mr. H. T. Brickwell, who has long been associated as business-manager with Mr. Terry, were beyond reproach, for, by a very simple arrangement, the holders of numbered seats had no difficulty in finding them, and those who owned carriages, or had hired cabs, had them in attendance with the least possible delay directly the performance was concluded. The principal item in the bill was the farcical comedy, translated from the German by Messrs. Ogden and Cassell, adapted for the English stage by Mr. Edward Terry and entitled *The Churchwarden.* London playgoers were introduced to Mr. Churchwarden Daniel Chuffy in December last, when Mr. Terry commenced a season at the Olympic, and he proved so eminently amusing that we have no doubt many will now avail themselves of the pleasant opportunity to renew so desirable and diverting an acquaintance. Mr. Chuffy, it will be remembered, is quite a model of all the proprieties until he ventures to London and goes through sundry exciting adventures at a restaurant with a strange young lady. The escapade is harmless enough, but after it Mr. Churchwarden Chuffy's existence is to him a misery. He lives in a state of constant dread lest something or somebody should 'let the cat out of the bag' and expose his departure from the paths of moral rectitude. 'What would Mrs. Chuffy say?' is a question that seems ever present to his mind, and it is out of his fears that the fun for the audience springs. Mr. Terry is quite an adept in the art of depicting comic fright, and on Monday evening, even while those who were seated in front were saying 'How extravagant!' they were holding their sides with laughter. Mr. Lionel Brough had been imported into the cast, and his impersonation of Mr. Bearder, M.P., the Churchwarden's patron, was marked by many quaint and humorous touches. Miss M. A. Victor succeeded Miss Maria Jones as Mrs. Amelia Chuffy, and proved highly diverting, as also did another newcomer Mr.

T. P. Haynes as the restaurant waiter Alfred—a character
that was played at the Olympic by Mr. J. G. Taylor.
Nathaniel Gaddam, the Churchwarden's chum, was again
well represented by Mr. T. C. Valentine; Mr. J. W. Erskine
was again seen to advantage as the young lover Frank Bilton,
and Miss Clara Cowper repeated her delightful representation
of Kate, the Churchwarden's niece. The comedy was preceded
by the comedietta written by Messrs. Bellingham and Best,
and entitled *Meddle and Muddle*. On this occasion this new
piece was played for the first time in London. The fun
springs from the confusion that arises when Mr. Meddle, a
retired tradesman, begins to interest himself in the secret love
affairs of, as he supposes, somebody else's daughter. Un-
consciously he assists in the scheme promoted by his own
child, who, without his sanction, favours the amatory pretensions of a young artist. Mr. Lionel Brough made amusing
the character of Mr. Meddle and was well supported, especially
by Miss M. A. Victor.

At the end of the comedy Mr. Terry was called to the footlights, and was received with enthusiasm. He apologised for a
few slight omissions incidental to the hurry of opening—
principally the electric light—and in response to complaints
from the gallery of an outer gate which opened outwards on
the incoming crowd, said the audience must blame the
Metropolitan Board of Works, who had insisted on this form
of gate. Having claimed to have done all he could to make the
theatre a safe one, he expressed his intention of making it also
a popular one. He intended, when the public were tired of
The Churchwarden, to submit a new comedy, called *The
Woman-Hater*, which had been successfully tried in the
provinces, and further, he promised a new comedy by Mr.
Pinero. Behind those works he had several novelties. Referring
to the kindly reception of himself and company, he said he
had received so many telegrams of congratulation from brother
and sister artists all over the kingdom that, if good wishes
could make a success, he had already achieved it. Mr. Terry
retired amidst loud plaudits. Skilled firemen, supplied by the
United Society of London Firemen, act as attendants in
various parts of the house, and are constantly on duty on the
stage.

Messrs. Chubb and Sons' panic door lock is one of the most
novel and, at the same time, principal features in the arrangements for the safety of the public at Terry's Theatre, it having
been fitted to all the emergency doors of the building. The
lock is contained in a panel which occupies a large surface on
the inside of the door, and anyone coming in contact with the
door must press the panel, thus causing the door to open
instantly. It is impossible for the officials of a building the
doors of which are fitted with the new lock to lock or fasten the
door so as to prevent egress at any time. From the inside it is
always possible to get out, while from the outside it is impossible for anyone to get in without the proper key. The
want of a lock of this character was pointed out to Messrs.
Chubb by Mr. W. Emden, the architect of the theatre.

In the lighting of this theatre gas and electricity (incandescent lights) are both employed. In the centre of the dome
over the auditorium is a brilliant sun-burner, ornamented with
wrought-iron scrolls and cut-glass drops. Round the dress
circle, balcony stalls, pit, and staircases are wrought-iron
brackets; the vestibule being lighted with old English
cylinder wrought-iron lamps, all made and designed for the
two kinds of illuminations employed. Above the brackets are
ventilating cones and shafts to carry off the vitiated air; the
flues are fitted with a revolving extractor on the roof. The
stage is fitted with a flash light arrangement, by which the gas
can be lighted instantaneously if the electric light should fail.
On the stage is fixed a patent automatic gas dip, by which it
is impossible for any length or row of lights to be shifted
without the gas being instantaneously turned off. The battens
are cased in specially designed wire fronts, as are also the
proscenium lights, hanging lengths, and ground rows. This
renders it impossible for any border cloths or inflammable
materials to come in contact with the gas jets. The meters are
fixed in a suitable building outside the theatre, and each is
fitted with a bye pass; thus preventing the house from ever
being in darkness. The contractors are Messrs. Holliday and
Greenwood, of Loughborough Junction, who have taken
especial care in the selection of the materials used that all
should be of the best quality. The whole of the wrought-iron
gas and electric light fittings, sun-burner, stage arrangements,

T

and ventilation appliances were manufactured and fixed by
Messrs. Vaughan and Brown, of Kirby Street, E.C.

Terry's was only the second London theatre to bear its
manager's name. J. L. Toole had re-christened the Folly Theatre,
Toole's, in 1882. Others later to follow their example were Daly's,
1893, Wyndham's, 1899, the Hick's (Globe), 1906. The Garrick,
1889, and the Irving Theatre Club opened in Irving Street, 1951,
were named after actors of the past.

After *The Churchwarden* the first big success of the theatre was
Pinero's *Sweet Lavender* produced 21 March 1888. A simple
romantic one-set play, it ran 684 performances and was said to
have made a profit of £20,000 for Terry, and to have cost £66 to
produce, with a top salary of £17 a week!

At a time when the rumbles of Ibsenism were crossing the North
Sea one detects the hand of Clement Scott in the unsigned
criticism in *The Theatre*, May 1888, which says:

> What an admirable retort witty Pinero is giving to the
> disciples of Zola and '*naturalisme*,' who think a play cannot
> be healthy without being insipid. In *Sweet Lavender* the
> dramatist introduces us to good women and honest men, and
> withal the play is as brilliant as a flash of light. The pure
> sentiment which brings tears to our eyes is well spiced with
> refined wit, quaint and even grotesque humour, in which
> nothing has been sacrificed to vulgarity to create laughter. But
> we do laugh, merrily and heartily, whilst wiping our eyes, and
> we are ashamed of neither, for this outward show of diverse
> feelings is only the just tribute to the author, who has written
> one of the best plays we have seen for a long time.

There is little of great importance to record in the next few
years of the theatre. Other less successful plays by Pinero, *The
Rocket* and *The Times* (both 1891), were produced with Terry in
the cast. In a programme of 'Five One-Act Plays by English Authors,' presented by Charles Charrington with his wife Janet
Achurch in 1893, it is interesting to find J. M. Barrie's first
dramatic essay, a dramatization of a scene from Thackeray called
Becky Sharp. (Thomas Hardy's *The Three Wayfarers* and Conan
Doyle's *Foreign Policy* were also on the bill.)

In 1894 Weedon Grossmith had a success with a farcical comedy by Arthur Law called *The New Boy*.

Edward Terry made a return to burlesque with *King Kodak* in 1894, his old partner from the Gaiety, Kate Vaughan, was in the cast, but it did not run. Burlesque as a type of entertainment was giving way to the newly invented Musical Comedy.

The theatre for a while could not find its own success and housed several transfers until *Jedbury Junr*. by Madelene Lucette Ryley ran over 100 performances (1896). Then a musical comedy by Basil Hood and Walter Slaughter *The French Maid*, with Kate Cutler, ran 480 performances from April 1897. Weedon Grossmith in a farce *The Lady of Ostend* (1899) and a revival of *Sweet Lavender* (1900), carry over the turn of the century.

In 1901 a satire on the successful *Sherlock Holmes*, then running at the Lyceum with William Gillette, was produced called *Sheerluck Jones; or, Why D'Gillette Him Off?* A programme note stated:

N.B.—No one arriving after 10 o'clock, and very few seated before that hour, can possibly understand the plot of the piece.

The Management desires to call the special attention of the audience to the novel light effects. For permission to reproduce these in the family circle by the method of rapidly opening and closing the eyes application to be made to the Acting Manager.

The light motives in the orchestra provided by Mr. Brigate Buccalossi.

Properties by their respective owners.

The costumes more by accident than design.

As the orchestra is only able to play one tune in the dark the indulgence of the public is requested should any similarity be detected in the musical finales to the various paragraphs.

It was a curtain raiser to *The New Clown* by H. M. Paull which starred James Welch.

Edward Terry made the transition to musical comedy in *My Pretty Maid* in 1902, but he was not in the cast of *My Lady Molly*, the most successful musical this theatre ever staged. It ran 342 performances from March 1903. It was by Sidney Jones and had Sybil Anundale, Decima Moore, Richard Greene and Walter Hyde in the cast.

Edward Terry returned to his theatre with *The House of Burnside* by Louis N. Parker in 1904, which did not run and proved to be his last play in this theatre, though he remained its proprietor.

Unfortunately the theatre fell on evil times, nothing stayed for long on its stage. Réjanè played a season in 1905 as did Mrs. Langtry and Weedon Grossmith.

The Heroic Stubbs by Henry Arthur Jones with James Welch (1906) and that most eccentric of managers, W. H. C. Nation (1907), preceded the last burst of success, *Mrs. Wiggs of the Cabbage Patch*, which ran 268 performances (including its transfer to the Adelphi).

James Welch, who had been lessee since January 1906, was hard put to keep the theatre open. A season of *The Follies* with H. G. Pelissier (1907) matinées of Ibsen's *Rosmersholm* with Florence Kahn (1908) and numerous transitory productions mark his tenancy.

The Passing of the Third Floor Back finished its run here in 1909 (from the St. James's), as did *Dame Nature* (1910, from the Garrick). After the production of *The Rejuvenation of Aunt Mary* with May Robson, which opened in August 1910 and ran till 8 October, the theatre closed.

It became a cinema at one time under the direction of Albert de Courville, advertised as Terry's Cinema in the Strand.

Edward Terry died in April 1912. He had lived to see the Victorian theatres all around him changed or pulled down. The Lyceum re-built as a Music Hall, 1904 (see *The Theatres of London*, Part IV, No. 5). The Gaiety, re-built and moved to another site (see Number 4). The three theatres lost in the Aldwych-Kingsway re-development were the Olympic (see No 12), the Opera Comique (see No. 13) and the Globe (see No. 5). The Tivoli (see No. 24) was soon to follow. The newfangled cinema was beginning to take over uneconomic theatres in London and the suburbs and even more so in the provinces.

Terry's remained a second rate cinema until 1923 when a Strand widening scheme came into operation. It was pulled down and the site bought for re-development. A new block, Norman House, arose on an enlarged site which included a Woolworth's and other shops with offices above (105-109 Strand). Woolworth's as we have noted (see No. 16), have always been on the look-out for theatre sites. This block was sold for £5,000,000 in March 1966, (it has a Crown lease expiring in 2018). A new block, Savoy Buildings, adjoining Woolworth's and straddling the old Fountain Court, leads steeply down to Savoy Hill. On the side of its entrance two commemoration plaques recall the past history, but not the existence of Terry's Theatre.

26
The Tivoli

The Tivoli Theatre of Varieties
Strand
In a site bounded by Adam Street and Durham Street (now Durham House Street) with buildings in John Street (now John Adam Street) at the rear

FIRST BUILDING

The Tivoli Beer Garden and Restaurant opened 1876.

SECOND BUILDING

The Tivoli, Theatre of Varieties (on a much enlarged site) opened 24 May 1890, with a Music Hall bill.
Under the management of The Tivoli Company Limited.
Interior re-modelled and re-opened 4 July 1891.
Closed 1914 and later demolished, with the adjoining building to the corner of Adam Street.
The ground remained vacant (except for temporary war time buildings) until 1922.

THIRD BUILDING

The Tivoli Cinema opened 6 September 1923, with *Where the Pavement Ends*.
Under the management of Metro-Goldwyn-Mayer.
Closed 1957 and demolished.
Peter Robinson's store now stands on the site.

IN THE MIDDLE OF La Grand Rue, what we now know as the Strand, just beyond the Palace of the Savoy, stood Durham House, the London residence of the Bishops of Durham. It is mentioned as early as 1232. The frontage was on the river, then the main traffic artery, and on the ground sloping up to the road were the stables. When the estate was split up the Strand part of the site was occupied by the New Exchange, built by Lord Salisbury in 1608. This building consisted of shops and a promenade, where fashion congregated. It is the location of the scene in Wycherley's *The Country Wife* when Pinchwife takes his wife, in boy's clothes, to see the pleasures of the town.

The venture was a failure and fell into disrepute as a haunt of vice and was pulled down, houses were built on the site.

In 1768 the Adam Brothers began to re-develop the whole area and built the Adelphi with its river terrace (see Number 11). The Strand frontage became houses and shops. It was in the middle of this block, bounded by Adam Street and Durham Street (now Durham House Street) at each end, and by John Street (now John Adam Street) at the rear, that the Tivoli Beer Garden and Restaurant was opened in 1876. It was a success and soon in the prevailing fashion singers and comedians were engaged to entertain the customers. Eventually it was decided to enlarge the premises, adjoining buildings down to Durham House Street were purchased and a company formed, The Tivoli Limited, to build a regular Music Hall: The Tivoli, Theatre of Varieties.

In *The Theatre* November 1888 we read:

The corner-stone of the Tivoli Theatre and Restaurant was declared 'well and truly laid,' on October 18, by Mr. H. J. Leslie, and promises to be, from the drawings exhibited by Mr. Walter Emden, the architect, a building that for beauty of design, both externally and internally, will surpass anything of the sort yet seen, and will be a great ornament to the Strand. The interior arrangements for the Music Hall are excellent, and the principal rooms in the Restaurant, such as the Palm-room, with its alabaster swans and cupids, and the Flemish room, with its exquisite carvings, will be the perfection of taste. There will also be a large Masonic Hall with its necessary accompaniments, while in the basement hairdressers' shops, &c., will be included in the plans for the

comfort of the visitors. The contractors promise that their
work shall be completed by Christmas.

The Era 5 April 1890 gives further details of the now almost
completed building, we are told:

> The Tivoli Company's handsome building for music hall and
> restaurant in the Strand is now nearing completion, and the
> end of the present month, or beginning of next, will witness
> its opening. Decoration and fittings are all that remain in the
> hands of the workmen, and these are so far advanced as to
> enable one to form a very good idea of the general effect
> when complete. Of the ornamentation in design there can be
> but one opinion, and that a distinctly favourable one, while of
> efficient execution there is already ample evidence. Both
> restaurant and music hall will contain all the elements of
> comfort and sightliness which, in places of this sort, go far
> towards securing popularity with the public. Entrance to both
> buildings is from the Strand, but there are excellent exits
> from the music hall into Durham Street. The entrance hall is
> spacious and well planned, and of elegant appearance, with its
> arcade of Indian arches and columns, filled in with arabique.
> On a level with the street is the balcony tier, which is a point
> of vantage for a general view of the house. It will here be
> seen that the Oriental character of ornamentation has been
> maintained throughout the building, and with admirable
> effect. An air of compactness and concentration over the stage
> is a striking feature, while, as a matter of fact, there is a very
> considerable amount of sitting accommodation as well as good
> promenading space. There are ten well-appointed boxes on
> the balcony tier—namely, on either side four small boxes for
> couples and one large one for four or six. In the area of the
> hall are a fair number of stalls in front, and an unusually large
> space for promenaders at the rear. There is a bar 50 ft long
> at the back, and a small one close to the stalls, both being
> shut off from the hall itself. The gallery has its separate
> entrance from the Strand, and an extra exit for use in case of
> emergency. There is a bar at the back of the circle and a good
> promenade. There are lounges in abundance, and a good view
> of the stage from all. The stage is small, but sufficient for the
> purposes required, and it has an adequate supply of dressing-

rooms. The music hall, like the restaurant, is heated with hot
water, and will be illuminated by electricity.

The restaurant is being decorated and fitted up with
unexceptionable taste. The buffet is decorated in Indian style,
the wall-space being covered with ornamented tiles of special
design, with Algerian marble bar and dado, and elegant
panels and intermediate niches with statues of Indian gods and
goddesses. The entrance vestibule is in oak panels, and the
staircase decorated in the François premier order of art. On the
first and second floors are the Palm Room and Flemish Room
respectively, both being large and elegant apartments;
graceful palm leaves being represented on the walls and
ceiling of the former, with a very fine dado of marble and
alabaster, and inlaid marble floor. The Flemish room is
executed in oak, and we hear the whole of the carving was
done at the Levant. In this room is a remarkably fine fireplace,
which was on view at the Paris Exhibition, and will doubtless
command much attention. On the third floor are a series of
private dining-rooms, artistically adorned in styles which
their names convey—namely, the Louis V Room, the
Japanese, the Arabian, and the Pompeiian Rooms; and, in
addition, there is a fair-sized Masonic Room. In the public
portions of the building there are, of course, suitable retiring
rooms, and every provision for comfort. There is a fourth floor,
in which is situated the culinary department, which is replete
with the most modern cooking appliances. There is ample
room on the basement and sub-basement floors for necessary
appliances, with which the visitor will not come in contact,
such as boilers, heating apparatus, storage, fittings, lifts to the
kitchen, &c. The total cost of the site and building has been
over a quarter of a million.

In due course the new Music Hall was opened on 24 May, as
reported in *The Era* 31 May:

The palatial theatre of varieties known as the Tivoli, and
advantageously situated in the Strand, was opened to the
public on the evening of Saturday last, and, as might have
been anticipated, was crowded in every part, early-comers
spending the time of waiting for the rising of the curtain in
admiring the rich and handsome decorations, which are in

T*

Indian style, and give the interior the appearance of an Indian temple. There was a little excusable grumbling about the seating arrangements in the large area, which does duty for pit, for the 'rake' of the floor cut off the view of the stage from a good many in the rear, the result being that some hundreds who should have been seated stood, and that the gangways were inconveniently blocked. Again, up above we noticed there were certain adventurous individuals who preferred to perch themselves on the balcony fronts to taking the places provided for them, and as there was nobody to order them otherwise there was a natural feat that some of them might in the course of the evening make an unwelcome dive into the stalls. A few uniformed officials stationed about the cheaper parts of the auditorium would correct this sort of thing, which, doubtless, when matters have settled down, will no longer give cause for uneasiness or complaint. Mr. H. F. Potter, the acting-manager, welcomed the more distinguished arrivals on Saturday evening, and punctually at the time announced the orchestra, directed by Mons. Max Maitret, started the overture, and then was commenced the long programme that had been put together in a short time, in the face of unlooked for difficulties. Mdlle. Bertoto, a Taglioni in miniature, 'opened the bill,' and with her transformation dances put the spectators in excellent humour—so excellent, indeed, that it was not kept in good restraint for the rest of the evening. There were many young gentlemen in the pit who seemed to prefer to hear their own sweet voices in preference to those who appeared upon the stage. They had been affected by the chorus of Mr. Harry Freeman's song called 'After me,' and so at every possible opportunity, and at opportunities that were not always appropriate, this 'after me' chorus broke forth and would not be denied. Mr. Harry Freeman was of the company. In the song referred to, he makes-up ugly and then boldly assures his hearers that he is wanted for a good many distinguished positions. There is a beauty show—'they're after me' he sings; a successor to Stanley is required—one who will sneak all Africa and bring it back—'they're after me' he declares; and he actually dares to assert further that her Majesty instead of looking to Germany should she have another princess to dispose of in

matrimony will look to him. Mr. Freeman secured one of the
big successes of the evening. Miss Florrie West, after telling
of somebody who 'wants another livener,' introduced her
Miss Tomboy impersonation with the song 'Who's coming
out to play? and romped in a way that seemed to be exactly
to the liking of a good many male admirers. Professor
Neiman gave what we suppose may be called appropriately
Valentine Vox's Christy minstrel show, and the fine singing of
Mr. Donnell Balfe was warmly cheered, the applause giving
evidence of the fact that a music hall audience will accept
something superior and refined when it is offered. Further
proof of this was afforded in the hearty reception given to
Miss Kate Chard, who to the programme contributed 'Love's
Old Sweet Song' and 'In Old Madrid.' Mr. Tom Costello
scored one hit with his impersonation of the tailor-made
masher, and another with an effort in a totally different
direction. His 'Comrades' is now well known, and is everywhere liked, and no wonder, seeing that Mr. Costello sings
it with marked feeling and expression. The pretty and dashing
Sisters Twibell gave with the customary chic their now well-
known medley of the most popular ditties of the day, and
followed this with a quaint Negro ditty with a very novel and
'fetching' dance. Mr. Sam Torr, in his merriest mood, gave
'Oh, won't it be joyful!' the 'it' relating to the time when all
policemen will speak the truth, when all jockeys will ride
straight, and when it will be lawful to take a wife for a month
on trial, his efforts being productive of much amusement.
Mr. Ben Nathan had to put up with considerable interruption
while delivering 'The Charge of the Light Brigade' according
to the lights of an Irishman, a Scotchman, a Frenchman, and
a London coster; but when the question was put the 'ayes'
had it, and he retired amid vociferous cheering. Chirgwin, the
musical Kaffir, hiding his white eye behind a Scotch hat as
large as a dining-room table, was very funny while he lasted,
but he didn't last half long enough. When suddenly he
disappeared, and it became evident that he would not return,
clamour arose, and did not cease until Mr. Ben Nathan at the
footlights had explained that Chirgwin was very unwell, and
that it was only at great inconvenience to himself that he had
been able to do anything at all. An 'extra turn' was supplied

by the Borani Brothers, whose tricks of contortion were
heartily applauded. Mr. M'Call Chambers having imitated
some of the dancers he had met at a ball, gave us 'The Village
Blacksmith' in dumb show, his pantomime being made
additionally eloquent by the assistance of the orchestra. An
exhibition of knockabout business by the Brothers Armstrong
created immense laughter, even the 'after me' enthusiasts
forgetting their chorus and roaring with merriment when,
one being found on fire, the other transformed himself into an
amateur fireman, fetched his engine and his watering-pot,
and proceeded to put out the conflagration. The Brothers
also did some marvellous things in the way of high-kicking.
Mr. J. W. Rowley started well with 'We drew his club money
this morning,' then gave a description of an Irish wedding in
a way that suggested a wonderful memory, and concluded with
the old, but still popular, 'Going to the Derby.' Even after
three songs the audience would have liked more from Mr.
Rowley, who at once 'caught on' with the Tivoli patrons.
Miss Jennie Williams, with flowing locks and pretty frocks,
offered flowers for sale, and tripped merrily and gracefully
on the light fantastic toe. Banjo playing in perfection was
exploited by the celebrated Bobee Brothers, and Miss Florrie
Leybourne, looking more charming then ever, revived with
lively choruses pleasant remembrance of her father, the late
popular comic vocalist, Mr. George Leybourne. The Brothers
James astounded the spectators with their extraordinary
gymnastic display, their chair feats fairly moving those present
to great enthusiasm. The bill was completed by the Sisters
Leyton, who danced well, and will please more with their
singing when they have learnt to sing harmoniously. The
attendance since the opening night has been enormous, and
already the directors are considering the propriety of converting the whole area into a luxurious lounge and of transferring
their humble patrons to the regions above. In the bill of the
week there have figured successfully, in addition to those
named above, The Sisters Levey, Miss Ella Dean, Mr. T. W.
Barrett, Tony Ryan, Lily Landon, and Mr. Charles Godfrey.

The new venture was not a success for some obvious reasons.
There was a court case and an auction arranged under a High

Court order to wind up the Company (it would seem that Barrett's Brewery forced the issue).

The property, as a going concern, was put up on 28 April 1891, but did not find a suitable buyer. *The Era* 2 May reported:

When Mr. William Joseph Hamnett, the auctioneer appointed by Mr. Justice Chitty, ascended his rostrum in Room D at the Mart, Tokenhouse Yard, E.C., on Tuesday afternoon, for the purpose of offering the Tivoli Theatre of Varieties for sale by auction, the room was uncomfortably crowded. Mr. Hamnett, confined his opening remark to a brief description of the property, the value of its position, the excellence of its building, and made no secret of its failure hitherto to attract the public. He said the place was built only a year ago at a cost of about £300,000, was freehold, and covered an area of nearly 8,000 feet. It was fitted up as a music hall in a most costly manner, and he had no hesitation in saying that it occupied a position second to none in the metropolis for the purpose for which it was erected. He was old enough to remember the Metropolitan, Edgware Road, being built and its early trials. He also pointed to the Alhambra and the Empire as instances of the great changes which had of late years come over the public mind with regard to such establishments, and as they were now realising splendid profits, there is no reason why the Tivoli should not be equally successful. It was useless to go into detail why the concern had been thrown into Chancery, nor would he discuss the reasons of its non-success. It might be due to over-capitalisation or to other causes. All he need say was that the Court had ordered its sale, and had fixed a sealed reserve price. In reply to questions, Mr. Hamnett said the ground rent of the small leasehold portion, chiefly covered by the staircase and lifts to restaurant, was £400 a-year, and the Marquis of Salisbury was the ground landlord. A representative of the Marquis's agent pointed out some slight flaw on the plan, and, having caused some irritation by his statement in reference to it, sat down. The bidding was commenced by Mr. T. Beard at £50,000, and rose rapidly to £100,000, at which sum it ceased. The auctioneer then opened the sealed envelope of the Court, and intimated that, as the reserve price had not been reached, the property would be withdrawn. A Bidder—What is the reserve? The Auctioneer—That is a modest question I cannot answer. For Lot 2, comprising the Salisbury Arms (3 and 4, Durham Street) and two dwelling-houses numbered 1 and 2 in the same street, no bid was made. We have been given to understand that the bid of £100,000 was made by Mr. Harrison, of Old Bond Street, and that since Tuesday the auctioneers have been offered by private treaty a considerably higher sum. Present at the sale we noticed Messrs. Sutton (Alhambra), Lake (Metropolitan), Robert Fort (proprietor of Theatre Royal, Margate), G. A. Payne (managing director of the Canterbury), James Kirk and C. H. Brighten (of the Oxford), Acton Phillips, sen. (Hammersmith Varieties), T. Beard, and Potter (Tivoli), A. Thioden, H. J. Didcott, L. Victor, G. W. Kenway, Herbert Sprake (Collins's), Captain Davis (late of Deacon's), C. Morton, Newson-Smith &c.

The Tivoli closed on 20 June and a new company was formed: The New Tivoli Limited. A fresh architect was given the task of re-modelling the front of the house and Charles Morton was called in as acting-manager to put the Music Hall on its feet. It re-opened on 4 July 1891. *The Era* of that date reported:

A wonderful transformation has been accomplished here by that well-known and popular theatrical architect Mr. Frank Matcham, and the habitués will hardly know the place again, so greatly has it been improved in its internal features, and so judiciously has it been re-decorated. Mr. Matcham has managed, by a few judicious alterations, and without inter-fering with the structural parts of the building, to very greatly improve the view of the stage from all sections of the house. The ventilation of the building has also been greatly improved, as Mr. Matcham has introduced a handsome sunlight of novel and effective design in the centre of the auditorium ceiling, from which a large foul air extract is carried outside the building. The electric lighting has been re-arranged, and a very complete scheme is the result. The lights are now distributed over the centre and sides of the ceiling, and are introduced in a very novel and effective way in the gallery and balcony fronts. Turning to the decorative features of the interior, it will be seen that considerable additions have been made to the fibrous plaster finishings and ornamentations, and that an effect of lightness and space has been gained by handsome mirrors on the walls. Use has been made of artistically designed and well-executed friezes and panels to heighten the general effect, and the whole of the auditorium has been re-decorated in gold and colour of a lighter and less severe style than before, the panels in front of the balcony ceiling being especially noticeable for their beautiful and artistic treatment. The entrances and saloons have been also thoroughly redecorated, but in different styles from the rest of the building—the balcony saloon being in Louis Quinze style, and the stalls saloon in Japanese. A special feature has been added by the introduction of a new arch over the proscenium opening, of Indian character and striking design. The whole of the interior has been entirely re-upholstered and re-furbished with luxurious carpets, tip-up seats re-covered with plush, artistically draped curtains and valances fixed to the boxes and principal entrances; the stage opening fitted up with handsome plush tableau curtains. The work has been carried out under the personal supervision of Mr. Matcham by the following well-known firms: Messrs. Campbell, Smith, and Co., the painted decorations; the Plastic Decoration Company, the fibrous plaster work; Messrs. Atkinson and Co., the upholstery and the rich draperies. The alterations are by Mr. Salter; the electric lighting by Mr. Harry South; and the new sunlight &c., by Messrs. Vaughan and Brown.

The following Saturday *The Era* reviewed the bill, after a description of the house:

We should, doubtless, have been able to give an equally enthusiastic account of the entertainment upon the stage had we enjoyed an opportunity of witnessing it; but we found, on presenting at the box-office the gilt-edged ticket which had been sent to us, that the courtesy of the management did not extend to the reservation of a seat. After a vain endeavour to see something of the artists on the stage through the serried rows of 'standing-room' patrons at the side of the stalls, we were thrown back upon the programme which we had purchased, and which informed us that the company engaged included Miss Effie Chapuy, Fred. Harvey, Ada

Reeve, George Beauchamp, Josephine Henley, Charles
Godfrey, the Two Macs. Minnie Thurgate, Albert Chevalier,
Ida Heath, the Brothers Horne, Jenny Hill, Prince Mignon,
Kara, Herbert Campbell, Fannie Marriott, Tom Costello,
J. W. Cheevers, the Eltons, Alice Maydue, Dutch Daly, the
Sisters Jonghmanns, Parker's performing dogs, and Revene
and Athas. Most of these artists we have recently seen at other
music halls, and we have every reason to hope that they
acquitted themselves at the Tivoli in a manner worthy of their
reputations. Mr. Angelo Asher directed a capital orchestra
in a capable manner that we have before praised, and towards
the close of the proceedings Mr. Morton answered a call to
the stage, and returned thanks for favours received.

After the false start all went well and the Tivoli became part of the
London music hall scene. Every star of the Golden Age appeared
on its stage until the decline began in the years just preceding the
first world war.

In 1910 some alterations were made when the buffet between the
main entrance hall and the restaurant were merged into the
theatre, making a new grand entrance hall and vestibule. Arches
were formed in the centre of the new hall, in Indian style, and the
grand circle saloon was decorated in the Louis XVI period.
Walter Emden, the original architect, was again called in and the
decorations were by J. M. Boekbinder.

On 7 February 1914 the Tivoli closed; a road widening scheme
necessitated re-building and plans were drawn up for the new
Music Hall to be ready for opening in the autumn. It was to have a
frontage in Adam Street, with the main entrance at the corner of
Adam Street and the Strand. The stage to be twice the size and
the capacity to be increased by fifty per cent. The rumbles of war
were in the air and plans were laid aside, and when hostilities
broke out in the autumn the old hall was left derelict. It was not
fully pulled down till 1916 when the whole island site was cleared.
Meantime it was used as a Recruiting Station for Kitchener's
Army. Then on the vacant site was built Beaver Hut, a temporary
structure to house the Canadian Y.M.C.A.

After the war a new Music Hall would have been an uncom-
mercial undertaking. The site was cleared in 1922 and the building
of a cinema, its frontage on the new line of the widened Strand,

was commenced by a company under the chairmanship of James White, to be leased to Metro-Goldwyn-Meyer. It covered the whole site and contained a Tivoli Dive Bar in the centre under the cinema retaining the old original licence. The architects were Bertie Crewe and Ganton and Ganton. On the opening night 6 September 1925 Kirkby Lunn sang the National Anthem and Little Tich, Malcolm Scott and Marie Dainton appeared before the film *Where the Pavement Ends* reviving memories of the music hall tradition of the old Tivoli.

The cinema suffered damage in the 1941 blitz and was not re-opened till 1943. In 1944 a memorial plaque to Marie Lloyd was unveiled in the foyer, presented by Sir Noel Curtis-Bennett. The cinema closed in 1957 and was demolished, in its place arose Peter Robinson's Department Store. A month after the new building was opened in August 1959, the plaque, rescued from the cinema, was re-dedicated by Bud Flanagan, keeping alive on the site the memory of The Tivoli Theatre of Varieties.

27
Toole's Theatre

The Lowther Rooms, The Polygraphic Hall, The Charing Cross Theatre, Theatre Royal, Charing Cross, The Folly Theatre

King William Street (now William IV Street)
Strand
In a triangular block bounded by Agar Street and Chandos Street with its stage door in Chandos Street

The Lowther Rooms, 1840, (used for lectures, masquerades, etc.)
Converted into the Polygraphic Hall, opened 12 May 1855, with *The Olio of Oddities*. An entertainment by E. L. Blanchard.
Under the management of W. S. Woodin.
Converted into a theatre and opened as the Royal Charing Cross Theatre, 19 June 1869, with *Coming of Age*, an operetta by Joseph Edwards Carpenter and E. L. Hime, followed by an opening address by E. L. Blanchard delivered by Madge Robertson, and *Edendale*, a drama in three acts by Charles Smith Cheltenam, concluding with *The Pretty Druidess; or, The Mother, the Maid and the Mistletoe Bough*, a burlesque by W. S. Gilbert.
Under the management of E. W. Bradwell and W. R. Field.
(The Royal was dropped from the name in 1872, but in 1874-5 it was advertised as the Theatre Royal, Charing Cross.
Re-constructed, re-decorated and name changed to the Folly Theatre and re-opened 16 October 1876, with a revival of *Man is not Perfect*, a comic drama by Benjamin Webster, followed by a revival of *Blue Beard*, a burlesque by H. B. Farnie.
Under the management of Alexander Henderson.
Re-constructed, enlarged and name changed to Toole's Theatre and re-opened 16 February 1882 with *Waiting Consent*, a comedietta by May Holt, followed by a revival of *Paul Pry*, a

comedy by John Poole and concluding with a revival of *Domestic Economy*, a farce by Mark Lemon.
Under the management of J. L. Toole.
Closed 28 September 1895.
Demolished the following year and the site absorbed into an extension (Out-Patients' Department) of the Charing Cross Hospital.

IN THE BUILDING SCHEME which re-constructed the western end of the Strand during the late eighteen-twenties and early eighteen-thirties, the area was re-planned and new streets constructed. Part of this re-development covered the ground behind St. Martin-in-the-Fields (making a new Adelaide Street) as far as Agar Street between Chandos Street and the Strand. This area was divided into two by the new King William Street (William IV Street). To the south, facing the Strand, a block contained, among other buildings, the Adelaide Gallery (later Gatti's Restaurant) and the Lowther Arcade (through the centre). There was a small room adjoining the arcade used for lectures and entertainments, in 1851 it called itself the Royal Music Hall, and eventually was used as an oratory by the Fathers of St. Philip Neri. This block still remains except for the central portion, re-built as Coutts Bank (see Number 11) and Gatti's, now the Nuffield Centre.

To the north a triangular site was formed, its apex at the top of Queen Adelaide Street, and bounded by Chandos Street, Agar Street and King William Street. Most of this was used to build the new Charing Cross Hospital in 1831, but a certain part of King William Street, at the eastern end, was covered by private houses and shop premises. One of these, Number 24, was rated in 1833 as a house, Club room and shop, but by 1840 it was calling itself the Lowther Rooms and Hotel. The notorious Blake's Masquerades were held here in the forties. In the early fifties a committee was formed, under the patronage of Lord Shaftesbury, to convert the property into a working men's club. There appears to have been a fair sized upstairs room which probably extended over several of the downstair properties. From time to time during its history various houses seem to have been merged together.

The first real history of the building, as a place of entertainment, comes in 1855 when William Samuel Woodin converted the premises into the Polygraphic Hall. Woodin, who had had a successful career as a ventriloquist, presenting his entertainment in various halls in London and the provinces, decided the time had come for him to establish himself in a permanent London home. *The Times* Monday, 14 May 1855 records his opening of the previous Saturday:

The new room which Mr. W. S. Woodin opened on Saturday bore every sign of established prosperity. It is situated in King William Street, Charing Cross, and has hitherto not been especially celebrated, but Mr. Woodin lifted it from obscurity by his own name, and the word 'Woodin,' written in gas above the door, marked out the house among less distinguished edifices. On entering, the visitor found himself in the presence of spacious stalls, clad in rich crimson velvet, and requiring that their occupants should be in full dress, an area in which the exigencies were less severe, and a row of handsome private boxes. Let us add that if he arrived after 8 o'clock he found all these places full, and might deem himself fortunate if he were allowed to stand by the door. The stage is even more striking than the salle, apparently supported, as it is, by craggy rocks, and decorated with rich hangings. Altogether, the whole thing denoted that Mr. Woodin was sure of his position, and could afford to construct, paint, and decorate for himself on a more costly scale than he had ventured on heretofore.

However, not only was the room new, but Mr. Woodin inaugurated it by a new entertainment, entitled the *Olio of Oddities*. His old entertainment called the *Carpet Bag and Sketchbook*, was, it may be remembered, in itself somewhat flimsy fare, and, though by his talent for impersonation and the quickness of his transformations he raised it to a popularity which few amusements of the sort have attained, we could constantly feel that all his salt was required to give flavour to so much insipidity. The lecturer, in fact, perpetually triumphed over his lecture. But the *Olio of Oddities* is a very different affair. It is smartly written throughout, and the types of character introduced are by no means of that hackneyed kind that looks like a perpetual reproduction of one of the late Mr. Mathews's old 'At Home' books. Moreover, the variety of personages introduced is exceedingly great, and this the author has attained, not by extending the entertainment, but by removing every character from the scene as soon as its pecularities are developed, and never pausing on an exhausted pleasantry. Formerly Mr. Woodin delighted his audience; and no one made any inquiry about the literary provider. Now, we feel that the author of the entertainment—Mr. E. L. Blanchard—merits some share of the acquired honours.

While Mr. Woodin is provided with better material to work upon he also displays great improvement on his own part. His former delineations were seldom more than amusing sketches, but his best characters in the new entertainment are highly-coloured portraitures, rendered the more remarkable by the shortness of the time during which each remains before the public eye. In the course of one song entitled a 'Chapter of Critics,' Mr. Woodin ducks his head under the table at intervals of about a minute in length, and after each duck rises as a new figure. First, he is a veritable portrait of Dr. Johnson, with dress, stomach, and voice all complete; then he is a slim, fashionable connoisseur of music, with large whiskers and eloquent shrugs; next he rises with a red beard and an Anglo-foreign aspect, to discourse technically on pictorial art; afterwards he is an occupant of some dress circle, who thinks Shakespeare 'slow' and adores the ballet; in another second, he is an old connoisseur of the pit, who mumbles over the palmy days of the drama; and lastly, he is a visitor to the one-shilling gallery, proud to patronize his favourite actor, quick to recognize a friend among the audience, and determined to enjoy everything. We did not test these personages by Sterne's stop-watch, but we shall go not far wrong in stating that they were all—the aggregate all— represented, both as to dress and characteristic peculiarity, in less than 10 minutes, and that the mechanical dexterity of the changes, admirable as it was, was the least meritorious part of the achievement. The traditional figure of Dr. Johnson and the nervous excitement of the London *gamin*, intoxicated not by ardent liquor, but by an overpowering sense of felicity, indicate a profound conception of character and a power of accurate delineation that are perfectly marvellous, when we take into consideration the number of directions in which they are employed, with scarcely a moment's interval. These 'Critics' are all half-length figures acted behind a table, but Mr. Woodin also introduces several completely-dressed figures, who step to the front of the stage, and excite wondering inquiry how they could have got their clothes on, and how Mr. Woodin, who has just been talking in his own (remarkably fashionable) coat and continuations, has so completely changed his age, dimension, and sex—one or all, as the case may be—that not a vestige of his former nature is visible to the eye. The ladies of such entertainments are generally rather caricaturish, and unwittingly betray a masculine foundation, but Miss Clara Chattaway, who is Mr. Woodin's chief heroine, is the complete *belle* of a modern room. The full dress, the ringlets, the smalltalk, the affected laugh, the manner in which she arranges herself at the piano, are all perfect.

We are not going through the long list of Mr. Woodin's personages, partly because it is a long list (including something like 50 changes), partly because we do not wish to destroy the charm of novelty to the future patrons of his performance. We will only remark that we are least satisfied with the character of an Astley's clown, with which he concludes the entertainment. In the first place, the necessity of a rapid change brings with it the necessity of a mask, which gives the figure a very lifeless apperance; and, in the second place, Mr. Woodin has previously shown that he can do so much better things that his amateur clownery, which is not to be compared with that of Mr. J. Robins, makes a somewhat pointless finale. If the Clown be transferred to an earlier part of the entertainment, and a little judicious weeding is employed here and there, the *Olio of Oddities* will be rendered perhaps the best characteristic monologue ever presented to a public.

He was to remain in possession of the New Hall giving seasons between his tours, for over ten years. When he was not in residence other one man entertainments and lectures occupied the hall and from time to time, it also became the home of many amateur dramatic performances. In September 1857 a ten month season of Raynor and Pierces' *Christy Minstrels* commenced, they returned from February to August 1860 and in 1864 the Matthews Brothers' *Minstrels* appeared.

It was eventually sold to Messrs. E. W. Bradwell and W. R. Field who also acquired adjoining houses and re-constructed the premises, turning them into a theatre which they opened as the Royal Charing Cross Theatre on 19 June 1869. *The Era* the following day reported:

Associated with a well-chosen title, which has the double advantage of never having been employed before in con-nection with a place of dramatic amusement, and of clearly indicating the locality in which the establishment is situated, another new Theatre was last evening added to the already greatly-extended list. The Charing Cross Theatre, of which Messrs. E. W. Bradwell and W. R. Field are the Lessees, is a handsome and commodious structure, occupying the site of the Polygraphic Hall, King William Street, Strand. The size of the new Theatre closely approximates that of the Strand, although it is estimated to hold a larger number of persons. There is no gallery. The auditorium comprises stalls, pit, dress circle, upper boxes, where bonnets can be worn, and eight private boxes, which are so arranged as to command a perfect view of the stage. The seats are roomy and spring-stuffed, covered in blue leather, and lifting up in the new approved method. The boxes are hung with blue satin damask, matched by the proscenium drapery, which is looped up with cords held up by female figures. The prevailing style of decoration is white and gold, with light tints, pale pink being most prominent. The general appearance of the house is exceedingly elegant, and more has been done to combine artistic with ordinary theatrical decoration than we have usually observed. The lunettes of the panels, most artistically painted in oil by Mr. T. Ballard, represent Music, Dancing, Acting, Poetry, Painting, and Sculpture. Ventilation is effectually secured by an ornamental dome of light perforated tracery, and from the centre of the ceiling is hung a handsome sun-light, with pendant glass. The size of the Theatre is about thirty feet from front to front of box rest, the height from floor to ceiling is about forty feet, and the opening of the proscenium twenty feet. All the staircases and approaches are either in stone or concrete, and ample accommodation has been provided for exit from each division of the house. The constructive portion of the work has been executed by Mr. C. N. Foster. The *carton pierre* and *papier mâché* ornamentation has been ably provided by the well-known firm of White and Co., of Great Marylebone Street, who have similarly furnished four other Theatres in the Metropolis. The general design and decoration, due to Mr. E. W. Bradwell, will be found to prominently exhibit the well-known inventive resources and refined taste of that experienced decorative artist; and the whole has been carried out under the supervision of the architect, Mr. Arthur Evers. A new act-drop, representing the Mall in St. James's Park at the time of Charles the Second, and c leverly painted by Mr. J. E. Meadows, completes the charming aspect of the interior, which, it may be here said, is admirably adapted to the conveyance of sound.

The programme for the opening night consisted of three new pieces, each of which obtained a most gratifying reception from the very appreciative and fashionable audience which filled the building in every part. At half-past seven the performances began with a lively little operatic sketch, written by the popular lyrist Dr. J. E. Carpenter, and composed by the well-known vocalist and musician Mr. E. L. Hime. The operetta, which is entitled *Coming of Age*, is obviously suggested by Frith's celebrated picture bearing the same name, and exhibited in the Royal Academy in 1849. The picturesque scene, painted by Mr. A. H. Groom, shows the group of dependants bringing the address of congratulation to the steps of the old Elizabethan mansion, where stands the future representative of the noble house just arrived at man's estate. The costumes, by Miss Thompson, and arrangements, under the efficient direction of Mr. T. W. Edmonds, formerly of the Princess's Theatre, are faithfully illustrative of the well-designed picture of the famous Academician. As a vehicle for some tuneful lyrics, the prelude is very pleasing, and the airs are likely to linger in the memory of the auditors. Mr. E. L. Hime, who conducted the operetta, was congratulated at the conclusion, and the curtain again rose responsive to the applause. The National Anthem was then sung by the whole of the company in a most creditable manner, the solos being taken by Miss Hughes and Miss Cicely Nott; whilst Mr. Stanley Betjemann and Mr. George R. Temple rendered the third verse conjointly, some of the occupants of the upper boxes evincing a strong desire to supply a choral accompaniment. After this Miss Madge Robertson came forward, and, after receiving an enthusiastic ovation, delivered amidst much applause the address, which had been written for the occasion by Mr. E. L. Blanchard.

Then followed a new and original three-act drama, by Mr. C. S. Cheltnam, entitled *Edendale*. The story of the piece, which is remarkably well written, is singularly slight, but it is full of interest, and has the special merit of breaking fresh theatrical ground. The working out of the slight story displays no less ingenuity than delicacy of treatment on the part of the dramatist, and the dialogue throughout is characterised by high literary merit. The performers, moreover, were excellently qualified for the parts assumed. The heroine, Ada, introduced Miss Ernstone (from the Manchester Theatre Royal), an actress of unquestionable power of intelligence, and who, in a character most difficult to personate effectively, quite won the sympathies and gained the warm approbation of the house. The future career of this young lady will be watched with interest. Miss Hughes, one of the most useful actresses a Manager could secure, threw much force and feeling into the pathos required from Mrs. Vandeleur, and it will be, perhaps, not disagreeable to the fair representative of the mother of Ada to say that the only deficiency was that of age. It required a vivid remembrance of the custom in Virginia of marrying at fifteen to believe that the honours of maternity could be fairly claimed in the manner shown. Miss Kathleen Irwin again delighted the audience by a bright, vivacious, and perfectly natural embodiment of the youth Ferdinand, whose boyish frankness and impetuosity was illustrated with excellent effect. Mr. J. G. Shore represented Esmond Fairholt with a manly dignity and spirit eminently characteristic, and especial praise is due to Mr. George R. Temple, who, in the last act, played the gentlemanly American, Jackson Goodchild, with an ease and buoyancy which brought this most complimentary illustration of transatlantic character

into a strong light. Mr. Flockton was efficient as the elderly
Colonel Vaudeleur, and Mr. W. Stacey was the Irish soldier,
Phil Magrath. The serious interest of the drama is agreeably
lightened by the clever performance of Miss Fanny Garth-
waite as Zoe, a Negro servant, and of Mr. R. Barker as a more
dissatisfied representative of the dark races. The scenes
between them, written with great point, were played without
the least exaggeration. Mr. Julien Hicks has placed a very
picturesque scene on the stage, and the appointments and
costumes are tasteful and appropriate. The applause was,
throughout, indicative of a genuine success, and the call for
the author brought Mr. Cheltnam upon the stage under much
more favourable circumstances than usually attend dramatists
who have to squeeze their way before the footlights. It was
past eleven before Mr. W. S. Gilbert's new, witty, and
eminently whimsical musical extravaganza could be brought
before the house; but the audience would not disperse until
they had enjoyed the concluding entertainment, and their
resolution was perfectly justified by the agreeable nature of
the result. *The Pretty Druidess; or, The Mother, the Maid, and
the Mistletoe Bough*, is a travesty of the story of the opera of
Norma. The story is perverted with great ingenuity, the lines
are as remarkable for correctness of rhythm as for their
abundance of puns, and the parodies are written with unusual
care to some of the prettiest melodies in the operatic and
lyrical repertory. Miss Hughes, who sings with admirable
skill and taste a grand scene, is excellent as the High Priestess
Norma; and Miss Kathleen Irwin completed her triumph of
the night by revealing herself as an accomplished vocalist no
less than a pleasing actress as the fair Adelgisa. Miss Cicely
Nott played Pollio, and sang her incidental music, notably a
parody on 'Rise, Gentle Moon,' with good effect; Miss Cruise
was diverting as Flavius; and Mr. R. Barker as the mysterious
Oroveso, who, on the restoration of his long-missing card-
case, discovers himself to be Julius Caesar, largely contributed
to the mirth of the audience. Although it was nearly half an
hour after midnight before the curtain fell, the jokes rattled
rapidly off through continuous laughter, and Mr. Gilbert at
the end was summoned to receive the congratulations of the
house. The entertainments, in short, gave the utmost satis-

faction to the audience, the talents of the company collected by the Lessees indicated the judgement with which the resources of Provincial Theatres had been estimated, and the first night of the Charing Cross Theatre had been pronounced an augury of a brilliant season, conveying the assurance of much future gratification being here in store for the London public, and of an adequate pecuniary reward being within reach of the Lessees.

The Theatre settled down to provide the mixed programmes of the light pieces which were then in vogue at the smaller theatres. The management of the theatre was in the hands of Edward Hastings for later seasons, and in 1872 the title Royal was dropped from the bills. Though the companies were first class, no new play of particular note was produced in these early years.

In November 1872 John S. Clarke became the proprietor and manager, an American, he left home to make his career in this country. He was married to the daughter of Junius Brutus Booth and was consequently brother-in-law to John Wilks Booth the assassin of Abraham Lincoln, a circumstance which he felt deeply and hoped would not be held against his work in this country. He achieved a big reputation in classical comedy and had a long run with *The Rivals* in this theatre. A press notice reprinted in the programme states:

> This theatre has undergone great alterations. These have been in excellent taste, and the house now is one of the prettiest in London. Its interior is as bright as may be, and the decorations have an unusually elegant and attractive effect. On the scenery, too, as well as before it, great pains have been bestowed and the manner in which the stage is turned to account reflects highest credit on the management. Those who have watched Mr. Clarke's career will not be surprised to find he has opened with a classical comedy. His preference for our older dramas has been marked. Almost all his successes have been in standard pieces, and we owe Mr. Clarke thanks for his systematic attempt to elevate the drama.
>
> *The Rivals*, at the Charing Cross Theatre, has passed its fiftieth consecutive performance—an event, without precedent, since no old comedy unaided by either burlesque or pantomime has achieved such a run.—*Sunday Times*, January 5.

Though he remained proprietor till 1876 he let the theatre to
other managers. (At times it was advertised as the Theatre Royal,
Charing Cross.) In 1874 Lydia Thompson and her husband
Alexander Henderson took the theatre and London saw H. B.
Farnie's burlesque *Blue Beard* for the first time. (She had played
it 470 times in America.) A programme note says:

> After an absence of six years, Miss Lydia Thompson returns
> from America, bringing with her the most gratifying evidences
> of her financial prosperity and the kindly and generous feeling
> entertained for her by every class of the community in that
> country. In response to the following very flattering invitation
> from all the leading Theatrical Managers in the United
> States, she will play one year more from next March a series
> of farewell engagements, commencing in Philadelphia previous
> to her final retirement from the stage.
>
> This arrangement enables Miss Thompson to appear for a
> short supplementary season in London, and she trusts to
> renew her old terms of popularity with a public by whom she
> was always so warmly encouraged from her first appearance
> as 'Little Silver Hair' at the Haymarket Theatre as a child
> of 11 years of age, up to the time previous to her departure to
> America.

In the company were also Lionel Brough, Alfred Bishop and
Willie Edouin. The following year Ada Cavendish was here in her
most famous character Mercy Merrick in a revival of Wilkie
Collins's *The New Magdalen*. The opera bouffe and comic opera
held the stage with Kate Santley. A French season with Déjazet
and burlesque under John Hollingshead's management bring the
story up to 1876 when Lydia Thompson returned from America
and her husband took over the theatre completely, re-christened
it the Folly Theatre, re-constructed and elaborately decorated it,
according to the 'grand opening night' programme on 16 October
1876. *The Era* 22 October said:

> Seeing that in again taking possession of the little house
> hitherto bearing a name derived from the locality (Charing
> Cross) in which it is situated Mr. Henderson has expressed
> his determination to 'shoot folly as it flies,' and to make the
> establishment the home of fun, we think he has been very

happy in the choice of a title. During the recess sundry marked improvements have been effected in the interior of the building under the able direction of Mr. E. W. Bradwell, the designs for reconstruction and decoration being furnished by Mr. Thomas Verity. The entrance to stalls and balcony has been much enlarged, and the comfort and convenience of the visitors thereby greatly promoted. A new act-drop has been furnished by Messrs. Grieve and Son, and, altogether, the house now presents a bright and attractive appearance.

The main attraction of the evening was a revival of *Blue Beard*. At the Christmas of 1876 another burlesque was produced: *Robinson Crusoe* also by Farnie. This was also a big success and Henderson continued to present opera bouffe and burlesque until 1879. His greatest success was with *Les Cloches de Corneville*, produced on 28 February 1878, it ran in all 705 performances (but not all were at this theatre). Lydia Thompson returned herself with *Stars and Garters* later in the year, and *Les Cloches de Corneville* moved to the Globe. She remained with a series of burlesques including *Tantalus; or, There's Many a Slip Twixt Cup and Lip* and *Carmen; or, Sold for a Song*, until March 1879.

The theatre was then taken by Selina Dalaro a 'Queen of Opera Bouffe' and among her successes were *La Périchole* by Offenbach.

In 1879 the theatre was leased by J. L. Toole. He opened with his company on 7 November with *A Fool and his Money* and a farce *Ici on Parle Français*.

John Lawrence Toole who, *The Dramatic Peerage* (1892) tells us:

. . . is the worthiest successor on the modern London stage to Wright and Buckstone, is the second son of the late James Toole, who for many years filled the appointment of Civic Toast Master, and was born within the sound of Bow Bells on March 12th, 1830, and educated at the City of London School, where he was distinguished by his powers of elocution. At the age of twenty he entered a wine merchant's office, but his tastes in life not being in accord with the quality of spirits dominant therein, he spent the greater part of his time at the City Histrionic Club, whose members frequently gave performances at the Walworth Institute and other similar places. On one of these occasions Charles Dickens was present, and was so delighted with the young city clerk's acting that he strongly advised him to adopt the stage for his profession. Acting on this good advice, John Toole left his desk and made his first appearance at the old Theatre at Ipswich, where a greater master than he, the great Garrick, first donned the buskin and ascended the stage. This *début* was in 1852, but Blanchard used to aver that he saw Toole make his real *début* when he came upon him one day, a chubby lad of six summers, in a farmyard at Erith, delighting a group of rustics. With pinafore tucked up and hat at the back of his head, he was taking off their country ways and mimicking the sounds of the farmyard in the drollest and most self-confident manner. After the Ipswich engagement ended, Toole gained experience, first under Charles Dillon at the Queen's Theatre, Dublin, and then at Belfast, Edinburgh and Glasgow. After this he opened his career on the London stage in 1854, at the St. James's Theatre, where he played the part of Pepys in *The King's Rivals*, and Weazle in *My Friend the Major*. At this time his old friend and manager Charles Dillon took the Lyceum, and invited Toole to join his company during his season there, which he did for a time, but when Benjamin Webster opened the Adelphi he migrated to that house, and played the first comedian leads in the plays produced there. In 1874 Toole starred the United States, having by this time achieved for himself a great reputation, and on his return to London joined for a while the Gaiety Theatre Company. Five years later he became lessee of the Folly Theatre, and started on a career of management, which made for its owner fame and fortune. [He left nearly £80,000 when he died in 1906.] His gray, twinkling eyes watch contemporaneous life closely, and his fertile brain draws inspiration from the world around him. His acting is marked by a fidelity to life, which is predominant in every character he portrays, whether it be in the broad region of farce or in those more important parts where tears and laughter find alternate abode. Funny on the stage beyond comparison, he is equally so off its boards, and has fathered more jokes and witticisms than a dozen volumes could record. In private life he is kind and very warm-hearted, and in his vast circle of friends, which include all classes of society from Royalty downwards, he has not a truer one than his brother actor Henry Irving. Following the fashion, Toole published in 1888 his reminiscences, which are as interesting as they are amusing.

When Toole took over the Folly Theatre and became a manager, his rules for the ladies and gentlemen of his company were set forth on a printed notice displayed at the stage door; it read as follows:

REGULATIONS:

Punctuality at Rehearsal.

Rehearsal Calls and Notices to be placed in the Hall Lobby.

Ten Minutes grace allowed after Call at First Rehearsal.

Each person should be at the Theatre every night sufficiently long before the commencement of the Performance to allow ample time for Dressing.

Each Member of the Company under-studying a part to be in the Theatre at Seven o'clock each evening.

No one to stand in the Prompt Place.

No one to stand at the Wings during the Performance.

The Business as arranged at the last Rehearsal to be strictly adhered to.

All Parts are to be returned within one week after the production of the Piece.

Smoking is absolutely prohibited in every part of the Building.

Members of the Company never to be in the Box Office.

The Address of every Member of the Company is to be entered in the Address-Book at the Stage Door.

No Member of the Company to sit in front of the House during Rehearsal.

Any applications for Free Admissions to be made to the Manager.

The Theatre Time is the Stage Clock.

No one to perform elsewhere, except by special permission.

No Stranger to be admitted behind the Scenes under any circumstances, or to be in any of the Dressing Rooms without permission.

All complaints to be made to Mr. George Loveday.

Mr. Toole will be glad to hear any suggestions with regard to the comfort of the Members of his Company.

There are no Fines of any kind, as Mr. Toole trusts to the *esprit de corps* of the Folly Company to carry out his wishes.

His management proved a success, and his next new production was H. J. Byron's comedy *The Upper Crust*, which was to remain in his repertoire for the rest of his career. After a revival of *Dot* a stage version of Dickens' *Cricket on the Hearth*, in 1880 and some now forgotten pieces, he went on tour, leaving R. C. Carton to present a Summer season in 1881, with his wife Katherine Compton and himself in *Imprudence*, the first comedy written by Pinero. When the season finished the theatre remained closed until 16 February, 1882 when it re-opened as Toole's Theatre. This was the first theatre in London to follow the American habit of calling itself after its actor-manager or owner (see Terry's Theatre Number 23). It held between 650 and 700 people. The new laws introduced for the public safety had caught up with the theatre and re-construction had become necessary. The opening was described in *The Era* 18 February:

On Saturday last the eminent and deservedly popular comedian Mr. J. L. Toole invited a number of his friends to inspect the alterations that have converted the old 'Folly' into the new 'Toole's' Theatre, and to pass judgment on the decorations and embellishments and the other aids to comfort and enjoyment that have been provided by means of a liberal outlay. They met with the approving verdict of all whose privilege it was to attend; the spacious vestibule, the elegant *foyer*, the beautifully decorated staircases, the broad exits and entrances, and the convenient verandah without meeting with special commendatory remark. The verdict thus pronounced was most cordially endorsed on Thursday evening by the large audience that assembled to lend *éclat* to the opening, to enjoy the amusing programme that had been selected, and by enthusiastic cheers to give the popular lessee that encouragement which by his enterprise, his liberality, and his talent he has so fully merited.

The opening item in the bill was the comedietta, in one act, by May Holt (Mrs. Fairbairn), called *Waiting Consent*. This little and amusing piece, which has already been favourably received in the provinces, was very well played by Miss Ada Mellon, Mr. Elmore, Mr. E. D. Ward, and Mr. G. Shelton, the last-named making a decided hit as a comic waiter re-joicing in the name of Scorcher. The comedietta was followed

by the comedy, in three acts, by John Poole, called *Paul Pry*.
How Mr. Toole plays the inquisitive hero of this comedy all
the laughter-loving world knows. On his first entrance, made
up in that fashion that must be familiar, his apologetic query,
'I hope I don't intrude,' was followed by a roar of acclamation
that must have been as sweet music to his ears, and must have
convinced him once more of the firmness of the hold he has
on the goodwill of London playgoers. The busybody who will
be in all that is going on, who will interfere with what does
not concern him, and who, while prying and poking his nose
into the affairs of other people, works so much mischief, and
yet, when reproached, thinks himself the victim of base
ingratitude, and affirms from time to time that he will never
again attempt to do anybody a service, has never had a more
amusing representative than Mr. Toole, and it will suffice
now to say that, on Thursday evening, whenever he was upon
the stage, the house was fairly convulsed with hilarity.

At the end of the comedy Mr. Toole stepped to the footlights, and, when the further hearty cheering that greeted him
had subsided, he proceeded to fulfil the promise held out
by the programme, that he would 'say a few words to his
friends.'

He said—

'Ladies and gentlemen, I am reminded by the programme
that at this stage of the evening's entertainment I am to have
a few words with you, but I hope they will not be disagreeable
ones on this occasion of your first visit to me in my new home.
Excuse me if I am personal, but I think you are all looking
very well. In fact, I never saw you looking better, and I really
think that you will always look better in this theatre than in
any other, and I hope you will come often, for the oftener you
come the better looking you will be. I confess I am rather
fond of company. I have, as you know, engaged one. Some
prefer to call it a staff, though why they should be called a
'staff,' when there is not a stick among them, I do not know.
I've had so much to do in preparing this little temple for
your reception that I have not really had leisure to study
speeches, and so must say just the few words that come to me.
If any of you have any complaints—I am not referring to
indisposition—I am sure I shall always be ready to receive

v

and give them attention. I have done what I can. You see what I have done for the pit. I hope to pit this little theatre against any in London. There is the new *foyer*, which I need hardly say I have had constructed expressly *for yer*. A friend who was here on Saturday observed that my ceiling whacks most ceilings. Then he had a good look at my stairs, and, as I don't mind your having a stare at my good looks, I shall not, of course, object if you do the same. Let me invite your attention to the large number of my doors. It is not perhaps an agreeable subject, but I may here say that I have made, with the valuable aid of my friend Mr. J. J. Thompson, the architect of the house, arrangements that will enable you all to get out in the street in a moment whenever you wish. The exits are indeed so many that really there is almost an exit apiece for you; and not only have I provided against fire, I have protected you against water—I mean rain water—by that extensive verandah which you have seen outside. Ladies and gentlemen, I wish I could convey to you what I have felt in receiving all the kindly messages and congratulatory telegrams both from private friends and public personages which have reached me to-night—among the former Mr. Byron, Mr. Henry Irving, Mr. Sims Reeves, and numerous others. As regards the future, we are now rehearsing a new piece by Mr. Byron, and others are arranged for with Mr. Robert Reece and Mr. Burnand. And now, let me thank you once more for all your kindness present and past. I am proud of the kindly association between us, and let me assure you that it will be my endeavour to the end to add to the friendly feeling that exists between myself and the public.'

Mr. Toole, on retiring, was greeted with more enthusiastic applause, and presently returned to delight those who remained with his comical portraiture of John Grumley, in the broadly-sketched farce, in one act, by Mark Lemon, called *Domestic Economy*. The house roared and roared again over the difficulties of the husband who fancies that he can do the domestic work and mind the shop better than his wife, and for ourselves we confess that it is not often we have such good cause for merriment as we found here. All the others engaged worked admirably, and if laughter and enthusiasm are worth anything we may say that on this occasion they were suggestive

of the great success which thousands now hope will attend
Mr. J. L. Toole in 'Toole's Theatre.'

How necessary were these new precautions for safety was proved
the following month when, at the first performance of the next
production, *The Era* 18 March reported that:

> The first night's performance was interrupted by an accident
> which happily was not attended by any serious results.
> During the second act, on Monday, some burning was
> suddenly observed in the canvas of the back of the scene—a
> closed-in dining-room interior. With excellent presence of
> mind Mr. John Billington instantly assisted the efforts of the
> fireman at the theatre behind in beating out the fire and
> tearing away the smouldering portion, and this was accom-
> plished in a few seconds. Though there was at first sight some
> little cause for alarm, the audience kept their seats with
> commendable composure; and greeted with loud applause
> Mr. Toole's assurance that there was 'no danger,' and that if
> there were, 'seven or eight fire-engines were always at hand in
> case of necessity.' Thereupon the performance proceeded
> without further interruption. The accident we learn arose
> from a slight leakage of gas at the screw joint of one of the
> pipes, which, igniting, formed a jet of flame extending beyond
> the protection of the wire 'battens,' and thus coming in
> contact with the back of the scene.

For the next thirteen years Toole appeared at his theatre for long
seasons, and in between other managements took the theatre
while he was on tour in the provinces. He also went to Australia
from February 1890 till the spring of 1891. His plays were those
he had made famous during his earlier years, and new farces,
burlesques and light comedies by authors such as Pinero, F. C.
Burnand, Herman Merivale and J. M. Barrie (whose *Walker,
London* was produced in 1892). Visiting companies included
Daly's from New York in 1884.

Toole maintained a good stock company, and many newcomers
had their early opportunities under his management, including
Seymour Hicks, Irene Vanbrugh, Eva Moore and Mary Brough.

In 1895 Toole, who had become a sufferer from gout, was
forced to give up for a time. His last new play *Thoroughbred* by

Ralph R. Lumly opened 13 February 1895 and he had to leave the cast the following week. His understudy played for a short time and the play closed. He re-opened on 3 September and it was announced that he would 'play a brief season of four weeks, at the end of which time his lease of the theatre expires.'

The theatre had been bought by the Governors of Charing Cross Hospital for eventual expansion and the L.C.C. were demanding alterations. The theatre closed on 28 September. The last night is described in *The Era* 5 October 1895:

On Saturday evening was given the last performance under Mr. Toole's lesseeship, and on this special occasion the pieces selected for representation were the recent success, Mr. Ralph R. Lumley's *Thoroughbred*, and the old favourite *The Birthplace of Podgers*. In both pieces Mr. Toole acted with much spirit, and his humour proved to be as rich and effective as ever. The reception accorded him was enthusiastic in the extreme. He was again and again recalled, and at the conclusion of the performance he spoke as follows:

'Ladies and Gentlemen,—I can only do what I have so often done—thank you for the very friendly and generous way in which you have received the ladies and gentlemen of my company and myself. I am giving up this theatre, as my lease expires to-night. I rebuilt it fourteen years ago at considerable cost, and I am not inclined to make another large outlay on alterations. I start on Monday for a tour of the principal cities for a few months, and shall visit Newcastle, Glasgow, Edinburgh, Dundee, Aberdeen, Inverness, Peterhead, Brechin, Perth, Liverpool, Manchester, Dublin, Cork, Belfast, Limerick, and Chester. After Christmas my movements are a little uncertain. Some friends have said that I produced *Thoroughbred* in order to prepare myself as a Nigger for an engagement on Margate sands, but I assure you this is not so. The last week I have been favoured with visits from two delightful actresses—Mrs. Keeley and Mrs. Alfred Mellon. Had I been able to induce them to return to the stage, I would have altered my line of business, and studied Romeo and Claude Melnotte, as it would have given me the greatest happiness to have made love to both those dear ladies. I have acted in most of the American, Australian, and New Zealand theatres, but oddly enough I have not explored the suburbs of London. I think of having a tour round London, and visiting Islington, Camberwell, Croydon, Hammersmith, Ealing, Stratford, Kilburn, Holloway, &c., provided I get engagements. I've already had some friendly offers. One gentleman wrote and said if I was disengaged he could give me a situation as flute or a tambourine player in the orchestra; but I think I should prefer the drum, that being an easier instrument to study. But wherever I may be my card will most likely be on the walls, and I sincerely hope, like Paul Pry, you will just drop in and see me. With my heart of hearts I thank you for all your loving kindness.

Toole toured until the following year, then retired to Brighton where he died on 30 July, 1906.

In the same paper the next week the following paragraph appeared:

Toole's Theatre has not yet been disposed of by its owners, the Governors of Charing Cross Hospital. Mr. Toole's lease was at a low rental, but he spent several thousand pounds in improving the property, and the 'requisitions' of the London County Council will cost, if they are carried out, at least another £3,000. The Beefsteak Club, which occupies the top floor of the theatre, has been granted a yearly tenancy by the Hospital.

No new tenant willing to spend the necessary amount turned up, and a proposed re-building to plans by C. J. Phipps fell through. The L.C.C. notified the Lord Chamberlain and the Licence for theatrical performances was withdrawn, a manoeuvre which seems to have satisfied both the L.C.C. and the Hospital, who needed the site for an extension.

A paragraph appeared in the press in February 1896:

Toole's Theatre is condemned at last, not only by the London County Council, who impose 'requirements' that would cost as much as its real rental value, but by its owners, the Charing Cross Hospital, who, after enduring its existence in one form or another for nearly forty years, and drawing a good annual income from its occupants, have at last announced that it is a dangerous and unsatisfactory adjunct of their hospital property. As a matter of fact it never was a theatre except in name, and had all the vices of a small, inconvenient building, tinkered from time to time into the resemblance of a playhouse. Under many names it succeeded in getting a succession of energetic tenants by virtue of its central position and the scarcity of better theatres. When comic opera and burlesque were the staple of its entertainment, the dressing-room accommodation must have defied every rule of decency, in spite of Lord Chamberlains' and municipal regulations.

In the spring of 1896 the theatre was pulled down, the Out-Patients' Department of the new extension to the hospital now covers the site.

28
The Trocadero
Palace of Varieties

New Private Subscription Theatre, The Royal Albion Theatre, The New Queen's Theatre, The Theatre of Arts, The Argyll (Subscription) Rooms, The Royal Trocadero and Eden Theatre, Trocadero Restaurant

Great Windmill Street

Tennis court and vaults built 1744 by Thomas Higginson. Later used for miscellaneous entertainments, exhibitions and private subscription theatrical performances, under various names.
Re-constructed and opened as the Argyll Subscription Rooms, October 1849.
Under the management of Robert Bignell.
Closed 30 November 1878.
Re-constructed as a Music Hall, The Trocadero Palace of Varieties.
Opened 30 October 1882.
Under the management of Robert Bignell.
Closed 24 February 1894.
Converted into the Trocadero Restaurant with the addition of premises in Shaftesbury Avenue and opened 5 October 1896.
Became Tiffany's, July 1965.

THE HISTORY OF the ground on which the Trocadero music hall stood is given in the *Survey of London*, volume 31. We find there that 'in 1744 John Cartwright of the Parish of St. James's, gentleman, leased a plot of ground on the east side of Windmill Street (later Great Windmill Street) to Thomas Higginson of St. Giles in the Fields, gentleman, for ninety-nine years. The lease was granted in consideration of the charges and expenses which Higginson "hath already been put to in erecting and building the Tennis Court and Vaults" which were then nearing completion. The ground had a frontage of 49 feet and a depth of 116 feet.' This ground had previously been occupied by half-a-dozen small cottages and was to become numbers 7-9.

Thomas Higginson remained in possession until 1761 and was followed by other tenants, Mary Rogers, James Ashley, Robert Handy, William Quentery and William Tyler, and presumably they all carried on the building as a Tennis Court.

During the eighteen twenties and thirties the building was used as a circus, a theatre, and for miscellaneous exhibitions and entertainments.

In January 1822 Senior Christopher Lee Sugg, a conjuror and ventriloquist gave 'A Display of the wandering sounds, after the manner, by which, in the year Anno Domini 1264, Pope Celestimus and Pope Boniface caused great tumults. The former being frightened out of his Popedom by the latter's power of ventriloquy.'

The following year the Lord Chamberlain allowed Charles Adams 'to have Horsemanship and Rope Dancing for his Benefit at the Tennis Court' for four weeks. By 1829 the premises were 'a house, tennis court and billiard room' and the next year, according to the Rate Books, part of the premises was converted into a theatre, the New Private Subscription Theatre.

Cooke's Royal Circus was there in 1831, and in December 1832 calling itself The Royal Albion Theatre, burlettas, farces and dramas were being performed by subscription to evade the licensing laws, no money being taken at the doors. By the end of 1833 there was a new regime and name, the New Queen's Theatre, with W. Elliott as proprietor; who had been turned out of the Queens Theatre in Tottenham Street (see *Theatres of London*). Though he had a temporary licence, the threat of closure by order of the Patent theatres was always hanging over the premises.

Between 1833 and 1835 it changed its name back and forth between the Queen's and the Albion, and for a time in November 1834 was the Theatre of Arts. The entertainments and the artists concerned were of no importance and have left little trace of their presence on the theatrical scene. In August 1835 the Lord

Chamberlain's attention was drawn, by an informer, to a season given by Sarah Booth of Covent Garden Theatre, and the Magistrates stepped in and closed the theatre, and in December Cooke's Circus was again in residence.

The rooms sunk to being used for boxing displays, Leigh's *New Picture of London* (1841), talks of 'Sparring, which is boxing in gloves, takes place at the Tennis Court, Windmill Street, Haymarket. The exhibitions are previously advertised, and the price of admission is generally 3s.'

The 'Theatrical' interior (most likely, according to a picture, an elaborate fit-up), was probably dismantled at the time of the closure in 1836.

In the next decade mechanical wax works and a 'grand centrifugal railway' were shown by John Dubourg, who in 1846 called the building Dubourg's Theatre of Arts, later for *Tableaux Vivants* he called it the Ancient Hall of Rome.

The original lease was due to expire and the freehold was bought by Sir John Musgrove in 1842, and in 1849 he leased the rooms to Robert Bignell, a wine merchant, who had been associated with Musgrove, probably using the vaults of the original building.

In partnership with Bignell were George French Bryer and Charles Emile Laurent. They re-decorated and partially re-built the rooms and opened them as Assembly rooms called the Argyll Subscription Rooms. (Not to be confused with the more famous Argyll Rooms in Argyll Street, Regent Street, which closed down in 1830.)

Laurent became the first lessee, he lived in Brompton and the other two partners resided on the premises. Bryer soon left the partnership and Laurent ran the Rooms for Bignell who at this time was concerned with several other business and family problems.

An advertisement in *The Times* in 1850 gives an idea of the kind of entertainment provided (by then the word subscription had been dropped).

ARGYLL ROOMS, Great Windmill Street, St. James's, licensed pursuant to Act of Parliament; sole lessee Charles Emile Laurent, 57, Brompton Square.—LAURENT'S SOIREES MUSICALES and DANSANTES OPEN every evening, with his celebrated and unrivalled band. Principal *cornet à piston*, M. Boulcourt from Paris, artiste attached to M. Strouss's orchestra at the baths of Vichy, France. Admission 1s. Doors open at half-past 8. Dancing to commence at 9, and terminate at half-past 11 precisely. N.B. Due notice will be given of the first series of concerts that will take place at the above rooms.

Though all sounded respectable on the surface, the rooms soon began to gain a dubious reputation, Henry Mayhew in *London Labour and the London Poor* (1862) notes it as a centre for prostitution. In 1863 Bignell became sole proprietor. He had the rooms completely re-decorated by Dellicort of Paris and re-opened on 5 September. The following year he acquired the freehold, two extra rooms were added and the building re-fronted, in all he is said to have spent £40,400.

W. H. Holden in *They Startled Grandfather* (1950) quotes the London Correspondent of *The New York Times*, D. J. Kirwan, on a visit he paid to the Argyll Rooms:

Where he paid a shilling for admission and found himself 'in a carpeted room, handsomely and tastefully furnished and decorated'. The saloon was a large one, lit up with splendid chandeliers, and in the gallery was a band of fifty musicians in evening dress. 'Women, dressed in costly silks and satins and velvets, the majority of them wearing rich jewels and gold ornaments, are lounging on the plush sofas in a free and easy way, conversing with men . . . and, as no virtuous woman ever enters this place, there is no danger of meeting those who own a sisterly or still dearer tie . . . Across the lower end of the room an iron railing is stretched, and this keeps the vulgar herd from mingling with the élite of the abandoned women who frequent the Argyle.' The bars were furnished with great splendour, the calls for champagne were incessant, and the women called the champagne 'fizz' and the ale 'swill'.

To the right of the gallery bar was 'a handsomely fitted up alcove', on which were painted pictures of Europa and the Bull, Leda, and Bacchus and Silenus; and here Mr. Kirwan espied 'a stout, florid-faced woman, vulgar in appearance, with incipient moustachios at the corners of her lips. She is covered with jewellery, and her fingers, fat, red, and unshapely, glitter with diamonds. This was the famous Kate Hamilton, who was at one time the reigning beauty of her class, and had now degenerated into a vile pander. She is surrounded by a cluster of girls, and they are all in animated discussion with her'. Mr. Kirwan was introduced to Kate, whose first question was: 'Will you stand some "Sham"?' and the next, to enquire after some New York politicians and sporting men who had patronised her own night house. 'While we are standing looking at her and her friends, the room is darkened, the gas being almost extinguished, and a chemical, light-coloured flame irradiates the room like a twilight at sea, and the entire female population rush below to join in the last, wild, mad shadow-dance of the night. Around and around they go in each other's arms, whirling in the dim, uncertain, grave-yard light, these unclean things of the darkness, shouting and shrieking, totally lost to shame—their gestures wanton as the movements of an Egyptian Almee and mad as the capers of a dancing dervish.

Bignell himself seems to have led quite a life after he lost his first wife in 1849. He found a young girl, Kathleen Crouch, and in 1858 took her to Paris on a visit, from which she did not return, becoming notorious as 'Cora Pearl'. She was followed by Sarah Squirer, promoted from maid to mistress (one of their two daughter's descendents was to sell the freehold of the building to J. Lyons in 1921). It was not surprising that the authorities received complaints, and for a short time Bignell lost his licence. He was continually being warned; at length in October 1878 he was raided by the police, and lost his licence completely.

The Argyll Rooms finally closed on 30 November 1878. The last years and closure are described by H. G. Hibbert in *A Play-goer's Memories* (1920), he says:

In the seventies the Argyll Rooms was like a modern night club, without its perfunctory condition of election to member-ship. You just bought a ticket and went in—to mix with the *demi-reps* and the *demi-mondaines* who danced and drank till morning, to the accumulation of a vast fortune for its last proprietor, one Bignell. Several times he was threatened with the loss of his licence, and at last it went. The golden youth contemplated a lusty last night, but there was no last night.

As the hour for the function approached the police formed a cordon round Windmill Street and drove back the angry roisterers.

Bignell, who had pleaded previously the loss of his licence 'would have been the total ruin of myself and family' was not quite ruined when the blow fell, but must have, as *The Era* said in 1882 'suffered a very great loss, seeing that his attempts to run the place as a restaurant and as a Billiard Saloon met only with failure'. He then hit on a brilliant idea; he converted the rooms into a Music Hall to seat 600 and applied for a licence, which was granted. Under its new name, The Trocadero Palace of Varieties, it opened on 30 October 1882.

The Era 4 November, 1882 records this event:

This establishment, the latest addition to the music halls of the metropolis, was opened on Monday evening, and, as was anticipated, there was an immense audience assembled, in spite of unpropitious elements, and evidently gratified at being able to 'assist' at the inauguration of a new style of entertainment in a building which, under another name, must be known at least by report throughout the civilised world.

The interior of the building has been entirely remodelled and redecorated at considerable expense, and it is evident that every effort will be made to secure the comfort, as well as to promote the enjoyment, of all who may be tempted to patronise the place by the excellent entertainment placed upon the handsome stage, which has been erected at that end of the building where a band of picked musicians, in the years gone by, were wont to discourse sweet sounds, inviting to waltz and schottische and galop. Music is not to be neglected now, and we are pleased to be able to state, at the outset, that there is engaged a very capable orchestra, which gave Monday's throng a taste of its quality by a very fine performance of a selection from *Lucrezia Borgia*. So important an event as the re-opening of so famous a place could not be allowed to pass without a display of loyalty, and thus the vocal portion of the proceedings was started with the National Anthem, led by 'the Sims Reeves of the music halls,' Mr. Alexander Lumsden, enthusiastic cheering attending. That old and esteemed

favourite Mr. Jonghmans had a most cordial greeting, and
fairly electrified his audience by his fine, spirited, and really
artistic rendering of 'The Gallants of England' and the
'Toreador' song from *Carmen*. Miss Marie Gilchrist found
ready favour in her clever transformation dances, to which
we have repeatedly referred in terms of commendation. Her
changes of costume and character are effected with surprising
rapidity, and the honours attending her were certainly well
earned. Mr. and Mrs. Ranson proved somewhat tame and
uninteresting as comic duettists; as, too, did Mr. H. Leander,
whose so-called comic songs were slightly dismal; but there
was plenty of good material to atone for these drawbacks.
Miss Ada Izon sang with considerable spirit 'I wish you'd
change your mind' and a battle song, in which she appeared
to be very anxious that somebody should 'Let the trumpet
sound' and proclaim the glory of our arms in Egypt. The
three Brothers Le Fre, in their rivalry for the favour of a damsel rejoicing in the name of Betsy, displayed much agility;
as did the Kellino troupe in their clever acrobatic display, the
concluding feature in which the adult of the party balances
and whirls round a couple of youngsters seated at the end of
the long pole which he supports on the soles of his feet calling
forth great applause. Messrs. Vern and Volt contributed an
amusing Nigger sketch, one of these gentlemen contriving to
get much fun out of a pair of skates. Miss Patti Heywood,
in her customary dashing style, sang 'Get away!' 'That is the
fellow, I'm sure!' and 'What my love is like,' accompanying
the last-named with some neat dancing. Messrs. Geraghty
and Gilligan introduced imitations, faithful and otherwise, of
certain popular music hall artists; and there was abundant
admiration for the 'Royal Infants,' the Misses Temple and
Frampton. On Monday there was quite a *furore* occasioned
by the stalwart proportions and beautiful dresses of these
ladies; but on Tuesday, although they met with favour, there
was no unseemly demonstration or interference with the
business of the artists who followed. These were the Four
Eccentrics. They are well named. The most remarkable of the
four is a long, lean gentleman, who seemed able to look into
first-floor windows, and to play with the tops of lofty trees.
He indulges in a boxing match with a very small and ill-

shapen Nigger, and the result is most laughable. The victory
is not all on the side of the giant, for the dwarf is so elastic of
leg that he actually contrives to get at his opponent's cheek
with the sole of his boot. All four gentlemen are wonderfully
agile, and we give up the impossible task of describing the
extraordinary antics in which they indulge, and content ourselves with saying that to see them is to wonder and to roar
with irrepressible laughter. Miss Marie Loftus took favour
by storm in her cleverly rendered song 'I'm so shy.' The
Bictorellis displayed their versatility by excellent playing on
guitar and concertina and by some skilfully executed acrobatic
feats. M. Zidney introduced some good feats of jugglery, and
scored a great success in his barrel dancing display. Mr. J. H.
Milburn sang acceptably of 'Romping in the Clover,' and
danced in his own peculiar fashion; and among others contri-
buting to the long and liberal programme were the Murray
Quartette, vocal comedians and dancers; the Sisters Belverne,
comic duettists; and Mr. Abbott and Miss Amy, vocalists
and dancers. The management, we should add, has been
intrusted to Mr. H. Hart, who is ably assisted by Mr. Charles
Merion; and the excellent orchestra is under the direction of
Mr. A. A. Asher.

Despite an auspicious opening the hall did not prosper; its biggest
success came in 1886 when Charles Coburn sang 'Two Lovely
Black Eyes', which drew London for fourteen months. By this time
the re-development of the top end of the Haymarket, where it
joined Tichborne Street, (which vanished with the enlargement of
Regent Circus into Piccadilly Circus) and the construction of
Shaftesbury Avenue were well under way.

The original London Pavilion was pulled down in 1885 and
re-built further back, Great Windmill Street was cut in two and
the Trocadero found itself in a little short street facing the side
of the new London Pavilion, and with a corner building between
it and the new Avenue.

In 1888 Bignell died and his trustees let the Music Hall to
Sam Adams, who had run the London Pavilion. He continued
with more success until he too died in 1893. The famous music
hall agent, Hugh Jay Didcott, in partnership with Albert
Chevalier, then took over until 24 February 1894 when their

company went bankrupt, and they closed. Several slight changes of name occurred during its short career including the Royal Trocadero and Eden Theatre.

In 1895 Bignell's daughter sold a ninety-nine year lease to J. Lyons and Co., who converted it into a restaurant. They gradually acquired the adjoining properties on the corner of Shaftesbury Avenue, and then the whole block (Avenue Mansions) stretching up Shaftesbury Avenue. They opened up party walls between the old Music Hall and their new acquisition making them into one large Trocadero Restaurant with its main entrance in Shaftesbury Avenue, re-fronting the old hall to match the existing buildings. By 1902 the project was complete and in 1921 Lyons acquired the freehold from Bignell's grand-daughter.

Early in the twenties Lyons were pioneers, at the Trocadero, of entertainment during meal-time, and in 1924 they engaged Charles B. Cochran to present Cabaret, in the Grill Room, which comprised substantially what had been the Music Hall.

Cochran 'Supper Time' Revues, under various titles, were a big success, with popular variety acts and 'Mr. Cochran's Young Ladies' in residence. Old favourites re-appeared, including Ada Reeve, Massine danced in ballet, and Anna Neagle (then Marjorie Robertson) was 'discovered' as a dancer. In October 1936 Charles Coburn returned to the scene of his triumph, and with Wilkie Bard and the daughters of Little Tich and Marie Lloyd, to celebrate the fortieth anniversary of the Trocadero Restaurant. With war time interruptions, Charles Cochran remained to provide a cabaret for the Golden Jubilee in 1946.

Changed tastes and dining habits brought about the decline of the restaurant by the fifties and Lyons sold a lease to Mecca Ltd., who re-opened the restaurant in July 1965 as Tiffany's, for dancing and light meals: 'The most excitingly romantic place in town.' Later a Casino was added and the Grill Room became a bowling alley. Another chapter in the long history of entertainment on the site began.

Appendices

Architects of the Lost Theatres of London

The numbers are those of the theatres in the main section where further details of interior decoration, etc., are to be found

1 THE ALHAMBRA THEATRE

1854 The Panopticon, T. Haytor Lewis
1858 The Alhambra Palace (*conversion*), T. Haytor Lewis
1860 The Alhambra Music Hall, William Beverley
1864 The Royal Alhambra Palace, J. H. Rowley
1881 The Alhambra Theatre (*re-construction*), John Perry and Frederick Reed
1883 The Alhambra Theatre Royal (*re-building*), John Perry and Frederick Reed
1888 and 1892 Re-decorated and re-constructed, Messrs Clark and Pollard
1897 The Charing Cross Road Extension, W. M. Brutton
1937 The Odeon (*Cinema*), Andrew Mather and Harry Weedon

2 DALY'S THEATRE

1893 Spencer Chadwick, C. J. Phipps
1938 The Warner Theatre (*Cinema*), E. A. Stone and T. R. Somerford

3 THE EMPIRE THEATRE

1882 The Pandora Theatre (*uncompleted*), Thomas Verity
1884 The Empire Theatre, Thomas Verity and A. E. Bull Façade from the Royal London Panorama (1881), M. L. Dumoulin

1893   Leicester Place vestibule and side entrance, Frank
       Verity
1905   Interior re-construction, Frank Verity
1928   The Empire (*Cinema*), Thomas W. Lamb and Frank
       Matcham
1962   The Empire (*Cinema and Ballroom re-construction*),
       George Coles

4 THE GAIETY THEATRE

1864   The Strand Musick Hall, E. Bassett Keeling
1868   The Gaiety Theatre (*re-construction*), C. J. Phipps
1903   The Gaiety Theatre (*new building*), Ernest Rüntz
       and George M'Lean Ford

5 THE GATE THEATRE STUDIO

(*a*)   Floral Street
(*b*)   Villiers Street

6 THE GLOBE THEATRE

1867   Sefton Parry
1870   Reconstruction, Walter Emden

7 THE ROYAL AMPHITHEATRE, HOLBORN

1867   Thomas Smith

8 THE HOLBORN EMPIRE

1857   Weston's Music Hall, Finch, Hill and Paraire
1887   The Royal Music Hall (*re-building*), Lander and
       Bedells
1897   New façade, Ernest Rüntz
1906   The Holborn Empire (*re-building*), Frank Matcham

9 THE HOLBORN THEATRE ROYAL

1866   Finch, Hill and Paraire

10 THE IMPERIAL THEATRE

1876 The Royal Aquarium Theatre, A. Bedborough
1898 The Imperial Theatre (*conversion*), Walter Emden
1901 The Imperial Theatre (*conversion*), Frank Verity

11 THE KINGSWAY THEATRE

1882 The Novelty Theatre, Thomas Verity
1900 The Great Queen Street Theatre (*re-construction*),
      John Murray (of Murray and Foster)
1907 The Kingsway Theatre (*re-construction*), Frederick
      W. Foster

12 THE LITTLE THEATRE

1910 Hayward and Maynard
1920 Reconstruction, Hayward and Maynard

13 THE OLYMPIC THEATRE

1806 The Olympic Pavilion, Philip Astley
1818 Re-construction, Mr. Leatherbridge
1849 Re-building, F. W. Bushill
1883 Re-construction, C. J. Phipps
1890 Re-building, Bertie Carewe and W. G. R. Sprague

14 THE OPERA COMIQUE

1870 F. H. Fowler

15 THE OXFORD

1861 E. L. Paraire
1869 Re-building, E. L. Paraire
1873 Re-building, E. L. Paraire
1893 Re-building, Wylson and Long
1921 New Oxford Theatre (*reconstruction*)

16 THE PANTHEON

1772 James Wyatt
1791 The King's Theatre, Pantheon (*conversion*), James
      Wyatt

1795   Re-building, Crispin Claggett
1812   The Pantheon Theatre (*conversion*), Nicholas Cundy
1834   The Pantheon Bazaar (*conversion*) Sydney Smirk

17 THE PRINCESS'S THEATRE

1828   Royal Bazaar
1830   Queen's Bazaar (*rebuilding*)
1840   Re-construction, Duncan and T. Marsh Nelson
1880   Re-building, C. J. Phipps

18 THE QUEEN'S THEATRE

1850   St. Martin's Hall, Richard Westmacott (the younger)
1862   Re-building
1867   The Queen's Theatre (*conversion*), C. J. Phipps

19 THE ROYAL STRAND THEATRE

1803   Reinagle and Barker's Panorama
1831   The Strand (Subscription) Theatre (*conversion*), Charles Broad
1858   Royal Strand Theatre (*re-construction*), J. Reynolds
1865   Re-construction, John Ellis
1882   Re-building, C. J. Phipps

20 THE ROYALTY THEATRE

1840   Miss Kelly's Theatre and Dramatic School, Samuel Beazley
1850   Royal Soho Theatre (*interior re-construction*), William W. Deane and S. J. Nicholl
1861   New Royalty Theatre (*interior re-construction*), M. Bulot
1883   Royalty Theatre (*interior re-construction*), Thomas Verity
1895   Interior re-construction, Walter Emden
1906   New Royalty Theatre (*interior re-construction and frontage re-modelled*), Messrs Smee and Cobay
1911   Royalty Theatre (*renovation*), Herbert H. Gissing

21 ST. GEORGE'S HALL

1867 John Taylor

22 THE ST. JAMES'S THEATRE

1835 Samuel Beazley
1869 Interior re-construction, James Macintosh
1879 Interior re-construction, Thomas Verity
1900 Interior re-construction and extension, Austin Blomfield and Emblin Walker

23 THE SANS SOUCI THEATRE

1792 (a) Strand (interior), Charles Dibdin
1796 (b) Leicester Place, Charles Dibdin

24 THE SHAFTESBURY THEATRE

1888 C. J. Phipps

25 TERRY'S THEATRE

1887 Walter Emden

26 THE TIVOLI

1890 Walter Emden
1891 Re-construction, Frank Matcham
1923 Cinema (re-building), Bertie Carewe and Ganton and
Ganton

27 TOOLE'S THEATRE

1869 The Charing Cross Theatre, Arthur Evers
1876 The Folly Theatre, Thomas Verity
1882 Toole's Theatre, J. J. Thompson

28 THE TROCADERO

1849 Argyll Rooms
1882 The Trocadero Palace of Varieties

Alphabetical List of Architects

ASTLEY, PHILIP   The Olympic Theatre, 1806
BEAZLEY, SAMUEL   The St. James's Theatre, 1835; Miss Kelly's Theatre and Dramatic School, 1840
BEDBOROUGH, A.   The Royal Aquarium, 1876
BEDELLS, *see Lander*
BEVERLEY, WILLIAM   The Alhambra Music Hall, 1860
BROAD, CHARLES   The Strand Subscription Theatre, 1831
BRUTTON, W. M.   The Alhambra Theatre, Charing Cross Road
BULOT, M.   The New Royalty Theatre, 1861
BUSHILL, F. W.   The Olympic Theatre, 1849
CHADWICK, SPENCER   Daly's Theatre, 1893
CLAGGETT, CRISPIN   The Pantheon, 1795
CLARK, E.   The Alhambra Theatre Royal, 1888 and 1892 (with Pollard)
COBAY, *see Smee and Cobay*
COLES, GEORGE   The Empire (Cinema and Ballroom), 1963
CAREWE, BERTIE   The Olympic Theatre, 1890 (with W. G. R. Sprague); The Tivoli (Cinema), 1933 (with Garton and Garton)
CUNDY, NICHOLAS   The Pantheon, 1912
DEANE, WILLIAM W.   The Royal Soho Theatre, 1850 (with S. J. Nicholl)
DIBDIN, CHARLES   The Sans Souci Theatre, 1792 and 1796
DUMOULIN, M. L.   The Empire Theatre (Façade from Royal London Panorama), 1881
DUNCAN   The Princess's Theatre, 1840 (with T. Marsh Nelson)
ELLIS, JOHN   The Royal Strand, 1865

PERRY, JOHN and FREDERICK REED — The Alhambra Theatre, 1881 and 1883

PHIPPS, C. J. — The Queen's Theatre, 1867; The Gaiety Theatre, 1868; The Princess's Theatre, 1880; The Royal Strand Theatre, 1882; The Shaftesbury Theatre, 1888; Daly's Theatre, 1893 (with Spencer Chadwick)

POLLARD, *see Clark and Pollard*

REED, FREDERICK, *see Perry and Reed*

REYNOLDS, J. — The Royal Strand Theatre, 1858

ROWLEY, J. H. — The Royal Alhambra Palace, 1861

RÜNTZ, ERNEST — The Royal Music Hall, Holborn, 1896; The Gaiety Theatre, 1903 (with George M'Lean Ford)

SMEE and COBAY — The New Royalty Theatre, 1906

SMIRK, SYDNEY — The Pantheon, 1834

SMITH, THOMAS — The Royal Amphitheatre, Holborn, 1867

SOMERFORD, T. R. — The Warner (Cinema), 1938 (with E. A. Stone)

SPRAGUE, W. G. R. — The Olympic Theatre, 1890 (with Bertie Carewe)

STONE, E. A. — The Warner (Cinema), 1938 (with T. R. Somerford)

TAYLOR, JOHN — St. George's Hall, 1867

THOMPSON, J. J. — Toole's Theatre, 1882

VERITY, FRANK — The Empire Theatre (Leicester Place entrance, 1893, and reconstruction, 1905); The Imperial Theatre, 1901

VERITY, THOMAS — The Folly Theatre, 1876; The Empire Theatre (Pandora Theatre), 1882; The St. James's, 1879; The Novelty Theatre, 1882; The Royalty Theatre, 1883

WALKER, EMBLIN — St. James's Theatre, 1900 (with A. Bloomfield Jackson)

WEEDON, HARRY — The Odeon (Cinema), 1937 (with Charles Mather)

WESTMACOTT, RICHARD the younger — St. Martin's Hall, 1856

WYATT, JAMES — The Pantheon, 1772 and 1791

WYLSON and LONG — The Oxford, 1893

Alphabetical List of Theatres

(The numbers are those of the theatres in the text.) The prefix
Royal where used indiscriminately has been omitted, its use will
be found noted under each particular entry.

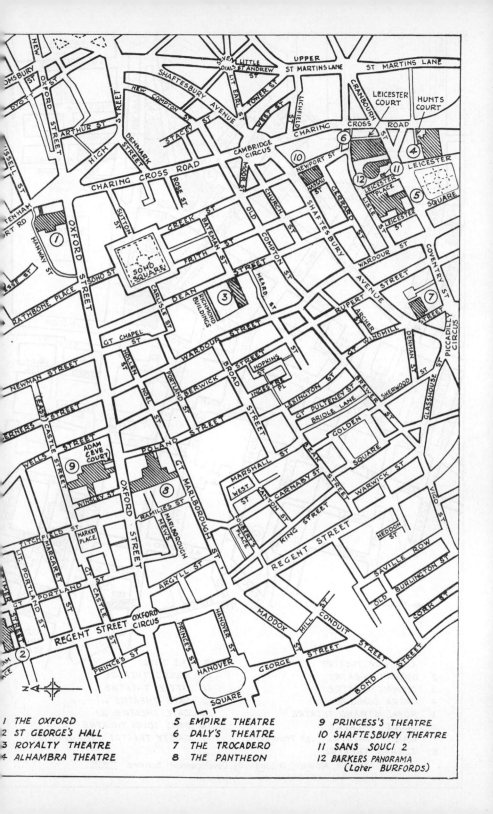

1 THE OXFORD
2 ST GEORGE'S HALL
3 ROYALTY THEATRE
4 ALHAMBRA THEATRE

5 EMPIRE THEATRE
6 DALY'S THEATRE
7 THE TROCADERO
8 THE PANTHEON

9 PRINCESS'S THEATRE
10 SHAFTESBURY THEATRE
11 SANS SOUCI 2
12 BARKERS PANORAMA
    (Later BURFORDS)

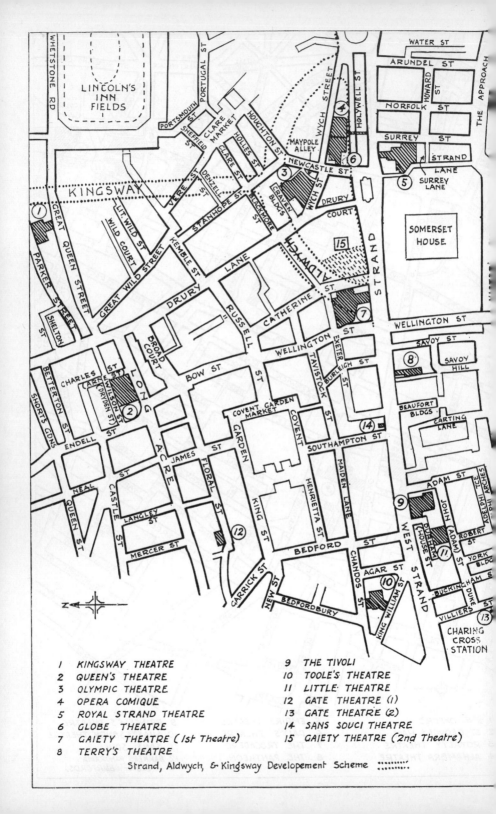

1 KINGSWAY THEATRE	9 THE TIVOLI
2 QUEEN'S THEATRE	10 TOOLE'S THEATRE
3 OLYMPIC THEATRE	11 LITTLE THEATRE
4 OPERA COMIQUE	12 GATE THEATRE (1)
5 ROYAL STRAND THEATRE	13 GATE THEATRE (2)
6 GLOBE THEATRE	14 SANS SOUCI THEATRE
7 GAIETY THEATRE (1st Theatre)	15 GAIETY THEATRE (2nd Theatre)
8 TERRY'S THEATRE	

Strand, Aldwych, & Kingsway Developement Scheme ∷∷∷∷

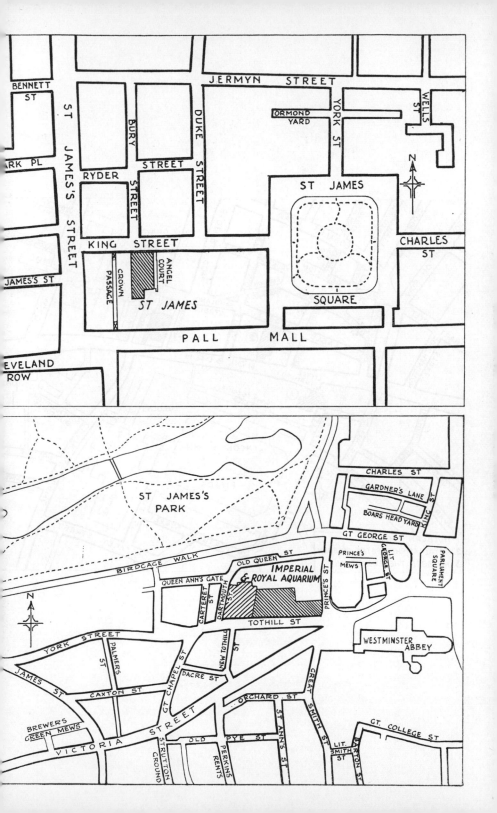

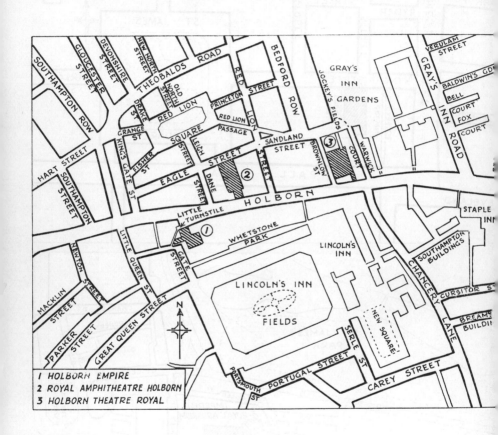